Politics in Francophone Africa

Politics in Francophone Africa

Victor T. Le Vine

LYNNE
RIENNER
PUBLISHERS

BOULDER
LONDON

Published in the United States of America by
Lynne Rienner Publishers, Inc.
1800 30th Street, Boulder, Colorado 80301
www.rienner.com

and in the United Kingdom by
Lynne Rienner Publishers, Inc.
3 Henrietta Street, Covent Garden, London WC2E 8LU

Library of Congress Cataloging-in-Publication Data
Le Vine, Victor T.
    Politics in Francophone Africa / Victor T. Le Vine.
       p.   cm.
    Includes bibliographical references (p.) and index.
    ISBN 978-1-58826-249-3 (hardcover : alk. paper)
    ISBN 978-1-58826-551-7 (paperback : alk. paper)
      1. Africa, French-speaking West—Politics and government.   2. Africa,
French-speaking Equatorial—Politics and government—1960–   I. Title.
    JQ3360.L425   2004
    320.966'0917'541—dc22
                                                             2004001833

British Cataloguing in Publication Data
A Cataloguing in Publication record for this book
is available from the British Library.

Printed and bound in the United States of America

      The paper used in this publication meets the requirements
 ∞   of the American National Standard for Permanence of
      Paper for Printed Library Materials Z39.48-1992.

Contents

Part 4 Connections

Tables and Figures

Acknowledgments

The colleagues, friends, and others, both in and out of Africa, whose help I should acknowledge are literally too numerous to list. I do owe a particular debt of gratitude to the many African friends and colleagues who over the years helped guide my steps in francophone Africa and whose unfailing generosity and hospitality I can never hope to repay.

A number of colleagues read parts of the manuscript at various times and offered valuable criticism and suggestions. I am most grateful to them as well: my old and very good friend René Lemarchand, plus William Foltz, Anthony Kirk-Greene, Crawford Young, William Roger Louis, Richard Joseph, Achille Mbembe, Naomi Chazan, (the late) Gwendolen Carter, Mark DeLancey, Jennifer Seely, and Richard Sklar. They are, of course, not responsible for any errors of fact or interpretation in these pages, and if I neglected to take some of their good counsel or heed some of their criticisms, that failure is mine alone. Very special thanks are also due Martina Baillie, whose remarkable editorial talents enabled the final version of this book to take shape and by whose technical alchemy the manuscript was transmuted into proper electronic form.

There is one person to whom I literally owe this enterprise itself and to whom I wish to pay particular tribute: the late James S. Coleman of UCLA, who in 1956 set me and other friends and colleagues on the path to Africa. During the 1950s, Jim Coleman, at once mentor and friend, fired the enthusiasms and imaginations of the small group of second-generation Africanists to which I have been privileged to belong. A leader among the first group of distinguished U.S. post–World War II Africanists (which included David Apter, Carl Rosberg, Gwendolen Carter, Alphonse Castagno, Carl Brown, Ruth Schachter Morgenthau, Gus Liebenow, Gray Cowan, and Helen Kitchen), Coleman offered us the extraordinary opportunity to be present at the creation of more than twoscore African nations. By his example and instruction he taught us the art of engaged but professional observation and analysis of politics on the continent. This book began with my own work in the Cameroons in 1959, which I undertook at Jim's urging, and has been in the writing through more than forty years of professional work in and with Africa.

Francophone Africa

Introduction

This book is about politics in fourteen African states that, before 1958–1961, were part of France's African empire. Twelve of the fourteen operated under the umbrella of what were then generally known as the administrative federations of French West and Equatorial Africa, Afrique Occidentale Française (AOF), and Afrique Equatoriale Française (AEF). French West Africa included Mauritania, Senegal, Guinea, the Ivory Coast (now officially Côte d'Ivoire), Mali, Upper Volta (now Burkina Faso), Dahomey (now Benin), and Niger. The UN Trust Territory of Togo, which was under French administration, operated in part under the aegis of the AOF but, because of its special international status, was treated as a separate political and juridical entity. The AEF group was made up of Chad, Ubangui-Shari (now the Central African Republic), Gabon, and the French Congo (now the Republic of Congo, or Congo-Brazzaville*). The UN Trust Territory of Cameroon (now the Cameroon Republic, or Cameroon)[1] was ruled by France under a set of dispensations similar to those that governed Togo.

France's African empire at one time also included French Somaliland (which was renamed the Territory of the Afars and Issas after 1966, then became the Republic of Djibouti in 1977); the great island of Madagascar; and three North African territories—Morocco, Algeria, and Tunisia. It also included several islands and island groups near Madagascar (the present Comoros Federal Islamic Republic plus Mayotte/Maore, the Îles Glorieuses, Réunion, the Îles Tromelin, Juan de Nova, Bassas da India, and Europa), of which all but the three islands of the Comoros Republic still belong to France.[2] A neighbor of Cameroon and the old AEF states, the

---

* In this text the Republic of Congo will be referred to as Congo-Brazzaville. The country formerly known as Zaire will be referred to as the Democratic Republic of Congo (or DRC).

Republic of Equatorial Guinea, a former Spanish colony, is tied monetarily to the Communauté Financière Africaine (and the CFA franc), but is only marginally involved with the politics of its member states, that is, to the extent that refugees from the Equatorial Guinean regimes of the late Maçias Nguéma and his nephew Teodoro Obiang (Nguema Mbasogo) still reside in Cameroon and the ex-AEF countries and agitate against Teodoro's dictatorship.

In any event, we will not deal with this latter group of states and territories, principally because their politics and political histories are largely peripheral to those of the fourteen of our focus. The modern political destinies of the Maghreb states (Morocco, Algeria, and Tunisia) in particular have connected them largely with the Arab world of North Africa and the Middle East rather than with sub-Saharan Africa. (Madagascar is a partial exception: it played a role in the preindependence politics of French Africa, and its leaders continue to meet with their West and Equatorial African peers at the francophone summits and the venues of the Francophonie organization.) Finally, the ex-Belgian colonies of the Democratic Republic of Congo, Rwanda, and Burundi are also officially francophone, but for most purposes they also lie outside our purview.

Why focus on Togo, Cameroon, and the twelve states of former French West and Equatorial Africa? The reasons are many and complex, but for now suffice it simply to stress that the fourteen share not only what amounts to a colonial past, but also social, political, and economic linkages born of common and sometimes shared postindependence political experiences, plus a set of surprisingly resilient and durable ties to France itself.

That such links to a former colonial metropole should persist some forty years after independence is not at all surprising: Belgium continues to play a role in the politics of its former dominions;[3] Portugal remains an active presence in Angola, Mozambique, and Guinea-Bissau;[4] and Britain does the same in its former colonies in West and East Africa. For example, when Sierra Leone's government, ECOMOG, (the Military Observers' Group of the ECOWAS, the Economic Organization of West African States), and the UN (which had sent peacekeepers) were unable to end Sierra Leone's three-year civil war, they turned to Britain, whose troops finally forced the surrender of warlord Foday Sankoh's rebels in 2001. In like fashion, in 2002–2003 French intervention ended—at least temporarily—a military mutiny and near–civil war in Côte d'Ivoire. This resulted in an agreement that melded—again, more or less temporarily—the rebels and the government into a new regime. Spain retains ties to one of its former colonies, Equatorial Guinea, though not with the other, now called the Western Sahara, which it surrendered to Morocco and Mauritania when General Franco died in 1975.

What is surprising in the case of the fourteen states that are the subject of this study is the strength and salience of their ties with France: involved are educational and cultural exchange, including the diffusion of French popular culture, particularly in urban areas; trade and investment; technical and financial assistance; French financial arrangements; periodic "Francophone" leaders' conferences chaired by the incumbent French president; membership in the international francophone cultural organization, La Francophonie; and the presence of some one hundred thousand Frenchmen living or doing business in the fourteen states while maintaining multiple links to France.[5]

Occasionally one or another of these states calls for French military intervention in a local conflict, and units of the French Force d'Action Rapide (FAR) have been stationed at some eight francophone African venues.[6] For example, between May 1996 and April 1997, France repeatedly used elements of its 1,300-soldier force in the Central African Republic, plus additional troops from France itself, to support the country's civilian president Ange-Félix Patassé, whose government was threatened by recurrent mutinies within its army.[7]

In the aggregate these past and present ties have tended to perpetuate a sense of connection among a variety of politically and economically active populations in the fourteen states and, thereby, among the fourteen political systems. It is not, of course, simply that French remains the lingua franca of the educated, the elites, and high politics, though the common language has obviously continued to facilitate these relationships; it is that when added up, these connections and continuities amount to a loose but durable political community. Admittedly one can make too much of all this. Indeed, France no longer wields the big stick it once did, and francophone African leaders periodically pick fights with their French friends. Furthermore, the old institutional and economic links have declined as France itself, beginning with the tenure of President François Mitterand and continuing during that of President Jacques Chirac, has been pulling back from its African commitments, and these fourteen states have been cultivating new connections with other members of the European Community, other African states, and a growing number of recently acquired non-African trading partners. Yet a loose and surprisingly durable base of political commonality persists and thus provides the principal reason for studying these fourteen states as a group.

This is the perspective, of course, that considers the French-African connection to be more or less benign. The opposing view sees the long relationship in a highly critical light, in which official France, in league with French corporations and businessmen-politicians and with the willing cooperation of a variety of corrupt and venal African leaders, maintains these links with the ultimate purpose of exploiting Africans and African wealth.While the first perspective reflects the reality of a variety of salutary Franco-African relationships, it is also the image official France has sought to project. The other view, in the eyes of its proponents, reflects the hidden reality of the connection, one that portrays francophone Africa as the *pré carré* (backyard) and *chasse gardée* (private hunting preserve) of official and corporate France and its African clients. The second, opposing view has been represented in the work of investigative journalists like Georges Chaffard, Antoine Glaser, Stephen Smith, and François-Xavier Verschave in the pages of the periodical *Jeune Afrique,* as well as in the academic efforts of Jean-François Bayart and the journal *Politique Africaine.* Granted, much of this work comes from the French left-wing tradition of *engagé* politics, but because so much of it is based on solid research, is often unblinkingly truthful, and is convincingly argued, I turn to it later, in Chapters 8 through 11.

Although it is true that after independence each of the fourteen states went its own particular political and economic way, the French connections remained both between the states and France and among the states themselves. Francophone leaders stayed in touch with one another, even to the point of creating—sometimes successfully, sometimes not—formal political and economic links between their countries. These include the ill-fated Mali Federation (1959–1961, mainly joining Mali and Senegal), the Council of the Entente (founded in 1959, which loosely connects Côte d'Ivoire, Benin, Togo, Burkina Faso, and Niger), the Central African Customs Union (the Union Douanière et Économique de l'Afrique Centrale, UDEAC, founded in 1964, which included Chad, Cameroon, the Central African Republic, Congo-Brazzaville, Gabon, and Equatorial Guinea), and the West African Economic Community (Communauté Économique de l'Afrique de l'Ouest, CEAO, founded in 1974 and including Benin, Burkina Faso, Côte d'Ivoire, Mali, Mauritania, Niger, and Senegal). These connections represent only the more visible, institutionalized part of a much larger array of continuous formal and informal postindependence interstate linkages.

It was a francophone country, Benin, that in 1989 finally led the way in the surprising resurgence of democratic politics on the continent, begetting similar processes in Mali, Niger, Congo, Chad, Cameroon, Togo, Mali, and Côte d'Ivoire—all francophone countries as well. While the results of this "redemocratization" process have been disappointing, the point is that the process diffused first to the francophone countries, an effect surely brought about by the existence of a community of political interest among the fourteen states. (Chapter 8 addresses the issue of redemocratization.) At the very least, the existence of that community is a hypothesis worth testing; at most, it establishes one set of analytic concurrences, a field of commonalities, that makes valid comparative analysis possible.[8] In all, then, there is ample justification for this study. But how to approach the subject?

The latest general work in English on francophone Africa is the 1997 volume edited by John Clark and David Gardinier, *Political Reform in Francophone Africa,* a series of essays taking its cue from Benin's 1989 national conference and its effects elsewhere in francophone Africa. Another recent such volume is that edited by Anthony Kirk-Greene and Daniel Bach, *State and Society in Francophone Africa Since Independence,* the revised product of a 1988 symposium on francophone Africa held at St. Anthony's College and the Maison Française, Oxford.[9] The book organizes eighteen contributions under four broad categories: political systems, economic and financial dynamics, external relations, and literature and philosophy. Patrick Manning's excellent history, *Francophone Sub-Saharan Africa, 1880–1995,* is presented under three general rubrics (economy and society, government and politics, culture and religion), with two chapters on each set of topics, that is, one dealing with events before 1940, and the other with those after. In the second edition of this book, published in 1998, Manning added a chapter called "Democracy and Dependence, 1985–1995," which extended the story ten years further.

Manning resisted organizing his book under country-specific rubrics, and I follow suit mainly because the monographic and periodic literature on the fourteen states is by now extensive enough in both English and French to satisfy readers wishing to explore in detail the politics, society, and economy of each. (The bibliography references the most important and useful of those works.) Instead, I've chosen to organize the book under a series of themes. Some of them offer broad historical analysis; others present arguments about some comparable, as well as territorially specific, facets of politics; and still others convey topical analysis and the results of comparative empirical research. It is, admittedly, a mixed bag, but one that I hope will prove both useful and interesting as it is unpacked.

The book begins with a set of three related chapters: the first on the physical and human contexts of politics, the second on the general character of the colonial legacy bequeathed to the fourteen states at independence, and the third on the growth of political and institutional life from the end of World War II to independence. The second set of three chapters addresses the interface of society and politics, speaking first to the growth of transterritorial and national political cultures, then to the intersection of ideology and political style, and finally to the role of religion and ethnicity in the politics of the fourteen states. The third set of chapters explores themes on the structures, processes, and exercise of power in the fourteen states. Chapter 7 discusses the variety of governance experiments from 1958 to 2003. Chapter 8 examines the remarkable redemocratization surge during the early 1990s. Chapter 9 looks at who rules and leads in the fourteen states, and Chapter 10 throws some light onto their political shadows—the "parapolitics" of the systems themselves. The final chapter considers some important facets of political economy and the linkages of the fourteen states to the international economic and political contexts in which they operate, including, notably and critically, those with France itself.

I freely admit that no single theoretical or methodological perspective informs these chapters, and I acknowledge that I have borrowed extensively from the work and ideas of friends and colleagues, as well as using my own studies and research to address the questions and issues raised in each chapter. Over forty years as a student of African politics, scholar-researcher, part-time journalist, visiting professor and lecturer throughout Africa, participant-observer, and eyewitness to extraordinary change have taught me that there are no simple or definitive answers to most Africa-related questions. Thus my own continuing doubts about the interpretations and answers presented here will be evident throughout the work, and I hope they will be accepted as honest uncertainties, not evasions.

Notes

1. The name Cameroon derives from Rio dos Camarões, or River of Shrimp, given to what is today the Wouri River by Portuguese explorers, the first Europeans to sail up the estuary of the Wouri in ca. 1472.

The Spanish called the river Rio Camerōnes; the Germans named the territory Kamerun when they annexed it in 1884. It passed to the French and British in 1916, and the French called their part Cameroun, the British named theirs the Cameroons (the British held two disconnected pieces). As League of Nations mandates in 1921–1946, and later as UN trust territories, the names were anglicized to be French Cameroon and the British Cameroons. When the French Cameroon became independent in 1961, it formally became La Republique du Cameroun, or the Cameroon Republic.

The British Cameroons, under the League of Nations and the UN, consisted of the Southern Cameroons and the Northern Cameroons. In 1961, as a result of a UN plebiscite, the Northern Cameroons joined Nigeria, the Southern Cameroons joined the Republic of Cameroon. The latter became the Federal Republic of Cameroon, until 1972 when the federation was dissolved and the whole was renamed the United Cameroon Republic. The "United" was dropped in 1982 when Paul Biya succeeded to the Cameroonian presidency.

To complicate matters further, an Anglophone secessionist group, the Southern Cameroons National Council (SCNC), announced the former Southern Cameroon's secession, renaming the territory the Ambazonia/Federal Republic of Southern Cameroon. Ambazonia derives from "Ambozes," what the folk at the mouth of the Wouri (now Douala) used to call the area. They insist on calling the francophone Cameroon by its French name, La République du Cameroun. The SCNC has not yet managed to secede the territory, but has given the central government a lot of grief.

2. Juan de Nova, Bassas da India, Europa, and the Îles Glorieuses, located in the Madagascar Channel, are uninhabited; all are administered by the French overseas department of Réunion but claimed by Madagascar. The Îles Tromelin, east of Madagascar in the Indian Ocean, are claimed by both Mauritius and Seychelles. The

island of Mayotte (Maore) is geographically and culturally part of the Comoros group, but in 1976 its inhabitants opted to remain part of France after the rest of the Comoros became an independent state in 1975. The leaders of the Comoros Republic apparently hope the citizens of Mayotte will someday change their minds; the green Comoros national flag includes a half-moon with four, not three, stars between its cusps.

3. Rwanda, Burundi, and the Democratic Republic of Congo all send representatives to the meetings of the French-sponsored international Francophonie organization, as well as to the periodic Franco-African summits. Until its relations with Burundi soured in 1985—in part because of the misuse of some fifty million francs allocated by the French Ministry of Cooperation for the 1984 Franco-African Summit in Bujumbura—France had a special relationship with that country. France had a similar relationship with the military regime in Rwanda (under President Habyarimana) when it helped arm the Rwandan army and trained many Rwandan soldiers and militiamen. During the early 1990s, French military "assistants" tried to prevent the regime's collapse and, when it did collapse in 1994, helped its remnants to escape to the DRC.

4. In 1996, after a twenty-year period of limited connections, Portugal reasserted her political and economic ties with her former African colonies by giving them pride of place in a new Community of Portuguese-Language Countries (CPLP). See Matloff, "New Kids on Trade Bloc: Portugal and Ex-Colonies."

5. McNamara, *France in Black Africa;* Chipman, *French Power in Africa;* Andereggen, *France's Relationship with Sub-Saharan Africa;* Corbett, *The French Presence in Africa;* Mortimer, *France and the Africans, 1944–1960: A Political History;* Frederick Quinn, *The French Overseas Empire.*

6. FAR was dissolved on June 30, 1998, and its units incorporated under the new overall structure for land forces, the Commandement de la Force d'Action Terrestre (CFAT). The FAR, which consisted of two divisions, two brigades, and several specialized regiments, saw action in Lebanon (1983), Chad (1986), Rwanda (1990), the Persian Gulf (1990–1991), Cambodia (1992–1993), and the former Yugoslavia (1992).

7. See Leymarie, "Gendarmes et voleurs en Centrafrique," 25.

8. The problem of making valid comparisons about African politics is an old one recently revisited by Chris Allen, who argues for the existence of a limited number of different event-sequences within individual state histories and of "the political forms that feature in them" ("Understanding African Politics," 303). I agree with much of his analysis, but insist that francophone, anglophone, lusophone (Portuguese-speaking), and even hispanophone African countries represent analytically discrete ensembles for comparative analysis, always given sufficient—and empirically demonstrable—commonalities among the component units.

9. The French edition was *Etats et sociétés en Afrique francophone.*

Part 1

Contexts

1

The Human and Geographical Contexts of Politics

A map of Africa provides a beginning for our study: these fourteen states of francophone Africa occupy more than half of the northwestern quadrant of the continent. French colonialism made the states neighbors: each of the fourteen shares a border with at least two other francophone states, two of the states (Niger and Burkina Faso) border five others, and one (Mali) borders seven others. The states share more than these common frontiers, reminders of past colonial administrative convenience. The facts of geography and climate make them neighbors in ways no drawing of political boundaries can ever change. They share climatic zones, shorelines, rivers, savannahs, plateaus, deserts, and even soil types and vegetation, factors that largely determine their present economies and, of course, influence their politics.

Ethnicity

Above all, the fourteen states share people. Political frontiers are rarely drawn to accommodate communal spaces, and they certainly were not in the case of these fourteen states. Only a few incorporate the majority of a large ethnic group: Senegal contains almost all of the Wolof, Burkina Faso has almost all the Mossi, Mali contains most of the Bambara, Cameroon includes practically all the Bamiléké, and Chad contains the majority of the Sara. However, the Fulani (also known as the Foulah, Fulbé, and Peul), perhaps ten to fifteen million strong in West Africa, are dispersed throughout the savannah zone stretching from Mauritania to Chad and contribute sizable numbers to the populations of Mali, Guinea, Niger, Cameroon, and Chad. (See Appendix A.) Other large ethnic groups, such as the Fang, Ewe, Fon, Hausa, Malinké, Yoruba, Tukolor, and Bakongo, are represented in two or more states.

In no state of the fourteen is there a complete coincidence of ethnic

11

concentration and political frontiers, even though in some of the states members of a particular ethnic group tend to dominate politics. This is the case for the Mossi in Burkina Faso, the Sara in Chad, the Maurs/Moors in Mauritania, and the Fang in Gabon. Of course, such dominance is never without challenge, and almost all of the fourteen states have more or less recently experienced some form of political conflict between members of rival and sometimes traditionally hostile ethnic groups.

The ethnic picture, then, is one of extraordinary diversity. Some 117.6 million people live in the fourteen states. They speak some three hundred distinct languages and hundreds of dialects, and they constitute well over five hundred different ethnic groups varying in size from a few thousand members to "nations" of over a million or more. Ethnologists and ethnographers argue about the exact number of these groups, since any estimate depends almost entirely upon whose taxonomy is used. Regardless of how the issue is resolved, the facts of great diversity and the large number of groups remain uncontested. Any attempt to render an ethnic map of one of the states produces something resembling a badly constructed patchwork quilt. (See, for example, the continental "ethnic map in Murdock's *Africa: Its Peoples and Their Culture History.*)

This complexity is one of the reasons why, faute de mieux and despite the objections of those who argue that ethnic designations are mainly colonial constructions, the linguistic denominator has become the standard classificatory device for distinguishing between the groups.[1] The largest and most important of these linguistic families, such as the Mande of Guinea and Mali, the Akan of Côte d'Ivoire and Ghana, the Volta of Burkina Faso, the Hausa-Fulani of the savannah belt, the Beti-Fang (Equatorial Bantu) of Cameroon and Gabon, and the Bakongo of Congo-Brazzaville and Gabon (and the Democratic Republic of Congo), all serve to reinforce the prevailing pattern of interterritorial ethnic linkage. (The basic demographic and ethnic data are presented in Appendix A.)

Religion

There are other commonalities. Islam is the confession of the overwhelming majority of people in the broad band of desert and savannah from the Atlantic coast to the borders of Sudan and the Democratic Republic of Congo, including much or most of Mauritania, Guinea, Mali, Burkina Faso, Niger, and Chad, as well as substantial northern areas of Senegal, Côte d'Ivoire, Togo, Benin, and Cameroon. To be sure, it is not the same brand of Islam throughout the region. Though nominally Sunni in orientation and connected to the Maliki legal school, it is divided into various confessional denominations (*tariqa,* also called *confrèries* or brotherhoods), styles, and syncretisms. Nevertheless, Islam in sub-Saharan Africa, as in Northern

Africa, has given a number of states a great deal to share: a religious bond, sometimes a cement for national values (Mauritania, for example, styles itself the Islamic Republic of Mauritania), and contributions to a rich history of empires, kings, and even protonationalist heroes such as Samori Turé, al-Hajj 'Umar Tal, Rabeh, and 'Uthman dan Fodio. Muslim leaders' and groups' contribution to contemporary politics in the fourteen states has been considerable, and the ruling political parties of at least two of the states (Mauritania's Republican Democratic and Social Party [PRDS], and the Cameroon People's Democratic Movement [CPDM]) began as associations representing primarily regional Muslim interests. In all, there are over sixty million Muslims in the fourteen states, and Muslims constitute more than half the total population in six of them (see Table 1.1). Islam matters politically, sometimes crucially, throughout francophone Africa.[2]

Christianity, particularly Roman Catholicism, has similarly created important transnational political and cultural links. Francophone West and Equatorial Africa now boasts four cardinals (Bernard Agre, Côte d'Ivoire; Bernardin Gantin, Benin; Hyacinthe Thiandoum, Senegal; and Christian Tumi, Cameroon) out of the sixteen for the continent and Mauritius. The twenty-two archdioceses (five in Cameroon, four in Côte d'Ivoire, three in Burkina Faso, two in Benin, and one each in Congo-Brazzavile, Chad, Mali, Togo, Guinea, CAR, Senegal, and Gabon) serve large Catholic populations, and their prelates all actively foster wide interterritorial Catholic contacts. What was probably the first, and has probably been the best, general francophone West African newspaper, *Afrique Nouvelle,* was published in Dakar during the 1950s and 1960s by the Paulist fathers. It disseminated not only news and excellent political commentary bearing broadly on West Africa, but also considerable material dealing with the life of the Church in all of francophone Africa.

The contribution of several Catholic and Protestant theological seminaries, particularly the Catholic ones, should not be overlooked in an assessment of the transterritorial political role of Christianity. During the post–World War II period the seminaries of Ouagadougou, Yaoundé, Brazzaville, and Dakar schooled several generations of francophone Africans, of whom a considerable number went into politics. Although few confessional Christian political parties have made much headway in francophone Africa,[3] the Church has frequently been involved in politics. Two prominent founding-father politicians of Equatorial Africa were once priests: the "Abbé" Foulbert Youlou, former president of Congo-Brazzaville; and Barthélemy Boganda, former premier of the Central African Republic. Both were suspended from ecclesiastical duties for becoming involved in politics.[4] (Boganda went even further: he married his secretary and was then defrocked in 1946.)

Several of the fourteen states now have, or have had, branches of the

Table 1.1 Religious Affiliations

Country	Estimated Population (in millions)[a]	Religion as Percentage of Population			
		Traditional	Catholic	Protestant	Muslim
Benin	6.78	58.8	23.18	3	15
Burkina Faso	12.6	37	11.8	0.5	50
Cameroon	16.5	35	25	15	30
CAR	3.64	22	23	15	50
Chad	6.7	6	8.9	<1	85
Congo-Brazzaville	3.6	38.4	42.6	17	2
Côte d'Ivoire	17.4	25	16.5	3.5	60
Gabon	1.74	42	50.17	<0.5	<1
Guinea	7.77	8	2.6	n.d.	85
Mali	11.3	8.1	1.86	n.d.	90
Mauritania[b]	2.8	n.d.	0.15	n.d.	>95
Niger	10.9	10	0.18	1.5	88
Senegal	9.9	2.93	5.3	<0.5	92
Togo	5.8	16	22.3	4	55

Sources: World Christian Handbook, 1998; *Annuaire des dioceses d'expression française, delegations apostoliques pour l'Afrique occidentale, l'Afrique centrale, et Madagascar*, 1994; *Africa South of the Sahara, 1999; World Factbook*, 2002; *UN Demographic Yearbook*, 1999; UN High Commissioner for Refugees, *The State of the World's Refugees*, 1999; "Statistics by Country by Catholic Population," 2002; "Report" (on Muslims in each country), Islamic Web, 1998.

Notes: a. Muslim estimates as of 1998. Other estimates as of July 2002.

b. Ever since some sixty thousand people (mainly non-Muslim blacks) were evicted from Mauritania—and sent mostly into Senegal—during the 1989–1990 Senegal-Mauritania border conflict, no reliable figures have been available on the number of non-Muslims remaining in Mauritania, which may be anywhere from near zero to no more than 5 percent of the total population. For a discussion of the larger issues of ethnic and racial identity in Mauritania, see Marchesin, *Tribus, ethnies, et pouvoirs en Mauritanie.*

n.d. = no data available.

Reliable data on religious affiliation are available only where censuses have recorded such information. The above percentages represent the best current (1998–2002) estimates rounded to the nearest 0.5 percent and do not include seasonal migrant populations, which are sometimes quite sizable, or refugees. In 1999, according to the UN high commissioner for refugees, at least 900,000 refugees from Liberia and Sierra Leone were in Guinea and Côte d'Ivoire and some 400,000 were in the other twelve countries.

Pan-African Union of Believing Workers (Union Panafricaine des Travailleurs Croyants), itself affiliated with the French Confederation of Christian Trade Unions. The African branches of the latter grew from the organization of Christian workers, but they soon included Muslims because there were few Muslim-member trade unions.[5] This is yet another way in which Christianity[6] and Islam, both originally alien to Africa, have come to serve as important transnational links between francophone African states.

Demographic Trends

A series of demographic surveys conducted in francophone sub-Saharan Africa between 1958 and 1966 help us to flesh out these skeletal comments about the basic human context of the fourteen states.[7] Though these surveys were not replicated, later local studies and surveys, UN data, and the country-specific monographic literature provide the relevant data for the 1966–2002 period. According to the earlier surveys, the total population of the fourteen countries in 1960 was around 35,270,000; by 1968 that number had increased to around forty-one million, a rise of about 15 percent in six years despite a persistently high infant mortality rate of 180 per thousand. By mid-1995 the total population had more than doubled—and almost tripled since the base year of 1960—to almost ninety million. If these figures are correct, the projected fertility levels given by the surveys, averaging between four and seven births per woman, exceed the high death rates, producing a net average rate of population increase of about 2.2 percent per year from 1960 to 1968, and around 3 percent per year from 1968 to 1999. By the turn of the millennium, the AIDS pandemic had begun to impact the fourteen states, as it had most sub-Saharan countries. The available data for Côte d'Ivoire, one of the epicenters of the infection in West Africa, suggest a slight downturn in fertility rates with an upturn in the number of AIDS-afflicted newborns.

Even with AIDS factored in, the fourteen states still have growing populations but, as it also turns out, not highly mobile ones. In most of the countries 75 percent or more of the people counted were living in the same locale where they were born. The percentage was less for women due largely to traditions regulating exogamy. In the urban centers, however, fewer people were town-born and town-reared (the modal percentages were between 55 and 65), and indeed, the larger the urban center, the lower the percentage. The data confirmed high urban influx, and such migration tended to be constant over time, rather than seasonal or occurring in large waves. The great migrations are those registered annually in the west, where large numbers of workers from the landlocked countries of Mali, Burkina Faso, and Niger move west and south to find work in the agricultural areas of the coastal states. (Burkina Faso, for example, experiences a more or less annual seasonal shift of between 350,000 and 500,000 workers south to Côte d'Ivoire, Ghana, Guinea, and Benin.) The extent of these migrations is nowhere more apparent than in Côte d'Ivoire: unofficial estimates suggest that at least one-fifth of the country's 15.4 million people are "foreigners" (i.e., non-Ivoirian by birth).

These seasonal migrations are sometimes dangerous. Periodic waves of xenophobia, usually generated by political or economic tensions, have afflicted Côte d'Ivoire (as well as Ghana, Guinea, and Nigeria) and have resulted in expulsions, beatings, and killings of migrants. During 1999 and

2000, migrant or temporary-resident Burkinabé again became victims, this time as the targets of an officially sanctioned minicampaign of ethnic cleansing connected with the candidacy of Alassane Ouattara for the country's presidency. (The twentieth century's last civilian president, Henri Konan Bedié, as well as General Robert Gueï, who replaced Konan Bedié in December 1999, both disqualified Ouattara, claiming he was Burkinabé and not a genuine Ivoirian. Konan Bedié, General Gueï, and Laurent Gbagbo, the civilian leader who helped chase Gueï from office on October 24, 2000, all championed "Ivoirité": the primacy of Ivorians over others. Street violence marked Ouattara's disqualification, and his followers again took to violence on October 26, as they would periodically thereafter, when it became clear that Gbagbo would continue his predecessors' policies.)

In September 1996, in response to Gabon's own wave of homegrown xenophobia, the Gabonese government imposed fees as high as $1,200 per person on immigrant workers from Mali and Burkina Faso. The predictable result was that in January and February 1997 thousands of migrants in Gabon were forced onto trucks and ships, having abandoned their homes and belongings. All this occurred in a country that had always imported workers from neighboring states because its own population growth remained flat.

Urbanization

Africa remained the least urbanized of the continents through the last decades of the twentieth century. In 1920 only about 4 percent of the population of our fourteen francophone states lived in towns of over 100,000 inhabitants, and an average of only 9 percent lived in towns of populations over 10,000. Rapidly changing demographics have altered this landscape. Between 1920 and 1960, the number of urban centers of more than 10,000 inhabitants increased over fourfold, from twenty-two to ninety-two, while their total population grew about fivefold, from 790,000 to over 3,736,000. In 1960 only seven cities had over 100,000 inhabitants; by 1970 that number had grown to thirteen and their total population had risen to 2.8 million. By 1998 there were eighteen cities with over 100,000 inhabitants, and their total population was over sixteen million. (See Tables 1.2 and 1.3.) It is not unlikely that by 2025 half of the continent's population will be urban.

Compared to rural populations, according to the studies, urban populations had higher ratios of men to women and of adults to children. A higher proportion of urban than rural adults were unemployed or underemployed. Urban residents were better educated, had smaller families, and had lower death rates than their rural counterparts. Finally, people in cities in large towns were primarily monogamous, and both men and women tended to marry younger.

Table 1.2   **Population Estimates of Major Cities (over 120,000), 1960 and 1998**

City (Country)	Type of Capital	Estimated Population, 1960	Estimated Population, 1998
Abidjan (Côte d'Ivoire)[a]	De facto capital; Commercial capital	250,000	2,793,000
Bamako (Mali)	Seat of government; Commercial capital	130,000	919,000
Bangui (CAR)	Seat of government; Commercial capital	80,000	650,000
Brazzaville (Congo-Brazzaville)	Seat of government; Commercial capital	130,000	1,004,000
Conakry (Guinea)	Seat of government; Commercial capital	110,000	1,558,000
Cotonou (Benin)[b]	De facto capital; Commercial capital	78,000	1,060,000
Dakar (Senegal)	Seat of government; Commercial capital	250,000	2,000,000
Douala (Cameroon)	Commercial capital	150,000	2,000,000
Lomé (Togo)	Seat of government; Commercial capital	73,000	750,000
Ndjamena (formerly Fort Lamy) (Chad)	Seat of government; Commercial capital	58,000	826,000
Nouakchott (Mauritania)	Seat of government; Commercial capital	20,000	735,000
Ouagadougou (Burkina Faso)	Seat of government; Commercial capital	59,000	824,000
Porto Novo (Benin)[b]	Seat of government	20,000	330,000
Yamoussoukro (Côte d'Ivoire)[a]	Seat of government	20,000	120,000
Yaoundé (Cameroon)	Seat of government	50,000	1,119,000

Sources: Legum and Drysdale, eds., *Africa Contemporary Record,* 1969–1994; *Africa South of the Sahara;* "Afrique: Images incertaines," 1992.

Notes: a. At the behest of President Houphouët-Boigny, Côte d'Ivoire's capital was legally changed to his hometown, Yamoussoukro, in 1983, although the seat of government remained in Abidjan.

b. Even though Porto Novo is the official capital of Benin, Cotonou functions as its administrative center, with most government offices and embassies located there.

Urbanization in the fourteen states remains very much a coastal phenomenon. The great ports—Dakar, Abidjan, Douala, Conakry, Lomé, Cotonou—are among the fastest-growing urban centers, and the greatest increase in the number of towns with populations over ten thousand during the past thirty years has been shared between national administrative centers and the coastal areas. Modern politics in Africa took shape primarily in the growing colonial towns, and today national politics in the fourteen states is still largely determined by what happens in what for most of the countries is not only the largest town, but also the only town of any consequence—the capital. In only two of the countries is the largest town a place other than the capital: Douala is Cameroon's main port, and Cotonou is Benin's. Only Cotonou and Yamoussoukro challenge the supremacy of a capital city. Porto Novo, the official capital of Benin, is linked to Cotonou, the de facto capital, by a short causeway, and by tradition and in practice it

Table 1.3   Urbanization Patterns, 1965–2000

	Urban Inhabitants as Percentage of Population				
Country	1965	1970	1975	1980	Rural/Urban Ratio, 2000
Benin	9.7	11.9	14.6	17.0	58/42
Burkina Faso	3.1	4.7	6.1	7.3	81/19
Cameroon	6.5	7.4	8.5	9.4	51/49
CAR	12.6	16.6	19.8	22.0	59/41
Chad	5.8	8.1	10.2	13.0	76/24
Congo-Brazzaville	26.8	29.9	32.2	34.6	63/37
Côte d'Ivoire	14.0	18.8	23.1	25.5	49/51
Gabon	8.6	11.4	14.9	18.0	19/81
Guinea	8.5	10.6	12.6	14.6	70/30
Mali	5.5	7.1	7.8	8.4	78/22
Mauritania	n.d.	2.3	3.0	5.1	42/58
Niger	1.5	2.4	3.8	4.5	79/21
Senegal	24.1	27.2	29.2	30.2	55/45
Togo	7.8	10.3	15.4	18.2	67/33

Sources: World Bank, *African Development Indicators, 1996; Development Data Group, 2001;* World Bank, *World Development Report 1996, 2001;* "Afrique: Images incertaines," 1992.
Note: n.d. = no data available.

is virtually a part of the larger town. Yamoussoukro was decreed the capital of Côte d'Ivoire in 1983 by the state's founding-father, Félix Houphouët-Boigny, who was born there. After Houphouët-Boigny died in 1993, his successor, Konan Bedié, returned most governmental functions to Abidjan.

The critical role of the capital towns is underscored by the fact that successful military coups in eleven of the states were largely organized and launched in the capitals of those states, as were unsuccessful coup attempts in four of them. This should come as no surprise: the most important military garrisons are usually located within or on the outskirts of the capitals, one more testament to the fact that the capitals almost invariably concentrate national political, economic, and social activity.

Much earlier, soon after the end of World War II, it was the larger towns that provided the small worker base for francophone Africa's politically potent trade unions, and it was primarily the towns that gave the nationalist parties their first militants and mobilizable masses. As the political crucibles of francophone Africa, the towns not only served their own countries, but spread ideas, organizations, and politically conscious members of the new intellectual elite across national borders in a continual process of mutual exchange and political cross-fertilization.

For example, Dakar and Cotonou–Porto Novo exported trained civil servants abroad in such numbers that their often involuntary repatriation after independence created serious difficulties for their home countries. In particular, Benin, called Dahomey until 1975, sent hundreds of trained civil servants to its neighbors, and it was often said only half in jest that the only truly valuable export the country had ever had was intellectuals. While the trained Dahomean and Senegalese were abroad, they helped spread political ideas and a political activism no less intense than that practiced by their French counterparts. The Dahomean civil servants' presence in Abidjan in 1958 precipitated Ivoirian labor unrest and some violence.[8] When these intellectuals came home, those who could find jobs swelled the ranks of an already oversized bureaucracy, and those who could not find work joined the ranks of an unhappy, intellectual, unemployed claimant class who in Dahomey, often in league with their employed colleagues, put insistent pressure on successive governments, helping to bring down more than one of them (e.g., that of Hubert Maga in 1963, the rotating presidency in 1965, that of Emile Derlin Zinsou in 1969, and that of Justin Ahomadegbe in 1972).[9]

Rural Areas

Important as the larger towns are to the political life of the francophone countries and, as John D. Hargreaves notes, despite the extraordinary social and political changes fostered by urbanization,

> These changes do not produce any sharp and sudden cleavages between urban and rural society. Migration is a continuing and two-way process; the new groupings in towns are superimposed upon families, households, and "tribal" associations which maintain close links with traditional ways of life and particular villages and families. Along these channels new ideas and expectations are disseminated into the countryside. The towns thereby influence the vastly greater section of the population which, though affected with varying intensity by commercial development and government policy, remains essentially rural in domicile and outlook.[10]

Indeed, despite the extraordinary concentration of political, economic, and social influence represented by West Africa's urban cultures, the majority of its people are still rural in residence, economic activity, and, above all, social and political outlook. It is the village, with its networks of intense kinship and ethnic relations, as well as its pervasive—and compelling—residues of traditional authority structures, that remains central to the lives of most people in francophone Africa. The political implications of this fact are well stated by W. Arthur Lewis, who argued that the bulk of the population are farmers living on the land, with only peripheral political interest: "Insofar as they expect anything from politicians, it is what constituents expect everywhere from their representatives—jobs, testimonials, contracts, financial help, advice in the courts, and so on. Party labels and programmes mean nothing to them."[11] Consequently, unless it can somehow maintain effective organization down to the village level, the local or, more likely, the national political party makes its presence felt only on the infrequent occasions of elections, visits of ministers or other dignitaries, or national holidays, when dances, displays, demonstrations, and speechmaking provide diversion from the ordinary course of village life.

From 1970 to 1990, only the political parties in Guinea, Mali, and Cameroon made any serious effort to keep in touch with the rural rank and file. Then, at least from 1990 to 1998, such contacts accelerated in countries affected by the wave of redemocratization (see Chapter 8). Typically the political link between the village and the national center is provided by the locally elected deputy, the prefect or subprefect, the tax collector or agricultural agent, the *notable,* or the businessman with interests in the capital. Their interventions tend to be sporadic, and seldom are these individuals as important for the daily life of the rural community as the local chief, the clan or family heads, and the leaders of traditional and modern associations and societies. This does not mean that the national government is unimportant to rural Africans in the fourteen states; the state, after all, is usually the primary source of money for local improvements and public amenities. Nevertheless, the national government's influence is rarely continuous, and it is seldom strong enough to overcome the dominant tendency for political and social loyalties to focus on the family, the clan, the village, or the ethnic group.

If national integration, an ostensible goal of all francophone African governments, is to mean anything, it will require subordinating, if not supplanting, precisely these parochial political loyalties, which still prevail despite all efforts to supersede them. And if Hargreaves is correct, then, contrary to expectations, even the attractions of towns and cities have not undermined parochial loyalties very much. Paradoxically, even though population growth in the major cities and towns has been exponential, increases in the number of *permanent* urban residents have been barely noticeable. The lure of the town is primarily an economic one; people move in and out with fluctuations of economic opportunity—or perceptions of such opportunity—and the village most often remains the emotional and social focus of the rural migrant's identifications.

In broad terms, francophone Africa's rural populations may be divided into two groups according to their primary economic modes: the nomadic and seminomadic herders of the desert and desert fringe, and the sedentary agricultural and hunting peoples spread throughout the remaining territories. In most of Mauritania and in the northern parts of Mali, Niger, Cameroon, and Chad for much of the latter half of the twentieth century, nomadic and seminomadic communities, such as those of Tuareg, Berber, and Arab people, moved with their herds in constant quest of water and pasturage. Others lived in isolated groups eking out a meager existence around a few oases. During the last two decades of the twentieth century, the town dwellers and sedentary farmers of both Mali and Niger have come into conflict with their desert populations, usually to the detriment of the latter.

The dominant economic activity of the savannah peoples—the Fulani, the Hausa, and so on—is pastoralism, but they herd cattle rather than camels, and in the desert fringe more or less permanent settlements, which are often the center of a complementary but limited subsistence agriculture, tend to be the rule rather than the exception. Many of these settlements were created in the wake of earlier imperial or religious conquests. In northern Cameroon, for example, Ngaoundéré, Garoua, Maroua, and Yagoua became important as outposts of 'Uthman dan Fodio's early-nineteenth-century empire, the capital of which was Sokoto; similarly, Ouagadougou, Timbuktu, Djenne, and Zinder were all once important military-political centers of earlier western Sudanic conquest states.[12]

It is in these desert, semidesert, and savannah areas that some of the most conspicuous survivals of precolonial authority systems can be found. So strong are some of these systems that central governments either move to destroy them and face unknown consequences, or make it possible for them to cooperate profitably with the national center. In Cameroon, for example, the political strength of the northern traditional magnates is attested by the continued presence of several emirs and *lamibé* (plural of *lamido,* the term for a northern Cameroon Fulani chief) in the national legislature. In 1969 the government of Chad's president N'Garta (François) Tombalbaye, facing mounting rebellion by desert tribes, found it expedient to reassert the positions and prerogatives of the "three great sultans," of Ouaddai, Kanem, and Baguirmi.[13] While these northern nomadic, pastoral, and semiagricultural peoples are important, they represent less than a quarter of the fourteen states' total population; the majority is constituted by the settled peoples of the coastal, forest, and plateau areas. (Few hunting and gathering peoples still survive in the fourteen states; their population probably does not exceed fifteen to twenty thousand.[14])

The majority is sedentary, agricultural, and largely village oriented, and its basic rural-agricultural orientation has even greater significance for the states' economies than it has for their modern political systems. To begin with, agriculture is the primary occupation of most of the people of Senegal, Côte d'Ivoire, Benin, Burkina Faso, Togo, Cameroon, the CAR, Congo-Brazzaville, and Gabon. Moreover, that agriculture is overwhelmingly either of the subsistence variety or oriented to local markets for internal consumption. Even the most successful export-agricultural economies of the fourteen states—those of Senegal, Côte d'Ivoire, and Cameroon—

devote on average a mere 5 percent of cultivated land to the growing of export crops.

According to the annual reports of the Franc Zone secretariat for the years 1985–1996 and of the World Bank's Development Data Group for 2000, on average approximately 72 percent of the economically active people of the fourteen states have been engaged in essentially rural pursuits: forestry, pastoralism, and agriculture both for subsistence and export. The lowest percentage, at 50 percent, is that of Congo-Brazzaville, where the oil-export sector dominates; the highest, at 90 percent, is that of Burkina Faso, whose economy rests precariously on subsistence agriculture and the remittances of its labor émigrés.

Geography

With the exception of Togo and Benin, which are coastal but remain relatively poor, the wealthiest and most economically advanced states of the fourteen are those with coastlines. It was along the coast that the first French colonies were created; and like technology and infrastructure, economic and sometimes political development penetrated the hinterland at a slow pace. Six of the nine coastal francophone states—Senegal, Congo-Brazzaville, Côte d'Ivoire, Guinea, Cameroon, and Gabon—have for some time consistently ranked relatively high among African states on a number of economic indices; in each case, a combination of exploitable resources; the labor power of skilled and unskilled workers, some of them engaged in migrant labor; and supportive infrastructure are utilized to stimulate national economic growth.

Mauritania, a poor country that still depends on agriculture and livestock, and whose primary export was once a very limited amount of peanuts, capitalized on its coastal position to exploit a rich deposit of iron ore at Zouerate near Fort Gouraud, along the north-south border with Western Sahara. Iron ore now amounts in value to about 40 percent of its total exports, down from 50 percent before 1990. The decline in world demand for this ore eventually led to cutbacks in production during the 1990s. Similarly, it is fair to assume that a coastal position is what made it economically feasible for Guinea to exploit the Fria bauxite deposits and to attract foreign capital for the Boke mining project. Today, some 85 percent of Guinea's exports are accounted for by the mining sector.

Just as coastal position does not guarantee economic or political preeminence, an inland position does not preclude significant economic development or political importance. The Central African Republic, landlocked and economically underdeveloped in relation to its neighbors Congo-Brazzaville and Cameroon, has been able to use its diamond production to good economic effect; some 54 percent of its export earnings come from it.

And Burkina Faso, as difficult to reach as the CAR, became for a time (1983–1987) very influential in inter-African affairs because of the dynamism of its young military leader, Captain Thomas Sankara, who will be discussed later. Nevertheless, the physical isolation of Mali, Burkina Faso, Niger, Chad, and the CAR, accentuated by the tenuousness of road and railway links with the coast, has posed serious problems for the economies of all these countries. The very high cost of goods, services, and transport, a consequence of physical distance and poor communications with the coast, has tended to discourage development that might be considered feasible for the coastal countries.

A bag of cement, for example, costs at least three to four times as much in Ndjamena as it does at the point of disembarkation, Pointe-Noire. Given optimal transport, dry weather, and no delays, to reach Ndjamena the bag first travels 315 miles by rail to Brazzaville, then 685 miles by boat up the Congo and Oubangui Rivers to Bangui, and then about 700 miles by truck over bad roads to Ndjamena, a total distance of 1,700 miles. And it takes at least three weeks, at the very best, to accomplish the trip by road. The use of air freight is economically feasible only if the goods carried are themselves of high value or if their shipment is subsidized, as in an attempt during the 1970s to fly dressed beef from Ndjamena to Douala, Brazzaville, and other points south. The venture initially proved profitable, but was abandoned after five years because the supply of cattle proved insecure. Hence, given the high cost of importing plumbing and electrical equipment, officials may think twice about constructing a public building in Ndjamena, or they may consider using local materials if these are available.

Economic indicators could greatly improve, at least for Chad, when the expected revenues from its Doba oil field begin to come in. The oil field was discovered in southern Chad some twenty-five years ago, and the thousand-kilometer-long (621-mile-long) oil pipeline running from Doba to Kribi (on the Cameroon coast) came on line in October 2003. The pipeline benefited from a $3.7 billion World Bank loan (the Bank's largest-ever investment in sub-Saharan Africa), and the main developers of the oil field (Exxon-Mobil, Malaysia's Petronas, and Chevron-Texaco) have promised the governments of both Chad and Cameroon considerable revenue (up to $2 billion and $500 million, respectively) during the 25-year production period. The two governments signed an agreement with the Bank and the developers stipulating that the bulk of the revenues (oil and pipeline for Chad, pipeline for Cameroon) would go toward improving the lives of the countries' citizens. It remains to be seen if the two governments, both of which already rank high on any list of the world's most corrupt regimes, will in fact honor their promises, or if Chad will become a smaller version of Nigeria, where great oil wealth has led to economic, social, and political disaster. Niger, also an inland state, is the world's third largest producer of uranium ore (over 3 million tons in 2002); fluctuations in the international market for uranium have kept returns to Niger at one-third what they were prior to a 1980s slump. Niger's per capita income in 2002 was only $820.

The concentration of wealth along the coast has had measurable economic and political repercussions not only for the inland, landlocked states, but also for the coastal states with sizable hinterlands. For example, a development gap of embarrassing proportions exists between the southern parts of Cameroon and the Sahelian hinterland, generating growing discontent among northern populations,[15] who have long tended to see themselves as the poor cousins of their wealthier southern counterparts. The Cameroonian government has tried with some success to bridge the gap by pushing the Transcameroon Railway to the north and by improving the north-south road links, but the problem continues to bedevil the government, much as similar coast-hinterland gaps have posed difficulties for Senegal, Guinea, Côte d'Ivoire, Benin, Togo, and Congo-Brazzaville.

These dichotomies between the coast and the hinterland, between the coastal state and the landlocked state, highlight the very real differences in climate, rainfall, soils, and vegetation between the primary agricultural and industrial areas along the coast and the savannah-Sahelian areas inland. These differences contribute to the concentration of agricultural and other production along the coast and the related differentials of income and wealth. And with the concentration of wealth, urban centers, ports, and modern infrastructure has also come the concentration of political power.

The rivers of francophone Africa also have important implications for the politics and economics of the fourteen states, as does Lake Chad, which is bounded by Niger, Cameroon, Chad, and Nigeria. The Senegal River rises in the rugged hills of the Fouta Djallon, extends into Mali and Guinea, then forms the boundary between Senegal and Mauritania. Questions of riparian rights, especially those connected with Malian plans for a dam on one of the upper branches and Senegalese plans for dredging the lower reaches of the river to permit access for vessels with deeper draught, caused the reactivation of the old Senegal River Commission and the creation in 1968 of the Organization of Riverain States of the Senegal River (OERS: Organisation des Etats Riverains du Senegal). In a very real sense, new uses for the Senegal River created the possibility of interstate cooperation and the reactivation of political links corroded by older rivalries and hostilities connected with the former Mali Federation and with the Guinean and Malian radicalism of the 1960s and 1970s.

The Niger, which rises in Guinea and then flows through Mali and Niger before entering Nigeria, is navigable outside of Nigeria in some three sections for a total of two thousand kilometers (1,243 miles). A great deal of traffic is carried by the river, up to as many as one million tons of merchandise per annum. Problems connected with riparian rights, as well as various proposals for improvement of the river, also stimulated the formation of an interstate group. Members of the Niger River Basin Commission include not only the riparian states of the Niger itself, but also Cameroon and Chad, through which the Benue, the Niger's principal tributary, flows.

The third great river system of paramount importance to its riparian states is the Congo and its tributaries, which involve Congo-Brazzaville; Cameroon, where the tributary Sangha rises; and the Central African Republic, as well as the Democratic Republic of Congo, or former Zaire, for whom the Congo River is the veritable lifeline. At one time the Belgians and the French thought of the Congo basin as one immense navigable river system until their enthusiasm was dampened somewhat by the discovery that rapids, falls, and whitewater areas block navigation at crucial points. It is impossible, for example, to travel by boat from the mouth of the Congo to Brazzaville. However, one long navigable stretch on the Congo and the Oubangui, one thousand kilometers (621 miles) from Brazzaville to just below Bangui, has been the principal link between Congo-Brazzaville and the Central African Republic, permitting the export of these two countries' products, as well as those of Chad. Chad's products travel by road to Bangui, and goods transported along the river to Brazzaville are then carried via the Ocean-Congo Railway from Brazzaville to Pointe-Noire. Since 1997, however, travel on this segment of the river has proven perilous, given the persistent civil war in the Democratic Republic of Congo and the presence of competing armies, militias, and bandits on and around the river.

Before an extensive FAO/UNESCO (Food and Agriculture Organization/United Nations Educational, Scientific, and Cultural Organization) study was completed in 1979, little was known of the development potential of Lake Chad. Since then, plans and projects have been going forward that are intended to benefit the four states bordering the lake: Nigeria, Niger, Chad, and Cameroon. In 1964 these four states formed the Chad Basin Commission to support the development of cattle, fish, agricultural, and water resources; to work toward tsetse fly eradication; and to coordinate water, rail, and road systems in the vicinity of the lake. The efforts of the commission notwithstanding, the future of the lake, once one of the world's largest inland bodies of water, looks very bleak. NASA satellite observations have confirmed that over the thirty-nine years from 1963 to 2001 the lake shrank to one-twentieth of its former size, and given increased demands on the remaining water, plus recurrent drought conditions, it may not have long to live. While it remains, however, it has the potential of causing political trouble for its neighbors.

Lake Chad and the Congo, Senegal, and Niger Rivers have all been important for political reasons in the past. They barred passage to some and offered the means whereby migratory and conquering peoples could spread, and their periodic inundations provided the basis for agriculture and sedentary political systems. Today, however, they are no longer the primary pathways for conquest or migration. Instead, they are used for navigation, trade, hydroelectric power, and irrigation. Despite occasional political setbacks, the rivers and the lake have made possible the growth of multinational cooperative ventures and associations, and one of the most important consequences of such cooperation has been the creation, tightening, and reassertion of political and economic links among the fourteen states.

Notes

1. See, notably, Greenberg, *Studies in African Linguistic Classification.*
2. One history of Islam in West Africa to the end of the sixteenth century is Cuoq, *Histoire d'islamisation.* For an examination of Islam in the West African sociopolitical context, see Sanneh, *The Crown and the Turban: Muslims and West African Pluralism.* Discussions of Islam in francophone Africa include, notably, Gouilly, *L'Islam dans l'Afrique occidentale française;* Marty, *Études sur l'Islam;* and Marty's studies of Islam in Côte d'Ivoire (*Études sur l'Islam en Côte d'Ivoire,* 1922) and Dahomey (1926). A recent study of Sufi orders in Senegal is worth consulting: Villalón, *Islamic Society and State Power in Senegal: Disciples and Citizens in Fatick,* as are two useful collections, Lewis., ed., *Islam in Tropical Africa,* and Kritzeck and Lewis, eds., *Islam in Africa.* In the latter collection, the articles by Vincent Monteil, Pierre Alexandre, John A. Ballard, Nehemiah Levtzion, and Alfred G. Gerteiny bear directly on French-speaking Africa. Overall the most useful work on the history of Islam in Africa, designed as both a textbook and reference book, is the 2000 volume *The History of Islam in Africa,* edited by Levtzion and Pouwels, in which eight full sections are devoted to West Africa and the Sudan. A good summary discussion of African Islam is Quinn and Quinn, *Pride, Faith, and Fear: Islam in Sub-Saharan Africa,* and an accessible summary discussion of religion on the continent is Ambrose Moyo's chapter, "Religion in Africa," in Gordon and Gordon, *Understanding Contemporary Africa,* 3rd ed..
3. The French Catholic–oriented party, the Mouvement Républicaine Populaire (MRP) had *filiales* (branches) throughout French West and Equatorial Africa, and during the 1946–1950 period the Démocrates Camerounais party began as an attempt to mobilize the Catholic faithful in the Yaoundé area. For an overview of this process in Cameroon, see Ngongo, *Histoire des forces religieuses au Cameroun: De la Première Guerre mondiale à l'Indépendance (1916–1955).* The continental picture is well drawn in Glélé, *Religion, culture, et politique en Afrique Noire.*
4. Much to the embarrassment of the local hierarchy but to the delight of his followers, Youlou loved champagne, and he took to wearing clerical garb of the brightest of colors. De Lusignan, in *French-Speaking Africa Since Independence,* said of Youlou that he affected "[Christian] Dior cassocks of white piqué" at official receptions and "even wore a pale blue one on the first anniversary of independence in 1961, on August 15—the Feast of the Assumption" (93). I met Youlou in 1965 after he escaped confinement in Brazzaville and spent some time talking with him. Since I'd heard about his sartorial tastes, I took particular notice of his appearance and was not disappointed. His secretary told me that it was especially for our meeting that he had put on a designer soutane in off-green silk, a huge pectoral cross, and stylish, shiny shoes. I was impressed but, other than offering a word of admira-

tion for the cross, refrained from comment. During an earlier conversation on a flight from Ndjamena, he reiterated his old charges that he'd been the victim of an unjustified, "lamentable" (Youlou's word) double conspiracy by the Frenchmen who (he said) ran the Congolese Church and by the Chinese, whom he blamed for his overthrow. He later amplified these charges in his 1969 book, *J'accuse la Chine.*

5. For additional discussion of the growth of trade unions in French-speaking Africa, see Berg and Butler, "Trade Unions," 340–381; Martens, *Trade Unionism in French-Speaking West Africa During the Colonial Period;* and Person, "Les syndicats en Afrique Noire," 22–46. A useful recent collection that includes commentary on francophone Africa is Kester and Sidibé, *Trade Unions and Sustainable Democracy in Africa.* One of the reasons for the paucity of studies on trade unions in francophone Africa after 1965 is that the unions were among the first set of autonomous associations to be absorbed by the single-party state, whether the state was run by civilians or the military. The unions then became yet another organizational adjunct of the single party, alongside such groups as formations for women, students, lawyers, and so on. Thereafter, even if the labor unions were permitted some degree of autonomy, they were almost invariably reduced in influence, scope, and operational effectiveness.

6. The literature on Christianity in Africa is voluminous. For francophone Africa before 1960, useful summaries are found in Thompson and Adloff's two volumes, *French West Africa* and *The Emerging States of French Equatorial Africa,* published in 1958 and 1960, respectively. Also recommended is Taylor, *Christianity and Politics in Africa,* and Sanneh's two volumes, *Christianity in West Africa: The Religious Impact* and *The Crown and the Turban.* The better monographic literature on our fourteen states usually contains sections on religion or religious politics. Among the more interesting and active nexuses of Christian confessional politics is that among Cameroon, Burkina Faso, Benin, Côte d'Ivoire, and Senegal.

7. The data cited in these paragraphs derive principally from Gendreau, "Les populations des pays d'Afrique Noire d'expression française et de Madagascar," 195–208; and Brass, "The Demography of French-Speaking Territories," 342–439.

8. See Zolberg, *One-Party Government in the Ivory Coast,* 245–247, and Carter, *Independence for Africa,* 106–117, for accounts of the expulsion of Dahomean and other "strangers" from Abidjan in the fall of 1958. Unrest and acts of violence on a lesser scale again took place against "foreigners" in Abidjan in November 1969. Thereafter, Côte d'Ivoire saw numerous reprises of antiforeigner violence, which became particularly virulent, even bordering on ethnic cleansing, after the death of Houphouët-Boigny in 1993, when his successors, Konan Bedié, Robert Gueï, and Laurent Gbagbo, stirred up xenophobic anger against northern Muslims, particularly Burkinabé.

9. In 1965 there were over eighteen thousand civil servants in Dahomey, making up 47 percent of all Dahomean wage earners, and annually consuming almost 65 percent of the government's operating budget. In addition, that year there were some three thousand civil servants on the lists of the unemployed.

10. Hargreaves, *West Africa: The Former French States,* 124.

11. Lewis, *Politics in West Africa,* 22.

12. See Trimingham, *A History of Islam in West Africa,* and Hiskett, *The Development of Islam in West Africa.*

13. Tombalbaye's decree was reported in *Le Monde,* September 1, 1969.

14. The figure is my own estimate; it includes Pygmies and various Oubanguian/Central African tribes. For details, see Balandier, *Sociologie actuelle de l'Afrique Noire,* and Murdock, *Africa: Its Peoples and Their Culture History.*

15. See Hugon, *Analyse du sous-développement en Afrique Noire.*

2

The Colonial Context

The history of France's penetration of and influence in Africa is so large a subject that even the official government historians of French colonialism have done little more than scratch the surface. The analytical problems are daunting: reasonable examination of the subject entails not only disentangling the main lines of the story from the morass of official French mythology, but also relating that story to the history of European, Asian, Arab, and U.S. activities on the continent. Michael Crowder has made an excellent start for the West African region,[1] but the French part of the story has yet to be told fully in its proper contexts.

This is not to say that the literature on French colonialism is sparse; far from it. There exists an impressive array of encyclopedias, books, monographs, studies, and so on by French, British, U.S., and other scholars, officials, explorers, missionaries, and travelers.[2] Official histories abound: shelves of books dealing with *"l'oeuvre français," "la mission française,"* and *"la colonisation française,"* reveal a continuing preoccupation with the apologetics of colonialism in its French variants. Until the beginning of the twentieth century, the French produced most of the studies of their own colonies. During the second half of the twentieth century, however, in the spirit of postwar anticolonialism or simply in the interest of scholarship, non-French academics have joined French scholars and publicists in beginning to challenge the established and largely self-congratulatory wisdom of French colonial historiography.[3] The facts of French colonialism in Africa, then, must be seen without blinders and in context.

Enter the French

Until the middle of the nineteenth century, French activities in west and central Africa were almost exclusively coastal in nature, as were those of the other colonial powers. The French roamed freely up and down the coast, establishing trading posts and "factories" (agencies), and competing with Portuguese, English, Dutch, Danish, Brandenburger, Hamburger, Swedish, Spanish, and later (during the eighteenth and nineteenth centuries), U.S. mercantile interests. From the latter part of the fifteenth to the middle of the nineteenth century the great maritime nations of Europe practiced what could be styled beachhead colonialism. They operated from small trading bases, floating hulks, minor forts, and petty settlements, and brought out gold, ivory, gum arabic, spices, palm oil, and, most important, the human treasure of the slave trade, which after 1492 fed the plantation economies of the New World for some three hundred years.

The first French traders to operate along the African coast came from Dieppe, and their successors from other French ports such as Rouen and Bordeaux. They probably began to sail south to Cape Verde and beyond during the fifteenth century. Reluctant to challenge the Portuguese, who were already established as the major naval power in the area, they touched land along the Senegalese coast at the mouth of the Gambia River and along the Dahomean beaches, and some may even have gone as far south as the estuary of the Congo.

It was not until the seventeenth century, on the initiatives of royal ministers Cardinal de Richelieu (1585–1642) and later Jean-Baptiste Colbert (1661–1683), that the French state began granting trading charters in specified areas as part of the attempt to extend France's power and wealth. The first venture was private in nature. In 1626 the Compagnie Normande de Sénégambie was founded in Rouen, and following an unsuccessful attempt in 1638 to establish a trading base near the mouth of the Senegal River, the company relocated within the sandbar at the river's estuary in 1659, where it founded the fort and trading post of Saint-Louis on the island of N'Dar. Saint-Louis de Sénégal, together with the small island of Gorée, captured from the Dutch in 1677, became the nexus of growing French activity along the coast. During the nineteenth century the settlement was the base from which the French expanded throughout West Africa, but until that time the Senegalese outpost was no more than a beachhead—strategically important and commercially profitable, to be sure, but a beachhead nonetheless.

In 1687, the French established a small post at Assinie, on the Ivory Coast, putting ashore an advance party of a half-dozen traders and a priest. The Assinie colony lasted until 1705, when it was abandoned after considerable attrition due to disease and Dutch attacks. The fate of the Assinie post illustrates neatly the vicissitudes encountered by all the European traders operating along the West African coast: climate, disease, and occasional violence by African and European neighbors often made settlement and trade a difficult, unpredictable, and perilous affair.[4] Nevertheless, the French persisted, and during the eighteenth century they gradually established a spotty presence along the coast, setting up trading posts at Grand Bassam, Whydah (Ouidah), and Porto Novo on the Ivory and Dahomean coasts. French traders visited the delta of the Niger, the mouth of the Sanaga at Douala, and the Congo estuary, as well as several islands, bays, and other river mouths at which small trading communities operated under constantly changing European flags. The failure of French commercial and political ventures along the East African coast, centered about Kilwa and Zanzibar during the eighteenth century, in part explains the attention the French concentrated on Senegal.[5] The Senegalese base ultimately proved most successful, and as a result it became the launching pad for France's West African activities.

Whatever the fortunes of the French commercial ventures along the Guinea coast, Senegal remained the key to France's colonial future in West Africa.[6] Initially, French activity in the area varied considerably: exploration; some privateering, particularly against the Portuguese; trade in gum arabic, ivory, gold, and spices, and the occasional quick profit in the growing slave trade. Saint-Louis gave the French access to the gum arabic of the Mauritanian forests even though the principal intermediaries in the trade, the Trarza Maurs, often preferred to deal with the Dutch along the coast to the north rather than with the French at Saint-Louis. On the coast south of Cape Verde, it was Gorée that opened Rufisque, Dakar, and Joãl to French traders. In 1679, Germain Ducasse, a special envoy from the King of France, signed treaties with the Serer and with the Damal of Cayor, which brought the Senegalese coast from Cape Verde to the Gambia River, as well as territory six leagues into the interior, into the French sphere of influence.

By the end of the seventeenth century, French interests officially turned to converting the Senegalese ports into entrepôts for the export of slaves to France's burgeoning sugar plantations in the West Indies. To this end, as well as to secure additional trading advantages in gum, gold, and spices, Colbert and his successors granted charters to a series of privileged companies. For various reasons—including the fact that the West Indian planters preferred Guinea coast slaves to those from Senegal—almost all the companies did poorly along the Senegal coast, and most went bankrupt, then shifted their operations to the Guinea and Dahomean coasts or began dealing in other commodities. Not even the Compagnie de Sénégal, one of the best-organized and best-financed of these enterprises, survived the financial hazards of the Senegalese trade.[7]

As the difficulties of the slave trade along the Senegal coast forced French slavers south and east into uneasy competition with slavers of other countries, the Senegalese posts were put onto a different economic footing and given a new identity and purpose. According to John Hargreaves: "Still, French companies did profit from the gum trade; also in much lesser degrees from dealing in gold, ivory, and hides, as well as from their disappointingly modest business in slaves. This relative diversity, as well as the possibility of limited penetration inland, gave their Senegalese establishments a distinctive character."[8] Early attempts at penetration of the Senegalese interior met with little success. André Brue, twice governor of the concession, traveled up the Senegal as far as the mouth of the Falémé River, then tried to interest the coastal traders in the opportunities that, he claimed, lay in the hinterland. They remained largely unconvinced, preferring their relatively secure coastal trade to the dangers of the hinterland and, for that matter, to the agricultural schemes proposed for the area.

Nonetheless, during the eighteenth century the Senegalese towns of Saint-Louis and Gorée grew both in size and in an importance that was as much due to the culturally and biologically Afro-European character of the population as to the trade conducted there. Africans were integrated into the two settlements in four principal ways: through employment by Europeans, through moving from the status of salaried employee to that of self-employed trader, through interracial marriage and concubinage, and through moving from Portuguese to French areas of influence. Already during the eighteenth century, Senegal had become the laboratory of an assimilation that did not become official policy until the latter part of the next century. This "protoassimilation" occurred in the context of, among other things, the introduction of Catholicism (though only a minority of Senegalese subjects converted), and the limited introduction of European governmental institutions, including some hybrid judicial arrangements. Probably most important, assimilation meant that "Senegalese consciously accepted values and standards derived from their European rulers, and in return claimed the rights which they believed such acceptance should bring."[9]

Innovative as the Senegalese experiment may have been, by the latter part of the eighteenth century official French policy shifted toward the more immediately lucrative trade on the Guinea coast. Between 1763 and 1779, as partial consequence of French wars in Europe, the British annexed Senegal, creating the Senegambian crown colony. The French monarchy regained Senegal in 1779, only to lose it again to the British in 1809 as a result of the Napoleonic wars. The territory was ultimately returned to France in 1814 following the settlement of the Treaty of Paris.

For the next forty years France concentrated on establishing its presence along the coasts south and east of Senegal. In 1828, a French post was established in the Casamance, below the mouth of the Gambia River. In 1842 Admiral Bouët-Willaumez erected a permanent settlement on the Ivory Coast over the ruins of the old Assinie mission. Six years later the French navy installed a naval antislavery station near the site of present-day Libreville, and for several decades France maintained trading and missionary posts there and at the mouth of the Ogooué River. Then, in 1851,

France signed a treaty of peace with the Abomeyan king, Ghezo, which opened the way for its expansion beyond the precincts of its old base at Whydah. By mid-century France had established itself all along the coast from Saint-Louis to the Ogooué River. The beachhead phase of colonialism was drawing to a close, and the stage was set for the next phase: penetration inland and the celebrated scramble for colonies.

The character of French interests in sub-Saharan Africa had changed, partly as a result of developments in France and Europe, and partly as a consequence of changes within the beachheads and in West Africa generally. Most important, Europeans' attitudes about the slave trade had shifted: they had once accepted the trade as necessary to the development of Europe's New World colonies, but now they had come to regard it as heinous and immoral. Britain, chastened by the loss of her U.S. (slaveholding) colonies, emboldened by her success over Napoleonic France, and pushed by abolitionist interests, made the trade illegal for its citizens in 1808. In 1815 the restored French monarchy was persuaded by British and European abolitionist groups to forbid its subjects to engage in the trade (an earlier, unsuccessful effort to abolish the trade had been made by the Convention of 1794). For the next fifty years the British engaged in a sustained effort to persuade both Europeans and Africans to stop the trade, and various British then multinational naval squadrons patrolled West African waters to intercept slavers and discourage the trade.[10]

The effort was not altogether successful because the patrols were too few and too spread out to be very effective, but the net effect of the anti-slavery campaign was a change in the character of West African commerce. From the primary emphasis on human export, it shifted gradually, first to spices, precious metals, ivory, and other natural resources, and then to products of agriculture such as peanuts and palm oil. The introduction of peanut cultivation in Senegal completely transformed the basis of that colony's economy; by 1842 Gorée was exporting 853 tons of peanuts annually, and by 1850 Senegal was producing as many as five thousand tons each year.[11]

The beachhead colonies were changing in other ways as well, and none more than those on the Senegal coast. The French Revolution of 1789 and its immediate aftermath had provoked a brief period of radical reform in Senegal, but that experiment had to be abandoned during the British interregnum. By 1840 the habitants of the colony had adopted French as the language of instruction in the schools, had created a *conseil général* in Saint-Louis, and had built up a set of social and political institutions that linked the fortunes of the French and their mixed-race subjects. The French Revolution of 1848, which ushered in the short-lived Second Republic, also had an effect on Senegal: by popular vote nearly five thousand electors in the colony returned a mulatto, Durand Valentin, to the French National

Assembly. The Second Empire later put an end to the attempt at overseas representation, the memory of which nevertheless remained a sign of the increasing political and social sophistication of the Senegalese communities.[12]

In the final analysis, however, it was the shift in the basis of trade that changed the character of French enclaves along the West African coast. Trade in slaves, precious metals, ivory, gum, and oil did not require more than a beachhead entrepôt and a few agents to do the bargaining. But trade in peanuts, palm oil, cotton, and indigo required that settlers be willing to create plantations and to retain a measure of permanence that could accommodate the seasonal and labor-intensive character of such crops. The beachheads were becoming bases and, in Senegal, settler colonies.

The Scramble and Territorial Conquest

What accounts for the extraordinary expansion of the French from their coastal beachheads, into the hinterlands of the western Sudan and to their acquisition, within about fifty years, of a territorial empire covering four-fifths of West Africa? To be sure, the coastal areas showed moderate economic promise, but they were hardly healthy enough for settlers until the beginning of the twentieth century, when the introduction of quinine made it possible for Europeans to survive malaria. The vast hinterlands were even less hospitable: they tended to be dry and, more important, populated by people who regarded Western incursions with general suspicion and often violent hostility. The standard arguments that attribute the colonial scramble to an economic determinism that required capital outlets abroad and colonial markets for European goods are attractive at first glance, but hardly persuasive in light of the facts.[13]

It is true that the desire for profit drove much of the colonial activity and that governments in Europe and the United States gave official encouragement first in the form of free trade policies and later in the form of protectionist policies that led to considerable expansion of European and U.S. exports between 1875 and 1914. Yet, concludes Phillip Neres, "only a small percentage of this increase can be accounted for by exports to the newly acquired colonies in Africa, whose populations were too poor to be able to absorb new products on any appreciable scale."[14] Furthermore, the countries of Europe that produced great surpluses of capital preferred to invest in each other or in Russia and the United States, where substantial economic growth gave promise of much greater returns than could be had in Africa, where social and economic infrastructure were insufficient to attract risk capital.[15]

The coastal traders, including those operating on the Dahomey coast, where profits were largest, were specifically traders, not capitalists. "The fundamental trait of this commerce," notes Henri Brunschwig, "is, in effect, that these traders did not invest in Africa." Even the large concessionary companies operating in the French Congo operated with relatively limited capital; they sought to extract as much profit as possible with minimal investment. Again, Brunschwig put his finger on the key distinction: Most of these societies "did badly and quickly disappeared," but even "those that succeeded did not display a capitalist spirit in the modern sense of the term."[16]

Karl Kautsky, the eminent Austrian socialist, first suggested in 1915 that the French and English roles in the scramble resulted from competition between the two countries for control of Egypt and the lower Nile valley, that is, the strategic European passage to the East. The British historians Ronald Robinson and John Gallagher later developed the connection further, on the basis of much more evidence than was available to Kautsky.[17] According to this argument, the famous Fashoda Incident, when British and French soldiers raced to the town of Fashoda on the upper Nile, became emblematic of British-French imperial competition. But the argument is not convincing. In rebutting the Egyptocentric theory of imperialism, Jean Stengers, a Belgian historian, has pointed out that neither the governments nor the colonial interests of either country ever saw their sub-Saharan African activities in that light.[18] Indeed, if Egypt and the Nile were the prize, there were more direct ways to Cairo, Alexandria, and the Isthmus of Suez than via Dakar or the settlements at the mouth of the Ogooué.

The more reasonable explanations are at once more complex and more direct. To begin with, the great rush for territory did not get under way until 1875. Prior to the last three decades of the nineteenth century the extension of French authority along the West African coast tended to follow the progress of French trade and, more important, could be measured by the extent to which influential French traders persuaded their government to guarantee peaceful conditions for their enterprises. One noteworthy example is that of Victor Régis and his brother Louis, who operated along the West African coast from 1833 to the mid-1870s. Victor Régis appears to have been principally responsible in 1843 for the hoisting of the French flag on the Ivory Coast, where it remained until 1856. Representing himself to the Dahomeans as an official agent of France, he established a factory (trading post) at Whydah in about 1841. In 1862 he secured consular status for his agents in Whydah, and in 1863 France established a protectorate at Porto Novo with, according to Hargreaves, "the sole purpose of securing for Régis substantial imports of spirits and entry into Yorubaland free of the heavy duties levied at Lagos."[19] Of course, a good many traders followed their own commerce and not the flag, preferring to remain relatively unconcerned about which state controlled a trading post so long as they were unmolested and were treated fairly in their competition with traders of other countries and in their dealings with the local African intermediaries.

The beachheads grew slowly in number and size over the years; by 1870 established beachheads protected by the French flag numbered only about fifteen: Saint-Louis, Gorée, Rufisque, Dakar, Casamance, Assinie, Whydah, Grand Bassam, Porto Novo, and a few ephemeral posts along the Ivory Coast, the Bight of Biafra, and the lower Congo. The most significant of these establishments was, of course, Senegal, and it is from Senegal that the first tentative penetrations of the interior were launched.

From 1815 on, many French people began to consider empire an essential element of national prestige. However, colonial expansion did not become widely popular in metropolitan France for another thirty years, until Louis Faidherbe, aided by excellent press-agentry, moved to consolidate the inland colony and then push east along the Senegal River and across to the Niger. Faidherbe, who governed Senegal from 1854 to 1861 and again from 1863 to 1865, extended French writ over most of Senegal, even seeking a kind of indirect-rule arrangement with the Muslim states of the Futa Toro and Cayor. He hoped to gradually create an empire in what he deemed the rich hinterlands near the bend of the Niger, by peaceful means if possible, by force if necessary. Faidherbe's efforts were only a precursor of the later push inland during which a handful of French officers commanding units made up almost wholly of African conscripts carved out an empire for France. By 1900 those conquests had made France the second largest colonial power of the day.

The real motives for France's part in the scramble lay in European politics: humiliated by their defeat in the Franco-Prussian War, the French developed a "febrile nationalism"[20] that saw in conquest and victories over their colonial competitors a way to regain national face lost in the disaster of 1871.[21] Young French naval and military officers, often acting beyond the instructions of their superiors, seized what they saw as opportunities for glory as they pushed inland, and in the process they destroyed or reduced to impotence the African states that stood in their way: the Toucouleur empire of El Hajj Omar; the realm of Samori Touré; the kingdom of the Mossi; Rabeh's Chadian empire, and the domains and states of Bornu, Cayor, Ségou, Abomey, Futa Jalon, and Zinder. It was all represented as splendid and heroic, and it enabled unabashed imperialist Jules Ferry, a minister in various French governments, to urge his countryfolk on to even greater colonial heights: "Nowadays it is whole continents which are being annexed; vast areas are being divided up and especially that huge black continent so full of fierce mysteries and vague hopes. . . . Washing our hands of colonial responsibilities . . . amounts to the bankruptcy of our rights and our hopes."[22]

By 1881 the holy city of Timbo in Guinea was occupied and a military command had been created at Kayes, the headquarters for water transport on the upper Senegal. In 1883, after an advance up the Niger Basin, the French occupied Bamako, and eight years later, Ségou, the last stronghold of Samori's empire. Timbuktu fell to the French in 1893, and soon thereafter, in quick succession, the Mossi capital of Ouagadougou, and then Zinder, in what is now the Republic of Niger. To be sure, the French advance was resisted at almost every step by the military forces of the polities encountered on the way. Some of these armies, like those of Samori and Ahmadou (el-Hajj 'Umar Tal's son), even had modern weapons in limited supply. But neither those weapons nor the undoubted bravery of the Africans availed against the French: "French superiority in weapons was such that though Africans had larger forces, they were unable to resist with any success. Furthermore, chiefs almost never joined cause against their common enemy. Indeed, to gain temporary advantage over a traditional enemy, they sometimes allied themselves with the French. But the essential point is that the French imposed their rule on French West Africa largely by force of arms rather than by treaty."23

While French civilians also played an important role in securing footholds for France along the Guinea coast, it was ultimately military conquest that decided the outcome. The strongest of the coastal states, Abomey, was subordinated by a combination of diplomacy and force. In 1874 Tofa, the ruler of Porto Novo and a nominal vassal of Glélé, the Abomeyan king, accepted French support in maintaining his dynastic claims. In 1883 the French proclaimed a protectorate over Porto Novo and occupied the neighboring port of Cotonou. Six years later, Glélé was succeeded by Gbehanzin, who was determined to reassert his control over Tofa and check the French advance north. Over time, Gbehanzin became too much of a threat to the French, so in 1892 a military column headed by Colonel Maurice Dodds finally occupied Abomey, the royal capital. Gbehanzin remained king for two more years at French sufferance, but was finally deposed in 1894.24 Tofa died in 1908, leaving his heir little more than the regalia of office.

Throughout the period of conquest, the French actively competed with other European states, first for control of the beachheads and by 1890 for territorial possession. During the last thirty years of the century, the British secured Gambia, Sierra Leone, Nigeria, and the Gold Coast, and the Germans established protectorates in Togo and Cameroon. Equatorial Africa fell to the French by a combination of belated good fortune, diplomatic maneuver, successful competition with the Belgians, and military conquest. The good fortune came by way of an 1874 decision in which the British cabinet refused a French offer to trade its Gabonese outposts for Gambia.25 The French unwillingly stayed on in Gabon, and this provided the opportunity for Savorgnan de Brazza, a naturalized Frenchman of

Italian birth, to push into the Congo basin and lay the groundwork for France's equatorial domain.

For a time de Brazza and Henry M. Stanley were in active competition in the lower Congo basin, de Brazza exploring for the French along the western bank of the river and Stanley exploring on the eastern side on commission from the Belgian king, Leopold II. The rivalry between France and Belgium in the area was temporarily settled by the Congress of Berlin in 1884, but it was not until 1908, when the Belgian government assumed Leopold's title and made the Congo a Belgian colony, that the boundaries of the area became more or less settled. De Brazza spent two years at home, and when he returned to Africa in 1886, he aimed for Chad. The French government and a French Comité de l'Afrique Française underwrote his efforts with subventions and encouragement, and he launched a number of exploratory expeditions, several of which met with disaster. One such mission, led by Jean-Baptiste Marchand, pushed all the way north and east to Fashoda on the upper Nile in an unsuccessful attempt to prevent the British from gaining control of that area.[26]

The French missions north continued despite all the setbacks. Finally in October 1899 the military mission led by Emile Gentil inflicted an early, though incomplete, defeat upon Rabeh, the Bornouan adventurer who had carved out a Chadian sultanate in the face of the German, French, and British colonial advance. It was not until April 22, 1900, that a 1,500-man force headed by Commandant François-Joseph Amédée Lamy finally chased Rabeh from the field at Koussouri.[27] The battle was a costly one: Lamy and most of his officers were killed, Rabeh himself was killed, and his army of five thousand was decimated. France could now link her West and Equatorial African domains into one great empire, to be complemented later by the fruit of her conquests of the Maghreb, and after 1916 by the addition of the western parts of the former German Togo and Kamerun, which became League of Nations mandated territories.[28] Although pacification of the hinterland territories was not complete until the second decade of the twentieth century, by 1920 France had emerged from the scramble with one of the largest territorial empires ever assembled.

The French Colonial System

In contrast to the possessions of France's colonial competitors, with the exception of Algeria, French colonies were never settler colonies. Charles A. Julien noted that, at the height of French colonial power, on the eve of World War II, "In Indochina there were only 42,000 Frenchmen in a population of 23,000,000; in Equatorial Africa the proportion was 5,000 to 3,423,000. Only in Algeria, because of its proximity to France and the similarity of its climate, were there as many as 988,000 French out of 7,234,684 inhabitants."[29] In 1938 there were 26,000 French people in French West Africa out of 15 million inhabitants. The unwillingness of French people, whom Julien describes as "stay-at-home by nature," to populate their colonies reinforced the strong French bias toward centralized control of the empire. This tendency helped give the French colonial system another of its dominant characteristics: the fortunes of the colonies were more strongly tied than those of other colonial powers to the political situation prevailing in the metropole at any given time. It was for this reason that regime changes, shifts in colonial philosophy, and even debates about colonial ends and means were so clearly reflected in virtually every part of the empire. This helps to explain some of the differences in administration among the various colonies and the frequent contradictions between policy and practice that eventually contributed to the dissolution of the empire.

During the expansion of the seventeenth and eighteenth centuries, encouraged by a monarchy intent on centralizing power and unifying populations, France transplanted its institutions overseas while insisting that its colonies remain assimilated politically to the metropole. The ancien régime, however, saw its dependent native peoples in a different light: they might be converted to Christianity—itself a form of assimilation—but otherwise they were usually regarded in purely instrumental terms according to the extent to which they contributed, or could be made to contribute, to the metropole's economic interests. In such a context, slavery could be accepted, as well as conflicting doctrines favoring the social and political advancement of the native peoples.

After the French Revolution of 1789, France incorporated both the institutional and the moral assimilationist policies of the ancien régime into the Constitution of 1795, but with an important difference: the constitution was to apply to both French citizens and natives with equal force, slavery having been abolished in 1792. Kenneth Robinson has called this the "policy of Identity," the colonial expression of the revolutionary-egalitarian phases of French history.[30] In its African reflections it gave political form to the protoassimilation already underway in Senegal before the Revolution. After 1848 the "policy of identity" was evident in the right of the citizens of the *quatre communes* of Senegal (Dakar, Saint-Louis, Gorée, and Rufisque) to elect a deputy to the French National Assembly, as well as in Senegal's educational system—"predominantly public, free, secular, and conducted in the French language."[31] It was also expressed in local governmental institutions variously adopted throughout Africa.

Napoleon I returned to the ideas of the ancien régime; he reestablished slavery and gave new life to the old mercantilistic impulses. Succeeding regimes of the Restoration (1814–1830) and the July Monarchy (1830–1848) vacillated between policies of harsh subjugation and moderate laissez-faire. However, the more enlightened doctrines of assimilation managed to survive, appearing finally to triumph during the ill-fated Second Republic (1848–1851).

Once French ideas of assimilation had taken hold, they appealed strongly, almost irresistibly, to later generations of French thinkers and politicians.[32] The reasons for this are relatively simple. The Revolution of 1789 proclaimed the Rights of Man to be universal values, and legislation made them part of the package of French citizenship that was conferred on all persons living on French soil, domestic or overseas. Under such circumstances, pride naturally went hand in hand with the assertion that French citizenship, thus endowed with the heritage of freedom, was both a noble and inimitably precious gift. Thus, *assimilation* was always self-referential: it meant assimilation *to* or *into* French civilization, not the other way around; it was France's unique gift, and the candidate for assimilation was expected to receive it with gratitude.

As it turned out, revolutionary pride was just a short step from the ultimate rationale of assimilation, the *mission civilisatrice*—France's "civilizing mission": given the self-evident superiority of French culture, law, administration, and language, assimilation was not only a worthy goal, but a *duty* that accompanied colonial expansion. Thus the leaders of the Second Republic, who saw in their work the moral reincarnation of the victories of 1789, once again abolished slavery, turned all natives into citizens, and provided for parliamentary representation of the colonies. Under the Second Republic the *quatre communes* of Senegal became the proud African example of the vitality and rightness of assimilation, and whatever else may have been wrong with French rule, there is little doubt that the Senegalese of Saint-Louis, Rufisque, Gorée, and Dakar considered themselves favored over all colonized peoples.[33] Assimilation, today condemned as the crassest kind of cultural chauvinism, was once hailed by both colonizers and colonized as an expression of the finest sentiments of the human spirit. It seldom occurred to French colonial policymakers and thinkers that Africans might not wish to be assimilated, and the fact is that most of those subjugated by France did not seriously begin to question the doctrine until after World War II.

With the fall of the Second French Republic and the rise of Napoleon III's Second Empire (1851–1870), the ideological pendulum swung the other way, and the advocates of unfettered domination again won the day. The right of political representation was suppressed, and the state asserted its prerogative to rule the colonies by decree. Authoritarian administration and a separate system of legislation for the colonies, two of the legacies of the Second Empire, remained basic to colonial principle and practice until 1939.

Under the Third Republic, France created its second colonial empire, consolidating its control over much of North Africa, the Sahara, and what

3

Political Life
and Institutions,
1944–1960

The Brazzaville Conference and
the Constitutional Reforms of 1946–1947

Early in 1944 General Charles de Gaulle embarked upon a grand tour of French Africa, now liberated and under the rule of his provisional government in Algiers. He hoped not only to provide visible proof of the reality of Free French rule, but also to reassert what had become to him a matter of principle: that France and its empire were an indissoluble whole and that their historic link had been reforged in the war against the Axis. He was greeted by cheering crowds in Rabat, Dakar, Conakry, Abidjan, Lomé, Cotonou, Douala, Libreville, and, finally, Brazzaville, where, on January 30, he opened a conference of forty-four French colonial administrators and political and trade union leaders. The conference's charge was to lay down the broad lines of postwar French colonial policy; its mission was to give substance to de Gaulle's new assimilationism, to suggest ways in which, according to Colonial Commissioner René Pleven, "the peoples of our Empire who shared French sorrows might also be fully associated with our rebirth."[1]

De Gaulle had good reason to be grateful to France's African allies. By the end of August 1940, not three months after the fall of metropolitan France to Hitler's armies, Cameroon and Equatorial Africa had "rallied" to de Gaulle's Free French movement, and "for two and a half years, Brazzaville, capital of French Equatorial Africa, was also the provisional capital of what claimed to be the government of France." (The AOF territories remained loyal to the Vichy government of Marshal Petain until 1942, when the Allied invasion of North Africa severed the connection.) Over two hundred thousand Africans had fought in Allied armies, and the Cameroon-AEF base had permitted General Jacques-Philippe Leclerc to launch an extraordinary expedition across the Sahara to attack the Italians in Libya and take part in the last stages of the Allied North African campaign. It can be said without exaggeration that France owed the people of its African empire, both black and white, not only its physical rebirth, but more important, its restored self-confidence. As Edward Mortimer has aptly put it: "Perhaps nothing did so much to salvage French self-respect after 1940 as the readiness of many Africans to regard themselves as Frenchmen and fight for France's liberation."[2]

If gratitude and the desire to reassert old ties had been the only motives of those who met at Brazzaville, the outcomes of the conference might have been different. In the background, however, were other significant factors: the colonial powers had been humiliated militarily in the war, having lost large portions of their territory to the Japanese, Germans, and their collaborators; the wartime allies, expressly and by implication, had committed themselves in such declarations as the Atlantic Charter to considerable postwar political devolution in their empires, if not to "self-determination" itself (even Winston Churchill promised independence to India in return for wartime support); and in French-speaking Africa accumulated grievances of the past, reemphasized by Vichy French misrule in North Africa and the AOF, came to be articulated by a growing number of African intellectuals on whom the Free French depended heavily for local support. De Gaulle and his aides undoubtedly recognized the need for reconsidering imperial relations, and they sought to give early expression to their understanding. In the background, too, was the admittedly conservative bias of the French *colons* in Africa. They had little stomach for colonial reform, and they sought to minimize the impact that changes in colonial policy might have on their privileged position. But this much, at least, stood as a clear charge to the conference: in de Gaulle's words, "to determine on what practical bases it would be possible to found stage by stage a French community including the territories of black Africa."[3]

While the Brazzaville recommendations had great importance for the future, the fact that the conference included no African political leaders necessarily limited its horizons. What African views were expressed were channeled through Félix Eboué, a Guyanese of African descent, who was governor-general of the AEF and one of the most influential participants in the conference. Eboué, who had long been active on behalf of colonial reform, presented a report that included documents submitted by *evolué* groups in Brazzaville and two statements by Fily Dabo Sissoko, an AOF intellectual and *chef de canton*. Eboué maintained a marked antiassimilationist bias, and the recommendations of the conference suffered from a certain lack of precision that partly concealed an uneasy compromise between Eboué and the assimilationists. Under de Gaulle's watchful eye the conference emerged with a program that it styled "recommendations," ostensibly with the purpose of establishing a French constituent assembly after the war. Its main points were as follows:

1. Categorical rejection of any idea of autonomy or self-government for the overseas territories or of any weakening of the imperial connection;

2. Representation of the colonial peoples first in a new constituent assembly and later within the centerpiece of the new system, a colonial parliament, or, to use the conference's phrasing, "preferably" in a "Federal Assembly";

3. Creation within the colonies of representative assemblies with mixed European and African membership that would perform limited budgetary and advisory functions;

4. Retention of higher executive and administrative powers in French hands, leaving to Africans mainly the task of carrying out rules and orders from above;

5. Creation of some sort of imperial citizenship; and

6. Suppression of the *Indigénat* "as soon as the war ends" and elimination of forced labor within five years after the end of the war (though the conference did recommend a one-year period of compulsory public labor service for Africans of twenty and twenty-one years of age who had been "recognized as suitable, but not called up for military service").

The conference also urged the rapid extension of social services, particularly education, with special emphasis on technical education; the development of colonial resources with a view to improving African living standards; industrialization, including the establishment of pilot state factories; the development of communications; and improvement of agricultural techniques and equipment, including the sending of a mission to the Soviet Union to study collective farms. Despite equivocation on the crucial questions of French citizenship, the *Indigénat,* and forced labor and the uncertainty about the possibility of a federal relationship between the metropole and the colonies, the conference represented the most important change in French colonial policy since the creation of the AOF and AEF federations some forty years earlier.

Stimulated by the recommendations of the conference, political groups already active in the new postwar atmosphere of free association began to make their demands known in Paris through African sections of metropolitan parties (in the case of the socialists), communist *sympathisants,* student groups, and the like. In August 1945 the provisional government extended the right of all the territories of French Africa to send representatives to the French National Assembly. This was followed by legislation guaranteeing freedom of assembly in French Africa and by the passage of the centerpiece of postwar French colonial reform, the first *Loi Lamine Guèye* (May 7, 1946—named after its author, Senegalese lawyer Lamine Guèye). Later restated as Article 80 of the 1946 constitution, it made all inhabitants of the overseas territories French citizens with the same rights as French nationals. With one stroke the legal distinctions between *citoyen* and *sujet* were swept away, and a revised penal code consequently replaced the hated *Indigénat*. The new guarantees also produced a mass electoral base for postwar representative institutions in France and Africa and stimulated the organization of political groups eager to participate in them.

The first postwar constituent assembly met in Paris in the fall of 1945 with sixteen elected representatives from Africa in attendance. One half had been elected by French citizens (the first electoral college), the other half by *sujets* eligible to vote (the second electoral college). The draft constitution that issued from the assembly's deliberations contained several far-reaching colonial reforms, the most important of which, Article 41, implied that the colonies would be free to choose their constitutional relationship with France. This first draft document, the so-called April Constitution, was rejected by an electorate composed wholly of French citizens, many of whom were frightened both by the prospect of an all-powerful National Assembly and by the communist resurgence in France. Conservatives in France and abroad pointed to growing disturbances in the colonies—riots in Cameroon and Senegal, strikes in many cities, radical nationalist agitation in Madagascar, bloody confrontations in Algeria, and near civil war in Vietnam—to warn that the proposed colonial reforms would only lead to further troubles, though it is unlikely that the proposals had much influence on voters in the colonies themselves. In June 1946 the second constituent assembly convened, its members considerably sobered by the rejection of the first draft. As expected, the liberal colonial clauses of the April Constitution were thrown out and a new text was drawn up, despite African protest.[4]

In its final form the October Constitution—adopted, without enthusiasm, by referendum in October 1946—recast the empire in a new form, styled the French Union, that incorporated the AOF and AEF territories into the unitary structure of the Fourth French Republic. Only Togo and Cameroon, nominally protected by their special international status, escaped the net, becoming the Associated Territories. The rest were designated as the *Territoires d'Outre-Mer* (TOM). Both the TOM and the Associated Territories were represented in the French Parliament, which remained the supreme legislature, and in a large Assembly of the French Union, whose powers were mainly consultative. The supreme executive of the French Union became, in effect, the executive of the republic, with the French president at the head. Thereafter, the French government typically included an African or two in the cabinet.

This guarantee of at least nominal African representation at the top decisionmaking levels could hardly conceal the fact that the October

Constitution had restored most of the colonial powers enjoyed by the French government before 1945. An elected assembly (called the *conseil général* until 1952) was created in each territory and granted limited consultative, or advisory, powers, but principal executive responsibility in each territory continued to rest with a professional governor, who reported directly to the French government and whose powers were limited only to the extent that he had to seek (but not necessarily heed) the advice of his territorial council, on which Africans sat by right. The AOF and AEF federations were preserved as administrative forms, with greatly diminished powers. Each federation had its own so-called legislature—a *grand conseil*—to which the territories elected representatives, but again, its powers were more rhetorical than real.

The new arrangements satisfied no one. It was clear that domination, not consent freely given, was to be the basis of the new union. The territories' legal position was said to be *susceptible d'évolution* (open to change), but their status could be changed only by an act of the French Parliament. Colonial conservatives thought the arrangement too lax; Africans who had supported the October Constitution because they feared much worse might follow if they did not deemed it too rigid and considered it a betrayal of the explicit and implicit promises made at Brazzaville. Despite the *Loi Lamine Guèye,* electoral laws not included in the constitution retained restrictions on voting rights, and for some territories (the AOF, excluding Senegal, because its *quatre communes* had been enfranchised since the revolution of 1789, and Togo under special UN rules) a two-college system that gave French nationals grossly disproportionate representation in the various elected bodies. The constitution conferred citizenship on everyone, but it did so in such deliberately ambiguous terms that it appeared to many African leaders that their newly won civic rights had been severely compromised from the start.[5]

Granted that the new set of colonial structures and relationships tightened, rather than loosened, France's hold on her colonies and that the liberal promises of the April Constitution found few echoes in the October version; on balance, many small steps and a few giant strides had been taken toward decolonization through assimilation, a goal actively sought and approved by almost all African leaders and by all French leaders but the most intransigent colonial conservatives (see Appendix B). For the first time an active African presence drawn from all African colonies instead of just Senegal could make itself felt on the highest French decisionmaking levels. For the first time, in the local assemblies, Africans had access to territory-wide forums, where even if they could not legislate, they could articulate the interests of increasingly politically conscious African publics.

From the time of their first sessions, the assemblies had African majorities, and from 1946 on no colonial governor could afford to disregard the sentiments and demands expressed in them. For all the ambiguities surrounding citizenship in the French Union, the *Loi Lamine Guèye* still provided the basis for an electorate that grew in number from election to election, and it stimulated a profusion of parties, associations, and political groups throughout French Africa. The earnest assimilationism of de Gaulle and his successors, institutionalized in the French Union, also found expression in programs of financial, economic, technical, and social assistance that between 1947 and 1956 provided 70 percent of all public capital investment, plus over one-third of recurrent administrative and military expenditures of the West African TOM.[6] The percentages were even higher in the AEF territories. Finally, the most oppressive features of colonial rule—forced labor and restrictions on the right to form political and trade union groups and to publish newspapers—were theoretically abolished and, in practice, increasingly eliminated throughout French Africa. It is fair to conclude, then, that the Brazzaville Conference and the 1946 constitution had brought unprecedented changes. More important, once made, the changes were irreversible. Postwar colonial policy gave political reality to the assimilationist ideal and ultimately prepared the way for the elimination of the empire itself.

The pace of reform slowed considerably during the next ten years; colonial conservatives in France thought too much had been given away by the 1946 constitution and sought to stem what they feared might be a rising tide of sentiment for independence. Thus, the few measures to liberalize the political status of Africans that were introduced during this period were granted grudgingly and often in the face of considerable opposition in the French Parliament. The so-called Second Lamine Guèye Law, which was designed to ensure African civil servants equality of pay and treatment, went through Parliament in only six months in 1950. By comparison, the Overseas Labor Code, which granted African wage earners equal status with French workers with respect to minimum wages, family allowances, length of the working day, collective bargaining, and paid vacations, spent over five years in the legislative process before its final adoption in December 1952.[7] It was only because of insistent pressure from both French and African labor leaders that it passed at all. Another important reform, the municipal law for the TOM, took even longer to get through Parliament: initiated in the Assembly of the French Union in 1948, it didn't become law until November 1955.[8]

This municipal law, which represented the first attempt to create local government institutions throughout French Africa outside of Senegal, provided for the creation of some thirty-five local governments (twenty-six *communes* in AOF, six in AEF, three in Cameroon), with mayors and councils chosen on the basis of a single electoral roll or college. Though French administrators oversaw the new municipal functions, it was the elected African mayors and their mostly African councils that set overall policy.

The *Loi-Cadre* Reforms

The conservative French reaction, expressed in an *immobilisme* that repeatedly stultified the efforts of African deputies in Paris to bring about political reform in the African TOM, bred a counterreaction. The African leaders turned to the creation of their own Africa-based political parties, the cultivation of African electorates, and a nearly wholesale disassociation from the metropolitan parties with which they had at first actively collaborated in both Africa and France. Besides, successive French governments were distracted by a series of crises that had begun to threaten the stability of the metropole itself. No sooner had the Mendés-France government extricated the country from its disastrous war in Indochina in July 1954, than the Algerian revolt broke out in November of the same year. During 1955 things got worse in Algeria.

By August massacres in Morocco had brought that territory to the edge of a general insurrection. A worried French government agreed to grant Morocco independence, while quiet pressure in Tunisia forced France to promise that country independence in 1956. A year earlier Togolese nationalists had won for their UN trust territory special autonomous status within the French Union and a large measure of self-government. Finally, in January 1956 the French general elections resulted in the formation of a liberal center-left coalition government made up of socialists, radicals, and the UDSR—the Union Démocratique et Sociale de la Résistance, a nonparty resistance grouping (see Appendix C). This government, headed by socialist Guy Mollet, included Félix Houphouët-Boigny, leader of French Africa's most important party, the Rassemblement Démocratique Africain (RDA), and, as minister of Overseas France, Gaston Deferre, who had long advocated substantial reforms of the 1946 system. Their joint efforts produced a legal and constitutional milestone for the African TOM: the so-called framework law, the *Loi-Cadre,* adopted in June 1956.[9]

Whereas previous French governments had acted as if the 1946 reforms gave too much political latitude to the sub-Saharan African territories and had granted concessions only when it was impossible to avoid doing so, the Mollet government, and in particular Deferre, saw that international and African events of the previous ten years not only had made the 1946 constitution outdated, but had put the whole body of France's African policies in jeopardy. The AOF and AEF federations had grown even weaker, while increased control from Paris had only whetted the appetites of African politicians for greater control over their own destinies. Two other developments had begun to undermine French aims: one, a territorialization of politics wherein local politicians sought to mobilize against the administration in each TOM; and the other, a move toward a West African federalism that would incorporate the AOF structures and create an increasingly powerful African political counterweight to the metropole itself.

Houphouët-Boigny had been involved in the former movement and had been imprisoned for a time for his activities. Yet his opposition to the federalists, who had become stronger by 1956; his desire to maintain the territorial advantages of the RDA; and Deferre's promise to decentralize control all appeared to him to be fulfilled in the *Loi-Cadre*.

The *Loi-Cadre* enunciated "principles," and these were worked out in legislation, promulgated by decree on March 30, 1957, that went even farther than either Houphouët-Boigny or Deferre expected:

1. The dual electoral college was abolished and universal suffrage instituted.

2. Elected assemblies in each territory were given enlarged powers, including crucial control over local budgets.

3. Each territory was to be governed by its own executive, a council of government *(conseil de gouvernement)* that was to be elected by the local territorial assembly and presided over by the governor *(chef du territoire)* or, in his absence, by the vice president of the council *(vice-président du conseil)*, the leader of the elected councillors. (In practice, of course, the governor was always French and the vice president of the council, a sort of premier, always an African.) The councillors were to be styled *ministers,* and even though the council was not responsible to the assembly, they and the vice president had to resign if they lost the confidence of the legislature. In everything but name, responsible parliamentary government had been introduced in the African TOM.

4. The governor—now *chef du territoire*—represented the prerogatives of the metropole and was responsible to Paris for foreign affairs, defense, public liberties, and culture. But, as Henri Grimal has pointed out, "his role was not clearly defined, and depended on the interpretation of the texts [the statutes regulating his powers]."[10]

The immediate effect of the *Loi-Cadre* was, as Deferre had hoped, to discourage further revolt and institute much-needed reforms. And it did more. It gave Houphouët-Boigny's RDA a new lease on life and fortified his refusal to have his home base, the Ivory Coast, become the rich "milch cow" for a federation of poor neighbors; he preferred to have his links with Paris without intermediaries. Most important, it ushered in a period of dyarchy during which Paris and the territorial governments shared power in the African TOM, together laying the institutional base from which the territories would move toward independence.

Deferre had hoped that the *Loi-Cadre* would be the last major change in the status of the African TOM for a long time. Indeed, in early 1957 no major African leader thought seriously of independence. But once again events outpaced expectations. By early 1958, the federalists regained their momentum to such an extent that Houphouët-Boigny lost control of his party, and the RDA split apart. A new party, the Parti du Regroupement Africain (PRA), was formed in the spring of 1958, and some of its leaders—such as Sékou Touré of Guinea, and Modibo Keita of Soudan (later Mali)—began to demand more than a federal union with France, threatening independence instead. "If France lets slip by the opportunity to realize the Franco-African community," said Modibo, "Africa will, inevitably, take the only path compatible with its dignity, that of independence."[11]

From the Community to Independence

In May 1958, in the train of events that brought the Colonels' Revolt in Algeria and a constitutional crisis at home, de Gaulle returned to power after ten years in retirement. Almost immediately he announced that a new constitution—that of the Fifth Republic—would be submitted to a popular referendum the following September. He now proposed to the TOM a new, stronger association: the Franco-African Community. In form this was to be a federal republic with France at its head and with its other members, formerly overseas territories, now autonomous states. Two examples already existed: the trust territories of Togo and Cameroon, which had become autonomous republics in 1957.

There is little question that de Gaulle's stock had never stood higher in Africa than at this point. His return gave new hope to the federalist cause. It seemed to many African leaders that the terms of the promised association would permit the territories not only to work out their individual ties to Paris (a path preferred by Houphouët-Boigny), but even to achieve independence if the separate arrangements could not be made (an outcome favored by Sékou Touré, Modibo, and now Léopold Sédar Senghor, the Senegalese *vice-president du conseil*). In any case, the capital of confidence in French liberalism, once devalued in the aftermath of the *Loi-Cadre* reforms, took a turn upward. Still, de Gaulle had no illusions about the situation. He sensed the radical turn in African politics, and he recognized that the Algerian tragedy and the cumulative setbacks to French pride in Indochina and North Africa had bred a French reaction at home against continued support of "ungrateful" colonies and a desire to avoid further humiliations by cutting possible future colonial losses.

It was against this background that in late August 1958 de Gaulle undertook another African tour, this time to explain the issues in the coming referendum. His hope was to bring the African leaders and electorates to a "spontaneous," that is, voluntary, acceptance of a new union with France. The key question for Africans was whether they would preserve the right to opt for independence if they voted yes in the referendum. At the same time, however, few were willing to face the economic consequences of the immediate independence that a no vote entailed. The dilemma was well expressed by the Malagasy leader Hubert Tsiranana in a press conference on August 21: "When I let my heart talk, I am a partisan of total and immediate independence; when I make my reason speak, I realize that it is impossible."[12] At first de Gaulle confronted the problem in guarded, elliptical phrases. Only later, after he had met with some visibly unenthusiastic African leaders and had realized that the cheers in Conakry were not for him but for Sékou Touré, was he prepared to insert into the new constitution a reference to "free determination," a provision of "evolutionary" character. In Conakry he told the crowds that they could choose independence if they wished but that France would "draw its conclusions" if they did. With his back turned on de Gaulle, Touré famously replied that Guinea preferred "poverty in freedom to wealth in slavery!" De Gaulle's implied threat was as clear to Touré as to other African leaders. Nevertheless, by the time de Gaulle left, all except Touré were convinced that even though the new constitution did not meet all their expectations, "they could now reasonably ask their peoples to vote for it as a step towards, not an alternative to, independence."[13]

The referendum of September 28, 1958, approved the new constitution. In the African territories, the yes votes varied between 78 percent (Niger) and 99.97 percent (Ivory Coast). Only Guinea voted no by 95 percent and immediately became independent. The French government—that is to say, de Gaulle—"drew its conclusions": in less than three months French administrative services, troops, and even most French civilians left the country, destroying or sabotaging offices, installations, and plantations on their way out.[14] De Gaulle, who regarded the Guinean no as a personal affront and who undoubtedly wished to present Guinea as a horrible example *pour encourager les autres,* refused to recognize the new state before it could prove that it was indeed able to "cope effectively with the responsibilities and expenses of . . . sovereignty."[15]

The new federal system was a federation of unequals in which France dominated. The African members of the Community were Madagascar, seven states in the AOF, and four states in AEF. Togo and Cameroon, because of their international status, did not vote in the referendum and remained outside the new organization. All members of the Community now became "autonomous," which meant that they could govern themselves except in those matters reserved to Community control: foreign relations, defense, currency, common economic and financial policy, and strategic matters.

The Community was governed by an executive council headed by the president of France and composed of the heads of government of the component states and the French ministers charged with Community affairs. Four advisory ministers to the French government were to be selected from the executive council to guard African interests within the French cabinet. A senate of the Community with 186 French delegates and 98 delegates from the component states was also created, but it had purely consultative powers. The executive council, dominated by its French members, similarly lacked any powers of decision. Only the president, who was charged, in the words of the constitution, with formulating "those measures necessary for the direction of common affairs," had any real power. In short, though it ostensibly possessed federal organs, the Community could never evolve toward a true federalism: French control precluded such a development. The authors of the constitution had, from the first, avoided creating a true federal system that might have profited the Community at the expense of French independence. Nevertheless, the door to independence had not been closed. Articles 78 and 86—the price of the African yes—permitted transfer of Community functions to a state through bilateral accord with France and wholesale transformation of the status of a state if demanded by both its legislature and its electorate.

It should be emphasized that the African leaders who supported the new constitution and recommended a yes vote in the referendum did so for reasons that differed from de Gaulle's. The federalists, recognizing the ephemeral nature of the Community, saw in it an open dispensation to form their own *African* federation, which they could then lead to independence within a Franco-African confederation. Accordingly, they began to plan a new West African grouping to be called the Mali Federation. It would include Senegal, Soudan, Upper Volta, and Dahomey.[16] Houphouët-Boigny, on the other hand, defended the Community because he wished to preserve Ivoirian particularism and prevent the creation of federal links between African states at Ivoirian expense. Hence, in May 1959, with French help, he torpedoed the four-country Mali Federation plan by persuading Dahomey and Upper Volta to join the Ivory Coast and Niger in an economic union without political pretensions, the so-called Conseil de l'Entente. Houphouët-Boigny's counterploy came in time to prevent the creation of a four-country federation, but too late to discourage Senghor and Modibo, who proceeded to make their truncated federation a reality.

By the end of the year Senghor and Modibo had gone even farther and persuaded de Gaulle to grant the Mali Federation independence without requiring it to withdraw from the Community and lose French aid. De Gaulle, by this time, had no choice but to give in with good grace; had he refused, the Mali Federation would have declared its independence anyway and left the Community. Besides, the momentum of events in Africa had made any other choice untenable. Guinea had survived his brutal chastisement, albeit with Eastern European and Ghanaian help; an independent Ghana projected a dynamic image of African self-government, and its example was difficult to disregard; and the two trust territories of

Cameroon and Togo had each been promised independence, on January 1 and April 24, 1960, respectively. Though by granting Mali independence he risked alienating Houphouët-Boigny, de Gaulle went ahead, and on June 20, 1960, the Mali Federation proclaimed its independence as a member of the Community. In an address broadcast on June 14, de Gaulle underlined the realities of the situation:

> As a result of the progress accomplished in our territories, of the training that we are giving to their elites, of the movement for emancipation that is carrying along all the peoples of the earth, we have recognized the right of those who depended on us to settle their own future. To refuse them would be to contradict our ideals, to risk interminable conflicts, to draw upon ourselves the condemnation of the world, and all for a resistance bound to fail in the end.[17]

By agreeing to the independence of Mali de Gaulle had, against his will, signed the death warrant of the Community. A last-ditch effort to preserve the French empire, the Community had been so badly designed that it could neither function nor last. The executive council, whose African advisory ministers to the French government were not named until July 1959, held only seven meetings and decided nothing. The senate met twice, first in July 1959 and then again a year later, and spent most of its time elaborating its by-laws. And a Community court of arbitration set up in March 1959 had no cases to decide. In 1960 the French African states all became independent under Article 78 of the constitution (transfer of Community functions) following the signing of bilateral assistance accords with France.

By 1962, only France, the Malagasy Republic, and the four equatorial states of Gabon, Congo-Brazzaville, the Central African Republic, and Chad remained in the Community, though their membership was more a matter of courtesy and sentiment than anything else. "In fact, this community never had a real life; its institutions never functioned (the Senate of the Community ceased to exist as of March 16, 1961)." Although "the French representatives in the various capitals received the title of ambassador, the states themselves dealt with France through the French Ministry of Foreign Affairs. All that remained was a Ministry of Cooperation, whose functions were to grant and distribute economic aid and technical assistance."[18]

The Mali Federation died even before the Community did. As it turned out, the will to unity was not strong enough to overcome fundamental differences between Senghor and Modibo Keita. They disagreed about the allocation of federal resources, about ties with France, about party activity in the two states, about the organization of the economy, and about Senghor's candidacy for the federation's presidency. Modibo, a Muslim and a Marxist, wanted pooled resources, a planned economy, a single party, and restricted ties with France. Senghor, a Catholic and a Francophile, sought a distribution of resources to permit greater Senegalese development, favored a multiparty parliamentary system, and wanted close ties with France. Modibo opposed Senghor's candidacy to the presidency because he felt a Muslim should head the predominantly Muslim federation. On the night of August 19, 1960, Modibo and his followers made an unsuccessful attempt to seize the federation government and take control of Dakar, its capital. Senghor immediately arrested and deported Modibo and his principal aides, then on the next day proclaimed the dissolution of the federation and the independence of Senegal. Shortly thereafter France recognized Senegal, and Mali turned to militant Marxism and an alliance with Guinea and Ghana.

Party Politics

Political parties on the European model did not make their appearance in French Africa until after World War II. The decisive factors in their formation within AOF (as well as in AEF and the trust territories), according to Phillip Neres, were "the granting of a sufficiently substantial measure of power to local assemblies; the opportunity provided by the presentation of Africans in the *Assemblée Nationale* in Paris to encourage nationalist politicians to come together; and the introduction of institutions and procedures—such as an electoral system—which made it possible for parties to impact on the [territories'] sovereign power."[19] The wave of extraordinary constitutional and structural reforms between 1944–1946 created the framework on which political parties might build and perform. Léon Hamon put it pithily: *"L'origine de la vie politique africaine est parlementaire. Ce n'est pas le parti qui a précédé l'élu, c'est l'élu qui a précédé le parti"* (The origins of African political life are parliamentary. The party did not arise prior to the elected representative; the elected representative preceded the party).[20] Of course, all this does not mean that there was no organized political activity in French Africa before 1944; to the contrary, there was a good deal. But most of it—again, the exception being the Senegalese *communes*—had little effect on the Parisian centers of colonial decisionmaking.

A few short-lived newspapers were published before the war by literate Africans, particularly in Dakar and Abidjan. One of the most important, *L'Eclaireur de la Côte d'Ivoire,* appeared briefly in 1935, and again in 1936. The Popular Front government in France during the mid-1930s stimulated the creation of a Senegalese section of the Socialist Party, as well as the rise of trade unions in Soudan and Senegal in 1937. At about the same time a political discussion group, the Foyer du Soudan, was formed in Bamako. Various French Marxist, procommunist, and leftist groups developed African ties during the days of the Popular Front and flourished in

Dakar, Abidjan, Conakry, and, for a brief time, Bobo Dioulasso during the early 1940s, culminating in the formation of the *groupes d'études communistes* (GECs—communist study groups). Senegal, where Blaise Diagne and Lamine Guèye developed political groups in the 1920s and 1930s, came to influence intellectuals elsewhere in the AOF, not only by the example of its vigorous political life, but by the success of the federal Ecole Normale William Ponty near Dakar, which between 1918 and 1945 turned out some two thousand trained teachers, civil servants, and "assistant doctors." "From among the Ponty graduates," notes Ruth Schachter Morgenthau, "came most of the postwar *parlementaires* and a very large proportion of the rival postwar party leaders."[21] Finally, of the many *amicales* (social clubs), veterans organizations, sports clubs, and youth groups throughout the AOF, a few in each territory developed overt political orientations.

Until 1945 official restrictions on associations, publications, and free speech kept political activity in the AOF outside Senegal on the level of minor infractions whose effects were usually restricted, diffused, and muted. The situation was similar in the AEF. Members of the educated elite in Pointe-Noire, Brazzaville, and Libreville became involved in various ephemeral groups protesting discriminatory treatment by the colonial administration and demanding privileges akin to those enjoyed by the *assimilés* of Senegal. During the 1920s and early 1930s a number of syncretistic, messianic religious movements and cults offered resistance—usually passive, but occasionally violent—to French authority. The Baya revolt of the religious leader Karinou; the reintegrative cult of Bwiti; the *amicalisme* of André Matsoua among the Balali; and, most significant, the messianic cult of the prophet Simon Kimbangu were mainly active in rural areas, but sometimes (as in the case of Bwiti and Matsouanism) attracted urban leaders. Again, however, the tribal and millennial cults proved little able to influence French policy. More often than not they were ignored, unless trouble arose, in which case they were put down by force.[22]

Some of the prewar groups and movements in AEF, AOF, and the mandates were undoubtedly protonationalist in character; that is, they articulated anticolonial feeling and asserted African, as opposed to European, rights and interests. On the whole, however, they tended to be poorly organized, and they usually operated only among the small, urban educated elite, rarely (with the exception of the religious and tribal movements) attracting anything like a mass following. In the final analysis, it was World War II and the consequent relaxation of political controls, coupled with the reformist spirit of French leaders, that provided the principal impetus for the rise of political parties in French Africa.

The first French reformist groups to become active in Africa were the trade unions, which set up African *filiales* (branches) in the wake of the labor reforms of 1937. Then, in the early 1940s, came the political study groups, organized among educated Africans by French teachers and officials affiliated with the French Communist and Socialist parties. The groups, as well as the parties themselves, "provided invaluable training in political organization and strategy for the new African leaders and their supporters."[23] The elections to the first and second constituent assemblies brought still other French parties to Africa, and the new African representatives began to ally themselves with the main French parties in order to increase their influence. Lamine Guèye and Senghor of Senegal, Sourou-Migan Apithy of Dahomey, Jean-Félix Tchicaya of Moyen-Congo (or Middle Congo), and Yacine Diallo of Guinea became *apparenté* (formally affiliated) with the socialists; Houphouët-Boigny of the Ivory Coast and Gabriel d'Arboussier, and Yacine Sissoko of Soudan with the Communist Party (Parti Communiste Français, or PCF); and Louis-Paul Aujoulat and Alexandre Douala Manga Bell of Cameroon with the Catholic left-of-center Mouvement Républicaine Populaire (MRP).

Many African leaders already considered the October 1946 constitution a betrayal of the promises made by de Gaulle and the Brazzaville Conference. Now a conservative French pressure group, the Etats Généraux de la Colonisation Française, formed in July 1946 to lobby for colonial interests, appeared to seven of the leading African deputies (Houphouët-Boigny, Fily Dabo Sissoko, Jean-Félix Tchicaya, Lamine-Guèye, Yacine Diallo, Apithy, and d'Arboussier) to be a revival of colonialism. In a September 1946 manifesto these leaders called on all African organizations seeking genuine African economic and political democracy to meet in Bamako to discuss their common problems.

Eight hundred delegates from study groups, trade unions, elite organizations, and nascent political parties in each territory attended the Bamako Congress on October 18–21, 1946. The congress passed resolutions denouncing colonialism and supporting the positions taken by the African deputies in the constituent assembly. It proceeded to organize a new, interterritorial party, the Rassemblement Démocratique Africain (RDA). John Ballard argues that had there not been official French opposition to the congress, at this point the RDA might well have grouped together all the developing political forces in French Africa. As it was, "the Socialist Minister of Overseas France (Marius Moutet) feared that the French Communist Party would capture control of the Bamako Congress and so he threw the entire weight of the colonial administration against the Congress."[24] As a result, the Senegalese socialists led by Lamine Guèye and Senghor did not attend, and the important Senegalese mass base was lost to the new organization. Moreover, the deputies of Soudan (Fily Dabo Sissoko), Guinea (Diallo), and Dahomey (Apithy) were persuaded to reject membership in the party.

In hindsight, it is clear that Moutet had seriously miscalculated: though he had succeeded in keeping all French parties except the communists away from Bamako and had persuaded the African socialist leaders to boycott the meeting, the absence of the socialists left the communists free to form an alliance with the new party and its president, Houphouët-Boigny. Senghor soon perceived his mistake, but by then it was too late to undo the damage. For the next twelve years he sought with little success to find ways to overcome the disadvantage at which he had placed himself and his followers.

The new French National Assembly, elected in November 1946, contained several RDA deputies who, as if to underline Moutet's blunder, allied themselves with the communists, an *apparentement* that lasted until 1950. Whatever else the alliance may have meant, it was not an illogical choice, given the illiberal tendencies of the hour: of all the French parties, the Communist Party was the only one that supported the RDA's demands for further colonial reforms and for substantive implementation of the reforms of 1946. In December the RDA won seats in all the territorial assemblies. For now, however, they obtained a majority only in the Ivory Coast, Houphouët-Boigny's stronghold.

During the next three years, the RDA built itself into a mass organization with *sections* throughout the AOF (except in Mauritania), as well as in Moyen-Congo, Chad, and Cameroon. By 1955, it had become the dominant party not only in the Ivory Coast, but also in Guinea and Chad and, to a lesser extent, in Upper Volta, Niger, and Moyen-Congo. Only its *sections* in Dahomey and Senegal remained relatively insignificant. Undergirding the party's electoral successes was its organization, consciously modeled on that of the French Communist Party (see Appendix E). Each territory had its own *section* that was guided by a *comité directeur* (executive committee), which coordinated the activities of regional *sous-sections* (subsections) and local *comités de quartier* and *comités de village* (residential area and village committees). The party *sections* sought to develop a mass following in both urban and rural areas in each territory, using trade unions, tribal associations, women's organizations, student groups, and other voluntary formations to broaden its appeal and spread its ideas. Interterritorial control was put in the hands of a *comité de coordination* (coordinating committee) set up by the party congress, though this committee met rarely. The party's internal links were instead maintained chiefly by its deputies in Paris. The party's congress was supposed to meet on an annual basis, but only three interterritorial RDA meetings were held in Africa between 1946 and 1958.

For all its organizational and tactical similarities to the French Communist Party, the RDA never became a branch of the PCF, even though it voted with the communists in the French National Assembly and defended their policies until 1950. Indeed, the RDA's alliance with the PCF, as well as the militantly communist stance of its secretary-general, the brilliant Malian mulatto lawyer, Gabriel d'Arboussier, tended to increase difficulties for the RDA both in Africa and Paris.

With the outbreak of the Cold War in 1946, the French communists, choosing to follow the Moscow line, became the odd men out of the French political system. Within two years the anticommunism within the French government and of most French politicians began to have adverse effects on the RDA. Its leaders were harassed by the government and accused of subversion, and attempts were made throughout Africa to weaken or eliminate the party. In the Ivory Coast, where the RDA was strongest and had the support of wealthy African coffee and cocoa growers, the conflict between the party and the administration erupted into violence. In 1949 and 1950 a series of outbreaks led to the deaths of fifty-two Africans in various parts of the territory and to about three thousand arrests. The worst incident occurred on January 30, 1950, at Dimbokro, where thirteen people were shot by troops. A frightened French government reacted by trying to arrest Houphouët-Boigny, and on February 1 it issued a decree banning all RDA meetings throughout Africa.

Although the warrant for his arrest was never executed, Houphouët-Boigny was shaken by events in the Ivory Coast. He now faced three related problems: mounting criticism both within and outside the RDA over the communists' seeming domination of the party, a large number of resignations from the party, and the obvious fact that an alliance that had seemed tactically natural in 1946 had become a liability. Quietly he began negotiations with the French government. In exchange for dropping the RDA's communist affiliations, he won the removal of the hostile French governor of the Ivory Coast and several of his key aides. On October 18, 1950, the RDA deputies announced their *désapparentement* (disaffiliation) from the communists.

As expected, the move split the party. D'Arboussier bitterly denounced Houphouët-Boigny for his "betrayal": "It seemed to me to be absolutely contrary to my honor as an African even to seem to abandon our progressive and Communist friends . . . just at that moment when the reaction against them was at its most violent. I affirmed . . . that taking such a decision was the first step toward changing the anticolonial orientation of our movement."[25] In a letter written two years after the event, d'Arboussier recalled that he had refused to sign the declaration of October 18. The Cameroonian and Senegalese *sections,* plus the left wing of the Niger *section,* sided with d'Arboussier and were eventually expelled from the party. Within five years, all three of these groups had resorted to revolutionary violence. Also, a number of trade unions affiliated with the communist-dominated French Confédération Générale du Travail (CGT), as well as some youth and student groups, turned against Houphouët-Boigny's new line. The rest of the *sections*—that is, the bulk of the party—went along with Houphouët-Boigny, seeking to reestablish its bona fides in Paris and to mend its broken fences in Africa in the face of continued, albeit diminished, official suspicion and hostility. That hostility, translated into electoral chicanery during the 1951 French National Assembly elections, cost the party all but three of its seats. Remaining as RDA deputies were Houphouët-Boigny, Mamadou Konaté, and Tchicaya.

The RDA's shift from opposition to collaboration bore immediate fruit in the Ivory Coast, where Ivorian and French commercial interests cooperated to persuade the French government to subsidize the sale of coffee and cocoa on the French market. Elsewhere, in Guinea and Soudan, for instance, the local French administrations rejected collaboration, forcing the territorial *sections* onto their own resources to prove their mass support and win electoral recognition. As it turned out, the most serious threat to the RDA came not in Africa, where no other party could effectively compete with it on an interterritorial basis, but in the French National Assembly, where in 1948 seven non-RDA African deputies formed a new parliamentary party, the Indépendants d'Outre-Mer (IOM).

Throughout its short life (1948–1957), the IOM was little more than a pragmatic coalition of local political leaders. By dint of parliamentary maneuvering and by moving in and out of temporary alliances, the IOM members sought to benefit from their anticommunist, anti-RDA position, and did so for a time. The IOM never succeeded in building an interterritorial organization, though by the time it held its first and only congress at Bobo-Dioulasso, Upper Volta, in February 1953, it had assumed the title of "movement" and had managed to win the elections of 1951, with the obvious help of the French administration. What gave it its strength was its leadership, which included Senghor, who won control of the divided Senegalese socialists in 1951 by defeating Guèye; Apithy, leader of the dominant Union Progressiste Dahoméene; Nazi Boni, a radical young leader from Upper Volta; and Aujoulat, the Catholic lay missionary from Cameroon who briefly (1949–1953) served as undersecretary for Overseas France. The IOM became, and until 1956 remained, a pivotal group in the French National Assembly, and at times it was able to make or unmake French governments by its vote. In 1951 even the RDA tried, unsuccessfully, to merge with it.

The IOM began to fall apart in 1956, when several of its deputies lost their seats to the RDA and the group's number of representatives dropped below the fourteen required to form an autonomous parliamentary bloc eligible to be consulted when a new French government was being formed. Within a year Senghor was leading his remaining forces into another attempt at an interterritorial party, the Convention Africaine, which in 1958 was replaced by the profederalist Parti du Regroupement Africain (PRA).

The PRA, which also lasted a year, briefly united all non-RDA parties outside Mauritania, then sought to merge with the RDA but was rebuffed. Ephemeral, with little political influence, these embryonic interterritorial parties are interesting mainly because they represented Senghor's continuing determination to offset the African socialists' failure to participate in the RDA by creating a counterweight based in Dakar. One other such short-lived party, the Mouvement Socialiste Africain (MSA), was founded in January 1957 and led by Lamine Guèye. It lasted until February 1958, when it merged with the PRA.

Between 1952 and 1956, the RDA slowly and painfully rebuilt its electoral bases despite harassment by the administration and challenges by local parties. The RDA's staying power was due in part to its excellent organization, in part to the pragmatism of its leaders, and in part to its attractive program, which sought increased powers for the territorial assemblies and more effective democracy overseas without demanding real autonomy or full self-government. Its tactical key was collaboration with the French administrations, the fruits of which were reaped in the National Assembly elections of 1956, when the RDA recaptured most of the seats available, mainly at the expense of the IOM. It was at that point that Houphouët-Boigny, named a member of the French cabinet, took a leading role in the drafting of the *Loi-Cadre*.

The *Loi-Cadre* reforms came into force following the March 1957 elections to the territorial assemblies, in which the RDA solidified control of the Ivory Coast, Guinea, Soudan, and Chad. In Gabon and Upper Volta, RDA leaders became heads of coalition governments, and the party dominated the *grand conseils* of both AEF and AOF. Yet this greatest success of the party was to be its last. The RDA had reached its zenith too late. The federalist controversy, coupled with the effects of the *Loi-Cadre,* splintered the party beyond hope of recovery. Sékou Touré and Modibo Keita, nominally within the RDA ambit but already federalist in orientation, began moving their parties toward independence. Senghor, first through the Convention Africaine and then through the PRA, adopted a radical line in favor of greater independence in federation and succeeded in attracting the more radical RDA groups, which were impatient with Houphouët-Boigny's Francophilic vacillations.

The reappearance of de Gaulle on the French scene and the new constitutional arrangements attending the birth of the Fifth Republic only hastened the demise of the party. By the end of 1958 the RDA was an interterritorial party in name only. Most of its component sections had grown into mass parties with territorial orientations, and in Senegal, Dahomey, Cameroon, Centrafrique (former Ubangi-Shari), and Moyen-Congo, non-RDA parties were in firm control. Guinea's Parti Démocratique de Guinée (PDG) left the RDA when the country declared its independence in 1958.

The final blow came in 1959, when Senghor and Modibo created the Parti de la Fédération Africaine, which included former RDA affiliates in Soudan, Senegal, and Dahomey.

By the end of 1960 all of the AEF and AOF territories plus Cameroon and Togo had become independent. The RDA had disappeared as an interterritorial force, remaining only in the names of its former *sections* in the Ivory Coast, Mali, Upper Volta, Niger, and Chad. In each country the number of political groups had been sharply reduced through amalgamation, elimination, and forcible incorporation of opposition groups into the governing party. The one-party system became the accepted political mode in Senegal, Mauritania, Mali, Guinea, Ivory Coast, Togo, Upper Volta, Niger, Chad, the Central African Republic, and Gabon. Where minor or even opposition parties continued to have some life, as in Senegal, Cameroon, and Congo-Brazzaville, their early demise was inevitable.

The RDA held the dominant role in the territorial and interterritorial politics of most of French tropical Africa between 1946 and 1956, and its leaders paved the way to the creation of African-centered mass political parties in the TOM. The party provided both ideological and programmatic content to the emerging nationalisms of francophone Africa, and it developed a set of leaders and cadres ready and willing to take the reins of power when it became possible to do so. Finally, for the first six years of the Fourth Republic, the RDA's deputies were the watchdogs of African interests in a French Parliament that was dominated by colonial conservatives and little inclined to take African demands seriously.

The RDA was not, of course, the only party to emerge in French Africa after 1946. The situation was extremely complex because in addition to the interterritorial groups, there was an extraordinary array of local parties and groups organized on personal, ethnic, religious, sectional, regional, occupational, ideological, and even class bases. There were six interterritorial parties, but the total number of territorial groups is almost impossible to compute. Morgenthau lists 115 of them for the AOF alone;[26] Aristide Zolberg's detailed study of the Ivory Coast mentions at least fifty groups active in the territory between 1946 and 1960, many of which were *filiales* or *sections* of French and other non-Ivoirian organizations;[27] and my own study of Cameroon lists 117 political parties and associations active during the same period.[28] In each territory only a handful of political parties and groups survived the almost constant process of group formation, amalgamation, coalescence, absorption, and disintegration, not to mention official repression—or sponsorship, which could be just as politically disastrous—as well as election campaigns and the fraud and manipulation that all too often accompanied voting, vote counting, and the writing of election rules.

For all the complexities of the party scene, during the 1946–1960 period the French West and Equatorial African parties fell roughly into four overlapping categories:[29]

1. The socialists' parties, which included the Socialist Party of Senegal before 1951; the two parties, headed by Senghor and Lamine Guèye, respectively, that grew out of the split of that year; and the various socialist parties in Soudan, Guinea, and elsewhere. Included also are the several *sections* of the MSA (1957–1958), as well as smaller "one-man shows" (Morgenthau's phrase), such as Charles Okala's Cameroun Socialist Party.

2. The interterritorial parties, of which the RDA, IOM, and PRA were the most important. Only the RDA, of course, succeeded in establishing relatively durable interterritorial links.

3. The various parties that were organized on a territorial basis. Some of these were first grouped within the IOM, others grew from former *sections* of the interterritorial parties, and most arose as a response to purely local circumstances.

4. The radical revolutionary parties of Marxist and communist inspiration. These included Niger's Sawaba, Upper Volta's Parti National Voltaique, Senegal's Parti Africain de l'Indépendance, and Cameroon's Union des Populations du Cameroun. The main parties in this group grew out of the 1950 RDA-communist split; others arose as a result of radical trade union, student, or intellectual group activity.

Further, five distinct phases of party development can be discerned during this period: (1) the "metropolitan" phase, roughly 1944–1946, when French political parties and groups carried the weight of African party and political group formation; (2) the "early radical" phase, 1947–1950, dominated by the struggle between a radical RDA and the French administration; (3) the "moderate" phase, 1950–1956, during which the RDA retreated from its oppositional stance and various right-wing parties began to emerge locally; (4) the "territorialization" phase, 1956–1959, marked by the disintegration of the RDA and the reinforcement of local, territorial political groupings; and (5) the "consolidation" phase, which overlaps with the territorialization phase, roughly 1955–1960, when single-party and single-party-dominant systems developed in almost all the African territories.[30]

This period also saw changes in and finally the severance of the old "metropolitan axis."[31] Until 1946 France and France alone determined what would and would not happen in its colonies; local events and local politicians—even those from Senegal—had little or no effect on the direction and content of the policies under which the colonies were ruled. But during the period of rapid decolonization almost everywhere in Africa and Asia that followed in 1946–1960, Africans seized the initiative and, through the complicated give-and-take of Franco-African political relations, finally asserted the right to rule themselves. And it was the francophone African political parties and their leaders, as much as any other factors, that made the transition possible.

Notes

1. Commissariat aux Colonies, *La Conférence Africaine Française, Brazzaville,* 19, cited in Morgenthau, *Political Parties in French-Speaking West Africa,* 38. The text of the conference's principal recommendations may be found in Hargreaves, ed., *France and West Africa,* 235–240.

2. Mortimer, *France and the Africans, 1944–1960: A Political History,* 27–28. Mortimer's account of the background of the Brazzaville Conference is the best discussion of the subject in print.

3. Ibid., 50.

4. For further discussions of the substance and context of the making of the constitution in 1945–1946, see Morgenthau, *Political Parties,* 71–104.

5. Article 81 states: "All French nationals and subjects of the French Union are citizens of the French Union, a title which ensures them the enjoyment of the rights and freedoms guaranteed by the Preamble. . . ." Article 82, seeking to clear up any doubts as to whether "subjects" had been granted membership in the French Union or French citizenship, stated that "citizens who do not enjoy French civil status preserve their personal status [i.e., under traditional rules] so long as they do not renounce it. This cannot, in any case, constitute grounds for refusing or restricting the rights and liberties attached to French citizenship." This masterpiece of constitutional obfuscation permitted, among other things, the creation of dual electoral rolls and considerable political flexibility in the later elaboration of statutes and decrees involving the rights and obligations of TOM inhabitants.

6. Berg, "The Economic Basis of Political Choice in French West Africa," 394–395.

7. Grimal, *Décolonisation,* 338.

8. See Mortimer, *France and the Africans,* 185–187.

9. For discussions of the *Loi-Cadre* and its consequences, see Grimal, *Décolonisation,* 346–352; Mortimer, *France and the Africans,* 233–261; Ansprenger, *Politik im Schwarzen Afrika: Die modernen politische Bewegungen im Afrika französischer Prägung,* 253–260; Morgenthau, *Political Parties,* 65–73.

10. Grimal, *Décolonisation,* 366.

11. Ibid., 352. Grimal quotes a communication from Modibo Keita to the minister of Overseas France. The translation is mine.

12. Crowder, "Independence as a Goal in French West African Politics," 32.

13. Mortimer, *France and the Africans,* 315. The formation of the Community and the political context of its creation is discussed in the following sources: Mortimer, *France and the Africans,* 303–335; Ansprenger, *Politik im Schwarzen Afrika,* 319–329; Morgenthau, *Political Parties,* 301–329 and passim; Deschamps, "La F.O.M. et la Communauté"; Ehrhard, *Communauté ou sécession?* Y. Guena, *Histoire de la Communauté;* Néra, *La Communauté;* Dugue, *Vers les Etats-Unis d'Afrique;* Foltz, *From French West Africa to the Mali Federation,* 88–96.

14. An unidentified American present in Conakry at the time was quoted as saying that the French departed "lock, stock, barrel, and toilets," a reference to the flush toilets the French allegedly tore out of the governor's residence and carted off to France. Reliable Guinean informants have sworn to me that the story is true, but I have my doubts.

15. Mortimer, *France and the Africans,* 331, citing Boubacar, *Porte Ouverte sur la Communauté Franco-Africaine.*

16. Foltz, *From French West Africa,* is the best account of this union; Dugue, *Vers les Etats-Unis d'Afrique,* contains useful sections on the Mali Federation.

17. Mali, Ministere d'Information, "Discours historique de Général de Gaulle de 14 juin 1960," mimeographed copy, 1965. My translation.

18. Grimal, *Décolonisation,* 365. My translation.

19. Neres, *French-Speaking West Africa,* 54.

20. Hamon, "Introduction à l'étude des partis politiques de l'Afrique française," 152. My translation.

21. Morgenthau, *Political Parties,* 19. Morgenthau's book is the standard work on the subject. Other sources on AOF parties include Hamon, "Introduction"; Ansprenger, *Politik im Schwarzen Afrika*; Foltz, *From French West Africa;* Blanchet, *L'itinéraire des partis africains depuis Bamako;* Hodgkin, *African Political Parties;* Milcent, *L'A.O.F. entre en scène;* Schachter, "Single-Party Systems in West Africa"; Mortimer, *France and the Africans.*

22. The literature on political groups in the AEF is somewhat sparser than that for the AOF. Useful summaries are in Ballard, "Four Equatorial States"; Thompson and Adloff, *The Emerging States of French Equatorial Africa,* 43–51, 343–526, and passim; and in Ansprenger, *Politik im Schwarzen Afrika.* Balandier's *Sociologie actuelle de l'Afrique Noire* remains the best discussion of reaction to colonial rule in AEF, and in particular of the messianic and millennial movements in that region.

23. Ballard, "Nationalist Movements in West Africa, (ii) The French Territories," 469.

24. Ibid., 470.

25. *Lettre ouverte à Félix Houphouët-Boigny par Gabriel d'Arboussier,* published in pamphlet form in Dakar and Paris, May–June, 1952. My translation.

26. Morgenthau, *Political Parties,* 417–426.

27. Zolberg, *One-Party Government in the Ivory Coast.*

28. Le Vine, *The Cameroons from Mandate to Independence,* 235–247.

29. I adopted—and adapted—the first three of my four party categories from Hodgkin's article, "Political Parties in French West Africa," 157.

30. My first three developmental phases were also suggested by a comment in Hodgkin, "Political Parties in French West Africa."

31. The phrase is also Hodgkin's. See his "The Metropolitan Axis," 5–6.

Part 2

Society and Politics

4

Political Cultures

Imagine a traveler who speaks both French and English undertaking an automobile trip from Brazzaville, on the west bank of the Congo River, to Nouakchott, some 2,500 miles west by northwest, as the crow flies, on the Atlantic shore. Assuming feasibility—during the 1960s such a trip was possible; in 2003 it is probably no longer so—the traveler would probably pass through Gabon, perhaps Equatorial Guinea, Cameroon, Nigeria, Benin, Togo, Ghana, perhaps Burkina Faso, Côte d'Ivoire, Guinea, Gambia, and Senegal before arriving in Mauritania. Our traveler would prudently detour around Liberia, Sierra Leone, and Senegal's Casamance region because of unsettled conditions (local violence, active banditry, absence of services for travelers, and so on) in these places. If Côte d'Ivoire still has an active rebellion at the time the journey is begun, our traveler may have to have a military escort, take his or her chances, or bypass that country as well. At the end of the road, if the traveler makes it all in one piece, some interesting comparative observations will have been gathered, including, perhaps, the following:

First, although villages and towns tend to look much the same from country to country in their physical aspects, large towns and cities in francophone Africa look and feel different from those in anglophone Africa. For one thing, cities like Brazzaville, Yaoundé, Douala, Cotonou, Lomé, Abidjan, Conakry, and Dakar appear to have a solidity and permanence about them, whereas anglophone African cities such as Enugu, Lagos, Accra, Freetown, and Banjul appear to have grown haphazardly. They are seemingly impermanent and are certainly more difficult to navigate. This is not to say that large francophone African cities and towns do not have their unplanned *quartiers*—indeed, the shacks and shanties of bidonvilles are evident in almost all of them and are witness to the continuing influx of migrants from the countryside and often from neighboring countries. Still, the new growth tends to build up within and around the old core patterns, which are evidence of French forethought about the process. One possible explanation for the difference is that the French, who built Brazzaville and the other francophone African cities, expected to remain indefinitely and thus brought to their construction notions about rational city layout, if not planning. The large cities in anglophone Africa, on the other hand, usually had no such underpinnings and were mostly allowed to grow without restraint. Another explanation is that there are differences between French and English urban political cultures and that these differences find reflection in the configuration, layout, growth, use, and demography of both countries' colonial cities.

Second, apart from linguistic differences the tone and content of political talk both within and between states, and particularly between anglophone and francophone states, tend to vary considerably. In francophone Africa, for example, officials are less willing to provide specific information about their work and their concerns, and at least for the first twenty years of independence politicians were more likely to reflect the rhetorical and ideological styles of their contemporaries in France. Debates, such as there are in francophone parliaments, still sound much like debates in France's National Assembly, while in anglophone parliaments the style, decorum, and ritual of the Mother of Parliaments in Westminster continue to find frequent echo. That expression of political-cultural difference also finds its way into less clearly demarcated precincts such as university curricula, styles of governance, and official ritual. Clearly, differences in political cultures and in the way politics are expressed help account for the larger institutional differences between states and territories.

Third, bureaucrats in the francophone states use French methods of organizing their work and dealing with the public, and courts often seem at first glance to be African duplicates of French judicial chambers and *parquets*. Throughout francophone Africa most judges come up through the ranks of the magistracy, a profession on the French model requiring special schooling that turns out judges, not simply lawyers. In anglophone Africa the judiciary often follows British models: many high court judges, for example, still wear periwigs and are addressed as "M'Lord," and lawyers, who often still are divided functionally between barristers and solicitors, may cite the Common Law and British case law in their pleadings.

These few observations relate to both the general and the political cultures of the countries concerned. Observations about similarities and differences in the way cities and towns are built and inhabited, about the manner in which people go about their business, and about their language and their social and economic habits all pertain more to the general than specifically to the political culture. Those observations relating to attitudes and opinions about politics and government, to the way in which decisions are made, to the impressions that politicians seek to make, and to the special language and symbols they use all pertain to the political culture, itself a distinct part of the general culture. One of the keys to understanding the politics of the fourteen states is that of political culture, the set or sets of attributes that, when identified and described, offer clues to, if not explanations of, political behavior. These attributes can be identified in francophone Africa and described with some measure of accuracy, though full empirical justification, admittedly, would be more difficult to obtain.

Richard Dawson and Kenneth Prewitt provide a useful definition of political culture:

> The phrase "political culture" summarizes a complex and varied portion of social reality. Among other things, a national political culture includes political traditions and folk heroes, the spirit of public institutions, political passions of the citizenry, goals articulated by the political ideology, and both formal and informal rules of the political game. It also includes other real, but elusive, factors, such as political stereotypes, political style, political moods, the tone of political exchanges, and finally, some sense of what is appropriately political and what is not.[1]

Reduced to its essentials, according to Lucian Pye and Sidney Verba, political culture is "the pattern of distribution of orientations members of a political community have toward politics. This patterned collectivity of orientations influences the structure, operation, and stability of political life."[2]

Our traveler might also have noticed that among the states visited there is a basic lack of consensus on the underlying values, beliefs, and attitudes that animate the political system. On close inspection the political cultures in the fourteen states of our study usually appear to be indistinctly defined, normatively chaotic, and unstable in composition. However, the fact that national political cultures are still in the process of being created in these countries despite the fact that more than forty years have passed since they attained independence does not mean that in each there is a political-cultural vacuum being slowly filled, like an empty bottle receiving distillations drop by drop. Exactly the reverse is true. In every state old and new political cultures coexist, each rooted in the sociohistorical experiences of the individuals and groups constituting the polity. The combination represents the confluence of exogenous and endogenous experiences, as outlined in Chapters 1–3, and therefore presents a picture of considerable analytic complexity. If, however, the several political cultures are sorted out on the basis of their social constituencies and origins, the political-cultural components in each state can be organized in roughly the following manner:

1. Elements of the political culture of an interterritorial elite deriving principally from the shared preindependence experiences, in both France and Africa, of older members of the countries' ruling groups (the "founding

fathers" generation of leaders).[3] These are reinforced by contemporary intergovernmental contacts and political and economic ventures in Africa and elsewhere. One such international venture, the eponymous Francophonie, created by France in 1970 ostensibly to foster French language and culture, has brought francophone African political and cultural leaders together some dozen times since 1986 at various international venues. So also the biannual meeting of francophone heads of state, a gathering usually chaired by the incumbent French president and held each time in a different francophone capital. (The resemblance of these meetings to the British Commonwealth conferences chaired by the queen did not escape former French president Georges Pompidou, who allegedly referred to the francophone states collectively as "the Commonwealth of the French spirit."[4])

2. An evolving national political culture. Though still largely the domain of the political elite, this evolving culture continues to be diffused as a mass political culture. It is most visible in the larger towns and the capital cities, especially among the bourgeoisie, that is, the professional and occupational middle classes.

3. A variety of parochial political cultures shared by members of the ruling groups and still relevant to millions in rural and semirural contexts as well as to those in the cities' ethnic *quartiers.* Some of these parochial cultures are of relatively recent, colonial-era construction; others have older, precolonial roots.

4. An eclectic political counterculture linked to and partly derivative of the national and parochial political cultures, in which attitudes and behaviors that challenge or derogate political authority are expressed.

This simple analytic quartet only begins to define the dimensions of the contemporary political cultures of francophone Africa. There are several crucial related aspects implied in the categories that need further comment, starting with origin and historical context, before we go on to the salient structural, notional, and operational components of the political cultures themselves.

Commenting on the interpenetrated cultural heterogeneity of francophone Africa, French sociologist Pierre Alexandre observed that "the ruling group is characterized by simultaneous participation in one totally non-African culture and several variegated indigenous ones."[5] The "totally non-African culture" to which Alexandre refers is, of course, that of France, and his observation, which deals with general cultures, is equally valid for political cultures. France, above all other contributing sources, provides the modern political orientations and values of the francophone African states, as well as the institutional referents in which they operate. Recall that the basic dynamic underlying the construction of the French empire, as of most great historical empires, was simple in the extreme: sub-jugation by military conquest, followed by domination by military then civilian bureaucracies, and finally political integration by social and politi-cal assimilation. It was during the latter two phases of French empire build-ing that the political culture of France became at once a model and the object of diffusion among France's colonial wards.

French political culture itself changed, sometimes radically, during the life of the empire. The French Revolution of 1789, which altered the basic premises of French political life, had repercussions in the Senegalese colonies, as it would later on contemporary politics in several other of the fourteen states. The ideas of assimilation emerged at this time as an exten-sion of the political values of civic liberty and equality. Later the First Empire of Napoleon undermined these values in the colonial context, if less so at home.

The Revolution of 1848 reasserted the values of 1789, and the Senegalese colonies regained both representation in France and civic equal-ity with French communities. Yet while the Senegalese *communes* strug-gled to retain the institutional and legal expressions of the metropolitan political culture in the half-century that followed, France proceeded with the military subjugation and then domination of what became the western and equatorial empires with relentless determination. By the time the German protectorates of Togo and Kamerun had been incorporated into the French empire at the end of the World War I, bringing that empire to its ter-ritorial zenith, assimilation had been shunted aside in favor of association, which saw assimilation as a long-range, indeterminate process.

In the meantime, France had begun the creation of an auxiliary elite of civil servants, teachers, and technicians who were destined to execute the basic tasks of colonial administration in the territories outside the Senegalese enclave, where a semiassimilated elite had come into being ear-lier. At the same time, in such growing colonial towns as Conakry, Bobo-Dioulasso, Niamey, Douala, Brazzaville, and Libreville, an African petty bourgeoisie had begun to emerge (as it had earlier in Senegal), and its members were rubbing shoulders with the French traders, planters, agents, and clerks who formed the base of the European substratum of French colo-nial society. Through the latter groups came infusions of French mass polit-ical culture much as French elite political culture was transmitted through the French colonial civil servants, professionals, and teachers.[6] During the 1920s and 1930s, the emergent African middle class began to produce what Immanuel Wallerstein called the "new" modern elite, the politically con-scious members of the modern elite who had internalized the egalitarian values of French political culture, both elite and mass, and had started to use them to criticize the premises of the colonial system.[7] The intellectual basis of the new modern elite's challenge to the French colonial system was absorbed, once again, from French and European political-cultural sources: the Marxist-Leninist critique of imperialism, as interpreted by the French left, and the liberal values of Léon Blum's Popular Front government.

Finally, the traditional political cultures almost certainly changed much more slowly and more reluctantly under the impact of the pervasive French administrative system, religious proselytization, and the penetration of the French *petit colons* and members of the African middle class and elite into the hinterlands. Indeed, the tenacity of traditional mores and values and the traditional authority systems' resistance to change permitted the traditional political cultures to influence, in varying degrees, the social and cultural makeup of the new African elites.

This sketch cannot pretend to do justice to the complex of social and political strands that, over time, began to weave the pattern of multiple political cultures that characterizes today's francophone African states. Crucial in that development was the gradual diffusion of key French political values and ways into Africa, the gradual social and political restructuring that accompanied French penetration and occupation, and the growth of indigenous, syncretic political values and orientations in the French colonies. Figures 4.1 and 4.2 summarize that process schematically by suggesting the social location and interaction of the principal political cultures at various points in time. Figure 4.1 describes the situation immediately preceding and partway into World War II, and between 1944 and 1960, before territorial politics pushed what had been a fairly general set of political cultures into disparate compartmentalized sets. In this figure the key analytic distinctions are two sets of dichotomies, elite political cultures versus mass political cultures and French political cultures versus African political cultures; a generalized schema combining social and political structure; and a series of lines suggesting patterns of diffusion of key political values and orientations. Figure 4.2 summarizes a combination of the analytic distinctions presented in Figure 4.1 and the post-1960 situation suggested by the triad of French administration, religious proselytization, and elite penetration.

The differences that emerge from a comparison of Figure 4.2 with Figure 4.1 are quite striking:

1. Between 1944 and 1960 a transterritorial political culture had emerged among the new modern political elite in the French African territories. It was based upon a common French educational experience in the French *lycées,* elite schools such as the Ecole Normale William Ponty in Dakar, French university education, and so on; shared political values and a common practical political education in French metropolitan legislative institutions, local legislatures and executive councils, and the French bureaucracy; contact with or participation in French political parties and trade unions or their affiliates; and involvement with or participation in

Figure 4.1 Transmission Patterns of Political Cultures, 1944–1960

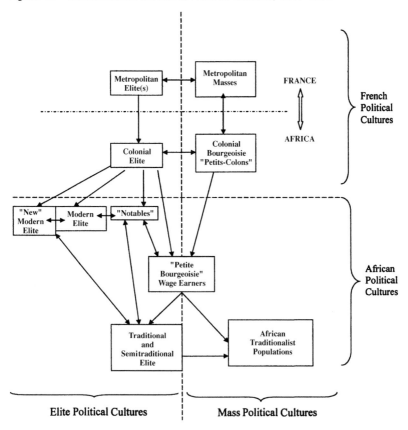

Source: Le Vine, "The Political Cultures of French-Speaking Africa," 1971.

transterritorial African political parties, movements, and associations. After 1960 the number of the transterritorial elite's members declined as the older, preindependence nationalists left government, were displaced, or died. Nevertheless, a significant number remained active into the 1970s and 1980s, and the relative ease with which the top leaders of our group of fourteen countries continue to communicate with one another is as much due to the lessons about their shared political culture learned from the "founding father" generation as to their common language.[8]

2. A genuine national political elite, which had absorbed both older and younger members of the earlier, modern elite, had made its appearance as the standard bearer of an emergent national political culture. (The old and new elites in French-speaking Africa will be examined more closely in Chapter 9.) The growth of this new political culture was due partially to the development of territorially oriented political styles and symbols, partially to the growth of

Figure 4.2 Structure and Sociopolitical Bases of Political Cultures, Post-1960

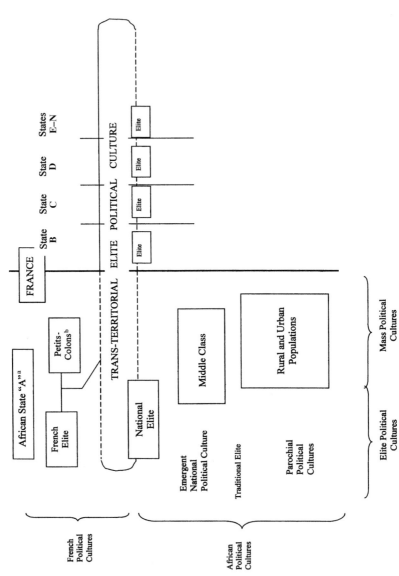

Notes: a. One state is generalized; the pattern is more or less replicated in others.
b. Principally in Côte d'Ivoire, Senegal, and Gabon.

local political parties and groups, and partially to the sheer increase in the number of individuals recruited to fill the elite positions created and made available after independence. Along with this enlargement of the national elite came the continuing effort to spread the salient aspects of the new national political culture through the instruments of mass education and popular mobilization: public schools, the single or dominant party, age-grade and women's associations of official inspiration, professional and occupational associations, and the institutions of central government. Further, as the middle class grew in size and influence in each country, it acted as an agent for the spread of the elite political culture and, more recently, as the nexus from which mass components of the new national political culture could grow.

3. The parochial political cultures, already under attack by the colonial governments and the new political elite, declined in salience even further after 1960. The process of co-optation of the traditional elite into the national elite increased. Where such co-optation was not possible, the members of the traditional elites became increasingly isolated and subordinated to the demands of the national government and its agents. Nevertheless, the old political values remained sufficiently important in the rural areas—and in the immigrant *quartiers* of the cities and larger towns—to force their recognition by members of the national elite anxious to spread the elements of the new national political culture. Moreover, the parochial cultures retained their salience for quite another reason: some of their elements were incorporated into the national ideologies being fashioned by the national elites, though translated or revised for heuristic political reasons. Léopold Sédar Senghor's negritude, Sékou Touré and Modibo Keita's brands of African socialism, and Ahmadou Ahidjo's "socializing humanism," for example, all claimed partial inspiration from basic traditional African political values—regardless of whether such connections actually existed.

4. By 1960 French political culture no longer provided a normative model for the francophone African political elites. French political styles, ideas, attitudes, and values had been absorbed into the emergent national political cultures, but French political culture's influence as the basic model of modern political orientation usually ended with independence and the departure of most members of the older French administrative elite. For some groups in the new states, such as university students, French political culture continued to have considerable appeal, but in their case the connection was often via the perfervid, ideologically superheated political world of the radical student left. Just how salient that relationship could be was amply demonstrated in May 1968, when the French student revolt in the metropole had almost immediate echoes at the Universities of Dakar and Abidjan. Furthermore, the national elites became responsive to the political cultures of their anglophone neighbors and were involved in the pan-African movement, and in the process of establishing their international identity they came into close contact with the political cultures of other

important countries such as the Soviet Union, China, the United States, Yugoslavia, and Israel.

In short, the national political cultures developed particular dynamics of their own, an autonomy often more real than the independence of their general cultures, which still responded to French styles, mores, intellectual fashions, and social orientations. Paradoxically, after 1960, while the general modern culture of the new states could be described as Franco-African, their political cultures had become Afro-French, with the accent on the first word. Members of the elite went to Paris for vacations, to shop the latest styles, to be culturally titillated, and even to be educated, but no longer to gain political inspiration, though that was not excluded. It could be argued that while de Gaulle remained in power his influence—and thereby that of France—remained enormous in francophone Africa; still, the fact remains that the *political* lessons he taught had been learned by African leaders long before 1960.

Content of the Political Cultures

It is easier to assert that political cultures exist than to define their content. The very idea of the political system presupposes that its participants have certain values, orientations, and attitudes of some durability, or there could not be a system in the first place. The problem is to specify these values and attitudes, to indicate how widely they are shared, and to show how they are expressed in the behavioral modes and institutional structures of the political system. By using the available techniques of empirical verification—observation, analysis of attitude, and opinion testing and sampling—it should be possible to discover not only what people think about their leaders and political issues, but also what their base values and orientations are about political matters.[9] Unfortunately, except for some scattered surveys and inquiries, there are no broadly based comparative studies of the political attitudes of either leaders or mass publics in francophone Africa. Studies that do exist on this subject deal with special populations—secondary-school and university students; industrial, manual, and day laborers; political leaders.[10] Thus we have to rely largely on the more synoptic political studies and the monographic literature developed during the last twenty-five or so years. Because these sources are quite rich and are evocative of what we seek, despite paucity of empirically derived data, it is possible to generalize from them a number of propositions about the content of the political cultures in the fourteen states of this study.

Political institutions, behavior, styles, and processes are based to a considerable extent on what people consider proper, right, or reasonable in political life; on their beliefs about politics; and on their orientations to political objects. In short, political life owes much of its content to political values, beliefs, and attitudes. If, as I have argued, each francophone African state contains several overlapping sets of political cultures, we should be able to suggest what operational values, beliefs, and attitudes govern the participants in each.

French Political Culture

French political culture permeated transterritorial elite political culture, and the resulting set of values, beliefs, and attitudes dominated the elite arena and, to a lesser extent, were diffused in the emergent national political cultures.

One of these values was an emphasis on centralization of power, manifested in colonial times by the close ties to the metropole, the creation of the AEF and AOF "federations," and the tight hierarchy of colonial officialdom running—at least theoretically—from the minister of colonies down to the *commandant de cercle* (see Appendix D). In its contemporary translations, this base value is expressed not only in the preambular rhetoric of the various constitutions ("La République de ———, une et indivisible") and in national mottoes and symbols, but also in the unitary structures of the states themselves. To a considerable extent the fourteen states have copied or adapted the French system of *départements* and *préfectures* and operate local governments as adjuncts of the central ministries. Even one of the two exceptions, the Cameroon Federation, kept that format for a dozen years, from 1961 to 1972.[11] The other exception, the Senegambian union, which federated francophone Senegal and anglophone Gambia, lasted seven and a half years, from February 1982 to September 1989, when it broke apart.

The operation of single-party systems in such countries as Guinea under Sékou Touré, Mali under Modibo, and Gabon, Mauritania, Cameroon, Burkina Faso, and Togo probably has owed a good deal to this predisposition as well. It may also be the case that the widespread informal organization of power at the top into patrimonial structures—of which Cameroon's elite "northern barons" (wealthy or powerful men from northern Cameroon, most of them ethnic Fulani, who served former president Ahidjo) and "southern barons" (mostly ethnic Beti, serving incumbent Paul Biya) are prototypical—tends to translate into centralizing government institutions. The value of centralization of power and its ideological correlate, national unity, also found popular resonance in traditional collectivism, which was often used by the new leaders to help shore up their power and political legitimacy.

Another value that was manifested at least during the early years after independence was an emphasis on human equality, with respect not only to African-European relationships, but also to relations within the African community. This value was commonly expressed in the statement, *"Il n'y a pas de surhommes"* (There are no supermen), a saying that articulated a broadly leveling attitude toward those categories of *surhommes* that were left over from the colonial period, were created by the colonial regime, or, frequently, were a product of the two: chiefs, *grands marabouts,* fief-holders, and, up to a point, intellectuals. Those belonging to such categories must be valued like everyone else, by their service to the community and the state.[12] As a base value, it can be argued, equality has profound African roots; however, as a *political* value, it assuredly represents one of the most potent products of the French Revolution. Assimilation, whatever its defects in practice, rested on a solid foundation of egalitarian ideas. It need hardly be added that after independence this value suffered grievously at the hands of rulers seeking to establish cults of personality of their own— the long list of those rulers in our fourteen states includes Sékou Touré, Modibo, Gnassingbé Eyadéma, Thomas Sankara, Jean-Bédel Bokassa, and Marien Ngouabi. We will return to them in Chapter 9.

A third value was a belief in the efficacy of the state as a rational structure, often coupled with a belief in its untrustworthiness as a moral agent. The French, as Thomas Hodgkin points out, were "in the habit of contrasting what they describe as their 'Cartesian' approach to the problems of African government with the 'Empiricism' of the British."[13] While the generalization is only partly true, it does reveal a sense in which the French chose to regard their own behavior and policy as something based on rational, logical premises. In practice, of course, neither French policy nor French administration, whether at home or in Africa, operated as neatly or rationally as the French would like others to believe. Yet French officials' *belief* that their ways were rational was strong enough to be transmitted to their African successors.

Today in the fourteen states, trust in *la planification* (centralized government planning) is responsible for plans and projects that sometimes owe more to logic than to reality, and every ministry operates—or at least is expected to—on the basis of elaborate hierarchies of responsibility and control. At the same time, among the general ranks of the citizenry just as among the politically literate, a relatively high level of distrust of the motives of government and its agents may be found both within and outside of the structures of government. The indeterminate "they"—*ils*—crops up constantly in ordinary conversation, and even the most popular of regimes must constantly reassure its followers of its moral trustworthiness. The *incivisme*—lack of civic responsibility—of which the French often accuse themselves (not infrequently with some degree of pride) is a perennial theme in African presidential discourses, often spun out in campaigns to illuminate and overcome laziness, apathy, and nonparticipation.

Finally, value was placed on the antinomy of pluralism and nationalism, the former manifested in the remarkable efflorescence of political parties and in democratic and quasidemocratic electoral activity from 1945 to 1960, and the latter in the efforts to harness the new political pluralism to the goals of autonomy and national independence.[14] As it turned out, more often than not independence (which had been advertised as a fulfillment of the democratic promise of nationalism) ushered in the single-party state, authoritarianism, constriction of pluralistic politics, and a new nationalism that was quickly harnessed to the centralizing needs of the new regimes and to celebrations attending the incarnation of national identity in the new ruler or rulers. Still, during the 1945–1960 period, this was electoral politics *à la française,* adopted by the new African elite and enthusiastically adapted to African milieux. And the candidates' messages—particularly those of politicians on the Franco-African left—translated postwar French ideas about nationalism and self-determination into local idioms. This was a memorable, exciting time, made all the more so by the extension of the franchise and the consequent participation of thousands who had never previously been involved in modern politics.

It cannot be denied that seventy-five years of French rule in our fourteen states (and longer, to be sure, in Senegal's *quatre communes*) left an unmistakable imprint on their modern politics. So did World Wars I and II; so did the states' several transitions to independence; and so, arguably, did the fifteen political years preceding those events. It is not too far-fetched to put the case, as I do in Chapter 8, that its sheer intensity made that fifteen years' experience part of our states' political-cultural gene pool, and that the experience was compelling enough in memory to be recalled in 1990 to inform those seeking a democratic renewal for their countries.

African Political Context

Five sets of orientations owe their elaboration to the African political context, though they may have French or other foreign roots. They are, with particular permutations, part of the content of the emerging national political cultures.

The first orientation is a clear preference for single-party rule, at least before 1990. Hodgkin writes of "the idea . . . of the governing party as the most effective—though not the only—embodiment of the popular will, through which popular needs and demands, in all their variety, should be expressed, and to which the organs of the State (e.g., the Administration) and associations (e.g., trade unions), must ultimately be subordinate."[15] The idea was most clearly defined in Guinea, where Sékou Touré applied older ideas (in particular Lenin's) about the monistic state and oligarchical organization to justify the supremacy of the Parti Démocratique de Guinée (PDG).[16] In a similar vein, the *marxisant* military rulers, beginning with

Ngouabi of what was until 1990 the People's Republic of the Congo (Brazzaville) and former Malian president Modibo Keita, strongly argued for the primacy of the single party. Since then the idea has been more or less explicitly expressed in most states ruled by civilians (Côte d'Ivoire until 2000; Mauritania before 1978; Chad until 1975; Niger before 1974 and in 1993–1996; and Senegal until 1981, Cameroon until 1990, and Gabon from 1968 to 1990), and in several of those ruled by military juntas (Togo, Burkina Faso, and the Central African Republic).

A corollary attitude is hostility toward autonomous groups—at least those that have not been brought under one of the auxiliary organizational umbrellas of the single party. The belief is that autonomous groups interfere with the general will as expressed by the ruling regime unless they become aligned with that regime. Thus it is hardly surprising that centralizing, and especially single-party, regimes tend to be generally hostile toward any part of civil society that may present an autonomous political challenge, however slight. This helps explain why throughout the fourteen states police forces operate with few restraints, and indeed may even be encouraged in their brutality by the regimes in power as they suppress political opposition.[17] I discuss how this works out in practice later, in Chapter 7.

A second orientation involves the primacy of ethical ideas. The African, so the argument goes, is animated above all by consideration of the ethical content of life. One need only glance casually at the principal daily newspapers in Brazzaville, Dakar, Douala, Conakry, Abidjan, Lomé, and Cotonou to note the extraordinary concern with justifying government decisions and the behavior of public officials in normative terms. A thing is to be considered right not just because it will bring about this or that desired consequence, but because it is *morally* right.[18] Needless to say, this belief is advanced regardless of the moral standing of the incumbent ruler or regime, or the international condemnation the regime earns for its behavior.[19]

A third orientation is toward achievement—of education, of political power, of public office—as that which confers leadership rights upon the holder. Well-educated younger members of the political elite in five countries surveyed in 1965 expressed the sentiment that their superior level of education conferred upon them both membership in the elite and the right to rule; older members in positions of authority argued that their leadership of nationalist movements and the fact that they had acquired power similarly justified their right to continue ruling.[20] A belief in democratic legitimacy—nonascriptive achievement through election—prevailed during the nationalist period, 1945–1960, and regained currency during the redemocratization period I describe in Chapter 8. At the turn of the millennium such achievement remains an article of democratic faith and part of the prevailing political culture in the democratic polities surviving the 1990–1995 redemocratization initiative (Mali, Benin), in the older democracies (Senegal, Botswana, Mauritius), in the newer democracies (Ghana, Mozambique, South Africa, Malawi, Namibia, Kenya), and in the revived democracy of Nigeria. It is symbolically potent enough as to remain part of rhetorical legitimating cover—invoked in constitutions, for example— almost everywhere else, regardless of the reality on the ground.

A fourth orientation is toward collectivism. Hodgkin writes of the "relevance to the contemporary situation of African values inherited from the precolonial past—e.g., collectivism: that the individual defines himself by his relationship in/with/to the groups of which he is a member. Such values are regarded as a common African (or 'Negro-African') stock. Hence they can be made the basis for mobilizing policies (e.g., *investissements humains*). Corollary: rejection of purely European institutional models."[21] Senghor, Sékou Touré, and Ahidjo developed such ideas, and they have been echoed by other leaders, including Julius Nyerere, Milton Obote, Jomo Kenyatta, and Kwame Nkrumah.[22] Here, of course, is an allegedly conscious borrowing from traditional political cultures, often pointed to with pride as being of continuing vitality and a useful source of true African values.[23] Traditional collectivism was also made to serve as an ideological basis for modern African forms of socialism and as part of the rationalization of the one-party state in Guinea and elsewhere in francophone Africa. Most important for such centralizing structures, as Joseph Ki-Zerbo and his colleagues point out, "traditional collectivism" can be used "to deny all forms of individualism in postcolonial Africa."[24] They cite Sékou Touré to make the point:

> Africa is fundamentally communocratic. The collective life and social solidarity give it a basis of humanism which many peoples will envy. These human qualities also mean that an individual cannot imagine organizing his life outside that of his family, village, or clan. . . . Intellectuals or artists, thinkers or researchers, their ability is valid only as it coincides with the life of the people, it is integrated into the activity, thinking, and hopes of the populace.[25]

Of course, the idea is not new; Sékou Touré used it to make the point that the new collectivity for Guineans—the new "communocracy"—was his single party and his new Guinée.

Finally, there is an orientation toward pan-African ideas. Hodgkin writes of "a cluster of 'pan-African' ideas, including the assertion, on assumed historic grounds, of a sense of African solidarity; emphasis upon the common interests of and the need for mutual aid between African States and Peoples; the demand for noninterference by external powers in the affairs of the African family."[26] These ideas find expression not only in support for and participation in various cooperative and collaborative inter-state ventures—from attempts at political union, including the ill-fated Mali Federation and Ghana-Guinea-Mali Union, to functional organizations such as the Conseil de l'Entente—but also as relatively widely diffused political values within the elite and the emergent national political cultures.

In 1963 some of the Organization of African Unity's more radical founding members, including Ghana, Mali, and Guinea, proposed that the OAU become the basis for an African political union. It never became that, but it remained until 2001 as one of the larger expressions of the pan-African idea. That the idea still has some ideological legs was manifest during a special meeting, sponsored by the OAU in Ndjamena in February 2001, at which several African heads of state renewed their commitment to join in an all-African political union. It was not clear how far all this would be carried since the meeting was sponsored and paid for by Colonel Muammar al-Qaddafi, but at least the idea still had enough salience that even so disreputable a herald as Qaddafi could rally some African leaders to its standard. As it turned out, and in spite of widespread misgivings about Qaddafi's motives, the new African Union became a reality in 2001.[27]

Parochial Political Cultures

We can identify a final set of orientations that, according to Amadou Hampaté Bâ, remain vital within the parochial, or largely indigenous, political cultures of francophone Africa. Hampaté Bâ argued (in terms similar to Sékou Touré's, though much different in meaning and intent) that what he styled "traditional civilization" is, before anything else, a civilization of hierarchy and responsibility. The life of the community includes everyone; it guarantees the reciprocal responsibility of each to all. No person can be alone, for he exists as a member of a community. He leaves it only by his own choice or if he is cast out from it (surely the worst punishment of all). Traditional life, then, is an ordered life in which each person has his place and knows it; the social hierarchy defines the political sphere and so irrevocably allocates responsibility to each member of the community.

Though this concept is admittedly somewhat idealized, it does correspond to the perception that many elite participants in the national political culture have about the "traditional" mores in which most were reared. It is the communalistic values of these parochial cultures that have found their way into the political language of francophone African leaders. To what extent these traditional values affect the behavior of participants in the modern political culture remains something of an open question. Prima facie evaluation, however, suggests that the traditional sense of hierarchy fits with the French sense of rational structure and that the values of order and reciprocal responsibility complement the centralist ideas of national unity and the primacy of the governing party. In other ways, the connection is much better established. For example, Pierre Fougeyrollas, who surveyed industrial workers in Dakar and Thiés, found that although the diffusion of democratic ideology had undermined support for traditional ideas of hierarchy and caste, such things as the sense of community continued to be highly valued.[28] French-speaking African university students surveyed by Jean-Pierre N'Diaye in 1961 and by Fougeyrollas in 1965 seemed to display "a need, more diffuse and perhaps more profound, to return to African sources, something which the educational system ought to take into consideration."[29] As presumptive members of the national elite they had to assert their "Africanness"—as distinct from their Western cultural outlook—by incorporating the best of the traditional outlook. Georges Balandier repeatedly notes the reinterpretation of traditional sociopolitical mores in the contemporary context.[30]

Developing National Political Cultures: Heroes, Myths, and Political Education

Before independence the national political cultures of French-speaking Africa grew almost unnoticed by their participants. To be sure, some nationalists, like Sékou Touré, Modibo, and Ruben Um Nyobé, had already developed vague ideas of what a Guinean or Malian or Cameroonian state and nation might be like, but none had given any indication in speech or writing—beyond opaque references to African personality and the political millennium to follow emancipation—of what such nationhood entailed. The emerging political cultures incorporated without plan or rhyme the elements we have noted: aspects of French political culture with the greatest relevance to the nationalist cause, syncretic values and behaviors derived from traditional political cultures and the growing urban middle class, plus specifically local political experiences, orientations, and symbols. However, once the disconnected parts of these polities were brought together within the framework of new and sovereign states, the processes whereby individuals learned to be citizens, previously the charge of the French or occurring without conscious direction, suddenly became the responsibility of independent governments. In short, political socialization, hitherto largely a latent function of the system, became, in Gabriel Almond's and James Coleman's term,[31] manifest; it became a new focus for the new governing elites. Such an emphasis was both logical and unavoidable; the foundations of the polity—the *new* polity—had to be built both by the creation of political consensus and by validation of the authority of the state and its rulers.

In other words, the shape and content of the national political culture, of which political socialization, patterns of legitimacy, and consensus were aspects, now had to be both planned and systematically guided, it was argued, so that the foundation, once laid, remained firm and stable. The question was—and remains—how best to achieve this end.

It is hardly surprising that there has been little agreement on this question in francophone Africa. The ideological differences between leadership groups in our several countries, at the very least, would guarantee this. However, some common elements can, again, be discerned. For example, it is universally officially accepted that both youth and adults must be taught those behaviors and orientations most conducive to stable civic loyalty.[32] Thus, political education almost always becomes the responsibility of the state. The schools, the governing political party, auxiliary political associations (of labor, youth, women, and so on), the institutions of government, all become active agents in the task. Nor are the symbols of nationhood neglected: every state adopts its own flag, with each color and image given patriotic meaning, to be displayed and saluted with appropriate ritual.[33] Every state endows itself with a national anthem, similarly the object of ritual devotion, though usually, as is not uncommon elsewhere, few people recognize the music and fewer still know all the words. (For a short time in 1969 and 1970, there was even some confusion about the anthem of the People's Republic of the Congo. The government had the Communist "Internationale" played over and over on the radio and on ceremonial occasions, though the real anthem was allegedly a song called "Les Trois Glorieuses." The lyrics for the latter song did exist, but until 1970, apparently, no one had written music for them.[34]) Schools received new history and civics texts, and campaigns, usually carried out by the organs of the national party, were instituted to instruct citizens on their duties and obligations to the state.

In all it was political education according to a pattern already well known in most older states, though it varied considerably in extent and impact from state to state in francophone Africa. In Côte d'Ivoire, for example, it appears that beyond providing the usual schoolbooks and ceremonial trappings, the government was doing relatively little to develop widespread civic consciousness or to mobilize the population to its ends. Undoubtedly, the restricted nature of participation in the country's only political party, the Parti Démocratique de la Côte d'Ivoire (PDCI), as well as the enormous shadow President Houphouët-Boigny cast over the political landscape, had much to do with situation.[35] By way of contrast, Guinea appeared almost frenzied in its campaigns to promote the proper political consciousness and to mobilize the population to the government's ends. There the Parti Démocratique de Guinée, also the only party, periodically organized what can only be called political circuses to launch such endeavors as road works, national service *(investissement humain)* projects, new maternity clinics, and a campaign against corruption. Paradoxically, all this activity seemed by 1966 to have become counterproductive; one authority described a "decline of the Guinean revolution" that was marked by increasing alienation from the regime on the part of some and apathy on the part of many others.[36]

Myths and Personality Cults

One common phenomenon throughout francophone Africa—as in most other African states—has been the attempt to provide national myths of historical origin and thereby quasitraditional legitimacy for the new polities. Local historians explore the precolonial and colonial past, often in a conscious effort to offset what they claim is the Eurocentric emphasis of historiography by non-African chroniclers. The target bête noire of some of this discourse, naturally, was the famous French textbook, allegedly used in Africans schools, that was said to have begun with the words, *"Nos ancêtres les Gaulois"* (Our ancestors the Gauls).[37]

The reconstructed emphasis is instead on the glories of past kingdoms and empires (Macina, Mali, Ghana, Songhai, etc.); the rich traditional past; and probably most important, the heroic role of such colonial-era resistance leaders as Samori Touré, el-Hajj 'Umar Tal, and Rabeh. Fily Dabo Sissoko, Hampaté Bâ, and Ibrahima Mamadou Ouane have celebrated the life and exploits of el-Hajj 'Umar; Arbab Djama Babikir has eulogized the Chadian leader Rabeh; Senghor has poetically praised Shaka, the Zulu king; and Pierre Bamboté has made a more recent hero, Patrice Lumumba, the theme of a long and passionate anticolonial poem.[38]

Similarly, national histories or parts thereof that draw heavily on the precolonial past have been produced by such scholars as Fily Dabo Sissoko and Ahmadou Hampaté Bâ (Mali), Joseph Ki-Zerbo (Burkina Faso), Cheikh Anta Diop (Senegal), A. Akindele and C. Aguessy (Benin), Boubou Hama (Niger), and Engelbert Mveng (Cameroon).[39] Some, in their quest of what Vincent Monteil has called the "decolonization of history,"[40] have extended their search for a national historical myth to the broader continental context. Ki-Zerbo's short history of Africa is such an attempt, as is Cheikh Anta Diop's complex argument by analogy that ancient Egyptian civilization (and thence, by derivation, Western civilization) owed its beginnings and content to the Negro race.[41] Surprisingly, some have even used colonial history for nationalist mythmaking, as did the Cameroonian radical left when it used the German spelling *Kamerun* to evoke the supposedly golden political era of German rule, 1884–1916, when the two Cameroons, British and French, were united as one.[42]

Less common, but no less a part of the attempt to develop specifically national political cultures, has been the glorification and sometimes near-deification of the great national leader, usually (not surprisingly) the president of the republic. In schoolbooks, in the press, and in the official propaganda of government and party, such leaders as Senghor, Houphouët-Boigny, Mokhtar Ould Daddah, Sékou Touré, Modibo Keita (until 1969), Léon M'ba of Gabon, and less recently deceased figures such as Ouezzin Coulibaly (Burkina Faso) and Barthélemy Boganda (CAR) became the particular objects of hero-worship. They were hailed as the fathers of their nations; considered wise in the ways of understanding the best interests of their peoples; and, in the case of someone like Sékou Touré, endowed with an almost supernatural aura. A poem by a young Guinean writer is reminiscent of the personality cults formerly built around the likes of President Nkrumah of Ghana, Kim Il-sung of Korea, Enver Hoxha of Albania, and Mao Zedong of China:

> Sékou Touré
> Many thanks to thee, Touré
> The liberation of Guinée
> Hardly surprises us.
> Does not the famished sense from afar
> The aroma of the tasty dish?
> Sékou Touré
> O Divine gift to Guinée
> Hail to thee, be blessed
> thou benefactor of Guineé
> Apostle of the good cause
> O child prodigy.[43]

Barthélemy Boganda, who met his death in an airplane crash in 1959, would have been the Central African Republic's first president but for his unfortunate demise. A laicized (defrocked) priest, he permitted tales about his putative invulnerability, even immortality, to circulate widely. Shortly before his death, a large crowd waited on the shore of the Ubangui River to see Boganda cross by walking upon the waters. He failed to appear, but apparently a good many people still believed that he could have made the miraculous crossing.[44] The Boganda myth continues to exercise a strong hold on many people in the CAR, and it has frequently been used by his successors in their appeals for national unity.

The father of the country, the great historical hero, the national myth of origin, the flag, the national anthem, and the national ideology are part and parcel of the search for a national identity rooted in a political culture. Insofar as they become the content of the effort at political education and are internalized by the citizenry, they help to create both political consensus and that sense of legitimacy so necessary for the growth and continuity of the new state.

The Subtexts of Political Culture: Opposition and Identity

The three political cultures with which this chapter mainly deals are represented by behaviors and ostensible attitudes and values that are identifiable in the public domains of politics. To use James C. Scott's felicitous distinction, these are the open transcripts of politics from which we read political events and their meanings.[45] Yet every open transcript may contain a hidden transcript, a subtext in which political actors intend meanings much different from those they express up front. Here is the domain of everyday resistance to authority, or evasion or flight from the exactions of power, of political activity that functions by keeping the state and its instrumentalities at arm's length. It is also where the slow anger of the oppressed finds expression in the astonishing variety of the acts so brilliantly described in Célestin Monga's *Anthropology of Anger.*[46] What Scott and Monga reveal could be called a political counterculture; in any case it is another repertory of values and ideas that must be added to the other three sets of expressions in order to complete the picture. (These subtexts often appear as "informal" politics, which are examined in some detail in Chapter 10.)

Now, to call this form of political culture a subtext is not to suggest that it is simply a mirror image of the national political culture. It is more complex than that. While mirror-image, dichotomous pairs of political behavior do exist—acceptance/rejection, participation/departicipation, obedience/disobedience, involvement/avoidance, etc.—and they do begin to describe the repertory of oppositional politics, the subtexts in question operate much less reactively than the pairs imply. Perhaps the French term *incivisme* (literally, the avoidance of civic duty and responsibility) comes closer to the mark: it suggests not only reaction, but also an array of possible ways in which the obligations and duties of civic membership, of citizenship, can be rejected, evaded, avoided, or finessed. Here there is no rendering unto Caesar; what Caesar gets is the fake smile, the manipulative obsequiousness of a Good Soldier Schweik,[47] the counterfeit coin of false loyalty, or simply absence at the roll call.

What are ostensibly organized manifestations of *civisme* frequently have intended or unintended "Schweikish" subtexts. I offer four snapshots from my trips to francophone Africa:

Brazzaville, 1981: a small military formation of youngsters in shorts, green shirts, and red bandanas marching with socialist resoluteness on their way to "fight laxity, absenteeism, and laziness on the job" brings to mind a similar encounter later in 1987 with a determined formation of elderly folk in Xi'an, China, armed with flyswatters and going off to "struggle against the winged fly menace." The youngsters are shoeless, and every so often the formation loses one or two marchers so that what began as a consider-able demonstration of solidarity ends with only those unable to peel off during the march. I recall that the elderly Chinese did not defect from their march, but that for all their determination they did not appear to be enthusi-astic about the event.

Conakry, 1971: trucks drive slowly up and down the back streets pick-ing up otherwise unemployed young men; each is offered four hundred CFA and a beer and agrees to be taken to the national stadium to hear and cheer some visiting dignitary giving a speech about nobody knows what. The forty-five-minute speech is in Arabic and is given by a Libyan notable (not Qaddafi), but everyone cheers lustily and applauds anyway. The pre-vailing sentiment is that the affair lasted too long and that two bottles of beer, not one, should have been offered the attendees. It also turns out that a number of those collected for the event had jumped off the trucks, beer in hand, when they slowed down at intersections on the way to the stadium.

Bangui, 1965: the government announces a campaign (named *Kwa ti Kadro*) to take place on successive Sundays, during which the people will voluntarily turn out to beautify their towns and villages by cutting grass and foliage *(defrichement)* along the main roads. On the first Sunday every-body turns out, machete in hand, including the president, his cabinet, the diplomatic corps, a visiting political scientist, and masses of citizens. Grass and scrub is vigorously hacked, and beer is handed out. On the second Sunday about half of the original number shows up (but there is no beer), and on the third nobody comes to cut foliage. Though the originally cut areas grow back to their pre–*Kwa ti Kardo* height in about three weeks, the campaign is declared a success. As far as I know, it is never repeated.

Lomé, January 1981: President Eyadéma decrees two days of celebra-tions to commemorate his "miraculous" escape from an airplane crash on January 24, 1974 *("les journées de Sarakawa")*. There are formations parading with signs thanking God for having saved Eyadéma, three brass bands, lively sales of the presidential comic-book biography, and a steady procession of notables from around the country bearing written and oral expressions of thanksgiving, joy, and good wishes for a long life of contin-ued illustrious achievement. The solemnity of the occasion is marred by the appearance of a *défile* of rowdy market women in front of the presidential palace; the women expose themselves and hurl sexual insults at the guards. I am given to understand that veiled comments belittling the president's virility were made by the women during the march.[48]

In part this is a repertory learned during colonial times, when it was almost expected that colonial subjects would find ways to deceive, to thwart, to get around—and to flatter—their colonial masters. It was a reper-tory composed of a thousand and one acts of defiance, protest, avoidance, and subversion of colonial authority. At its most overt, it was violent, but open rebellion, deliberate disobedience, and mutiny were more often than not costly and futile. At its most subtle, it was expressed in the ability to manipulate colonial authority, whether by presenting "straw chiefs" to touring district officers, as in Delavignette's story,[49] or by mobilizing opposition in protected environs such as churches or schools, or in the confidence games played by the prototypical "users" of the colonial system as portrayed in Hampaté Bâ's delightful Wangrin.[50] In between there were flight to avoid forced labor; women's uprisings (such as the 1929 Aba revolt in Nigeria and the 1959 Ahnlu revolt in British Cameroon—both outbreaks of disobedience with which European colonial authorities found it particularly difficult to cope); the multiplication of rebellious millennial Christian sects (e.g., Lotin Same in Cameroon in 1922–1923 and Kimbanguism, Matsouanism, and Kakism in the Moyen-Congo during the 1930s); and sporadic strikes (during the 1920s and 1930s).[51]

When independence came, as the new African governments learned to their chagrin, it proved difficult to persuade all the newly enfranchised citizens to switch from habits of disobedience and resistance to those of civic loyalty and obedience. Independence, as it turned out, did not mean that the new citizens would automatically start paying taxes, join the dominant or single party, and respond enthusiastically to the new regime's calls for acts of support. The residue of the old habits of resistance remained in the body politic as a sort of recessive political gene set, mutable into and becoming part of a new *incivisme* that was ready to emerge should the new rulers begin to behave like the old—which, unfortunately, occurred all too often.

How does this mutation occur, what forms does it take, and when does it begin new subtexts of *incivisme*? How should these next subtexts be read? What opportunities for expressing the new *incivisme* have the new regimes provided? Here again, Monga and Scott are excellent guides. Although the new subtext differs from state to francophone state, it is possible to extract several common countertextual themes from the dense transcripts of our fourteen states' political experience:

1. *Nationalism as political entitlement.* Over forty years of effort to create national political cultures notwithstanding, in some states parochial loyalties remain strong enough to fuel demands for recognition of particular political identities, or at the extreme, separation or secession. Two of our fourteen states are specially affected: Senegal and Cameroon.

In Cameroon the anglophone western region has emerged not only as the nexus of the main opposition to the Biya regime, but also has given rise to several secessionist movements determined to gain independence for what used to be the British Cameroons trust territory. In 1961, as a result of a UN-sponsored referendum, the former British Southern Cameroons federated with the Republic of Cameroon; the federation turned into a unitary state in 1972. Since the end of the federation a continuous undercurrent of resentment against the government in Yaoundé—first the Ahidjo regime and now that of Paul Biya—has fueled anglophone separatism.[52]

In Senegal the government in Dakar has been unable to end a separatist rebellion in the southern Casamance region. The rebellion itself developed from a political movement of the Diola (not be mistaken for the Dyula)—a largely Muslim ethnic group constituting some 60 percent of the Casamance population—that finally turned violent in 1982, long after the Mouvement des Forces Démocratiques de la Casamance (MFDC) had proclaimed Casamance's independence in 1947. Though the MFDC and the government had already signed five cease-fire agreements since 1982 (the latest two in 2001) and many refugees from Casamance had begun to return from Gambia and Guinea-Bissau, at midyear 2002 there was still some violence, particularly that initiated by one of the hard-line breakaway sections of the MFDC.[53]

Aside from the particulars of both cases, which confirm that separatist sentiment in both countries already existed prior to independence and remains alive today, what is striking is that the separatist groups use words and symbols that were common nationalist coin during the 1940s and 1950s. Their propaganda and publications demand the "self-determination" of "oppressed" and "exploited people" subjugated by an "alien" "colonialist" or "tyrannical" regime.[54] It is not unreasonable to suggest that these ideas became part of these countries' political culture during the nationalist period and have remained as part of Cameroon's and Senegal's repertory of political ideas during the half century since they were first articulated.

2. *Political change through popular mobilization.* This, of course, is part of the repertory of nationalist ideas accepted broadly throughout Africa. Nationalists played and replayed variations on the theme that the nation comes into being in part as a result of the active participation of its people and that, consequently, mobilization—through the vote, political parties, movements, political associations, trade unions, and so on—impels, even propels, political change. Actively propounded during the nationalist period, the idea operated almost everywhere to overcome the counterintuitive reflex that voters often brought to the modern political arena from their own traditional milieux: that political change was dangerous and that abandoning hierarchy, obedience, obligation, and veneration of the elders inevitably led to political disaster or anarchy. As it turned out, of course, most Africans were willing to accept the risks inherent in nationalist ideas and embraced the democratic futures promised them by their leaders.

Now, while independence may have seemed the fulfillment of the democratic promise, what it brought, paradoxically, was rejection of the pluralist mobilization thesis and a demand by the new rulers that *their* hierarchy replace all others, that citizens obey *their* commands, and that citizens act in conformity with *their* new structures of authority and social organization. Political change was dangerous, they affirmed; it threatened newly won freedoms and possibly opened the door to civil strife or anarchy. In effect, it was back to the traditional square one, save that now loyalties and obediences had to be shifted from the chief, the tribe, the clan, and the village to the new national leaders and their regimes. This has been the message brought by most postindependence regimes in Africa—by one-party regimes, military juntas, dictators, and authoritarian leaders or cliques, and certainly by those in our fourteen states—during most of the forty-odd years since independence.

What is remarkable is how much of the older message—in particular, the pluralist mobilization thesis—survived in the face of a half century of pressure exerted by the machineries of the state that were operated by rulers determined to stamp out ideas and voices other than their own. Censorship, loss of employment, internal exile, and official harassment, plus arbitrary arrest, imprisonment, "disappearance," torture, and death squads were all deployed by one or more of our fourteen states as part of their regimes' armories of repression. How else to explain the remarkable series of national conferences, beginning in Benin in 1990, that ushered in the "redemocratization" experiments of the 1990s? It took considerable courage for leaders of civil society in Benin, Cameroon, Gabon, Mali, Niger, Congo-Brazzaville, Togo, Zaire, Madagascar, and Chad to confront the authoritarian rulers in their respective countries and reassert the pluralist mobilization thesis—both when they successfully removed the incumbent ruler, as in Benin, Niger, Mali, Congo-Brazzaville, and Madagascar, and when they failed and often paid a high price for their presumption, as happened in Cameroon, Togo, Zaire, Gabon, and Chad. Again, that the idea had become part of these countries' political cultures made it that much more available when the opportunity to act on it presented itself.

3. *New forms of resistance:* villes mortes. During the 1990s, when regimes throughout the continent were under pressure from oppositions to allow multiparty politics, elections, and other forms of democratic political participation, those, like the regimes of Togo and Cameroon, that were determined to keep the redemocratization process at bay at first gave way by legalizing opposition parties and then sponsoring multiparty elections. This was the official text, a response designed to give the appearance of reform. The regime's subtext came in the form of "informal repression," that is, violence carried out by third parties. In Cameroon these third parties included northern Cameroonian Fulani chiefs, the *lamibé*, who were involved in murderous attacks on members of opposition groups; as well as thugs hired or sent out by the ruling party, the Rassemblement Démocratique du Peuple Camerounais (RDPC); and police, gendarmes, and

local officials in mufti.[55] In Togo a similar pattern unfolded, though without the reaction of civil society that developed in Cameroon.

What was remarkable was the response in Cameroon: though the regime had legalized oppositional multiparty activity in December 1990, it met escalating demands for a multiparty system and a Cameroonian version of a national conference with increased repression and violence. Finally, in May and June 1991 the opposition increased its pressure on the regime by introducing a new tactic, *villes mortes,* or Operation Ghost Towns, a campaign of civil disobedience by which it sought to disrupt all public activity in towns and cities. When the regime responded with even greater force, the campaign escalated, and over a six-month period in 1991 strikes were observed systematically in Douala, Bamenda, Bafoussam, and other towns in the west. Joseph Takougang and Milton Krieger estimate that two million people throughout the country participated in the movement.[56] The toll from government-sponsored violence was high: between two hundred and four hundred people are believed to have been killed during the months of the *villes mortes* strikes.[57] A similar tactic was tried in Congo-Brazzaville later that year, but it never had the impact of the Cameroonian movement.

Even though the Cameroonian regime managed to survive the economic and political damage of the campaign and prevented a national conference from convening, *villes mortes* was a brilliant tactic that was born almost spontaneously in civil society and came close to forcing the regime to make critical concessions to the opposition. Though it failed to bring the regime to its knees, it now remains as part of Cameroon's new national political culture, a reminder of the regime's vulnerability and the inherent possibilities of informal resistance.

4. *New forms of resistance: the Internet.* Today almost everywhere in the world the political repertory of oppositional parties and groups includes Internet Web sites. No matter whether the group is small and relatively inconsequential or large and powerful, and regardless of what it seeks or professes, the Internet offers it a relatively cheap way of presenting itself to domestic and international audiences. That no self-respecting political group will do without an Internet address is obvious; what is not obvious is the Internet's democratizing effect in giving equal space to every group and a presentation effect limited only by the imagination and the forensic and public relations skills of its Web masters. Regimes have no inherent advantages on the Internet: they cannot easily force opponents off or censor their material; they cannot drown them out or overwhelm them with size or bulk or noise level. Quite literally, the Internet is unfair to establishments.

To be sure, all this has little political consequence in countries where the use of the Internet is limited by poorly developed electronic infrastructure, the relatively high cost of personal computers, and the fact that access to the Internet tends to be self-limiting because the technology is available mainly to those who are computer literate and can afford personal computers. However, electrification has progressed considerably in Africa during the last thirty years, bringing power and TV and, increasingly, wired and wireless telephones. In our fourteen states political Web sites are typically deployed for governments and their sponsored parties, and only a handful of parties have created Web sites for themselves. That number, however, grows year by year: whereas in 2000, excluding governments and their parties, there were only eight party Web sites for our fourteen states, in June 2002 a rough survey turned up over two dozen such sites on the Internet.

A measure of the change is the Cameroonian and Burkinese sites deployed or refurbished for the May and June 2002 elections in the two countries. In Burkina Faso thirteen parties presented candidates in the legislative elections of May 5, and there were four Web sites, including that of the government party, compared to one official site in 2000. In Cameroon there were seven main parties presenting candidates for the June 30 elections: four, including the government party, had Web sites, and three more sites were posted by secessionist groups operating outside the country. That eight out of the twenty groups presenting candidates had Web sites is already a considerable proportion for Africa, and it suggests steady future growth for an increasingly potent new medium for oppositional voices.[58] The Internet has also become part of the new political culture.

Aili Marie Tripp observes that the democratic experiments of the 1990s not only gave women unprecedented opportunities to participate in politics, but may also have added yet another page to the volume on changing political cultures on the continent.[59] C. M. Toulabor goes even further: he argues that these changes and amendments to both the national and the wider African political culture at the turn of the millennium, "despite the slowness of concrete results" attending political change, "brought forth a new political culture . . . throughout the continent, one which has begun to favor the African democrat. This new political culture takes shape over the warm remains of that which preceded it, the culture of dictatorships, where the autocrats, often mediocre and corrupt, operated like dominant males at the head of [blinkered] herds of gnu."[60]

Toulabor also reminds us that to the erosion of regime power from internal conflict and "subterranean" (informal) resistance "must be added the 'gray' literature, the tracts, the graffiti, and the informal political debates so loved by Africans. These activities played a decisive role in Senegal's political alternations during the spring of 2000, as in Côte d'Ivoire during the winter of 2000–2001. The appearance of these phenomena, practically nonexistent—or, insofar as they existed in Senghor's Senegal, seriously controlled—a dozen years ago," represents "an important social and political change."[61] Most important, stresses Toulabor, is that the new political cultures appear to have triggered new ideas about good government and, as the national conferences were witness to, a renewed interest in democratic governance. If so, it is good news for the fourteen states.

Notes

1. Dawson and Prewitt, *Political Socialization,* 26.
2. Pye and Verba, eds., *Political Culture and Political Development,* "Introduction," 7.
3. For details about this generation, both continent-wide and in francophone Africa, see my "Leadership Transition in Black Africa: Elite Generations and Political Succession."
4. Philippe Decraene, long *Le Monde*'s principal Africa correspondent, in a letter to the author, May 5, 1968.
5. Alexandre, "Social Pluralism in French African Colonies and in States Issuing Therefrom: An Impressionistic Approach," 206.
6. For a discussion of the social bases of French colonial Africa see the seminal article by Balandier, "La situation coloniale—Approche théorique," 44–79.
7. Wallerstein, "Elites in French-Speaking West Africa: The Social Bases of Ideas," 1–33.
8. See my *Political Leadership in Africa: Post-Independence Generational Conflict in Upper Volta, Senegal, Niger, Dahomey, and the Central African Republic,* 4–7.
9. Merkl, "Political Cultures."
10. Foster and Clignet, *The Fortunate Few;* Fougeyrollas, *Modernisation des hommes: L'exemple du Sénégal;* J. Guilbot, *Petite étude sur la main d'oeuvre à Douala;* Hauser, *Absentéisme et instabilité de la main-d'oeuvre;* N'Diaye, *Enquête sur les étudiants noirs en France;* Tardits, *Porto Novo: Les nouvelles générations africaines entre leurs traditions et l'Occident;* Le Vine, *Political Leadership in Africa.*
11. See Johnson, *The Cameroon Federation,* and my *The Cameroon Federal Republic.*
12. Hodgkin, "Political Forces in French-Speaking West Africa," 8.
13. Hodgkin, *Nationalism in Colonial Africa,* 33.
14. This dichotomy is explained and illustrated in Joseph Ki-Zerbo, Ali Mazrui, and Christophe Wondji, with A. Adu Boahen, "Nation-Building and Changing Political Values," 468–498.
15. Hodgkin, "Political Forces."
16. See Andrain, "The Political Thought of Sékou Touré," 103–147.
17. The annual country compilations by such human rights organizations as Amnesty International and Human Rights Watch detail the brutal lengths to which local and national police forces go to suppress political dissent and dissenters. During the past twenty years I have been involved as expert witness or consultant in several dozen U.S. Immigration and Naturalization Services cases in which petitioners—men and women who fled from countries including Congo-Brazzaville, Guinea, and Cameroon—sought sanctuary under U.S. law. Their depositions tend to be harrowing, detailing official mistreatment including rape, torture, imprisonment under inhumane conditions, forced starvation, repeated beatings resulting in maiming and broken bones, murder of the petitioners' relatives, and death threats against the petitioners themselves, all inflicted by police, gendarmes, or soldiers because

the petitioners had nonviolently opposed the regime in power.

18. As I was writing this, a September 7, 1970, copy of *Togo-Presse* lay at hand. The headline story had to do with visits by groups of village elders and *chefs de quartier* to President Eyadéma during which they brought messages and resolutions of support. The occasion undoubtedly was orchestrated as part of a campaign to show how the country was behind the president following the discovery of an unsuccessful plot against the government (August 15, 1970). The whole newspaper story was suffused with high moral tone: the themes of national reconciliation, charity, cooperation, and *prise de conscience* (moral rededication) were stressed throughout. A picture of a bitch suckling some kittens had been displayed by one of the delegations and was reproduced by the paper with the caption "Even animals understand the benefits of union and reconciliation."

19. In 1999 Cameroon ranked first in Transparency International's annual list of the most corrupt political systems. I was informed by friends in Cameroon that President Biya was furious and that he insisted he was still the moral exemplar he had claimed to be at the beginning of his terms in office in 1982, when he was presented to the nation as *"l'homme de la rigueur"* (the man of moral rigor/uprightness). An example of his regime's official praise-singing is Florent Etoga-Eily et al., *Paul Biya ou l'incarnation de la rigueur.*

20. See my *Political Leadership in Africa,* 12–19.

21. Hodgkin, "Political Forces."

22. Nyerere's *Ujamaa*—"familyhood"—has traditional roots, according to Nyerere. See his *Ujamaa—Essays on Socialism,* especially chapter 1, "Ujamaa— The Basis of African Socialism," 1–12. For broader treatment of this theme, see Wauthier, *L'Afrique des Africains, inventaire de la négritude,* especially "Pélerinage aux Sources," 35–112; and Christian Vieyra, "Structures politiques traditionelles et structures politiques modernes," 210–212 and passim.

23. See Hampaté Bâ, "Les traditions Africains, gages de progrès."

24. Ki-Zerbo, Mazrui, Wondji, and Bohen, "Nation-Building," 468.

25. Sékou Touré, cited in Ki-Zerbo, Mazrui, Wondji, and Bohen, "Nation-Building," 468.

26. Hodgkin, "Political Forces," 9.

27. The African Union, which replaced the Organization of African Unity (founded in 1963) at the inaugural Assembly of Heads of State and Government of the African Union held in South Africa from June 28 to July 10, 2002, was apparently Qaddafi's brainchild. The African Union was launched in July 2001 at Lusaka after forty of Africa's fifty-three states had ratified its Constitutive Act, adopted in Lomé on June 12, 2000. Given widespread misgivings about Qaddafi's motives for his initial sponsorship of the new organization, plus continuing evidence of strained relations with sub-Saharan African states (e.g., the brutal eviction of thousands of sub-Saharan African workers from Libya in 2000), the future path of the new organization remains unclear.

28. Fougeyrollas, *Modernisation des hommes*, 42–130 passim.

29. N'Diaye, *Enquête sur les étudiants noirs en France;* Fougeyrollas, *Modernisation des hommes,* 158.

30. Balandier, especially his *Sociologie actuelle de l'Afrique Noire,* and *L'Afrique ambigue,* in translation as *Ambiguous Africa.*

31. Almond and Coleman, eds., *The Politics of the Developing Areas,* 28.

32. For further discussion of the concept of "political education" as an aspect of political socialization, see Dawson and Prewitt, *Political Socialization,* 76–78.

33. Green, yellow, and red appear to be favored; Cameroon, Congo-Brazzaville, Benin, Mali, and Senegal use only these colors. Red often symbolizes "the blood of patriots," green the tropical rainforest or verdant fields, and yellow the desert or savannah. Blue, deemed by some militant nationalists to be an imperialist color, appears in the flags of Gabon, the CAR, and Chad; in these cases it represents bodies of water (the Congo and Chari Rivers, Lake Chad).

34. The whole silly business persuaded some foreign observers to conclude that Congo-Brazzaville had indeed gone communist. "Les Trois Glorieuses" refers to the three days of popular demonstrations in 1963 that led to the overthrow of the regime of the Abbé Foulbert Youlou and ushered in the era of revolutionary politics.

35. Potholm, *Four African Political Systems,* 267.

36. Victor D. Du Bois, "The Decline of the Guinean Revolution."

37. I never saw a copy of that book but was assured it existed.

38. For a discussion of this aspect of the historical search, see "The Hero Cult," in Wauthier, *The Literature and Thought of Modern Africa,* 95–103.

39. The late Father Engelbert Mveng (d. 1995), once minister of culture in Cameroon, even wrote his doctoral thesis on sub-Saharan Africa in the literature of classical ancient Greece. For a summary, see his "L'Afrique: Emergence d'un continent, peuples, et civilisations de l'Afrique antique."

40. Monteil, "La decolonisation de l'histoire."

41. Ki-Zerbo, *Le monde africain noir—histoire et civilization;* Cheikh Anta Diop, *Nations nègres et culture;* Cheikh Anta Diop, *The African Origin of Civilization: Myth or Reality.*

42. I examine this phenomenon in "The Politics of Partition in Africa: The Cameroons Myth of Unification."

43. The original follows:

Sékou Touré,
Grand-Merci à toi, Touré
La libération de la Guinée
Ne nous surprend guère.
L'affamé ne sent-il pas de loin
Le fumet du plat salutaire.
Sékou Touré
O don Divin à la Guinée
Salut à toi, soit béni
O toi, bienfaiteur de la Guinée
Apôtre de la bonne cause
O l'enfant prodige.

From the poem "Independence" by Djely (Diely) Mamoudou Kandé, printed in *Présence Africaine,* December 1959–January 1960, p. 95, cited in David Apter, *The Politics of Modernization,* 297. The translation is mine, but perhaps there is a problem not so much with the translation, as with the intent of the author. Apter accepted the poem at face value as a paean to Sékou Touré, and I am inclined to do so as well. However, the French term *grand-merci* usually expresses irony and is translated in the English colloquial as "Thanks, but no thanks!" If that is in fact what the poet intended, then the whole poem is really an exercise in snide irony. I tried to find out if this is the case, but though Kandé was still active in 1986, I was unable to contact him.

44. The story was related to me by several reliable informants in Bangui in 1965.

45. Scott, *Domination and the Arts of Resistance.*

46. Monga, *The Anthropology of Anger: Civil Society and Democracy in Africa.*

47. Hasek, *The Good Soldier Svejk.* Svejk, or Schweick, who had been a dog broker before he was conscripted, arranged to become a "batman," or officer's orderly, in the Austro-Hungarian army, and from that position he worked a series of schemes, cons, and self-serving deceptions of his superiors.

48. I take a point of personal privilege here: I experienced, or took, each of these "snapshots" during visits to the locales mentioned. Eyadéma's DC-3 crashed near Sarakawa in north-central Togo. The comic-book biography, officially commissioned and sold through the president's party (the RPT, Rassemblement du Peuple Togolais) suggests that the Sarakawa accident might well have been the result of sabotage committed by European interests seeking to prevent the Togolese government from acquiring a majority share in the Kpéme phosphates company (Serge, *Histoire du Togo: Il était une fois—Eyadéma*). I happened to be in Lomé on a visit from Ghana and observed the festivities. A French friend with access made it possible for me to watch the procession of obsequious well-wishers tender their plaques, scrolls, petitions, and gifts to the president himself. It was all very monarchical.

49. Delavignette, *Freedom and Authority in French West Africa.*

50. Hampaté Bâ, *The Fortunes of Wangrin (Etrange destin de Wangrin).*

51. For a summary account of these various forms of disobedience and resistance, see Hodgkin, *Nationalism in Colonial Africa,* chapters 3 and 4.

52. For the recent history of anglophone Cameroonian opposition, see Takougang and Krieger, *African State and Society in the 1990s: Cameroon's Political Crossroads.* The separatists, in the tradition of the longtime opposition party, the Union des Populations du Cameroun (UPC), continue to make their case outside the country through publications of various kinds and on the Internet.

53. Apart from documents issued by the MFDC and the Senegalese government, there is not much reliable information on the Casamance rebellion. Two sources, however, stand out: United Kingdom, Foreign and Commonwealth Office, "The Casamance Conflict, 1982–1999," and Amnesty International, "Climate of Terror in Casamance."

54. See, for example, the Web sites of several Cameroonian separatist organizations, each of which gives the Southern Cameroons a new name, ostensibly for the separate country each envisions: "The State of Southern Cameroons," by the Southern Cameroons National Council/Southern Cameroons Peoples' Conference (http://www.iccnet.cm/cam_actu/act_pol/p00011801.htm); "The Federal Republic of Southern Cameroons," by the Southern Cameroons Provisional Administration (http://www.southerncameroons.org); and "Republic of Ambazonia (ex-BSC)," probably by the same people sponsoring the "Federal Republic of Southern Cameroons," but with a Web site listing some forty "Murdered Victims" of the Cameroon regime, including Augustin Ngom Jua, former West Cameroon prime minister, allegedly poisoned in 1977 by the Ahidjo regime (http://www.human-rights.de/ambazonia/). (The entry for Jua in DeLancey and Mokeba, *Historical Dictionary of the Republic of Cameroon,* gives 1979 as the year of Jua's death and is silent on the reason for his demise.) The MFDC Web site, available in both English and French, is at (http://www.ifrance.com/Casamance), and a limited amount of printed MFDC material circulates clandestinely in Dakar and openly in Paris.

55. For a fuller exposition of this thesis, see Linda Kirschke's "Informal Repression, Zero-Sum Politics, and Late Third Wave Transition." Kirschke is also

the author of a report for the freedom-of-the-press NGO called Article 19, "Northern Cameroon: Attacks on Freedom of Expression by Governmental and Traditional Authorities," in which she provides details of the *lamibés'* activities.

56. Takougang and Krieger, *African State and Society,* in particular 115–130.

57. Kirschke, "Informal Repression," 392, citing Eboussi Boulaga, *La démocratie de transit au Cameroun,* 84. Opposition sources claim even higher casualties; what I've been able to gather from various official and unofficial sources suggests that the number of dead may be close to six hundred and of the wounded around eight hundred.

58. There was nothing very scientific about my survey of party Web sites. Working from lists of political parties for the fourteen states and concentrating on those actually contesting elections, which would give them a reason to put up a Web site, on June 23 and 24, 2002, I searched the Internet (using Google as my search engine) for each one.

59. Tripp, "The New Political Activism in Africa."

60. Toulabor, "Naissance du democrate Africain," 4. My translation.

61. Ibid.

5

Ideology and Political Style: The Uneasy Marriage of Thought and Action

"In what myth shall we look for consolation?"
Onwuchekwa Jemie, "Biafra," 1972

The African nationalists' task, as suggested earlier, was twofold: to win the political kingdom and then to consolidate it.[1] The first imperative required that African political leaders have the skills of persuasion, agitation, and the manipulation of symbols likely to influence their followers on the one hand and the metropole and its representatives on the other. These were skills suitable to what was, in francophone Africa, largely a process of peaceful colonial disengagement. Some francophone leaders did use the language of revolutionaries, but with few exceptions the recourse to metaphors of violence was for effect, rather than for purposes of bargaining or persuasion. Only the neo-Marxists and the *marxisant* groups (Cameroon's Union des Populations du Cameroun [UPC], Niger's Sawaba, and Senegal's Parti Africain de l'Indépendance [PAI], for example) meant much of what they said or were willing to suit violent action to their words.

The second task, consolidation of independence and power, proved at once more formidable and subtler than the first. Here what was required was a political style appropriate to construction rather than opposition, to the confrontation and solution of problems that before independence had been the charge of embarrassable colonial administrations. The lesson sometimes was a hard one to learn since, as it turned out, the political skills and rhetoric that had won support before independence generally failed to do so afterward.

Viewed thus, the analysis of ideology and political style in francophone Africa requires that we distinguish between two political contexts— colonial and postindependence—each of which called for a unique ideological language and political style. Ideology and political style must also be

119

distinguished one from the other since any connection between the two can be neither assumed nor inferred.

Lucian Pye and Sidney Verba argue that *political style* refers to two aspects of political belief systems: one, "the way in which beliefs are held" as distinct from the "substance of beliefs," and two, "those informal norms of political interaction that regulate the way fundamental beliefs are applied in politics."[2] Pye and Verba stress the political belief systems themselves and only secondarily their connections to political behavior. Taken in its broadest sense, however, it is the translation of beliefs into behavior, or in Pye and Verba's terms, "the way in which political beliefs are held," that distinguishes one political style from another. In other words, *political style* refers to a complex of related political beliefs and behaviors—in sum, ideology—that also serves to distinguish one political actor or set of actors from other actors or sets of actors.[3] Thus, insofar as ideology informs political behavior it has empirical political consequences in political style. An ideology may be sufficiently pervasive or dominant to become the operational code of political actors or of a regime; in that case, political behavior fits political beliefs, and an official ideology may come to be expressed in government policies, programs, and the like. In the real world, of course, such a fit is never perfect, and more often than not, what leaders proclaim is not what they do.

There is one further difficulty connected with the term *ideology:* it generally refers to an explicit system of political beliefs that have operational consequences in the real political world. An ideology in this ideal sense should be a political weltanschauung—coherent, manifest, and explicable. Yet, again, in the real world of African politics, and certainly in the case of francophone Africa, there has been little real ideology and, rather, much *ideologizing;* that is, the use of cascades of ideological language that might but usually do not fit into any systematic, internally consistent array of political beliefs to which the label *ideology* could be applied.

The Ghanaian political scientist B. D. G. Folson goes even further: he argues that nationalism, for example, be it affirmative or reactive, is suspect as an ideology because "there is hardly any African leader who is not a nationalist, and yet some have systems of ideas that are recognizably ideological, whilst others have not." Moreover, "there are too many contradictions in nationalist rhetoric and realities in Africa for it to be able to provide that system of ideas with any consistency without which one can hardly speak of ideology." Ideological assertions remain suspect even if one argues, as does Folson, that in Africa only the socialists—including the Marxist-Leninists and "Afro-Marxists"—insist on the universal importance of ideology and propose that "socialism has emerged as the characteristic ideology in Africa."[4] At all events, nationalism remains a residual category incorporating a wide array of programs, demands, and objectives focusing on the symbols of independence, removal of alien influences, and national identity. In this view, the test of ideology is consistency and the systematic coherence of the ideas involved. By that standard, the nationalisms of Africa fail as ideologies—though not as a set of ideological themes. But if for argument's sake we adopt the view that within the range of African ideologizing the socialists and Afro-Marxists probably have the most focused ideological sets, we can ascribe ideological import to a whole range of admittedly diffuse, but nonetheless politically significant ideas and programs without doing violence to logic or reality.

In the fourteen francophone countries only Sékou Touré, Modibo Keita, Léopold Sédar Senghor, and (perhaps) Thomas Sankara have made anything like an effort to spell out coherent ideological systems, and only in Mali, Guinea, Benin, Congo-Brazzaville, and Burkina Faso can it be said that the official word has been more or less reflected in the policies, programs, and practices of government. Certain political symbols and varieties of political language have spelled out the belief systems and the pragmatic, heuristic political concerns of some leaders and their regimes, but such language usually bears little relation to government policies. As Ahmed Mahiou, referring to political parties, puts it succinctly, "Is it then legitimate to speak of African ideology since the course of African parties seems to be basically pragmatic? Yes, if ideology is simply understood as the expression of future projects or as a program of action." If Mahiou is right, then the meaning of the term is reduced even further. Consider, for example, socialist ideology. Mahiou himself recognizes the difficulty: "There has never been such a blooming of 'socialisms' since African states attained independence to the point that it may be asked if there are not as many ideologies as there are parties."[5]

What is left after this distillation? Certainly political style, taken in its broader meaning and granting the empirical difficulties of definition, remains an important way of describing how politicians, political groups, and regimes go about their business. Further, if we no longer insist that political rhetoric somehow exactly match political action, we can discuss ideological language and ideological themes in political language with the understanding that they may or may not be related, depending on circumstances of time, place, and political context. And finally, ideology emerges as a kind of more or less focused language, a convention that enables us to describe a fairly wide variety of ideas, orientations, and programs—including nationalism and socialism.

Nationalism, Francophilism, and Other Dilemmas

If one simply regards the colonial situation through the eyes of a dialectician—even those of a Marxist dialectician—then the origin and growth of nationalism in francophone Africa (as elsewhere on the continent) can be seen as a natural reaction to the colonial situation.[6] Nationalism in such a formulation becomes an "ideology of rejection" *(une ideologie de refus),* the logical, dialectical affirmation of an identity and self-determination for the submerged subject to whom political rights have been denied.[7]

There is much to such a formulation, particularly since the first stirrings of nationalism in francophone Africa seem to have come in the form of open resistance to the imposition of French rule. The rebellion of Lat-Dior, the *damel* of Cayor (in Senegal); the struggles of the Abomeyan kings against the French; and the resistance of el-Hajj 'Umar Tal, Samory, and the Bornuan Rabeh all certainly appear, in that light, to represent attempts to resist the encroachments of colonialism and to preserve authentic African political values. The protonationalist agitation of religious groups in the Congo area and the resistance to forced labor and to the excesses of administrators in the Cameroons, Dahomey, and Congo all help to bolster this thesis. It is also supported by the literature of anticolonial protest—from the West Indian René Maran's *Batouala* (which in 1921 won the Prix Goncourt, one of France's most prestigious literary prizes), to the writings of Mongo Beti and Ferdinand Oyono[8]—and by the post–World War II push for independence, accompanied by manifestoes, declarations, and party programs with very specific anticolonial content.

The dialectical formula of nationalism as rejection and anticolonialism, appealing though it may be, is nonetheless only partially valid. What it overlooks, particularly in the francophone African context, is the political schizophrenia of many of the leading nationalists themselves, a condition manifested in both their language and their behavior as nationalists. To begin with, the African elites' rejection of colonialism in francophone Africa was usually conditional, partial, and, until very late into the decolonization process, hesitant. With the exception of a few radical and revolutionary nationalists, the thesis of political independence from France had few advocates until 1957 and 1958, and even those in support displayed little enthusiasm for the idea. The language of local nationalist leaders tended toward familiar boilerplate denunciations of the evils of colonialism, but when Senghor, Philibert Tsiranana, Félix Houphouët-Boigny, Mamadou Konaté, and Barthélemy Boganda spoke of independence, what they meant was autonomy within some form of French political community, not complete rejection of France and all it had meant to them.

For some, of course, the reason for the leaders' hesitance was a matter more of the economic consequences of an abrupt separation than Francophilic sentiment. The Malagasy leader Philibert Tsiranana put it precisely at a press conference in Tananarive on August 21, 1958: "When I let my heart talk, I am a partisan of total and immediate independence; when I make my reason speak, I realize that it is impossible."[9] Though economic considerations played a role in framing francophone African responses to de Gaulle's 1958 proposition of new ties to France, it must be stressed that almost from the earliest days of the political awakening in French-speaking Africa, the dominant theme in political discourse was the quest for the fullest realization of *French* political values as these were expressed in the French Revolution and in the colonial doctrines of assimilation. It was only after World War II that the assertion of an African identity mingled with the earlier theme, and even then it was expressed in integrative rather than mutually exclusive terms.

In other words, those Africans who expressed their discontent with the colonial situation more often than not came to do so within the framework of an all-too-familiar dilemma: they felt themselves to be part French, having learned the language and the basic political ideas of their criticism from the French. But they were also African, and as Africans had tasted the bitter frustrations and anger of the colonized. Thus they could rage at the French for the more repressive, cruel aspects of the French colonial system, but could never fully bring themselves to reject a political and social culture whose language, ideas, and mores they had, to varying degrees, made their own.[10] As a consequence, the language and ideas of francophone African nationalism evoked as much the nationalists' sense of having been betrayed and rejected by France and the French as it reflected their own rejection of French colonialism as a system of political and economic domination. Albert Memmi, one of the French theorists of anticolonialism, explained the failure of French colonialism in just such terms: "It was the colonized who first sought assimilation, and it is the colonizer who denies him."[11]

Initially the sense of betrayal was muted among the *evolués* of the AOF, and the promise of assimilation remained an article of faith among those expressing discontent with the political status quo. Here is Galandou Diouf, an important early Senegalese political figure, in 1915 upbraiding the French for betraying their own values: "Forgetting their own and their ancestors' past, certain undesirable Frenchmen from the metropole would like to try keeping us under the yoke of slavery, despite all the liberties generously granted us by the great French revolution. The French Republic, gentlemen, freed us as it did you; if we were most recently slaves, you were among the first to be freed from bondage."[12] Of all the francophone African intellectuals, it is Senghor who most clearly expresses the tense counterpoint between rejection of French colonialism and love of France. His "Prière de paix" (Prayer of Peace, 1948) speaks directly and eloquently to the feelings involved:

Lord, the mirror of my eyes clouds over
And there is the serpent of hate raising his head in my heart, the serpent
    I had believed dead. . . .

Kill it, O Lord, for I must continue on my way and I want to pray particularly for France.

O Lord, among all the White nations, place France on the right hand of the Father.

Oh! I know she is also part of Europe, that she has stolen my children as a robber from the north takes cattle, to enrich her lands with sugar cane and cotton, for the Negro's sweat is manure.

That she also brought death and the cannon into my blue villages, that she set my people against one another like dogs fighting over a bone.

That she treated resistance as banditry, and spat on the heads that dreamt of greatness.

Yes, Lord, forgive France who preaches the straight path but takes the crooked one herself.

Who invites me to her table yet tells me to bring my own bread, who provides with the right hand, but takes half away with the left.

Yes, Lord, forgive France who hates occupiers yet imposes occupation so heavily on me.

Who opens the triumphal gate to heroes and treats her Senegalese as mercenaries, making them the black watchdogs of the Empire.

Who is a Republic, yet places the country in the hands of the big companies.

And of my Mesopotamia, of my Congo, they have made a great cemetery beneath the white sun.[13]

Examples abound, but one more will suffice to make the argument. In 1938 Paul Hazoumé, the distinguished Dahomean ethnologist, writer, and, later, nationalist politician, published *Doguicimi,* a historical novel that vividly recreates the court life of the Abomey kingdom destroyed by the French in 1892. The book celebrates Dahomean tradition and the values of African life, those themes of the nationalist argument that asserts the depth and richness of African life in contrast to the cultural values of the West. Yet Hazoumé ends the novel with an epilogue in which he argues that his heroine, Doguicimi, would have welcomed the arrival of the French, who, "you thought, seemed to combine the essential qualities that would enable them to stop the endless wars of the Dahomeyan kings, the slave trade, and the human sacrifices that were laying waste to the country more than they were enriching it."[14] He suggests that Doguicimi would have rejoiced that the French, rather than British, became the eventual occupiers of the country because they brought "peace, liberty, and humanity." To be sure, Hazoumé was regarded by some of his younger intellectual contemporaries as overly Francophilic, but the African-French ambiguity is visible in his novel as it was in his political life. In 1915 Hazoumé had been coeditor (with Emile Zinsou Bodé) of a clandestine monthly, *Le Récadaire de Benhanzin,* which attacked an obnoxious French governor, Charles Noufflard. After 1945 he became an influential member of the Indépendants d'Outre-Mer (IOM) in the French Parliament and an active participant in the Dahomean nationalist arena.[15]

Doudou Thiam, a former Senegalese foreign minister, not only argued that this inner conflict delayed the development of nationalism in francophone Africa, but represented it as a salient point of difference between francophone and anglophone African nationalism:

> In fact, nationalism, whose concrete form is the demand for independence, arose much earlier in English-speaking African countries. This is because British colonial policy did not pass through the detour of assimilation. African leaders in British territories knew, very early, that it would be a vain hope to seek to invade the House of Lords or the Commons. They knew that they could not recover their dignity or exercise their liberties except within the framework of independence; in contrast, French-speaking Africans reasoned in terms of "French dignity," "French liberty," and "French equality." But it must be noted that, whatever the road taken, the results were the same in both cases.[16]

Thiam brings us back to nationalism in its more conventional form, as the assertion of the right of political self-determination for dependent peoples. The end of the process, as Thiam rightly notes, was independence, pursued with visible reluctance in some cases, with enthusiasm in others, but independence nonetheless. Bearing in mind the underlying ambiguities of the Franco-African relationship, we can now turn to other themes in the ideologies of francophone African nationalism.

Thomas Hodgkin, surveying the language of nationalism in Africa, suggests some eleven recurring "common themes."[17] His list (see Appendix F) is useful not only because its themes were expressed to some degree in most of francophone Africa, but also because it includes some of the most important verbal symbols used in the oral and written literature of nationalism. What Hodgkin does not do is distinguish between the symbols' extensive changes in meaning as they were used by the nationalists themselves; nor does he explain why those differences occur. An understanding of francophone nationalism requires that these matters be clarified because these differences, and the reasons for them, help account for one of the realities of Africa after the 1960s: a shift from a situation of ideological efflorescence to one in which ideology has played a decreasing, and often minor, role in politics.

This is not to imply some sort of African "end of ideology"; for some time into the decades of the 1970s and 1980s, some of the more persuasive and interesting ideologues (such as Julius Nyerere, Sékou Touré, and Senghor) continued to produce exegeses on their own themes, and a few fresh voices (like those of Sankara in Burkina Faso and Marien Ngouabi in the Central African Republic) came onto the scene. Rather, it is that other political realities—authoritarian military and civilian regimes, struggling or stagnant economies, persistent ethnocommunal strains—led to the devaluation of most ideological currencies in favor of ad hoc or pragmatic ruling styles. The old symbols and rhetorics are still around, but they have largely lost their old salience, and, more important, their power to engage popular affect and action has substantially diminished. However, after 1989 democracy unexpectedly reemerged as a potent ideological symbol, challenging the assumptions of those who had come to accept the autocracies and kleptocracies of the 1970s and 1980s as the African norm.

During the period between World Wars I and II, what ideological expression there was among educated Africans tended to be relatively unfocused, congealing from time to time around questions of abuse by colonial authorities; the relationship between the colonies and metropolitan France; pan-African ideas developed by African exiles or blacks from the West Indies and North America; or, as in the case of Senegal, the activities of political groups and of French, mixed-race, and African politicians in the *quatre communes*. There were religiopolitical agitations (as those in Moyen-Congo, the Ivory Coast, Guinea, and Cameroon) brought about by local religious schisms or by such external influences as the Garveyite movement. African intellectuals in some of the early political movements of anglophone inspiration (like the Aborigines' Rights Protection Society and the National Congress of British West Africa) also had some impact on the French colonies, but again, it weighed little on the ideological scales. In any case, if there was nationalist ideologizing, it tended to be muted, or at best protonationalist (a term that suffers from post hoc, ergo propter hoc assumptions).

Although the interwar period was hardly an auspicious time for the growth of nationalist sentiment, in the period from 1945 to 1960 nationalism became *the* basic political orientation of francophone African politicians, though it was never simply a broad duplication of thematic material over time or across territorial frontiers. Three related sets of factors help distinguish among the varieties of nationalism in francophone Africa during the post–World War II period:

1. The predispositions of the nationalists themselves, e.g., their values, experiences, and attitudes;
2. Certain situational variables such as politics in the metropole, the favorability of the international climate, constitutional and institu-

tional reforms in the colonies, and the territorialization of politics from 1946 on; and

3. The nature of the audiences to which nationalist appeals were directed and the nationalists' perceptions about the impact of those appeals.

Each set of factors is worth exploring in its own right.

The Nationalists' Predispositions

It has been emphasized here that except in the case of some socialist and *marxisant* political leaders and groups, independence became a viable ideological icon in most of francophone Africa only after 1957. It may well be the case that African Francophilism contributed a good deal to the fact that endorsement of a goal embraced openly and with fervor elsewhere on the continent took place so late and with such little enthusiasm. As late as April 1958, when the Fourth Republic had already entered its death throes, the majority of francophone African politicians—Senghor, Lamine Guèye, Yacine Diallo, Modibo, Hubert Maga, Houphouët-Boigny, Philibert Tsiranana, Boganda, and Sékou Touré—still sought associational formulas that would somehow preserve viable links between France and its empire in sub-Saharan Africa. They had shared in the birth of the Fourth Republic, helped to write its constitutions and laws, and participated in its legislatures and political parties; not a few had been members of French governments. Even the last government of the Fourth Republic, that of Félix Gaillard, contained four African notables: Maga (Upper Volta) was undersecretary of state for labor, Modibo Keita and Hammadoun Dicko (Soudan) were secretaries of state in the prime minister's office and the ministry of education respectively, and Houphouët-Boigny became minister of public health and population.

Senghor, who had served in Edgard Faure's government (1952), was offered a cabinet post but declined, making it known that he would not serve so long as the Algerian war continued.[18] It is fair to assume that Senghor would hardly have bothered to make the excuse if he had already fully committed himself to independence; he may well have already thought about it, but his position had not yet crystallized to the point where he could see independence as a real goal. The events between May and September 1958 that brought de Gaulle to power and the Fifth Republic into being were still ahead; only then could Senghor think of using the constitutional referendum of September 1958 as a first step to independence. Even Sékou Touré, who had already crafted the institutional and political base for an independent Guinea, in early 1958 could still "talk of liquidating the colonial system, of the struggle for emancipation, or decolonization, but avoid pronouncing the key word of our time, 'independence.'"[19] Of course, it was not long before Sékou Touré and Guinea opted for independence, and within two years the rest of the ex-AOF and AEF territories had done so as well. But the fact remains: commitment to independence was long delayed and was not easy for any of the old Francophilic politicians.[20]

That the symbols of independence were ambiguous does not mean that other symbols, such as those of self-determination, autonomy, and self-government, were similarly so. Those were clear enough because the whole thrust of francophone African political development, particularly after 1956, had been to create increasingly self-governing, territorially distinct units in which the French connection remained discreet, to be brought out in the open and used forcefully only in extremis. What did divide francophone African politicians were questions about the modalities of autonomy and, before 1958, about the nature of their association with one another vis-à-vis France. Except in the case of a few of the more venturesome leaders—like Sourou-Migan Apithy, Sylvanus Olympio, and Djibo Bakary—autonomy did not also mean independence.

Not all francophone African leaders were schizophrenic about independence, and not all were equally affected by the ambivalence. Far from it. It is interesting to observe that the francophone African politicians active during the early days of the Fourth Republic's constitution making and party formation, the Rassemblement Démocratique Africain (RDA) leaders, as official radicals, given their alliance with the French communists, remained wedded to the proposition that, as D. Bruce Marshall puts it, "an underlying harmony of outlook and interests between France and the colonies" could develop "a freely consented union" among them.[21] The communists' position, articulated by (among others) Aimé Césaire of Martinique and Lamine Guèye of Senegal remained unchallenged until 1949, when some RDA members began talking privately about independence as a possible option.[22] Earlier, during the final debate of the French Union provisions in the first 1946 constitutional draft, Apithy (the Dahomean socialist who had refused to join his political party to the RDA) was the only West African deputy to pursue the ideas of autonomy *and* possible secession from France.

By the early 1950s, however, the idea began to gain some currency, particularly among the more radical—i.e., *communisant*—African leaders in both France and Africa itself. Their shift in disposition was due in part to reversals in the French communists' political fortunes, in part to a change in Moscow's attitudes in favor of rapid decolonization, and in part to their perception that their chances in Africa would be improved if they stimulated a quasi-revolutionary mood. Further, there is little doubt that Kwame Nkrumah's visible and exhilarating successes in Ghana whetted radical appetites among trade unionists and student groups in France, as well as among francophone African leaders increasingly frustrated by the official French conservatism on colonial questions. However, it took a combination of such sentiments and the very special circumstances of Cameroon and Togo to force the issue out into the open.[23]

The two territories had special status as United Nations trusteeships under Charter provisions that explicitly envisioned political devolution leading to self-government or independence, encouraging a nationalism more sharply focused on independence than was possible elsewhere. As one consequence of that special status, a cohort of politicians appeared who could operate in an ideological climate different from that in the rest of francophone Africa. Thus, in Cameroon it was possible for the local RDA branch, the *marxisant* UPC, to demand almost immediately after the group's founding in 1948 rapid progress toward independence under the terms of the UN Charter. By 1955, almost all Cameroonian political parties had co-opted the independence symbol for their own programs.

In Togo it was not leftists who first made independence a primary objective, but, ironically, the leaders of a political party, the Comité d'Unité Togolais (CUT), that had originally been formed under government auspices as a cultural club. The CUT, led by Sylvanus Olympio and Augustino de Souza, became the Togolese branch of the RDA in 1946 and at once declared itself in favor of both unification with the British Togoland Trusteeship and early independence.[24] The French administration, which had different (that is, associational) plans for Togo, proved able by 1955 to put its "own" politicians (Nicholas Grunitsky and Antoine Meatchi) into office. But by then it was already too late to turn the clock back: the new Togo Statute of 1954 went further in the direction of self-government than any previous French dispensation and, for that matter, further than France had been willing to allow anywhere else in its African dominions. In 1956 Togo became an "autonomous republic," and even the most Francophilic of the Togolese leaders, like Grunitsky, began to press for early independence.

By 1955, then, the meaning of *autonomy* had begun to change for francophone African leaders. Not only could they now ask, "If Togo, why not the AOF?" but the more radical among them could now inquire, "If autonomy, why not independence?" The rest hardly needs recapitulation: by the end of 1958 Sékou Touré and Guinea had already taken independence, Senegal had voted yes in the 1958 constitutional referendum as a first step to independence, Mali and Modibo Keita were preparing for independence, and the once lonely voices that had earlier demanded independence were joined by a chorus that included both ardent Francophiles and radicals of the *marxisant* parties in Upper Volta (Sawaba) and Senegal (Parti Africain de l'Indépendance [PAI]).

Contextual Differences

Because of their legal status as UN trust territories, Togo and Cameroon represented very special political situations. For one thing, the normative reinforcement provided by the UN commitment permitted Togolese and Cameroonian nationalists to operate much more freely outside the francophone colonial consensus than would have been possible otherwise. For another, the very structure of those situations—close international monitoring through UN bodies and visiting missions; ready access to international anticolonial forums through petitions, delegations to the UN, and representations to visiting missions; and the constraints placed on French colonial administrations and policy by these factors—all encouraged the proliferation of parties, groups, and associations, almost all of which cast their appeals and programs in territorial or parochial terms. In Cameroon over one hundred such formations of varying duration and strength appeared between 1946 and 1960.[25]

As a consequence, pan-African ideological themes found little echo in either territory save in the loftiest, most general declarations. Local nationalists preferred to focus on such symbols as self-determination (presumably guaranteed by the UN Charter), ethnic unity (in Togo in relation to the Ewe), reunification (of British and French Togo and of the British and French Cameroons), reconciliation (of moderate and radical political elements in Cameroon), and, of course, independence. Further, as David Apter and James Coleman remark, the anticolonial majority in the UN helped preserve African fragmentation by opposing the creation of administrative unions that would unite trust territories with neighboring colonies ruled by the same government and by delaying the integration of the trust territories with their soon-to-be-independent neighbors.[26] Although support for the latter point is dubious,[27] the effect of the dominant UN orientation, at least for Togo and Cameroon, was to reinforce the trend toward territorialization of politics in francophone Africa.

This last fact—political fragmentation—constitutes another important variable for the development of ideology, as does the growth of internal political institutions in the territories themselves. Both situations narrowed the focus of ideological discourses to fit territorial boundaries, while at the same time diversifying them to meet local concerns, such as the winning of seats in territorial assemblies; the mobilizing of populations for political action; and (with the creation of local ministries after 1955) the seizing, reinforcing, and holding of political power. Apter and Coleman make the point with precision: "Committed to a strategy of constitutional agitation and non-violent change," the nationalists "were obliged to adapt the style, scope, and tempo of their political action to the unique situation and institutional complex with which they were presented." Among other imperatives, it was necessary to "create in the popular mind some concrete image of the new community being created," a sense of "territorial personality."[28] Thus, in Cameroon a historical "Kamerun myth" became part of Cameroonian nationalist ideology, the Union Soudanaise (the Soudanese branch of the RDA) strove to build a sentiment of "Soudanness," and the Bloc Démocratique Sénégalaise emphasized the special character of Senegalese life. This is not to say that francophone African nationalists failed to deal with the larger transterritorial and pan-African ideological themes (anti-imperialism, African personality, African unity, etc.); rather, with the nationalization of ideology, their more pragmatic concerns dictated the use of language tilted toward immediate, visible interests on the local level.

Finally, French politics and policies shifted and changed. The post-Brazzaville aura of colonial reform; the RDA's alliance with the French communists; the presence of Africans in French councils, legislatures, and ministries; the eight-year (1946–1954) conservative hiatus on colonial matters; the Vietnamese and Algerian conflicts; the return of the socialists to power in France during the mid-1950s; and the political resurrection of de Gaulle and his policies all had visible effects on francophone African politics and its ideological by-products.

Audiences and the Impact of Ideology

A third and related distinction of the formation of African nationalism is the adaptation of ideological language to meet the expectations of various audiences. The notion is not a new one: it is almost common sense that the choice and use of affective symbols by politicians depends not only on the politicians' values and ideas, but also on their assessment of their audiences' responses. We can distinguish among various ideological modes and even partly explain their uses by asking who the audiences are.

Negritude is the key symbol in a set of ideas usually associated with Senghor. First developed during the 1930s by a group of black expatriate colonial intellectuals including Senghor, Aimé Césaire, and Léon Damas, it grew into an ideology that asserted certain unique racial characteristics of the black, or more precisely, the "Negro-African world." Senghor's famous Oxford Statement encapsulates it: "the sense of communion, the gift of mythmaking, the gift of rhythm—such are the essential elements of Negritude, which you will find indelibly stamped on all the works and activities of the Black man."[29] Originally conceived as an answer to the alienation of black intellectuals unable to come to terms with the fiction of promised assimilation, negritude, at different stages of its formulation, stood for different things: a critique of imperialism, a rebirth of black civilization, a new path for African progress, "an ideology for African unity, a methodology for development, justification for rule by indigenous elites, a defense of the dignity of cultured Blacks."[30] As part of the official ideology during Senghor's presidency of Senegal, it was also expected to provide a moral basis for programs of social action and economic development.

Most important for our purposes, however, is that negritude was originally addressed not only to black expatriates but also to French intellectuals. Irving L. Markovitz stresses the importance of this fact and assesses its consequences:

> In Senghor's hands . . . Negritude became above all an appeal to the French. Its success had little to do with any forceful revolutionary appeal. Rather, Negritude served as a type of "passive resistance." It "worked" because it contained a moral appeal to the French intelligentsia couched in terms of their own culture and tradition. Negritude attracted not only intellectuals of the Left, such as Jean-Paul Sartre, but also the more general French intellectual and political establishment. The appeal succeeded because Negritude, from its origins, was conceived within the scope of the French colonial myth. French colonial policy had never maintained that the colonial peoples were racially inferior or inherently different in any manner. Like the Greeks, the French had always proclaimed to the peoples of the world that when they had achieved the level of French civilization, they would be equal. Negritude attempted to show that this level was attained. It was a demonstration in abstraction, erudition, and sensitivity. Negritude may have been rebellion, but not revolution.[31]

Viewed from this perspective, some of the criticisms leveled at negritude—that its assertions have no empirical foundation in biology or psychology, that it was a form of reverse racism, that it corrupted the African heritage by toadying to French sensibilities, and so on[32]—seem beside the point. Granting the ambiguities of the ideology, including those grafted onto it by Senghor's own polymorphic explications,[33] it is important to emphasize that negritude helped mobilize French intellectual sentiment on behalf of African aspirations and gave the French left a viable set of ideas and heroes to champion. Above all, it touched a sensitive core of political conscience long stultified by the colonial policies of the Fourth Republic's politicians by bringing to light the glaring discrepancies between assimilationist theory and actual colonial practice. And in the process it also gave black intellectuals a new set of reintegrative symbols that they could use in their own search for political and social validation.

Negritude remained an important component of Senghor's ideological line, but because it was couched in language and embodied ideas far removed from the ordinary concerns of most Senegalese, its appeal was limited to foreign and African intellectuals—and, over time, to a dwindling part of the latter at best. Markovitz takes a similar view: "Senghor's doctrine remains inaccessible to the mass of the population. Significantly, all the populist revolutions of the past have had simple slogans like 'Land, Bread, and Peace.' To insist upon talking in the most sophisticated terms to unlearned men about 'Negritude,' 'African Socialism,' 'Economic Development,' and the 'Civilization of the Universal,' on the grounds of not talking down to them, is not to talk to them at all."[34] Were it not that Senghor was also a consummate politician who balanced, reconciled, and shifted the various personalities and groups on whom he relied for his power and who mixed his philosophical metaphors with visible programs of economic and political redistribution, he would have remained only a poet and visionary.

Senghor never found a dramatic way to communicate with his Senegalese constituency as a whole, but his highly pragmatic political style permitted him to mix socialist programs with endorsement of capitalist ventures, poetry with economic planning, and subtle ethnic maneuvering with appeals to his intellectual elite. Senghor's audiences changed over the long period of his presidency, and with them the symbolic mix in his ideologizing. Negritude, once a passionate affirmation of African identity and equality and one of the most powerful political weapons in his armory, became a far less significant arrow among the many in his rhetorical quiver.

A kind of stylistic-ideological counterpoint emerged after Senghor appointed Abdou Diouf as prime minister in 1970; Diouf eventually succeeded Senghor as president in January 1981. Diouf had a civil-service background and exhibited something in which Senghor put great stock: "technicity," the expertise and practical skills needed for development. Diouf was always his own man, but in a subtle fashion he played the role of embodying an important part of Senghor's pragmatic alter ego. While Senghor remained on the scene, the style of the regime reflected an interesting dialectic compound of the two men's outlooks and behaviors. Diouf stayed in office until March 2000, when the Senegalese voted him—and the ruling Parti Socialiste—out of power. By then, however, both Diouf and the party had distanced themselves considerably from the ideological stances of Senghor's regime. Diouf's successor, Abdoulaye Wade, a highly educated secular lawyer and economist and a longtime opponent of the old regime, completed the ideological estrangement from Senghor's foundations. If Wade professes anything akin to an ideology, it is his own vague brand of liberalism, which espouses free-market principles and privatization while rejecting excessive centralized government power. In any event, there is nothing like an official ideology here yet.

African Socialisms, Communisms, and Marxisms

The literature on the subject of "African socialism" is extensive. It includes contributions by self-styled African socialists and Marxists, as well as by a host of non-African polemicists, publicists, propagandists, and analysts of every political persuasion and national origin.[35] Part of the reason for this interest in the subject was the happy discovery by non-African ideologues of the left that Africa represented lightly settled ideological space into which they could project their own doctrinal analyses, disputes, and pre-conceptions. Thus, sober discussion about the growth of revolutionary con-sciousness among Pygmy peoples finds a place beside celebration of the significance to Africa of the Mongolian revolutionary experience.[36] Moreover, the wider international context within which post–World War II decolonization took place—the presence of the United Nations, the impact of European socialist and communist parties on colonial policies, the emer-gence of communist China as a major influence on "Third World" poli-tics—provided yet more ready-made opportunities for ideological interven-tion. Most important, of course, is that the language of socialism had long been part of the conventional political discourse of most leading African politicians. Even some military rulers—Ngouabi of the CAR, Mathieu Kérékou of Benin, and Sankara of Burkina Faso—who were little prone by temperament or training to adopt such language came to adopt some of the rhetoric. But the question remains: Why socialism?

First, as Fenner Brockway points out, many "founding father" African leaders were socialists because they belonged to an age group that conclud-ed its student days around the end of World War II, when socialism experi-enced a popular resurgence in Europe.[37] In 1945 the Labor Party was swept into power in England, and a coalition of socialist, communist, and radical Christian parties governed France until 1947. Thus, as Gilbert Comte argues, Marx (at least in the eyes of French socialists) once again became a respectable source of intellectual authority. Before the war,

> when a sensitive African like Léopold Senghor dreamed of liberty, he did so in the language of Jean-Jacques Rousseau, as it appeared in the republi-can phraseology of the Senegalese Socialist Party. At a time when the cap-ture of Berlin by the Red Army eclipsed the storming of the Bastille, the cohort *(classe-d'age)* of a Sékou Touré, a Modibo Keita, found itself affected mainly by the heroes of the moment. In its eyes, Lenin and Stalin seemed much more the revolutionary heroes than Messieurs de Lafayette and Danton.[38]

It was not that these young men had not been exposed to either socialist or communist ideas before the war; from 1922 on, Lenin had tried to extend the idea of the proletariat to colonial peoples, and the Communist International had developed considerable interest in the fate of black people in general and the American Negro in particular. The young African intel-lectual in Paris during the 1920s and 1930s could hardly escape contact with the panoply of communist and socialist ideas. Moreover, the Senegalese wing of the French Socialist Party had locally attracted many bright young activists. But neither communists nor socialists had developed much of an ideology of colonial liberation before or during the war, and indeed, both parties in France operated within, not outside, the French colonial myth. It took World War II and its extraordinary events to crystallize what would become an ideological consensus on the anticolonialism issue. Such an appeal could not fail to touch the sensitive ideological nerve of younger members of the African intelligentsia, be they in Africa or Europe.

Marxism, in both its socialist and communist guises, had considerable appeal to leaders in Third World areas also because, according to Adam Ulam, it promised both emancipation from the evils of the colonial present and future well-being based on the construction of new societies that combined equality and scientific-technological plenty. "Marxism," wrote Ulam, "to a remarkable degree reproduces the social psychology of the period of transition from a pre-industrial to an industrial society."[39] If Ulam's argument is that the appeal had special salience to the colonial (and ex-colonial) intellectual, it is well taken. Marxism, in this sense, offered at least an ideological shortcut to an African affirmation of a future in which Africans, not Europeans, were to be at once the molders and the beneficiaries of the new society. Moreover, coupled with some variant of Lenin's thesis on imperialism, Marxism was seen as a new weapon with which to force concessions from reluctant colonial policymakers.

Finally, the anticolonial discourse of the Marxist-socialist left, particularly after 1940, provided an unrivaled arsenal of slogans, clichés, and affective symbols for the emergent African elite. The language of the Marx of the Communist Manifesto, of Lenin, and of Mao (and later, of Fidel Castro, Che Guevara, and Frantz Fanon) is above all a language of political catalysis, designed—consciously or not—to be used by the intellectual vanguards to legitimize and justify their revolutions to themselves and each other, to be simplified into affective symbols capable of mobilizing mass support and action, and ultimately, to maintain the proper course of the new order once achieved.

No other modern political language has been so potent in its impact and so rich in the variety of its symbols: it was (and, to a lesser extent, remains) the language par excellence of those who are impatient to change their world. It implied a "scientific" method of social reconstruction and analysis, a claim made by Senghor, Sékou Touré, Mamadou Dia, Modibo, and the later "Afro-Marxists" of Congo and Benin for their brands of African socialism; it provided an ambiguous, and hence politically useful, set of labels with which to mark and vilify enemies (e.g., *imperialist, neocolonialist, bourgeois remnant, antirevolutionary, lackey, stooge,* and so on), who, depending on the circumstances, could be the French, the English, the Americans, the Germans, political opponents, or ideologically uncongenial African neighbors; it offered a simple theory of foreign domination (Lenin's imperialism thesis in various permutations); it celebrated rational and technical solutions to the problems of underdevelopment, such as centralized planning and state ownership of the means of production; it legitimized the role of the political vanguard and rationalized its prime construct, the single-party state; and if necessary it justified the use of violence against "class enemies" and governments that were labeled "oppressive" and "lackeys of neocolonialism." Above all, the language appealed to nationalist sentiment because it spoke directly to important nationalist themes: national liberation and a simple identification of capitalism with imperialism.

Again, the language had much greater immediate appeal to African intellectuals than to the African masses. The mobilization of their peers was at least as important to the intellectuals as the mobilization of the masses; without the former, a nationalist cadre of sufficient size and conviction to affect the masses could hardly be created. Still, the translation of Marxist-socialist themes along national ideological lines required simplification of the symbols.

The new users of the language found a sympathetic international audience as well as a set of symbols with which they could relate to one another. "The newly converted," argues Gilbert Comte, "demanded of Marxism above all motivating ideas *(idées-forces)* recipes, intellectual fetishes capable of hastening their own advancement. They did not always penetrate to the exact meaning of an ideology accepted as a temporary ally." More often than not they saw the language and its symbols in instrumental terms and played the Marxist card as a tactical choice—something that "did not necessarily also involve adherence to a credo."[40]

It is hard to avoid the conclusion that the orthodox Marxism-Leninism of the PAI, the FEAN (Fédération des Etudiants de l'Afrique Noire, based in Dakar), Sawaba, and the Cameroonian UPC owed much of its doctrinaire character to the fact that these groups' primary supportive audience was the French Communist Party, the far left in Western Europe, the Americas, and Asia, as well as leaders in Eastern Europe, whence they derived much financial, logistic, and political aid for their several brands of revolutionary action. The ideological commitment of such Marxist-Leninist ideologues as Majhemout Diop (principal spokesman and leader of the PAI) and Félix-Roland Moumié (leader of the exiled wing of the UPC after 1958) can be traced much more easily to their experiences as students (Diop in Paris, Moumié in Dakar), to their contact with communist teachers, and to their affiliation with radical left-wing organizations than it can to tactical considerations.[41]

Yet even a cursory look at the ideological evolution of these four groups demonstrates that the shape, the content, and the key symbols of their doctrines closely followed the contours of their political fortunes. For all of them alliance with and the support of the French Communist Party meant endorsing that party's contradictory positions on decolonization. For all of them, parroting the official Soviet line meant that a conduit to material favors from Moscow and Eastern Europe could be kept open. Once the Sino-Soviet conflict erupted into the open, the exile UPC split into pro-Soviet and Maoist wings, with the latter taking up Maoist revolutionary theses and being rewarded with trips to Peking, guerrilla training in China, money channeled through third parties, financial support to attend various leftist congresses throughout the world, and some living expenses.

It can also be argued that African socialism is distinguished more by its proponents and uses than by its content. As "an eclectic formula" that is articulated in a variety of ways by a heterogeneous array of political leaders and that "accepts certain facets of classical capitalist and socialist conceptions of economic change and organization, but rejects other facets,"[42] it generates what Bernard Charles terms "a singular logomachy."[43] Mamadou Dia, an eloquent exponent of socialism as the favored method of development, himself denounced the constant use of socialist vocabulary as an ideological cover for the "mystification" of the people. Similarly, the PAI and other cognate groups, in the name of Marxism-Leninism, accused African governments of betraying "true" socialism. Student organizations such as the Fédération des Etudiants Noirs en France (FEANF) even saw in socialism *à l'africaine* a myth that masked neocolonialism. Others, like the Malian Mamadou Konaté, insisted that the essential part of the African socialist formulation is the word *African:* "socialism is a secondary term that could well be replaced by another such as communitarianism."[44] The examples are endless.

Still, the interesting question is not necessarily "What does African socialism mean?" but "To whom are those calling themselves African socialists speaking?" The answer is clear: they are speaking primarily to each other—to African intellectuals, particularly students, and to leaders, parties, organizations, and governments of the left outside of Africa, and only secondarily to their own people. For the latter, to whom the doctrinal differences between various types of socialist ideas were (and are) essentially meaningless, the socialism of their leaders came wrapped in symbols, slogans, and clichés. More important, they were embodied in the policies and programs that affected everyday life. It is style that has always made the difference.

This does not mean that socialist-Marxist ideologizing in francophone Africa only adds up to the crass manipulation of symbols in the service of political opportunism, though unquestionably there was some of that, especially in the period before independence. Rather, African socialism has had some definable content, and its translation into government policy deserves further examination. The crystallization of African socialism into official postindependence ideologies is an important matter for consideration, as is the sudden mass conversion of African Marxists into African free-marketers.

Ideological Particularism and the Decline of Ideology

Trusteeship status, the growth of local institutions, the need to create new national political images and symbols, and changes in French politics and policies all helped narrow ideological concerns to fit territorially specific situations. The proliferation of political parties, groups, and associations in the ex-AOF and AEF territories, then the decline in their number, both during the 1945–1960 period, also played a role. Closely corresponding with that development was an efflorescence, then decline in ideological expression.

Well into 1946 the principal political associations operating in French Africa were local branches of newly resurgent metropolitan parties such as the French Communist Party (particularly through their several *groupes d'études communistes*), the socialist French Section of the Workers' International (Section Française de l'Internationale Ouvrière, or SFIO), the left-of-center Catholic-inspired Mouvement Républicaine Populaire (MRP), and the Gaullists. A number of local groups of purely African inspiration also operated in several of the territories, but only those with administration sponsorship or metropolitan affiliation could garner much support. Africans at the two 1946 French constituent assemblies allied themselves with the socialists and the Union des Républicains et Résistants (URR), an affiliate of the communists.

The political defeats the Africans suffered at the second constituent assembly, plus the revival of colonial reaction in France in the form of the conservative Etats Généraux de la Colonisation Française, persuaded these representatives and their cohorts in Africa that an organized African front was needed not only to counter this move toward colonial recidivism, but also to seize the electoral opportunities provided by the territorial and metropolitan legislative bodies created under the new French constitution. Thus, the formation of the Rassemblement Démocratique Africain (RDA) in September 1946 marked the first attempt to create an *African* base for African electoral politics, as well as to offer African alternatives to the *colon-* or administration-dominated local branches of French parties. The RDA's manifesto, with its call for African emancipation and the formation of an African "united front," also clearly marked a point of departure for the subsequent elaboration of African ideological themes.[45] Finally, even though the RDA originally described and regarded itself as a "movement," it quickly went on to organize itself in all but two (Togo and Mauritania) of the fourteen territories of our study.

Whatever the other reasons for its creation, the RDA served to open the organizational floodgates. To its territorial affiliates were added, at various points in time, the local affiliates of the several other interterritorial groupings. Included were the Indépendants d'Outre-Mer (IOM, founded in 1948, eventually with five branches in Africa) and its successor, the Convention

Africaine (CAF, 1957, with five branches); the Mouvement Socialiste Africain (MSA, founded in 1957 to unite the several SFIO locals, with nine affiliates) and its successor, the Parti du Regroupement Africain (PRA, uniting the CAF and MSA in 1958, with twelve affiliates); and the Parti de la Fédération Africaine (PFA, 1959, with six affiliates, all formerly part of the RDA or PRA). Beyond these parties and their various local and interterritorial permutations, over 250 other territorially specific parties, associations, and other political groups active between 1948 and 1960 can be counted in the fourteen states. No true count of the actual number exists, and my estimate may be quite low.[46] In any case, the number represents local party activity in full bloom, accompanied by programs, manifestoes, symbols, declarations, statements, and the like on a wide variety of local themes. The transterritorial parties provided ideology wholesale; the local ones did so retail, offering an array of choices to suit the local political markets.

The future status of the two UN trust territories, Togo and Cameroon, became a matter for party ideologizing, in each case complicated by nationalist calls for "reunification" of the two parts "arbitrarily sundered" by colonialism. Ewe irredentism added an extra ingredient for Togo, and in Cameroon interethnic and interreligious antagonisms gave rise to groups voicing highly parochial demands. Senegalese complexities—including Senghorian socialist vacillations, conflicts between trade unions and the regime, fallout from the continuing Senghor–Houphouët-Boigny antagonisms, the involvement of the Muslim brotherhoods in politics, and disagreements on national policies on issues such as relations with France—all served to give Senegalese ideologizing a special flavor of its own.[47] Even neighboring Mauritania, relatively untouched by the major ideological and organizational schisms of the AOF, faced a series of severe internal difficulties: tribal rebellion, north-south racism, and chaotic party formation, each of which fueled the several major Mauritanian parties with locally focused ideological themes.[48] It was not that the great themes—independence, autonomy, national construction, socialism, etc.—had no echoes in these and other AOF-AEF countries; indeed, they were already well-nigh universal ideological stock-in-trade. Rather, by 1958 local concerns loomed much larger for local politicians than they had earlier, and to the more conventional, vague symbols of African nationalism the politicians added much more specific ones designed to appeal to local audiences and to mobilize support for local organizations and electoral campaigns.

If the 1956–1958 period can be considered the apogee of party formation, it also marks the penultimate preindependence phase for the parties themselves. By this time power had begun to devolve upon a dominant or single party in virtually all of the fourteen states.[49] This circumstance was also attended by a sharp reduction in the ideological output of the dominant parties. Most of their leaders were too busy consolidating internal power or preparing for independence to worry too much about framing a national ideology; after all, they had won the battle, and now that they were firmly ensconced in power (or about to be), they had little need to develop new issues or symbols with which to mobilize support against their enemies or the soon-to-depart French. The old nationalist symbols were simply repeated by rote, and if there was anything new in the declarations of the national leaders, it involved rationalizations for their monopoly of power or praise of national unity and harmony. In some territories the opposition, now driven underground or into exile or politically emasculated, continued to insist on the salience of the old issues, but in the euphoria of the transition to independence their voices were scarcely heard, and where they were heeded it was usually only by their supporters outside the territory.[50]

Independence, once achieved, changed the tone and style of ideological output. Under independence, ideology was now official ideology, the monopoly of the state, articulated by the head of state and through the ruling party where there was one. While such output often contained statements about government policies, programs, and initiatives, as well as exhortations to the citizens to support them, the bulk of the output tended to revolve around two main sets of themes, both essentially self-serving and meant to aggrandize and reinforce the power and image of the regime.[51]

First, the ruling party asserted a role in guaranteeing the principle of national unanimity by ensuring communication between the political center and the periphery and promoting national solidarity through vertical institutional structures and links. Thus "the party aids the Chief of State . . . by creating a tight cluster of loyalties to the State."[52] Whether it was Ahmadou Ahidjo's Union Nationale Camerounaise (or the Mouvement Populaire Démocratique Camerounais of his successor, Paul Biya), Sékou Touré's Parti Démocratique de Guinée, Senghor's Union Populaire Sénégalaise, Houphouët-Boigny's Parti Démocratique de la Côte d'Ivoire, or Omar Bongo's Parti Démocratique Gabonais, the structures and propaganda after independence were much the same: a hierarchy of institutions from village cells/*bureaux/offices* to national party congresses and secretariats, tending to parallel the formal hierarchies of official administration, with the head of state usually also acting as the party's secretary-general. If the ruler changed, so did the name of the party, and perhaps its outlook as well, but its general structure and generic tasks as a ruling party remained.

Second, the head of state, whether as prophet–founding father *(prophète-père-fondateur)* or presidential monarch, played a role as the symbol of national unity and the incarnation of the national will. In these manifestations he was the apex of the regime (that is, *his* regime). He commanded the ruling party, which in turn (at least in theory) subordinated the state. It was here, more than with the first thematic set, that style became at least as important as substance because what was produced was a more or less developed cult of personality. The president's picture was everywhere; the official print and electronic media vied daily to present favorable versions of his words, image, and activities; congratulatory books and articles about him were commissioned; he became a required part of the national primary and secondary school curricula; and his praises were sung wherever and whenever he, the party, or the government showed a public face. He accumulated praise names. Some are fairly common, like *timonier* (helmsman), *père de la nation* (father of the nation), and guide; others were specific to one person, such as the titles heaped on Sékou Touré: Guide and Supreme Spokesman of the Revolution; Our Well-Beloved Secretary-General; The Great Son of Africa; The Liberator of Oppressed People; The Terror of International Imperialism, Colonialism, and Neocolonialism; Doctor of Revolutionary Sciences.[53]

To bring the leaders to the people and further sanctify their image, during the 1970s and 1980s a number of francophone regimes even contracted for a kind of popular but official mythmaking: the production and distribution of French-style hardcover and softcover color comic-book biographies of their leaders. Those portrayed included Senghor, Gnassingbé Eyadéma, Bongo, Ahidjo, Sékou Touré, and Houphouët-Boigny, as well as King Hassan II of Morocco and Mobutu Sese Seko of Zaire.[54] Even this was not enough for some of the leaders, who strove to have their names become icons by tying them to some real or rhetorical political characteristic: thus Cameroon's Biya had himself touted *L'Homme de la Rigeur* ("Man of Rigor") to reflect his call for public "rigor," "discipline," and honesty, and Chad's N'Garta (François) Tombalbaye had himself styled *L'Homme de l'Authenticité* ("Man of Authenticity") to reflect his 1968–1973 "cultural revolution" policy of *authenticité,* or *tchaditude.* Tombalbaye also forced his civil servants to change their Christian names to "authentic" Chadian ones and had them undergo "traditional" Yondo male initiation rites or their functional equivalent in non-Sara areas. The names of many towns were also changed to Chadian ones; notably, Fort Lamy became Ndjamena, and Fort Archambault, Sarh.[55]

There was much less than met the eye in all this profusion of ideological display. Save for Sékou Touré, who was prepared to elaborate his own version of "African socialism," and the continued exchanges of the Senegalese socialists (Mamadou Dia, Doudou Thiam, Majhemout Diop, etc.) about the proper content of their doctrines, most of the terrain was occupied by paper-thin versions of the single-party, personality cult templates already familiar elsewhere on the continent.

The "Iron Surgeons" of the Left and Afro-Marxism

If the ideological ground remained relatively barren during the long period when kleptocracies, single-party regimes, and unadorned military rule dominated the political scene in francophone Africa, the appearance of so-called Afro-Marxist regimes in Congo-Brazzaville (1969), Benin (1974), Madagascar (1975), and Burkina Faso (1983) brought new ideological and stylistic themes to the fore.[56] These new regimes were difficult to label, not just because their ideological output made it difficult to distinguish them from the African socialist systems, but because all four were also military dictatorships and ranged on a scale of ideological commitment from *"très sérieux"* to *"pas sérieux"* ("very serious" to "not serious"),[57] and in application from dogmatic to pragmatic. Such judgments as could be made about their level of seriousness were put in further doubt when their leaders (excepting Burkina Faso's Sankara, who was murdered in 1987), and those of the other Afro-Marxist regimes (excepting Ethiopia), underwent almost instant conversion to free-market principles in the wake of the collapse of communism in the Soviet Union in 1989. The next development was even more dramatic than the post-1989 conversions: the unexpected wave of African "redemocratization" set off by Benin's national conference of 1991, which brought democracy back into both ideological parlance and practice.

What made the Afro-Marxist regimes in Burkina Faso, Congo-Brazzaville, and Benin so arresting was their almost complete break with the first wave of African socialist experiments, such as those led by Sékou Touré in Guinea and Modibo in Mali. Those earlier regimes had elaborated broad, long-range socioeconomic development programs ostensibly grounded in African traditions; the latter were represented as rescue missions, deliberate interventions by Marxist "iron surgeons" to halt and reverse seemingly dangerous political and economic deterioration in the three countries. These regimes made no sentimental evocations of the African past; their chosen instrument was Marxist-Leninist doctrine, rigorously applied.

Sankara's *Discours d'orientation politique* (pronounced October 2, 1984), which lays out the main policy lines of his regime, identifies as "enemies of the people" those "retrograde forces which draw their strength from the traditional feudal structures of our society. . . . These reactionary forces most often have recourse to the decadent values of our traditional culture still alive in [our] rural milieux."[58] Marien Ngouabi, in Congo-Brazzaville, said he had little use for "romanticized evocations of a mythical African personality. . . . The true spirit of the Congo people is in the Revolution of 1968."[59]

In any event, both Sankara's and Ngouabi's prescriptions included the creation of structures of tight, centralized political and economic control and popular mobilization through extensive ideological campaigns, all under the penumbra of a hard-edged, muscular Marxism that emphasized the (essentially Leninist) role of the vanguard formations—including, of course, the arbiters of power, the uniformed vanguard—in turning the country around.

The Afro-Marxist regime in Congo-Brazzaville, which Crawford Young calls the "dean" of such regimes, had its start in the Trois Glorieuses, the three days of riots and general strike on August 13–15, 1963, which toppled the corrupt and incompetent government of the Abbé, Foulbert Youlou. The army, which had refused to back Youlou in his last hours, in league with trade union leaders and the Marxist Union de la Jeunesse Congolaise (UJC—Union of Congolese Youth), some of whose leaders were prominent in the local version of the French communist-dominated Confédération Générale du Travail, conferred the presidency upon Alphonse Massamba-Débat, a socialist former teacher and government official.

Propelled by "revolutionary democrats"—political figures, intellectuals, teachers—prepared "to lay the foundations for socialism by following a non-capitalist path of development"[60] and by elements of radicalized youth (found also in Benin), Massamba-Débat declared Congo-Brazzaville to be on the socialist path, launched the Mouvement National de la Révolution (MNR) as the country's sole legal party, aligned the country with the more radical African states, and developed active ties with the Soviet Union, China, and Cuba.[61] In the end, Massamba-Débat proved unable to cope with the turbulent ideological, factional, ethnocommunal, and personal politics of the country, much less give new impetus to its economy. What finally undid him, however, was his promotion of two paramilitary formations, a party militia and the youth wing of the MNR (Jeunesse du Mouvement National de la Révolution [JMNR]), which was quickly commandeered by the most radical elements of the party. Supported politically, financially, and logistically by the friendly embassies of the Soviet Union, Cuba, Vietnam, and so on, the two groups began pushing for ever more radical Marxist solutions to Congo-Brazzaville's problems and a greater voice in the councils of the MNR. In the end, they posed so serious a threat to the role and existence of the army itself—they were even planning to create a new, ideologically pure "people's army"—that the Congolese army finally brought Captain Marien Ngouabi to power in August 1968.[62]

Between 1969 and 1972 Ngouabi dismantled the MNR; set up a new Marxist-Leninist vanguard party, the Parti Congolais du Travail (PCT); adopted a red flag; launched several far-reaching structural reorganizations (including an augmented public economic sector); promulgated two new constitutions; and proclaimed the Congo People's Republic. For all its glittering militant Marxist trappings, however, the Ngouabi regime exemplified not Afro-Marxist transformation, but the triumph of style over substance. Samuel Decalo, a notably perceptive analyst of Congo politics, points out that although Ngouabi himself became an eloquent ideological exponent of the new rhetoric, "his personal outlook had always been moderate,"[63] and it remained so during his years in power. Crawford Young agrees, suggesting that his (Ngouabi's) rhetoric "was a patina over his quite moderate personal convictions," a pragmatic weapon with which he sought to assert the authenticity of his regime, hold true believers in his camp, and (unsuccessfully, as it turned out) combat the ideological conflicts and conspiracies that beset his regime.[64] Though Ngouabi affected the air of a "charismatic and dashing figure . . . at times donning camouflage fatigues (along with loaded grenades and pistols) to lecture on the prevalence of enemies of the state . . . [his] ziz-zag leadership of Congolese socialism was in most respects no different from Massamba-Débat's—nor were his travails in office any less or different."[65]

The imagery and the rhetoric that became the principal output of the regime hardly concealed the realities: the socialized sector was a financial disaster, French and expatriate capital continued to control the heights of the economy, and most Congolese understood and cynically accepted the glaring contradictions involved. Young, who apparently visited Congo-Brazzaville in the late 1970s after Ngouabi's death, offered an apt description of the situation:

> Even the casual visitor to Brazzaville is struck by the innumerable contradictions of the People's Republic. The red flag of socialism flies aloft, while the supermarket below overflows with Rhodesian beef and elegant French cheeses. Slogans adorn the walls, as in Eastern Europe, but their content is not very Marxist: eternal glory to the fallen comrade Marien Ngouabi, down with corruption, long live the work ethic. The rhetorical level of the state media is shrill: the private conversations of ranking government officials is relaxed and moderate. Ideological spokesmen hurl thunderbolts at capitalism and imperialism, while economic delegations tour Western financial centers, assuring would-be investors that these imprecations are only verbal. Marxism-Leninism is at once ubiquitous and evanescent.[66]

I was in Brazzaville in 1981 on a U.S. State Department–sponsored lecture tour, and I can confirm Young's observations. What I also noticed was that the Congolese were not very *sérieux* about their Marxism. For example, following a lecture at Marien Ngouabi University, I was invited to a reception in my honor at the home of the information minister. The house itself was a beautiful old colonial mansion overlooking the Congo River, and the minister greeted us at the door wearing his Gucci shoes and Pierre Cardin suit. We sipped Moët et Chandon champagne and ate canapés slathered with Beluga caviar, courtesy the ideologically friendly embassy of the USSR. It was not long until, loosened by the champagne, we got to "tutoyer-ing" (using highly familiar language). With a wink, I asked the minister if all this represented the lifestyle of a dedicated socialist. Roaring with laughter, he claimed he hadn't heard anything so funny in a long time. "Ah," he said, with a broad smile, *"nous nous débrouillons!"* ("We try to make do!")

Ngouabi himself finally became a victim of Congo-Brazzaville's vicious factional wars and was assassinated on March 18, 1977, probably by close military friends though it was Massamba-Débat, implicated in the plot, who was executed for the deed. Ngouabi became the object of an extraordinary posthumous personality cult propagated reluctantly by his immediate successor, Joachim Yhombi-Opango, and enthusiastically by Yhombi-Opango's successor, Denis Sassou-Nguesso, who ruled the People's Republic from 1979 to 1991, when it was replaced by the nonsocialist Fourth Republic in the 1991–1993 wave of democratization. (Sassou-Nguesso, by then shorn of his Marxist pretensions, retook power in 1997.)

When Colonel Mathieu Kérékou led Dahomey's fifth successful military coup on October 26, 1972, displacing civilian president Justin Ahomadegbe, it was clear that neither he nor any of the other coup makers had any interest in ideology, much less Marxism-Leninism. In fact, his first major speech, the 1972 *Discours-Programme,* had little ideological content, and in a mid-1973 interview he made a point of his ideological neutrality, stressing only his nationalist commitment: "Our earnest desire is that the Dahomean revolution will be authentic. It should not burden itself by copying foreign ideology. You see, we do not want communism or capitalism or socialism. We have our own Dahomean social and cultural system."[67] But a year later, on November 30, 1974, he made a speech in which he announced, to everyone's "complete surprise,"[68] the official choice of a socialist development path and a Marxist-Leninist ideology.

Why this sudden and unexpected reversal? Like much of francophone Africa, Dahomey, now Benin, had a socialist and even radical tradition of thought among students, intellectuals, educated trade unionists, and some junior military officers who had been in touch with those currents; most officers, including Kérékou, were much more involved in military-civilian than ideological politics. In any event, leftist politics in Benin never developed either the numbers or the passionate commitment that characterized the left in Congo-Brazzaville. The most perceptive analysts of Benin's politics (Samuel Decalo, Christopher Allen, Crawford Young, Dov Ronen) all agree that Kérékou's resort to the Marxist-Leninist path had less to do with his own convictions—he was, and remains, an ideological moderate—than with an attempt to break with the old and destructive ethnic-personalist politics of the past, establish the legitimacy of his regime, squelch the radical left, and jump-start a floundering economy.[69]

In short, the turn toward socialism was the Ngouabi solution, and as in Congo-Brazzaville it failed, eventually weakened by economic decline, the failure of the nationalized sector, foreign (mainly French) pressures, and the progressive alienation of all the constituencies that had initially supported the move to the left (intellectuals, trade unionists, civil servants, students, and finally the army itself). Not even Kérékou's virtual disavowal of his own socialist programs in the wake of the Soviet collapse in 1989 could halt the erosion of support. Thus it was not surprising that the 1991 national conference could demand, and get, his resignation. (Perhaps Kérékou's drabness and lack of charismatic appeal spared him Ngouabi's fate. Unlike Ngouabi, Kérékou understood when to leave. He withdrew with much of his dignity intact, then reappeared in 1996 and was elected president by democratic mandate; he was now apparently a convinced democrat and an advocate of free-market economics.)

In any event, by 1977 Kérékou had organized a single party, the People's Revolutionary Party of Benin (PRPB), complete with women's, youth, and trade union auxiliaries; created a network of some five hundred local Committees for the Defense of the Revolution (CDR) designed to mobilize the population and (after 1975) to be a base from which members of the PRPB were to be recruited; established diplomatic relations with the People's Republic of China, North Korea, and Libya; and launched various ambitious programs designed to greatly expand the public sector, all under the guidance of the National Revolutionary Council (Conseil National de la Révolution [CNR]) and the Military Council for the Revolution, led by Kérékou himself. However, all the new structures and the regime's attempt to mobilize the citizenry and revitalize the economy failed to accomplish their purposes; in the end, as in Congo-Brazzaville, Marxism in the People's Republic of Benin became an eclectic mixture of ideas and dogma expressed more in official rhetoric than in government performance. Again, it was the outward symbols and the language of radicalism that took center stage. "Every visitor to Benin," observed Chris Allen, "stresses the ubiquitous excesses of official language down to revolutionary equivalents of the courtly phrases beloved of French civil servants."[70] The Beninois revolution, as it turned out, failed to change hearts and minds and turn the economy around; it did, however, produce almost twenty years of relatively stable rule, and because it never developed into a genuine dictatorship, it left few scars on the country.

Thomas Sankara's regime in Burkina Faso was a different matter.[71] Sankara came to power in what was then Upper Volta by military coup on August 4, 1983; he was murdered on October 15, 1987, probably on orders from his best friend and successor, Captain Blaise Compaoré, and the two other "historic chiefs" of the 1983 coup, Major Jean-Baptiste Lingani and Captain Henri Zongo. Between those dates (some four years, two-and-a-half months) he led a remarkable effort to completely transform the political, economic, and ideological face of his country, an effort that, though largely unsuccessful, left a populist legacy—and a Sankarist "quasi-messianic cult"[72]—that his successor could neither appropriate nor expunge. On each anniversary of Sankara's death hundreds, sometimes thousands of people gather at his grave in Ouagadougou to honor him and, often openly, denounce Compaoré as "the brother who killed his brother."[73]

In 1983 Sankara had briefly served as prime minister in the government of Major Jean-Baptiste Ouedraogo, himself brought to power in 1982 with the help of the same group of radical young officers—Sankara, Compaoré, Lingani, and Zongo—that removed him in 1983. "Named Prime Minister by Ouedraogo, Sankara frankly admitted that he and his colleagues were revolutionary 'ideologues' who were determined 'to reform Voltaic society, to clean it up, and to purify it."[74] Though the four initially denied being Marxists or followers of Ghana's military ruler, Flight Lieutenant Jerry Rawlings, or Libya's Muammar al-Qaddafi, it became clear after the 1983 coup that their protestations had been a tactical subterfuge and that, in fact, they had taken Marxism-Leninism as their guiding star and owed many of their ideas, policies, and ideological formulas to both Qaddafi and Rawlings.[75] For one thing, Sankara's October 2, 1983, *"discours-guide"* (guidance speech, also known acronymically as the DOP, *discours d'orientation politique*), which laid out the new regime's main programmatic and ideological lines, had been drafted by several of the ruling council's communist members. For another, the four officers' Marxism dated back at least to the 1970s, when all four had almost certainly been members of a clandestine formation, the Regroupement des Officiers Communistes (ROC), and in touch with Upper Volta's several tiny but influential civilian, self-styled Marxist and communist organizations, themselves in and out of clandestinity and proscription since the 1960s. And finally, five of these organizations or their offshoots became, at one time or another, part of Sankara's ruling council, the CNR.[76]

Although the CNR was ideologically front-loaded with Marxist-Leninists, that did not mean they were agreed on ideas or policy; far from it. The CNR was almost continually plagued by bitter internal ideological divisions, and if Compaoré is to be believed, it was Sankara's unwillingness to create a single national Marxist party, coupled with his attempt to translate his own loyalists into a dictatorial junta at the expense of the "historic chiefs," that led to his death.[77] It is also the case that compared to Kérékou's Benin, Sankara's Burkina Faso produced a much greater volume of Marxist rhetoric, certainly on a par with Ngouabi's Congo-Brazzaville, and as turgid and formulaic. But it was not its Marxist rhetoric that made Sankara's regime interesting; rather, it was the eclectic translation of those words into structures and policies, the regime's undoubted mass appeal, and above all, the quixotic style that Sankara brought to the task of transforming the country.

Sankara *was* different. His enthusiasm, his ability to connect with his audiences, his image (young, slim, mustachioed, smiling, accessible, seemingly guileless, energetic, a hero of the short war with Niger, clad in military beret and pressed battle fatigues, sometimes carrying and playing his trademark guitar) all served to evoke the adjective *charismatic* in an African political world seemingly devoid of the kind of charismatic leaders who trod the African stage at independence. His closest competitor in this regard, Ngouabi, turned out to be more charismatic dead than alive. Even Sankara's successors (and probable assassins) grudgingly used the word *charismatic* to describe him. His style, personality, and audacious project—to transform Burkina Faso virtually overnight—were sufficiently seductive to dazzle otherwise cynical foreigners of both the left and right. Guy Martin, one of the most perceptive academic observers of francophone Africa, became convinced that Sankara's was "a genuine popular revolution,"[78] and Babou Paulin Bamouni, Sennen Andriamirado, and Jean Ziegler (who founded the Thomas Sankara Society) each wrote an admiring book about him and his revolution.[79]

Sankara launched his "revolution" with his October 2, 1983, DOP, which also served as the country's unofficial constitution during his rule. The DOP, which identified both the worthy "revolutionary" Voltaic people and the "enemies of the people," launched the key institutions of the regime, that is, the CNR, called the "supreme power" in the DOP and composed of the military and civilian leaders and the top "revolutionary" groups, plus the country-wide Libyan/Ghanaian-style CDRs, which were constituted as the "authentic popular organization in the exercise of revolutionary power" and located in "the villages, the *quartiers* of the towns, and the workplaces."[80] Shortly after issuing the DOP, Sankara renamed the country Burkina Faso, which means "Land of Dignified People," and initiated the series of programs designed to create a clean and honest regime, exclude all former politicians from power, deprive the Mossi chiefs of their "traditional" power, and pull the Burkinese from the general poverty afflicting the country.

Elliott Skinner enumerates some of Sankara's early moves:

> He championed women's rights, and in an effort to win their allegiance, decreed 22 September 1984 as the day for husbands to do the family shopping so that they would know what this task entailed. He banned prostitution, and in an unprecedented action, named women to about one quarter of the ministerial posts: they were put in charge not only of family affairs, health, and culture, but also of such key ministries as the environment and the budget. Then in an effort to deal with beggars . . . Sankara took them off the streets, and established "solidarity compounds" where they could be taught trades.[81]

That was only the beginning. In an effort to cut back government spending and have the government live within its means, he cut the wages of civil servants, curtailed their allowances for housing and transportation, and called on them to make sacrifices comparable to those of the peasants—including spending time in the fields, planting and harvesting crops. He also cut their numbers, both by dismissing some of them outright (some four thousand) and by lowering the retirement age from fifty-five to fifty-three (which accounted for another 4,500 departures).

Military pay was also cut, but it was harder to get the officers to give up some of their more expensive prerogatives. In any event, these measures were immensely popular except among those affected and those who remained—their loss of support that would later come back to hurt Sankara. That loss of support was further accelerated by the 1983 creation of the Popular Revolutionary Tribunals (Tribunal Populaire de la Révolution, or TPRs) system, which tried cases of political and economic crime committed by civil servants or public officials in the performance of their duties. The TPRs were also initially popular, but as they and the CDR became increasingly heavy-handed in their operations, they helped contribute to the general erosion of confidence that characterized the regime by 1987. The regime also put all voluntary organizations under strict control and reduced the influence of the trade unions, which were led by some of the most radical members of the CNR. Above all, it undertook to mobilize the peasantry by redistributing land taken from the chieftaincies, and through the CDR it launched a massive *"investissement humain"*[82] campaign designed to transform all of Burkina Faso's seven thousand villages into centers of planned agricultural production and development.

Sankara and his colleagues sought nothing less than a total reconstruction of Burkinabe society through a massive redistribution of the country's wealth and an equally all-encompassing *"prise de conscience révolutionnaire"* (revolutionary awakening) of its citizens. And Sankara, who sought to make his own austere and simple lifestyle an example to his people, was everywhere, enthusiastically exhorting, scolding, lecturing, getting his hands dirty, and engaging his audiences in the repartee and antiphonal exchanges for which he had become famous. By all reports it was a bravura performance, and for at least the first three years of his regime, it earned Sankara genuine popularity and general acceptance of his aims and programs. It was also something of a rarity: ideology really became flesh (or so it seemed); this was part of the myth that melded into the personality cult that attached to him both in life and in death.

In the end, even though many of Sankara's programs could be adjudged successes, he could not rescue his country from its economic and social woes or change the basic social fabric of his society. Perhaps he took too much upon himself and became erratic and unpredictable in the process, a victim of his own hubris. In any event, by the time he was murdered he had not only alienated his closest comrades-in-arms, but also most of the very constituencies that had supported him at the outset of his journey: the trade unions, the leftist intellectuals, the students, the civil servants, and above all the peasants, who were victimized by the CDR and who failed to find the better life promised in his rescue packages. Even his unwillingness to create a ruling Marxist-Leninist party and thereby avoid the problems common to single-party regimes backfired: institutionalized rule was already in the blood of his closest colleagues. Save for the single-party question, the similarities to Kérékou's and Ngouabi's regimes were striking; it turned out that for all their zeal and energy, the Afro-Marxist regimes of francophone Africa (as elsewhere) collapsed when tested against the seriousness of the leaders' commitments and the social, political, and economic realities of their respective countries.

However Marxist or Marxist-Leninist their ideological language, however close their ties to the Soviet Union and other communist states, and however much those regimes doted on them, these leaders never really deserved to be called communist or even Afrocommunist. For one thing, their lead parties and structures were not official parts of that complex of organizations that included the South African Communist Party and looked to Moscow for ideological and tactical guidance.[83] Second, and more important, those that were also military regimes (six of the seven Afro-Marxist states, including Congo-Brazzaville, Benin, and Burkina Faso) could never successfully overcome the contradictions posed by their origins and their espousal of the Leninist concept of party supremacy. Crawford Young puts it succinctly: "For those germinating in military circles, the army is quite ambivalent about placing full power in the hands of a party that is not a simple emanation of the junta."[84] Given that the Marxist political field is usually in part preempted by radical left-wing civilian movements, Young continues, "it is in practice very difficult to disperse these formations, especially to secure their voluntary self-effacement before a monopolistic political instrument under military hegemony." This was true in Congo-Brazzaville, Benin, and Burkina Faso, though in the latter, and despite some steps in that direction, Sankara never got around to creating the single ruling party before he was murdered, preferring to put his faith in the efficacy and mobilizing capacities of the CNR-CDR tandem.

The next ideological experiments were those accompanying the African democratic revival of the 1990s. Why did the military Afro-Marxist regimes collapse so quickly after the fall of the Soviet Union in 1989, and why did they metamorphose, some almost overnight, from Marxist-Leninist to capitalist, free-market systems? There are three sets of possible answers.

One set has to do with the rulers, or the ruling elites, and proposes that they were never *très sérieux,* that their Marxism was never more than skin deep and that it was adopted (wholly or in part) for pragmatic political reasons. There is good evidence that that was the case with Kérékou and Sassou-Nguesso, though perhaps less so with Ngouabi and Sankara, both of whom may have been convinced Marxists at the outset of their careers even if they probably were not at the end. And certainly the immediate successors of the latter two were never Sankarists or Ngouabists, except rhetorically, and very loosely at that.

A second set posits that the so-called Marxist-Leninist regimes themselves turned out to be failures, unable to deliver on their promises of material and social well-being, something that was objectively true of all the Afro-Marxist regimes. Some of that evidence is presented in these pages, as is evidence of the futile attempts of the Afro-Marxist leaders and their successors to halt their countries' slide into economic, social, and political disaster. It would have been difficult in 1988 and 1989 not to have noted the parallels between the collapse of the Soviet system and those of its junior acolytes in Africa.

The third set argues that several contextual realities that faced the Afro-Marxists when the Soviet Union fell contributed to their rapid changeover. First and foremost, the collapse of the Soviet Union meant that there would no longer be profitable trade with and aid from the ideologically compatible East, that it would no longer be possible to capitalize on Cold War antagonisms to extract or extort aid and comfort from the West, and that all useful financial and material assistance would henceforth come only from the West and its international agencies. Further, whatever satisfactions could be derived from being part of an international or African socialist family had ended: communist parties had become orphans, left to fend for themselves, or had become domesticated or simply were changing ideological color, as did many parties and regimes. It no longer paid to be in a club with mainly dinosaur members: Cuba, North Korea, and mainland China itself becoming paler by the decade.

These add up to some very practical, pragmatic reasons for the African Marxist leopards to change their spots, and to do so quickly. The pragmatic predisposition was probably already there, as was the overwhelming evidence that the ideological and political world had changed—Sankara and Ngouabi died before they could change with it, but Kérékou and Sassou-Nguesso survived because they did change, and in time.

Notes

1. I deliberately use Kwame Nkrumah's famous biblical paraphrase here. "Seek ye first the political kingdom" became his party's slogan, and the full paraphrase—which included "and all other things shall be added unto you"—was engraved on the base of the Nkrumah statue erected in front of Ghana's Parliament

House. When Nkrumah's political kingdom was overthrown in 1966, so was the statue: toppled, it was broken into pieces, and the fragments were taken away by children, local adult residents, and tourists. In francophone Africa, as almost everywhere else on the continent, the political kingdom that was seen before independence as the answer to all political prayers proved difficult to govern after it was won.

2. Pye and Verba, *Political Culture and Political Development,* 545.

3. Otherwise, from a behavioral perspective, "political style can be viewed as an aspect of role-performance—the quality of leadership behavior, defined by cognitions, expectations, and norms, both as that performance is *projected* by a leader, and as it is *perceived* by others" (Le Vine, "Changing Leadership Styles and Political Images: Some Preliminary Notes," 631).

4. Folson, "Ideology and African Politics," 2.

5. Mahiou, *L'avenementt du parti unique en Afrique Noire,* 342. My translation.

6. The first part of this section is adapted from my 1986 essay, "Political-Cultural Schizophrenia in Francophone Africa."

7. See, for example, the Marxist statement of this thesis in Majhemout Diop's *Contribution à l'étude des problèmes politiques en Afrique Noire.* A nondoctrinaire socialist view is expressed by Mamadou Dia in his *African Nations and World Solidarity.* The theme of nationalism as an ideology of rejection is also developed in more conventional French writing, such as P. F. Gonidec's 1971 and 1984 surveys of the institutional-political structures of francophone Africa, *L'état africain,* and Mahiou's *L'avenement.*

8. On this point, see Moore, "Literary Protest in French-Speaking Africa."

9. Cited in Mortimer, *France and the Africans, 1944–1960,* 314. The context was the beginning of de Gaulle's August 21–26 tour of francophone Africa on behalf of his new constitution, to be put to the voters in France and overseas France in September that year. The francophone African voters would be asked if they wished immediate independence or a new form of loose constitutional attachment to France.

10. The French psychologist Dominique O. Mannoni, attempting to examine the roots of the 1947 revolt in Madagascar, used the evocative metaphor of the Prospero-Caliban relationship to explain the respective roles of the French and the colonized Malagasy in the conflict. As interpreted by Mannoni, Caliban in Shakespeare's play *The Tempest* is clearly the archetypal colonized, both a semi-slave and a second-class citizen, but also loved and the object of Prospero's civilizing ministrations. Caliban's "rebellion" stems from a compound of love, desire, and hate and therefore is incomprehensible to Prospero, who proceeds to punish him with the utmost severity (Mannoni, *Prospero and Caliban: The Psychology of Colonization*).

11. Memmi, *The Colonizer and the Colonized,* 125.

12. Cited by Johnson, *The Emergence of Black Politics in Senegal,* 148.

13. Senghor, *Chants de l'ombre, suivis de Hosties noires,* translation by Shirley Kay, in Wauthier, *The Literature and Thought of Modern Africa,* 156–157. The fourth stanza is even more revealing (I offer my own translation here):

Ah! Lord, banish from my memory that France that is not France, that mask of pettiness and hate from the face of France,

That mask of pettiness and hate for which I have nothing but hate—and I can well hate Evil,

Because I have a great weakness for France.
Bless this repressed people who twice knew how to free its hands, and dared
    proclaim the royal accession of the poor,
Who made of slaves free men, equal, fraternal,
Bless this people who brought me Your Good News, Lord, and opened my heavy
    lids to the light of faith,
Opened my heart to knowledge of the world, showing me anew the rainbow
    faces of my brethren.

14. Hazoumé, *Doguicimi: The First Dahomean Novel,* 382. Of particular
interest is Richard Bjornson's excellent introduction (xvii–xliv), which not only discusses Hazoumé's opus but places it in its historical and political context.

15. The incident is discussed in Ballard, "The Porto-Novo Incidents of 1923:
Politics in the Colonial Era," 63–64. For further details on Hazoumé's role in
Dahomean politics, see Glélé, *Naissance d'un état noir: L'évolution politique et
constitutionelle du Dahomey de la colonisation à nos jours,* and Bjornson's introduction in Hazoumé, *Doguicimi.* The name of the journal refers to the official mes-
senger of the last, exiled king of Abomey, Béhanzin. A *récade* was a short, curved,
decorated staff carried only by royal messengers—*récadaires.*

16. Thiam, *La politique étrangère des états africains,* 12–13.The translation is
mine.

17. Hodgkin, *African Political Parties,* 23–24.

18. Mortimer, *France and the Africans, 1944–1960: A Political History,* 284.

19. Quoted in Lacouture, *Cinq hommes et la France,* 336–337, cited in
Mortimer, *France and the Africans,* 287. Francophone African students studying in
France were among those for whom independence had unambiguous appeal. See,
for example, "Les étudiants noirs parlent," and in particular an article by
Majhemout Diop, "L'unique issue: L'indépendance totale; La seule voie: Une large
mouvement d'union anti-imperialiste" (The only goal, total independence; the only
way, a great unified anti-imperialist movement).

20. For an illuminating discussion of the entire issue, see Crowder,
"Independence as a Goal in French West African Politics."

21. Marshall, *The French Colonial Myth and Constitution-Making in the
Fourth Republic,* 243.

22. Crowder, "Independence as a Goal," 26, citing the introduction in
d'Arboussier, *L'Afrique vers l'unité.* This represented a considerable change from
the communists' earlier positions, particularly during World War II, when the Parti
Communiste Français (PCF), worked within the Komintern to prevent the imperialist Allies (France and Britain) from losing the support of their colonies. This included opposing or putting down leftist nationalist, or even communist, formations in
Algeria, Morocco, Madagascar, and the AOF-AEF regions.

23. The specific question of the relationship of trusteeship status to politics in
Cameroon is explored in Gardinier, *Cameroons: United Nations Challenge to
French Policy;* Le Vine, *The Cameroons from Mandate to Independence;* and
Rubin, *Cameroun: An African Federation.* The Togolese situation to 1956 is dis-
cussed in Coleman, "Togoland." See also Welch, *Dream of Unity: Pan-Africanism
and Political Unification in West Africa,* especially chapters 2 and 3.

24. "Unification" was part of a complex of issues involving the ethnic politics
played by Ewe leaders in both the British and French Togolese territories. It may
well be that the demands for an independent Ewe state voiced by some Ewe leaders
put additional pressure on Sylvanus Olympio, himself an Ewe, to demand early

independence for a reunited Togo. If so, it serves to reinforce the point that special circumstances and individual predispositions help explain some of the variations in nationalist theses. Olympio's background also helps explain why he was never afflicted by the Francophilic ambivalence that so colored the actions of many of his contemporaries. Born in 1902 of an influential family of Portuguese-Brazilian-African antecedents, Olympio first attended German schools in Togo when Togo was still a German protectorate, then later, in 1922, he completed his studies at the London School of Economics. From 1926 to 1946 he worked for the (British) United Africa Company, rising to become district manager, the highest post ever reached by an African in that expatriate firm. His British and anglophone experiences and his long espousal of the cause of Ewe unification, as well as the overt French hostility that greeted his revival of the CUT in 1946, could hardly have engendered excessive Francophilism in him. To be sure, he later made his peace with the French, but as prime minister and later as president of Togo he could afford to do so. Ras Makonnen, a former advisor to Nkrumah and an old-time pan-Africanist politician, nonetheless placed Olympio, whom he knew personally, among the "French elite." Though Olympio was related through his wife to his political enemy Nicholas Grunitsky, he was often seen as being "too French" and an "outsider," or, because of his family's origins, was despised as a descendant of slaves. It was all, according to Makonnen, a social "morass" (Makonnen, *Pan-Africanism from Within,* 226–236 and passim).

25. See the list in the appendix to Le Vine, *The Cameroons.* Admittedly, fewer than a dozen such formations emerged in the two Togoland territories during this same period, but that was mainly due to the fact of Ewe political dominance (the Ewe represented over 30 percent of the population) and the relatively high degree of consensus on Ewe demands.

26. Apter and Coleman, "Pan-Africanism or Nationalism?" 92.

27. There is no evidence that any reputable Cameroonian leader ever considered integration with the AEF as a possibility. Some French politicians may have favored such a move, but official circles conscious of the territory's special status never seriously advocated the idea. Integrating British Togoland with Ghana did have some currency in both Ghana and the territory, but prior to 1956, when a UN plebiscite in British Togoland resolved the question in Ghana's favor, most Ewe politicians, hoping for ethnic unification, opposed a union with Ghana, and even more opposed a union with the territories of the AOF.

28. Apter and Coleman, "Pan-Africanism," 93.

29. Lecture given at Oxford University on October 26, 1961, reprinted in part in the journal *West Africa.*

30. Markovitz, *Léopold Sédar Senghor and the Politics of Negritude,* 42.

31. Ibid. Textual footnotes are omitted.

32. On the last point, see, for example, the attack by Ezekiel Mphalele, cited in Markovitz, *Léopold Sédar Senghor,* 66–68. Mphalele amplifies his ideas in *The African Image.* Another interesting critique is by Abiola Irele, "Negritude or Black Cultural Nationalism," 321–348.

33. Consider two examples: Senghor, "Negritude and the Concept of Universal Civilization," and Senghor, "Negritude et civilisation Greco-Latine ou democratie et socialisme." Senghor also wrote "Latinité et négritude," and I heard him lecture on "Negritude et l'humanisme" in Yaoundé in 1961 during a francophone heads-of-state conference.

34. Markovitz, *Léopold Sédar Senghor,* 34.

35. Rather than attempt a survey of the literature here, I direct the interested

reader to the selected bibliography in Rosberg and Callaghy, *Socialism in Sub-Saharan Africa: A New Assessment,* 417–426. The source notes in Ottaway and Ottaway, *Afrocommunism,* and Keller and Rothschild, *Afro-Marxist Regimes,* can also be mined for references to the more recent literature. Understandably, there is very little new published material on these subjects after 1989, and what there is tends to be retrospective.

36. On rural Africans and their revolutionary potential, see Orlova, *Afrikanskyie Narodi: Kultura, Khosaistvo, Byit* (The Peoples of Africa: Culture, Economy, and Daily Life). The Mongolian reference is Tsebendal, "The Revolutionary Party and Social Changes," 3–11.

37. Brockway, *African Socialism,* 18–19.

38. Comte, "Le Marxisme et l'Afrique," 85. My translation.

39. Ulam, *The Unfinished Revolution,* cited in Markowitz, *Léopold Sédar Senghor,* 122. Brockway, in *African Socialism,* 35, also argued that socialism has particular appeal to Africans because of its communalistic bias. It can be applied and reinterpreted successfully to meld with African ideas of family and communal action and responsibility. Socialism, argued Brockway (citing the Ghanaian sociologist K. E. de Graft-Johnson), may well be the extended family writ large.

40. Comte, "Le Marxisme et l'Afrique," 85.

41. Some of my observations about the PAI are derived from Foltz, "Senegal"; Traoré, Lô, and Alibert, *Forces politiques en Afrique Noire,* 91–99; and Majhemout Diop's own book, *Contribution à l'étude.* The story of Sawaba and its leader, Djibo Bakary, is told by Chaffard in "La longue marche des commandos nigériens" in his *Carnets secrets de la décolonisation,* vol. 2, 269–342. For the UPC's story, see Le Vine, *The Cameroons;* Joseph, *Radical Nationalism in Cameroun: Social Origins of the U.P.C. Rebellion;* and Mbembe, *La naissance du maquis dans le Sud-Cameroun (1920–1960).* The early course of the West African radical parties is covered in Morgenthau, *Political Parties in French-Speaking West Africa.*

42. Kilson, "The Politics of African Socialism," 18.

43. Charles, "Le socialisme africain, mythes et réalités," 857. A logomachy is a conflict about words and their meaning.

44. Ibid., 858, citing Konaté 1963. The African socialist thought of Konaté, as well as that of various African socialist ideologues, is well summarized and analyzed in the two-volume work by L.V. Thomas, *Le socialisme et l'Afrique.* Yves Bénot, a French Marxist who has lived and worked in Guinea and Ghana, argues that most African socialism reinforces European neocolonialism. See Bénot, *Idéologies des indépendences africaines,* 191–306 and passim.

45. The final resolution of the Bamako Congress, later reprinted in *Le RDA dans la lutte anti-imperialiste* (undated pamphlet, Paris, ca. 1948, no publisher given, cited in Mortimer, *France and the Africans, 1944–1960,* 105, 106; Hodgkin, *African Political Parties,* 177; and Hodgkin, *Nationalism in Colonial Africa,* 205) has given rise to some misunderstandings about the RDA's initial ideological positions. The document begins with a phrase more than just reminiscent of the Communist Manifesto: "La réaction agite devant l'opinion un epouvantail, celui du mouvement des peuples d'O.M. vers la liberté" (Reactionaries evoke a specter to haunt public opinion, that of the movement of the people of the Overseas Territories toward freedom). The word *rassemblement* (rally) in the RDA's name was clearly of communist inspiration because it implied a broad coalition of anticolonial groups, and so were such phrases as "to do away with a typical instrument of the trusts" (i.e., the double-roll electoral college); "to triumph over reaction"; and "to defeat the repeated efforts of the colonialist reactionaries to reduce African representa-

tion." Yet despite the boycott by the socialists, denunciation by the French government, and the communists' strong support of and involvement in the Bamako
Congress and the presence of their verbiage in the final resolution, the Congress
was hardly a communist gathering. As Mortimer correctly notes, the Congress supported the French Union (created by the 1946 constitution) and said nothing about
independence for the territories. In fact, at its last session, "Houphouët made a
speech stressing the 'indefectible attachment of the African populations to republican and democratic France,' and the proceedings ended with Konaté and [Fily
Dabo] Sissoko leading the 'Marseillaise' in slightly awkward unison." Mortimer,
France and the Africans, 110.

46. Using the sources cited in Chapter 3 (especially Decraene, *Tableaux des
parties politiques de l'Afrique au sud du Sahara;* Coleman and Rosberg, *Political
Parties and National Integration in Tropical Africa;* Hodgkin, *African Political
Parties;* and Morgenthau, *Political Parties in French-Speaking West Africa*), as well
as the available monographic literature, I counted some 247 groups, parties, "movements," associations, and the like. Much depends on how *political party* is defined.
My count includes what Ruth Schachter Morgenthau calls "one-man shows," several parliamentary factions, and at least fifteen extraparliamentary, ethnically based
groups mobilized, but not used exclusively, for electoral purposes.

47. Traoré, Lô, and Alibert, *Forces Politiques en Afrique Noire,* 1–105.

48. For Mauritanian party politics in the early 1960s, see Gerteiny,
Mauritania, in particular chapters 11 and 12. A more recent (and succinct) survey is
Soudan, *Le marabout et le colonel: La Mauritanie de Ould Daddah à Ould Taya.*

49. Between 1958 and 1960 ten of the fourteen states had at least nominal
two-party systems, but in only six was the opposition represented in parliament
(Congo-Brazzaville, Upper Volta, CAR, Chad, Niger, and Togo). The other four had
nominal two-party systems in which the opposition was not represented in parliament (Senegal, Mali, Gabon, and Mauritania). Two states (Cameroon and
Dahomey) had nominal multiparty systems, and by 1958 Guinea and the Ivory
Coast were already single-party systems. In the twelve states with more than one
important party, no opposition party or combination of opposition parties had
sufficient electoral strength to challenge the dominant party in any significant manner.

50. The lot of the opposition exiles was often unhappy and frustrating.
Supported by such so-called radical states as Guinea, Ghana, Algeria, Egypt, Libya,
and Morocco for reasons usually having little to do with the exiles' own aims,
dozens of politically disaffected Cameroonians, Senegalese, Ivoirians, Nigerois, and
Dahomeans (among others) flitted between friendly capitals, engaged in guerrilla
training, and pandered to Russian or Chinese sensibilities in exchange for money,
arms, or propaganda outlets. They plotted and bickered amongst themselves and
were in turn exploited by their hosts. At one point Sawaba, PAI, and the UPC exiles
had offices and facilities in both Conakry and Accra; at another, the exiles found
their way to the United Nations as petitioners for "national liberation movements."
Some died naturally in exile, some were murdered abroad (like the Cameroon
UPC's Dr. Moumié, who was poisoned in Geneva), others eventually found their
way home to face trial or receive pardon, and a good many simply remained as
exiles, having established themselves permanently abroad. Ghana was an important
center for their activities, and as a consequence President Kwame Nkrumah earned
the enmity of most of his francophone neighbors, often for good reason. In 1965 I
was an eyewitness when a Ghana-trained Nigerois commando attempted to assassinate then-president Hamani Diori while he was at prayer outside the Great Mosque

in Niamey. For details of the exiles' Ghanaian activities, see Thompson, *Ghana's Foreign Policy, 1957–1966: Diplomacy, Ideology, and the New State.* A number of UPC exiles were still in Accra when I was teaching at the University of Ghana in 1969–1971.

51. The two sets of themes are drawn from Asso, *Le chef d'état africain: L'éxperience des états africains de succession française,* 124–185.

52. Ibid., 126.

53. Cited by Jackson and Rosberg in *Personal Rule in Black Africa,* 213. For a discussion of the use of praise names and other symbols of leadership as part of political-stylistic expression, see my article "Changing Leadership Styles."

54. These comic books were produced by a French-Belgian advertising firm in accordance with a preset formula that was then scripted by the individual regimes. The books are usually titled *"Il était une fois"* ("once upon a time"), followed by the president's name. They measure twenty-two by thirty centimeters, run about thirty pages in length, and usually provide a capsule history of the country leading to the birth of the president, then cover his youth and education (which usually included a memorable confrontation of some sort with the colonial authorities), his rise to prominence and leadership, and his international prominence (usually he is shown with world leaders with whom he has met or who have come to pay him court). They end with portrayals of his accomplishments as leader. The books lay no claim to historical accuracy; they present simply what the regimes wanted people—especially young people—to believe about their president; they are exercises in political mythmaking. I bought the copies in my collection from street vendors, at the party headquarters in Lomé, and at bookstores. Some were distributed, at a price, by party officials. Those in my collection include the books on Senghor, Eyadéma, Ahidjo, Bongo, King Hassan II, and Mobutu Sese Seko; there may be more, but I've not seen them.

55. For details and references, see Decalo, "Regionalism, Political Decay, and Civil Strife in Chad," 47–48. Mobutu took credit for coining the authenticity motto, instituting his authenticity campaign in Zaire in 1971. Tombalbaye was apparently inspired by that example. I was told by a Chadian colleague that Tombalbaye always claimed to have thought of the program first and deeply resented the fact that Mobutu never acknowledged its Chadian parentage.

56. Keller and Rothchild *(Afro-Marxist Regimes)* and Ottaway and Ottaway *(Afrocommunism)* agree on a common list of these regimes: Angola, Benin, Congo-Brazzaville, Ethiopia, Madagascar, and Mozambique. I would add Burkina Faso for reasons discussed in the text. The Ottaways distinguish between "African Marxist" and "African Socialist" states. During the mid-1980s the latter group included (according to the Ottaways) Guinea, Zambia, Tanzania, and the island republics of Cape Verde, São Tomé and Príncipe, and Seychelles. The Ottaways prefer to label the former group *Afrocommunists* because not only did those regimes adopt Marxist-Leninist doctrines and policies, they also, like the "Eurocommunists," chose political and doctrinal autonomy rather than direct attachment to the Moscow communist center. I prefer *Afro-Marxist* because, given their reluctance to go all the way and attach themselves formally to communist networks and states, the *communist* label is harder to pin on them. This group includes Sankara's National Revolutionary Council (Conseil National de la Révolution, or CNR), three of whose four component organizations called themselves communist: the Union of Communist Fighters—Restructured (Union des Luttes Communistes—Reconstruite, or ULCR), the Union of Burkinabé Communists (Union des Communistes Bukinabés, or UCB), and the Union of Communist Groups (Union

des Groupes Communistes, or UGC). Composed primarily of intellectuals and old hard-line leftists, these small elite formations were more rhetorical than real.

57. I frequently heard the adjective *sérieux* used in Benin and Congo-Brazzaville as a judgment on the extent to which those who led these regimes were themselves willing to live up to the Marxist moral codes they advocated.

58. My translation. Text reprinted in Englebert, *La révolution burkinabé*, 224.

59. My translation from mimeographed excerpts of Marien Ngouabi's "Remarks to a group of militants," dated January 12, 1970, provided by the Bureau National de Presse.

60. Young, *Ideology and Development in Africa*, 29.

61. The story of "Les Trois Glorieuses" and that of the subsequent Congolese regimes is told in excellent summary detail in Radu and Somerville, "Congo." A fuller account is Bazenguissa-Ganga, *Les voies du politique au Congo: Essai de sociologie historique*. My discussion of the Afro-Marxist regimes also draws from Crawford Young, *Ideology and Development in Africa*, 2–96; Decalo, "Ideological Rhetoric and Scientific Socialism in Benin and Congo/Brazzaville"; Decalo, *Coups and Army Rule in Africa: Motivations and Constraints*, 2nd ed., chapters 2 and 3; Robinson, "Grassroots Legitimation of Military Governance in Burkina Faso and Niger: The Core Contradictions"; Guy Martin, "Ideology and Praxis in Thomas Sankara's Revolution of 4 August 1983 in Burkina Faso"; and Le Vine, "Military Rule in the People's Republic of Congo."

62. "The JMNR, 35,000 strong by 1968, was an unruly but potent body. The Party militia, which received Cuban training, numbered 2,000, nearly matching the Army itself. . . . The seizure of power required a bloody assault on the hard core of the JMNR militia, with the result that 100 of its 300 members were killed" (Young, *Ideology and Development*, 35).

63. Decalo, *Coups and Army Rule*, 256.

64. Young, *Ideology and Development*, 36.

65. Decalo, *Coups and Army Rule*, 256.

66. Young, *Ideology and Development*, 32–33. I visited Brazzaville briefly in 1971 and for a longer period in 1982, and I can confirm Young's description and observations. My observations from my 1982 visit are discussed in "Military Rule in the People's Republic of the Congo."

67. Quoted by Allen in "Benin," 63, and by Ronen, in *Dahomey*, 116. My discussion of Benin also relies heavily on Decalo, *Coups and Army Rule;* Decalo, "Ideological Rhetoric"; Young, *Ideology and Development*, 22–96; and Ronen, "People's Republic of Benin," chapter 8, in Harbeson, *The Military in African Politics*.

68. Young, *Ideology and Development*, 43.

69. Chris Allen, "Benin"; Samuel Decalo, "Full Circle in Dahomey"; Dov Ronen, *Dahomey;* and Crawford Young, *Ideology and Development*.

70. Allen, "Benin," 63. Decalo, "Ideological Rhetoric," 241, provides an apt description: "The regime's penchant for the *trappings* of a Marxist-Leninist state were manifest in the great attention given to the superficial and tangential: the promulgation of an edict concerning the proper 'revolutionary' way of ending letters ('Kindly accept the assurance of my revolutionary commitments'), a drive against 'neo-colonialism' in clothing, continuing diatribes about the lack of 'Socialist morality' in attendance at nightspots (whose hours were curtailed because they were seen as a 'hotbed of reactionary forces') and in weddings lasting until midnight, the change in Dahomey's name and flag in November 1975, etc." (emphasis in the original). A brief visit I made to Cotonou in 1976 confirmed both

Allen's and Decalo's subsequent descriptions. There were also pictures of Kérékou everywhere, revolutionary slogans on the walls, and pervasive cynicism voiced by the Beninois with whom I spoke—save that by 1976 the Marxist bloom had already withered on its stem, and *pragmatism* had become one of the key words in informal political discourse.

71. The main sources for this section are Martin, "Ideology and Praxis"; Baxter and Somerville, "Burkina Faso"; Ziegler, "Dans la Haute-Volta du capitaine Sankara"; Skinner, "Sankara and the Burkinabe Revolution: Charisma and Power, Local and External Dimensions"; Cherlonneix, "La voie burkinabé vers le socialisme?"; and Englebert, *La révolution burkinabé.*

72. Galy, "Le Burkina-Faso à l'ombre de Sankara," 4–5.

73. The phrase is cited by Galy (ibid.), who attended the 1996 graveside demonstrations in Ouagadougou hosted by the Thomas Sankara Association. Sankara and Compaoré had indeed been like brothers as well as best friends, since both had been reared by Sankara's father. Galy noted that most of the Sankarists in attendance were young people; the association's president claimed that 80–90 percent of the country's high school students were Sankarists. The 1997 event was even larger, of sufficient scope and importance to attract the foreign press. Earlier that year, in March, correspondents from both the *New York Times* and the *Washington Post* visited the gravesite and commented on the Sankara myth and legacy (Howard W. French, "In Burkina Faso, a 9-Year-Old Assassination Won't Stay Buried," *New York Times,* March 10, 1997; "Remembering Africa's Anti-'Big Man,'" *Washington Post,* March 17, 1997.

74. Siradiou Diallo, "Haute-Volta: Qui sont les nouveau dirigeants?"

75. Sankara became good friends with Rawlings, who came to power in Ghana in 1981 and who for a time had himself become an ardent admirer of Qaddafi and his Green Book. Qaddafi considered Sankara a valued protégé, and the two were also close until 1985, when Qaddafi began taking political liberties with his Burkinabé colleague, like dropping in unannounced on Sankara anytime he felt like it. Arguably Sankara's CDRs—Comités pour la Défense de la Révolution— were based on Qaddafi's system of direct popular rule, whose key is a network of local committees, or "congresses."

76. The five organizations were the Groupe Communiste Burkinabé (GCB— 1985 splinter of the Parti Communiste Révolutionnaire Burkinabé [PCRB]); the Parti Africain de l'Indépendance-Ligue Panafricain pour le Développement (PAI-LIPAD—remnant of the transterritorial PAI of the 1960s); the Parti Communiste Révolutionnaire Burkinabé (PCRB—originally Maoist, then Albanian in orientation and never part of the CNR); the Union Communiste Burkinabé (UCB—since 1985); and the Union des Luttes Communistes-Reconstruite (ULC/R—the old student movement, restructured since 1983). Pierre Englebert calls them "*groupuscules,*" or minigroups *(La révolution burkinabé);* for descriptions, see the glossary in Andriamirado, *Il s'appelait Sankara,* 183–187.

77. For the official texts, see Andriamirado, *Il s'appelait Sankara,* 166–172; and Burkina Faso, Direction de la Presse Presidentielle, *Le Burkina Faso du Front Populaire, An I,* 6–18.

78. Martin, "Ideology and Praxis," 84.

79. The books are Bamouni, *Burkina Faso: Processus de la révolution;* Ziegler, *Thomas Sankara: Un nouveau pouvoir africain;* and Andriamirado, *Sankara le rebelle.* The term *charismatic* fits Sankara because it refers not so much to leadership style as to a relationship of nearly unquestioning devotion between followers and a leader. The leader's style helps him connect with his followers, who

take his stylistic evocations as proof of his appeal. For further discussion of this subject see my 1977 essay, "Changing Leadership Styles," 631–638.

80. The quotations above are from the DOP, reproduced in Englebert, *La révolution burkinabé.*

81. Skinner, "Sankara and the Burkinabe Revolution," 444.

82. The term *investissement humain,* meaning literally "human investment," refers to programs in which people are mobilized to accomplish economic objectives. These programs were part of the policy repertory of a variety of African regimes of almost all ideological varieties. Some were successful, including several of those initiated in Sékou Touré's Guinea, but most failed because they appeared to require the equivalent of involuntary labor. The CAR's 1965 Kwa Ti Kadro urban weed-cutting project is one such program.

83. David and Marina Ottaway argue that the Angolan, Mozambican, and Ethiopian regimes, the principal "Afrocommunist" regimes they describe, believed in a single scientific socialism, class conflict, the dictatorship of the proletariat, a small vanguard party to lead the revolution, the acceptance of coercion and violence as necessary to socialist transformation, and close ties with communist states abroad *(Afrocommunism).* Of these three regimes, the Ethiopian Derg undoubtedly had the closest links to Moscow, to the point of embracing Soviet-style scientific socialism and being considered a client by Moscow. Yet the Ethiopians, like the Angolans and Mozambicans, shied away from actually proclaiming themselves communists, and indeed, as Edmond Keller suggests, "the choice of the scientific socialist path by the Derg . . . was based more on pragmatic than ideological considerations" (Keller, *Revolutionary Ethiopia,* 198). That judgment applies equally to the Afro-Marxist regimes, excepting perhaps Sankara's Burkina Faso, and takes them even further from qualifying as communist.

84. Young, *Ideology and Development,* 27–28.

6

Ethnicity, Religion, and National Politics

A 1968 symposium on "Institution-building in Africa" bore the evocative title, Nations by Design.[1] Certainly, the virtually simultaneous appearance of thirty-six African states between 1951 and 1969 supported an image of unparalleled activity by constitutional and political architects working feverishly to realize some sort of historical blueprint. Design there certainly was, and the marked institutional and constitutional similarities among the fourteen states of our study reflect considerable planning, albeit more often Parisian than African in inspiration. Yet whatever the nature of the design or the intent of the planners, the fact remains that fourteen, not one or two, political units emerged in postwar west and equatorial francophone Africa. The African codesigners, with some conspicuous exceptions, opted for and sought the creation of truly national political systems. However, even those with wider visions—the designers of the Mali Federation, for example— failed to turn to the essential task of combining the diverse ethnic, religious, and cultural elements of their polities into viable Senegalese, Mauritanian, Dahomean, Guinean, or Malian mixes. The sheer cultural and social heterogeneity of the fourteen states has made that task extraordinarily difficult in some cases, and at least onerous and worrisome in all. It becomes useful, therefore, to look briefly at two key aspects of this diversity—ethnicity and religion—as they relate to the political process.

Ethnicity and Politics

Two points must be made at the outset: First, ethnicity in its institutional aspects, such as systems of chiefs, traditional councils, and customary courts, is a gradually declining force in contemporary francophone African politics. Second, ethnicity in its affective dimensions, such as tribal loyalty, identity, the basis for the distribution of political spoils, and a nexus of support for various political actors and groups, remains a vital, sometimes even

161

dominant element in the politics of our fourteen states. The two propositions are not contradictory: the institutions of ethnicity that are visible and
incorporated in roles, offices, and formal processes could be and are the
object of constant—and increasingly destructive—attacks by legislatures,
bureaucracies, and national governments; the affective ties of kinship, linguistic commonality, traditional culture, and tribal solidarity are almost by
definition much more resistant to the political, social, and economic
designs of contemporary nation-builders (or pillagers, as in Chad, Côte
d'Ivoire, the Central African Republic, and Congo-Brazzaville).
Institutions, however adaptable to change, can and do give way before
determined makers of new rules; but to change attitudes, orientations, and
loyalties requires a much more massive and long-term campaign than most
current African regimes are able to launch. In short, "traditional" institutions can be made to bend under governmental pressure unless they are too
strong, but basic social and political orientations can usually be changed
only over time, with great effort, and under the right conditions.

It was the chiefs who gave way first to the integrative demands of the
new national political cultures. The colonial system had already managed
to emasculate all but the most powerful, and even these latter, who had
become too useful or too costly to dislodge, nonetheless remained in office
only at the sufferance of the French. The institutional and constitutional
changes of 1946 and 1956—particularly the latter, which gave authority
over chieftaincy matters to territorial executive councils—served to undermine the chiefs even further. Thus the new men began to seek, as Pierre
Alexandre puts it, "structures which would bring about a reintegration of
African society in the existing circumstances."[2] The stress was on the word
existing, and the chiefs could only lose thereby. Finally, the acceleration of
economic development, which introduced new economic values onto the
local scene, drained young men away from the villages and permitted the
alienation of land held under customary tenure, undermining the economic
basis of chiefly rule.

In the postcolonial situation the net effect of these changes constituted,
to cite Alexandre again, a "revolution" in the position of the chiefs: "First
of all, from the customary point of view, their role as the living incarnation
of the traditional group disintegrated. Then, administratively, their de facto
position in the colonial hierarchy made them share its unpopularity. Last,
and most important, the political reforms favored the advancement of new
personalities whose authority and prestige eclipsed those of the chiefs."[3]
Though Alexandre's generalizations hold true for most of francophone
Africa, there were notable differences in the manner and circumstances of
the chiefs' reaction to their changing status. Some were able to adapt themselves to the new situation and even take an active, if not a major, part in
the revolution. Félix Houphouët-Boigny, who combined his role as tradi-

tional *chef de canton* with those of head of an agricultural organization and modern politician, is a telling example of such adaptability. Some chiefs, particularly those located where there had been little or no economic development, generally in areas farthest from the coast, managed until recently to keep their authority intact and sometimes even to reinforce it by using the new electoral systems and administrative structures to their advantage. However, their residual power waned as political parties grew stronger, and today almost everywhere, instead of the party seeking the support of the chiefs, "the chiefs seek the support of the party,"[4] all the more so, of course, if there was or is a dominant single party.

Thus, for example, the active collaboration of the Fulani *lamibé* (plural of *lamido,* traditional chiefs in northern Cameroon) with the Cameroon National Union was based upon the realization of the former that if they did not willingly support President Ahmadou Ahidjo (himself a northerner) and his party, they might well be swept aside. In similar fashion, the *lamibé* made their peace with Ahidjo's successor, Paul Biya, to the point of becoming vigilantes for his national party, the Rassemblement Démocratique du Peuple Camerounais (RDPC). In some cases, the chiefs had earlier sought to stem the tide by organizing political groups in defense of their prerogatives. The Union des Chefs et des Populations du Nord Togo, the AOF's Union Fédérale des Syndicats des Chefs Coutumiers, and several patron parties in Senegal, Mali, and Guinea (until 1956) are examples of this reaction.[5] As it turned out, none of the chiefs' associations survived beyond 1957.

Exceptions aside, by 1957 the new territorial executive councils were faced with chieftaincies and chiefs ranging all the way from those in nearly complete degradation to those retaining a considerable degree of their former customary prestige and, very often, their authority. Given the necessity (to recall Alexandre's phrase) of finding structures that "would bring about a reintegration of African society in the existing circumstances," the new national leaders could do one of two things. They could "provide for a progressive adaptation of traditional society to modern life, so as to limit social traumas." In this case "government adopts a conciliatory attitude. It decides (where possible) to integrate the chieftaincy into the new political and administrative system."[6] In effect, the government would make an open offer of co-optation by which chiefs could be retained where they still operated effectively, or could be removed and replaced by civil administrators when they no longer performed any useful function. Or they could "adopt, according to French practice, a single regime applied indiscriminately to all situations, either fitting all the chieftaincies into a uniform pattern or else categorically abolishing them."[7]

The second alternative appears to have been initially chosen by most of the francophone states, since it corresponded most closely to both their adoption of the French administrative tradition and to their espousal of ideologies stressing the detrimental effects of tribalism, of which the chiefs were often said to be the principal exponents. But only Guinea carried this alternative to its logical conclusion, in December 1957 completely abolishing all of its 247 cantonal chieftaincies by transferring the chiefs' powers to district councils *(conseils de circonscription)*. Guinea's village chiefs suffered a similar fate.[8] Mali under Modibo Keita followed Guinea's lead in 1960, but did not go the whole route. It permitted the nomadic tribes, whose support was considered essential to the regime, to keep their chiefs so long as the chiefs accepted party guidance and were able to keep order among tribes that were notoriously difficult to administer.[9]

The more accommodative mode, which combines the rationale of the first alternative with the statutory uniformity implied in the second alternative, exists in a variety of ways, depending always upon the political exigencies of the situation. Senegal, the Côte d'Ivoire, and Cameroon provide examples of the range of current arrangements.

In Senegal cantonal chieftaincies were eliminated by law in 1960. Village chiefs remain, but they are named by the minister of the interior (whether or not they are selected according to traditional practice) and fall under the direct supervision of the *chefs d'arrondissement* (local heads, all in the civil service). These village chiefs act as village administrators and stay in office as long as they behave themselves and, even more important, as long as they remain in favor with the local leaders of the ruling Senegalese party.

Côte d'Ivoire, at least during Houphouët-Boigny's years in office, eliminated neither cantonal nor village chiefs, but simply integrated many of them into the country's civil service. Their numbers have, however, dwindled over the years, and the chiefs who remain do so because they can be used by the regime to mobilize local populations to its ends or because they command economically important resources.

In Cameroon a unique hybrid of French and British practices regarding the chiefs continues to hold. On the whole, Cameroonian traditional chiefs remain very influential, particularly in the northern and western parts of the country. In the anglophone provinces, many traditional chiefdoms have remained viable, cohesive units, mainly because they operated for many years under British administrative protection. For this reason the federal constitution (1961–1972) provided West Cameroon with a House of Chiefs as part of the West Cameroonian legislature. In East Cameroon, heir to a French administrative tradition, the local chiefs, with their councils, performed administrative functions at the lowest levels. All, however, were subject to confirmation by the government and were expected to fit into the regime's policies and plans. The political importance of the chiefs was attested by their numbers in the country's three legislative bodies: in 1970, a typical year, they constituted four (of fifty representatives) in the Federal Assembly, eight (of one hundred) in the East Cameroon Assembly, and a combined number of twenty-three (one in the Legislative Assembly, twenty-two in the House of Chiefs) in the bicameral West Cameroon Legislative Assembly of fifty-nine members. Moreover, both the House of Chiefs and West Cameroon's customary courts were expressly guaranteed by the constitution.

For all their constitutional security, the chiefs have remained under attack from various quarters. Many young Cameroonians, particularly those with a secondary or higher education and those who live in the larger towns, resent the chiefs and tend to consider them irrelevant anachronisms. The chiefs among the Bamiléké, probably the most enterprising as well as turbulent of Cameroon's peoples, have been under attack for decades, and not a few were the object of violence perpetrated by the once-proscribed Union des Populations du Cameroun (UPC). Aside from overt verbal and sometimes physical attack on the chiefs, subtle government action has undermined them even further. For example, a primary-school civic education text published under official auspices and used throughout the country describes in detail every local, state, and national political and administrative institution. In all its 270 pages, however, there is not a word about traditional chiefs, not even of the West Cameroon House of Chiefs formerly entrenched in the constitution. There is, however, a two-page chapter with a reading titled, "Le tribalisme, le clanisme, et le racisme sont les fleaux de la nation" (tribalism, clannishness, and racism are the nation's plagues).[10]

In sum, the chiefs, both Robert Delavignette's "real" village heads and those who derive legitimacy more from official than traditional sources, are a diminished—and diminishing—force in contemporary politics. Even the great savannah chiefs in northern Cameroon and Chad (*lamibé,* emirs, and sultans), who continue to enjoy some continuing political influence, must admit to themselves that with Biya instead of Ahidjo in the presidency their days are probably numbered, and that their chieftaincies may one day be simply permitted to wither on the vine or may be kept on as a tourist attraction, much as is the court and person of the *moro naba,* paramount chief of the Mossi.

The present *moro naba's* ancestors once ruled a great empire; he, his "palace," and his court in Ouagadougou remain as a subsidized curiosity, a sad reminder of the decline and degradation of the chieftaincy.[11] While it is true that the *moro naba* still retains influence among the older generation of Mossi, his fortunes, and those of his subordinate chiefs, wax and wane as the governments of the day use him or abuse him to improve their respective political fortunes. The old skills in finding ways to keep power and privilege by mobilizing Mossi constituencies for the regime no longer paid off after the death of Thomas Sankara in 1987; indeed, Elliott Skinner's gloomy 1989 forecast about the Mossi aristocracy's future still appears to be on track: "What is clear . . . is that the ability of that political organization to survive and to adapt is not unconditional. Like all human institutions, the Mossi political organization will in time cease to exist because it can no longer adapt."[12]

If the chiefs, as the institutional embodiment of ethnicity, have fared badly, it is because they are, after all, only the ephemera of a phenomenon relatively unmoved by social, constitutional, and economic engineering. Ethnicity in this deeper sense refers not simply to the corporate arrangements—villages, clans, tribes, etc.—that chiefs embody in their sacral and temporal roles, but to identifications, loyalties, and values understood better on the affective, or emotional, level than on any other. In Clifford Geertz's felicitous terms, ethnicity on this plane becomes a "primordial attachment stemming from the 'givens'—of social existence."[13]

When the group referent is the family, these attachments animate kinship relations; when the referent is the state, they are found in sentiments of patriotism and nationalism. In the case of ethnicity, the referent is that indeterminate group sometimes defined by common origins, sometimes by language and shared culture, sometimes by a shared myth, or by all of these plus, perhaps, common institutions. Or ethnicity may be defined simply by an ineffable "we-ness"—denoted in the group's name for itself—that serves to set "us" off from "them."[14] For our purposes, ethnicity in its affective dimensions has political consequences, and it is these, rather than the phenomenon of ethnicity itself, that interests us here.

Ethnicity has simple but highly important social and political consequences for the individual. To begin with, and perhaps most significantly, it defines the public side of personal identity; that is, it provides those criteria, the physical or behavioral markers of identity, by which it becomes possible to recognize and be recognized by all those people with whom useful relationships can be created and maintained with the least friction. Here, obviously, language is a key criterion, and appearance (dress, hairstyle, ornamentation, etc.) is only slightly less so. In this sense ethnicity also prescribes the limits of political relationships, defining who can be trusted, those with whom reciprocities must be exchanged, those to whom obligations are owed or who must be obeyed, etc. That an individual should identify herself as, say, a Mossi, a Sara, or an Ewe means not only that she will find herself most at ease among Mossi, Sara, or Ewe people, but also that she may, for example, take on a generalized distrust for some other group or groups, or in an election may vote for Candidate A rather than Candidate B because Candidate A "is one of us."[15]

Such "primordial" attachments and their personal implications do not, of course, transfer unchanged from the individual to his or her group, or from the group to the level of the polity. At the very least the implications and consequences differ enormously in scale and content. Consider, for example, distrust, which at the personal or group level may simply lead to avoidance, but which, when translated to the level of the polity, may become xenophobia and result in public violence.

A case in point is the recurrent violence against "strangers," and later among Ivoirian ethnic groups themselves, which began in Côte d'Ivoire in October 1958. In that year Ivoirians in Abidjan, incited by an organization calling itself the Ligue des Originaires de Côte d'Ivoire (LOCI, led by jobless young returnees from French universities and schools), turned violently on resident non-Ivoirian Africans, particularly Dahomeans, Togolese, and Voltaics. The government was incapable of controlling the situation, and after three days of disorder at least six persons had been killed, many more had been injured, and perhaps five hundred houses had been destroyed or damaged. Some twenty thousand "stranger" Africans finally found refuge in the old port under police protection. Similar events occurred elsewhere in Côte d'Ivoire, and finally perhaps twenty-five thousand persons had to leave the country.

Whatever the real motivations of the LOCI or the ostensible economic threat posed by the alien Africans, it is clear that ethnic distrust fomented against Ewe, Fon, Yoruba, and Mossi had been transformed into pseudonationalist xenophobia, and with disastrous results.[16] Apparently xenophobia is one of the easiest nationalist weeds to cultivate. The expulsion of "aliens" and "strangers," allegedly for solid economic reasons, has become commonplace. In 1969 and 1970, Côte d'Ivoire once again expelled Voltaics, Ghanaians, Togolese, and Dahomeans, certainly under less violent conditions than in 1958, but accompanied by a drumbeat of xenophobic sentiment reminiscent of the earlier expulsions. Following the death of Houphouët-Boigny in December 1993, his immediate successor, Henri Konan Bedié, as well as the other leading military and civilian successors to the Ivoirian presidency (General Robert Gueï and Laurent Gbagbo) all fanned anti-Voltaic xenophobia in their attempts to thwart the presidential candidacy of former prime minister Alassane Ouattara, himself of partial Voltaic origin. In the process, thousands of Voltaics were driven from their homes or sent packing back into Burkina Faso, and uncounted hundreds were dispossessed brutally or were murdered.

The violence spread during the mid-1990s and came to involve the governments and militias of neighboring Liberia and Burkina Faso, and finally civil war broke out in September 2000. By late 2003, despite various attempts by France and friendly African governments to bring an end to the fighting, the war and the interethnic killing were continuing apace.[17]

The two Congos have also driven out each other's nationals, and between November 1969 and mid-1970, Ghana forced out almost two hundred thousand "aliens" of Togolese, Dahomean, Nigerian, and Voltaic origin.

The Ivoirian case reminds us that, as a basic given of modern African politics, ethnicity can be and often is mobilized to nationalist ends, good or bad. Much less clear in that situation is the fact that modern nationalist politics—which are by definition territorial politics—have tended to redefine ethnicity by giving it national boundaries. A consequence of the nationalist focus has been to encapsulate and thereby to sometimes exacerbate interethnic hostilities. Where some sort of constructed "ideology of national consanguinity"[18]—nationalism or patriotism—has been unable to override the primordial attachments of ethnicity, ethnicity itself becomes a prime basis for political conflict. And this, it cannot be repeated too often, is the case to some degree in most francophone African states. The evidence for this proposition is almost overwhelming: the single-party system notwithstanding, ethnicity has been and remains a prime focus for political loyalty; political goods are more often than not distributed on ethnic grounds or are believed to be distributed on this basis; and where ethnic groups have developed highly valuable stakes in the new polities, the exercise of and competition for political power comes to be defined primarily in ethnic terms, in spite of all calls for discipline, cooperation, and national unity.

In a few states governance is possible only—and usually just temporarily so—as the result of some sort of compromise, coalition, or shifting balance between strong ethnic interests. Benin and Congo-Brazzaville exemplify this situation. In Benin, at least since 1951, national politics have been dominated by the rivalry of parties and politicians representing the three major and dominant ethnic groups: the Bariba in the north and the Fon and Yoruba in the south. During the 1960s Hubert Maga symbolized the interests of the Bariba and the other northern groups, while Sourou-Migan Apithy represented the Yoruba in the southeast, and Justin Ahomadegbe the Fon of the southwest and south-center. Between 1957 and 1969 the three leaders combined and recombined in various patterns of government and opposition: Apithy formed Dahomey's first government in 1957; Maga followed as the first president of the independent republic of Dahomey (with Apithy as vice president) until 1963, when he was deposed by Colonel Christophe Soglo; a short Soglo interregnum was followed by a duumvirate of Apithy as president and Ahomadegbe as prime minister (while Maga was in prison), which lasted until the end of 1965, when the military reintervened and threw both out; three military regimes were then followed by a short period of civilian rule under Emile Derlin Zinsou, an able southerner without a developed ethnic constituency; in December 1969 Zinsou gave way to Lieutenant Colonel Paul-Emile de Souza, who called general elections, invalidated them, and finally, in frustration, adopted in 1970 a tricephalic presidential commission composed of Maga, Apithy, and Ahomadegbe as copresidents, with the chairmanship rotating every two years. Maga became the first chairman of the commission.

It turned out that the durability of this tricephalic formula depended not only on the extent to which the three presidents could agree to bury their long-standing personal differences but, more crucially, on the degree to which the ethnic constituencies they represented could restrain their mutual jealousies and distrust.[19] Predictably, it didn't work, and Colonel Mathieu Kérékou ended the tricephalic presidency by coup d'état in 1972. The most recent installment of the Dahomey/Benin story ended in a set of surprises: Kérékou managed to quiet the country's fractious ethnic elements, but otherwise ran the country into the ground, so that in 1990 he was removed nonviolently by a national conference that also ushered in a democratic political system. That system appears not only to have held ethnic conflict in check, but also to have tolerated the return of Kérékou to the Benin presidency, this time as an ostensibly reformed democrat.

Similarly, the political fortunes of Congo-Brazzaville depend very largely on the outcome of the intermittent hostilities between the Bakongo, who inhabit both sides of the lower Congo River and extend as far south as northern Angola, and the Mbochi and other related peoples from the central and northern part of the state. In February 1959 Balali (a branch of the Bakongo that accounts for about 20 percent of the country's population) supporters of the Abbé Foulbert Youlou's Union Démocratique de Defense des Interêts Africains (UDDIA) and Mbochi supporters of Jacques Opangault's branch of the Mouvement Socialiste Africain (MSA) clashed on the streets of the Poto-Poto section of Brazzaville in savage, bloody battles. Youlou eventually became president; he was the only candidate of a national coalition of parties, and he preached national reconciliation and urged his fellow citizens to "de-ethnicize" (*déséthniser*) themselves.

Youlou's coalition soon fell apart as Opangault's Mbochi followers accused the president of favoring the Balali and as Youlou increasingly turned to strong-arm tactics to consolidate his rule. A military-civilian uprising unseated Youlou in 1963, and he was succeeded by another Balali, Alphonse Massamba-Débat, former speaker of the National Assembly. Massamba-Débat ruled until 1968, when he lost the support of both the army and the militant left-wing youth movements and trade unions he had encouraged during his tenure. The Congolese army, led by Captain (soon President) Marien Ngouabi, took charge and in 1969 established a rhetorically revolutionary "Peoples' Republic," which promised to use Marxist-Leninist principles to bring about the "triumph of the proletarian ideals of the Congolese people" and to practice scientific socialism so as to expose feudalism and fetishism and to eliminate exploitation.

For all its Marxist rhetoric and antitribalistic orientation, the Ngouabi regime, according to a contemporary observer, "has not resolved the problems of ethnic division, but has simply reversed the roles. Non-Bakongos dominate key position in the Ngouabi regime and his own Mbochi tribe from the north is well represented. All of at least 18 government officials tried for treason since the summer of 1968 have been Bakongo."[20] The later political history of Congo-Brazzaville, notwithstanding an honest attempt to create a democratic system during the early 1990s, has been one of increased interethnic tension and violence, to the point that the main ethnic groups and their leaders "took the Somali route" by creating militias that terrorized the country and each other, leading to civil war and, in 1997, to what amounted to a new military dictatorship under General Denis Sassou-Nguesso, a northern Mbochi. At mid-2003 he was still in power, and interethnic violence continued to be a feature of Congolese life.[21]

In these examples the ethnic groups involved are numerically large but unequal in size compared to one another. If sheer numbers were all that counted in the ethnic scales, then the Bakongo and Fon, who make up 47 and 40 percent of their countries' populations, respectively, should each dominate their local scene. In truth, it is not the size of an ethnic group that determines its importance, but the extent to which it has become politicized, the quality of its political spokespeople, the effectiveness of the organizations that derive from it, the economic resources it commands, and the skill with which its politicians and political groups play the game of alliance and counteralliance.

The Congolese-Beninois pattern of continuous interethnic confrontation in the postindependence political arena is perhaps unique in francophone Africa. This pattern nevertheless exists, with variations, in a good number of other countries, notably Nigeria, the Democratic Republic of Congo, CAR, Kenya, Sudan, and Uganda. Less unusual, but still relatively uncommon, is the situation in which one ethnic group has achieved dominance over the others, be it by an early monopoly of political power, as with the Sara in Chad, or through the imposition of an enforced equilibrium, as in Burkina Faso, where the military regime of Colonel Sangoulé Lamizana, himself a Samo from the northwest, maintained the supremacy of the Mossi in modern political roles.

A superficially similar though actually different situation obtains in Togo. The Togolese and Burkinabé situations are alike in one respect: power was seized by a military elite drawn largely from elements outside the dominant ethnic group. But while Colonel Lamizana and his northern and other non-Mossi officers simply made sure that the Mossi would no longer exercise power at the expense of the country's smaller groups, Togo's mainly Kabré junta, led by Colonel Gnassingbé Eyadéma, imposed what many southern Togolese saw as northern rule. Particularly resentful were the Ewe, who make up 20 percent of Togo's population and had grown accustomed to dominating the country's politics and economy. At one time during the late 1940s the Ewe almost managed to convince the United Nations to create a pan-Ewe state including most of southern Togo and the southeast part of what is now Ghana. The Ewe hold Eyadéma responsible (and justly so) for the assassination of Sylvanus Olympio, an Ewe and the country's first president, and despite the fact that Eyadéma has Ewes in his cabinet and in key governmental posts, it is fair to say that most politically articulate Togolese Ewe consider themselves in a sort of political bondage. Obviously, in all these cases, ethnicity continues to have high political salience.[22]

A more common pattern is one that varies considerably from country to country but has at its core more or less successful attempts to find a supraethnic basis for national politics. It worked for a time in Mali, Côte d'Ivoire, Gabon, the Central African Republic, Mauritania, Niger, and Cameroon, but that consensus broke down in Côte d'Ivoire following the death of Houphouët-Boigny in 1993; it collapsed in the CAR in 1998–2001 in the face of repeated army mutinies; it disappeared in Mauritania in 1989 when the regime began attacking, then forcibly expelling tens of thousands of black and non-Moorish Senegalese on the Mauritanian side of the Senegal River; and it was cast aside in Cameroon after 1982, when northern partisans of former president Ahidjo sought to remove Ahidjo's successor, Paul Biya, and Biya began favoring his ethnic Beti/Bulu brethren in the allocation of political and economic resources. In any event, in each country, for various reasons, it was possible for a time to deemphasize ethnic conflict through the promotion of a national ethic of some persuasiveness, through the integrative efforts of a party-state, or by a process of cultural assimilation in which the primordial "givens" of ethnicity were in the process of being transformed into "elements which contribute to the formation of distinct incipient patterns of national integration" (as in Mali and Côte d'Ivoire, according to Zolberg).[23]

What went wrong? The easy answer is that in each case, despite significant public and private efforts to create ethnic peace, effective social and institutional checks on ethnic aggrandizement, xenophobic attacks on "aliens" or "strangers," and the sponsorship of discriminatory and exclusionary policies were simply never put in place, or failed to work if they were. A less satisfying though probably more realistic answer is to admit that aggravated interethnic conflicts are extraordinarily difficult to resolve and that some are never satisfactorily settled. However, where measures to achieve ethnic peace prevail, there also exists either a superordinate integrative myth accepted by most citizens or institutional devices to damper incipient ethnic conflict by providing credible doses of distributive justice, or both. Or, as in Côte d'Ivoire and perhaps Cameroon, relative economic prosperity and a well-oiled patronage machine can keep the lid on old or incipient ethnic conflicts. The solution of acceptable dosages of redistribution is that established, perhaps inadvertently, in the democratic institutions and laws of Benin and Mali.

Thus, while it may be possible to subordinate ethnic claims to national purposes or to find a degree of interethnic peace, ethnicity remains, more often than not, as fuel for political conflict in most of our fourteen states. Obviously Mauritania is still troubled by differences between its "black" and "white" Moors and, even more important, by the major cleavage between the remaining, primarily black, sedentary inhabitants of the Senegal River Valley (the "Black Africans") and the dominant Moors. Since at least 1990 the Cameroonian state has been unable to satisfy the demands of its anglophone citizens or to cope with the hostility of its aggressive, enterprising Bamiléké population, numerically the country's largest ethnic group. Gabon's Fang majority is still regarded with suspicion by the country's minority groups. In all these states ethnicity remains a significant factor in national politics, whether as a catalyst in conflict or as a source of insistent demands on national political resources.

A final pattern, exemplified by Senegal and perhaps Guinea, is the relatively unusual situation in which political conflict has largely shifted from ethnic to other bases. The Casamance conflict apart, Senegal has over a dozen ethnic groups, of which the most important are the Wolof, Serer, and Tukolor. Two factors, however, have served to minimize interethnic conflict: urbanization, which during the past 150 years has made the old *quatre communes* highly successful ethnic assimilators; and Islam, which is the religion of over 92 percent of all Senegalese people and provides a strong element of social commonality.

One consequence of these developments, according to William Foltz, has been to make Senegalese politics clan-oriented and to permit client-group relationships to influence political life profoundly. The Union Progressiste Sénégalaise (UPS, later, the Parti Socialiste), which controlled the government for forty years under the leadership of President Senghor and his successor, Abdou Diouf, until it was replaced in March 2000 by Abdoulaye Wade and his Senegalese Democratic Party (Parti Democratique Socialiste, or PDS), was heavily dependent upon alliances with religious and clan leaders for its tenure and cohesion. Of particular importance to the Senegalese government has been its links to the Muslim brotherhoods (the *tariqa*), religious orders that, because of their economic power—the Muslim Mouridiyya control most Senegalese peanut production—became important interest groups in the state. How President Wade will work with the powerful brotherhoods is not yet clear, though there are indications that he seeks the same kinds of relationships as his predecessors.

Another, broader consequence of this shift has been the development of new bases of political conflict: government versus trade unions, government versus students in the secondary schools and the university, and urban versus rural. The last of these was evident in 1971, when the government-*tariqa* alliance almost broke down in the wake of the Mourides' unwillingness to plant or harvest peanuts, the country's main export crop.[24]

Guinea is something of a special case. For a time—at least until 1961—it seemed as if the regime had been relatively successful in subordinating the old, divisive ethnic particularisms to national objectives and interests. The single party—the Parti Démocratique de Guinée (PDG)—was deliberately made an active agent for ethnic integration; the government insisted on and achieved reasonable ethnic balance in the PDG base committees and in the distribution and rotation of civil servants; the army was turned into an ethnically neutral organization; and in all its educational and propaganda activities the regime stressed themes designed to minimize ethnicity and maximize national unity in the face of the country's internal and external enemies, real and imagined. Further, to emphasize the point, all organizations with an ethnic or regional base were banned by law.

Recent evidence, however, suggests that not only has a retribalization of Guinean politics taken place, but old ethnic rivalries, papered over or quiescent during the first few years after independence, have taken on new dimensions.[25] Guinea's weak economic position appears to have persuaded both the poor and well-to-do members of the political elite to reinforce those family and ethnic ties most likely to secure their positions. In a situation of general economic scarcity political resources tend also to become scarcer, and the *situation acquise* itself becomes a valuable resource to be defended by all means available. In the Guinean context then, as elsewhere in Africa, a preferred defense lies in the cultivation of ethnic, clientelistic, brokerage, and family networks of support and reciprocity. Moreover, as the regime became increasingly embattled and authoritarian, and as the revolution began to lose its dynamism, the top Guinean leaders came to rely more and more on their most trustworthy ethnic allies—the Malinké.

The Malinké constitute about 34 percent of Guinea's total population and are the country's largest ethnic group. By 1968 they made up 40 percent of all civil servants and 56 percent of the members of the PDG Bureau Politique National, and in the majority of the administrative regions, Malinké officials and party apparatchiki were in control. Cabinet posts increasingly went to Malinké politicians, usually at the expense of Fulani, whom Sékou Touré had on occasion accused of disloyalty, and for good reason Guineans frequently accused Touré himself of surrounding himself with faithful cotribalists and members of his own family to ensure his tenure in office. Of that group, Ismaïl Touré, Sékou's half brother, is remembered for being his chief torturer and executioner.

In all this it became evident that the Fulani and the forest peoples were the objects of calculated discrimination. In fact, probably half of the over six hundred thousand Guineans who went into voluntary exile—at least between 1961 and 1984, when Sékou Touré died and General Lansana

Conté took over—were Fulani, as were most of the leaders of the several external opposition groups. Also, though the picture is still far from clear, reliable evidence suggests that a majority of those arrested and tried in the long wake of the abortive Portuguese-Guinean exile invasion in November 1970 were also Fulani and forest people. Thus, Guinea, which had promised to be one of the few African states to transcend its ethnic politics, presented the disquieting picture of a retribalization of politics following domestic economic and political difficulties, a phenomenon painfully visible in post–civil war Nigeria and Democratic Republic of Congo.

Admittedly, during the early years following his 1984 coup d'état, Conté calmed the ethnic fears raised by his predecessor and refused to play the deadly games of ethnic favoritism and division that had characterized the Sékou Touré regime. Nevertheless, given Conté's age (early seventies), his poor health, and his determination to contest the December 21, 2003, presidential elections, the old ethnic demons that have been lurking in the background appear to have become restive, and another violent change of regime could well loose them once again. By late 2003 there was much that put a peaceful succession in doubt: a continuing refugee crisis in the southeast; persistent ethnopolitical rebellions in the peripheral regions; evidence of questionable loyalty within the armed forces; repression of the opposition, including the continued imprisonment of one of its main figures, Alpha Condé, since 1998; and unofficial partisan involvement in the ethnic imbroglios of both the Ivoirian civil war and the violence in neighboring Liberia and Sierra Leone. On December 29, 2003, the government of Guinea officially announced that President Conté had won a landslide victory in the December 21 elections, receiving 95.6 percent of the votes cast. The large margin of Conté's victory had been widely expected; the mainstream opposition parties had boycotted the elections, the balloting had been shunned by international observers, and two million new voters had suddenly appeared on the electoral roll (increasing the number of registered voters from three to five million) during the month before elections. Conté's health remained precarious; because of his diabetes and heart disease, he was barely able to walk. He made only one public appearance during the election campaign and cast his vote while sitting in the front seat of his official car. By the end of 2003, he had not designated a successor.

Religion and Politics

In modern Africa "the relation of religion and politics is posed squarely by Christianity, which postulates the legitimacy of a separate organization or organizations of the citizenry for religious purposes—organizations which do not derive their right to exist from the state and which have claims upon the loyalties of individual citizens."[26] Islam, in which the problem of the relation of the individual to society is avoided because it combines both secular and sacral life for its believers, nonetheless becomes involved in modern politics where it coexists in the same polity with Christianity or other religious communities, or where a secular, nonreligious ethic competes for the loyalty and obedience of the citizen. It is rare, however, that traditional African religion poses serious political problems in the modern state, and for good reason:

> For one thing, it tends to be highly decentralized and institutionally fragmented, with little in the way of a professional clergy or hierarchy. Its very permeation of traditional life, combined with the general overlapping of functions within traditional society, has meant that it has failed to create such specifically religious social institutions as schools and hospitals, which for other religions often become a source of religio-political controversy. Many of the traditional religions have become so localized . . . that any possibility of their becoming a source of tension with a national state is remote. . . . Finally, it can be held that African traditional religion . . . is social rather than personal in its moral and ethical import, emphasizing shame rather than guilt or sin; and that therefore it is not as likely to provide a source of conflict between individual moral beliefs (conscientious scruples) and the demands of the state as are the moral codes of other religions.[27]

Victor Ferkiss, an early student of the relationship between religion and politics in Africa, provides a useful framework for our discussion. He suggests that religiopolitical interaction can be best examined under three main rubrics: (1) church-state relations, particularly, in the African context, interaction in a pluralistic state where religious leaders and institutions come into direct contact with the state through various educational, welfare, intellectual, and economic activities they direct; (2) the role of religious ideas, insofar as they affect politics through the activities of religiously oriented political parties, through the direct intervention of religious leaders in politics, and through the activities of a religiously trained political elite; and (3) ethnoreligious conflict, including "the role of religion in the formation of interest groups which have as their special cohesive factor the tendency of individuals to identify with their co-religionists."[28] In some instances such groups may also operate wholly or partially within an ethnic-group identity, thus reinforcing their solidaristic claims.

Church-State Relations

Mauritania is unique in our group of countries as a state that has declared itself an Islamic republic. Article 2 of its constitution, which also guarantees equality before the law for all, regardless of religion, race, or social condition, proclaims that "Islam is the religion of the Mauritanian people." The implications of this statement are far-reaching, though not unusual in

Muslim states: by law the president of the republic and the president of the supreme court must be Muslims, and given the fact that Islam is also a juridical system, Islamic law (here the Maliki code) and Islamic jurists coexist with secular legal precepts and practitioners. Moreover, the Islamic state, by tradition, need not accord primacy of place to Islam; rather, the state is *the* institutional expression of a faith that prescribes—and thereby combines—devotional, social, legal, and organizational aspects of life. Finally, though Christians are tolerated in Mauritania, Christian schools, agencies, and, in particular, missions, are not.[29]

In other francophone states where Muslims make up a majority or a large part of the population, problems of church-state relations do arise, particularly where it appears that governments give Islamic establishments special consideration or privileges. During Modibo Keita's regime in Mali, for example, it was claimed that the government, despite its overtly Marxist orientation, directly and indirectly supported specifically Islamic institutions such as the hajj, the pilgrimage to Mecca (through subsidy of airplane flights for pilgrims); the Koranic schools; Ramadan and the main Islamic festivals; and the Sufi orders and their leaders, the marabouts. The teaching of Arabic in government schools in Senegal, construction of a special railway extension to Touba, the Mouride center of worship in Senegal, and the use of government radio and TV to broadcast religious programs in Mali, Senegal, Niger, and Cameroon are other examples of such support. At all events, however cozy the mosque-state relationship appears to be in Senegal, Mauritania, Mali, and the other Sahelian states, the several Muslim establishments in these countries share similar problems, all of which impact the mosque-state relationship, including:[30]

1. Succession crises among aging leaders, notably those of the Mouridiyya and Tijaniyya brotherhoods in Senegal and Mali;
2. Urbanization, unemployment, and juvenile delinquency among Muslim youth in Dakar, Nouakchott, Bamako, Ouagadougou, Niamey, and Ndjamena, often associated with a heightened vulnerability to extremist religiopolitical sects and organizations, such as those arising in northern Nigeria during the late 1990s and early 2000s;
3. Destructive agricultural practices and environmental degradation, especially in Senegal among the Mouridiyya;
4. Shifting power alignments among and within the brotherhoods and with the state, a particular problem in democratic Mali but also elsewhere in the region; and
5. Social tensions relating to caste and class within the brotherhoods themselves and between followers and secular institutions in society.

Of the 111 million inhabitants of the fourteen states we are considering, perhaps 11 percent are Roman Catholics, and another 4 percent belong to various Protestant and Protestant-derived sects. Because of their smaller number, their dispersed administrations, and their diversity, the Protestant churches have made little impact on the politics of the fourteen states, save in the relatively marginal areas of voluntary agency education, social welfare, and health. Besides, the Protestant churches are generally local implants, more concerned with their position vis-à-vis competing sects and with getting along with government than with becoming actively involved in political life. When their leaders and members cross national lines, as they do at international conventions, conferences, and retreats, they tend to avoid political issues in their discussions. Almost the sole exceptions to this rule have been the various Christian messianic and syncretistic cults of the Lower Congo area. These were once highly important in politics, but their influence is minimal today. However, the Catholic Church, which operates both transnationally and nationally, has developed highly cohesive and well-organized national clerical hierarchies, and enjoins its devotees to loyalties that occasionally can and do clash with the demands of national governments; it has often found it very difficult to keep out of politics.

Thus, where there are large Catholic populations, and often therefore extensive church hierarchies, church-state relations have sometimes run into considerable difficulties. Some of these difficulties arise from the fact that during colonial days the Church enjoyed a favored position and was often seen by Paris and colonial administrations as a valuable adjunct to the French *mission civilisatrice*. With independence, according to Victor D. Du Bois,

> The governments of the new states, forced by internal pressures to "decolonialize" their national institutions and give them a more African character, show little inclination to accord special consideration to the Roman Church. Even the numerical importance of Roman Catholics in the political hierarchies of the former French territories has been no assurance that their governments would necessarily be pro-Catholic in their policy. Though they consider themselves faithful sons of the Church, the Catholic heads of state in Gallic Africa have been reared in a French republican tradition having as one of its basic traits over the years an abiding anticlericalism. They have thus tended to perpetuate in their own countries a belief in the separation of Church and State.[31]

The Guinean regime carried anticlericalism much further than any other francophone African state. Characterizing the Church as an alien body whose activity undermined the unity of the state and thwarted the attempts of the party to mobilize Guinea's citizens, Sékou Touré called the Church a relic of colonialism that "wants a victory over the Guinean people."[32] Following Catholic protests about the nationalization of Catholic schools in 1959, Touré expelled the archbishop of Conakry, a Frenchman, and in blunt terms demanded the Africanization of the Guinean clergy: "No Catholic prelate will be accredited to Guinea unless he is an African."[33] The new archbishop of Conakry, Monseigneur Raymond-Maria Tchidimbo, a Guinean, lasted out ten years of uncertain relations with the government until he was allegedly involved in the abortive Portuguese-Guinean exile invasion at Conakry of November 22, 1970, tried, and sentenced to life imprisonment. (Tchidimbo was released in 1979.) It was perhaps inevitable that church and state should clash in Guinea, considering the regime's Marxist proclivities. Both the Church and Tchidimbo were caught in the near-hysterical xenophobia following the November 1970 invasion; Touré had always considered—and probably not without justification—the Guinean Catholic clergy as part of the covert opposition to his rule.

In Cameroon the Catholic Church has been repeatedly involved in politics, sometimes as a supporter of the regime, sometimes appearing to be a threat to it. The Parti Démocratique Camerounais (PDC), one of the lineal precursors of the present ruling party, was formed in the Yaoundé area and drew heavily for its electoral strength on the 350,000 Catholics in the Yaoundé archdiocese. The Democrats derived strong support from the local clergy, who in 1955 openly denounced the Marxist Union des Populations du Cameroun (UPC), the political party that had tried to launch a nationwide revolt in May of that year. After the first Cameroonian government of André-Marie Mbida, a Democrat and a Catholic, was replaced in 1958 by that of Ahmadou Ahidjo, a Muslim northerner, at the head of the northern-dominated Union Camerounaise party, the Church withdrew from open participation in the political arena, though it continued quiet support for the Democrats until the Cameroonian archbishop Jean Zoa ordered that they cut these ties. Relations between the Church and the state have remained strained despite the fact that in the area of institutional arrangements, particularly those concerning education, rapport has been good.

Archbishop Zoa angered the regime when in 1962 he and the local Catholic newspaper criticized the government for its hand in the accidental death of a number of political prisoners. Later, in 1970, Albert Ndongmo, bishop of Nkongsamba, was tried and convicted of complicity in an attempt to assassinate the president and for actively aiding the remaining UPC guerrillas in the country. The Ndongmo affair proved an acute embarrassment for both the government and the Church, particularly since both had sought to prevent a head-on clash and because by 1970 Zoa and President Ahidjo had come to a workable, if not cordial understanding. The uproar caused by Ndongmo's trial caused a deep split within the Cameroonian clergy and managed once again to sour relations between church and state.[34]

When Cameroon president Ahidjo retired in 1982 and was replaced by Paul Biya, a southerner and a Catholic, observers optimistically predicted a honeymoon between the Church and the state. Initially relations were warm, but over time they cooled considerably as the Church took notable exception to policies of the Biya regime, particularly as it became increasingly arbitrary and authoritarian in dealing with its opponents. At the turn of the millennium it was daggers drawn between the archbishop of Douala, Cardinal Christian Tumi, and the regime; in 2000 the cardinal had called the regime to account for a series of apparent extrajudicial murders by the security forces in Douala.[35]

Probably the Church's most successful intervention in politics occurred in 1965 in Upper Volta (now Burkina Faso), where Cardinal Paul Zoungrana of Ouagadougou and his hierarchy conducted a quiet campaign that significantly contributed to President Maurice Yaméogo's downfall. In 1965 Yaméogo had sent his local wife back to her village and had ostentatiously married an Ivoirian beauty queen of Voltaic origins. The wedding reputedly cost the Voltaic treasury at least two hundred thousand dollars. Yaméogo then took his new bride on a Brazilian honeymoon at government expense. The president's behavior shocked the cardinal and galvanized the hierarchy against the free-spending president. The weight of the clergy's anger was manifested in the government's embarrassingly poor showing in the municipal elections of 1965 and in the open support the clergy gave the presumably more moral military regime that took power soon after Yaméogo returned home.[36]

The contemporary examples of involvement by the Church hierarchies in local politics in Guinea, Cameroon, and Burkina Faso remain relatively discrete cases. In most other francophone African countries with large Catholic populations, church-state relations range from excellent (Senegal, Benin, and Côte d'Ivoire), to good (Mali), to a formally polite but not quite hostile coexistence (Togo). Twenty of the twenty-two francophone African archbishoprics are now occupied by African prelates, and Catholic schools, welfare agencies, and hospitals have generally managed to adapt quietly to the secular, national demands of the various governments. What is more, such political prudence is exercised not only by the Church hierarchies themselves, but also by the large Catholic populations, whose political potential is very difficult for any regime to ignore. In sum, the prevailing pattern is one of accommodation, but with the understanding that in a case of open conflict the state's interests will be served first, and by forceful intervention if need be. The success of the Church's accommodation can be seen in the fact that a Christian clergyman presided over at least five of the eight francophone African national conferences convened during the 1990s.

The Political Effects of Religious Ideas

Religious ideas affect politics in a variety of ways, direct and indirect. They flow, first of all, from the obvious institutional sources: churches, mosques, religious leaders, missions, holy books, and the like. They are also transmitted, perhaps with more reserve, through religious schools, associations, agencies, and social organizations. And finally, they find expression, with more or less emphasis on their source, in political parties and trade unions and in the actions and policies of political leaders and, sometimes, governments.

Only one francophone African state has openly espoused one religion over all others, and that is the Islamic Republic of Mauritania. By doing so, Mauritania deliberately broke with the French secular consititutional tradition that the other francophone states had adopted, and positioned itself politically closer to the Arab states of North Africa and the Middle East (in fact, joining the Arab League in 1973). A much more common embodiment of religious ideas has been through religiously oriented political parties and organizations. Although religiously oriented parties are usually no match for the more broadly based nationalist mass parties, they existed in several francophone African countries prior to independence. Some were openly Muslim, representing the efforts of Muslim minorities to preserve their interests in the face of secular nationalism or the centralizing efforts of government. Thus, the Parti de Solidarité Sénégalais, which was outlawed in 1959, represented the traditionalist maraboutic interests of the Tijaniyya *confrérie*. A similar, though nameless, religious opposition (to the Rassemblement Démocratique Africain [RDA]) in Côte d'Ivoire developed around the almamy and the mosque in Bondoukou. Elsewhere Muslim parties developed that, while not devoting major attention to religious issues, gained much of their support because of feelings of Muslim solidarity. As it turned out, some of these groups also represented regional interests against secular parties with largely Christian or mixed ethnic and religious clientele. The MSA in Chad, the Union Camerounaise, and the Groupement Ethnique du Nord-Dahomey (founded by Hubert Maga in 1951) were three such parties.

During the preindependence period, the Catholic Church inspired and supported groups in Upper Volta (the Union Voltaique), Cameroon (the Bloc Démocratique Camerounaise in its early days), and the Ivory Coast (the Action Démocratique et Sociale de la Côte d'Ivoire, supported indirectly through its link with the Ivoirian branch of the Confédération Africaine des Travailleurs Croyants, the Catholic trade union). In other areas, it appears that the Church's influence was exerted primarily to prevent undesirable developments rather than to gain political power. It took an active part in the struggle against the communist-dominated UPC in Cameroon, and in Dahomey and the Ivory Coast the Catholic hierarchies openly agitated against the RDA during the period of its ties with the French Communist Party.

Somewhat more indirect religious influence has been exerted through trade unions, such as the Confédération Africaine des Travailleurs Croyants, of French Catholic inspiration. Equally significant, though again indirect, has been the contribution of some influential members of the Catholic laity. According to Ferkiss, "The thinking of the predominantly Catholic group of economists called 'Economisme et Humanisme' has had much influence in Senegal and Mali; the economic development plans for these states were drawn up by the group's Father Lebret."[37] In this connection newspapers and other materials published by religious groups are important. For example, the influential weekly newspaper, *Afrique Nouvelle,* was published for nearly twenty years in Dakar under the auspices of the Paulist fathers. Cameroon has had two Catholic papers—a weekly, *L'Effort Camerounais,* and a monthly, *L'Essor des Jeunes.* Also, for a time (between 1965 and 1969), a Protestant weekly, *La Semaine Camerounaise,* was published in Yaoundé. Exactly how influential such publications are is difficult to assess, but it is true that *Afrique Nouvelle* was read widely throughout francophone Africa and that the Church-related journals, particularly those also publishing national news, are read widely by religiously diverse audiences.

Least measurable of all is the political impact of religious men: leaders and politicians with religious training or orientation. Of the political involvement of some clerics there is little doubt; we noted the unhappy fates of Archbishop Tchidimbo and Monseigneur Ndongmo, as well as the roles played by Cardinals Zoungrana and Tumi and by Archbishop Zoa in their countries' political life. Somewhat more ambiguous—at least from the standpoint of relating politics and religion—are the careers of two priests, Foulbert Youlou and Barthélemy Boganda. Youlou, who eventually became Congo-Brazzaville's first president, incurred the wrath of his superiors for his political activities. They forbade him to preach or administer the sacraments, though he was not defrocked, and he continued to wear cross, cap, and cassock, often in flamboyantly colored silk, until his removal from office in 1963. Boganda, who had not only entered politics but had married his secretary as well, was defrocked, but he continued to trade on his religious aura until his death in 1959. Youlou, it should be recalled, also had the enormous advantage of being considered the successor to André Matsoua, the Congolese cult leader who died in prison in 1939.

To what extent did the religious vocation of Youlou and Boganda affect their political ideas? There is really no way of knowing for sure, but one thing is unambiguous: their religious roles—however conceived—affected their political behavior and certainly their political careers. Neither Boganda nor Youlou was particularly concerned with his religious mission once he entered politics, but each unabashedly used the enormous popular respect for the Church and the cloth to political advantage. Both successfully manipulated religious symbols for political purposes (clerical garb, crosses, baptism, disciples, acolytes, etc.), and both did little to discourage stories that credited them with having supernatural powers.

As to secular leaders with marked religious backgrounds, the conclusion is also ambiguous. Senghor, an active Catholic communicant, for example, appears to have been influenced by the seemingly contradictory mix of the ideas of the Jesuit paleontologist Pierre Teilhard de Chardin, Karl Marx, and African tradition. In Cameroon at least four important politicians—Paul Biya, André-Marie Mbida, Charles Okala, and Reuben Um Nyobe—may have been influenced by previous religious training. Biya, who took over after Ahidjo resigned the presidency in 1982, had once attended the seminaries at Okono and Edea, giving every indication that he expected to join the Catholic priesthood. He finally wound up at the secular Lycée Leclerc in Yaoundé and the Sorbonne in Paris and thereafter pursued a nonreligious political path. Mbida was Cameroon's first premier (1957–1958) and helped to found Cameroon's only Catholic-based party, the Démocrates Camerounais. Mbida's strong religious convictions may have contributed to his downfall: his government's actions against insurgent Marxists were deemed so excessive and his attitude so stubborn that he lost the support of the parties forming his ruling coalition. Um Nyobe, who had once studied at a Protestant seminary, was one of the cofounders of the procommunist UPC movement. Um's political rhetoric was at times a peculiar blend of biblical and Marxist language, and even Um's principal lieutenant, Dr. Félix-Roland Moumié, a *médecin africain* with an Ecole William Ponty medical degree, once penned a strange document purporting to prove that God favored movements of national liberation.[38] And Charles Okala, formerly head of the Cameroon branch of the MSA and later the country's first foreign minister, clearly showed his Catholic seminary training by bringing to public debates a style and a rhetoric more Jesuit than socialist.

Diffuse as the evidence may be, there is little question that religious ideas have affected politics in our fourteen states in the past and will continue to do so. Modern politics almost invariably developed first among the Christianized populations on the coastal margins, and as a consequence the nontraditional political elites of francophone Africa came to be overwhelmingly composed of men with Christian religious backgrounds. It was only later, toward the end of the 1950s, that Muslims began to be represented in modern politics in any significant numbers.

Ethnoreligious Conflict

Ferkiss calls ethnoreligious conflict "perhaps the most-deep seated and permanent aspect of the influence of religion in African politics. Religion-oriented political parties may decline, church-state institutional conflicts may be resolved (probably in favor of the state), and establishments of religion may disappear from the scene, but as long as religion is a means of self-identification, even among those who do not know or care much about its formal ideology, spiritual or temporal, it will have a role to play in African politics."[39] When ethnicity underlies or reinforces religious identification, the mixture takes on added political potency. Two ethnoreligious phenomena, the Muslim brotherhoods of the Western Sudan and the Christian messianic and syncretistic sects of the Lower Congo area, exemplify the deep-seated, politically volatile nature of this variety of political conflict.

During the late nineteenth and early twentieth centuries Dioula traders spread Islam from its bastions in the savannah and desert fringe south into the forest regions. They were followed by the marabouts (religious teachers) of the major Muslim *tariqa,* or brotherhoods (*confrèries* in French), such as the Qadiriyya and Tijaniyya. In the process of diffusion, a large number of additional Muslim brotherhoods sprang up, since any individual who had acquired a reputation for saintliness or Koranic learning might become a marabout and found a new order. Despite the proliferation of the *tariqa,* however, the majority of Muslims in francophone Africa came to belong to either the Qadiriyya or the Tijaniyya. By and large, the brotherhoods have stayed out of politics, either having made their peace first with the colonial authorities and later with the new regimes, or simply restricting themselves to purely religious matters. The Mouride (Mouridiyya) order of Senegal, an offshoot of the Qadiriyya that is about two million strong, and the much smaller Hamallists, centered in Mali and an offshoot of the Tijaniyya, to which about 60 percent of Senegalese belong, have been conspicuous exceptions to this rule.[40]

The Hamallist Brotherhood, founded in the early 1900s as a reformist Tidjani sect centered at Nioro in Mali, spread as a movement of social and religious protest through the Sahel and Sudanese zones. As it spread, it first came into conflict with the more conservative Qadiriyya for trespassing in areas where the latter order had large followings; with the Tijaniyya the conflict was for doctrinal reasons. Between 1924 and 1939 Hamallists provoked attacks against members of the Qadiriyya. In 1930 the French, persuaded by Tidjani leaders that the Hamallists were covertly anti-French and a threat to the established order, exiled several Hamallist chiefs, including the head of the order. In 1940 Hamallists were held responsible for a bloody massacre of members of the Qadiriyya. That incident was followed by severe French repression: thirty-three leaders were shot, and six hundred rank-and-file adherents were exiled to various parts of West Africa. After

World War II the Hamallists helped the RDA to mobilize support in the savannah areas. Since the decline of the RDA the Hamallists have lost influence and followers, and today they maintain only a marginal existence in Mali, Burkina Faso, and Niger.[41]

Not so the Mouridiyya. Founded in 1886 by Amadou Bamba (1850–1927), a marabout notable for his piety and learning even in a land of marabouts, the order grew from a handful of disciples to a membership of over seven hundred thousand in 1971 and well over one million in 2001. Its mosque at Touba, some two hundred kilometers east of Dakar, is the largest in sub-Saharan Africa, and its leaders are among the richest and most influential people in rural Senegal. The Tijaniyya in Senegal exceeds the Mouridiyya in membership, but of the dozen or so *confrèries* in Senegal, the Mouridiyya is easily the most influential, partially because its members grow and market the bulk of Senegal's primary export crop, peanuts.

The Mouridiyya is particularly interesting not only because of its undeniable economic leverage in the economy, but for four other reasons as well: it includes most Wolof-speaking Senegalese, thus it has both religious and ethnic strength; it propagates what amounts to a Muslim variety of the Protestant ethnic, which distinguishes it from the other *confrèries;* it is tightly organized, operating through sophisticated hierarchies of sheiks (spiritual guides) and marabouts, all the way up to the khalif-general (the head of the order) resident in Touba; and finally, it has been intimately involved in Senegalese politics, once as one of the main props of President Senghor's regime, but also more recently in muted but nonetheless visible opposition to it until Senghor's retirement in 1982. What this adds up to is a highly disciplined, cohesive, ethnoreligious political interest group with enormous real and potential political influence within the Senegalese system.[42]

Along with the other Senegalese orders, the Mourides received both moral and financial support from the colonial administration, who relied on the marabouts to keep their *talibé* (followers) submissive to colonial authority. The regime of President Senghor continued the practice of supporting the marabouts, even though many of them opposed independence, and formed what amounted to an *entente cordiale* with the Mourides. Four Mouride leaders with close relations to the khalif-general were appointed to the cabinet and the UPS executive, and the government advanced $340,000 to the late grand khalif al-Hajj Falilou M'Backé, for work on the Touba mosque. The marabouts could usually command government trucks and tractors for their agricultural activities, and they found it easy to get government guarantees for some of their financial activities. In return the order provided party militants, support to the government when it sought traditional legitimacy, and a steady, reliable supply of groundnuts and groundnut products. On occasion it provided even more visible support to the regime. In 1962, in the wake of the power struggle between Mamadou Dia and Senghor, the Mouride marabouts rallied the brotherhoods to reinforce a weakened Senghor government. And between May and June 1969, when it seemed as if the regime might collapse under a combined assault by striking workers and rampaging students, the publicly announced refusal of the Mouride leadership to permit its *talibé* to join the general strike did much to defuse a dangerous situation and end the strike.

The 1969 strike, however, marked the brotherhoods' last major, overt gesture of support on behalf of the government. By 1971, they too had joined ranks of the discontented. At root was a catastrophic decline in the production of peanuts, from 1.1 million tons in 1955–1956, to less than six hundred thousand tons in 1969–1970. The decline was due as much to a precipitous reduction in the price paid to producers (which resulted, in turn, in part from the reduction and then elimination of French support prices, itself an outcome of France's membership in the European Common Market) and the fact that the government paid the producers not in cash but in chits (IOUs) supposedly redeemable in trade, as it was to a serious drought. As it turned out, few merchants were willing to redeem the chits, and increasing numbers of peanut growers turned from peanuts to other food crops.[43]

The shift in production had the support of the Mouride marabouts, already somewhat estranged from the regime following the death of eighty-one-year-old Muhammadou Falilou M'Backé in August 1968. During May and June 1971 the government desperately sought to heal the breach by redeeming a large amount of the chits and by promising the producers a five- to six-CFA-franc increase per kilo (over the 1970 price of fifteen to seventeen CFA per kilo) for the 1971–1972 crop year. Whether these measures would be enough to regain the Mourides' confidence was unclear, but it was clear that henceforth the *tariqas,* and the Mourides in particular, would no longer give automatic support to the government; nor would they necessarily come to its relief in times of political trouble. The Senegalese government's relations with the Mouridiyya improved markedly with the election of Abdoulaye Wade to the presidency in 2000. Wade, himself a Mouride, has undertaken a number of highly publicized visits to Touba and the venerable khalif-general, Cheikh Saliou Mbacké. Among other benefits to the order, he has inaugurated a paved road from Touba to Mbacké, home of the Mbacké clan. Withal, Wade has been careful to maintain political distance between himself, the Mourides, and the other religious orders. Saliou, for his part, has publicly promised that he would never interfere in national politics.

It would be an error to ascribe more political influence to the Senegalese Muslim brotherhoods than they actually command. In the past, it is true, they played an important, even crucial role in the country's politics. Senegal's decisive vote in favor of the Constitution of 1958 would not have been possible without the marabouts, who, to use Cheikh Tidiane Sy's words, "in the name of the power they received from God,"[44] effectively commandeered a *oui* vote from their *talibé*. They could not, however, prevent acceptance of the independence constitution of 1960, and once they made their peace with the regime, they became solid and dependable props of the government. Foltz has argued that during the ensuing years, their actual political influence declined, though they did retain powerful negative influence on the government.[45] Negative or positive, the influence of the brotherhoods has remained considerable, especially that of the Mouridiyya. How much they will count in the scales during the next decade is an open question, but at present no government in Senegal can afford to disregard either their economic power or the sheer weight of cohesive numbers they represent.

Some of the syncretistic, prophetic sects of the Lower Congo area also profoundly affected preindependence politics in Moyen-Congo (now Congo-Brazzaville) and, to a lesser extent, in Gabon. Almost all were of Protestant inspiration and appeared during the economically and politically unsettled periods that marked the two world wars and the worldwide economic depression of the early 1930s. Some of the most important of these movements, such as Kimbanguism, Matsouanism, and Kakism, represented important centers of anticolonial sentiment or were, to use Thomas Hodgkin's phrase, protonationalist "safety-valves" when other forms of political protest were either lacking or prohibited.[46] Others, such as the groups known as Dieudonné, Zoka-Zoka, and Labi, were simply separatist churches with few political overtones. After 1946 the most important of the sects took on additional significance, becoming vehicles for prominent AEF politicians, who mobilized them as ethnoreligious bases in conflicts of party and personality.

The messianic sects of the Lower Congo were part of a wider phenomenon of Protestant church separatism throughout the African continent. Some were almost purely local variants of groups established by missionaries of the Seventh Day Adventist Church, the Salvation Army, and the Jehovah's Witnesses. Some, like the United Native Church of the French Cameroons, were inspired by the back-to-Africa movement of Marcus Garvey, whose agents were active on the West African coast after World War I. Most of the separatist groups, however, were of purely African inspiration, offshoots of the more ordinary churches established by the Protestant missions active in sub-Saharan Africa. A few sects were overtly anticolonialist, such as Lotin Same's United Native Church and the little church communities associated with John Chilembwe, who led the Nyasaland Shire Highlands uprising in 1915. The majority, like the Harrisites in Côte d'Ivoire and western Ghana and the multitude of syncretic sects in South Africa, were much less overt in their opposition to colonial authority, preferring to submerge political expression in their rituals, symbols, and millennial doctrines. The Lower Congo sects, however, were unique both in their impact upon preindependence politics and the extent to which their members tended to be drawn from the same ethnic group.

The oldest of the AEF sects is Bwiti, which developed among the Fang of Gabon and extended into the Cameroons in the early years of the twentieth century. During the 1930s the sect became violently xenophobic, but after World War II it lost much of its extremism when one of its cult leaders, Léon M'ba, returned from exile to seek his political fortunes amid the changed political atmosphere of the 1940s and 1950s.[47] M'ba eventually became mayor of Libreville, then in 1957 head of the Council of Government, and in 1960 president of an independent Gabon. M'ba's rise to power certainly owes a good deal to his ability to manipulate the Bwiti-Fang combination, building on this foundation an effective organization that enabled him first to unite the Fang and then to successfully challenge political opponents who had support in the rival Mpongwe tribe.

In 1921 Simon Kimbangu, a Bakongo catechist of the British Protestant mission at Thysville in the Belgian Congo, claimed to have been touched by grace and rapidly became known as a healer and worker of miracles. Kimbangu announced that he was not only a prophet, but also the Son of God, and with his twelve disciples spread a doctrine that utilized both Christian and traditional elements. Because he stressed biblical passages that appeared to incite the oppressed to revolt, he soon alarmed the Belgian authorities, who arrested and tried him, then exiled him to a prison in Elizabethville, where he died thirty years later.

If the Belgians thought the removal of Kimbangu would cause his movement to atrophy, they miscalculated; Kimbangu became a martyr in the eyes of his followers, and his sect spread like wildfire among the Bakongo and beyond. Virginia Thompson and Richard Adloff explain the reasons:

> Kimbangu became the symbol of resistance to the colonial administration and also to the Catholic missionaries, who were believed to have cooperated with the government in trying to eradicate the sect he founded. He became the prophet of a golden age that was soon to dawn in central Africa after white colonialism had been eliminated, and was venerated as the founder-martyr of a religion that had been directly revealed to a Negro without any alien intermediation. In the eyes of the Bakongo, Kimbangu was gradually elevated to a position similar to that of Moses for the Jews, Mohammed for the Arabs, and his followers, like the early Christians, lived in expectation of an imminent second coming of their Messiah.[48]

Kimbanguism had its principal impact in the Belgian Congo, but it also spread among the Bakongo in the French Congo. The French exiled three of its most turbulent leaders to Chad in 1923. Despite these harsh counter-measures, however, the movement remained active in the Brazzaville area. Of all the Bakongo sects, Kimbanguism retained the greatest vitality: it claimed over three million believers, mostly in Zaire, in 1970, and in July of that year it was admitted as a full-fledged member of the World Council of Churches.

I have devoted more attention to Kimbanguism than the scope of its activities in Moyen-Congo might seem to warrant because the movement set the tone, provided many of the ideological predicates, and profoundly affected the growth of its most important successor cults: Amicalism, Kakism, Lassyism, and Ngol. Amicalism, often referred to as Matsouanism, is the religious sect that developed in Moyen-Congo around the person of André Matsoua, a Bakongo clerk who actively criticized French colonial policy and practice between 1926 and 1929. During this period Matsoua actually lived in Paris, where he founded a mutual aid society for Bakongo residents in France—the Société Amicale des Originaires del AEF, whence the name of his movement. Amicalism took root first in Bangui and Libreville, and then most successfully in Moyen-Congo, where two of his emissaries undertook a dues-collecting and propaganda tour between 1928 and 1929. Matsoua's activities in Paris, plus the resistance in the AEF offered by his followers, who were estimated to number about thirteen thousand in 1929, led to his arrest and trial in Brazzaville in 1930. He was found guilty of sedition and financial fraud and exiled to Chad. Like Kimbangu, Matsoua soon became a martyr in the eyes of his followers, and a quasi-religious aura came to surround his person.

It was not long before Kimbanguists and Matsouanists in Moyen-Congo—most of them Balali Bakongo—found common cause, and the former group came to lend active support to the growth of the latter. During the 1930s Matsouanists engaged in passive resistance to the French authorities, refusing to grow new crops as demanded by the administration, refusing to pay dues to the government-sponsored Sociétés Indigénes de Prévoyance (Indigenous Savings Societies, in effect local savings and self-help associations), and even opposing a population and animal census. In April 1941 Matsoua was rearrested, this time for allegedly disseminating pro-German propaganda. Two years later he died in prison and was buried secretly by the authorities. Matsoua's death gave his movement a dead, rather than a living martyr, and Matsouanism soon became a full-fledged religious cult, complete with doctrines of revelation and millennial rebirth of the prophet.

For a time the movement became politically quiescent, only to reemerge in 1956 when its members found a champion in the Abbé Foulbert Youlou, a Balali whom the majority of Balali accepted as Matsoua's spiritual and political heir. At this point the internal politics of the French Congo become so complicated as almost to defy description: personal rivalries between Youlou, Stéphane Tchitchellé (a Vili and mayor of Pointe-Noire), Jean-Félix Tchicaya (a Vili and the RDA leader in the Congo), and Jacques Opangault (a Mbochi and a socialist); tribal rivalries between the Balali, Mbochi, and Vili on behalf of or against the principal politicians; and competition, often turning into violence, between the main political parties and leaders, supported by one or another or a combination of ethnic groups.

In this context the Matsouanist-Balali combination proved crucial to the rise of Youlou, providing him with a mobilizable base for his political party, the UDDIA. Similarly, Tchicaya used and was used by another sect, the Kakists, for their reciprocal political ends, and both Tchicaya and the other Vili politicians found supporters among the followers of Zépherin Lassy, whose predominantly Vili sect, Lassyism, operated in the Pointe-Noire area. The Matsouanists participated in the riots of January 2, 1956; the Brazzaville Balali-Mbochi riots of February 17–19, 1959; and the riots of June, July, and August 1959. In the months up to and including February 1959, the Matsouanists turned out to vote or riot for Youlou or his UDDIA; thereafter, when the Youlou government began to demand obedience and payment of taxes, they turned out against his regime and the UDDIA. The August 1959 Matsouanist-government confrontation was the most bloody of the year: following Youlou's forcible deportation of five hundred of their number to the Fort Rousset region, at least thirty-five people were killed and seventeen injured during their attack on government forces. Youlou won his test of strength against the Matsouanists, reducing much of their local power, but the movement remained very much alive. It appears to have given support to the coup that overthrew Youlou in 1963, and one of the first acts of the revolutionary regime was to remove all restrictions imposed on the sect.

Kakism, named for the khaki uniform worn by its adepts, was launched in 1941 by Simon Mpadi, who claimed to be Kimbangu reincarnated and was Matsoua's local deputy. The sect, born in the Belgian Congo, found many followers among the Mbochi in the French Congo and, for a time, among the Vili. Ngol, which developed in northern Moyen-Congo and from there spread to Gabon, is interesting because of its name, which derives from the name of General Charles de Gaulle and the Congolese word *ngolo,* meaning power and strength, and because during the 1940s it attracted large numbers of Bakongo youth in revolt against the traditional power of the tribal elders. The cult faded away as its leaders were imprisoned or exiled for resorting to violence; furthermore, de Gaulle's visible support of the French authorities made the sect's use of the de Gaulle symbol both confusing and counterproductive.

All of the AEF's messianic sects came into being as spontaneous reactions to alien religious and political domination. Utilizing the ubiquitous networks of ethnic commonality, the most important of the sects grew in membership and influence until, during the first postwar decade, the AEF's emergent political elite began to court them and, in exchange for votes and mobilizable bodies, provided political protection for their proselytizing and organizational activities. They reached the height of their political influence during the late 1950s, then went into decline after independence as they attempted to resist the new African regimes or were seen as potentially dangerous foci of autonomous political power. Most important for our discussion is that their characteristic mix of religion, ethnicity, and political purpose has had, and may again have, great political impact on the polities in which they operate.

Ethnicity, Religion, and Political Culture

Aristide Zolberg notes the important political paradox that dominant mass nationalist parties often operated, both as irresistible bandwagons for the previously unpoliticized and as a spur to political fragmentation. No sooner had a party such as the Convention People's Party (CPP) in Ghana or the Parti Démocratique de la Côte d'Ivoire (PDCI) in the Ivory Coast established what amounted to territorial hegemony, than notables previously uninvolved in politics, or even political entrepreneurs within the dominant movement, began to stake out new or opposing constituencies. Zolberg writes:

> What strong reason could be elicited from the masses for not identifying with the dominant movement? For the most part, it entailed an appeal to primordial loyalties, usually in the form of ethnic affinities—using this term to include subgroups within a larger one—or kinship relations. This tendency was reinforced by the fact that as political participation was extended, the new electorate included more of the rural population, composed much less of transitionals than of traditionals, who would naturally be more responsive to the appropriate stimuli. As the political sphere was enlarged, there was a general politicization of primordial ties.[49]

Zolberg put his finger on a phenomenon common to the newly independent African polities: ruling parties, in order to survive, not only had to cultivate the economic, social, occupational, and ideological constituencies on which their power rested, but also had to seek the support of hitherto unpoliticized populations. Such appeals tended to be couched in ethnic terms, and in the process they brought new ethnic-based players into the game, either to join the dominant party or to go on their own with their own organizational bases. It is not that dominant and/or ruling parties did not also rest on ethnic bases but, given the ethnic pluralism of most of the fourteen states, ruling parties themselves had to mix and match among the varied social, economic, and ethnic interests they represented. Thus, expanding political participation, on which the new polities fed, was not without its cost to ruling parties: it opened political space to potential competitors and, frequently, to opponents.

Where dominant mass parties developed in situations of considerable ethnic pluralism (as in Côte d'Ivoire, Senegal, Cameroon, and Guinea), they tended to become coalitions of ethnically-based groups and parties. The dominant parties also contained parliamentary cliques—what Ruth Schachter Morgenthau called "one-man shows," revolving around some prominent political figure—as well as including the leaders of important trade unions, occupational groups (such as lawyers), or patron-client networks. While the dominant parties and the new rulers strove to be socially and politically all-inclusive and sought truly national integrative symbols, however, it was on the ethnically-based groups that they built their electoral support. The result, more often than not, was that they achieved neither national integration nor full penetration to the ethnic core of those whom their efforts had mobilized.

That core, more or less quiescent during the period of greatest nationalist fervor—immediately before and after independence—remained available for mobilization if, as happened in Dahomey, Togo, the CAR, and Congo-Brazzaville, the dominant party began to disintegrate or found itself unable to cope with postindependence problems. One interesting observation, though based on impressionistic evidence, supports this contention. It appears that in virtually every francophone state experiencing a coup d'état or some sort of traumatic political upheaval, the period preceding the event is marked by attempts on the part of the most astute civilian politicians to consolidate or rebuild personal support in their local—hence ethnic—constituencies.[50] In sum, notwithstanding attempts to create national integrative mechanisms such as single-party systems, ethnicity continues to be one of the most important political touchstones in the francophone African states.

The creation of truly national political cultures thus lies in the different strategies political elites adopt in their quest for national unity. One strategy appears to be to try to build a system resting squarely on a dominant ethnic group, but to ensure that other groups in the polity receive a reasonable share of the political and economic goods distributed by government, whether through regular patronage channels or as rewards for political acquiescence or quiescence. Houphouët-Boigny, who built his party upon a rural Baoule foundation; N'Garta (François) Tombalbaye, who ruled with almost solid Sara support; and General Lamizana, whose principal prop was the Mossi group, all adopted this strategy. In Côte d'Ivoire, Chad, and Burkina Faso, despite the usual ritual condemnations of "tribalism," the governing elites have made no real attempt to "de-ethnicize" (Youlou's phrase) politics, preferring instead to use the ethnic facts of life when that could benefit them politically, sometimes defusing incipient conflict, sometimes inciting ethnic xenophobia, as the post-Houphouët rulers of Côte d'Ivoire did after 1993.

Of these three leaders Tombalbaye appears to have been least successful in this strategy during his time in office. The revolt that began in Chad in 1969 was at least partially due to long-standing unresolved grievances of northern Muslim peoples against the political and economic monopoly enjoyed by the Christianized Sara. During 1970 and 1971 Tombalbaye tried to find a way to stem the revolt by means of a combination of military and political moves, including recognition of the traditional legitimacy of the "three great Sultans" of Ouaddai, Baguirmi, and Kanem, and the release from prison in April–May 1971 of some old political enemies, followed by their reincorporation into the party and government. It didn't work: the 1975 coup that toppled and killed Tombalbaye and brought General Felix Malloum to power was engineered in part by northern politicians playing the religion card.[51] As for Houphouët-Boigny, his patronage system needed his presence to work; it quickly collapsed after his death in 1993.

A second strategy has been a genuine attempt to find a supraethnic national political ethic, be it through pragmatic, ethnically neutral policy choices or through the elaboration of a highly charged national ideology. Cameroon exemplifies the pragmatic, de-ethnicized path. President Ahidjo, a northern Fulani, took great pains to deemphasize ethnicity in all areas of government policymaking and output. Though his cabinet reflected a judicious mixture of representatives of the most important ethnic groups—Bamiléké, Fulani, Bassa, Tikar, Bulu, Douala, Bamoun, etc.—he was still criticized for favoring "his northern barons," as Biya was later accused of giving "his" southern "Beti barons" the pride of political place. Guinea is the obvious example of the latter strategy. Not only did Sékou Touré develop a full-scale ideological framework for Guinean unity, but he reinforced it from time to time by fomenting a national xenophobia against real or pretended external enemies and their alleged internal (ethnic) agents. Biya has not been able to make his own version of Ahidjo's *dosage* (ethnic balancing) work, and Sékou Touré's grand supranational ideology failed both to convince his countrymen and to restrain the ethnic conflict he generated with his dictatorial policies.

A third strategy, available in predominantly Muslim countries, has been to deemphasize ethnicity by stressing the unity of all believers and thus their obligation to the state that exemplifies and supports that unity. Mauritania, Mali, and Niger have chosen this road, but to different degrees. While Mauritania has made Islam the moral and ideological basis of the state, Niger and Mali have kept secular state structures and have used the

Islamic bond to reinforce government and as a weapon against possible ethnic and sectarian particularism. Sékou Touré also called upon Islam to find religious rationalization for his ideology, admittedly not always an easy task.

There are other strategies for dealing with the ethnic givens: an emphasis on clan politics as a substitute for ethnic politics as in Senegal, and the "conquering tribe" situation as perhaps in Togo and (sporadically) Congo-Brazzaville are two examples. The salient point is that in ethnically plural polities—as are most of the francophone countries—the emerging national political cultures almost invariably contain an important ethnic component. This is to be neither deplored nor applauded; what is important is the composition of the mix, whether it induces conflict, and whether or not such particularisms aid or impede the attainment of national political goals.

A similar set of observations can be made about religion and politics, though the evidence does indicate that ethnicity is likely to have a higher and temporally longer political salience than religion—unless, of course, one finds the highly unusual situation where, as in Senegal, loyalty to religious orders trumps ethnicity. Where church membership is high or sectarian rivalries acute, and where there is active competition between religious bodies for converts, religion cannot but affect the political scene. Groups such as the Catholic Church, the messianic sects of the Lower Congo, and the Muslim brotherhoods have already displayed considerable willingness to become involved in politics. Actively proselytizing groups such as the spiritualist churches in urban ghettoes and the burgeoning Islamic Ahmadiyya sect, whose propensity for capital investment, the building of schools, and the sponsorship of business enterprise reminds one of the American Church of Jesus Christ of Latter-Day Saints, have already begun to interact with political authority, albeit up to now peacefully and cooperatively.[52] Whatever the nature of religious involvement in political life, the emerging political culture almost always reflects it.

Postscript: "The Venomous Flowers of Ivoirité"

The phrase *venomous flowers of ivoirité* is René Lemarchand's; he uses it to describe the toxicity of the Ivoirian political construct that is intended to draw a spurious ethnic distinction between so-called real Ivoirians (initially meant to be largely synonymous with people of Baoule identity) and people originating in Burkina Faso, who from 1995 on have become the objects of official persecution. "Like the Hamitic myth in Rwanda," writes Lemarchand, "*ivoirité* was first invented to distinguish, then to discriminate and denigrate and ultimately to kill."[53] Elsewhere Lemarchand argues that Ivoirité was primarily used by southern Ivoirian politicians "as a political tool—first to expel the foreign immigrants (mostly from Burkina and

Mali), then to disqualify the northern candidate to the presidency (Alassane Ouattara), and ultimately to prevent the northerners as a whole from becoming full participants in the political and economic life of the country."[54]

Ivoirité is a political construct concocted out of whole cloth by former president Henri Konan Bedié and some of his ideologues, and it has only the most remote connection to genuine ethnicity, save that it was one specific way by which to preserve the privileges of the Baoule political elite that Houphouët-Boigny had gathered and Konan Bedié hoped to inherit fully, to knock Ouattara out of political contention, and to revive and play upon the periodic xenophobia of the southern Ivoirian peoples. Chasing Burkinabé and Malians out of the country had been done before, with good effect, and it appears that Konan Bedié, seeking to nail down the succession and turn the national unease that followed Houphouët-Boigny's death to his own advantage, hit on a fictitious Ivoirian identity as the vehicle for his ambitions. It certainly worked: Konan Bedié was able to move swiftly into the presidential palace by decree and, later, via the 1995 elections; and the "northerners" (or more generally, in the quasi-scientific jargon evoked at the time, *allochtons,* or foreigners, as distinguished from *autochtons,* or natives) took the blame for all of the country's ills.

The unintended consequences of what began as a political ploy to benefit the Baoule politicians, were, of course, extremely grave, leading ultimately to mounting interethnic violence, the flawed presidency of Gbagbo, General Gueï's short-term coup, and, into 2002 and 2003, civil war and the entrance of French and West African "peacekeeping" troops. In the process perhaps six hundred thousand people fled or were uprooted from their homes, tens of thousands were forcibly evicted from the country, and thousands died at the hands of their neighbors, local militias and mercenaries, and government troops. Early in 2003 a power-sharing pact was negotiated by the French at Marcoussis, France, but by midyear it had begun to break down, and the civil war looked to resume.

Venomous flowers, indeed.

Notes

1. Rivkin, ed., *Nations by Design.*
2. Alexandre, "The Problem of Chieftaincies in French Africa," 15. Much of the first half of this discussion on chiefs, unless otherwise attributed, is based on Alexandre's paper. A useful summary is Kirk-Greene, "'Le roi est mort! Vive le roi!': The Comparative Legacy of Chiefs After the Transfer of Power in British and French West Africa."
3. Alexandre, "Problem of Chieftaincies," 15.
4. Ibid., 17.
5. See Ruth Schachter Morgenthau's discussion of this phenomenon in her *Political Parties in French-Speaking Africa,* 332–334.

6. Sy, *Recherches sur l'éxercise du pouvoir politique en Afrique Noire,* 61. My translation.

7. Alexandre, "Problem of Chieftaincies," 19.

8. See Suret-Canale, "La fin de la chefferie en Guinée." This article appears in English translation as "The End of Chieftaincy in Guinea."

9. Sy, *Recherches,* 66.

10. Bala, *J'aime mon pays: Le Cameroun.* The position of chiefs in contemporary Cameroon is discussed by Willard Johnson in his *The Cameroon Federation,* 214–217. See also Gonidec, *La République Fédérale du Cameroun,* 27–28.

11. In 1959 the *moro naba* Kougri, seeking to persuade the Upper Volta Constituent Assembly to maintain the privileges he and his subchiefs enjoyed, gathered three thousand warriors and besieged the building in which the Assembly was meeting. The French, who had little sympathy for the niceties of the situation—or for the plight of the *moro naba*—dispersed Kougri's bowmen and spearmen with a brisk police charge and a few shots. The Constituent Assembly was also unimpressed and proceeded to strip the *moro naba* of all except his ceremonial powers. A later regime restored some of the authority of the *moro naba* and his highest-ranking subordinate chiefs, but that did not halt the decline of the institutions of Mossi power. The story is told in Skinner, *The Mossi of Burkina Faso,* 206–238 ("Epilogue").

12. Ibid., 237.

13. Geertz, "The Integrative Revolution: Primordial Sentiments and Civil Politics in the New States," 163.

14. An ample literature on ethnicity already exists. See ibid.; Zolberg, "Patterns of National Integration"; Wallerstein, "Ethnicity and National Integration"; Mercier, "Remarques sur la signification de tribalisme actuel en Afrique Noire"; Delavignette, "Resurgences tribales dans les régimes présidentiels en Afrique Noire Francophone." Also see my essay, "Conceptualizing 'Ethnicity' and 'Ethnic Conflict': A Controversy Revisited."

15. This assumes a free election in which voters cast their ballots without constraint, something relatively unusual in Africa until the 1990s. However, even in democratic elections, ethnic preferences do not always translate into ethnic voting, as Jennifer Seely demonstrates in her 2003 APSA paper, "It's All Relative: The Importance of Ethnicity in Benin's Elections."

16. For further details, see Zolberg, *One Party Government in the Ivory Coast,* 245–247; Carter, *Independence for Africa.*

17. The most reliably accurate and extensive analyses of Côte d'Ivoire's recent internal conflicts have been those by the International Crisis Groups (ICG). In particular, see its situation report, *Côte d'Ivoire: The War Is Not Yet Over.*

18. I am grateful to Professor K. E. De Graft Johnson, my colleague at the University of Ghana, for introducing me to this term. Citizenship establishes a legal fiction that relates otherwise unrelated people to one another within a larger corporate group, the nation. The content of the fiction is a sort of juridical kinship, and its intent is to create bonds that recall, if they cannot duplicate, the affective ties of blood, family, and kin. Thus, nationalism and patriotism become the ideological expression of this fiction of kinship. According to this argument, ethnicity, as a halfway house between kinship and nationalism, can block the translation of primordial attachments from kin to nation. Of course, if ethnicity can be translated into nationalism, the elements of an integrative ideology of consanguinity can be found to cover the change. The greater the number of contending ethnicities in the polity, however, the more difficult the transformation. The modern rulers' problem is to find the most effective means to accomplish this shift.

19. The convolutions of Dahomean politics are well traced in Glélé, *Naissance d'un état noir;* Ronen, *Dahomey;* and Adjovi, *Une élection libre en Afrique: La presidentielle du Bénin (1966).*

20. House, "Brazzaville: Revolution or Rhetoric?" 20. The fullest accounts of Congo-Brazzaville's politics are Bazenguissa-Ganga, *Les voies du politique au Congo: Essai de sociologie historique;* Wagret, *Histoire et sociologie politique du Congo-Brazzaville;* and Ballard, "Four Equatorial States."

21. For details of Sassou-Nguesso's rise to power, see Bazenguissa-Ganga, ibid., 259–298; and for the facts on the "Somalization" of Congolese politics, see Congolese Human Rights Observatory, "Congo-Brazzaville, l'Arbitraire de l'Etat, la terreur des milices."

22. The pre-1965 standard histories are by Cornevin, *Histoire du Togo,* and *Le Togo, nation-pilote.* Ewe nationalism and the 1956 UN referendum are well covered by Claude Welch in his *Dream of Unity: Pan-Africanism and Political Unification in West Africa,* 37–147. Though the official story was that Olympio had been accidentally killed, Eyadéma as much as admitted having pulled the trigger.

23. Zolberg, "Patterns of Integration," 466.

24. For background on Senegal, see Foltz, "Senegal," and Lavroff, *La République du Sénégal.* For informed commentary on the election of Abdoulaye Wade, see M'baye, "Alternance historique dans l'ex-pré carré français: Au Sénégal, les chantiers du changement."

25. The argument is persuasively presented by Claude Rivière in his "L'intégration des éthnies guinéennes." Rivière's analysis is based heavily on Bernard Charles's doctoral thesis, *Cadres guinéennes et appartenances ethniques,* a survey of 2,382 members of the Guinean elite in positions of authority in the government, the PDG, and the trade union between 1958 and 1966. The data cited in this and the following paragraph are from Rivière's study.

26. Ferkiss, "Religion and Politics in Independent African States: A Prolegomenon," 6–7.

27. Ibid., 6.

28. Ibid., 3.

29. See Gerteiny, *Mauritania,* and Piquemal-Pastre, *La République islamique de Mauritanie.*

30. These categories are paraphrases and adaptations from Quinn and Quinn, *Pride, Faith, and Fear: Islam in Sub-Saharan Africa,* in particular chapter 3, 89–107.

31. Du Bois, "Catholicism's Problems in French Black Africa," 4. At independence nine of the fourteen states were ruled by Christian heads of state. All but one of these nine rulers (Tombalbaye of Chad) were Roman Catholics. The remaining five heads of state were Muslim. In 1971 there were seven Muslim, eight Catholic, and one Protestant heads of state among the fourteen countries (including all three copresidents of Dahomey, but not Kwame Nkrumah, who was copresident of Guinea in name only.) By 2003 the mix was eight Christians and six Muslims.

32. See the January 6, 1962, issue of *West Africa,* p. 11, cited in Ferkiss, "Religion and Politics," 12.

33. *Horoya* (the official government paper), Conakry, September 2, 1961, cited in Du Bois, "Catholicism's Problems," 6.

34. I discuss church-state relations and the Ndongmo affair in *The Cameroon Federal Republic.*

35. Tumi's homilies on the matter, his exchange of letters with the government, his press interview, and other commentary on the conflict between Tumi and

the regime are detailed in the pages of Pius Njawe's electronic journal, *Le Messager,* particularly issues beginning November 6, 2000. (See *Le Messager*'s Web site for texts: http://www.wagne.net/messager/).

36. See Du Bois, "The Struggle for Stability in Upper Volta."

37. Ferkiss, "Religion and Politics," 22.

38. The text of this curious document is in my *The Cameroons from Mandate to Independence,* 285.

39. Ferkiss, "Religion and Politics," 24.

40. For further details about the Hamallists, see Alexandre, "A West African Islamic Movement: Hamallism in French West Africa."

41. For the broader context of West African maraboutism, see Gouilly, *L'Islam dans l'Afrique Occidentale Française;* Monteil, *L'Islam noir;* and Trimingham, *Islam in West Africa.* See also Monteil's "Marabouts."

42. The best studies on the Mouridiyya are by Marty, *Les Mourides d'Amadou Bamba;* O'Brien, *The Mourides of Senegal;* and Copans, *Les marabouts de l'arachide.* Various Senegalese orders are examined in Behrman, *Muslim Brotherhoods and Politics in Senegal;* and Coulon, *Le marabout et le prince (Islam et pouvoir au Senegal).* The Mourides' "Protestant ethic" consists of the doctrine that hard work, thrift, and sobriety, plus unquestioned obedience to marabouts and regular payment of labor and cash tithes to the brotherhood, guarantee salvation. The great mosque at Touba, commenced in 1927 after Amadou Bamba's death (and incorporating his tomb) and completed in 1964, was built almost wholly with labor and money donated by the faithful. As a consequence of these doctrines, the Mouride marabouts have joined the ranks of Senegal's most influential capitalists. Professor Mark Karp suggested to me that, given the Mouride example, Max Weber's classic argument about the relationship between the Protestant ethic and the rise of capitalism must now be broadened to include non-Protestant—qua Protestant—societies.

43. The background to Senegal's economic problems, characterized by Senghor as "la malaise paysanne," is discussed in "Senegal: Ten Years After," 664; and Jean-Pierre N'Diaye, "Sénégal: L'heure de verité."

44. Cited by N'Diaye in "Sénégal: L'heure de verité."

45. Foltz, "Senegal," 47–49.

46. See Thomas Hodgkin's admirable summary, "Prophets and Priests," 93–114, in his *Nationalism in Colonial Africa.* The political role of the groups in AEF politics is well covered in Thompson and Adloff, *The Emerging States of French Equatorial Africa,* 301–314, 479–492. The most detailed examination of the prophetic sects is by the French sociologist Georges Balandier, particularly in his *Ambiguous Africa* and his *Sociologie actuelle de l'Afrique Noire,* 2nd ed.

47. James A. Fernandez, an authority on the Bwiti cult, argues that its politicization was over-interpreted by "an administration ever-sensitive to any threats to their authority. . . . Insofar as the Bwitists gave support to nationalist movements and incipient political parties, the great majority did so to preserve their rights of worship" (Fernandez, "Microcosmogony and Modernization in African Religious Movements," 11).

48. Thompson and Adloff, *Emerging States,* 310.

49. Zolberg, *Creating Political Order,* 21–22.

50. I was in Upper Volta, Dahomey, and the Central African Republic during the spring of 1965, some six months before each of those countries experienced its coup d'état, and was struck by the extent to which this phenomenon recurred. In the CAR in particular, deputies who previously hadn't visited their constituencies more

than once or twice a year—and then only briefly—now had begun to spend long periods among them. Had I had the wit to see it then, I might have concluded that they knew—or smelled—something I didn't. I wonder if this might be a useful test of the degree to which politicians sense impending political crises. One of my students to whom I expounded this theory suggested (without being unkind to the politicians) that it be called the "rats and the sinking ships" test.

51. Kelley, *A State in Disarray,* 13–14 and passim.

52. Ahmadiyya, an offshoot of Shia Islam, has been branded heretical by orthodox Islam because its founder, Mirza Ghulam Ahmad (c. 1839–1908) claimed to be a prophet after Muhammad. The sect claims some ten million followers worldwide, of which an estimated twenty-four thousand are in Côte d'Ivoire and perhaps fifty thousand in Mali. For further details about Ahmadiyya membership, see www.adherents.com.

53. Lemarchand, "The Venomous Flowers of Ivoirité," 21. The title's literary allusion is to Charles Baudelaire's famous collections of poems, *Les fleurs du mal* (The Flowers of Evil). The NGO Community of St. Egidio, on the occasion of being awarded the 2003 Eburnie prize (founded by Houphouët-Boigny), approvingly noted that certain religious leaders had invited Ivoirian farmers "to prepare an abundant harvest by beginning to uproot the weeds—weeds which emit the nauseous smell of cadavers, (weeds) whose sap is a poison that brings on a killing drunkenness: Ivoirité. . . . The wise man's [Houphouët-Boigny's] heritage did not include Ivoirité."

54. "Comments by René Lemarchand, Professor Emeritus of Florida University, on Paul Collier's Press Conference of May 14, 2003." Available at http://www.zef.de/download/articles/2003_lemarchand_collier.pdf.

Part 3

Structures, Processes, and Power

7

Experiments in Power, 1958–2003

Guinea became independent in October 1958. Its early transition was the result of its *non* vote cast in the September 1958 referendum on the Fifth Republic. A *oui* meant acceptance of Charles de Gaulle's new constitution and membership in his "Community"; rejection entailed almost immediate independence. The latter option was taken up by all the rest of our fourteen states within two years of 1960, but without the brutal consequences visited on Guinea by a peevish de Gaulle.[1] In any event, the leaders of all fourteen states—most already in office as premier or *président* or *vice-président du conseil*—negotiated the terms of their transitions, and except for Cameroon, where the January 1, 1960, independence celebrations took place against a background of rebel gunfire, the transitions took place peacefully amidst general rejoicing.

All fourteen states were also endowed with constitutions at independence—most of them modeled after that of the French Fifth Republic—which, in addition to their provisions for a strong executive presidency, "explicitly embodied democratic norms, presumably in fulfillment of the promises made by the founding fathers to the citizenry they had led to independence." However, "the founding fathers, for all their ideological, stylistic, and personal differences—and their ostensible commitment to democratic pluralism—all agreed on the desirability of establishing strong central governments. In francophone West Africa, each successful party set about creating structures and institutions that would make it virtually impossible for any other to come to power by legal means. . . . The net effect was the establishment of a form of presidentialism even more powerful than the original Gaullist model."[2] This holds true in French Equatorial Africa as well. The less significant and less proximate effect was the creation, almost immediately after independence or within five years, of single-party regimes—that is, regimes that govern with an exclusive or dominant single political party. Two modal patterns, according to Ruth Berins Collier, describe how the new regimes came about:

1. In Côte d'Ivoire, Mauritania, Senegal, and Guinea "dominant parties during the pre-independence period mobilized the population to build sufficient electoral support so that the party could either eliminate opposition parties through total electoral victory or absorb the opposition through mergers. One-party regimes in these countries were thus formed before independence."[3] (The Central African Republic, Niger, Mali, and Upper Volta also came to independence with dominant parties, but their leaders later adopted single-party regimes through various forms of coercion.)

2. There were neither dominant parties nor one-party regimes in Dahomey, Togo, Chad, Gabon, and Congo-Brazzaville at the time of independence, "but within the next few years all attempted to form one coercively through some type of ratification election."[4]

Collier overlooks the fact that in both patterns the new constitutions, as rule-setting institutional contexts, played a catalytic role in the making of the postindependence regimes. Where, as in the first pattern, the country came to independence with a dominant, or even exclusive, single party, the constitution provided the rules or the framework for the rules that enabled the new rulers to keep their opponents permanently out of power. Where, as in the second pattern, no single party was dominant at independence, the constitution, again the rule-setting institutional context, empowered the new rulers to create a single party, whether by passing enabling legislation or (as in Senegal, Mauritania, and Cameroon) by amending the basic document itself.

Although party system, civil-military relations, ideology, and the role of the chief executive are all useful ways to describe regimes because they focus on key or even critical aspects of politics and government, they miss the larger dynamics that animate them. Naomi Chazan and her coauthors make the point well:

> If the concept of regime indeed refers to the rules of the political game and its concomitant institutions, to the ways in which society is linked to the apparatus of the state, then regime types should be defined in those terms. The intent of rulers is less important than the latent principles that have guided their exercise of power. Regimes in Africa may vary according to seven main criteria: the structure of the relationship between the administrative, the political, the coercive, and the legal apparatus; the degree of elite cohesion; the extent of societal exclusion and/or inclusion; the rules and modes of social-governmental interaction; spheres of operation; longevity of institutional arrangements; and workability.[5]

On this basis, argue Chazan and her colleagues, some seven distinct types of regimes can be distinguished. With the understanding that these regime types are themselves quite fluid in practice and configuration, Chazan and her coauthors label them *administrative-hegemonic, pluralist, party-mobilizing, party-centralist, personal-coercive,* and *populist.*[6] Faute de mieux, the regimes in our fourteen states fit reasonably well under these rubrics and thus can be described by their terms.

Administrative-Hegemonic Regimes

As of 2003 the regimes in Togo, Cameroon, and Gabon provide examples of administrative-hegemonic rule, as did those in Côte d'Ivoire before 1993; Mauritania, 1960–1977; Senegal, 1963–1975; Upper Volta (later Burkina Faso), 1960–1983; Niger, 1960–1975; CAR, 1960–1965; and Congo-Brazzaville, 1960–1968. "These regimes were first established in the early 1960s and later sometimes adopted by military leaders," and "most other African countries, at various junctures, fall into this category."[7] Ten of our fourteen systems had or still have such regimes, the result of choices that appeared to promise both institutional workability and a reasonable measure of governmental stability. These regimes feature more or less pragmatic rulers who are willing to find ways of including key interest group (ethnic, regional, class, occupational) leaders in the decisionmaking process, as well as giving their judiciaries and bureaucracies, including the technical apparatuses, both room within which to function and some autonomy vis-à-vis each other.

Where auxiliary organs of one-party dominant regimes have been created, they are subordinated to the presidency but also allowed some political space, and the coercive apparatus—army, police—are controlled without being stifled. Civilian rulers in Africa have had good reason to be wary of their militaries, and it is always a problem to find the right mix of rewards, incentives, and controls that will keep them contented and loyal. When Cameroon president Paul Biya's special Republican Guard tried to overthrow him in 1984, Biya was able to call on the regular army to crush the revolt. Former president Ahmadou Ahidjo, who had created the Republican Guard and manned it with gendarmes from his hometown of Garoua, had probably inspired the attempted coup. Ironically, however, the methods Ahidjo had developed to keep his other generals and colonels happy—large budgets, inflated ranks, informal payoffs and perquisites, and so on—also worked for his successor, Biya, who was able to redeem the chits on them in the emergency.

At all events, the administrative-hegemonic regimes were—and still are—balancing acts, developed by ruling elites not so much out of weakness (though that may have been partly the case in Niger and Chad during the 1960s), but because the national or regional configuration of interest aggregates and institutional forces made such pragmatic choices workable. This does not mean that these regimes cannot deploy forceful or coercive measures to restrain or overcome challenges to the regime's version of balance. Most of the time they can. Suppression of the 1984 coup attempt in Cameroon, the failure of Mamadou Dia's 1962–1963 semicoup in Senegal, and Gnassingbé Eyadéma's successful 1991–1993 bypass of Togo's national conference are examples in point. Withal, it may well be the case that the more successful, or less precarious, the balancing act, the better the regime is able to fend off dangerous challenges. When the regime cannot fend off a challenge for whatever reason, it usually falls to a coup, as did the regimes in Chad (1975); the Central African Republic (1965); Mauritania (1978); Niger (1974 and 1997); and finally, the most stable of the fourteen at least up to 1993, Côte d'Ivoire (1999).

Three examples, drawn from Senegal, Côte d'Ivoire, and Cameroon, suggest how the francophone administrative-hegemonic regime operates— or operated until 1993 in the case of Côte d'Ivoire.

Senegal

Of all the francophone African states, Senegal has the longest experience with African political participation, going all the way back to Blaise Diagne's election to the French National Assembly from the *quatre communes* in 1914, a seat he held until 1934. Sheldon Gellar notes that "his election marked the ascendancy of Black African leadership in Senegalese politics, which had been previously dominated by French and Afro-French *(métis)* politicians. By 1920, the majority of local elective offices were also in African hands."[8] What this meant was that the balances and arrangements of Senghor's postindependence regime were already in place long before independence, including the alliance with the Mouride and Tidjani Muslim brotherhoods;[9] the configurations of clientelistic networks (the so-called clans) linking the movers and shakers of Senegalese society to each other and to salient interest aggregates outside the state;[10] the multiple pathways of French-African commercial and financial collaboration; the operating networks of black local and national politicians and officials; and the connections to a well-established, professional bureaucracy and judiciary ready to take over the tasks of governance. Senegal also had a citizenry seasoned and well schooled in electoral politics, led by an elite of ideological and political sophistication virtually unmatched in francophone Africa. This is the elite, formally in place since 1957, that led Senegal to independence and manned the first pluralist regime, of 1958–1962, which, after 1960, was officially headed by Senghor and Dia as president and prime minister, respectively.

This first regime was marked by turbulent electoral competition, the emergence of the Union Progressiste Sénégalaise (UPS, founded by Senghor and his former mentor, Lamine Guèye) as the country's dominant party, and the Senghor-Dia confrontation of December 1962–January 1963, from which Senghor emerged as undisputed leader of the country and Dia and his associates were tried and convicted for attempting a coup d'état. (Dia was sentenced to life imprisonment but in 1974 was pardoned by Senghor and released.) The first regime's troubles were not all internal: Senegal became independent on April 4, 1960, as part of the Mali Federation, which foundered five months later on the rocks of a power struggle between Senghor and his partner Modibo Keita, the leader of Soudan (later, Mali). On August 22, 1960, with support from the army and the Mouride marabouts, Senghor had Modibo Keita arrested in Dakar and shipped back to Bamako in a sealed railway car. By the end of September 1960 the Senegalese had formally seceded from the federation, proclaimed Senegal's sole independence, and taken the separate Senegalese seat in the United Nations.[11]

The second regime, under the Constitution of 1963, confirmed Senghor's version of presidentialism and permitted him to deploy his full configuration of balances and accommodations. Senghor not only dropped the office of prime minister, but arranged the electoral system to make the UPS the single governing party. The Senegalese 1963–1975 administrative-hegemonic regime was strong enough to shake off the violence that attended the 1963 elections, force the opposition to rally to the UPS in 1968 (for which several of its leaders were rewarded with ministerial posts and places in the UPS Political Bureau), and crush student and trade union strikes in May–June 1968. In 1970 Senghor restored the office of prime minister and named a young technocrat, Abdou Diouf, to fill it, and in 1976 he had the constitution amended to permit three specified "ideological trends *(courants)*" to field political parties and compete in national elections. Each *courant*—the "social democratic," "liberal democratic," and "Marxist-Leninist/Communist"—was allocated one party. The UPS, renamed the Parti Socialiste du Senegal (PSS), took the social democratic slot; the Parti Démocratique Sénégalais (PDS) of Abdoulaye Wade was allocated the liberal democratic position, and Majhemout Diop's resurrected Parti Africain de l'Indépendance (PAI) represented the Marxist-Leninist/Communist *courant.*

The reappearance of pluralist politics in 1975, albeit initially in a severely constrained form, did mark a regime change from one featuring hegemonic control by Senghor and the UPS machine to a freer and more democratic one. The new pluralist regime, still in play today, gradually made it possible to shift from the constrained, three-party "pluralism" to a more genuine multiparty system (the 1993 presidential and parliamentary elections were contested by eight parties), allow for peaceful succession from Senghor to Diouf in 1981, and preserve the dominance of the PSS and its balancing arrangements in the system.

Despite Diouf's attempt to give himself greater permanence as president—in 1998 he persuaded the Parliament to pass a law allowing him to become president-for-life—he gave way gracefully when on March 19, 2000, free and fair presidential elections ended forty years of PSS rule and put his long-time rival, Abdoulaye Wade, into the Senegalese presidency. The coalition of nineteen opposition parties united behind Wade proclaimed what it called an "electoral coup d'état," launching Wade, his new government, and Senegal into the ranks of genuine African democracies. By end of 2003 the Wade government had done most everything right: it took a leading role in the creation of the African Union, which replaced the discredited Organization of African Unity in 2002; it pushed for democratic governance elsewhere on the continent—and was believed; it began to mend fences with its neighbors and was able to deal with the long-term consequences of the breakup of its confederal tie with Gambia;[12] and it took on the more serious and still unresolved challenge of a popular insurrection in the Casamance.[13] The rise of an important, though not yet formidable, Islamic opposition presented yet another vector of uncertainty to the regime.[14] Another challenge is the country's gradual economic downturn, which threatens to place the country in the ranks of the UN's "least developed countries," something for which Diouf had lobbied so Senegal might become eligible for increased international development aid.

It is fair to suggest that the post-1975 (or more accurately, the 1981–2000) pluralist regime was in fact a mixture, with a semicompetitive party system, a quasi-democracy, resting upon the relatively stable patrimonial/clientelistic relationships of the earlier administrative-hegemonic regime. However, adding the Wade regime to the Senghor-Diouf ensemble, and forgiving Diouf his flirtation with permanent power, all in all Senegal offers a remarkable and rare African example of democracy sustained and strengthened.[15]

Côte d'Ivoire

Given that Félix Houphouët-Boigny dominated Côte d'Ivoire politics from 1946 to his death in 1993, there is some justification for confuting his regime with him, his leadership style, and his governments. He may well have been the model for Bernard Asso's prototype of the African "presidential monarch": prophet-founder of the state, symbol of the nation, and "autocrat in a divided society."[16] This, after all, is the ruler who not only had the national capital moved to his hometown, Yamoussoukro, but had erected there one of the world's largest churches, the Vatican-style basilica of Our Lady of Peace of Yamoussoukro, originally taller by thirty-seven feet than St. Peter's in Rome.[17] Robert Jackson and Carl Rosberg, in a seminal work on African leadership, also use the term *autocrat* to describe him, and Virginia Thompson bluntly characterizes his regime as "one man, one party government."[18]

However apt these descriptors, they speak more to Houphouët-Boigny's ruling style than to the character of the regimes he led. Houphouët-Boigny not only was a presidential monarch and autocrat, but was, above all, a manager, a consummate juggler of political institutions, men, interests, and power. The case can be made that if there is a model of the successful administrative-hegemonic regime in Africa, Houphouët-Boigny's Côte d'Ivoire was it.[19] To be sure, the regime began to totter in the late 1980s with the beginning of the precipitous decline in world prices for coffee and cocoa, the country's mainstay exports; with the recurrent health problems of Le Vieux ("the old man," Houphouët-Boigny); and with increasing manifestations of discontent and the threat of general instability following his death in 1993. For now, however, our focus is on the regime during its political apogee.

It is fair to say that Houphouët-Boigny began building his regime in 1946, when he launched his Parti Démocratique de la Côte d'Ivoire (PDCI) as the territory's branch of the newly founded transterritorial Rassemblement Démocratique Africain (RDA), whose president he also became. Founder of the Ivory Coast's first major political party (the Syndicat Agricole Africain, in 1944), member of the 1945–1946 French constituent assemblies, and deputy to the French National Assembly (a post he was to hold for fourteen years), Houphouët-Boigny quickly moved to make the PDCI the dominant political force in the territory. Official French harassment and prosecution of the PDCI because of its ties to the French communists (1947–1950) only served to enhance his and his party's popularity.[20] He broke with the communists in 1950, further strengthened his hold on the party and the country's electorate, and went on to cumulate official positions at four levels (municipal, territorial, AOF, and French): in 1951 he was reelected to the French National Assembly, was named mayor of Abidjan and entered Guy Mollet's government as a minister of state (1956), and was elected president of the Grand Council of French West Africa as well as president of the Ivory Coast Territorial Assembly (1957).

In 1959, after the Ivory Coast voted *oui* on de Gaulle's 1958 referendum, Houphouët-Boigny resigned his French cabinet position to become prime minister in his own Ivoirian government. As a principal coauthor of the French *Loi-Cadre* of 1956, which sanctioned the creation of territorial African-led governments, he not only marked a victory over the AOF federalists and Senghor, but also helped set up the institutional footings of his own regime. (See Chapter 3 for details on the *Loi-Cadre*.) By the time of independence in August 1960 the opposition parties that remained had folded or merged into the PDCI, and in November of that year Houphouët-Boigny was elected the Ivory Coast's first president without opposition. He was reelected in the same fashion every five years from then to 1990.

Jean-François Médard offers an apt description of Houphouët-Boigny's leadership persona:

> What distinguishes the President . . . is his popularity, even his exceptional personal legitimacy. . . . For once, and for him, one can apply the disreputable term "charismatic leader." But this charisma, which he has succeeded in "routinizing," evokes more the authority of a father than that of a tribune, or the leader or mobilizer of the masses. . . . To the observer, his popularity rests on the spontaneous testimony of the little people of Abidjan: the "little ones" *[les petits],* who are highly critical of the ruling class and the administration, spare the President, for whom they have genuine affection. Like the Frenchmen of the *ancien régime,* they appeal to the king to be better informed: they reckon that the President can't know everything that happens, but that when he is informed, he will intervene. This capital of confidence gives Houphouët [a set of] decisive trump cards: it permits him to master crises and challenges to his rule by placing himself above conflict, in the position of referee.[21]

The key contours of Houphouët-Boigny's regime can thus be identified; they are, in addition to Houphouët-Boigny himself, the PDCI machine, centralization of power in Abidjan, the use of patronage and targeted redistributional benefits to create and maintain a sizable "state bourgeoisie,"[22] ethnic balancing, manipulation and periodic scourging of the small political coterie at the very top, co-optation of oppositional elements and unruly interest aggregates, close ties to France and a large resident French population, a relatively thriving economy, and control over the army.

The PDCI, originally used to create and retain a loyal electorate, over time became more the organizer of the population than its mobilizer, more one of the important cogs of the regime than its engine. Until 1990, when Houphouët-Boigny conceded the existence of opposition parties and permitted competitive elections, the PDCI offered a useful but supernumerary, nationwide grass-roots support structure for the ruling class and the presidency. It acted as the official personnel recruiter for the country's elected bodies, particularly the National Assembly; provided a way by which to exclude other parties (all Ivoirians were automatically members, their dues being deducted from their income according to their ability to pay); and created a reservoir of loyalists who could be tapped when votes or expressions of support were needed. Though it presented itself as a mass party, its leadership, concentrated at the regime's elite level, never exceeded more than 150–200 persons, all them exclusively party, not government, officials.

As Michael A. Cohen has pointed out, the regime deliberately concentrated power in Abidjan as part of its strategy of maintaining strict control of the distribution of political goods, be they material (money, offices, development projects, public services, infrastructure improvements) or symbolic (location of the annual independence day festivities, traditional and ethnocultural revivals and celebrations, etc).[23] Centralization of power in Abidjan and the use of patronage and targeted redistributional benefits also made it possible for Houphouët-Boigny and his regime to control and manage the networks of patronage that kept the societal periphery, the party, officialdom, and the political elite both quiescent and acquiescent. Originally the party was the main channel for patronage, but after independence, given centralization of the levers of power, it became possible to create a distinct Ivoirian political-administrative-economic elite—a state bourgeoisie of wealthy businessmen, top officials and politicians, bureaucrats, party officials, Baoule ethnocrats, and privileged resident Frenchmen—held together by the networks of patronage shared by its members.

Ethnic balancing was manifested by the presence in both Houphouët-Boigny and Konan Bedié's cabinets of individuals from, if not representing, each of the major ethnic groups in the country, as well as an almost institutionalized system of ethnic candidatures to the National Assembly. Administrative ranks, however, were almost completely Ivoirianized, and the top rank of politicians and officials have been almost all native Ivoirians; members of the foreign-born African population (some 30 percent of the total) simply were not allowed to scale to these heights. Thus, between Ivoirians and non-Ivoirians, and particularly between African Ivoirians and African non-Ivoirians, a balance was preserved that was satisfactory to Ivoirians. The African non-Ivoirians were a mass of seasonal migrant workers and residents existing at the bottom of the socioeconomic scale and were periodically the objects of violent xenophobic attacks. At least some of the non-African residents, including about one hundred thousand Syrian-Lebanese and thirty to forty thousand Europeans, mostly urbanized, shared in the general prosperity, if not always the status, of the state bourgeoisie.

The small political coterie at the very top was manipulated and periodically scourged. For a long time this group was what could be called the presidential entourage, composed of *les anciens* of the preindependence period and those who were drawn into the entourage later on. These were the men generally found heading the most important presidential ministries, the legislature, the party, and the statutory councils; their names recur in successive cabinets, and they made up the circle from which Houphouët-Boigny's successor was expected to be drawn. The original group included such stalwarts as Abdoulaye Sawadogo, Mathieu Ekra, Mamadou

Coulibaly, Alphonse Boni, Camille Alliali, Jean-Baptiste Mockey, Philippe Yacé, and Auguste Denise, with the last three constituting what became Houphouët-Boigny's inner circle. From time to time Houphouët-Boigny shook up the entourage by creating or eliminating positions, reshuffling his cabinet and bringing in younger technocrats (e.g., Konan Bedié in 1966, Alassane Ouattara in 1990), or purging overly ambitious members (e.g., Mockey and Mockey's closest colleagues in 1963).

To the last, Houphouët-Boigny refused to name his dauphin, though at the end the contest came down to Prime Minister Alassane Ouattara and Assembly President Henri Konan Bedié. When Houphouët-Boigny died in 1993, Konan Bedié moved quickly to fill the presidency, using the lever of a 1990 constitutional amendment that permitted the National Assembly's speaker to become president in the event of a vacancy. Ouattara, dismissed from office in 1994, returned to challenge Konan Bedié for the presidency in 1995; he was disqualified under a hastily passed law that decreed that a presidential candidate had to be the child of two Ivoirian parents; although Ouattara's mother was Ivoirian, his father was born in Burkina Faso.

While Houphouët-Boigny's regime never hesitated to use coercion to suppress its challengers, whether they were local ethnic separatists (like the Sanwi in the early 1960s), student demonstrators, strikers, or alleged plotters, it always avoided using excess force or causing loss of life. Usually it sought dialogue with its opponents, often led by the president in an open or closed forum, a process frequently resulting in the co-optation of the challengers. During the early 1970s, for example, discontent among the younger, urban-based regional elites became so severe that Houphouët-Boigny sponsored a "Year of Dialogue" in 1974. Then in 1975 the PDCI party congress significantly expanded the number of ministerial positions, increasing the number of young technocrats and leaving only six *anciens*. In 1978, in the wake of student demonstrations, new dialogue with student leaders resulted in the reorganization of the student union and its incorporation into the PDCI. Jennifer Widner notes that Houphouët-Boigny also responded to discontent by co-opting "radicals" into the cabinet or the political bureau of the PDCI at frequent intervals, "usually after convening 'days of dialogue' or a national seminar. The president installed younger technocrats in positions of power in 1966, 1970–71, 1975, and 1977, sometimes displacing long-time friends and allies and sometimes simply augmenting the size of governing bodies. These changes opened the upper ranks of the political elite in order to accommodate the interests of the new political entrepreneurs, including student leaders once jailed."[24]

Close ties to France—particularly since 1951—and the large resident French population in West Africa helped to support what was until recently a relatively thriving economy, known until 1986 as the "Ivoirian miracle."

In addition, the regime maintained control over the army by keeping it small, well fed, well paid, and well equipped and by balancing it with a sizable gendarmerie. The army faltered only three times during the Houphouët-Boigny era: its generals stirred in 1963 when Minister of Defense Jean Konan Banny was inculpated in the so-called Mockey Plot;[25] it went on alert in 1990 when conscripts demanding higher pay occupied Abidjan–Port Bouët International Airport, invaded the Plateau (Abidjan's business district), wounded several civilians, and confiscated automobiles; and it became extremely nervous in March 1993 when elements of the elite Republican Guard mutinied in Abidjan and Yamoussoukro, taking three officers hostage. Houphouët-Boigny himself intervened the first two times to calm nerves and restore order, as did Prime Minister Ouattara, under the president's authority, on the occasion of the third. (I do not, of course, include here the first real military coup, in 1999, because that took place some six years after Houphouët-Boigny had passed and his aura had long dissipated.) The regime also ensured the loyalty of its administrative bureaucracy by safeguarding the pay and prerogatives of its more than thirty thousand jobs and by including them in the state bourgeoisie—that is, near the top of the sociopolitical food chain. Much of this landscape—including the PDCI and its electorate, the administrative bureaucracy, the leadership core, the framework of the state bourgeoisie, and the basic networks of patronage that fed them all—was already in place some ten years before independence.

Whatever else can be said of the post–Houphouët-Boigny leaders (Henri Konan Bedié, December 1993–December 1999; General Robert Gueï, December 1999–October 2000; Laurent Gbagbo, October 2000–present), they were never able to acquire as much power or manage the system as well as it was run during the zenith of the Houphouët-Boigny years. For one thing, even though the economy has recovered somewhat from the disastrous 1986–1991 fall in cocoa and coffee prices (they dropped 59 and 72 percent, respectively), all of Houphouët-Boigny's successors faced the discontent of huge numbers of unemployed and poor citizens who had formerly been able to survive relatively well when the accumulated wealth at the top trickled down to them. For another, certainly none of the three successors—Konan Bedié, Gueï, or Gbagbo—proved political matches to Houphouët-Boigny, and all labored at an obvious disadvantage under the long shadow cast by Le Vieux. Resort to unnecessary electoral and statutory chicanery may have helped Konan Bedié win the presidency in 1995, and thereafter, having to cope with the constant demands of his technocrats and discontented members of the elite, he became increasingly authoritarian in his attempt to keep an already shaky roof of power over the house that Houphouët-Boigny had built. Further, Konan Bedié's attempt to disqualify Ouattara from running for president and his efforts to fan anti-Burkinabé xenophobia under the color of an artificial ethnic distinction called Ivoirité made things even worse.

Thus, when retired general Robert Gueï, the former chief of the general staff, was recruited to head the coup launched by junior officers on Christmas Eve 1999—the first successful military coup in the country's history—many, perhaps most, Ivoirians hailed it as a "good coup" and praised Gueï for seeking reconciliation with the opposition parties, restoring order, and styling his regime a "transitional government," and thereby promising an early return to civilian rule. Gueï's honeymoon didn't last long. He proved no more willing to countenance the possibility of a Ouattara presidency than had Konan Bedié, and he reopened the Ivoirité issue by including in a new constitution (adopted by referendum in July 2000) wording that barred non-Ivoirians from seeking the presidency.[26]

The July 25 vote on the new constitution came two days after soldiers who claimed they hadn't been paid for supporting the December coup rioted in the streets of Abidjan, and six months after the price of cocoa (Côte d'Ivoire's main export) dropped even further. Gueï proved unable to push the country into economic recovery and only barely managed to cajole his soldiers back to their barracks. In September a group of disgruntled soldiers attempted to assassinate Gueï but failed. By October 26, despite all Gueï's efforts to stay in power, his string had run out and he was forced out of office by what amounted to a popular uprising against his rule. The occasion was a botched presidential election. Gueï had set the dates for the election as October 5–22. Ouattara, who had been forced to flee the country, had been disqualified along with fourteen other presidential hopefuls, leaving Gueï and Gbagbo as the main candidates. Ouattara's partisans actively boycotted the poll and were frequently involved in violence with the other parties and the security forces. The last straw was the army's October 23 announcement that it was suspending public statements about the vote count (the official electoral commission had announced that Gbagbo was in the lead) and its October 24 proclamation that Gueï had won. The next day widepread rioting swept the streets of Abidjan, and Gbagbo claimed victory in the poll. On October 26 Gueï, unable to control the violence, fled the country by helicopter.

By the end of the month the dust had settled. Gbagbo had been officially proclaimed president and had even arranged a meeting of reconciliation with Ouattara, who, fearing civil war, had called off further demonstrations by his partisans and ended demands for a rerun of the election. Gbagbo also kept his promise to lift the legal ban on Ouattara: on June 30, 2002, Ouattara was legally certified as an Ivoirian citizen, though it was not clear whether under the 2000 constitution he could challenge Gbagbo at the next presidential elections in 2005.

Gbagbo's victory in the 2000 presidential election did little to restore calm to the country. In January 2001 another coup was attempted and failed, and during the next twenty months Ouattara and Gbagbo gradually strengthened their reconciliation, which reached its culmination in August 2002 when Ouattara's Rassemblement des Républicains (RDR) opposition party was given four ministerial posts in the government. On September 19, 2002, some seven hundred soldiers in Abidjan, unhappy at being demobilized, mutinied. The disturbance grew into a full-scale rebellion during which former military ruler Gueï and his wife were murdered, gangland style, by a loyalist death squad. At the same time, rebels calling themselves the Mouvement Patriotique de Côte d'Ivoire (MPCI) had begun an offensive against the government. By the beginning of 2003, the rebels had broken at least two cease-fires; had congealed into three groups, each with a "patriotic" name; and had seized control of the northern half of the country, including the key cocoa-industry town of Daloa.

A feature of the new rebellion was the entrance—and metastasis to the three Ivoirian groups—of free-floating guerrillas from neighboring conflicts in Guinea, Liberia, and Burkina Faso. The "friendly" guerrillas had come in, whether on their own or by invitation is not clear, ostensibly to help their coethnic, cotribal, conational allies, but it quickly became clear that their agenda included looting, rape, and general violence. Also, in addition to the 1,400 ECOWAS (Economic Organization of West African States) peacekeepers already present by the end of 2002, some four thousand troops had been sent in by France to help stabilize the situation. As a consequence, a pact was signed in Paris between Gbagbo's government and the main rebel groups for a power-sharing arrangement; this was the so-called Marcoussis Agreement. By midyear 2003, however, the Marcoussis pact had begun to unravel despite the presence of French and ECOWAS peacekeepers, a May cease-fire, and cooperation between Gbagbo and a new prime minister, Seydou Diarra. The UN's first quarterly report on Côte d'Ivoire expressed disquiet at reports about the activity of rebels who were opposed to the new arrangements in Abidjan, and on August 4 UN Secretary-General Kofi Annan cited disturbing signs that both sides were rearming.[27] Given what the previous ten years had brought the country, there was little ground for optimism about its immediate political future.[28]

Cameroon

Like those of Côte d'Ivoire and Senegal, Cameroon's administrative-hegemonic regime was the creature of its first president; unlike Senghor's and Houphouët-Boigny's, however, Ahidjo's regime had to be constructed almost from scratch shortly before and after independence was achieved on January 1, 1960. Ahidjo, who had been involved in territorial politics since 1947, came onto the national Cameroonian political scene first as secretary, then as vice president, then as president of the territorial (later, legislative) assembly, and then as minister of the interior and vice premier in André-Marie Mbida's 1957 government. When the French forced Mbida to resign in 1958, Ahidjo became prime minister. To give himself an electoral constituency and institutional backup for his new positions, Ahidjo helped found the Union Camerounaise (UC), initially a legislative alliance of south-center politicians and mainly northern Muslim-Fulani socioeconomic magnates. Ahidjo carried the UC into independence, and it became one of the bases of Cameroon's subsequent one-party, administrative-hegemonic regime.

There was no dominant party during the 1946–1960 period, when more than a hundred political parties appeared and disappeared, combined and recombined. Whereas Côte d'Ivoire's PDCI was given a boost to primacy by becoming the territorial branch of the RDA, Cameroon's RDA branch, the *communisant* Union des Populations du Cameroun (UPC), never became the country's ruling party, having turned to rebellion in 1955—a rebellion from which it and the country did not finally emerge until 1971. Constrained by both the UN's trusteeship rules and a prickly French territorial administration, bedeviled by the UPC rebellion, and riven by sharp partisan disagreements, the territory found no single leader able to command its political heights or to create the foundation for a regime of the kind associated with Senghor and Houphouët-Boigny. Ahidjo arrived relatively late onto the national scene, and he could begin building his regime only when Mbida, one of only a handful of local politicians with a more or less legitimate claim to the title of founding father, was forced to step aside in 1958.[29]

The Federal Republic of Cameroon (1961–1972), which united the former British Southern Cameroons Trusteeship and the Republic of Cameroon, presented problems of political, economic, and social integration, but none so serious as to deflect Ahidjo from his regime-building task. By judiciously distributing patronage and by co-opting and rewarding a number of federalist anglophone politicians (beginning with John N. Foncha, whom he named both prime minister of West Cameroon and vice president of the federation, as well as Solomon Tandeng Muna, who became federal vice-president in 1970). By 1972, Ahidjo was able to engineer the gradual legal, institutional, and political integration of the two systems.[30] Using a combination of guile, selective patronage, legal manipulation, and coercion, in 1962 Ahidjo forced from the field the last eastern opposition parties, which had been cobbled together in the ad hoc Unified National Front. In June 1966 Ahidjo was able to announce an agreement under which the UC and the three western (anglophone) parties were dissolved, all to be replaced by a single national party, the Cameroun National Union (CNU). The remaining account to be settled was the last elements of the UPC rebellion. This Ahidjo did by relegalizing the UPC and then stifling it in his 1962 *coup de main;* by securing French military help against the UPC guerrillas; and finally by capturing, trying, and executing the last of the UPC *maquis* chiefs, Ernest Ouandié, during 1970–1971.[31]

By 1966, then, Ahidjo had put in place the main pillars of his regime: his single party, the UNC; an alliance between the northern "barons" and the principal southern politicians, tied together by the network of patronage and regional redistributive benefits controlled from Yaoundé; a well-paid security apparatus (army, gendarmerie, secret police) reinforced by French technical and logistical assistance; and a bureaucracy and judiciary secured by patronage and guarantees of jobs, emoluments, and perquisites. The regime was further seconded by a compliant national legislature that it maintained as a prebendal pasturage,[32] as well as by various other councils and public commissions filled by patronage appointees and charged with ratifying the regime's policies.

Ethnic balancing (in French, *dosage*) also figured prominently in the Ahidjo regime. The ethnic factor has been and remains critical to Cameroon politics, given the country's extraordinary ethnocultural heterogeneity[33] and a number of important ethnic and cultural cleavages operating in both the national and regional political arenas. These include the old north-south division based on historical ethnic and cultural distinctions between the mainly Muslim and Fulani peoples in the northern savannahs and the predominantly Christianized and non-Muslim populations in the south-central, southeast, and coastal areas of the country. In the north there is the split between the Islamized and the so-called Kirdi (pagan) peoples; in the south various permutations of identity politics involve the southwestern Bamoun and "Grassfields" peoples (mainly the Bamiléké); the center-south Ewondo-, Bassa-, Bulu-, and Beti-speaking peoples; and the coastal Douala. The federation attenuated the anglophone versus francophone dimension, as well as older western coastal versus highlands frictions.

Examples of the political salience of ethnicity abound: the UPC rebellion benefited from supportive constituencies first among the Bassa and later among the Bamiléké; Mbida's Démocrates Camerounais, one of the territory's leading parties during the mid-1950s, was first organized among Yaoundé's Catholic Ewondo-speakers; and Ahidjo's first party, the UC, effectively brought the power of the Fulani north to bear on national politics; and so on. At all events, faced with such a complex and always dangerous ethnic mix, Ahidjo's management of ethnic balances was a virtuoso performance. For some twenty-three years he successfully organized regional balances in his cabinets (though he did reserve critical ministries, such as Interior and Defense, to his northern barons); he rotated ministries and important offices among southern ethnic loyalists, including anglophones after 1961; and he made sure that the more important ethnic constituencies were always included in the regime's patronage loops.

Ahidjo's regime (like Senghor's and Houphouët-Boigny's) also benefited from a thriving economy, at least while the oil sector remained strong and helped make the country an important platform for foreign investments. And while Ahidjo himself was never able to generate charismatic appeal, he profited both from the image of reserve and stability he projected and from his regime's diffusion of the metaphors of him as political father and of the party as family.[34]

On November 4, 1982, Ahidjo unexpectedly stepped down from the presidency, turning the office over to his hand-picked successor, Prime Minister Paul Biya, up to that point only the fifth peaceful transfer of power in independent Africa (the two previous peaceful transfers were Senegal's Senghor-Diouf and Botswana's Khama-Masire transitions, in 1980). If Biya had expected a smooth, seamless transition and clear title to Ahidjo's administrative-hegemonic regime, however, he was soon proved wrong. In August 1983 the government announced that it had foiled a plot allegedly inspired by Ahidjo and involving several northern military officers and politicians. The principals were tried in February 1984, and all were sentenced to death, including Ahidjo in absentia; later their sentences were commuted to life imprisonment. Shortly after the trial, between April 6 and 8, 1984, the Republican Guard launched a bloody putsch against Biya, which was squelched. The attempted coup and the harsh suppression that followed—civilian casualties are said to have numbered in the thousands—shook the country; it was the most violent political event in the country's history since the end of the UPC rebellion in 1971. By mid-May the government admitted that 1,053 people had been arrested, but that over half had been set free, and that forty-six had been executed. Three others, unnamed but probably again including Ahidjo, were sentenced to death in absentia. Amnesty International claimed that as many as 120 executions were carried out.[35]

After the 1984 coup attempt Biya emerged frightened but alive from the impregnable basement bunker of the presidential palace, where he had taken refuge. The failed coup ended Ahidjo's attempts to retake power and enabled Biya finally to take full control of the regime, first by cutting the regime's ties with the remaining uncooperative northern barons and Ahidjo loyalists, and second by reshuffling the ethnopolitical cards and redistributing the key official positions to his own loyalists, especially members of his own ethnic group, the Beti. It was soon commonplace to hear that the northern barons were out and the Beti barons were in. Biya also launched a "New Deal," using what were intended to be the key slogans of his presidency, "rigor" and "moralization," signifying the struggle against all those factors (such as tribalism, sectarianism, clientelism, and so on) that affect public service, as well as the permanent endeavor against laxity, fraud, corruption, and the abuse of public office. He renamed the country from the United Cameroon Republic to simply the Republic of Cameroon; changed the name of the UNC to the Cameroon People's Democratic Movement (CPDM); moved younger technocrats into the cabinet and the top ranks of the bureaucracy; sought to mend political fences with the restive anglophones; and even, in 1990, restored multiparty politics and elections.

Though undeniably popular during the first five to six years of his presidency, Biya found public favor eroding in the late 1980s and the early and mid-1990s, in part because his regime was unable to cope with a sharp economic recession and in part because he and the regime became increasingly authoritarian and repressive. Matters came to a head just before and during the legislative and presidential elections of 1992, in which Biya was directly challenged by an anglophone politician, John Fru Ndi, and his Social Democratic Movement (SDM). The official results gave Biya 39 percent of the presidential vote, Fru Ndi 36 percent, and a third contender, Bello Bouba Maigari, 19 percent. International observers found considerable electoral fraud and intimidation by the regime, but Biya was declared winner by the Supreme Court. During the next six years, which included another presidential election won by Biya (and boycotted by the opposition), the regime came down hard on its opponents, using intimidation, beatings, imprisonment, arson, torture, and murder against the SDM's supporters.[36] Fru Ndi himself was continuously harassed and, for a time, placed under house arrest.

Even in the face of very real threats to his life and power, Biya did, all in all, manage to keep Ahidjo's administrative-hegemonic regime intact, though never at the levels of effectiveness it reached under Ahidjo. For whatever reasons, Biya never proved as guileful as his predecessor, nor able to find the effective, pragmatic balances between accommodation and coercion, reward and punishment that had been Ahidjo's hallmark as manager of his regime. Given the Biya regime's most recent challenges and the growing political disillusion in the country, whether the regime will survive in its present form is another question.

What is immediately evident in this review of the Senegalese, Ivoirian, and Cameroonian administrative-hegemonic regimes is the extent to which each owed its existence to a strong-willed, talented politician able to master the levers of power in his system. Senghor and Houphouët-Boigny, to be sure, each had a head start on local primacy, but coming to power late in the game did not prevent Ahidjo from forging a regime as effective as the other two. Nor was Ahidjo's lack of charismatic appeal—again compared to Senghor and Houphouët-Boigny—a disadvantage: he more than made up for it by creating his own official minicult of personality and institutionalizing the image of himself as founding father and political family head. All three were also masters of political guile and pragmatism, an attribute shared by the managers of the other contemporary francophone administrative-hegemonic regimes, Omar Bongo in Gabon and Eyadéma in Togo.

In all three of our examples, as in other long-lasting regimes of this kind, effective survival has depended on maintaining the complex balancing act that keeps potentially destabilizing factors—be they ethnic, religious, ideological, or economic—in reasonable equilibrium, and on acting forcefully when they threaten to get out of hand. By that criterion the six successors get marks that differ from those of their predecessors: Diouf appeared to have mastered the art, at least until he was defeated at the polls, and preliminary assessment suggests that Wade has as well. Both Konan Bedié and Gueï proved woefully inept, and the jury is still out on Gbagbo. Biya, who has tested the boundaries of coercion with variable results, has managed to stay in power while his legitimacy steadily erodes within the country's anglophone community.

Pluralist Regimes

In the taxonomy of Chazan and her colleagues, pluralist regimes are those in which "the relationship of public bodies to each other . . . has been based on a notion of the separation of powers, with multiparty political institutions and fairly vibrant representative institutions. In a few of these countries an effort has been made not only to pursue interest-group involvement but also to allow for a fair amount of autonomous nongovernmental activity. At least some notion of checks and balances has been retained, and therefore the very centralized political structures apparent in administrative regimes are not present in this more loosely organized context." The operating principle of pluralist regimes has been "a mixture of bargaining, compromise, and reciprocity."[37]

While more or less competitive electoral politics were practiced in colonial francophone Africa prior to independence and most of the francophone states emerged to independence with multiparty systems, none realized that initial promise. Before 1990, only three regimes in all of Africa were pluralist: those in Botswana, Gambia, and Mauritius. Thereafter a dozen others could be so designated, though some only briefly. Of these dozen at least five were in francophone Africa—Benin, Mali, Congo, Niger, and Chad. A number of analysts also included Senegal[38] because it appeared to move in the democratic/pluralist direction after Senghor's 1970 liberalization reforms, and more so after Diouf took over. The election of Abdoulaye Wade in 2000 left no doubt about the shift. However, according to Dwayne Woods, the Diouf regime's commitment to pluralism was somewhat clouded: "opposition parties are allowed to exist and social groups allowed to mobilize while the party in power refuses to concede on anything of substance."[39] This pattern, claims Woods, was also evident in Côte d'Ivoire. Still, although Diouf demonstrated the occasional authoritarian reflex, when Wade won the 1999 presidential elections, Diouf ceded power with grace and without visible reluctance.

All of this, plus the sudden, seemingly inexplicable reappearance of pluralist and democratic politics and regimes after 1990, as well as the national conference phenomenon that catalyzed that change, warrants a more extensive and separate discussion that is not appropriate in this summary review of francophone regimes. Chapter 8, on redemocratization, extends this discussion.

Party-Mobilizing Regimes

In francophone West and Equatorial Africa, only Guinea under Sékou Touré and Mali under Modibo more or less fit within the rubric of the party-mobilizing regime. The paradigmatic example of such a regime is that of Kwame Nkrumah in Ghana (1957–1965). Other examples, according to Chazan and her colleagues, are Zambia under Kenneth Kaunda, Algeria under Houari Boumedienne, Tanzania under Julius Nyerere, and Zimbabwe under Robert Mugabe. At least as far as Guinea was concerned, the designation is problematic because Sékou Touré's regime became increasingly tyrannical after 1975 and for the next ten years operated much more as a personal-coercive system than as a party-mobilizing one. During their own first several years as independent states both Guinea and Mali were governed by regimes that displayed significant populist elements, appearing to derive their legitimacy more from the personal, charismatic appeal of their leaders than from the party-institutional base those leaders were constructing. In any event,

> The party-mobilizing type of regime bears the imprint of some of the participatory elements of regimes in the pluralist category together with the monopolistic tendencies of the administrative-hegemonic regimes. . . . Regimes in this category reflect the organizational preferences of founding fathers with strong socialist predispositions. . . . The ordering of public institutions in these regimes . . . rested on a combination of strong one-party domination coupled with bureaucratic expansion under the control of an executive president. Unlike administrative-hegemonic regimes, the center of gravity in these regimes is in an ideological party . . . [and these regimes feature] the centralization of power around the leader and the party. . . . In these and other cases, coercive devices have been used to consolidate party-state control.[40]

Modibo's regime lasted only a little over eight years, from the formation of the government of the former French Soudan in 1959 to its removal by military coup in November 1968. Modibo himself was kept under house arrest until his death under mysterious circumstances in 1977.[41] In contrast, Sékou Touré's regime was one of the longest-lasting in francophone Africa. It was born in October 1958 in the wake of the country's *non* vote on the de Gaulle referendum, and it survived for twenty-six years until Sékou Touré's death in April 1984.[42]

Both men were dedicated Marxists. Sékou Touré was essentially self-taught, having learned both doctrine and practice during the course of his decade-long (1946–1956) involvement in Guinea's *communisant* trade unions; Modibo had earned his Marxist credentials through long association with the Parti Communiste Français (PCF). In the mid-1940s he had become a prominent member of the PCF-sponsored Groupe d'Etudes Communistes and had affiliated with local political parties that themselves supported the PCF in the French National Assembly. Both men had also forged local branches of the RDA—the Union Soudanaise (US-RDA) and the Parti Démocratique de Guinée (PDG-RDA)—into all-encompassing, single ruling parties in their respective countries.

In both countries the structures of power were much the same: at the top was the president, who was at once head of state, leader of the government, and secretary-general of the ruling party; under his command were both the functional ministries and bureaucracy and the apparatus of the party, with the key functionaries wearing hats in both state and party structures (see Appendix P on the structures of Guinean government). There was no question in either regime about where the power lay: the president was the "supreme guide of the revolution," the chief ideologist, the chief law-giver, and the *guide éclairé* (enlightened guide); the party was his instrument of social mobilization and national reconstruction; and the organs of government were intended simply to carry out the will of the president and his party.

Guinea and Mali each had a National Assembly elected by universal franchise. The Assembly was constitutionally meant to debate and vote on legislation proposed by the government. In neither Guinea nor Mali did the Assembly have any real power, however; election to it was part of the patronage package available to the regime, and it was used as such or functioned as a reward to superannuated or especially meritorious party faithful. The two legislatures rarely actually debated, much less rejected, proposed legislation.[43] In Guinea the Assembly's legislative role was minimal: it merely voted on—that is, approved—the budget (Article 16) and the laws (Article 9) that were initiated and drafted by the office of the head of state alone.[44] Since most legal measures were promulgated by decree in both countries, little was left for the legislatures to do, and their annual sessions were usually quite brief.

Sometimes the two presidents used the parliaments to make important announcements or to address the people, and despite their lack of substantive power, the deputies did use their respective rostrums to make speeches, most of which were innocuous or tended toward ideological homilies or fulsome praise of the president and his accomplishments. The Guinean National Assembly reached the nadir of its sycophancy on January 18, 1971, when it was asked to convene in emergency session to "try" more than 160 Guineans suspected of being implicated in the failed November 22, 1970, invasion of Conakry by Guinean exiles and Portuguese soldiers. The 160 had already been condemned and sentenced by the PDG party congress. The Assembly did not disappoint. Lansiné Kaba mordantly summarizes the proceedings:

> In the meantime, Touré published his long poem, "Adieu, les traitres" against political prisoners, and temporarily abdicated his constitutional right to grant pardon. He demanded that the Assembly be faithful to the decision made by the party at its extraordinary congress, and that each Deputy "bring the best of his contribution by the rigour and firmness he will add to the discussions; overlook subjectivity, sentiment, tribalism, and irresponsibility; and act as loyal interpreter of the people's demands." Every member ended his speech with thanks to "Comrade and Brother Ahmed Sékou Touré, the *Responsable suprème de la Révolution*," for trusting him and giving him the opportunity to show his allegiance to the Party and to the Enlightened and Faithful Servant of the People. As expected, the Assembly acting as a supreme court . . . faithfully enacted the orders of Touré: 92 were condemned to death and 67 to life imprisonment. The "plotters" were subsequently hanged in Conakry and other major towns on 25 January 1971, in a kind of P.D.G. carnival atmosphere.[45]

In any event, most of the time the legislatures were used to ratify decisions taken by the executive or the party and to proclaim the regimes' democratic character; such initiatives as emanated from the two parliaments tended to be resolutions commending the regime for this or that "historic" accomplishment, and minor and relatively unimportant emendations to laws that were usually passed unanimously.

It was hardly surprising that the Guinean and Malian legislatures played the minimal roles they did: they were part of the system of party-state control by which the elites strove to consolidate power and ensure uniformity. That system included the unabashed use of coercion, insistence on ideological conformity, and measures of social control that ran from preventing market women from operating their businesses to systematically undermining or suppressing recalcitrant or potentially recalcitrant social groups—for example, decreeing the elimination of traditional chieftaincies in Guinea. Coercion increasingly became the preferred method of social and political control in Sékou Touré's Guinea, so much so that one could argue with just cause, as does Kaba, that Touré's regime became an autocracy, and a particularly vicious one at that.[46]

If anything epitomized the coercive atmosphere maintained by the Sékou Touré regime during most of its existence, it was the institutionalized paranoia of the "permanent plot," developed as an argument by Touré himself to explain the crises of Guinean society and to justify permanent revolutionary vigilance and repression.[47] From the so-called Diallo Ibrahima assassination conspiracy of April 1960 to the supposed March 1984 plot to sabotage the twentieth OAU summit in Conakry (allegedly involving the governments of Algeria, Libya, and Madagascar, and announced by Touré barely two weeks before his death), Touré and his regime "uncovered" at least twenty plots and conspiracies, both major and minor, including that of the Guinean "fifth column" and coup plotters allegedly connected with the November 22, 1970, invasion of Conakry by armed Guinean exiles and Portuguese troops.[48]

Three facets of the so-called plots, besides their frequency, are striking. First, the evidence against the alleged plotters was frequently insubstantial compared to the magnitude of the official response. Second, the range of those accused was extraordinary. They included teachers, lawyers, merchants, officers and soldiers of the Guinean army, an entire ethnic group (the Fulani), Houphouët-Boigny and Senghor, American mercenaries, the United States, France, other African governments, and some of Sékou Touré's closest domestic collaborators and political allies. Finally, official retribution was ferocious and grand in scale; it often included not only mass arrests, detentions, and imprisonment, but also torture and executions. The carnival atmosphere surrounding the execution of the fifth-column plotters was mentioned above; public executions, usually by hanging, were common, and the regime considered them salutary education.

The "discovery" of each plot was usually accompanied by the announcement of the arrest of the plotters and often by the mass detention of hundreds of others as well. Frequently there would be "confessions" reminiscent of those extracted by Stalin during his purges, and the publication of lurid accounts of the misdeeds of the plotters. The prisons often functioned as death camps, particularly the notorious Boiro Prison in Conakry, which maintained a special section where the so-called "black diet"—execution by starvation—was carried out. The most famous victim of the black diet was Diallo Telli, formerly Guinea's minister of justice and at one time secretary-general of the Organization of African Unity, who was implicated in a vague June 1976 "plot against the Guinean Government." How many people were arrested in connection with the permanent plot or died in the regime's prisons is still a matter of conjecture; Amnesty International estimated that the dead ran into the "many hundreds," the imprisoned, into the thousands.[49]

The Guinean plots, whether real or imaginary, testified to the widespread oppositional activity from both the ideological left and right engendered by the regime,[50] as well as to the fact that there was no sector of Guinean society immune to the deadly paranoia of its leaders. That some of the real plots were hatched in neighboring countries was not surprising: in the twenty-six years of the Sékou Touré regime, as many as a million Guineans took refuge in Côte d'Ivoire, Senegal, Upper Volta/Burkina Faso, Sierra Leone, Portuguese Guinea/Guinea-Bissau, and Liberia, with the majority settling in the francophone countries. One notable exile was David Soumah, head of the local branch of the transterritorial African Confederation of Believing Workers (Confédération Africaine des Travailleurs Croyants [CATC]), who was one of many forced to flee on the night of May 2–3, 1958, when PDG militants went on a murderous rampage (Pierre Biarnès calls it a "pogrom"[51]) against workers and their leaders who had refused to join the PDG and its trade union arm. Soumah found his way to Portuguese Guinea and subsequently returned with the November 1970 "Portuguese" invasion.

While the Malian regime of Mobido could hardly begin to compete with Sékou Touré's in Guinea when it came to official violence (Miles Wolpin characterizes Modibo's regime as being engaged in "relatively mild repression"[52]), it did not hesitate to resort to violence when challenged: it called out the army to break up a demonstration by Bamako merchants in 1962, and it brutally put down a Tuareg uprising in 1964 during which two leading opponents of the regime, veteran politicians Fily Dabo Sissoko and Hamadoun Dicko, who had been imprisoned for instigating the merchants' "riot," were murdered.

Again, while the regime in Guinea continually honed its coercive apparatus, Modibo went part of the way by creating a Malian version of Mao's Red Guards, the Milice Populaire (People's Militia), an organization of teenage youth initially responsible for carrying out Mali's own Cultural Revolution by purging corrupt officials and politicians and promoting ideological education and the mobilization of youth. Eventually it also took on such tasks as border surveillance, night patrols, traffic control, and limited market intervention, duties usually associated with the military. By 1968 the Milice Populaire had grown from three thousand to nine thousand members, outnumbering the Malian military, and had become universally unpopular for the unabashed zeal and unchecked brutality with which it performed its tasks. There is no question that both the Milice's numbers and its behavior helped persuade the military to intervene in 1968, and the youths' excesses help explain why Lieutenant Moussa Traoré's coup was greeted with general approval and relief.[53]

Finally, both regimes were marked by their commitment to the revolutionary transformation—social, economic, and political—of their respective countries by what amounted to universal mobilization, to be accomplished through their chosen instruments, the leading parties and their manifold organizational extensions into civil society.[54] In both countries revolutionary fervor came to be expressed in terms of socialist doctrine, though with three significant differences. First, in Guinea socialism became Stalinist in complexion and behavior, with Sékou Touré as its living hero and universal expert;[55] in Mali it took on Maoist coloration, what with the Milices as Mali's own version of China's Red Guards and Modibo's 1967 dissolution of the Union Soudanaise's National Political Bureau in favor of a narrowly constituted and much more radical group called the Committee for the Defense of the Revolution. Second, Modibo's socialist vision as the regime's official line had been articulated before independence and continued to be thereafter, whereas it took Sékou Touré nearly ten years before he officially proclaimed Guinea's version of socialism.

Finally, when Mali launched its revolutionary program of socialist transformation, it lacked the rich resource potential available to Guinea (Crawford Young styled the program "building socialism without resources"[56]), while Guinea always had the economic cushion provided by its mining sector, which was run by Western capitalist firms. What that meant was that when the socialist plans of the Malian regime went awry, the regime immediately had to face the consequences of its failures, while Guinea always had the income from its bauxite mines and the exports of the Fria aluminum complex to feed its annual budgets, regardless of such costly policy missteps as the regime's early "human investment" program for rural agricultural and infrastructural work and its decision to ban all private business and trading. At all events, Guinea's maintenance of this early form of a "two systems, one nation" arrangement—part socialist, part capitalist (of which, at least until 1997 when Hong Kong joined permanently with mainland China, the Hong Kong–China coupling was the living exemplar)—probably helped Sékou Touré's Guinean regime survive as long as it did. However, the rampant corruption, mismanagement, and tyrannies of the system had so corroded the country that when Touré died in April 1984 his regime died with him. In Mali the soldiers ruled for thirty years until 1991, when they ceded power to a popularly elected regime; in Guinea, by mid-2003, nineteen years after Touré's death, the military was still in charge.

Party-Centralist Regimes

The proponents of the party-centralist regime type, explain Chazan and her colleagues, "have insisted on virtually absolute central control and direction and have generally been less tolerant of accommodation with local social forces or with most external actors. . . . Although the executive remained important, this pattern of institutionalization subordinated all other structures to the party mechanism."[57] While this regime type at first glance appears to describe the Guinean and Malian systems, at least in their later stages, it more closely fits the contours of the Afro-Marxist francophone states of Benin, Congo-Brazzaville, and Burkina Faso, where the "party mechanism" and ideological purity were emphasized much more than was the case in either Guinea and Mali. In both sets of regimes the repressive apparatus of the state and party was widely deployed and used, but, Ethiopia excepted, the Afro-Marxist regimes never allowed coercion to substitute for policymaking, as became the frequent practice in Guinea.

Because I discussed the character of the Afro-Marxist regimes at length in Chapter 5, I will not do so again here; instead, I will move on to the personal-coercive regimes, exemplified in francophone Africa by Jean-Bédel Bokassa's Central African Republic, which in 1977 became the Central African Empire.

Personal-Coercive Regimes

"Idi Amin's Uganda, Jean-Bédel Bokassa's Central African Republic, and Maçias Nguéma's Equatorial Guinea," writes Chazan and her colleagues, "provide the best examples" of the personal-coercive regime type, "although Liberia under Samuel Doe and Mobutu's Zaire in the 1980s also fall into this category." Arguably, Sékou Touré's Guinea in its later, most paranoid stages and Charles Taylor's brutal Liberian kleptocracy could also be included. "In these cases, the entrenchment of the regime has been predicated on the connection between a strong leader and the coercive apparatus. All other structures—the bureaucracy, the political machinery where it existed, the court system—have been subjugated to the whims of the leader backed by military force. Unlike the party-centralist countries, where a ruling clique dominates, in dictatorial regimes the predominance of the leader has precluded any firm pattern of regularized exchanges."[58] Samuel Decalo uses the phrase *personal dictatorships* to describe the Maçias Nguéma, Idi Amin, and Bokassa regimes, titling his book on the three *Psychoses of Power* in order to emphasize the abnormal, psychotic dimension of their rule—in part to describe the character of their regimes and in part to explain why they got that way.[59]

It is hard to argue with Decalo's analysis as it applies to Bokassa and the CAR, especially considering the monarchical turn the regime took in 1977 when Bokassa, reflecting on the 1974 death of Ethiopia's Haile Selassie, chose himself to fill the imperial void left by the departed negus, or king. The Bokassa regime lasted about three months short of fourteen years, from New Year's Eve 1965, when Bokassa staged a coup d'état to displace his cousin, President David Dacko, to September 20, 1979, when a seven-hundred-man French paratroop commando, in Operation Barracuda, flew into Bangui and returned Dacko to power.[60]

The Bokassa regime was the CAR's third since December 1, 1958, when the territory became an autonomous republic within de Gaulle's Community. Barthélemy Boganda, revered as the charismatic founder of what became the country's sole party, the Mouvement d'Evolution Sociale en Afrique Noire (MESAN), was invested as president by the first constituent assembly. Boganda, a defrocked priest who was also widely believed to have magical powers, died in an airplane crash in March 1959 and was succeeded as head of the government and MESAN by his cousin, David Dacko.[61] Reelected president in 1964, Dacko remained in power until Bokassa's coup. Dacko's first regime experienced no notable crises; it was remarkable only for its ineptitude and vulnerability to official corruption and for the extent to which it relied on foreign technical experts to help run the government.

Bokassa always claimed that he had staged his New Year's Eve coup to preempt one being planned by Commandant Henri Izamo, then chief of the gendarmerie, together with Commandant Georges Bangui, Dacko's senior military advisor, and Jean-Prospère Mounounbaye, commander of the presidential internal security brigade. Though Bokassa was never a wholly reliable informant, here he was probably telling the truth. On New Year's Eve he invited the unsuspecting Izamo over to his office, then arrested him; the others were arrested when they showed up for a New Year's party. Dacko, caught fleeing on the M'Baiki road, was placed under *résidence surveillée* (house arrest) after meekly penning his letter of resignation with a loaded gun pointed at his head. It is also very possible that one or two other plots were being hatched at the time, one by Jean-Christophe Nzallat, chief of President Dacko's *cabinet politique* (that is, his senior political advisor), and the other, also allegedly involving Nzallat, to storm the presidency using elements of a secret guerrilla force being trained on the outskirts of the capital by instructors from the Chinese embassy.

Be all that as it may, Bokassa's coup did neutralize his principal potential rivals for power and, as Dacko himself publicly asserted later, may have even saved his cousin Dacko's life. It is also fact that Bokassa had resented that the gendarmerie and the security brigade reported directly to Dacko and not to Bokassa himself, and he had complained that these units, kept by the president under his personal control, had more men and better equipment than the army itself.[62] Initially Bokassa's coup was well received in the country; after all, the forty-four-year-old lieutenant-colonel was well liked in the army and had distinguished himself during his long military career, having landed with the Allies in Provence, served in Indochina and Algeria, and earned some dozen decorations, including the Croix de Guerre, the Medaille Militaire, and the Legion d'Honneur. He had left the French army as a captain in 1961 and had returned to the CAR, where he moved up rapidly in rank to become army chief of staff in 1964.

He did strike one odd note in his postcoup declaration, announcing that "the bourgeoisie of the privileged classes is abolished" (*New York Times,* January 1, 1965). People smiled but let the matter pass without much comment.

Once in power, Bokassa reunited the army, police, and security forces under his single command. This was but the beginning of his passion for control over all aspects of political life in the CAR: more and more, as his rule became increasingly idiosyncratic and capricious, he accumulated titles, functions, offices, and decisionmaking powers.

> To the powers of the Presidency of the Republic, in 1966 he added permanent, direct control of various ministries . . . such as National Defence, . . . Interior, Information, and Justice, and occasionally, according to the problems with which he decided to deal personally, Agriculture, Transportation, Mines, Health and Social Security, Civil Service, Civil Aviation, etc. At the end of July 1967 he joined the General Union of Central African Workers, and the following August 23 had himself named General Secretary of Barthélemy Boganda's Movement for the Social Evolution of Black Africa [MESAN], whose torch he symbolically intended to take up.[63]

Ministerial portfolios were the lesser part of the titles and offices he took; the others included increasingly higher military ranks (from colonel to field marshal), presidential titles (president and president-for-life), and finally, in 1977, emperor. Even familiar titles were regulated at Bokassa's court: at one time he circulated an official list of those who were privileged to address him as "Papa."[64]

The empire that Bokassa inaugurated with his elaborate and bizarre coronation on December 4, 1977 (December 4 is the date on which Napoleon crowned himself, which is why Bokassa chose it), merits a chapter to itself, if only because it is difficult to describe without incredulity. It marked yet another step for the worse in the paranoid, capricious, and brutal path of Bokassa and his regime. Already noted for its excesses, the regime outdid itself for the coronation. Costing up to perhaps thirty million dollars, it was held in Bangui's basketball stadium, which was rededicated as the "Coronation Palace" for the occasion; Bokassa crowned himself and his wife while some 2,500 invited guests, but no real royals or presidents, looked on. France, which had helped underwrite the affair and had contributed, inter alia, a fine matched set of eight Belgian white horses to pull the coronation coach, sent Robert Galley, its ambassador and minister for cooperation, and René Journiac, presidential adviser on African affairs.[65]

To the murderous caprices of a president-for-life was added the savage megalomania of a self-crowned emperor, one who, now invested (as he is reported to have put it) with "unquestionable" power of life and death, could vent his occasional murderous rages at will. Not that he needed much encouragement: earlier, in 1971, furious that his war on crime had not prevented a wave of robberies in Bangui, including thefts from his own house, Bokassa had ordered his soldiers to kick and beat a group of some forty-six thieves "until you kill them," all in the presence of photographers and witnesses summoned for the occasion. When it was over, the witnesses counted at least ten dead and twenty wounded, and many of the wounded were left where they fell and later died. On Mother's Day in 1971 he ordered that all women held prisoner be released and that all men imprisoned for crimes against women be executed. Soon after his coup he had ten of his most prominent opponents (including Izamo and Mounounbaye) executed, and on occasion he reportedly fed condemned prisoners to his lions and crocodiles. When he had individuals executed or imprisoned for plotting his overthrow—more than a dozen such plots, real or imagined, were uncovered—he often eliminated all the members of their immediate family as well. The journalist Alex Shoumatoff, who attended Bokassa's trial, reported that one such case was discussed in detail in court, "that of General Martin Linpoupou, who was sentenced to ten years for plotting a coup in 1974; Bokassa had his brothers, cousins, and even his mother, killed."[66]

International outrage at Bokassa's excesses had already begun to grow before his coronation, especially over his treatment in 1977 of a white Associated Press correspondent, Michael Goldsmith, who had been arrested for allegedly sending coded messages abroad (the electricity had been temporarily interrupted, and the telex had sent gibberish instead of Goldsmith's cable). Accused of spying for South Africa, Goldsmith was savagely beaten by Bokassa himself, then was held in abysmal conditions for a month before being sent home—unbelievably with Bokassa's personal embrace, blessings, and benedictions.

The last straw was the two "massacres of the schoolchildren" in 1979, outrages that not even the French government, which had theretofore protected Bokassa, could overlook. Though the sequence of events and some of the facts are in dispute, the affair began with an imperial decree that all schoolchildren must wear uniforms. Bokassa's family owned the only uniform factory in the country. On January 19, there were demonstrations by several hundred children whose parents couldn't afford the uniforms. The demonstrations grew into disorders at various places in the city, and the soldiers, called out to maintain order, apparently opened fire and killed a number of people, including children. On April 18, after a vehicle belonging to the imperial guard—one version has it that it was Bokassa's own limousine—was stoned by schoolchildren, Bokassa ordered a roundup of the youthful protesters. About 180 children (the estimates range from one hundred to five hundred, depending on the source) were thrown into the infamous Ngaragbo Prison and the Kasai barracks. They were crammed into three tiny cells in Ngaragbo and stripped naked; by nightfall several children had already died of suffocation, and overnight soldiers finished beating the rest. Only a handful of the children (Shoumatoff has the number at twenty-seven) reportedly survived. Some accounts have Bokassa himself involved in the beatings, arriving at 8:00 p.m. to initiate the killing; others, including Brian Titley, cite reliable French sources that deny Bokassa was ever there.[67]

The arguments among the eyewitnesses, journalists, and commentators were about the details, not the main facts: dozens of children were dead, brutally murdered, victims of Bokassa's megalomania. The next move was France's Operation Barracuda. Even before the events of January and April 1979 Bokassa's empire had been teetering on the brink of ungovernability: it was a swamp of plots, attempted coups, high- and low-level corruption, contradictory policymaking, and unpredictability, all brought on by Bokassa's increasingly erratic and often bizarre style of personal rule, including the creation of a full-blown royal court, complete with elaborate titles of nobility and a complex court protocol. Earlier, in 1976, Bokassa had briefly converted to Islam at the urging of his friend Muammar al-Qaddafi and had forced several of his wives and his premier, Ange-Félix Patassé, to do likewise. For much of nearly four months, most of the government's predominantly Catholic personnel were thrown into panic, unsure about which religious devotions were permitted and which not. During this remarkable fourteen-year descent into near chaos, Biarnès reported, "the Central African government was reshuffled more than sixty times, that is, on average, once every three months."[68] Finally, although the economy actually improved somewhat during Bokassa's first three years in power, due mainly to heavy investments in infrastructure development, thereafter it was all downhill, a slide resulting as much from the increasing rapacity of the ruling elite (which, for example, began treating the country's diamond trade as its own) as from losses of productivity and the inability to conduct predictable foreign trade.

Overthrown on September 20, 1979, Bokassa found refuge first in Côte d'Ivoire, then in France in 1983. In 1980 a CAR court sentenced him, in absentia, to death. In 1986 he was persuaded to return home, where he was put on trial and again condemned to death in 1987. General André Kolingba, now the head of state, gave him a reprieve, commuting his sentence to life imprisonment, and then pardoned and freed him in 1993 shortly before being forced from office himself. Bokassa died of a heart attack in Bangui on November 5, 1996, and was given a state funeral.[69]

The election of October 1993, which brought Patassé to the presidency, was conducted under democratic rules, the first time this had happened in the CAR for more than thirty years. That Patassé could claim democratic legitimacy availed him little: his regime, like those of his predecessors, could not master the country's economic problems, including recurrent army and civil servant salary arrears, and it was beset by corruption, mismanagement, and general political ineptitude. These problems were compounded by no fewer than four failed coup attempts staged by Kolingba, plus one in 2001 led by Patassé's former army chief of staff, General François Bozize, who had tried to overthrow Kolingba too, in 1983. Finally, after four months of salary arrears, Bozize led a successful army coup on March 15, 2003. Patassé fled to Togo, and later a warrant was issued for his arrest, accusing him of murder and embezzlement. One feature of Patassé's regime that was much resented by Centrafricans and may have contributed to his downfall was the continuous presence in Bangui of over two thousand often unruly foreign troops—including Libyans, Sudanese, Djiboutis, Congolese, Gabonese, and Chadians—all ostensibly sent at one time or another to help Patassé keep power. By midyear 2003 Bozize's junta, which styled itself the National Transitional Council, was following a well-worn template: calling for national reconciliation, inviting former presidents Dacko and Kolingba for "dialogue," and promising to set the country aright.

Populist Regimes

Exemplified by Ghana under Jerry Rawlings and Burkina Faso under Thomas Sankara, the populist regime, emerging in the 1980s, "was in part a response to unpredictable dictatorial trends."[70] The Burkinabé version of this regime type, under Sankara, like Rawling's Ghana, sought to circumscribe the operations of the formal institutions of the state, including the civil service, certain public corporations, and the judiciary, with popular, even alternative sets of institutions operating at the grass roots, such as public tribunals, citizens' vetting committees, and national investigative commissions. It was thought that state institutions prone to immobility, corruption, and the unchecked exercise of privilege and authority would be matched by institutions that safeguarded the public's access to power. Thus "an essential tenet of the populist regime has been . . . a concept of social inclusion defined in nonelite terms."[71]

What Sankara sought, simply put, was empowerment of the Burkinese masses, something much more easily envisioned than achieved. The problem in Burkina Faso was that of translating ideology into practice, in particular convincing those at the top of the sociopolitical pyramid to allow their power to be diffused. For all the appeal of Sankara's message and his undeniable popularity, he found it impossible to appease the radical ideological factions in his regime, eliminate rooted patron-client networks, and overcome the resistance of entrenched factional alliances and economic-occupational interest groups. Caught in a web of factional and personal intrigue, he paid for his presumption with his life.

"The governments established along populist lines, as in the examples of Ghana and Burkina Faso, rapidly gave way to hegemonic-administrative forms."[72] Rawlings's three-month regime in 1979 and the early period of his "second coming" (December 1981 to about mid-1985) exemplified populist politics, but by 1992, when he ran for president the first time, his regime was already transitioning to a less ideological, less populist, and less activist form. Sankara's regime was unique: his successor, Blaise Compaoré, certainly had no ideological fire in his belly, much less a populist spark, and his regime made no effort, other than by mouthing Sankara's slogans, to replicate the earlier leader's populist message. Compaoré's regime became establishmentarian, as did Rawlings's, relying for power on well-worn institutions, solid administrative apparatuses, and the time-tested alliances with the social and economic groups—professionals, labor unions, civil servants, "traditional" magnates, market women, businessmen—that had always underwritten longer-lived civilian and military regimes.

Notes

1. For details, see Chapter 3; also Camara, *La Guinée sans la France,* 113–234.

2. Le Vine, "The Fall and Rise of Constitutionalism in West Africa," 184, 187.

3. Collier, *Regimes in Tropical Africa: Changing Forms of Supremacy, 1945–1975,* 155.

4. Ibid., 155. Collier's use of *regime* to describe the party configuration before independence is well warranted since *regime* does describe the arrangements, at least from 1958 on, by which the African officials and politicians held the keys to the territories' internal politics.

5. Chazan et al., *Politics and Society in Contemporary Africa,* 136.

6. Ibid., 137–151.

7. Ibid., 137.

8. Gellar, *Senegal: An African Nation Between Islam and the West,* 11. In 1918 Diagne was given a cabinet post in Georges Clemenceau's emergency government (commissioner for troop recruitment in West Africa); he was the first of a number of francophone Africans named to French cabinets.

9. There is a sizable literature on the Mouridiyya and the other Senegalese brotherhoods. The best include Copans, *Les marabouts de l'arachide, and* O'Brien, *The Mourides of Senegal,* specifically on the Mouridiyya; and two more general works, Behrman, *Muslim Brotherhoods and Politics in Senegal,* and Coulon, *Le marabout et le prince (Islam et pouvoir au Senegal).* (Marabouts are the religious teachers and leaders of the Muslim brotherhoods; their disciples are known as *talibé,* from the Arabic, meaning "student.") I can offer corroborative eyewitness testimony to the close ties between the marabouts and the regime: In the spring of 1965, while I was interviewing al-Hajj Falilou M'Backé, the khalif-general (leading reli-

gious authority) of the Mouride brotherhood, the phone rang. Speaking into a receiver brought him, Falilou M'Backé carried on an animated fifteen-minute conversation in Wolof. It was, he said to me after hanging up, his daily chat with his "beloved cousin," President Senghor, who kept him informed and who consulted him on "important matters." My interviews in Dakar had already suggested that among my elite informants Falilou M'Backé was considered the second most influential man in Senegal, in part because his alliance with Senghor gave both men additional political clout. Two of Falilou M'Backé's aides, with whom I spoke after the interview with the khalif-general himself, confirmed that Senghor called "nearly every day." They even contended that had it not been for Falilou M'Backé's support during Senghor's 1962–1963 confrontation with Mamadou Dia, Senghor would not have survived. Be that as it may, the alliance certainly benefited both parties: it gave the Mourides the protected internal markets and financial institutions they needed to consolidate and maintain their economic supremacy in the peanut production and export domains; it gave Senghor rural votes, clan links with not only Falilou M'Backé but also the leaders of the other three local brotherhoods, and access to the economic resources of the brotherhoods. John Waterbury (in *The Political Economy of Risk and Choice in Senegal*) contends that the brotherhoods no longer play the strong political role they once did; that may be, given the strengthening of the Senegalese economy and its diversification away from the domination of the peanut sector.

10. See Gellar, *Senegal,* 27–30, and Waterbury, *Political Economy of Risk and Choice.* Though Fatton insists that class is a better analytic tool for studying Senegal, he does give clientelism its due in his "Clientelism and Patronage in Senegal," 61–78.

11. The best account of the short life of the Mali Federation is Foltz, *From French West Africa to the Mali Federation.*

12. For a good review of the experiment, see Hughes and Lewis, "Beyond Francophonie? The Senegambian Confederation in Retrospect."

13. For background, see Barbier-Wiesser, *Comprendre la Casamance.*

14. Villalón and Kane, "Senegal: The Crisis of Democracy and the Emergence of an Islamic Opposition."

15. For a discussion of quasi-democracy, see Vengroff and Creevey, "Senegal: The Evolution of a Quasi-Democracy"; Gellar, *Senegal;* and Beck, "Senegal's 'Patrimonial Democrats.'" For informed commentary on the Wade victory, see M'Baye, "Alternance historique dans l'ex-pré carré français: Au Sénégal, les chantiers du changement" (Historic Turnover in a Former French Backyard: In Senegal, Factories for Change"), 22. On Wade's economic challenges, see, for example, Paringaux, "D'autres voies pour le developpement: Coopération su-sud au Sénégal," 12; and "Senegal's Slide from 'Model Economy' to 'Least Developed Country.'"

16. Asso, *Le chef d'état africain: L'éxperience des états africains de succession française,* 81–185.

17. Completed in 1989, the basilica was not consecrated by Pope John-Paul II until September 10, 1990. The delay was due, according to reliable rumor, to Rome's insistence that the cross on the dome be lowered to top out below that on St. Peter's Cathedral; this was apparently done. The basilica, reported to have cost an estimated $200 to $250 million (all, said Houphouët-Boigny, paid from his personal fortune), was designed to hold eighteen thousand air-conditioned worshipers, with another three hundred thousand accommodated on the marble plaza outside. I visited it before it was completed, and it is quite extraordinary indeed. The basilica's

plaza, also modeled after the Vatican's, is flanked by a colonnade à la Bernini, but without the statuary.

18. Jackson and Rosberg, *Personal Rule in Black Africa,* 149–152; Thompson, "The Ivory Coast," 259.

19. My discussion of the Côte d'Ivoire is drawn from my observations during several visits to the country and relies on accounts of Ivoirian politics in such works as Zolberg, *One-Party Government in the Ivory Coast;* Baulin, *La politique interieure d'Houphouët-Boigny;* Fauré and Médard, eds., *Etat et bourgeoisie en Côte d'Ivoire;* Zartman, ed., *The Political Economy of Ivory Coast;* and Bakary, *La démocratie par le haut en Côte-d'Ivoire.* A good recent summary of the circumstances and prospects of post–Houphouët-Boigny Côte d'Ivoire—at least until 1996—is Mundt, "Côte d'Ivoire: Continuity and Change in a Semi-Democracy." For my summary account of the tumultuous nine post–Houphouët-Boigny years in Côte d'Ivoire, I have relied on the accounts in *Abidjan Matin, Le Monde and Le Monde Diplomatique,* BBC-Africa, and some excellent reporting in the *New York Times* and other international publications. See also Cornewell, "Africa Watch, Côte d'Ivoire: Asking for It." The four elections during the December 1999–March 2001 period are analyzed by Christian Bouquet in "Côte d'Ivoire: Quatre consultations pour une transition."

20. For details of the official French campaign against the PDCI and Houphouët-Boigny (as well as on Ivoirian politics between 1944 and 1960 in general), see Morgenthau, *Political Parties in French-Speaking West Africa,* 166–218. For an interesting vignette of this affair, see Georges Chaffard, "Quand Houphouët-Boigny était un rebelle," 99–132, in his *Les carnets secrets de la décolonisation,* vol. 1.

21. In Fauré and Médard, *Etat et bourgeoisie,* 63. My translation.

22. Ibid., 212–216.

23. Cohen, "The Myth of the Expanding Centre: Politics in the Ivory Coast."

24. Widner, "Single-Party States and Agricultural Policies: The Cases of Côte d'Ivoire and Kenya," 6.

25. The Mockey Plot is the bizarre series of events in 1963 in which Jean-Baptiste Mockey, minister of state and one of Houphouët-Boigny's closest confidants, plus some seventy others, including seven ministers and six deputies, were charged with involvement in a plot to kill the president and seize power illegally. The alleged plot, according to the authorities, was linked with an earlier conspiracy, the 1959 so-called Black Cat Plot (named for the head of a black cat, one of the maleficent fetishes said to have been found at the presidential residence), itself linked to an alleged secessionist attempt by the king of the Sanwi people. Mockey had been charged and arrested in 1959, then later reinstated to office. In 1963 the six main leaders of the new plot, including Mockey, were condemned to death. The sentences were never carried out, and by 1967 all those detained had been released. Mockey himself returned to ministerial office in the early 1970s. The best explanation of these affairs is that Mockey and his ministerial colleagues may in fact have sought to mount a challenge to Houphouët-Boigny's leadership, though not, as charged, to assassinate him or conduct a coup d'état. The plot gave Houphouët-Boigny the opportunity to severely chastise Mockey for his presumption and purge the elite ranks of those with doubtful loyalty to him. A detailed though highly biased account is by Jacques Baulin, once an advisor to Houphouët-Boigny and later one of his fiercest opponents, *La politique interieure;* a good journalistic account is by Blaise Mombat, "Verités sur le 'Complot Mockey.'"

26. René Lemarchand characterizes the Ivoirité constructs as "venomous

flowers." Private correspondence with the author, December 10, 2003. For further details, see Chapter 6.

27. UN Office for the Coordination of Humanitarian Affairs, "Côte d'Ivoire: UNSG Releases First Report on Côte d'Ivoire."

28. A report in late 2003 by the International Crisis Group gave additional warrant for pessimism about Côte d'Ivoire's immediate future: "Côte d'Ivoire: 'The War Is Not Yet Over.'"

29. Politics in preindependence Cameroon is covered in my *The Cameroons from Mandate to Independence,* and in various chapters of Rubin, *Cameroun, An African Federation;* Johnson, *The Cameroon Federation;* and Welch, *Dream of Unity: Pan-Africanism and Political Unification in West Africa,* 148–249. The UPC story, which accounts for a very large part of Cameroon's political bibliography, is best served by the analyses in Joseph, *Radical Nationalism in Cameroun: Social Origins of the U.P.C. Rebellion,* plus the more recent and even more authoritative exploration by Achille Mbembe, *La naissance du maquis dans le sud-Cameroun (1920–1960).*

30. To be sure, not all anglophones were equally pleased to discover that the union meant domination by the francophone east. A core of anglophone resentment persisted into the 1980s and 1990s, when it emerged to challenge Ahidjo's successor, Biya. For a sympathetic treatment of the anglophones' problems, see Benjamin, *Les camerounais occidentaux,* which is officially banned in Cameroon.

31. Ouandié was also implicated in an alleged conspiracy against the state involving Bernard Ndongmo, the Catholic bishop of Nkongsmaba, and two others. The four were tried and condemned to death; Ouandié and two of the coconspirators were executed in 1971, and Ndongmo was remanded to the Church, which sent him to Rome and then to pastoral duties in Quebec. The whole affair was strange enough and the charges and evidence sufficiently incredible to suggest that it had been mostly cooked up by the authorities, who had hoped to undermine residual support for the *maquisards* among the southwest's Bamiléké people. All four of the accused were Bamiléké. A longtime opponent of the regime, the Paris-based Cameroonian novelist Mongo Beti (Alexandre Biyidi), wrote a spirited defense of Ouandié and the others in his *Main basse sur le Cameroun.*

32. This pattern was replicated in most of the administrative-hegemonic regimes of francophone Africa. Most of those elected to the parliaments were there as beneficiaries of patronage distributions, were being rewarded for loyal party service, or were being recognized for past political contributions. For details, see my "Parliaments in Francophone Africa: Some Lessons from the Decolonization Process."

33. In my *Cameroons from Mandate to Independence,* published in 1964, I identified some 201 ethnic groups in West and East Cameroon combined (pp. 5–14). The thirteenth edition (1996) of the *Ethnologue* (available at http://www.sil.org/ethnologue/countries/Came.html) identifies 279 living languages in Cameroon. On the assumption that language remains a key to ethnic identity, these data suggest the existence of well over two hundred ethnic groups in Cameroon.

34. For an extended portrait of Ahidjo, see my essay, "Ahmadou Ahidjo Revisited."

35. The story of the Biya regime up to 1997, including the transition from Ahidjo to Biya, is well told in Takougang and Krieger, *African State and Society in the 1990s: Cameroon's Political Crossroads.*

36. These assertions are corroborated by Amnesty International, Human

Rights Watch—Africa, and SDM documentation, and in more than a dozen sworn affidavits of mainly anglophone Cameroonian applicants for political asylum in the United States—cases in which I have been involved as expert witness on behalf of the applicants. All but one of these applicants were deemed sufficiently credible to be granted asylum by U.S. immigration judges.

37. Chazan et al., *Politics and Society,* 141–142.

38. Chazan, et al., *Politics and Society;* Fatton, *The Making of a Liberal Democracy: Senegal's Passive Revolution, 1975–1985;* Vengroff and Creevey, "Senegal."

39. Woods, "Côte d'Ivoire: the Crisis of Redistributive Politics," 230.

40. Chazan, et al., *Politics and Society,* 142.

41. Diarrah, in his vignette on the life and death of Modibo ("Les deux morts de Modibo Keita"), avers that Modibo was poisoned, probably by his jailers. Aside from journalistic accounts, the literature on Modibo and the early period of Malian politics is not extensive. The most useful studies are Foltz, *From French West Africa to the Mali Federation;* Diarrah, *Le Mali de Modibo Keita;* Snyder, *One-Party Government in Mali: Transition Toward Control;* De Lusignan, *French-Speaking Africa Since Independence,* 231–249; and Defosses and Dirck, "Socialist Development in Africa: The Case of Keita's Mali."

42. The useful scholarly and analytical literature on Sékou Touré and his regime is much more extensive than that on Modibo and his Malian system. Among the most informative works are Camara, *La Guinée sans la France*, which describes the separation from France and the institutionalization of the regime to 1963; and three works on Touré and the regime: Rivière, *Guinea: The Mobilization of a People;* Adamolekun, *Sékou Touré's Guinea: An Experiment in Nation Building;* and Kaké, *Sékou Touré, le héros et le tyran.* "Sékou Touré et la Guinée après Sékou Touré," *Jeune Afrique Plus,* no. 8 (June 1984), contains a number of sketches on the Touré regime, plus a long and revealing interview with André Lewin, France's former ambassador in Conakry and one of Touré's best friends. Charles, *Guinée,* 45–128, offers a biting critique of the regime in its early days.

43. Le Vine, "Parliaments in Francophone Africa," 142–152.

44. Rivière, *Guinea,* 95.

45. Kaba, "Guinean Politics: A Critical Historical Overview," 33. Kaké, in *Sékou Touré,* 205, reprints a photograph of four of the main "plotters" (Baldé Ousmane, Barry III [Ibrahima Barry], Magassouba Morita, and Camara Sékou) hanging from a bridge over a crowd of onlookers.

46. Kaba, "Guinean Politics," 25–46.

47. Touré, "Complot permanent," in *Défendre la Révolution,* 24–51. See Rivière, *Guinea,* 121–140 ("The Perennial Plot"), for a discussion of some of the plots and what they represented in the context of Guinean politics. Kaba, in "Guinean Politics," 45, insightfully compares Sékou Touré's permanent plot with Jean-Paul Marat's argument regarding a permanent conspiracy. (Marat was a leader of the powerful Montagnard faction of the French Revolution and frequently argued that the revolution was under continual conspiratorial attack from the aristocracy and other enemies. Reportedly he was subject to recurring bouts of extreme paranoia.) On the permanent plot in Guinea, see also Biarnès, "Guinée: Le complot permanent," chapter 10, 157–182, in his *L'Afrique aux Africains.*

48. The invasion was aimed at toppling the Guinean regime and freeing the Portuguese prisoners kept by Amilcar Cabral's revolutionary Partido Africano de Independencia de Guiné e Cabo Verde (PAIGC, whose headquarters were in Conakry), as well as killing Cabral himself. Ill-organized and eventually routed, the

invaders failed to remove the Guinean regime or to kill Sékou Touré or Cabral (Touré was upcountry, and Cabral was fortuitously abroad), though they did free a number of Portuguese and Guineans kept in detention in Conakry. The official Guinean account is found in Guinea, Government of, *L'agression portugaise contre la République de Guinée: Livre blanc.* Kaké, in *Sékou Touré,* 143–164 ("Face à la 'Cinquième Colonne'"), offers a detailed account of the invasion and its consequences. The best (though not necessarily the most reliable) account is probably that found in the UN Security Council's *Report of the Security Council Special Mission to the Republic of Guinea, Established Under Resolution 289.*

49. This is from an Amnesty representative who declined to be identified, with whom I spoke during a visit to Conakry in 1987. I also visited Boiro Prison, which was maintained as a witness to the evils of the late regime, and was shown Diallo Telli's cell and the torture chambers. Testimony by those who lived through torture at Boiro confirmed what I saw: the methods were crude but effective. They included suspension by the thumbs with electrical wire, a Guinean version of the *bastinado* (beatings of the soles of the feet), electrical shocks, whipping with barbed instruments, head dunking, and the so-called *cloche,* or bell, in which a metal bucket is put over the head then "resonated" with a stick. For details of Diallo Telli's ordeal, see Lewin, *Diallo Telli, le tragique destin d'un grand Africain.*

50. For all its official socialist militancy, Guinea was the subject of attacks from the left, including communists and *communisant* PDG party members. For example, the teachers' "plot" of 1961 probably represented the final denouement of the 1956–1958 "Mamou deviation," in which a local PDG branch in the town of Mamou launched a series of verbal attacks on the party leadership, including Sékou Touré, for alleged betrayals of revolutionary principles. Among the early opponents of the PDG were leaders of the Bloc Africain de Guinea, including Keita Koumandian, head of the Guinean teachers' union, and Koumandian had made common cause with the Mamou faction. For details, see Johnson, "The Parti Démocratique de Guinée and the Mamou 'Deviation.'" The climax of the right-wing challenge was reached in 1965–1966 with an alleged plot (the "Petit Touré" conspiracy) to overthrow the regime and establish a capitalist system. For details, see *Le Monde,* March 6–7, 1966; and Biarnès, *L'Afrique aux Africains,* 166.

51. Biarnès, *L'Afrique aux Africains,* 162.

52. Wolpin, "Dependency and Conservative Militarism in Mali," 600.

53. Apparently the military had continually sought assurances from Modibo Keita that the Milice Populaire (people's militia) would attempt neither to purge the military nor to disband it. Realizing that the Milice was fast becoming uncontrollable, Modibo was unable to make that assurance. Casting his lot with his half brother, Moussa, who led the Milice Populaire, Modibo therefore planned for a preemptive purge of junior army officers on November 25. The military uncovered the plot and staged its own coup on November 19 when Modibo was in Mopti. On his way back to Bamako Modibo was arrested by Moussa Traoré's soldiers. (Wolpin, "Dependency," 608–611; Billet, "The Precipitants of African Coups d'Etat: A Case Study of the 1968 Malian Coup." I have also drawn from Michael Schatzberg's 1972 paper, "The Coup and After: Continuity or Change in Malian Politics?")

54. The early years of both the Guinean and the Malian party systems—up to 1963—are detailed in Du Bois, "Guinea," and Hodgkin and Morgenthau, "Mali." Ideology and ideological praxis in Mali and Guinea are discussed in Young, *Ideology and Development in Africa.* For the Malian experience, see Wolpin, "Dependency and Conservative Militarism in Mali," 175; Snyder, *One-Party*

Government in Mali; Snyder, "The Political Thought of Modibo Keita"; Hazard, "Marxian Socialism in Africa: The Case of Mali"; and Grundy, "Mali: The Prospects of 'Planned Socialism.'"
   55. Kaba, "Guinean Politics," 35.
   56. Young, *Ideology and Development,* 174.
   57. Chazan, et al., *Politics and Society,* 144.
   58. Ibid., 147.
   59. Decalo, *Psychoses of Power: African Personal Dictatorships.* Decalo's discussion of the Bokassa regime (129–178) is one of the better short accounts of the thirteen years of Bokassa's dictatorship. Thomas O'Toole offers a useful vignette, "Jean-Bedel Bokassa: Neo-Napoleon or Traditional African Ruler?" and Biarnès, in *Afrique aux Africains,* 329–347, devotes a detailed chapter to Bokassa's regime. There is now a sparse bibliography on Bokassa himself and on his regime and its excesses. The least reliable authors are the journalists, many of whom have personal or ideological axes to grind—or perhaps the miasmic quality of the regime clouded the perceptions of those who covered it. Pierre Péan, a French journalist who has written extensively on francophone Africa, has written *Bokassa 1er,* and another French journalist, Bernard Loubat, who spent three weeks with the Bokassa entourage, reports on his conversations with the leader in *L'ogre de Berengo: "Bokassa m'a dit."* The best—most reliable and scholarly—two works available are Bigo, *Pouvoir et obéissance en Centrafrique;* and Titley, *Dark Age: The Political Odyssey of Emperor Bokassa.* The books on Bokassa and the CAR by Roger Delpey, *La Manipulation* and *Affaires Centrafricaines: Quand Centrafrique bougera, l'Afrique explosera,* are interesting but should be read with extreme caution: Delpey has a particular axe to grind with the French governments of ex-presidents Valéry Giscard-d'Estaing and François Mitterand for allegedly attacking him and his accounts of official French complicity and duplicity in the excesses of the Bokassa regime and the coup of one of his successors, General André Kolingba. Moreover, Delpey remained a friend of Bokassa, tried to "rescue" him from Abidjan, and may have been responsible for persuading him to return to the CAR in 1986. In 1985, while still in France, Bokassa himself brought forth his memoirs, titled *Ma verité* ("My Truth") and ghostwritten by Roger Holeindre, a longtime friend and admirer of Corsican origin, with a French publisher, Carrère-Lefon. However, the whole print run of ten thousand books (less a few pirated copies) was seized by the French government and incinerated at the request of former president Giscard on the grounds that it violated a law that forbids the published defamation of ex-presidents of the republic. I was allowed to read one of the pirated copies in Paris, and I can report, as does Titley (in *Dark Age,* 172–176), that aside from the more credible accounts and discussions, it also contains strange nonsense and speculations and some fantastic charges, including Bokassa's allegation that he had to arrange an abortion for his wife, whom he claimed had been impregnated by Giscard. Bokassa also alluded to the gifts of diamonds he had made to Giscard over the years, revelations about which, when published in the journal *Le Canard Enchainé,* caused a tremendous scandal in France and probably helped lose Giscard reelection as president. It is hardly surprising that Giscard wanted the book suppressed. Finally, mention must be made of the seminal work by university lecturer and holder of doctorates in literature and the humanities Pierre Kalck, who at one time was overseas administrator in the Ubangui-Shari territory, which was later renamed the Central African Republic, and who served as economic advisor to the pre-Bokassa CAR government. Kalck's *Réalités Oubanguiennes* was long the only work on the CAR's pre-1960 politics. His latest work is a useful 538-item annotated

bibliography of the CAR, in volume 152 of the World Bibliographical Series: *Central African Republic.*

60. At the time Bokassa was in Tripoli, allegedly seeking a deal with Qaddafi to establish a Libyan military base in the CAR (*Afrique*, no. 54, December 1981, 24). Hearing of the coup, Bokassa demanded asylum in Libya and was summarily refused and given an hour to leave. He next approached the Swiss, and they also turned him down. He then flew to France, claiming asylum under his dual French-Centrafrican citizenship. The embarrassed French rejected his claim, sequestered him and his twenty-six-person entourage on board his Caravelle for two days at Evreux military airport, and then, with visible relief, sent the ex-emperor off to Abidjan, where Houphouët-Boigny had been cajoled into giving Bokassa sanctuary. Houphouët-Boigny's agreement had been secured with promises that once in Abidjan Bokassa would live quietly and without ostentation, and above all that he would stay out of politics, particularly Central African politics. There are reports—still unverified, but credible—that Houphouët-Boigny was offered other inducements to take Bokassa, given France's embarrassment in the affair. On November 26, 1983, "twelve mercenaries and a group of supporters led by French writer Roger Delpey flew to Abidjan to pick up Bokassa, intending to take him to Bangui and restore him to power," but "Ivoirien troops, tipped off by French intelligence, surrounded the plane" (Shoumatoff, *African Madness,* 119). Incensed, Houphouët-Boigny threw Bokassa out of the country, along with fifteen of his children, his new wife, Augustine, and twenty other women. This time, because no other country was willing to take him, he was allowed to remain in France. Installed in a rented chateau at Hardricourt, near Paris, with several of his wives, numerous children, and a small retinue, forbidden to leave the premises and guarded by some sixty French policemen, Bokassa held minicourt there until 1986, when he was persuaded to return home secretly on the strength of advice that his former subjects joyfully awaited his return to the throne. His homecoming, as it turned out, was far from triumphant: landing in Bangui, he was immediately arrested and charged with numerous capital crimes, and he was subsequently put on trial. The prosecution used the same list of accusations that had been brought against him during the in-absentia trial in 1980. The fourteen charges included murder and complicity in murder, poisoning, beating children to death, cannibalism, misappropriation of state assets (including public funds, diamonds, and coronation jewels), threatening state security, and collusion with a foreign power (Titley, *Dark Age,* 185). Bokassa denied that he was a cannibal, but a parade of witnesses at his trial contradicted him. I think it possible, but not likely.

61. On the day Boganda died, I was told by eyewitnesses, hundreds of residents of Bangui had gathered at the riverside, expecting him to walk across on the river. Hearing of his death, many helped spread the rumor that he had not died and that he would return someday—and that if he had been present at the riverside that day, he would indeed have walked on the waters. Boganda had been defrocked in 1940 for marrying his secretary. He had quit the priesthood, and thereafter had devoted himself to politics. Boganda was twice elected as a deputy to the French National Assembly, and he also held the title of grand counselor to the *grand conseil* of the AEF. One of the peculiarities of CAR politics is that many of the country's top politicians are kin to each other. Not only were Dacko and Boganda cousins, but so also were Dacko and Bokassa, though once removed. Boganda's mother's uncle was Bokassa's father. When Dacko "retired" after being removed from office by Bokassa, he did so in his house in Bangui, amicably next door to Cousin Bokassa's.

62. I had interviewed Bokassa in May 1965 in connection with research on generational conflict in five francophone countries, and during our conversation he had voiced his frustration about the army's diminished role. Though Biarnès (*Afrique aux Africains,* 336) claims that "no serious proof" of the other plots "has ever been adduced," I can testify that the "Chinese army" was something of an open secret in Bangui. Stories about their ragtag condition and their volubility about their mission circulated widely in the bars, whorehouses, and markets they frequented. After the coup they apparently dispersed, and they were never heard from again. Nzallat, who had had me followed and twice held overnight for questioning by French "technical advisors," was killed near the frontier with Cameroon as he tried to flee the country. The Frenchmen involved told me that it was on his orders that I was also strip-searched at the airport upon leaving the CAR and some of my research documents were confiscated. Nzallat himself had earlier denounced Philippe Decraene, *Le Monde*'s excellent Africanist reporter, to me for writing "lies" about the CAR and had warned me about *"immixtion dans nos affaires"* (meddling in our affairs). I examine Bokassa's coup in "The Coup in the Central African Republic" and "The Coups in Upper Volta, Dahomey, and the Central African Republic."

63. Biarnès, *Afrique aux Africains,* 340. My translation.

64. He was familiarly referred to as "Papa Bok" at home and abroad. It is difficult to recite all his titles without remarking on his extraordinary record of self-promotion, as follows:

1966: from colonel to brigadier, president, prime minister, minister of defense
1967: to colonel-general and president, with two ministerial portfolios
1970: to full general and president, with three ministerial portfolios
1972: to full general, president-for-life, head of three ministries
1975: to field marshal, president-for-life, head of four ministries
1977: to emperor, field marshal, president-for-life, head of four ministries

65. At least one journalist reported that the horses were killed and eaten later that day; given everything else, the story is not improbable. I checked to find out what happened to the horses. No one officially knew anything about their fate, though one U.S. embassy member, who asked to remain anonymous, said that it was necessary to kill the animals because given the local climate and the presence of disease-bearing insects they would not have lived long anyway. I still don't know whether he was jesting, but others with whom I spoke thought it likely. A dozen or so grays, whose riders were taught equestrian etiquette in France, flanked the coach to and from the coronation. Their fate is also unknown.

66. Shoumatoff, *African Madness,* 104.

67. Titley's account is in his *Dark Age,* 112–113. Decalo, a usually reliable scholar, tells the story in his *Psychoses of Power,* 162–163, drawing from the sources he cites in his notes to those pages. He reports that on January 19 Bokassa asked for and received some three hundred Zairean troops to help restore order. With the Zairean soldiers at hand, "a ruthless counterassault commenced, employing mortars and machine guns. The brunt of the assault was aimed at the non-riverine ethnic quarters of the town and resulted in hundreds of deaths" (*Psychoses of Power,* 162). Titley disputes this account, particularly the contention that Bokassa brought in Zairean soldiers to attack targets in Bangui. On April 18, according to Decalo, Bokassa unleashed the imperial guard, which went on "a savage rampage in which hundreds of children were indiscriminately bayoneted" (*Psychoses of Power,*

162). Titley argues that this description, too, is an exaggeration. He also questions Decalo's account of the killings in prison, citing one account that eighteen bodies emerged from the prison and that other children, held in other venues, were released unharmed. Biarnès puts the figure at "more than 150 children—mostly schoolchildren and high school students . . . savagely massacred in a number of prisons in the Central African capital. . . . The Emperor himself, it was quickly proved, personally took part" in the killings (*Afrique aux Africains,* 346, my translation).

Bokassa's removal and departure was almost anticlimactic. Amnesty International had publicized the massacre at Ngaragba prison. France had repeatedly and privately urged Bokassa to resign. Then, in May, at the Sixth Franco-African Congress in Kigali, Rwanda, France asked for and obtained the creation of an African Mission of Inquiry to go to Bangui and inquire into the affair. The Mission of Inquiry's report appeared in Dakar on August 16 and concluded with "quasi-certainty" that Bokassa himself had participated in the massacre of the students. France almost immediately suspended all but the most necessary health, education, and food supports for Bangui. On the night and morning of September 20–21, Operation Barracuda, with Dacko on board one of the paracommando planes, launched its coup against Bokassa. The coup was peaceful, as Bokassa was in Libya seeking aid from Qaddafi. Despite his French passport, Bokassa was refused entry into France and was forced to remain at the airport: somewhat embarrassed by Bokassa's public appeals to his good friend Giscard d'Estaing, the French did manage to convince Houphouët-Boigny to allow the ex-emperor to be exiled in Abidjan, providing he behaved himself and stayed out of politics.

68. Biarnès, *Afrique aux Africains,* my translation.

69. There was little question but that Kolingba released Bokassa out of spite, having failed in his bid to recapture the presidency of the CAR. Kolingba apparently hoped that Bokassa's release would disrupt the second round of the CAR's 1993 presidential elections and thus give him renewed purchase on power. It was not to be: Patassé defeated Abel Goumba in the second round, "a contest," according to Titley (*Dark Age,* 206), "that went off without mishap." During the three years left him after his release in 1993, Bokassa gave interviews, allegedly became extremely pious, and embraced celibacy. He was survived by at least sixty children (out of hundreds he sired unofficially) and perhaps twenty ex-wives. I had drinks with one of his older sons, "Prince" Georges, in Paris. Georges had little reason to love his father: in 1972 he had spent two months in prison for defying his father's wish that he study engineering. Georges's judgment on his father was short and dismissive: *"Le vieux est fou!"* (The old man is crazy!)

70. Chazan, et al., *Politics and Society,* 148.

71. Ibid., 149.

72. Ibid.

8

Redemocratization

Beginning in 1990 what Samuel Huntington calls the Third Wave of democratization began washing over Africa.[1] Before 1990 only Botswana, Gambia, Senegal, and Mauritius had pluralist regimes; within five years some two dozen other states had launched democratic experiments, some more or less successfully, some with indifferent results, some without success. Some saw their experiments die at birth, and a few returned to military or dictatorial rule after brief democratic interludes. Michael Chege puts the case even more broadly: "Since 1990, most of sub-Saharan Africa's 45 states have seen attempts at transition from authoritarianism to democracy. The fate of these efforts runs the gamut from outright disaster to relative success, with stalemate being a frequent outcome (as in Nigeria, Zaire, Togo, Kenya, and Cameroon)."[2]

In the francophone Africa of our fourteen states, twelve undertook part of the experiment, with eight (Benin, Burkina Faso, Chad, Congo-Brazzaville, Gabon, Mali, Niger, and Togo) proceeding by way of the surprising institutional innovation of the African wave, the sovereign national conference. Another francophone state, the island republic of the Comoros, held its own national conference, and demands for convening one were made and denied in Cameroon, the Central African Republic (CAR), Côte d'Ivoire, and Guinea. Seven of the eight states that held national conferences (the exception being Chad) also held what Michael Bratton and Nicolas van de Walle call "founding elections," in which "for the first time after an authoritarian regime, elected positions of national significance are disputed under reasonably competitive conditions."[3] The four regimes that refused to hold national conferences nonetheless held founding elections, one of which, in the CAR, resulted in a change of regime in 1993. The military regime in Mauritania, which neither faced demands for a national conference nor held one, also held a founding election, in 1992, and together with Niger, Benin, Côte d'Ivoire, Gabon, Mali, Burkina Faso, and

Cameroon, later held a "second election," an exercise that, according to Bratton, "held out the possibility that democratic routines might be deepened."[4]

What emerges even from this cursory review of the ways by which the experiment was conducted is the participants' preference for institutional solutions. No mass cataclysms or bloody revolutions here; where radical changes did take place, as in Benin and Mali, they did so more or less peacefully through what amounted to civilian coups d'état in the case of national conferences, or by way of the ballot box in the case of multiparty elections. These were indeed experiments in the larger sense of that word: organized, rational, schematized, and very French in cultural inspiration. While public attention focused on the frequent heated exchanges between the sovereign national conferences and the local rulerships, much of that which turned out to be controversial had to do with the rules involved, the protocols of the conferences and the political agendas of those who set up and participated in the conferences and the elections. It remained, however, that neither a national conference nor a founding election could guarantee that the democratic experiment, however well launched, would ultimately succeed. In any case, the initial optimism was there, as was trust in institutional solutions.

Analytical Problems

The African Third Wave poses a variety of interpretative problems, not the least of which is the fact that it took both Africans and outside observers by surprise. Of course, viewing the phenomenon in retrospect evokes the suggestion that *surprise* is not the right word, that all the portents and indicators of the change were there to be seen beforehand. Nevertheless, almost all observers of the African scene during the late 1980s saw only continuing authoritarian rule, more military takeovers, and increasing internal conflict in Africa's short-range political future. That misdiagnosis remains to rebuke the experts, who, like the rest of us, are only now beginning to understand why the African Third Wave broke when it did; why it happened first in the francophone states; and how it came about, how it unfolded, and what its ramifications were.

Another arresting facet of the phenomenon also calls for explanation: for almost all but the four African states that had had more or less pluralist regimes from independence onward (Gambia, Botswana, Mauritius, and Senegal), this was not the first democratic experiment but was at least the second, the first having been that of the period before and just after independence. The first experiments were conducted when parties multiplied, open elections were held frequently, and independence constitutions promised democratic futures for their countries. Dahomey/Benin tried democratic governance five times, Ghana four; the CAR, Nigeria, Sierra Leone, and Uganda each tried three times, with variable results. The 1989–1990 wave was not truly the third wave for most of Africa, and Samuel Huntington's apt phrase needs to be qualified for these African cases. Thus the term *redemocratization* better describes the situation because many of the post-1990 experiments may well have owed their very existence to the first experiments, the memory of which had become imbedded (though later suppressed) as part of the political unconscious of those polities now undertaking their second—or third, fourth, or fifth—try at democratic governance. If that is the case, it is remarkable that for most states the nondemocratic hiatus lasted almost thirty years, certainly sufficient time to justify both the pervasive political pessimism that preceded the new wave and the surprise that it broke out when it did. Pearl Robinson, examining the francophone national conferences, perceptively goes back even farther, suggesting that their roots are to be found in French political mythology.[5]

The Reasons: External Factors

Samuel Decalo warns that "it would be ethnocentric and too facile to assume the pro-democracy pressures in Africa were merely knee-jerk reactions to events in eastern Europe." The psychological impact of the visible collapse of communism in Eastern Europe, the spillover effect of the democratization of Latin America, and the increase in democratization activity elsewhere in the world, do not, adds Decalo, tell the whole story: "The continent was already more than *ripe* for upheaval, and there were additional internal and external factors that played a crucial role in leading the democratic pressures to successful fruition."[6] Decalo is right, particularly about the latter set of facts. Nevertheless, the effects of the communist collapse must be given their due, and while the chain of causation is indirect and distant, it is nonetheless real and traceable.

The collapse of the Soviet Union and the breakdown of its communist base in 1989 led to the subsequent disintegration of the Soviet empire and had major visible effects in Eastern Europe. Extending outward, the shock waves of the Soviet collapse orphaned a number of foreign communist parties, not to speak of former Soviet clients that were left in the lurch and forced to fend for themselves. Hardest hit in Africa were the few functioning communist parties (in South Africa, Lesotho, Réunion, Benin, and Sudan) and the client "Afro-Marxist" regimes (Benin, Congo-Brazzaville, Ethiopia, Madagascar, Angola, and Mozambique) and their "vanguard" parties. The government of Mengistu Haile Mariam in Ethiopia, which had probably come as close as any African regime to being a Soviet satellite, lost its Soviet military and technical subsidies, as well as its Russian and Cuban advisors. Soon thereafter, in 1991, it fell to the joint Eritrean-

Tigrean-Oromo rebel forces. The new Ethiopian leaders quickly fashioned a quasi-democratic regime for the country, and in 1993 newly independent Eritrea began creating its own version of a democratic system, both of which efforts had been abandoned by 2003.

The other Afro-Marxist leopards, not so much from conviction as out of necessity, faced as they were with the prospect of having only the West to turn to for aid, financing, and international respectability, simply changed their political spots, embracing the West and market capitalism. Among the converts were the francophone regimes of Benin, Congo-Brazzaville, and Burkina Faso. This conversion, occurring in states with already shaky political and economic foundations, as well as regimes of uncertain reach, almost inevitably opened up political space that long-suppressed democratic forces could appropriate.

It may well be that the conversions further weakened the already unstable regimes of Mathieu Kérékou, Denis Sassou-Nguesso, and Moussa Traoré, leaving huge policy gaps and lowering the opportunity costs of oppositional activity. For example, by the end of 1989 Benin's Kérékou regime, after eighteen years in power, had plunged the country into a seemingly bottomless political and economic crisis, prompting Kérékou to convene a "Conference of the Vital Forces of the Nation" as a last-ditch effort to stave off disaster. Part of Kérékou's problem was the failure of his Marxist policies, a failure that became even more glaring with his attempt to change his ideological spots in December 1989. Among other troubles, public sector employees were experiencing frequent delays or nonpayment of wages and salaries. As strikes followed upon strikes and antigovernment demonstrations turned violent, the government finally called out the police and army to suppress them. Faced with political and economic bankruptcy, Kérékou finally called on his opponents to save his regime. The conference, which convened in February 1990, did save the country, but it exacted Kérékou's removal from power as its price for doing so.[7]

Further, the conversions removed props that had previously helped shore up these regimes: they had used their links to the socialist and communist states to give themselves international legitimacy, and their connections with each other to give themselves the reinforcement that being part of an African socialist or Afro-Marxist bloc provided. All of that disappeared with the Soviet collapse: no more of the Second World–Third World alliances and no more of the comforting ideological company of radical African regimes. Needless to say, there was now also little attraction in belonging to the truncated bloc of remaining hard-line communist states—Cuba, Vietnam, and North Korea. Mainland China was no real option, either; being pro-Beijing was a viable strategy only so long as the Russians and Chinese were involved in their own cold war in Africa; once that ended, the Chinese cut their commitments to the continent. Thus the connection between the Soviet collapse and the beginning of the 1990–1995 redemocratization surge in Africa is admittedly distant, but it is certainly not accidental.[8]

The Soviet collapse also signaled the end of the African segment of the Cold War, resulting in a sharp drop of American, Russian, and Chinese support for what had been pro-Western, pro-Moscow, and pro-Beijing clients on the continent. Like their African clients, the Russians wasted no time in shifting their ground. In 1988 and 1989 they were already engaged in promoting cooperation with the United States; a series of joint U.S.-Soviet symposia and conferences produced a jointly-edited volume on the theme: *Agenda for Action: African-Soviet-U.S. Cooperation.*[9]

In any event, the United States could finally end its increasingly embarrassing patronage of Zaire's Mobutu Sese Seko and Angola's Jonas Savimbi, and the Russians could not only disengage from Mengistu's Ethiopia, but also regularize their relations with the regimes in Angola, Mozambique, Congo-Brazzaville, and Benin. The mainland Chinese government, for its part, no longer felt it needed to compete for African favor with its old rival, Russia, so it scaled back or terminated support for a whole series of prestige projects with which it had been involved (e.g., the Tanzam railway, road building in Rwanda and Burundi, scaled-down African versions of Tienanmen Square's Great Hall of the People in Kinshasa and other African capitals, a Cameroon national party headquarters in Yaoundé, and so on). In 1996 Chinese president Jiang Zemin reconfirmed the new Chinese policy toward Africa at a meeting of the Organization of Africa Unity in Addis Ababa: he donated just three hundred thousand dollars to the organization (a paltry sum compared to former Chinese largesse), and he bluntly and pointedly stressed China's own domestic needs and underlined the importance of trade, as opposed to aid, and of such things as African-Chinese joint ventures as the ways by which China could best advance Sino-African friendship.[10]

The Soviet collapse was but one of several exogenous factors giving impulse to the wave of democratization in Africa. Another two developments, affecting particularly the francophone countries, amounted to a one-two punch to the solar plexus of the French-African relationship. First was France's official move in 1990 toward placing proactive democratic conditionalities—or at least it appeared so at first glance—on relations with its African clients. Second, in part a consequence of the first, was the increasingly unstable and unpredictable state of that which had been hitherto a set of special and durable political, financial, and technical French-African links.

For some thirty years after independence was attained by the francophone countries in 1960, France and her former colonies enjoyed extraordinarily close ties. Francophone Africa was characterized as a *chasse gardée* (private hunting preserve) in which French statesmen, politicians, and (largely corporate) businessmen developed cozy, mutually profitable relationships with their counterparts in Africa.[11] These relationships included the privilege of asking the Elysée (the French presidency) for troops to help put down local insurrections and disturbances; a *pré carré* (backyard) marked by a special monetary zone and its CFA (Communauté Financière Africaine, or African Financial Community) franc, pegged directly to and completely convertible with the French franc; frequent mutual visitations by French and African presidents; ready access to special budget-balancing accounts at the French Ministry of Finances and the regional CFA central banks; a large set of defense and technical military cooperation accords; the Ministry of Cooperation (operated out of the side pocket of the French presidency) and its aid packages; a special francophone-Africa-friendly advisor to the French president (the late Jacques Foccart and his successors); regular conferences of francophone heads of state presided over by the French president (like the British Commonwealth conferences with the queen in the chair); and a panfrancophone "cultural" organization, La Francophonie.[12] The connection was, in sum, a dense network of personal, private, public, official, formal, and informal relationships, all devoted to keeping green the multiple Franco-African linkages and to minimizing the presence of outsiders and potential interlopers (notably, Americans and other Europeans) on the *pré carré*. (See Appendixes G and H.)

By 1990, however, the *pré carré* was no longer the exclusive commons of the francophones, and the intimacies of the *chasse gardée* had begun to wear thin. For one thing, given France's growing role within the European Community and the increasing financial and economic obligations that role entailed, the sheer cost of maintaining the Franco-African relationships strained the French treasury and occasioned a growing volume of criticism in the French Parliament. Symptomatic was both the crisis-level debt affecting most African states, the francophone states included, which the French treasury balked at covering, and a related decline in French investment in Africa beginning in 1980, "from a net annual inflow of *circa* one billion dollars at the decade's beginning, to $53 million in 1985, and a net *outflow* of $824 million in 1988."[13] Moreover, observes Samuel Decalo, from the beginning of his presidency in 1981,

> François Mitterand had been itching to disencumber himself of residual unconditional "Gaullist" obligations to a multitude of oppressive, klepto-maniac client-states, whose heavy-handed domestic policies (e.g., Chad, C.A.R., Gabon) and swollen multiple Swiss banking accounts had increasingly tarnished France's reputation, and had drawn serious negative domestic political repercussions in Paris as well. The end of the Cold War and Africa's economic decline—that saw a massive erosion of France's economic presence in Africa, and in Africa's importance to France—provided the backdrop for the sudden new pressures from Paris on its client-states.[14]

Also, the corruption that had been standard operating procedure since 1960 was no longer tolerable: early in 1990 a senior French official suggested in *Le Monde* that France should disengage from Africa, which had become "the conservatory of the ills of humanity," noting that in 1988 the bank of France had purchased $1.8 billion worth of CFA currency fraudulently transferred to Europe "in full suitcases and diplomatic bags."[15] Mitterand now let it be known that governments introducing reforms would be preferred; he did so through his ministers and by the way his government placed severe International Monetary Fund (IMF)–World Bank conditionalities on aid and on budgetary and other subventions. The warning extended to the mutual-defense treaties, under whose terms, very loosely interpreted, France was committed to supplying arms and men to put down regime-threatening rebellions. Henceforth such support, if it was given at all, would go to those with good human rights records and visible movement toward democratic reforms. Under the circumstances, and because such warnings had been issued previously without effect, most francophone leaders did not take them seriously.

At the June 19–21, 1990, Franco-African summit in La Baule, France, Mitterand made the threat explicit, bluntly telling the African leaders that French aid would be reserved for countries moving toward democracy: French aid-giving "would be increasingly lukewarm with regard to regimes which comport themselves in an authoritarian manner" and "enthusiastic with respect to those who courageously take that step" toward democratization.[16] "African jaws dropped," reported *The Economist*. "What was the mother country up to? The answer was that the policy came not from Mr. Mitterand's own book: it had been cooked up by the European Community shortly before. Still, a harbinger of sorts" (July 23, 1994, p. 23). The figurative jaws need not have dropped because implementation of the new policy had already begun at least two years prior to La Baule, and though Mitterand may well have been prodded by the European Community's pressure on France's African clients, his disingenuous attempt to blame his European partners convinced no one. The policy was his, for good or for ill. And the policy was more than just "a harbinger of sorts": by 1995 the CFA franc had been dramatically devalued by half, and eight years later Mitterand's presidential successor, Jacques Chirac, made good on the threats with real cuts in French troops overseas, budgetary subventions, and official aid.

At all events, this time, in 1990 at La Baule, the African leaders listened. At home in Benin and elsewhere the message had already come through earlier, and there is little question that without explicit and implicit French support and the implied guarantee that French troops would not intervene, the national conferences might not have been organized and held. "For once," said a former French Ambassador to one francophone capital, "it was good to be able to tell those [leaders of the opposition] who contacted us that France stood by its democratic vocation. La Baule put us officially on the side of the angels."[17] The Development Ministry, for example, provided logistical support for elections in Benin (1990), the CAR (1992), and Niger (1993), as well as financial aid for judicial reform in Mali and Guinea.[18]

Eric Fottorino suggests that even if Mitterand himself was late in understanding the effects on Africa of the extraordinary series of events of 1989–1990, the Africans had already drawn their lessons:

> Even before the fall of the Berlin Wall, Africans . . . had had proof that no power, however strong, was forever. A "medical" coup d'état had chased [Habib] Bourguiba from his (presidential) seat in November 1987. The Tunisian neo-Destour (party), . . . which had been help up as a model of organization, had been much admired by single-party regimes. . . . Launched by young people, the violent disturbances of November 1988 in Algeria had pushed General Chadli [Benjedid] to inaugurate multiparty-ism. Later on, the execution of the Ceauşescus, overthrown in the wake of a "spontaneous popular demonstration" . . . made a strong impression on African oppositions. Had not the "Genius of the Carpathians" [one of Ceauşescu's praise-titles] developed strong ties with Mobutu (Zaire), Kaunda (Zambia), and again, Mugabe (Zimbabwe)? Then in February 1990 came Mandela's liberation. South Africa showed another facet of modernization by consecrating a prisoner held for more than twenty years. Would he have survived Gabonese, Guinean, or even Ivoirian jails?[19]

Had Mitterand simply recognized the obvious and decided to ride the Third Wave? After all, by the time La Baule took place, Benin and Gabon had already held their national conferences, mulitpartyism had appeared in Côte d'Ivoire, and even Mobutu had begun consultations intended to lead to political pluralism, though the latter, to be sure, qualified as a kind of "multimobutism." In truth, Mitterand had come late to this table, but he apparently believed what he said. After all, his emissaries to Omar Bongo during the January 1970 riots, when French troops evacuated French citizens from Libreville, had urged the benefits of political liberalization on the Gabonese president, and the French ambassadors in Benin and Zaire had cautioned the regimes in these two countries about the dangers of a popular explosion. By the time the La Baule conference convened, Mitterand had become convinced, perhaps naively,[20] that by blessing the new liberalizing currents France could both spur local reforms in Africa and improve France's overall standing there. The *chasse gardée* and *pré carré* notwithstanding, La Baule sent a clear and encouraging message to Africa's new democrats.

As it turned out, the La Baule message, however encouraging, was nei-ther clear nor unambiguous. On the one hand, the forces of democratization could take heart from French support for the national conferences and the subsequent founding elections, as well as from France's refusal to intervene to protect "old-friend dictators"[21] such as Hissene Habré in Chad (Déby's coup, December 1990) and Moussa Traoré in Mali (Toumani Touré's coup, March 1991). Both Habré and Traoré had scoffed at Mitterand's La Baule conditionalities, "and as if to attest to the fact that he understood France's new line, once installed in Ndjamena, Déby [Idriss Déby, the new head of state, who had been Habré's chief of staff] . . . pledged a prompt return to civilian rule and multiparty elections."[22] On the other hand, the signs of backtracking from France's professed commitment to political liberalization began to multiply, indicating that in the eyes of French politicians, when aid was being provided, economic conditionalities counted for much more than political ones.[23] Mitterand himself, at the 1991 Francophonie summit, suggested that "each country . . . should set . . . the terms and pace of its own reform"; this advice was underlined by ex–prime minister Pierre Bérégovoy at the 1992 Franco-African summit when he pointedly pledged "full" French support for *economic* reform.

It was also evident that in a crunch recalcitrant leaders in countries with major French business and political interests, such as Cameroon's Paul Biya, Côte d'Ivoire's Houphouët-Boigny, and Gabon's Omar Bongo would be preferred over democratic oppositions. Not only were democratic reformers not rewarded in these countries, but subsidies and aid actually increased to the regimes in power. In 1992, for example, Biya's regime received $436 million, compared to the $159 million given it in 1990.[24] Nor were promises to cut French troops in Africa and to revise the bilateral defense agreements honored, though the number of French technical assistance personnel in Africa was reduced by half. And finally, there were actions such as the dispatch of 150 French paratroopers to aid Idriss Déby's repressive regime in Chad; a brief intervention in Zaire in 1991 to protect French nationals and help Mobutu control his riotous troops; the sale of nine million rounds of ammunition to Biya's government; and, most worrisome, military and financial assistance to Rwanda's Juvenal Habyarimana beginning in 1990, as La Baule itself got under way, to help him equip his presidential guard and fight off invading Tutsi forces from Uganda. That aid turned to intervention in 1994 and arguably made the French complicit not only in the genocidal slaughter of Tutsis by the Hutu regime following Habyarimana's death, but also in the later protection of the flight of both Hutu civilians and the remaining Hutu *génocidaires* (genocidal killers) into Zaire—all with Mobutu's acquiescence.[25]

By 1995, when Jacques Chirac took over the French presidency, there may well have been sufficient confusion about France's vacillating support for democratization that it had begun to falter in francophone Africa—as the disappointing results of the "second elections" demonstrate. It had become clear that if a regime was important to French economic and political interests, France would not encourage its democratic opposition and, indeed, would turn a blind eye even to its more egregious human rights violations—as it did in February 1991 when the Ivoirian regime imprisoned key leaders of the opposition and in August 1991 when demonstrators in Madagascar demanding Didier Ratsiraka's resignation were massacred. It was also clear that under the right circumstances France would intervene militarily to help a client regime, though it would not save it if it was considered a lost cause (Rwanda in 1994, Congo-Brazzaville in 1997, Zaire in 1997, and the CAR in December 1996 after the third intervention). France also protected newly redemocratized systems (Benin and Mali, for example), though its unwillingness to intervene when Niger's Colonel Ibrahim Mainassara Barre seized power from the democratically elected government of Mahamane Ousmane in 1996 dramatically illustrated once again how far France had come—and had failed to come—since La Baule.

The Reasons: Internal Factors

No one who knows anything about the way the Third Wave broke in Africa can think that factors external to Africa were alone responsible for the event. While events such as the collapse of the Soviet Union may have helped provide a fortuitous moment and an opening for the forces of African democratization, those forces could not have pushed their agendas, much less succeeded, had it not been for other, mainly country-specific factors that impelled those forces to action. However, the evidence from our fourteen states, as from most of the others, is mainly circumstantial; in the flow of events it is almost impossible to pick out the key factor, the critical actor or actors, or the defining event that made the difference. Nevertheless, a survey of the states involved does reveal several striking patterns: that the wave broke first in francophone Africa, with Benin leading the way; that its key institutional innovation, the national conference, was of francophone inspiration; that it first affected states with regimes experiencing both severe economic malfunction and political crises of legitimacy; and that where a democratic transition was at least initially achieved, a firm institutional base—including a constitution, a multiparty system, a founding election, and a form of responsible government—was first laid down.

There is also evidence, admittedly largely circumstantial, that a kind of demonstration effect was at work: what happened in Benin appears to have emboldened Togolese seeking to challenge the regime of General Gnassingbé Eyadéma, and the striking success of the Beninois national conference apparently gave impetus to similar ventures in Gabon, Congo-Brazzaville, Mali, Togo, Niger, Zaire, and Chad—in that order. In some cases the Benin model was copied very closely as a means to political liberalization. Rémy Bazenguissa-Ganga, in his useful description and analysis of Congo-Brazzaville's national conference, agrees: "The case of Benin, which opened the way to a peaceful transition, . . . inspired the strategy of Congo's opposition, who found in it the justification for their struggle against the regime. That external model became an unavoidable point of reference even during the process when new leaders were being produced."[26] Using the Benin model, the opposition demanded that technocrats who had worked in international organizations be included in the conference, that the post of prime minister in the transitional government be given to someone with these qualifications, and that a prominent religious figure should preside over the conference. At all events, the Benin conference became hot news for both francophone elites and publics, and it was that much more imitable for being so visible:

> An instant media event throughout Francophone Africa, the story of Benin was carried live on Benin radio, rebroadcast on national television, given prominent international coverage on Radio France International (RFI), reported and analyzed by the government media and the independent press in every Francophone African country, and held up as a model of political reform by the Paris-based journal, *Jeune Afrique*. The text of this political drama was preserved by the Benin government news agency, which produced a two-hour video tape of conference highlights. Over 400 copies of the video had been sold by the end of 1991, and untold numbers of pirated copies began to circulate.[27]

In any event, the larger questions remain: Why should this have happened so late in the twentieth century? And why did the francophone states lead the way? It is tempting to speculate that the preindependence period in francophone Africa, with its proliferation of political parties, elections, and vigorous nationalist contestation, may have left an indelible "genetic" imprint on the political cultures of the states that reasserted itself some thirty years after independence. Since we do not yet have the intellectual technology to do longitudinal testing of political DNA, much less to isolate individual political genes, the issue remains moot. Nevertheless, the existence of some evocative pieces of circumstantial evidence about just such an inheritance suggests that there might be something to the metaphor. For one thing, it is interesting to note that the Benin national conference not only ended military rule, it also wrote a constitution that was similar—at least in the articulation of its basic principles—to the one with which its leaders had started at independence thirty years earlier. Further, during the thirty years since independence the dictatorial regimes of francophone Africa, whether run by soldiers or civilians, never had a free ride; they were almost always contested not just by in-house elements jockeying for power or seeking to appropriate it for themselves, or by ethnic or interest cartels with the same aim, but also by various individuals and formations articulating demands for political liberalization or for restoration of the democratic institutions with which their countries had been endowed at birth.

All too often those voicing such opposition suffered arrest, imprisonment, or even death for their presumption. This speaks volumes for the stubborn survival of democratic principles and the memories that fed them. The prisons run by Sékou Touré, Modibo Keita, Ahmadou Ahidjo, and Paul Biya, as well as by the military regimes in Mauritania, Niger, Mali, Burkina Faso, and Chad, not only housed common criminals but also held—by the score, if not the hundreds—political prisoners and those whom Amnesty International calls prisoners of conscience.

One of these chambers of horrors, Guinea's infamous Boiro Prison in Conakry, and Habré's *piscine* are perhaps the star witnesses to that repression. Boiro held some of the most notable military and civilian victims of Guinea's "perpetual plot," including Diallo Telli, former secretary-general of the Organization of African Unity (OAU), who died on March 1, 1977, of forced starvation—the so-called black diet—a fate shared by a number of others who, like Telli, had dared call for democratic reforms in his country.[28] The *piscine,* literally the shell of an old swimming pool converted into a bunker with a set of torture chambers, capped Habré's bloody superstructure of repression. Between 1982 and 1990, according to the 1991 report of the International Helsinki Federation for Human Rights, Habré and his political police, the Direction de la Documentation et de la Securité (DDS) executed approximately ten thousand people in Chad's capital, Ndjamena, alone (out of about forty thousand for the entire country during that period).

It is also the case that documentation on the Benin, Mali, and Niger national conferences reveal both implicit and explicit references to the French constitutional mythology still taught in their schools. One account in particular, which Pearl Robinson calls the "master narrative" of French political history, had become part of the elite political culture of those countries.[29] That story, of course, is how the Third Estate, or popular assembly, meeting separately in June 1789 as part of France's Estates-General, swore its famous *"Serment de jeux de paumes"* ("Oath of the Tennis Court")—that "wherever its members are gathered the National Assembly is in being"—in effect affirming itself to be the sovereign voice of all French people.[30] Shortly thereafter the deputies collectively declared themselves to be a constituent assembly, and after disposing of the king they proceeded to write a new constitution. (The master narrative also includes reference to the fact that many in the Third Estate were already steeped in Jean-Jacques Rousseau's ideas about popular sovereignty and the right of the people to renegotiate the social contract.) In any event, it does no violence to the facts to suggest that for many history-minded participants in the Benin and other national conferences, the parallel must have seemed both striking and apt, the more so since at the time France was celebrating the bicentennial of its own revolution.

We don't know exactly who or what finally prompted the idea of convening a conference of *"Les forces vives de la nation"* in Benin, but Kérékou made the suggestion official and public by endorsing it late in 1989. (Fabien Eboussi Boulaga thinks the idea was Kérékou's, that he saw in the formula the least dangerous of the unpleasant options before him.[31]) The Beninois journalist Emmanuel Adjovi, writing about Benin's 1996 presidential elections, asserts simply that the conference was "inspired by the Estates-General of the French revolution,"[32] but he offers no direct proof to support the contention. However, Albert Tevoedjre, one of Benin's senior statesmen and intellectuals, in his report to his country's national conference, left little doubt about what he deemed the source of its inspiration. Citing the calamitous state of Benin's polity and economy in 1989, he wrote, "Each of you saw this with such troubled heart and spirit that we decided to transform ourselves into an Estates-General of the nation, and to proclaim without ambiguity the sovereignty of our assembly and the executive force of our decisions."[33] Pearl Robinson forcefully makes the point that the "historic precedent of the Estates-General, transformed into a structural schema, became a principle for generating strategy on regime change in Francophone Africa."[34]

Still, however compelling and vital the story may have been as "a principle for generating strategy," by itself it was clearly insufficient to catalyze the movement for wholesale political liberalization on which the francophone states embarked. Even the spectacular success of the Benin conference was not immediately transferable elsewhere, *except* as a strategy, and then only with highly variable effect. According to Eboussi Boulaga, the Benin conference had "the beauty of the unique, the incomparable thing. The Benin model did not export. Its copies are always defective, not to say caricatures. The price of mimicry is artifice, which does violence to the specific historical givens of different countries. The national conference is not a panacea."[35] (For details on the National Conferences, see Appendix H.)

However, adding up the impact of both internal and external forces and factors, and including the generative salience of revived (perhaps "genetic") political memory, plus the empowering historical principle of the Estates-General, suggests the appearance during the late 1980s of an "enabling environment" (Pearl Robinson's apt term, also used by Decalo), in which it seemed that those seeking political liberalization, at least in francophone Africa, might finally succeed where they had previously failed repeatedly. The political and economic bankruptcy or near bankruptcy of incumbent regimes, the collapse of the old bipolar world order and the abrupt ending of the Cold War—a series of events that heralded political reform from Algeria to South Africa—and, of course, the bicentennial of the French Revolution, as well as the French government's more critical view of its former African wards, all undoubtedly affected the political calculus of francophone Africa's reformers: they could argue, justifiably or not, that their efforts were beginning to pay off. The political environment had become enabling.

The Conferences, Founding Elections, and Transitions

Identifying an enabling environment that gave the political reformers purchase for their hopes for change only takes the story to the edge of the changes that did take place, but doesn't explain why they happened as they did. Here there are two sets of connected stories, each of which contributes part of the explanation: one set covers those experiments that failed, and the other, those that succeeded.

First, the visible failures, which among our fourteen are Togo, Cameroon, Congo-Brazzaville, Niger, and, though it took a decade for its failure to become visible in the clear light of hindsight, Côte d'Ivoire. National conferences were convened in Togo, Congo, and Niger, but produced little or no lasting democratic change; in Cameroon and Côte d'Ivoire demands for convening national conferences were made, but were refused by the regime in power. Though at first glance the stories of these failures offer few features that suggest common ground for explanation, when they are examined more closely, some patterns do emerge.

Crucially, as Jennifer Seely has shown in her comparison of the national conferences and redemocratization processes in Togo and Benin, the power-political cards held by the major players varied enormously from one situation to the other, and so did their ability and willingness to play them.[36] Whereas Kérékou had few options left to play in Benin after he ceded the initiative to the opposition by agreeing to convene a national conference and assenting to its initial assumption of sovereignty, the opposition groups in Togo's national conference could never trump the decisive cards held by Eyadéma, who could (and did) call on the support of the army, mobilize his northern allies (Kabré and others), and manipulate the machinery of government to his own benefit. In effect, while the Benin conference had the leverage given it by a bankrupt and enfeebled regime, the one in Togo faced a regime that, though it was in trouble, was neither bankrupt nor lacking weapons with which to defend itself. Moreover, the groups in Togo, already riven by the old Ewe controversies and fearful of Eyadéma's reach, were never able to find a common front or to agree on common strategies. In both countries an enabling environment sufficient for the convocation of a national conference had been reached, but unlike the Beninois, the Togolese found themselves unable to take advantage of the opportunities it presented.

The central story of Seely's comparison not only captures the dynamics of the process, but also offers a useful model on which to base an explanation of its failures and successes. While the timing of the conference, the existence of an enabling environment, and the regime's possession or lack of the means and resources with which to control the situation were all factors contributing to the success or failure of the conferences themselves, perhaps just as critical, argues Seely, were the bargaining strategies employed by the participants in their attempt to wrest concessions or power from the regime and to map out a new political future for their country. The fact of the conferences themselves, and the participants' very presence therein were assets in hand before the conferences even began; what the participants then did with those assets and with the considerable political and social capital they brought with them as representatives of important civil constituencies largely determined the conferences' outcomes.

Although both conferences began with auspicious numbers and representation (Togo's had one thousand delegates representing more than two hundred organizations and constituencies; Benin's, 488 delegates representing almost four hundred constituencies, not including the Beninois category of "Personalities and Sages"), the Togolese, having taken inspiration from Benin's example, fatally overestimated Eyadéma's weaknesses, and rather than mustering and organizing appropriate bargaining strategies, they fell to squabbling among themselves. The Beninois got it just right, providing reconciliation for Kérékou, financial balm for the army and the civil service, and a fresh start for everyone. While both conferences were chaired by members of the clergy, which gave the meetings the proper moral tone and decorum, the Beninois were also able to reassure to their country by appointing a prominent World Bank official, Nicéphore Soglo, to head the interim government.

In Côte d'Ivoire and Cameroon demands for democratization were short-circuited by the regimes' refusal to convene national conferences and by maneuvers that in both countries amounted to the regimes' co-optation of the rhetoric of democratic political change without changing the realities on the ground. In Côte d'Ivoire the enabling environment took shape in 1990, during what turned out to be one of the last years of Houphouët-Boigny's extraordinary thirty-two-year rule. Le Vieux ("the old man," used as an honorific) had become Le Vieillard ("the oldster," spoken derisively), and the system of personal-cum-bureaucratic rule he had perfected had begun to unravel as his putative heirs started to jockey for succession. It didn't help that even to the very last Houphouët-Boigny had pointedly refused to designate his own dauphin and that the economic system he had nurtured was on the decline, not least because the French investment capital he had so assiduously courted was beginning to leach back out toward the metropole. At all events, those seeking democratic reforms, including intellectuals like Laurent Gbagbo, students and faculty on Abidjan campuses, transporters, and farmers' and teachers' syndicates,[37] had to compete for political space with the human pieces starting to come loose from the Houphouët-Boigny machine.

A so-called *appel à la rénovation* (call for renewal) with some five hundred signatures began to circulate in August–September 1990, demanding, among other things, the convocation of a "national convention for renewal" to be held prior to the next Parti Démocratique de la Côte d'Ivoire (PDCI) congress.[38] Following student demonstrations in 1990 and persistent demands for a national conference, on May 17–18, 1991, military *paracommandos* (airborne infantry) invaded the University of Abidjan's campus and killed several students, wounded a larger number, and issued a sharp warning about excess student activism. There was more protest, but it was already clear to the principal establishment figures contending for power—Philippe Yacé, Henri Konan Bedié, and Alassane Ouattara—that a national conference, much less democratic reforms such as multiparty elections, might not only hasten the disintegration of the Houphouët-Boigny system, but also complicate matters for the contending putative successors. In their need for stability during this trying time, the three found a paradoxical partner in Houphouët-Boigny, who needed to preserve the appearance of control. Consequently, when the growing opposition demanded that the regime convene an Ivoirian version of the national conference, Houphouët-Boigny was able to refuse and to have his refusal backed up by what was left of the establishment.

In the disintegration of Houphouët-Boigny's ancien régime the democratizers saw their opportunity for major changes in the system, but what they perceived as an enabling environment, Houphouët-Boigny's possible successors and Houphouët-Boigny himself saw as a mortal threat to a system both needed to remain unchanged, albeit for very different reasons. A national conference was never convened, and the political situation continued to deteriorate to the point where the authoritative *Le Monde Diplomatique* was able to announce confidently in its November 1992 issue the death throes of the regime: "End of the reign, end of a dream" *(fin de régne, fin d'un rêve).*[39]

The story of Cameroon also confirms the presence of an enabling environment and an active, dynamic opposition, but also of a regime that, though in political and economic trouble and faced with aroused popular anger, was nevertheless able to mobilize its supporters and use the levers of coercive power to prevent democratization.[40] Here the story begins with the constitutional changes of December 1990, which permitted multiparty activity and multiparty elections for the first time since 1964. Recall that when Biya succeeded Ahidjo as president in 1982, he appeared to promise the democratic reforms the Ahidjo regime had denied during its twenty-four-year run. As it turned out, Biya was no reformer; in fact, his regime became a southern version of Ahidjo's northern-dominated, authoritarian one. The opening to multipartyism in 1990 was little more than a move to placate growing opposition to Biya's regime. It took what was billed as the country's first democratic multiparty presidential election, held in April 1992, to confirm the authoritarian nature of that regime: after a campaign marked by violence and intimidation against his main rival, Biya was declared the winner by 39 percent to John Fru Ndi's 36 percent, in spite of massive irregularities and an unofficial count that clearly showed Fru Ndi had gained the majority of votes in both francophone and anglophone Cameroon.

At all events, the opposition's demand in 1991–1992 for a "sovereign national conference" on the Benin-Mali model got nowhere; instead the regime produced so-called constitutional reforms and promised an officially sponsored "Tripartite" conference at which, it was claimed, all outstanding grievances of the opposition would be redressed. The conference, convened by Prime Minister Sadou Hayatou and held from October 30 to November 13, 1991, brought together members of the government, leaders of opposition parties, and a group of Cameroon People's Democratic Movement (CPDM) partisans labeled notables. Amid unabashed prodding by the regime that reached the point of intimidation, the meeting produced a document, the Yaoundé Declaration, in which the signatories, representing forty of the forty-seven registered political parties, agreed to end the *villes mortes,* or urban civil disobedience, campaign and to abandon their demand for a sovereign national conference. In exchange, the regime relaxed police and security measures imposed during the *ville mortes* strikes, freed most of those recently imprisoned for oppositional activity, gave selective tax breaks to new friends of Biya, and opened the door to the return of some political exiles. It also agreed to further talks about constitutional and electoral reforms, but, unsurprisingly, little came of these latter promises. The regime had reason to be pleased with its efforts: it had successfully staved off the sovereign national conference (SNC), co-opted part of the opposition, and probably escaped involuntary retirement.

In Côte d'Ivoire and Cameroon it took full mobilization of the regimes' political assets and some nimble footwork to fend off demands for an SNC. The regime in the Central African Republic also avoided an SNC, but the price for doing so turned out to be that General André Kolingba had to depart anyway—he was forced out by the French.[41] In 1985 Kolingba had dissolved the military junta with which he had ruled since 1981, and in 1986 he had endowed the CAR with a new constitution. Kolingba obviously sought to endow his regime with new legitimacy, but the 1986 constitution, as those that preceded it, did little to reinforce his shaky regime. By the time the democratization wave hit the CAR in late 1990, Kolingba's military regime was in economic straits and under pressure to liberalize the political system, and the movement further unsettled the government. In 1991 the regime amended the constitution to provide for a multiparty system under which, in August of that year, it officially legalized nine new political parties in an attempt to counter the growing unrest in the country. Early in 1992 a loose amalgam of opposition groups and parties demanded that Kolingba convene a national conference; he refused, authorizing only a broad "national debate." The opponents, unable to concert their efforts and agree on a joint strategy, could not prevent Kolingba from convening the "debate" on August 1, 1992. The event was boycotted by the opposition parties, the Roman Catholic Church, and leading trade union officials. That same day the leader of the opposition Alliance for Democracy and Progress, Jean-Claude Congugo, was killed in a violent clash between prodemocracy protesters and security forces in Bangui.

Kolingba had avoided calling an SNC only to be undone by the excesses of his armed supporters. The French, who had supported Kolingba to this point, stationing some 1,500 French troops in Bangui and Bouar and providing the bulk of the CAR's foreign aid, were sickened by the violence and impressed by the strength of the opposition. They finally pressured Kolingba into calling for open, multiparty elections, which he lost on August 22, 1992, to an old foe, Ange-Félix Patassé, once the imperial Jean-Bédel Bokassa's prime minister but now a professed convert to democracy.[42] Kolingba tried a comeback in May 2001 in the form of an attempted coup d'état, but failed. The French stood by Patassé despite the eruption of a spate of mutinies in 2000–2001, even using its troops to help put down the Kolingba-inspired coup attempt and sponsoring a multinational peacekeeping force commanded by a Guinean general.[43]

By any democratizing criteria, of our fourteen states Benin, Mali, and Senegal emerged from the 1990s as unqualified exemplars of successful democratic transition, though only the first two leveraged their transitions with a sovereign national conference. Benin, of course, not only provided the template for the other national conferences, but more important, it set a vivid example "by demonstrating that a 'civilian coup d'état' was possible against a derelict regime incapable of mastering the profound socioeconomic crisis affecting the country."[44] In addition, French president Mitterand's affirmation at La Baule that thenceforth French aid would go to those favoring increased freedom was generally perceived as an open encouragement to promote democracy in Africa and as an additional endorsement of the Benin SNC and its results.

In Benin a weakened Mathieu Kérékou was removed by the SNC while the army stayed on the sidelines, and in Mali the army did the job of deposing the dictator Moussa Traoré four months before Mali's national conference convened in July–August 1991. While the Beninois army refused to support Kérékou when the chips were down, the army in Mali (led by Lieutenant Colonel, later Brigadier General Amadou Toumani Touré) went farther, becoming an active, even enthusiastic partner in the democratization process. It created a transitional government headed by a respected technocrat (Soumana Sacko, a senior United Nations Development Programme official), which, in turn, organized Mali's national conference.

In neither Benin nor Mali did delegates' intergroup bargaining ever become zero-sum contests, so both conferences were able to move to a successful conclusion without excessive difficulty. However, there were some critical differences between the SNC experiences in Mali and Benin, and in Congo-Brazzaville as well. First, in contrast to the Benin and Congo-Brazzaville examples, the Mali conferees did not feel the need to assert the conference's collective sovereignty, and it was understood that the Soumana Sacko–Toumani Touré government would remain in power until democratic elections could be held. (Amadou Toumani Touré had also made it clear that he would not participate in the elections.) Second, the Mali national conference was not primarily an arena for managing conflict between an incumbent regime and a competing opposition, as was the case in Benin, Togo, and Congo-Brazzaville. The Mali national conference played a much more limited role in the transition process, serving more as a consensus-building mechanism following the overthrow of Moussa Traoré's twenty-two-year-old dictatorship than as the main vehicle for political change.

However one judges the success of national conferences, clearly those in both Benin and Mali were successful, Benin's because it set the tone and rules for a democratic transition that was still valid over ten years later, and Mali's because it set the seal to a democratic system that, despite various difficulties facing the Alpha Oumar Konaré regime, has also lasted out the 1991–2002 decade.[45]

Senegal never had a national conference; nor did the Senegalese, who had enjoyed a so-called quasi-democracy for decades, ever demand one. But Senegal also underwent a democratic transition of sorts, though a much more gradual one, to be sure. It moved from Senghor's single-party Union Progressiste Sénégalaise (UPS) regime (1966–1976), which became the Parti Socialiste in 1976; to the de jure tripartite organization of ideological "tendencies" (1976–1981); to more or less open multiparty elections with repeated UPS victories following the Senghor-Diouf transition (1981–1991); through several bitterly contested national elections (1991, 1993, 1995, and 1998); to Abdoulaye Wade's remarkable March 2000 victory in the freest, most open presidential elections ever held in Senegal.[46] Despite difficulties with the economy and the open sore of the Casamance rebellion, Senegal certainly deserves inclusion in the list of successful democratic transitions.

For a time it appeared that the national conferences in Niger and Congo-Brazzaville might enable those countries also to join the ranks of Africa's stable democracies, particularly because both also underwent founding elections, one of the apparent prerequisites of the democratic transition.[47] But redemocratization efforts succeeded in neither state.

In Congo-Brazzaville the prospects for democratization had looked particularly good because the national conference appeared to followed the Benin script:[48] a troubled economy, a society riven by ethnopolitical conflict, military mutinies, recurrent student and labor strikes, and a military dictatorship (headed by Denis Sassou-Nguesso) increasingly unable to cope and turning finally to a national conference to extricate the head of state and the country from its troubles. As in Benin, the national conference, which was convoked as a Conference of Vital Forces of the Nation *(Conférence des forces vives de la nation),* rapidly became a sovereign national conference. In one of its first acts as such, it divested President Sassou-Nguesso of all but his ceremonial functions. The military (as in Benin), already fractured and debilitated by its own ethnic tensions and with a deteriorating command structure, was unable to affect events in the conference and simply stood aside as Sassou-Nguesso's regime collapsed around him.

On June 10 the conference adjourned, having disassembled Sassou-Nguesso's authoritarian structures, promised early multiparty elections, and put in place an interim government (headed by André Milongo, a World Bank official) and a new legislature, which later produced a new constitution to be submitted to referendum. This new constitution was duly adopted on March 15, 1992, and Pascal Lissouba was elected president on June 2, but not before army mutinies broke out again in February. On August 31, 1992, Sassou-Nguesso finally retired (temporarily as it turned out) after signing an agreement with Lissouba for a common government program. By the end of 1992 and the beginning of 1993 the main power figures (Bernard Kolelas, Lissouba, Sassou-Nguesso, Jean-Pierre Thystère-Tchicaya, Ambroise Noumazalaye, Joachim Yhombi-Opango, and so on) had begun again to recruit followers, both armed and unarmed, and in July 1993, November 1993, and January 1994, despite various externally generated efforts at peacemaking, there were repeated violent confrontations between armed ethnic and personal militias, and between militias and elements of the army.

By mid-1997 the country was again on the verge of economic and social breakdown, and a mini–civil war was raging in Brazzaville. On October 15, 1997, Sassou-Nguesso, with the help of Angolan forces sent to his aid, finally defeated Lissouba and retook power. Between January 5 and

14, 1998, Sassou-Nguesso, who for obvious reasons had hated the 1991 national conference, convened his own version, a *"Forum d'unité et reconciliation nationale"* with 1,500 handpicked "representatives of political formations and delegates of civil society." As expected, his forum endorsed his return to power and voted for a three-year transition to national elections. Those elections, in March 2002, overwhelmingly confirmed him in the presidency, also as expected. At the end of 2003 Sassou-Nguesso was still in office, and the SNC all but forgotten. Despite the cease-fire Sassou-Nguesso had negotiated with his principal opponents and their militias in 1999, sporadic militia violence broke out again in Brazzaville in 2003, and the majority of the more than two hundred thousand people displaced by the fighting in the capital had yet to return home.

Niger's was the fourth national conference to be convened during the 1990–1993 period. Beginning on July 29 and ending successfully three months later, it more or less followed the Beninois script: it met to deal with the progressively more onerous social, political, and economic problems cumulated during the military presidencies of Seyni Kountché (1974–1987) and his weakened successor Ali Saibou (1987–1990); it declared itself sovereign and suspended the constitution and national assembly; it muzzled the army then took it out of politics (the army had already announced in March that it would leave politics); it removed Saibou from power, leaving him only ceremonial functions; it restored multiparty politics; it reorganized the country's finances and economy; and in its constitutional role it began rewriting the constitution, which in its new form, with democratic institutions and guarantees and a much constrained presidency, was to be submitted to a referendum by the end of the year.

The happy consensus that prevailed at the end of the conference lasted only until January 1992, when another round of army mutinies broke out. The transitional regime was replaced in April 1993 by the democratically elected civilian government of Mahamane Ousmane, but the new government proved no more able than its predecessors to solve the country's outstanding problems: near financial and economic bankruptcy; demands for salary arrears or unpaid subventions from everyone from the military to civil servants to students; recurrent military mutinies; periodic shortfalls in crucial foreign aid; and a festering, vastly destabilizing Tuareg revolt still without resolution.

Ousmane lasted until January 27, 1996, when he was ousted by a military coup led by General Mainassara Barre, who was then murdered on April 9, 1999, by his presidential guard, headed by Major Daouda Malam Wanke, who then, in turn, assumed power, promising to restore civilian rule as soon as possible. To everyone's surprise, Wanke kept his promise and organized a free and open presidential election, which was won in November by Mamadou Tandja, a retired army colonel who defeated

Mahamadou Issoufou, prime minister in the only previous democratically elected government (that of 1993–1994), and Mahamane Ousmane, whom Mainassara had removed. While Tandja's election could not be claimed as fulfillment of Niger's democratic promise, it restored some measure of trust in government, appeared to have temporarily calmed Niger's restive soldiers, and most important, helped turn the major donors' aid taps back on, including that of the IMF, which granted a large loan. By August 2002, however, the generally parlous state of Niger's economy, including, again, nonpayment of pay arrears to government employees, led to new army mutinies in the east and in the capital. The rebellions were put down by loyal troops, but in June 2003 Tandja faced yet another crisis when he drove a controversial new electoral law through Parliament without consulting opposition parties. Tandja weathered the crisis, but not without putting Niger's democratic future in further doubt.

Summing Up: Possible Answers

When the African political landscape at the end of 2003 is viewed in light of the events of the preceding thirteen years, there is little argument now that the democratizing efforts of the 1990s produced highly variable results ranging from complete failure (Togo, Mauritania, Democratic Republic of Congo) to spectacular success (Benin, Mali, Senegal, South Africa). Overall, however, Arthur A. Goldsmith convincingly argues, the data "support a bona fide democratic tendency" throughout Africa: "more liberal rules of political engagement are being adopted," and there "is the growing number and competitiveness of elections in recent years"; the "overall indexes of political freedom, because they capture the previous two types of evidence, have been on the rise."[49]

Nevertheless, when each of those countries that had national conferences and founding elections during this period (twelve of them: Benin, Chad, Comoros, Congo-Brazzaville, Ethiopia, Gabon, Guinea-Bissau, Mali, Niger, South Africa, Togo, Democratic Republic of Congo) is viewed separately, the picture is less encouraging. Only three—Benin, Mali, and South Africa—have managed to institutionalize the democratic gains they made during the 1990s. Where, then, does that leave the national conferences? They were certainly innovative, exciting, and forceful means wherewith to bring democratic agendas to the attention of reluctant regimes; they gave voice and representation to hitherto unco-opted, active elements of civil society; and they were usually able to concert action to bring about wide-ranging political changes. Undeniably the SNCs not only opened new avenues for political participation, but more important, lowered the costs of oppositional activity for those who had theretofore feared to show open defiance of the regime in power or had remained outside the political system for the same reasons. Yet with the exceptions noted above, in the long run each SNC had less political effect than the sheer weight and import of the activity would have predicted, even though altogether they did contribute to the general improvement of the continent's democratic climate. What explains this ambiguous, and disappointing, outcome?

First, as Bratton and van de Walle observe,

> With the exception of South Africa, all national conferences resulted, not in compromise, but in a zero-sum victory for one side or another and the defeat of the losing side. Thus, in Benin, Congo, and Niger the incumbents collapsed at the conference itself; in Zaïre and Togo, the opposition achieved Pyrrhic victories at the conference, but made mistakes that would eventually play into the incumbent's hands and ensure his survival. The fact that the winners took all in African national conferences augured badly for democratic consolidation, because it suggested that transiting countries still lacked a political process for arriving at negotiated solutions, and a balance of power that would ensure that transition agreements had broad support, and therefore could be enforced.[50]

The point is a good one: zero-sum results reveal the absence, or failure, of compromise and may leave the losers not only with hard feelings, but also with thoughts of revenge. Sassou-Nguesso, if he spoke at all for leaders removed by SNCs, vividly recalled his own bitterness on the occasion and his "resolve" to vindicate himself, a vindication he achieved by retaking power in 1997.[51] Although Kérékou and Ratsiraka, both of whom returned to power in their own countries by changing their political coloration, have yet to publish autobiographies, it is not unreasonable to think that they would admit to similar feelings. Still, in neither case, nor indeed in any of the other SNC "civil revolutions" where incumbents were forced out, did the zero-sum result mean their death or imprisonment, a result always possible under the circumstances of the usual coup d'état. In fact, that leaders like Kérékou and Sassou-Nguesso were able to participate in the proceedings enabled them to negotiate a dignified exit for themselves, and even thus facilitate their eventual return to politics.

Second, the effects of an enabling environment are important. Both in the countries where democratizing efforts failed and in those where they succeeded, an enabling environment for democratization had clearly developed sometime during the 1989–1991 period, a moment in time when it appeared that such efforts might bear fruit. When they did not, it was due not so much to a lack of will or desire or to a failure to seize the opportunity, but in part to the strategically superior position in which the regime in power began the contest (as in Togo and Cameroon), or into which it maneuvered itself during the conflict (as in Côte d'Ivoire).

Arguably the failure of Togo's opposition to work together cost it dearly in its contest with President Eyadéma, but it is equally persuasive to argue that Eyadéma held the better cards from the beginning. Where the reformers succeeded—that is, where their efforts eventually led to more or less lasting democratic changes, including at least first and second founding elections, regular alternation in the country's top offices, and institutions providing both transparency and accountability in governance—not only did the enabling environment hand the democratizers some tactical advantages, but also, it turns out, both rulers and democratizers were able to capitalize on those advantages and cooperate for their mutual benefit. Benin and Mali (at least when viewed at midyear 2003) qualify as long-term successes: in Mali the military regime had been fortuitously removed before the push for democracy really began, and in Benin Kérékou had virtually nothing left with which to defend his position when the SNC voted his divestiture. In Niger, the CAR, and Congo-Brazzaville, the reformers benefited (at least at the time) from severely weakened regimes and rulers with few remaining options, including, critically, the use of brute force.

The elements of the several enabling environments came together in part by plan of the organizers, in part by historical accident and current circumstances (including, as noted earlier, the two-hundredth anniversary of the French Revolution), and in part because most of the countries involved underwent similar political and socioeconomic crises at the same time, a circumstance that was itself due to their coadjutant economic and financial relations with each other and Europe. While it is admittedly difficult to pin down all the elements of the several enabling environments contributing to African democratization, it is clear that democratization could not have occurred in the absence of such contexts. (For a view of democratic progress in francophone Africa, see Appendix G.)

Notes

1. Huntington, *The Third Wave: Democratization in the Late Twentieth Century.* This chapter has benefited from the insight and advice of Jennifer Seely, whose doctoral dissertation deals with the national conferences, particularly in Benin and Togo and generally in francophone Africa. I gratefully acknowledge her contributions.

2. Chege, "Between Africa's Extremes," 350. The tabular summary account of democratization attempts in all sub-Saharan African states in Wiseman, *The New Struggle for Democracy in Africa,* 20–31, confirms Chege's observation.

3. Bratton and van de Walle, *Democratic Experiments in Africa: Regime Transitions in Comparative Perspective,* 196.

4. Bratton, "Second Elections in Africa," 51.

5. Robinson, "Democratization: Understanding the Relationship Between Regime Change and the Culture of Politics."

6. Decalo, *The Stable Minority: Civilian Rule in Africa,* 279, 280. Decalo's emphasis.

7. For details, see Nzouankeu, "The Role of the National Conferences in the Transition to Democracy in Africa: The Cases of Benin and Mali"; and Allen, "Restructuring an Authoritarian State: Democratic Renewal in Benin."

8. Known communist organizations included the Communist Party of South Africa (CPSA; still banned at the beginning of 1990, but unbanned after Nelson Mandela's release in that year); the banned Egyptian Communist Party, the communist parties of Lesotho, Benin, Réunion, and Mauritius; plus formations in Sudan, Madagascar, Senegal, Tunisia, Algeria, and other states. (The Hoover Institution's 1991 *Yearbook on International and Communist Affairs* lists communist parties and organizations in Angola, Benin, Congo-Brazzaville, Ethiopia, Lesotho, Mozambique, Réunion, Senegal, Sudan, and Zimbabwe; it conflates parties with direct ties to Moscow or Beijing and "vanguard parties" operating as adjuncts of Afro-Marxist regimes. For a relatively comprehensive listing of leftist, Marxist, Marxist-Leninist, Stalinist, and Maoist organizations and groups in Africa, see Ray, *Dictionary of the African Left.*)

9. Gromyko and Whitaker, *Agenda for Action: African-Soviet-U.S. Cooperation.* I offer anecdotal corroboration: In January 1989, during a United States Information Agency (USIA)–sponsored speaking tour in Africa, I flew from Kigali to Bujumbura in a small plane with the Soviet ambassador to Bujumbura as the only other passenger. Since I speak Russian, we struck up an amiable conversation, and once we landed in Bujumbura, he enthusiastically attended two of my lectures. At every opportunity he spoke glowingly of U.S.-Soviet cooperation in Africa, "now that we no longer need to fear each other." We also toasted U.S.-Russian friendship on several occasions, all in the interest of our countries' joint and benevolent concerns for Africa.

10. "Toward a New Historical Milestone in Sino-African Friendship," excerpts from a speech before the 1996 meeting of the OAU, Addis Ababa, May 13, 1996. *Beijing Review.*

11. Devastatingly described by Antoine Glaser and Stephen Smith in their *Ces messieurs Afrique,* vol. 1: *Le Paris-village du continent noir.* The *chasse gardée* was literally real enough in the friendship between ex-president Giscard-d'Estaing and Emperor Bokassa, who several times hosted Giscard on his private hunting preserve—the prizes were wild boar and, apparently, diamonds—in the former Central African Empire. The Giscard-Bokassa relationship is discussed further in Chapter 9.

12. Of special relevance to this chapter are D. G. Lavroff, ed., *La politique africaine du Général de Gaulle, 1958–1969;* Decalo, *The Stable Minority,* 283–290; articles by Patrick Quantin, Jean-Luc Dagut, Jean-François Médard, Alain Ricard, Daniel Bach, Philippe Hugon, and Robin Luckham in "La France en Afrique," *Politique Africaine* 2, no. 5 (February 1982): 8–110; Bayart, *La politique africaine de François Mitterand;* Glaser and Smith, *Ces messieurs Afrique,* vol. 2: *Des réseaux au lobbies;* Glaser, *L'Afrique sans Africains: Le rêve blanc du continent noir* [Africa Without Africans: The White Dream of the Black Continent]; "France and Africa," *The Economist,* July 23, 1994, 21–23; Leymarie, "Inexorable effritement du 'modèle' franco-africain," 4–5; Leymarie, "En Afrique, Dieu n'est plus français" [In Africa, God Is No Longer French], 26–27; Leymarie, "En Afrique, la fin des ultimes 'chasses gardées,'" 4–5; Schraeder, "France and the Great Game in Africa"; Martin, "Continuity and Change in Franco-African Relations"; and two essays in Kirk-Greene and Bach, *State and Society in Francophone Africa Since Independence*: Coussy, "The Franc Zone: Original Logic, Subsequent Evolution, and Present Crisis," and Constantin, "The Foreign Policy of Francophone Africa: Clientelism and After." The special budgetary support system is discussed in Engberg, "The Operations Account System in French-Speaking Africa."

13. Decalo, *The Stable Minority,* 284. Italics in original.

14. Ibid., 285.

15. Ibid., 285, citing Whiteman, "The Gallic Paradox." For further details on corrupt Franco-African networks, see Glaser and Smith, *Ces messieurs Afrique,*

vols. 1 and 2; Bayart, *La politique africaine de François Mitterand;* and Péan, *Affaires africaines* and *L'argent noir.*

16. President Mitterand, from his "Discours de François Mitterand au XVIème sommet franco-Africain à La Baule." My translation. Officially the conference was the Sixteenth Conference of the Heads of State of France and Africa. La Baule is a coastal half-isle near Nantes. For a description of and commentary on the La Baule summit, see Fottorino, "France-Afrique, les liaisons dangereuses: La démocratie à contre-coeur."

17. Author's interview with an ambassador who declined to be identified, June 18, 1991. The ambassador acknowledged that subsequent events substantially diluted the message of La Baule, but he insisted that in 1990, at least, he and some of his peers did everything they could to encourage democratic forces in the countries to which they were posted.

18. Cited by Cumming, "French Development Assistance to Africa: Toward a New Agenda?" 390.

19. Fottorino, "France-Afrique, les liaisons dangereuses," 2. My translation.

20. Jean-François Bayart makes the point that Mitterand was sure that the African world was his and France's to remold: "More or less convinced that the 'neo-colonial' regimes were no more than puppets and only existed by grace of the aid that France provided them, the socialists [Mitterand and his party] cradled their illusions and overestimated the means by which they had come to power. . . . In these cirumstances, it was often the alleged marionettes who pulled the strings" (Bayart, *La politique africaine de François Mitterand,* 128, my translation). Bayart's point is well taken. As it turned out, however, Mitterand's government could and did stimulate redemocratization. Still, given the fierce resistance mounted by *"ces messieurs Afrique"* ("these gentlemen Africa"—French political and economic power brokers with long-standing, substantial interest in Africa), both within his own establishment and in Africa itself, he obviously overestimated the extent to which he could push real economic and political change among France's African clients.

21. Cumming, "French Development Assistance," 390.

22. Decalo, *The Stable Minority,* 286–287.

23. Cumming, "French Development Assistance," 391.

24. Schraeder, "France and the Great Game," 207.

25. The case for France's complicity is made by Verschave, *Complicité de génocide? La politique de la France au Rwanda.* See also Verschave's "Connivences françaises au Rwanda"; and Braeckman, "Le feu court sur la région des Grands Lacs: La présence militaire française au Rwanda."

26. Bazenguissa-Ganga, *Les voies du politique au Congo: Essai de sociologie historique,* 365. My translation.

27. Robinson, "The National Conference Phenomenon in Francophone Africa," 576.

28. When I visited the Boiro camp shortly after the end of the Sékou Touré regime, my guide, a former guard who swore he had never been involved in torture (*"Moi? Jamais, jamais tortionnaire!"*), said he was at the camp when Diallo Telli died. He claimed that from 1975 to 1977 almost one hundred political prisoners besides Telli had been killed by the "black diet," a figure I was unable to verify. For further details, see Lewin, *Diallo Telli, le tragique destin d'un grand Africain.* On the matter of the independence constitutions, see my "The Fall and Rise of Constitutionalism in West Africa."

29. See Robinson, "The National Conference Phenomenon in Francophone

Africa."

30. The Third Estate, as Robert R. Palmer points out in his *World of the French Revolution,* was not all that popular, heavily weighted as it was in favor of government functionaries, lawyers, merchants, and other professionals, of whom medical doctors were most prominent. As Palmer goes on to claim, "Had actual peasants, shopkeepers, and workmen been elected," the Third Estate when it convened "would have been more docile" (55). Despite the absence of complete data on the composition of the Benin, Mali, and Niger national conferences, the available evidence suggests a much broader base of representation than that which underlay the French Third Estate—at least insofar as the African assemblies included shopkeepers, members of peasant cooperatives and trade unions, and many women. Nevertheless, despite the broad base of constituencies on which the conferences rested, most of those attending represented the educated, politically-aware class of their respective countries.

31. Eboussi Boulaga, *Les conférences nationales en Afrique Noire,* 59–68.

32. Adjovi, *Une élection libre en Afrique: La presidentielle du Bénin (1996),* 13.

33. "Rapport-Général de la Conférence (presenté par M. Albert Tevoedjre, rapporteur-général)," in *La Nation,* 53. (My translation.)

34. Robinson, "The National Conference Phenomenon," 577–578.

35. Eboussi Boulaga, *Les conférences nationales,* 14. My translation.

36. The discussion in this and the following four paragraphs are based on Jennifer Seely's doctoral dissertation, "Transitions to Democracy in Comparative Perspective: The National Conference in Benin and Togo."

37. Jennifer Widner reminds us that much of Côte d'Ivoire's associational activity was subsumed under national syndicates operating under official aegis or that of the all-powerful Parti Démocratique de la Côte d'Ivoire (PDCI). Houphouët-Boigny occasionally consulted the syndicates' leaders during his "days of dialogue." One exception, notes Widner, was the transporters (Widner, "Political Reform in Anglophone and Francophone Africa," 64–66). Gbagbo even wrote a book challenging Le Vieux *(Le Côte d'Ivoire: Pour une alternative démocratique).* When a Gbagbo lecture was canceled by authorities, student strikes followed, and the speaker was forced to flee the country. The first officially sanctioned farmer's syndicate, the Syndicat National des Agriculteurs de Côte d'Ivoire (SYNAGCI) began operating in 1991; eventually its leaders joined the chorus of those seeking political reform. For details, see Widner, "The Rise of Civic Associations Among Farmers in Côte d'Ivoire."

38. "Le sursaut du PDCI."

39. "La Côte d'Ivoire, rejet du modèle, retour du réel" (Ivory Coast, Rejection of the Model, Return to Reality).

40. For details see Takougang and Krieger, *African State and Society in the 1990s: Cameroon's Political Crossroads;* and Mehler, "Cameroun: Une transition qui n'a pas eu lieu" (Cameroon: A Transition that Didn't Happen).

41. The somewhat jaundiced view of these developments is Verschave's *Noir Silence: Qui arrêtera la Françafrique?* 222–231. The CAR section of Verschave's account is subtitled "Centre à fric," a colloquial French wordplay on the name Centrafrique meaning "the boodle, or illicit money, center."

42. Richard Joseph comments on the apparent democratic conversions of rulers such as Kérékou, Eyadéma, Ali Saibou, Ratsiraka, and Blaise Compaoré, reinforcing the generally accepted view that they changed political coloration for tactical and strategic reasons, by and large to save their own political skins

("Democratization in Africa After 1999: Comparative and Theoretical Perspectives," 250–252). Given Patassé's own checkered past and his well-documented sycophancy of the imperial (and preimperial) Bokassa, it is difficult to take his democratic professions seriously. Though Patassé was briefly imprisoned prior to Bokassa's overthrow, Bernard Loubat claims the former prime minister was passed over in favor of David Dacko when the French were seeking replacement for Bokassa just before Operation Barracuda removed him in 1979 (*L'ogre de Berengo: "Bokassa m'a dit,"* 24.)

43. See also Wiseman, *Democracy in Black Africa: Survival and Revival,* 157–164; and Leymarie, "Gendarmes et voleurs en Centrafrique" (Policemen and Thieves in Centrafrique), 5–6. No one appears to have a good word for Kolingba, least of all Roger Delpey, a French journalist who claims to have been victimized by the French government because of his close relationship to Bokassa. Delpey argues that as former French president Giscard-d'Estaing was brought down because he got too close to Bokassa, so could François Mitterand be brought down for his support of Kolingba. Delpey's book on the Kolingba-Mitterand link is *Affaires Centrafricaines: Quand Centrafrique bougera, l'Afrique explosera* (Central African Affairs: When the CAR Moves, Africa Will Explode).

44. Raynal, "La démocratie au Niger: Chronique inachevée d'un accouchement difficile" (Democracy in Niger: Incomplete Chronicle of a Difficult Birth), 362n1. My translation.

45. The Malian story to 1988 is well told in Imperato, *Mali: A Search for Direction;* subsequent key sources include Diarrah, *Vers la troisième République du Mali;* Vengroff, "Governance and the Transition to Democracy: Political Parties and the Party System in Mali"; Nzouankeu, "La transition démocratique au Mali"; and "Le Mali, la transition." See also Docking, "Mali: The Roots of Democracy's 'Success.'"

46. The Senegalese progression to full democracy has been exceptionally well documented. The more important references of that development include the following: Fatton, *The Making of a Liberal Democracy: Senegal's Passive Revolution, 1875–1985;* Coulon, "Senegal: the Development and Fragility of a Semidemocracy"; Vengroff and Creevey, "Senegal: Evolution of a Quasi Democracy"; and M'Baye, "Alternance historique dans l'ex-pré carré français: Au Sénégal, les chantiers du changement." *Le Soleil en ligne* in 1998 carried an excellent dossier, "La vie parlementaire et son évolution au Sénégal d'hier à aujourd'hui."

47. The larger issues of democratic transitions in Africa and the role of the founding elections are discussed at length in Bratton and van de Walle, *Democratic Experiments in Africa: Regime Transitions in Comparative Perspective.* Raynal, "La démocratie au Niger," brings the Niger story to the opening of the national conference in 1993; for an excellent discussion of the politics of the conference and of the country during the early 1990s, see Gervais, "Niger: Regime Change, Economic Crisis, and Perpetuation of Privilege." See also Pierre Englebert's detailed recent history of Niger in *Africa South of the Sahara 1996;* and Decoudras and Gazibo, "Niger: Démocratie ambigue, chronique d'un coup d'état annoncé." There is also a very extensive literature on Congo-Brazzaville's political odyssey, including its attempt to democratize. The best source for that story is Bazenguissa-Ganga's impressive thesis, published as *Les voies du politique au Congo;* it includes detailed commentary on Congo-Brazzaville's national conference. An excellent, detailed analysis of the violent conflicts of 1997 is to be found in "Dossier spécial: Congo-Brazzaville, entre guerre et paix." Also valuable is the 1999 joint report of the

International Federation of Human Rights Leagues and the Congolese Human Rights Observatory, "Congo Brazzaville, 'L'arbitraire de l'état, la terreur des milices'" (Arbitrariness of the State, Terror of the Militias).

48. Bazenguissa-Ganga evokes not only Benin's SNC, but also the French 1789 model: "The debates of the Sovereign National Conference proceeded according to a model analogous to the 'society of ideas' [société de pensée] which controlled the French Revolution," a social mode in which the group "does not think: it talks," in effect, producing words creating ideology to be translated into action. (*Les voies du politique*, 383, my translation.) Without going into Bazenguissa-Ganga's reference to the "society of ideas," for me the interesting point of his observation is that like so many francophone African political analysts, he seems to have found reference to the Revolution of 1789 and the Third Estate irresistible. Not surprisingly, Sassou-Nguesso saw the SNC in a much different light. Emboldened by Benin's SNC and Mitterand's new policy line as announced in June 1990 at La Baule, Sassou bitterly accused his opponents of pulling off a "kind of political stunt" intended in the first instance not to promote democracy, but to bring him down. He was half right: the SNC was no stunt, but its organizers certainly intended to bring him down. (For Sassou-Nguesso's full argument see chapter 4, "Democracy's Price," in his autobiographical *The Mango-Tree, the River, and the Mouse*.)

49. Goldsmith, "Donors, Dictators, and Democrats in Africa," 418.

50. Bratton and van de Walle, *Democratic Experiments in Africa*, 175.

51. Sassou-Nguesso, *The Mango-Tree, the River, and the Mouse*, chapter 5, "Bitter Appraisal."

9

Rulers and Leaders

Everything depends on the temper of the chief. Naturally, when people learn that he is slightly diminished physically, that destabilizes the system. The courtiers begin to spin succession scenarios; the discontented begin to raise the tone [of their complaints]; and those who have been involved in pillaging [the state] become worried and look for ways to shelter their gains. All this creates a pernicious atmosphere which is not so much a consequence of [the leader's] illness, as it is of the fact that the system is highly personalized.[1]

Who Rules? Who Leads? Who Governs?

Since 1964, when Robert A. Dahl's pathbreaking study of New Haven, Connecticut, *Who Governs?* appeared, one of the key questions in political science has changed from "Who rules?"—that is, who occupies the formal positions of rulership—to "Who governs?"—that is, who *in fact* rather than simply officially—makes the important political decisions affecting governments, states, citizens, and peoples. The different meaning of the new question took the analysis of political leadership beyond the classic focus on those acting within the ambit of official positions, that is, those in positions defined by laws, constitutions, sets of rules, and the like, including monarchs, presidents, prime ministers, governors, and various other top officials.

Although, as Robert Jackson and Carl Rosberg argue, in most of sub-Saharan Africa personal rule—by "prince, autocrat, prophet, and tyrant"—predominates,[2] the point remains that the old answers no longer suffice and that it may turn out that more than one person is in charge, that power is shared or exercised by a collective or corporate group (a military junta, for example), or that someone other than the formal officeholder is actually in charge (recall Delavignette's "straw chief"). Sometimes it is the case that because of special circumstances so-called influentials, or *éminences grises,*—people formally in the lower official ranks or without formal office—are considered more powerful that those on the top official rungs. For example, during the 1960s the khalif-general of Senegal's Mouride brotherhood, Falilou M'Backé, was considered by many to be more powerful than all the president's ministers, and second only to Senghor in national influence.[3] Carrying the question, and the answer, even further, Cameroonian political scientist Pierre Flambeau Ngayap, in his study, *Cameroun: Qui gouverne?* posited a relatively small Cameroonian "ruling class" (a *classe dirigeante*) of 950, including public officials, legislators, party officials, police and military officers, and intellectuals, as well as directors and employers in the private, public, and "parapublic" economic sectors.[4]

Then there are some observers of francophone Africa, notably Stephen Smith and Antoine Glaser, who make the case that beyond particular African "ruling classes" or rulers, a group of rich and influential French entrepreneurs and officials around the French presidency—whom Smith and Glaser style collectively as *ces messieurs Afrique* ("these Africa gentlemen")—exercised an inordinate amount of influence on the national politics of our fourteen states from the 1950s to the beginning of the 1990s.[5] Finally, at another end of the analytic spectrum are the neo-Marxist, even Gramscian arguments that point to the activities of "hegemonic," even "predatory" or "criminal" African ruling classes, a view reflected in the work of Jean-François Bayart (also regarding Cameroon) and Robert Fatton Jr., among others.[6]

To inquire "Who rules?" then, is to pose an empirical question requiring more than the matching of people with formal, official positions. Not only must the question be asked separately of each system under consideration, but it must be rephrased as "Who governs?" to take account of influentials such as autonomous power magnates, traditional rulers with national constituencies, and other leaders capable of exercising "unit vetoes" or of critically affecting decisions and initiatives of those in official positions. That said, it remains that personal rule as defined by Jackson and Rosberg is still the most common form of rulership in our fourteen states; moreover, it is also the fact that a personal ruler tends to occupy the top official position, whether he is called head of state, president, prime minister (where the head of state is a figurehead or that role is purely ceremonial), head of government, or leader or chairman of a military junta. The lists in Appendices I and J mainly comprise these personal rulers (with the exceptions noted), and the analysis in this chapter focuses on them and the nature of their rule.

The exceptions must also be given their due here; they include the few chosen in democratic elections (such as Nicéphore Soglo and the reformed Mathieu Kérékou in Benin, Alpha Oumar Konaré and Amadou Toumani Touré in Mali, Mahamane Ousmane and Mamadou Tandja in Niger, Pascal

Lissouba in Congo-Brazzaville, and Abdoulaye Wade in Senegal) and those who have held office at the sufferance of others, as well as the less frequent cases in which rulership is shared by a military junta. There are also a very few recent instances of succession through democratic elections in our fourteen francophone states, in addition to those in South Africa, Botswana, Zambia, Kenya, Tanzania, Malawi, Nigeria, Ghana, Mauritius, and Madagascar: Abdou Diouf to Wade in Senegal in 2000, Nicéphore Soglo to Kérékou in Benin in 1996, Mahamane Ousmane to Tandja in Niger in 1999, and Konaré to Amadou Toumani Touré in Mali in 2002.

Machiavelli's Prince and Francophone African Rulers

I think it likely that Machiavelli would have recognized as kindred spirits many of the rulers and leaders of francophone Africa—though not always approvingly. With some conspicuous exceptions, these heads of state or government practiced, in the style and performance of their roles, that pragmatic behavior, justified as necessary for reasons of state, that Machiavelli advocated as the means whereby his prince should protect and advance his power, overcome his adversaries, and maintain the state he ruled.

Our fourteen states produced no truly exemplary rulers, though Senegal's Léopold Sédar Senghor—constitutional rhetorician, poet, essayist, philosopher, ideologist, *agregé,* member of the Academie Française, skilled diplomatist, and pragmatic politician—came as close as any. Several (Sékou Touré in Guinea, Modibo Keita in Mali, Thomas Sankara in Burkina Faso) developed, by virtue of their talents or force of personality, enthusiastic, even worshipful followings, earning the description charismatic early in their careers. Charisma, however, only lasts as long as the charismatic bond between leader and followers endures. Toward the end of his rule, Sékou Touré, seized by deadly paranoia, had become a hated and fearsome figure to his former followers; Modibo became a petty tyrant and Sankara a depleted ideologue, though the latter's assassination did preserve some of his aura. Another leader whose charismatic aura was preserved by his death was Congo-Brazzaville's *marxisant* military ruler Marien Ngouabi, who was most likely assassinated in 1977 by his closest associates; his aura arguably shone more brightly posthumously than before because his successors used it to legitimize their own rule.

Sometimes, if a charismatic relationship does not develop between a leader and his followers, then attempts are made to manufacture such a relationship by means of propaganda. Apparently the reverential reference Le Vieux ("the venerable one") was not deemed sufficiently inspiring by Houphouët-Boigny's official praise-singers, so they sought to inflate him to the rank of world-class thinker:[7]

Houphouët has truly become the sage of the world, a symbol, a legend; . . . he dared attack the bimillennial myth that the powerful are entitled to rule over the weak, the rich over the poor, both of which [ideas] generate injustice. . . . In him is united all the latent forces of the African continent's hereditary substance. . . . By extending Kant's thought, "Houphouëtism" links the nobility of a system [of philosophy] to an orientation and [system] of thought. . . . He understood how to make political honey from the pollen of theory. . . . [Houphouëtism is an ideology] halfway between [those] of the anarchic democracies and the "peoples" democracies . . . creating membership to avoid demanding obedience, . . . motivating people to work rather than imposing schedules.

While it is highly unlikely that anyone in the country, including the author of these lines, saw Houphouët-Boigny in that special light, we do know that he was feared by his enemies, courted by the French, and respected, if not loved, by most Ivoirians, a combination sufficiently potent to help keep him in power until his death.

At all events, most francophone African rulers tended to be relatively colorless as personalities, memorable only for excesses (if there were any) in their public or private lives or for the manner in which they clung to power or entered or left their high positions. They range from the dull but guileful, like Cameroon's Ahmadou Ahidjo and Senegal's Abdou Diouf, to the military nonentities that populated the 1978–1984 period in Mauritania, to Benin's surprising Kérékou, the military tyrant ostensibly turned democrat. The Central African Republic's Jean-Bédel Bokassa, of course, rose entirely out of the normal range, having elevated himself from colonel when he first took power on New Year's Eve 1965–1966, all the way to emperor in 1977, complete with ersatz imperial trappings and court.

According to the Machiavellian criterion of survival, of course, relatively few francophone rulers could be counted as completely successful. Among the sixty-seven rulers of our fourteen states, between 1958 and the end of 2003, long-term survival through a combination of craftiness, coercion, and the intelligent manipulation of people, circumstances, and resources was something accomplished only by Côte d'Ivoire's Houphouët-Boigny (thirty-six years, eight months), Senegal's Senghor (twenty-one years), Cameroon's Ahidjo (twenty-three years) and Paul Biya (over twenty years), Togo's Gnassingbé Eyadéma and Gabon's Omar Bongo (both thirty-six years by mid-2003), and Benin's Mathieu Kérékou (eighteen years, four months). Houphouët-Boigny, in power from 1959 to 1993, died in office of natural causes, a combination of circumstances relatively rare in Africa.[8] (Léon M'ba, Gabon's first president, also died of natural causes in 1967, as did Guinea's Sékou Touré in 1984.)

Nicéphore Soglo (Benin 1991–1996), Konaré (Mali, 1992–2002), Senghor (Senegal, 1960–1981), Abdou Diouf (Senegal, 1981–2000), and Ahidjo (1959–1982) all voluntarily and peacefully transferred power, a feat accomplished only six other times in sub-Saharan Africa, 1957–2003. (Senghor hand-picked Diouf, and Ahidjo picked Biya. In the latter case Ahidjo apparently tried, and failed, to return to power in 1983 and 1984. Diouf left office quietly and with dignity after losing the March 2000 runoff presidential elections to Abdoulaye Wade.) Eyadéma, who took full power in 1967, some four years after killing Togo's first president (Sylvanus Olympio), and Bongo, who succeeded M'ba in 1967, were both still in office by midyear 2003, and barring assassination, coup, or sudden fatal illness or accident, both will in all probability remain so for several more years. Bongo, who won his latest term in 1998 in a sham election, announced in March 2000 that he intended to stay in power until his current seven-year term expires in 2005.

Benin's Mathieu Kérékou came to power in 1972 via a coup d'état and remained in power for over eighteen years until 1991, when the Benin national conference forced him out of office. He then reconfigured himself from military dictator to democratic politician, and when he ran in the 1996 presidential election, he surprisingly won. Finally, four military dictators were still in power by the end of 2003 (Burkina Faso's Blaise Compaoré, since 1987; Chad's Idriss Déby, since 1990; Guinea's Lansana Conté, since 1984; and Mauritania's Maaouya Ould Sidi Ahmed Taya, since 1984), if only because they were crafty and brutal enough in their use of power to survive.

Congo-Brazzaville's Denis Sassou-Nguesso, an accomplished author and political survivor, deserves special mention. He took power by coup in 1979, then held on to office for almost fourteen years, as much by guile as by force, then had to relinquish it to Congo-Brazzaville's 1993 national conference. His democratically elected successor, Lissouba, was unable to contain the ambitions of his several military- and ethnic-based rivals, and in 1998, after a bloody twelve-month elimination contest, Lissouba was forced out by the eventual winner, Sassou-Nguesso. By the midyear 2003, Sassou-Nguesso's combined time in office had come to twenty-one years.[9] Return to power after a hiatus, whether that hiatus was forced or not, is not all that uncommon: in addition to Kérékou and Sassou-Nguesso, Madagascar's Didier Ratsiraka accomplished the feat. After having been forced to give up power in 1992 by a national forum, Ratsiraka, like Kérékou, transformed himself into a democrat and was reelected to the presidency in 1996. However, his attempt to gain yet another term in office went astray in 2002 when his principal opponent, Marc Ravalomanana, the mayor of Atananarivo, won a trial of strength. Ratsiraka, faced with an indictment for corruption and human rights violations, retired to the Seychelles. For the record, Benin's Christophe Soglo and Hubert Maga, the CAR's David Dacko, and Chad's Hissene Habré also returned to power after a hiatus.

Among the rest are several leaders—both civilians and military men—who held power for relatively long periods, but failed the peaceful survival test, fallen instead to military coups (Burkina Faso's Sangoulé Lamizana, after fifteen years; the CAR's Emperor Bokassa, after thirteen years; Chad's N'Garta (François) Tombalbaye, after fourteen years, eight months; Mali's Moussa Traoré, after twenty years, five months; Niger's Hamani Diori, after thirteen years, eight months; and Niger's Seyni Kountché, after fourteen years). Four of the military men (Lamizana, Bokassa, Traoré, and Kountché) ruled as dictators, and the civilians, Tombalbaye and Diori, became corrupt and tyrannical despite promising democratic beginnings in 1960. There is little question but that these rulers' excesses—including mass murder (Bokassa and Habré); gross corruption (Tombalbaye and Diori); and the use of widespread arbitrary arrests, imprisonment, and torture (Chad's Habré and various military regimes)—contributed to their downfall and that all of these leaders broke Machiavelli's rules that the wise prince carefully times and measures violence for its impact and avoids conspicuous display of wealth lest it arouse envy and resentment. On the other hand, Machiavelli does advise the prince to allow his subordinates to become wealthy because that ties them more closely to him—this strategy was pursued by Zaire's Mobutu Sese Seko and to a lesser extent by Togo's Eyadéma, who was able, at least until 1990, to buy the southern Ewes' political quiescence by allowing them unconstrained commercial leeway.

The rest of the rulers were in office for shorter periods and left power for a variety of reasons, including loss of election, rotation out by law, assassination, and coup d'état.

Seven leaders (out of the more than sixty listed in Appendix I) were assassinated during coups, usually by, or at the instigation of, their successors. The charge of fratricide, that he murdered his fellow officer and best friend Thomas Sankara, has continued to haunt Burkina Faso's Compaoré. Congo-Brazzaville's Ngouabi was almost certainly killed by his fellow officers. Credible eyewitness testimony and the assassin's own admission assigns the killing of Niger's Ibrahim Mainassara Barre in 1999 to Colonel Daouda Malam Wanke. The same is true of the shooting of Togo's Sylvanus Olympio by Eyadéma. Particular culpability is harder to assign in the killings of Chad's Tombalbaye, Mauritania's Ahmed Ould Bouceif, and Niger's Hamani Diori, though all died in the course of the military coups that removed them.

Most of the coups, some thirty-eight between 1963 and midyear 2003, required little more than a show of superior force to be successful. In fact, save for the occasional palace coup (which was more the rule than the exception in Mauritania), the usual coup followed what became an almost standard template for coups in Africa: seizure of the presidential palace and arrest or other removal of the president and his cabinet, then capture of the capital's airport and radio station, from which the successful coup makers announce the fall of the previous "tyrannical" and "corrupt" regime and proclaim a new "revolution" and a better, cleaner, and genuinely reformist government.[10]

More often than not, a successful coup is followed by a public holiday during which the people are encouraged to express their jubilation, and often soon thereafter the previous leaders, unless they have managed to flee the country, are condemned, tried, and punished. The bloody coup that overthrew the Tombalbaye regime in 1975, during which perhaps six hundred soldiers and civilians were killed or wounded, and the 1998–1999 mini–civil war that devastated Congo-Brazzaville and left Brazzaville in ruins were exceptional for the casualties produced, as was the failed coup attempt against Biya by Cameroon's presidential guard in 1984, in which up to a thousand people, mostly civilians, were killed or wounded during the loyal army's mopping-up operations in the capital, Yaoundé. Also exceptional was the case of Chad's Habré, who fled to Senegal after he was toppled from power in 1990. In March 2000 Habré became the first African ex-dictator to be charged with crimes against humanity; in July of that year, however, the Senegalese court before which he was to have been tried dismissed the charges, claiming that it had no jurisdiction because the alleged crimes were committed outside Senegal and that the case was international in scope.

Over the years fewer and fewer coups throughout the continent have been styled revolutions by their authors, and what had been almost obligatory postcoup public jubilation diminished in enthusiasm and levels of participation so that by the late 1980s people tended to stay at home rather than turn out to cheer the newest set of military rulers—unless, of course, they'd been ordered to celebrate. It is not difficult to understand why this should be the case. For one thing, the most recent military coup makers have not been ideologically motivated and thus have tended to explain their coups in utilitarian terms rather than to proclaim them movements of national liberation. For another, repeated or cascading coups (six in Benin, six in Burkina Faso, five in Chad, six in Congo-Brazzaville, six in Mauritania) appear to have engendered considerable public cynicism and to have blunted any residual enthusiasm for new governments. There has also been a noticeable increase in the levels of violence accompanying coups and mutinies, so prudence dictates staying at home until the smoke has cleared. Thus it is that postcoup jubilation has been nearly replaced by ennui, dread, or the general cynicism about politics increasingly found among African publics everywhere.

Machiavelli's ironfisted but pragmatic prince provides a generally useful—if cynical—standard for assessing the performance of our fourteen states' rulers, in particular by helping us understand one critical feature of their rulership: that except in the case of the democratic regimes, the prince tends to be a personal ruler with plenary powers. Most postindependence rulerships in Africa usually also operate as patrimonial systems, with all that that entails for decisionmaking and the distribution of political goods. In our fourteen states rulerships have combined personal with pragmatic elements so that very few fall into extremes of either psychopathic personal rule (as exemplified by Bokassa, Maçias Nguéma, and Idi Amin) or pragmatic ineptitude (of which Ghana's prime minister Kofi Busia, 1969–1972, is the exemplar).

Dictatorships, Personal Rule, and Patrimonial Rule

It should be understood from the outset that even the worst of the African tyrannies—the "personal dictatorships" of the CAR's Bokassa, Uganda's Amin, and Equatorial Guinea's Nguéma, described by Samuel Decalo in his *Psychoses of Power*[11]—could neither have operated by themselves nor committed the atrocities with which they have been charged without a corps of willing henchmen. Not surprisingly, these helpers were largely people whom the dictator thought he could trust above all others; they were usually recruited from his family, village, clan, ethnic group, and other close groups of associates. Whether benign or malevolent, personal rulerships are usually structured with the ruler in the figurative center, surrounded by a close coterie, inner circle, clique, or oligarchy of supportive figures who are willing to carry out his wishes and through whom the reins of his power pass. In our fourteen states the extent to which the inner circle mediates, circumscribes, or even restrains the power of the ruler depends on a variety of factors, including the degree to which the ruler owes his power to the inner circle and whether that circle contains relatively autonomous actors or represents powerful constituencies in the country at large. In any event, it all evokes the metaphor of the augmented, or extended, family or, in practice, patrimonial leadership.[12] This is the world of the Saudi royal family, Lebanon's political clans, Latin America's familial narcotics cartels, the Japanese Yakusa, and the leading Italian Mafia families, all circles of relationship in which fictive consanguinity weighs as much as the real thing.

Thus it was that Bokassa ruled largely with the aid of his Mbaika coethnics, who were heavily represented in his cabinet, his imperial entourage, and his security apparatus. He may well have understood, probably unconsciously, his symbolic role at the apex of his own patrimonial system: after he made himself emperor, he benevolently permitted his closest associates to call him Papa.

In Cameroon Ahmadou Ahidjo, despite practicing a calculated "ethnic balance" (*dosage*, in French) in composing his cabinets, relied most heavily on a group of coethnic "northern barons" (power brokers, magnates, chiefs, and politicians from the country's mainly Fulani north) to maintain his power. When Biya, a Beti-Bulu and a Christian from the south, succeeded Ahidjo, the new president's closest associates, not surprisingly, turned out to be a group of southern barons, of which the most trusted were also Beti and Bulu.

In Chad Tombalbaye's reliance on his mainly coethnic Sara inner circle became even greater after 1973, when he proclaimed that as part of his "cultural revolution" and "authenticity" campaign, all adult male government officials and employees in the country must undergo Sara initiation rites. Déby, who took power in Chad from Habré in 1990, relies heavily on his northern Zaghawa clan as his main power base.

The general pattern repeats itself with more or less fidelity across the francophone leadership spectrum, with ruling oligarchies here and there including family members (e.g., those of Tombalbaye in Chad, Bongo in Gabon, and Sékou Touré in Guinea), close ideological allies (e.g., part of the shifting group around Sankara), and other *fidèles* such as security chiefs and expatriates with specialized functions (e.g., Bongo's French and Moroccan security chiefs and Senghor's long-serving—1963–1990—Jean Collin, French-born minister of finance, minister of the interior, secretary-general of government, and *numero deux* in his regime).[13] The inner circles of patrimonial rule also contained the occasional *éminence grise* or *démi-grise* such as Jean Fochivé, internal security chief to both Ahidjo and Biya in Cameroon; Collin in Senegal; and the members of Bongo's shadowy "Clan des Gabonais."[14] Overall, however, though the presence of some extremely powerful people operating behind or partly behind the scenes should not be discounted, their influence has probably been overrated: the almost constant internal feuding that characterizes patrimonial leadership more often than not targets and frequently neutralizes those who get too close to the ruler.

It is also characteristic of patrimonial rule, particularly in Africa, that the ruling "family" organizes the distribution of political goods, including the financial and political spoils of office, so as to reward its *fidèles* and punish its enemies; sometimes this occurs to the extent of criminalizing the state or turning its elite into a kind of mafia. Among the most egregious practitioners of criminal patrimonialism have been the Bongo clan in Gabon, the old Houphouët-Boigny coterie in Côte d'Ivoire, and Ahidjo's "northern barons" and Biya's "Beti barons" in Cameroon. Such examples of unchecked criminal consumption often serve to whet the appetites of civilian and military aspirants to power who are anxious for their "turn at the table."[15]

This pattern of patrimonial leadership can also be found in military regimes that usually at first consist of conspiratorial elites come to power.

Almost by definition, successful military conspirators will at least initially be a relatively close-knit group, since one of the requirements of a successful coup is that the conspirators so trust one another that they are able to act in concert. The danger of failure, which entails the very real possibility of courts-martial and firing squads, tends to draw them even more closely together.[16] They are, then, brothers in arms in more ways than by simple *esprit de corps,* and that tends to carry over in the composition of military and military-dominated governments—again, at least initially. The almost obligatory, and by now standard, group photograph of a new military government is intended to project an image of stern unity and purpose: a muster of two, perhaps three ranks of erect, determined-looking, unsmiling officers (and sometimes noncommissioned officers as well) in identical battle or dress uniforms, with the leader or leaders of the junta front row, center.

The group usually gives itself a name that speaks to its collective identity and purposes; it calls itself not *government* or *regime,* but often *Council,* as in the Reconciliation Council of Major Daouda Malam Wanke, which took power immediately after Niger's president Mainassara, himself a former military officer, was assassinated on April 9, 1999. The junta led by General Robert Gueï (then chief of the general staff), which took power in Côte d'Ivoire on December 24, 1999, ran true to form: reaching into French revolutionary history, it promptly named itself the Comité National de Salut Public (CNSP—National Committee of Public Safety), proclaiming that it was only a *gouvernement de transition,* a crisis regime in office reluctantly and provisionally only until a new civilian government could take over in late 2000.[17] (Gueï was truer to his word than he probably wished to be: he was forced to flee Abidjan by a popular revolt on October 22, 2000, following his defeat at the polls and his attempt to declare himself the winner. He later returned to Abidjan, where he and his wife were assassinated gangland style in September 2002 during yet another attempted coup, probably by a loyalist (i.e., pro-Gbagbo) death squad.

Soldiers in Power

It is clear from watching soldiers take, hold, and exercise power in Africa that when in office they tend to perform much like civilian leaders in most things: they often operate personalist or patrimonial regimes, they can be as corrupt or inept as civilian rulers, they are as likely to turn to dictatorial methods, and their claims to the contrary notwithstanding, they do not necessarily manage the state more efficiently or productively. When it comes to policies, those formulated by soldiers are no more wise or beneficent or rational or effective than those promulgated by civilians. Nor, on the other hand, are military rulers necessarily any more tyrannical or duplicitous or stupid in office than their civilian counterparts. Where they do differ from civilian rulers, however, they do so significantly.

First, the fact that they come to power by means of the gun, not the ballot box, makes all the difference in the way they rule because they can command obedience with their guns and are hence accountable only to themselves. Then, as Mensah Adinkrah convincingly demonstrates, because they are trained to be specialists in violence, they tend to resort to violence as a labor-saving and cost-effective way of solving problems.[18] It may well be the case that many, if not most military coups in Africa can be explained by Thomas Hobbes's famous punning, card-playing axiom that "in the matter of government, when nothing else is turn'd up, clubs are trumps."[19] In effect, says Hobbes, when you have guns, and other solutions to your problems are not available, violence and the guns themselves may appear as the readiest resort. Besides, if Mao Zedong is correct, the most direct route to power is through the barrel of a gun.

At least some of the first generation of military coups in Africa, including those in our fourteen states, may be seen as well-meaning responses to the mismanagement, corruption, and performance failures of the first postindependence regimes they replaced. At least this is what the rhetoric of the first wave of military coup makers would have us believe: that they acted out of a sense of duty to the nation to rescue the national patrimony, to sweep aside corrupt or hopelessly inept governments, to restore pride and honest, effective governance. (A Voltaic lieutenant colonel, in a letter to me, even invoked classical Greek mythology to justify the first coup, in January 1966: he wrote of the Herculean task of "cleaning out the Voltaic Augean Stables.")[20] Once the stables were cleaned out, they usually promised to find the civilian *hommes valables* (good and true men) to whom the keys of executive power could soon be returned. Thus it was, with the militaries seemingly using the same default script, that a cascade of coups brought down the independence regimes in Togo (1963), Dahomey (1963), Congo-Brazzaville (1963), Upper Volta (1966), CAR (1966), Mali (1968), Niger (1974), Chad (1975), and Mauritania (1978).

Admittedly, the face of self-righteousness that the francophone militaries presented to the world after the first round of coups had some credibility in Congo-Brazzaville, Dahomey, Mali, and Niger, where the independence regimes had forfeited all semblance of legitimacy, whether through exemplary mismanagement, corruption at the top, repeated policy failures, or sheer ineptitude. In the eyes of most citizens of these countries, the coups were fully justified and the coup makers' explanations eminently believable. For example, in Congo-Brazzaville, the Abbé Foulbert Youlou ran a thoroughly venal and reactionary regime, in part by manipulating the complex ethnic and religious politics of the country to his own advantage and that of his Lari ethnic group, and in part by allowing French business and economic interests virtually free run of the country's resources. At the end of three days of massive demonstrations and strikes in August 1963, the army stepped in, removed Youlou, and installed a moderate socialist, Alphonse Massamba-Débat, in the presidency. Samuel Decalo observes that the demonstrations "bore a striking resemblance to the 1963 unionist-student upheaval that toppled Maga in Dahomey."[21] In both instances the military were taken at their word because they had no apparent political ambitions of their own and they claimed to have intervened only to prevent further violence and to restore order and good government.

As for the rest of the first wave of coups, the picture becomes much less clear on closer inspection, and the militaries' explanations begin to lose credibility as their behavior begins to reveal personal agendas, hypocrisy, or self-serving cynicism. Three examples, may suffice to make the case:

First, Togo's Eyadéma has always maintained that the January 1963 coup was needed to save Togo from economic ruin, ethnic discord, and the disastrous policies of the Sylvanus Olympio regime. The death of Olympio, Togo's first president, is always officially portrayed as accidental, the result of shots fired in the dark by one of the rebels as Olympio tried to climb a wall into the U.S. embassy.[22] In fact, the coup had little to with Togo's economy or Olympio's policies and everything to do with Olympio's refusal to integrate Eyadéma and the other three hundred demobilized Kabré veterans of France's colonial army into Togo's small (250-man) army. As described elsewhere, it was Eyadéma and several of his men who invaded the U.S. embassy's parking lot, dragged Olympio out from the car in which he was hiding, and shot him out in the street. Decalo cites a *West Africa* story (January 17, 1983) in which Eyadéma himself admits to killing Olympio, though the circumstances appear somewhat different.[23] At all events, the first version remains the official story, and it is one version of the general postcoup explanatory template. Needless to say Olympio's sons, Gilchrist and Bonito—and indeed, most ethnic Ewe in Togo—never bought the official story and remain determined to bring Eyadéma down if possible.

Second, there is the case of the first coup in Upper Volta, in January 1966. The regime of President Maurice Yaméogo was ousted by the Voltaic army not because Yaméogo was particularly tyrannical or corrupt (though he was later brought to trial for embezzlement), but because by the end of 1965 he had managed simultaneously to offend the chiefs and "emperor" of the Mossi ethnic group, the largest ethnic group in Upper Volta; the citizens and municipal authorities of Ouagadougou, who alleged government mis-appropriation of flood relief money provided by France plus punitive moves against the city's officials; the powerful trade unions because he had cut civil servants' salaries and had increased taxes; and the Church, in particular an outraged Cardinal Paul Zoungrana, because he, a nominal

Catholic, had packed his first his wife off to her native village, married an Ivoirian beauty queen, and taken a substantial part of the national treasury to pay for his honeymoon. Following tainted legislative elections in November, violent mass demonstrations led by the trade unions and students broke out at the end of 1965, and on January 3, 1966, the army, pressured by the rioters to take over, "assumed its responsibilities." Though the chief of staff, Lieutenant Colonel Sangoulé Lamizana, who headed the new junta, issued one version of the standard postcoup announcement, it was clear that the army had been reluctant to intervene and that Yaméogo's own moral obtuseness, combined with singular political ineptitude, had precipitated his fall as much as anything else.[24]

The third case is that of Bokassa's preemptive coup on New Year's Eve 1965. Bokassa claimed that he intervened to forestall a pro-Chinese coup by which the gendarmerie commandant, Jean Izamo, was to be installed as head of state, and to save the life of Dacko, the incumbent president and Bokassa's cousin. In fact, Dacko had been in trouble long before the coup: his domestic and foreign policies were in tatters, and his government faced bankruptcy because the Chinese, who had promised a substantial loan, had announced that they would pay in kind rather than in cash. The French, who sought to avert a leftist coup (such as the one in Congo-Brazzaville), conspired with Dacko to mount a charade-coup and install Izamo as head of state. Bokassa trumped them by arresting Izamo on New Year's Eve and taking power on January 1, 1966. "Rather than reveal its own machinations," writes Thomas O'Toole, "the French government remained neutral."[25] And not only had the Chinese reneged on their promise of aid, but also, through their embassy in Bangui, they had informally sponsored a ragtag guerrilla force with which, apparently, they hoped to mount their own leftist coup. Their principal collaborator was probably Jean-Christophe Nzallat, Dacko's *chef du cabinet politique* (principal political advisor), who was shot trying to flee the country.

At any rate, all of that also fell apart with Bokassa's preemptive strike.[26] Clearly, there was much more at work in the CAR in December 1965 than Bokassa was willing to admit. Above all, of course, there was the French plot, about which Bokassa remained mute because his silence could well guarantee French goodwill later on. He was right; the French embrace came within a year of his coup: France honored him for having been the most decorated African officer in its colonial army, and he was received by General Charles de Gaulle in November 1966. Subsequently he emerged as a close friend of French president Valéry Giscard-d'Estaing. He hosted Giscard on his private hunting preserve, and in 1976 the French government helped underwrite his imperial coronation. As for Bokassa's claim that he had struck in part to save Dacko's life, that was pure invention: while it is true that Dacko was in some danger when he tried to flee the country during the coup, once he was captured he was returned to Bangui, put under nominal house arrest, and later named a councilor to Bokassa's imperial court.

Because I have already told the last part of the Bokassa story, I need not reprise it here. However, a reminder of some of its extraordinary ironies is certainly appropriate at this point: in 1979, some thirteen years after Bokassa's coup, the French, embarrassed by his excesses, sent in paratroopers to chase him from his throne. The French also sent back Dacko with the *paras,* the same Dacko they had tried to force from power in 1965. And as the French subsequently learned to their chagrin, the price for supporting Bokassa proved higher than simply putting his cousin back in power. Rumor has it that they had to pay off Houphouët-Boigny to shelter Bokassa in Abidjan; when he had worn out that welcome, they had to put up with him and his family and retinue in a rented chateau near Paris; and when he tried to publish memoirs that further threatened the reputation of ex-president Giscard (and those of a number of Giscard's colleagues), they forced his publishers to stop printing more copies and had those already published consigned to the incinerators. I did see a pirated copy of the book, and I can confirm that Bokassa spared little malodorous detail in describing his relationship with the Giscard troupe.

Thus, although African military coup makers have almost universally presented themselves as selfless saviors of the national patrimony, very few, even among the ranks of the first wave of postindependence military rulers, qualify as such. This is not to say that neither devotion to duty nor a genuine sense of patriotism nor an honest belief that only the military could restore order ever played a role in the coups; these factors did sometimes play a role, perhaps more so in the early coups than in the later ones (Colonel Lamizana probably qualifies on all three counts.) In the other cases, however, all or part of the military gained a sense of its corporate interests and corporate capabilities, and unless it had been socialized to accept civilian supremacy, it sought power when those interests were threatened and the opportunity to intervene presented itself. Eyadéma certainly acted in part on behalf of his Kabré brothers in arms, and Bokassa in part to defend the army's interests against Dacko, Izamo's gendarmes, and the latter's French sponsors.

Once coup leaders are in power, more often than not the politics of the belly comes to the fore and military rulers and juntas frequently become as predatory and corrupt as their civilian or military predecessors. The behavior of successor military regimes (such as Compaoré's in Burkina Faso, for all its moral posturing and invocations of Sankara's memory) more often than not demonstrates that the new leaders are more interested in making the most of their time at the table than in pursuing national reconstruction. The clear evidence that Compaoré, along with President Charles Taylor in

Liberia, marketed—and profited from—diamonds mined illegally in areas under the control of Sierra Leone's rebel leader Foday Sankoh forcefully makes the point. Compaoré has also been implicated in the sales of diamonds illicitly mined by Angola's Jonas Savimbi and his UNITA guerrillas. Similarly, Guinea's Conté and his regime have been charged with profiting from the procurement of arms for Liberia's Taylor.[27]

A Portrait of Francophone Africa's Leaders

Who are these leaders, and what are their backgrounds, both as individuals and collectively?[28]

This portrait includes executive cabinets because they tend to contain individuals in the governing circle; it does not include parliaments, not because parliaments are not intrinsically interesting or politically significant, but because after the first decade of independence they increasingly became supernumerary appendages to the people at the top, losing such autonomy and legislative powers as they had enjoyed previously. In some instances they were also turned into prebendary pasturages or were kept on to provide symbolic legitimacy and adulatory choruses to the ruling clique or party (in Cameroon, Congo-Brazzaville, Gabon, Guinea, Côte d'Ivoire, Mauritania, Senegal), and sometimes they were simply dispensed with altogether (CAR, Chad, Benin, Mali, Niger, Togo, Burkina Faso).[29] It was not until the 1990s that, as part of the redemocratization phenomenon, francophone parliaments gained new life and real power, as they did in Benin, Mali, Niger, Congo-Brazzaville, and CAR.

The whole founding-father generation of francophone African leaders who led their countries to independence was not, its members' rhetoric notwithstanding, composed of fire-breathing revolutionaries, but of individuals more disposed to parlaying than to fighting. Even Sékou Touré, who offended de Gaulle to his face and persuaded Guinea to reject de Gaulle's 1958 constitution, later repented of his truculence and sought reconciliation with France. The founding fathers were almost all members of the political establishment, not outsiders seeking to wrest power from the colonial enemy by force. Among the ranks of the top leaders of our fourteen countries (presidents, vice presidents, prime ministers, and the like), there was not one who could claim to have spent hard time in a colonial prison for a political offense, and indeed, for the most part they had already occupied official positions, having served as nominal premiers, members of executive councils, elected deputies to local or French legislatures, and so on during the preindependence period.

Paradoxically, it was Houphouët-Boigny, confirmed Francophile, deputy to the French National Assembly, leader of the Rassemblement Démocratique Africain (RDA), and, later, good friend of France and French presidents, who came closest to being arrested, and that in connection with the riots and demonstrations in Abidjan in 1950 that took three lives.[30] At all events, dramatic circumstances of the kind in which Kwame Nkrumah was called to power from a Gold Coast prison cell never arose in our fourteen countries, and except in Cameroon, the transition to independence was accomplished smoothly, without violence, and under terms negotiated by the founding fathers and the French government. Appendix K provides information about this group's key members' occupational and political backgrounds.

While Appendix K gives prominence to those members of the founding-father generation who assumed their countries' top official positions at independence, the table does not include an important number of that cohort who played key roles in moving their countries to independence, in posting and advancing the nationalist agenda, in challenging French hegemony, and in creating the political parties, movements, and organizations out of which the postindependence associational mix was formed. Some of this latter group were active much earlier, and some during the late 1940s and the decade of the 1950s. These leaders should be considered part of the founding-father generation, if not by chronological delimitation, then by virtue of their achievements, so at least some of the most prominent of this latter group should be remembered at this point:

Senegal: Blaise Diagne, Lamine Guèye, Abdoulaye Diop, Gabriel d'Arboussier
Mali/Soudan/Upper Volta: Fily Dabo Sissoko, Joseph Conombo, Amadou Hampaté Bâ, Ouezzin Coulibaly, Mamadou Konaté
Dahomey: Emile Derlin Zinsou, Paul Hazoumé
Gabon: Jean-Hilaire Aubame
Guinea: Yacine Diallo, Saifoulaye Diallo
Cameroon: Alexandre Douala Manga Bell, André-Marie Mbida, Reuben Um Nyobe, Louis-Paul Aujoulat
Moyen-Congo: Jean-Félix Tchicaya, Félix Eboué, Jacques Opangault, Stéphane Tchichellé

Some members of this group were also involved in the two 1946 French constituent assemblies (Tchicaya, Guèye, Yacine Diallo, Ouezzin Coulibaly, d'Arboussier); helped found the RDA and its offshoots (Ouezzin Coulibaly, d'Arboussier, Tchicaya, Um Nyobe); sat in the French National Assembly or in the assemblies of the French Union or French Community (Aujoulat, Saifoulaye Diallo, Yacine Diallo, Ouezzin Coulibaly, Conombo, Aubame, Zinsou, Manga Bell, Mbida, Diagne, Guèye, d'Arboussier); or were members of colonial governing councils and French governments (Conombo, Saifoulaye Diallo, Aubame, Opangault, Tchichellé, Mbida,

Eboué, d'Arboussier). Hazoumé and Um Nyobe are included in this list because of their catalytic roles in the prewar and postwar opposition to French rule: Hazoumé as a teacher, anthropologist, novelist, and colleague of Louis Hunkanrin (Hunkanrin was imprisoned for his verbal attacks on the colonial administration); and Um Nyobe as founder of Cameroon's RDA affiliate and leader of the UPC revolt against French rule. Um Nyobe later led a revolt against the regime of Ahidjo.

The founding fathers of our fourteen states had been involved in politics for an average of thirteen years prior to independence; only three had come late to politics, Dacko (CAR, three years before independence), Youlou (Congo-Brazzaville, four years), and Moktar Ould Daddah (Mauritania, three years). The average age of the founding fathers and their cabinet members was a relatively young forty-three at independence, and the leaders were relatively well educated: about a third had had some higher education, and about half had completed at least high school or the equivalent. The "old school tie" of the Ecole Normale William Ponty near Dakar (companion of the African School of Medicine and Pharmacy) recurs: thirty-one (16 percent) attended Wlliam Ponty; for most of these (twenty), the school provided terminal education. (William Ponty, it will be recalled, is renowned as one of the AOF-AEF's cradles of nationalism.)

Of the 193 top-level leaders and cabinet members counted in Appendix K, 134 had come to politics from government posts (fifty-nine had been civil servants; forty-two had been teachers; and thirty-three, including six veterinarians, had worked in public health). Eleven had worked in law, seven as lawyers and four as paralegals, and sixteen, including six businessmen and three farmers, had worked in the private economy. Seven were "traditional" chiefs; eight, trade union leaders; and seven, civil and other engineers. Clearly, government posts offered the best springboards to politics, since many of these jobs provided prestige, some power, and, most important, access to the voting public.

The public health category requires additional comment. In this category are fourteen physicians (with French medical school degrees), and eight *médecins africains* (graduates of the African School of Medicine and Pharmacy in Dakar, whose skills and training approximated those of registered nurses in the United States). The latter group includes Houphouët-Boigny, who parlayed his reputation as a healer, his influence as a traditional chief, and his wealth and influence as a planter into a political career. It even appeared sometimes that doctors were valued far more as political prizes than for their medical expertise. The January 1961 Mali cabinet, an extreme example, contained no fewer than five medical doctors, and only one of them (Somine Dolo, minister of health) exercised functions having anything to do with public health.

The founding fathers' status as well-educated professionals and establishmentarians who used revolutionary rhetoric does not mean, of course, that they never had their active, even bitter disagreements with France and France's colonial establishment: many did, and several of the more important leaders came to the fore during periods of open confrontation with the French authorities. In Senegal it was the 1944 killing of veterans and the 1947 railway strike that helped turn Senghor and Guèye to nationalist politics; in Côte d'Ivoire it was the 1944 controversy over the use of forced labor that led Houphouët-Boigny to form his overtly political Syndicat Agricole Africain; and in Cameroon it was the 1945 strikes and demonstrations against the meeting of the extreme right-wing Etats-Généraux de la Colonisation Française that helped spark Cameroonian nationalism. The *marxisant* radicals of Senegal, Niger, and Cameroon excepted, the founding fathers successfully and peacefully negotiated the transition to independence, proving to be the kind of African *interlocuteurs valables* France had sought to help ease the pains of decolonization.

Though the founding fathers held sway during most of the first ten years after independence, the Togolese coup of 1963 began the cascade of succession events that transformed the fourteen states' leadership group. By 1974, of the 297 ministerial posts only twenty-two (7 percent) were occupied by members of the founding-father generation; even more significant, eight of the fourteen states had had military coups, which meant wholesale replacement at the top positions. There were also three relatively peaceful successions: Gabon's Bongo succeeded M'ba, who died in office in 1964, and in Cameroon in 1961 and 1972 top posts were reshuffled as that country moved in and out of a federal configuration.

Some fifteen years after independence the second largest pool for leadership recruitment (or, more often than not, self-recruitment) was the security forces, which provided 21.4 percent of all leaders and cabinet members. The civil service still provided 42 percent of leadership recruits, and education 12 percent. It is noteworthy that the successors, military men included, tended to be better educated than the founding fathers; 60 percent of the top leaders and cabinet members had attended university, and some of those had even had postgraduate schooling. Given the turnover after 1968 and the arrival of military men on the scene, one might expect the successors to have been substantially younger than the founding fathers were at independence; that was not the case: the successors' average age was 41.2 years in 1975.

By the end of the millennium, almost all of the founding fathers who had served as heads of state had died or had been forcibly retired in one way or another, and only a very few, like Senghor and Ahidjo, had left national politics voluntarily. None were left in power, but of the few who were still alive, one or two still lingered as shadows in the corridors of power. Senghor, rich in honors and still influential, survived into the new millennium (he died on December 22, 2001). Another old-time politician, Abdoulaye Wade, was elected president of Senegal in March 2000 at age seventy-four after more than half a lifetime of oppositional politics. Elsewhere on the continent almost all of the founding fathers of the 1960s and 1970s had also passed away, including such notable leaders as Julius Nyerere, Jomo Kenyatta, Kwame Nkrumah, and Hastings Banda.

The physical departure of the founding fathers sounded the death knell of civilian dominance in ten of our fourteen states: during most of the final twenty-five years of the twentieth century the military became the arbiters of power in Mauritania, Mali, Burkina Faso, Guinea, Benin, Togo, Niger, Chad, CAR, and Congo-Brazzaville, a circumstance reflecting the general trend toward the militarization of power on the continent. Conspicuous exceptions include some of the states involved in the democratization experiments of the 1990s; Robert Mugabe's Zimbabwe; post-Banda Malawi; post-Kaunda Zambia; Nigeria, where the heart attack of the military dictator Sani Abacha in 1998 fortuitously resulted in a return to democratic civilian politics; Kenya, where Daniel arap Moi bought off his military, stood off repeated opposition challenges, then finally ceded power to Mwai Kibaki, who won a landslide electoral victory in December 2002; and, of course, South Africa, which achieved civilian majority rule (in the 1994 elections) following the release of Nelson Mandela in 1990.

In several African states with ostensible civilian rule, the military have played key supportive or decisionmaking roles, making little attempt to conceal their involvement. Of our fourteen states, Cameroon offers the best example. In 1984 when Biya's presidential guard, instigated by ex-president Ahidjo, attempted a coup against him, it was the regular army that put down the rebellion and rescued Biya. He remains indebted to the army and to the security services, including, notably, his chief of staff, General Pierre Semengue. Whereas Ahidjo had been able to buy off his generals and colonels and keep his army tame for twenty-two years, since 1984 Biya has had to continuously monitor the military's political stake in the survival of himself and his regime. So far the partnership has worked, but if another crisis such as the one in 1984 erupts, all bets are off.

Taking Stock: The Leaders at the Turn of the Millennium

Forty-three years and six months after independence, none of the national leaders in our fourteen states could be styled *charismatic;* nor do any enjoy genuine popularity, much less generate popular excitement. The closest thing to excitement is the support given Senegal's Wade, who was elected on his own merits in a contest against an established leader, Abdou Diouf. In fact, those who have ruled with a significant degree of genuine public support, in addition to Wade, can be counted on the fingers of one hand:

Kérékou in Benin, Konaré and Mamadou Touré in Mali, and, perhaps, Mamadou Tandja in Niger. Had the wave of redemocratization successfully washed over Togo, Niger, CAR, Congo-Brazzaville, and Cameroon, the number of popularly elected leaders would have increased substantially, but by 2003 only two of the francophone countries where the wave originated, Benin and Mali, still had the genuine democracies it brought. In 1999 Niger chose Mamadou Tandja in an open election, thus retrieving some of its democratic credentials from the military, which had confiscated them in 1996. Major Daouda Malam Wanke had set the stage for the democratic restoration by staging a coup in which President Ibrahim Mainassara Barre was assassinated.

By midyear 2003 the military remained the principal arbiter of politics in eight of our fourteen states. It was still in firm control in Burkina Faso (Blaise Compaoré, since 1987), Chad (Idriss Déby since 1990), Mauritania (Taya, since 1984), and Togo (Eyadéma, since 1967). The military remained in charge also in Guinea, where Lansana Conté, a diabetic who probably has a diseased heart, contested the December 21, 2003, presidential election, which he (not surprisingly) won against Ahmadou Bhoye Barry, a virtual unknown put up to lend legitimacy to the electoral process.

In the CAR, Ange-Félix Patassé, freely elected after the 1993 national conference, managed to survive only by the sufferance of his army and with French and Libyan help. That help, and the army's sufferance, ended in March 2003 when the former army chief, General François Bozize, declared himself president and dissolved Parliament. Patassé, in exile in Togo, and like Chad's Habré, soon found himself the target of an international arrest warrant for crimes allegedly committed while he was president, including murder and theft. In Congo-Brazzaville Sassou-Nguesso, removed by the 1991 national conference, returned to power after winning a bloody free-for-all in 1998 but is still plagued by recurrent violence initiated by his various enemies. Finally, in Niger the military, which had sponsored two coups d'état after the 1991 national conference, also sponsored a presidential election in November 1999 in which a civilianized former general, Tandja, was elected. Tandja still had to contend with recurrent army mutinies well into August 2002.

Other than those confirmed by genuinely democratic elections (Wade, Kérékou, Konaré, Amadou Toumani Touré), the civilians who remained in office at midyear 2002 were there under questionable circumstances. Gbagbo and Tandja, for example, both owed their offices to military intervention, and Cameroon's Biya had created an authoritarian, personalist regime.

Seen against the larger backdrop of leadership change in sub-Saharan Africa, however, in the year 2003 the incumbents' regimes in francophone Africa were neither uniquely configured nor operating ruling systems much different from the norm. Three of our fourteen are democracies, which represents a net gain of two over the pre-1990 number. Elsewhere the democratic camp now includes Ghana, Nigeria, Malawi, Tanzania, Mozambique, Cape Verde, and, of course, South Africa; recently only Botswana, Senegal, Mauritius, and Gambia (before its 1994 coup) so qualified. The ranks of military rulers, thinned by the peaceful electoral departure of Jerry Rawlings in Ghana and Abacha's heart attack in Nigeria, now also include the leaders of regimes in Uganda, Guinea-Bissau, Rwanda, Burundi, Sudan, and Equatorial Guinea.

Since 1998 a new category of regime—the militarized civilian regime—has emerged as a transitional form between military and civilian rule. These are regimes that are ostensibly governed by civilians but operate with a very high level of military mobilization, activity often related to a recent or ongoing rebellion or war, recurrent coups, or widespread civil unrest. This category includes the regimes of Isaias Afewerki (Eritrea) and Meles Zenawi (Ethiopia), which were at war with each other in 1998–2000; those of Ahmad Tejan Kabbah (Sierra Leone) and interim head of state Gyude Bryant (Liberia), which were both under attack by rebels and until midyear 2003 at deadly odds with each other over rebel-related violence; the Democratic Republic of Congo, headed by Laurent Kabila and then, following his assassination, by his son Joseph, still embroiled in a civil and regional military conflict; Angola, just emerging from civil war following the death of Savimbi; and Sudan, still in the grip of its own seemingly interminable civil war. The closest to a militarized civilian regime in francophone Africa is Chad, with its recurrent northern-based military coups and rebellions, and paradoxically and distantly, democratic Senegal, still unable to quell the rebellion in its southern Casamance region.

Some of the other African civilian regimes are not much better off than the bureaucratic, hegemonic, personalist, and authoritarian regimes in Cameroon, Congo-Brazzaville, and the CAR. Moi of Kenya, until his departure in 2002, compared unfavorably with Cameroon's Biya, and it now turns out that at heart neither Eritrea's Afewerki nor Ethiopia's Zenawi was the democrat each claimed to be. Mugabe of Zambia, in the twilight of his career, has turned to mobilized xenophobic violence to hang on to power, and at midyear 2003 in Somalia and the Democratic Republic of Congo, anarchy remained the order of the day.

Three Predicaments of Rule:
Legitimacy, Food, and Succession

This chapter began with the assertion that most African regimes exercise variants of personal rule, as Jackson and Rosberg argue. This has certainly been the case with the military regimes, based as they are on a hierarchical command structure and despite their occasional resort to collective rule. Collective military rule, with a depersonalized junta speaking with the single oracular voice, just does not work, all good intentions notwithstanding. What begins as collective rule almost invariably turns into an elimination contest on the model of the Ethiopian Derg (with Major—later Colonel—Megistu Haile Mariam coming out on top in 1977) or a rough but less violent jostling at the table (as in the case of Mauritania and the emergence of Colonel Taya) or some other kind of internal contest whereby a single individual emerges to take the reins of power.

Civilian regimes are no more adept at collective rule than military ones. Imaginative schemes intended to balance ethnic or other collective interests, such as Dahomey's rotating presidency (designed for an initial 1970–1976 round), are ineffective. In 1972 Colonel Kérékou became impatient with the Maga-Ahomadegbe-Apithy biennial rotation and simply kicked out President Justin Ahomadegbe six months into the beginning of the second rotation and took power for himself and the army. And as the federal union between Mali and Senegal broke down in August 1960 with Modibo's attempted coup against Senghor, so did power-sharing arrangements between Senegal and Gambia (the Senegambian Federation, 1981–1988) and between anglophone and francophone Cameroon (the Cameroon Federation, 1960–1972).

The reasons for the breakdown of collective leadership, military or civilian, are obviously idiosyncratic to the particular situation, but they do appear to confirm the truth of an allegedly traditional francophone African saying often heard in West and Central Africa that: there can only be one crocodile in every pond *(un seul caiman dans chaque marigot)*. Though the choice of amphibian in the saying does suggest a Darwinesque survival of the fittest—or of the most predatory, which may amount to the same thing—the point is that whatever the *institutional* structures of rulership, and however they come into being, regimes tend to become personalist clusters. Thus, the figurative caiman, or crocodile, in Senegal turned out to be Senghor; in the Senegambian dispute, Abdou Diouf; in Benin, Kérékou; and in Cameroon, Ahidjo. And it is hardly accidental that regimes in Africa and elsewhere tend to be denominated by the names of their leaders—the Wade regime, the Biya regime, the Bongo regime, and so on. That being the case, of the many issues with which rulers have to contend, three are worth further discussion at this point: the question of legitimacy; the conundrum of the political economy of rule or, put more simply, of how to keep both the regime and the country fed; and the problem of succession.

Two recent books, one by Pierre Englebert, published in 2000, and the other by Michael G. Schatzberg, 2001, directly address the question of legitimacy in Africa, including our fourteen states.[31] They both remind us that, put simply, legitimacy has to do with eliciting the consent or, if that cannot be had, the acquiescence of the ruled to rulership. With it leaders can lead and rulers can rule because then those who are led or ruled follow more or less willingly. Although coercion (some of it egregious) is commonly, and apparently successfully, used by contemporary African regimes, it needs to be stressed that there is an almost inverse relationship between coercion and legitimacy, and it seems to be the case that rulers who consistently abuse their people find they have little legitimacy left to draw on when they need it. So it was when Kérékou, Mainassara, Sassou-Nguesso, and Ratsiraka needed the trust on which legitimacy rests: there was none to be found and each paid the political price accordingly.

Military rule, which by definition rests on the use or threat of coercion, also has its limitations; Napoleon is supposed to have observed that one can do almost anything with a bayonet except sit on it. Some military regimes come to power with popular approval, as has frequently been the case in Africa (in our fourteen states "popular" coups have occurred in Burkina Faso, Niger, Benin, Congo-Brazzaville, Côte d'Ivoire, Mauritania, Togo, Chad, and CAR). However, when popular approval and, with it, legitimacy begin to fade, military regimes often begin to share rule with civilians and eventually, if they manage to stay in power for a prolonged period, become civilianized themselves—a process the French style *embourgeoisement*.[32]

Thus Kérékou in Benin appears to have made a credible (at least to the Beninois) transition from soldier to civilian, as have ex-officers Ould Taya in Mauritania and Mamadou Tandja in Niger, not to speak of Olusegun Obasanjo in Nigeria. At first it also seemed that ex-admiral Ratsiraka in Madagascar had made such a transition, but given the results and aftermath of the 2002 presidential election (contested results and a near civil war, which Ratsiraka lost), his conversion may not have been complete or completely credible. More evidence of this is his hasty departure for Seychelles and a criminal suit charging him with various crimes, including provoking tribal hatred and civil war, brought before an official Malagache prosecutor in July 2003. In sum then, rulers who fail to attend to and replenish the store of legitimacy, however sparse, on which their regimes' power rests sooner or later get into political trouble.

How to avoid this erosion of legitimacy? One way, argues Schatzberg, is to tap into one of the moral matrices of legitimate governance, in which "the imagery of father, family, and food is culturally relevant and politically important, and . . . strikes a responsive chord throughout middle Africa." The president becomes "Father-Chief," a metaphor of "political paternity most fully elaborated in Côte d'Ivoire under Houphouët-Boigny, Zaïre under Mobutu, Cameroon under both Ahidjo and Biya."[33] Officials generously employed the term *founding fathers* to designate the leaders at independence, and the idea of family to describe the nation under its father-chief, or founding father. Both devices were evoked in order to confer legitimacy on the leader. Food in this context further enhances the father image: the father feeds the nation or, in any case, enables the people to be fed. Moreover, as the symbol of national well-being, he himself is expected to consume conspicuously, which may help explain the surprising tolerance throughout Africa for the extravagant consumption and corruption of leaders. (The point at which tolerated, legitimate "overeating" becomes wretched excess varies throughout the continent; we will touch on this in the discussion of corruption in Chapter 10.) Bayart's aptly named politics of the belly recognizes and responds to a political culture in which metaphors of food and eating describe both the structures of distributional politics and the ethical parameters of legitimate leadership.

There is more. Englebert argues that the relative levels of legitimacy attending African regimes relate directly to the developmental capacity of each state. He points out that the most economically productive states—Botswana, Mauritius, Seychelles, and South Africa—are also Africa's most legitimate, whereas the states with the most disastrous economic conditions have suffered disastrous drops in the level of legitimacy of their regimes (Liberia, Zimbabwe, Sierra Leone) or have for some time been unable to produce a legitimate government (Somalia, Democratic Republic of Congo). The relationship between legitimate government and economic success operates both ways, almost as a kind of self-fulfilling prophecy. Thus, legitimate governments are able to mobilize productive resources, evoke trust, collect taxes, and lower the opportunity costs of democratic participation. Legitimacy and good governance go hand in hand, and from that partnership economic development becomes possible; in that connection, economic success and failure are easy to identify and measure.

However, the relatively few African states that are genuinely successful or unsuccessful both politically and economically lie at opposite ends of a developmental continuum; most lie somewhere in between. In that middle range, the problem of legitimacy takes on a different configuration because the long-term survival of a group of authoritarian rulers—Eyadéma, Biya, and Bongo, among others—can only be explained by the operation of a complicated set of informal social contracts in which violations of human rights are tolerated as acceptable costs of achieving distributional preferences—another aspect of the infamous politics of the belly.

In Togo, Eyadéma's longevity in office and his ability to prevail over his democratically minded opponents in 1990–1991 has undoubtedly been due, to a considerable extent, to his informal contract with the country's southern Ewe population, described in 1971 as follows: "We [Eyadéma's northern Kabré] will run the country, and you [the Ewe] will have a free hand to make money in the south, providing you stay out of politics."[34] In Cameroon the understanding has been that the Beti barons (Biya's political-economic elite) will run the state and that, providing they do not interfere with Biya's regime, the Bamiléké and what is left of Ahidjo's northern barons will enjoy more or less unhampered economic activity. That contract appears to have been strong enough to withstand some northern defections during the 1983 and 1984 Ahidjo coup attempts, as well as Bamiléké pro–Social Democratic Front activity during the last two decades of the twentieth century, and to survive into the twentieth-first century to benefit from the lucrative Chad-Cameroon pipeline project. In Gabon the relatively small Gabonese population has left the Bongo *rentier* regime and the "clan des Gabonais" to run the state, in exchange for generous (by African standards) redistributional benefits from oil revenues and some entrée into the ranks of the Franco-Gabonese social elite.

In all three countries, though the regimes are execrated by their internal and external opponents, they are apparently tolerated, even supported by the majority of their populations. By midyear 2003 none of the three had yet reached the tipping point from legitimacy to illegitimacy, and barring the unexpected, each could expect additional years of rule.

Considering the sheer number of succession events that have occurred in our fourteen states—over seventy since independence—with very few exceptions (leaders in Senegal, Benin, and now perhaps Mali), rulers still have good reason to fear becoming victims of irregular regime change, though it is true that just under half of these events were peaceful, that is, occurring without major violence, and of that number ten were the product of free elections, many of which occurred during the past thirteen years. Constitutional succession, in which a transfer of power, other than by election, takes place in accordance with constitutional rules (which all of our fourteen have) when a head of state dies, resigns, or is incapacitated, is much more difficult to achieve, however: it happened only in Senegal in 1981 and Cameroon in 1982. Withal, the good news is that peaceful succession by free election has occurred with increasing frequency since 1990; the bad news is that the coup d'état is still the dominant form of regime succession in francophone Africa—as it is in most of the rest of the continent.

That African states as a whole, and our fourteen states in particular, have not yet managed to institutionalize modes of peaceful succession has both obvious and not so obvious consequences. Clearly, for example, military rulers who come to power via the usual route of coup d'état understand that unless they pay a good deal of attention to their own personal security and do everything possible to keep their subordinates well fed, well armed (at least with shiny new weapons), well paid, and regularly stroked with praise and other rewards, their own replacement via another coup is almost guaranteed. The problem is that coddling the troops becomes increasingly expensive, and worse still, it almost always comes at the expense of urgent civilian needs. And then there is the tendency for military regimes to resort to coercion as standard operating procedure, something that elicits grudging obedience at best, evasion and flight coupled with precipitous delegitimation at worst.

The civilian side of the military succession dilemma is represented by authoritarian regimes that have come to lean on their militaries to stay in power, even perhaps owing them their very existence, as is the case in Cameroon. The informal social contract in Cameroon, which keeps the regime afloat and from which the Cameroonian military profits, is at best precarious because it rests on a consensus of stakeholders—anglophones, Bamiléké, northerners—some of whom have recently shown themselves angry and disillusioned. Add to this the fact that recent Cameroonian elections have been of questionable validity, and Biya has all the more reason to worry about possible unscheduled succession events.

Postscript: An Extended Note on the Causes of Military Coups

The substantial literature that seeks to explain the causes, contexts, inspirations, motives and consequences of military coups in sub-Saharan Africa is divided roughly into three approaches. The first identifies a variety of factors that, singly or in combination, are said to establish cause-effect nexuses; the second identifies factors and variables according to which predictions about coups can be made; and the third, mainly represented in the work of Samuel Decalo, argues that the first two approaches are a waste of time and that causes are almost always particular to each coup and must be identified accordingly. The proponents of each approach profess and can honestly claim that theirs is empirically based and methodologically appropriate to its tasks.

My own review of the thirty-seven successful and fifty-one failed coups in our fourteen states between independence and midyear 2003 disposes me to question the second approach, partially accept the first, and largely embrace the third. For one thing, prediction à la Patrick McGowan and Thomas Johnson,[35] however methodologically sophisticated the analysis, has not been able to account for coups or coup attempts that occur in relatively prosperous, theretofore coup-free environments (e.g., Côte d'Ivoire in 1999 and Cameroon in 1984), or in political environments in which the military is a more or less permanent fixture in politics, and coups become almost standard operating procedure for succession (Mauritania, 1978–present; Dahomey/Benin, 1963–1991; Burkina Faso, 1966–present; Congo-Brazzaville, 1963–1993; Chad, 1975–present). In Dahomey, for example, it was a troika of colonels (Colonel Maurice Kouandété and Lieutenant Colonels Alphonse Alley and Paul-Emile de Souza) who acted as a collective arbiter of Dahomean politics from 1969 to 1972, and who inspired the ill-fated rotating presidency of Maga, Ahomadegbe, and Apithy, which Kérékou revoked in 1972. Who could have predicted Kérékou's coup in October 1972, save to hazard the reasonable guess that if the military had already intervened six times since independence, it might well do so again if things didn't work to its liking? (An acerbic biblical paraphrase was overheard in Cotonou at the time: *"Les colonels donnent et le colonels prennent: bénis soient les noms des colonels!"*—"The colonels give and the colonels take; blessed be the names of the colonels!")[36]

Decalo argues that every military coup presents its own set of empirical puzzles, and the researcher must examine it on its own merits to discover what causal elements are present in the record. I agree. It is fact that very few common causal elements can be found as threads running through the stories of two or more military coups. Yet though the threads are few, several coups are connected in part by possible and plausible demonstration effects. A number of interstate military forums, some of French inspiration; officers' training programs in France, Russia, and the United States; local and regional officers' courses run by expatriate military experts; international military publications; and so on all afford the francophone officers opportunities to talk to one another and share experiences. There may not be a good way to measure the cumulative effect of successful coups from, say, 1965 onward, but it makes sense to think that a kind of positive demonstration effect may have been at work in this larger picture as well.

It may also be that one of the corollary endowments of African independence, the national army required by every new government, turned out to be a poisoned apple in a number of instances. In almost every new country, the francophone states included, the new national security forces were constituted from the previous colonial security forces, plus, in francophone Africa, soldiers repatriated from the French army itself. It was a contingent of just such a group of repatriated soldiers in Togo that initiated sub-Saharan Africa's first postwar coup, killed its first incumbent president (Sylvanus Olympio), and launched Sergeant (later General) Eyadéma's long political career.

The military training and traditions of francophone officers, both abroad and in-country, do not stress discussion of a basic rule governing armies in a democracy, that is, unquestioning subordination to civilian authority. Not only is French political history replete with examples of overt military involvement in politics (including the 1958 reappearance of General de Gaulle, to whom the francophone Africans owed the independence option), but colonial rulers and regimes in our fourteen states operated in concert with their security apparatuses. Though the new civilian rulers may not have intended it that way, for the most part their armies and officers were political from the start, and if they were not, they soon became politicized as postindependence problems began to confront the new regimes and often threatened to overwhelm them.

Further, that several of our fourteen states' governments (e.g., those of Cameroon, Chad, CAR, and Gabon) had occasion at one time or another to call upon France and French soldiers to set political matters aright probably also served to reinforce the notion that military intervention could not only be a legitimate resort in times of crisis, but was sometimes even necessary in order to save the national patrimony. At least, so have coup makers argued after the fact, and though there is often a good deal of self-serving rhetoric and hypocrisy in such statements, there is reason to believe that at least some of them were both serious and sincere.[37] It remains also that highly politicized militaries, acting to protect their political turf and claiming resources they deem legitimately theirs, will use their weapons to secure both, particularly if that door to power has been left open by previous coup makers. As violence begets violence, so coups beget coups.

Another thread is the fact that many, if not most, of the coups in our fourteen states have occurred in times of crisis—at least in situations the military saw as crises. It is arguable whether the occasion for the Lamizana coup of January 1966, which removed the first Burkinabé president, Maurice Yaméogo, because he had misused public funds and outraged the Church, qualified as a crisis requiring a military solution, but apparently Lieutenant Colonel Lamizana, who feared further unrest in the streets of Ouagadougou, thought it was. So too the first Togolese coup, in which Eyadéma and his fellow noncoms responded to Olympio's refusal to enlarge the Togolese army with an assassination and a coup d'état. On its face Olympio's refusal was no crisis; Eyadéma's coup made it one. Moreover, it is often the case that those factors that precipitate a coup—its immediate and proximate causes—appear banal in retrospect, but seem large and threatening at the time. Be that as it may, the thread of crisis is visible in many coup situations—as it was during the December 24, 1999, mutiny in Côte d'Ivoire, Bokassa's coup on New Year's Eve 1965, Felix Malloum's 1975 coup against Tombalbaye in Chad, the death of Sékou Touré in April 1984, and so on.

Crises; politicized militaries in competition for resources; demonstration effects, including the accumulation of interventions; and, at least initially, some genuinely patriotic motives all appear to me to be commonalities for which reasonable empirical warrant can be established. Other putative causal factors cannot provide such warrant:

1. *Economic problems.* Coups or attempted coups have occurred in reasonably prosperous states (Senegal, 1961; Cameroon, 1983, 1984; Côte d'Ivoire, 1999), as they have in poor states or where economies have been in serious trouble (Benin in 1986–1989, Mauritania, Niger, Chad, etc.).

Whether economic factors are causal elements in political crises, including coups, remains in all cases an empirical question, though coups are frequently associated with weak economic performance.

2. *Exogenous intervention.* The French hand has certainly been visible in the CAR (for and against Bokassa, in defense of Patassé), Cameroon (counterinsurgency troops against UPC rebels during the 1960s), Chad (Operation Turquoise against rebels and Libyans and on behalf of Habré and Déby), and Gabon (for M'Ba in 1965), and there is no lack of accusations claiming that France, through the Elysée or its embassies or its military missions and Africa-based forces, was involved with or responsible for various attempted and successful coups. There may well be some substance to some of these accusations, but the bulk of the coups occurred without—and sometimes, in spite of—French involvement. (For a list of French interventions in Africa, see Appendix L.)

3. *Ethnic conflict.* While ethnicity is certainly an important factor in the civilian and military politics of many, if not most, of our fourteen states, ethnic conflict per se is rarely the main or even a major cause of military coups. Perhaps the state that comes closest to supporting the case for ethnic conflict as the cause of coups is Chad, where a major century-long breach between the ethnic groups of the predominantly Muslim north and those of the mainly Christianized south has helped produce a succession of northern-based rebellions and coups, including those by former presidents Goukouni Oueddei and Habré, and by the present ruler, Déby. That cycle may well begin anew: Déby's former defense minister, Youssouf Togoïmi, in 1998 raised his own flag of rebellion in the northernmost regions of Bourkou, Ennedi, and Tibesti.[38] It is possible, however, that in Chad the ethnic factor has now been displaced by what amounts to a continuous and deadly power struggle in which ethnicity has become simply a mobilizable resource for the contenders.

Elsewhere, in Mauritania, Togo, Benin, Cameroon, and Congo-Brazzaville, for example, powerful ethnic currents affect politics, but it is only in Congo-Brazzaville, where ethnic-based militias have contended for power, that a good case can be made for a causal connection between coups and ethnicity. In Mauritania the deadly antagonism shown blacks in the Senegal River Valley and the older tensions between "black" and "white" Moors have little or nothing to do with the country's recurrent coups. Rather, it appears that rivalry among its officers and a recurrent struggle for control of the country's meager resources are the main factors at work. Eyadéma's first coup in 1963 had little or nothing to do with his Kabré identity, but rather with his desire for a place in Togo's miniscule army. In Benin the old ethnic-based rivalry between former presidents Maga, Apithy, and Ahomadegbe may have helped trigger at least two military interventions, but ethnic rivalry played no role in Kérékou's downfall and resurrection. Finally, in Cameroon, while Ahidjo and some of his ex–northern barons may well have been behind the attempted coups of 1983 and 1984, what was involved was not an effort to gain ethnic supremacy, but simply a naked attempt by Ahidjo and his friends to recapture power.

While it is possible to indicate a variety of factors that may or may not have played a role in particular military interventions, it remains that continent-wide, longitudinal evidence offers little empirical warrant for broad generalizations about such events, and that convincing cause-effect conclusions are best sought in the details of each coup or intervention. One final general observation, however, is justified: with very few exceptions (South Africa, Botswana, Mauritius, and Benin), the military and/or security forces act as corporate players on the local political stages. The ideal democratic military-civilian relationship is to have militaries unconditionally subordinate to civilian power, to the point where to have a military establishment as a corporate player in politics becomes unthinkable. The African reality is far from the ideal, and it should come as no surprise that the African militaries as corporate political players not only seek power, but also deploy in politics the instruments of coercion allocated to them in their security roles. African democracies such as South Africa, Botswana, Mauritius, and Benin have come closest to depoliticizing their militaries, thereby placing them beyond the temptation to intervene on their own behalf.

Notes

1. Acheikh ibn Oumar, secretary-general of the opposition Democratic Revolutionary Council and former Chadian minister of state, commenting on the news that President Idriss Déby was ill. Cited by Tshitenge Lubabu in "Idris Déby: Le déclin. . . ." My translation.

2. Though Jackson and Rosberg (in *Personal Rule in Black Africa*) discuss several so-called charismatic leaders, the subject is fully and authoritatively covered in Willner, *The Spellbinders: Charismatic Political Leadership*. For an analysis of the manufacture and use of affective symbols of leadership, see my "Changing Leadership Styles and Political Images: Some Preliminary Notes"; and Kirk-Greene, "His Eternity, His Eccentricity, or His Exemplarity? A Further Contribution to the Study of H. E. the African Head of State." For a discussion of the "charisma" of Burkina Faso's Thomas Sankara, see Skinner, "Sankara and the Burkinabe Revolution: Charisma and Power, Local and External Dimensions."

3. In 1965, in conjunction with a study of intragenerational conflict in francophone Africa, I administered a questionnaire to the one hundred members of the Senegalese National Assembly. One of the open-ended questions asked the respondents to name the ten most influential political leaders in the country; another asked for the ten most influential leaders in four main "social" categories, including government and administration, commerce, trade unions, and political parties. I left space in the latter question for an "other" category." I had a 68 percent response rate

and almost all who responded listed Falilou M'Backé second or third in their answers to both questions. (The study was published in 1967 as *Political Leadership in Africa: Post-Independence Generational Conflict in Upper Volta, Senegal, Niger, Dahomey, and the Central African Republic.*) For detailed discussion of Falilou M'Backé and the Mourides, see O'Brien, *The Mourides of Senegal,* and Coulon, *Le marabout et le prince (Islam et pouvoir au Senegal).*

4. Ngayap, *Cameroun: Qui gouverne?* Ngayap's "ruling class" somewhat resembles Jean-François Bayart's larger and more amorphous Cameroonian "hegemonic alliance," save that while Ngayap uses the term *class* mainly as a descriptor for his elite group and describes that group's efforts at integration, Bayart expands the term's scope and ascribes a higher measure of class consciousness to it, calling the same group a "dominant class" and arguing that it was the product of its own "hegemonic project," the objective of which was to capture the Cameroonian state. See Bayart, *L'état au Cameroon.*

5. Glaser and Smith, *Ces messieurs Afrique,* vol. 1: *Le Paris-village du continent noir* and vol. 2: *Des réseaux aux lobbies.*

6. Bayart, *L'état au Cameroun;* Fatton, *Predatory Rule: State and Civil Society in Africa.* Fatton explicitly acknowledges his debt to the thought of Antonio Gramsci. Also, see Bayart, Ellis, and Hibou, *The Criminalization of the State in Africa.*

7. The quotation is from an article titled "Prestige de l'élite francophone," which appeared in the journal *Lumières noires,* 1990, and is cited by René Dumont in his *Démocratie pour l'Afrique,* 222–223. My translation.

8. Apparently, this circumstance is rare enough to be considered a mark of presidential success. Crawford Young reports that a number of Zairean intellectuals cited a boast by Mobutu Sese Seko on the occasion of his thirtieth anniversary in office that "he might ultimately become known as the late president, but never as the former president." He almost fulfilled his own prediction: he died shortly after he was ousted from power in 1997. (Young, "Zaire: The Anatomy of a Failed State," 97.)

9. For the basics of that conflict, see "Dossier spécial: Congo-Brazzaville, entre guerre et paix"; and Bazenguissa-Ganga, "The Spread of Political Violence in Congo-Brazzaville."

10. For two templates in print, see Ferguson, *Coup d'Etat: A Practical Manual;* and Luttwak, *Coup d'Etat: A Practical Manual.*

11. Decalo, *Psychoses of Power: African Personal Dictatorships.*

12. Perhaps the clearest definition of patrimonial leadership is in Bill and Springborg, *Politics in the Middle East,* 4th ed., 150–175. While their description applies specifically to the Middle East, at least the first four of their six major characteristics of patrimonial leadership (personalism, proximity, informality, and balanced conflict; the other two are military prowess and religious rationalization) apply almost mutatis mutandis to the African variety.

Personalism refers to the personal relationships of the leader or ruler, whether they are based on family, clan, or ethnic ties; friendship; loyalty; or reciprocal obligations. The paradigmatic example of how personalism works is Sékou Touré's regime. Ibrahima Baba Kaké (*Sékou Touré,* 168–174) identifies eleven members of Sékou Touré's immediate family on whom he relied and put into important official positions, beginning with Ismaël Touré, a half-brother and "number 2" in the regime. On his side of the familial ledger there was another half-brother, two half-sisters, a paternal first cousin, a nephew, and the husband of a sister; on the Keita side, the family of his wife, there was Andrée herself, two half-brothers, two husbands of two half-sisters, as well as various other family members on both sides, their allies, and other in-laws. The Gabonese regime of Omar Bongo operates in much the same fashion, that is, by giving relatives, clanspeople, and co-ethnics pride of official and unofficial place.

Proximity refers to the factor of physical proximity to the ruler; those closest to him tend to live and work near him and are required to be on ready call. Just as the royal Louis (XIV, XV, and XVI) configured their courts so that those closest to the king, on whom he relied most, lived at court or close by, so, for example, did Bokassa at his court in Berengo. Elsewhere, the inner circles to Sékou Touré, Omar Bongo, Houphouët-Boigny, Eyadéma are found within easy proximity of the presidential palace. Thus, proximity facilitates patrimonial rule.

Informality refers to the tendency of members of the coterie, oligarchy, or inner circle to be able to dispense with the formalities of access and address (Bokassa: "call me 'Papa'") and to have privileged access to the leader.

Balanced conflict refers to the successful patrimonial leader's ability to manipulate, even regulate, the pervasive divisiveness and personal rivalries that tend to be endemic to patrimonial rulership. As Machiavelli teaches us, the wise ruler uses such divisions to strengthen his position.

13. Collin became a Senegalese citizen in 1960 and married one of Senghor's nieces. He was considered by many to be one of the most powerful men in Senghor's regime. For a biographical sketch, see Wiseman, *Political Leaders in Black Africa*. For a detailed description of the extent to which Sekou Touré relied on his family as a key element of his inner circle, see Baba Kaké, *Sékou Touré*, 165–192.

14. Douglas Andrew Yates describes the "clan" as follows: "When we speak of a ruling class in Gabon, what we really mean is a small, secretive, tightly-knit organization of Franco-Gabonese elites otherwise known as the 'Clan des Gabonais'" ("The Rentier State in Gabon"). Also, see Pierre Péan's acid portrait of the "clan" in his *Affaires africaines*, 129–166.

15. We will return to the problem of political corruption in Chapter 10. The key recent discussion on the "criminalization of the state" is Bayart, Ellis, and Hibou, *Criminalization of the State*.

16. One is reminded here of Dr. Johnson's famous epigram that "when a man knows he is to be hanged in a fortnight, it concentrates his mind wonderfully"; in this case, the concentrator is the thought of the firing squad, the traditional punishment for mutineers and failed military conspirators. I have not been able to make a complete tally of soldiers and officers executed after failed coup attempts, but a rough initial count for the fourteen states to the end of the year 2000 comes to somewhat over four hundred. Clearly, in our region, a coup d'état is usually neither planned nor undertaken lightly. According to Decalo, *The Stable Minority: Civilian Rule in Africa*, 17, until 1990 only about a dozen African countries had experienced neither a successful nor an abortive military coup, including, in our group, only Côte d'Ivoire—which, however, had its first successful military coup in December 1999. Patrick McGowan and Thomas Johnson's 1984 tally of coups ("African Military Coups d'Etat and Underdevelopment: A Quantitative Historical Analysis") yielded twenty-four attempted (i.e., failed) coups between 1956 and 1984 in ex-French Africa, including Madagascar. My own updated (1984 to mid-2003) count, using McGowan and Johnson's criteria, adds another twenty-nine attempted coups for our francophone states, excluding Madagascar.

17. "La mutinerie des jeunes militaires ivoiriens se termine en coup d'état," *Le Monde*, December 25, 1999; "Le chef de la junte ivoirienne devoile ses ambitions,"

Le Monde, January 3, 2000. The phrase *"comité de salut public"* hearkens back to the French Revolution, when it was used to describe the special mobilization of Frenchmen that took place when the Revolution appeared under attack from all sides. It was also, of course, the name taken by the group of twelve men, led by Maximilien Robespierre, who ruled France from 1793 to 1795—the height of the Terror. When used in contemporary times, the phrase is meant to designate a special organization formed to meet a national crisis, here the military junta that took over when Ivoirian military mutineers threatened general instability. (The name *Committee of Public Safety* carries its own historical irony: three leaders of the original French group, Robespierre, Louis-Antoine Saint-Just, and Marie-Jean Hérault de Séchelles, became victims of the Terror they and the committee helped propagate.)

18. Mensah Adinkrah, *Political Coercion in Military-Dominated Regimes.*

19. Thomas Hobbes, "Of Punishment," in *A Dialogue Between a Philosopher and a Student,* 140.

20. This was a young officer I interviewed in 1965 in Ouagadougou under a promise of anonymity.

21. Decalo, *Coups and Army Rule in Africa: Motivations and Constraints,* 2nd ed., 55. Decalo's account of the coup that deposed Youlou and of military politics in Congo-Brazzaville remains definitive. In May 1965 I met Youlou on a flight from Fort Lamy (now Ndjamena), Chad, to Paris, and later in Paris. During the trip he defended his regime's record, claimed he was grossly misunderstood by his French friends (whom he denounced for failing to stand by him), blamed the Chinese Communists for his downfall, and predicted that the regime in office at the time (that of Massamba-Débat) would not last out the year. Youlou's case against the Chinese may be found in his *J'accuse la Chine.* Massamba-Débat lasted until 1968, when he was replaced with Captain Alfred Raoul, who was then replaced with Marien Ngouabi in 1969. Youlou himself died in 1972.

22. This explanation appears in all the official histories of Togo, including a French-style comic-book version titled *Histoire du Togo: Il Etait une Fois: Eyadema,* one of a series of similar comic-book-format history-biographies commissioned by various African leaders. (The collection includes similar canned biographies of Senghor, Bongo, Mobutu, Ahidjo, King Hassan II of Morocco, and Muammar al-Qaddafi.)

23. Decalo, *Coups and Army Rule,* 326. See also Decalo's excellent section on Togo in the same book, 205–240.

24. For details, see Guirma, *Comment perdre le pouvoir? Le cas de Maurice Yaméogo;* and Englebert, *Burkina Faso: Unsteady Statehood in West Africa.* The role of ethnic politics in Burkina Faso is detailed by Elliot Skinner in his *The Mossi of Burkina Faso.*

25. O'Toole, *The Central African Republic: The Continent's Unsteady Heart,* 49. O'Toole's account of the Bokassa coup is on pp. 49–50.

26. I was told about the Chinese plot by several informants when I was conducting research in CAR in 1965. Also see my "The Coups in Upper Volta, Dahomey, and the Central African Republic."

27. On Sankoh and his diamonds, see, for example Douglas Farah, "Diamonds are a Rebel's Best Friend." Compaoré's complicity in the illegal diamond trade, including those sold by Angola's Savimbi, is reported in Blaine Harden, "Africa's Gems: Warfare's Best Friend," *New York Times,* April 6, 2000, and in the special report to the UN Security Council, *Report of the Panel of Experts on Violations of Security Council Sanctions Against UNITA.* The Angolan connections are detailed

in Hodges, *Angola: Anatomy of an Oil State.* The charges of illegal weapons procurement may be found in Human Rights Watch's 2003 briefing paper, "Weapons Sanctions, Military Supplies, and Human Suffering: Illegal Arms Flows to Liberia and the June–July 2003 Shelling of Monrovia."

28. Substantial portions of the data and descriptions in this section are drawn from my "Leadership Transition in Black Africa: Elite Generations and Political Succession."

29. Le Vine, "Parliaments in Francophone Africa: Some Lessons from the Decolonization Process," 125–154.

30. That story is told in detail by Georges Chaffard in "Quand Houphouët-Boigny était un rebelle," in his *Les carnets secrets de la décolonisation* 1:99–132.

31. Englebert, *State Legitimacy and Development in Africa;* Schatzberg, *Political Legitimacy in Middle Africa: Father, Family, Food.*

32. For examples and analysis, see Feit, *The Armed Bureaucrats: Military-Administrative Regimes and Political Development.*

33. Ibid., 202.

34. This is a paraphrase of statements made during a conversation with a group of Togolese intellectuals, held on January 15, 1971, in Lomé, at the home of a French sociologist. I later read some of these statements to members of the Olympio clan (relatives of the murdered Sylvanus Olympio) in Accra, Ghana, and they agreed that the characterization was accurate.

35. McGowan and Johnson, "African Military Coups." See also Johnson, Slater, and McGowan, "Explaining African Coups d'Etat."

36. Interview with Major X (anonymity requested), February 6, 1971, during a visit to Cotonou.

37. From 1969 to 1971, while I was head of the political science department at the University of Ghana at Legon, I taught a series of seminars at the Ghanaian army's Teshie Officers' Training Center. Informal conversation after the sessions, at the officers' mess, enabled some very open exchanges to take place, including some very spirited defenses of intervention "to save the nation" by Ghanaian field officers. To my surprise, several officers even expressed admiration for the Turkish military and its self-appointed role as guardian of the polity. Conversations with various francophone officers over the years confirm these observations, though only the Ghanaians suggested the Turkish military as a possible role model.

38. Lubabu, "Idris Déby."

10

In the Shadow of the State: The Domain of Nonformal Politics

It goes almost without saying that there is more than one kind of politics. While the basic processes of politics remain the same regardless of context or the people involved, the politics of each leader, legislator, bureaucrat, political party, and election are different because the imperatives, stakes, and transactions themselves vary according to the subjects and objects of the processes and the demands of the institutional settings in which they occur. These are time-, place-, and subject-specific politics.

Another way of empirically distinguishing among different politics is according to the domains, or political spaces, in which they take place. Some analysts speak of "high" politics, or the politics of the state—the larger national arena of official institutions, structures, and processes—and distinguish them from "low," or "deep," politics, that is, the politics of citizens and their associations as they relate to the state and its institutions.[1] But there is also a third domain, the "parapolitical," or nonformal domain, which intersects both high and deep politics (the latter more than the former), but which is characterized by its inhabitants' purposive distantiation, even often relative autonomy, from the state and its formal institutions and agents. Here, political actors figuratively tend to look over their shoulders to see if the state is watching or is hovering nearby; in any case, they deliberately seek to keep their distance from it by employing strategies of subterfuge, evasion, concealment, enclosure, or flight. This is also the domain of what has been called private politics—the personal politics of kith and kin and, more to the point, of such often shadowy and illicit activity as political corruption; organized crime; and the working of secret and other informal associations, ethnic politics, and black markets and informal entrepreneurs; as well as the more benign activities of what has become an extraordinary array of NGOs (nongovernmental organizations) and the like.

All of this is in large part, though not exclusively, the politics of civil society, the politics with which most people have daily contact and that, in most countries, encompasses the greatest volume of political transactions. There is no way of estimating the relative proportion of the size of the parapolitical to that of the overtly official political domain, but it is fair to suggest that insofar as most people only occasionally deal directly with the official realm—unless, of course, they operate within in or work for it—most of their politics are in the parapolitical domain.

Ethnicity, "Tradition," and the Politics of Identity

Perhaps the most visible of the nonformal political domains has been that involving ethnicity (called tribalism in more common parlance), an inescapable factor in African politics at the national level, and often overwhelming at the local level. Jean-François Bayart remarks on what he calls "the shadow theater of ethnicity," an apt way of characterizing a cluster of behaviors and activities relating to identity, matters that can be identified and defined by their effects and that, in his view, operate "mainly as an agent of accumulation":

> In Africa ethnicity is almost never absent from politics, yet at the same time it does not provide its basic fabric. Put this way, the dilemma is naturally absurd. Manifestations of ethnicity inevitably involve other social dimensions, . . . and in the context of the contemporary State, ethnicity exists mainly as an agent of accumulation, both of wealth and of political power. Tribalism is thus perceived less as a political force in itself than as a channel through which competition for the acquisition of wealth, power, and status is expressed.[2]

Bayart is certainly right to qualify his definition by placing the ethnic factor "in the context of the contemporary state," the domain where, unquestionably, it has largely become instrumental in character. Almost everywhere, public office is seen as an open opportunity to practice what Bayart calls "the politics of the belly," that is, the politics of "feeding" one's own—usually defined as giving one's own kinfolk and coethnics privileged access to public goods.[3] Leaders are expected to "feed" their followers or, in any event, their constituents, ethnic affines, and kinfolk.

This feeding has characterized situations ranging from the economic ascendancy of the so-called Beti and Bulu barons in Paul Biya's Cameroon, to the making of Gabon into what amounts to a business that is largely jointly owned and controlled by Omar Bongo's family and the so-called clan des Gabonais, to the giving of pride of place to Félix Houphouët-Boigny's business and planter elite in the Ivoirian economy, to the installation of N'Garta (François) Tombalbaye's Sara clansmen and coethnics in key Chadian official positions. The latter practice was unabashedly duplicated by Tombalbaye's successors—Goukouni Oueddei, Felix Malloum,

Hissene Habré, and Idriss Déby—each on behalf of his own family, clanspeople, and coethnics. During his so-called Cultural Revolution's "authenticity" campaign, Tombalbaye even went so far as to impose a version of the Sara *yondo* initiation rites on southern officials in his single party. The politics of the belly also includes what the French call *dosage*—careful allocation of ministries and government offices according to ethnic criteria—a skill of which Ahmadou Ahidjo of Cameroon and Houphouët-Boigny of Côte d'Ivoire were undoubted masters.

Another dimension of ethnic politics, ethnicity translated in practice as identity and trust, is found both in the postcolonial and the precolonial state. This dimension is less visible than the instrumental aspects of ethnicity, but it is equally consequential.

Begin with the facts that most African states, including our fourteen, are ethnically plural, and that political dominance by a single ethnic group is almost never a foregone conclusion. In such a situation, and where elections help decide political outcomes, ethnically based political parties have often become effective instruments wherewith ethnic communities can claim their piece of the national resource pie, and people will vote for these parties and their candidates for that reason. People may also vote for them because they trust their "own" candidates more than other candidates who are not their own: this is trust not only in the sense that coethnics will make more reliable political agents, or that they can be reliably expected to give primacy to their constituents' interests, but also in that coethnics offer a relatively low-cost, secure bridge between home and the state. Having "our" man in Bamako, Dakar, Niamey, Ouagadougou, Yaoundé, Brazzaville, or Abidjan means not only that "we"—ethnically speaking—have a gateway to the national capital and its resources, but also that "we" are consequential and have an influential voice in the corridors of power.

It is not only in the national arena that the ethnic calculus is played out; where there is a high degree of competition for jobs and official favors, the ethnic joust extends to the lowest local levels as well.[4] This was also by and large the situation in West and Equatorial Africa during the preindependence period and the early years of independence, when the proliferation of ethnoregional parties testified to the attractions of such a strategy. It remains meaningful where patrimonialism is standard operating procedure and where electoral politics continue to play an important role in national politics.

Then there is the role that ethnicity plays, often in its "traditional" sociopolitical guises, in maintaining ethnocommunal solidarity, particularly in states undergoing political or economic crises. Whether an ethnic group is of relatively recent provenance (constructed during the colonial period) or has an established precolonial history, it can act as and often becomes a place of refuge in times of distress, whether that place is generalized, as among one's kinfolk, or is particular, as a village, town, neighborhood, or other locality.

Achille Mbembe writes of *"le politique par temps de disette"*—people and politics in times of scarcity—to remind us that "the crisis of governance observable in many African countries is born, in part, of the fact that bit by bit society disengages itself from the State, that it 'washes its hands' (Pontius Pilate–like) of the state and discovers that it can get along without it."[5] This is the more so because in times of prolonged national crisis African countries typically become impoverished and the citizens literally become hungrier as well—evoking and emphasizing another form of the politics of the belly, that is, one based on the real imperative of physically feeding oneself and one's family. The "imploding state" reciprocates and also disengages itself from society, leaving the countryside literally to fend for itself.[6] In the process, the countryside may also have to accommodate the hungry and frightened thousands fleeing from the main population centers.

The December 2000 coup in Côte d'Ivoire and its sequels, and the recurrent bloody unrest in Brazzaville and Bangui during the years 1999–2001, in which members of certain ethnic groups became the targets of violence, all created tens of thousands of refugees whose first instinct was to try to reach their "home"—that is, their ethnic sanctuary, in villages, towns, and other localities. Those who were unable to do so literally and figuratively became homeless, the charge of reluctant neighboring countries, international agencies like the UN High Commission for Refugees, and the occasional friendly neighboring state.

This is ethnic home as a refuge, ethnicity as the sanctuary in extremis. It is not too much to suggest that there may well be something akin to ethnic "early warning" antennae that, when fully extended and functioning well, send frequently targeted peoples or ethnic populations at risk scurrying home for shelter. Then too, there is physical protection in ethnicity used as a shield; Célestin Monga makes the point for Congo and Cameroon:

> Come to power, certain Heads of State hardly bother to conceal their intentions in this domain: either they recruit new soldiers from their (the rulers') tribe of origin—the postulate here is that one is better protected by one's own "brothers"—or they sponsor at their own expense the creation of tribal militias with baser duties such as the regular army might refuse to carry out (e.g., the assassination of political adversaries, acts of terrorism to intimidate populations, acts of high banditry to recycle funds of doubtful origin, etc.). In Congo, President Lissouba made no secret of the fact that the massive recruitment of soldiers which he undertook in 1995 was essentially destined to accommodate certain members of his tribe of origin. So too did he implicitly recognize that the three private [ethnic] militias which paralyzed the army and provoked the deadly events of 1992–1994, had been, if not created by, then at least operated

under the patronage of, the three big leaders of the Congolese political market: the "Cobras" of former President Denis Sassou-Nguesso, President Lissouba's own "Zulus," and the "Ninjas" of Brazzaville's Deputy Mayor Bernard Kolelas. Cameroon illustrates this schema as well. When he was first confronted by the first popular rising against his regime in 1991, President Biya encouraged the rise of private militias devoted to him ("the Self-defense Commandos"), the majority of whose members came from his home region. He thus had at his disposal a national army devoted to serving him—something which contributed to tribalizing political conflict.[7]

A key point, which Monga overlooks, is that in Congo-Brazzaville the leading politicians deliberately recruited young men's militias not mainly from Brazzaville itself, but from their home districts, where their coethnics were dominant. To put it simply, it was a matter of trust.

Even though Pascal Lissouba had brought considerable numbers of his coethnics into the army, when the 1997 semi–civil war broke out, he created his own militia, initially called the Mouvance Presidentielle and later known as Cocoyes and then Zulus, drawing from regions where he had the greatest ethnic support, that is Niari, Bouenza, and Lekoumou. The inhabitants of these regions had originally been ethnically Kongo, but the highly complex politics of Congo-Brazzaville had converted them into a people whose identity was designated acronymically by the first two or three letters of each district: Niari Bouenza Lekoumou became Nibolek, and this is what the inhabitants of these regions, and a portion of the Brazzaville populace, came to call themselves. Anne Sundberg explains that creation of the Nibolek "Zulus" became necessary because when the chips were down, Lissouba could not trust the army, since it had too many non-Nibolek in it, even counting the president's dedicated recent ethnic recruits.

Sassou-Nguesso, an Mbochi, created his own Mbochi "Cobras," and Bernard Kolelas, a Lari from the Pool region, created his own Lari (including some Vili allies) "Ninjas."[8] The fact that the young men came from outside of Brazzaville made looting "enemy" territory in town that much easier. This helps account for the several militias' continued presence on the scene after Sassou-Nguesso retook power in 1997: though Sassou-Nguesso was able to reconstitute the national army and gendarmerie, the Ninjas, Cocoyes/Zulus, and Cobras continued to be involved in the country's renewed internal violence during the next five years. In fact, the Zulus became so unreliable, having run out of looting opportunities and having been paid only sporadically, that ironically Sassou-Nguesso turned to Angolan troops, who were loaned to him for use as his personal bodyguard and to protect such key installations as the main airport.

The next step was inevitable: by December 2000 Sassou-Nguesso was strong enough—in command of a reconstituted and reasonably reliable army and gendarmerie—to order the ethnic militias to disarm, and some twenty-five thousand from all sides turned in their weapons. Many were taken into the army, but most disbanded—or so it seemed at the time. Shortly after Sassou-Nguesso's reelection to the presidency in 2002, the Ninjas reappeared in bloody confrontation with the Congolese army.

The recourse to ethnic militias in Congo-Brazzaville illustrates the uses of ethnicity, in Mbembe's evocative phrase, *par temps de disette*. It is an extreme example of destructive parapolitical creativity in the search for protection and trust. Just as trust, embodied in kinship and ethnic ties, is a paramount ingredient in the success of widespread (across Africa and up to France) francophone African commercial activity on the parapolitical margins of the law,[9] so is it vital to the more benign social structures that combine to make ethnic homes for millions of Africans, whether in difficult or prosperous times. When home means the family's natal town or village, the local chief and the "traditional" rituals that sustain them, the old usages and ways, then all of these combine to refresh the bonds of community and to provide that citadel, that safety zone, to which the beleaguered and the beset can repair. Bana, a small chiefdom in Cameroon's Bamiléké country,[10] is an excellent case in point. A visit I made there in 1980 revealed much about that aspect of its being.

Celebrating Bana: A Personal Narrative

If the data are to be trusted, the Bamiléké and their ethnic cognates make up around 30 percent of Cameroon's population. Their home country—designated as *le pays Bamiléké* (or *le pays dites-Bamiléké*—"the so-called Bamiléké country") by French and British ethnographers and generally accepted as such by the Bamiléké themselves—is a large, densely populated, hilly area located in Cameroon's southwest. Its inhabitants are mainly concentrated in the Southwest and Northwest Provinces, with significant numbers in the neighboring Littoral Province as well. The area contains about one and one-half million of the roughly four million Bamiléké in Cameroon, clustered in and around four main towns (Bafang, Banganté, Bafoussam, and Nkongsamba, the Northwest Province's capital) and in some ninety named chiefdoms of various sizes and importance, each with a main town to which the chiefdom gives its name and where the chief has his official residence or palace. The Bamiléké have made their mark on Cameroon by the vigor and commercial acuity of their people, the avidity with which their sons (and more recently, daughters) have taken to both modern education and politics, the press of their demographic expansion, the lingering effects of sporadic and sometimes deadly conflict with their Bamoun neighbors, and the fact that the radical nationalist rebellion that shook the country from 1955 to 1962 played out the second part of its guerrilla stage in the Bamiléké homeland. During the 1990s and early years of the twenty-first century many Bamiléké were again on the defensive as the Biya regime came to see some of their leaders and notables—with some justification—as part of its opposition.

By size and population Bana town is small to medium-sized; when I visited in 1980, it probably had no more than about ten thousand in residence. But, as I soon learned, it had importance far beyond what its size and population would indicate: it was a small commercial and political powerhouse that was able, as it turned out, to put on an extraordinary three-day extravaganza (on February 3, 6, and 7, 1980) commemorating, as Bamiléké tradition dictated, both the death and the funeral of its late king (technically, *fon*) Hapi II, and the enthronement of his successor, King Hapi III.

I was told that the royal family—by name Hapi or Happi, spelled either way—had invited some five thousand people to the second part of the event, the enthronement on February 7, including the sultan of Bamoun; a clutch of neighboring chiefs; high government officials; members of the diplomatic corps from Yaoundé; and important notables, friends (like myself), allies, and businesspeople from all over the country. From my vantage point it appeared as if almost all the invitees had come, plus, by right, a huge number of the Bana themselves from both near and far. (I had been invited because I was friends with one of the Hapi and a visiting Fulbright professor at the University of Yaoundé. To my considerable pleasure, the Hapi even sent a chauffeur-driven Mercedes to fetch me from Yaoundé.)

We witnessed the royal installation, the elaborate "traditional" *hommages* (honors) paid the new king, dancers in costume from all over the Bamiléké area, and various age-grade and traditional Bamiléké societies parading and dancing in their finery. We heard musical ensembles (both traditional and modern) and the sultan's trumpeters and his personal praise-singer in full throat, and we saw displays of royal art, masks, cloth, and costumes that were brought out only for the most important ceremonial occasions. An elaborate lunch (huge mounds of chicken, lamb, goat, yams, rice, vegetables, fruit) was set for three thousand of the guests on that third day, and we sipped orange squash (soda), beer, and chilled French Moët et Chandon champagne convoyed up from Douala a week earlier (I was told the wine needed a week to settle down after the bottles' bumpy, hundred-mile truck ride from the coast).

It was, in all, both stunning and memorable, representing a deliberate exhibition of wealth, power, and good fortune far beyond what one would expect of a chiefdom that normally presented a modest front to the world. Long after it was over, I asked my hosts and several well-informed Bamiléké friends to explain the discrepancy and the reasons for what seemed to me to be an ostentatious, even extravagant display. First of all, I learned that it was not the royal Bana treasury that paid for the event, but

Bana businesspeople and households throughout the country, many of whom vied with one another to see who could raise the largest sums. Second, my hosts explained to me in gentle rebuke that what was done was neither extravagant nor ostentatious, but befitting of the occasion, the guests, and the need to impress the visitors.

The event was an opportunity to remind the visitors that Bana was more than it seemed, that it could mobilize its hidden wealth to invite—read "command the presence of"—the great and powerful of the land. The presence of the sultan of Bamoun, a traditional grandee of national importance with whom the Bana had forged an informal alliance, emphasized the point. The message was that here was real influence, and that it could be translated into benefits for the Bana—and its friends—at the seats of local and national power. No one should forget, my interlocutors emphasized, that the Bana already had three of the Hapi in Yaoundé, individually and collectively representing Bana interests and ensuring that it would be heard by the government: Louis Kemayou Hapi, former mayor of Nkongsamba and ex-president of the eastern and national legislative assemblies; Jean-Claude Hapi, a son of the late King Hapi II and counselor at the presidency and the ministry of foreign affairs; and Daniel Kemayou Hapi, vice president of the court of appeals in Yaoundé.

Finally, and perhaps most important, the event was a way of renewing the ethnocommunal solidarities on which Bana stood and to reassert publicly what the ethnic home meant to both those "at home" and those "abroad." Pride, and even some arrogance, was certainly involved, as well as the renewal of trust and reinforcement of the subtler structures of ethnic kinship. It did not surprise me that not only the older Bana, but also other Bamiléké whom I encountered in Cameroon frequently spoke of retiring "at home": *au village, chez moi.*

My visit to Bana was in 1980, over twenty years ago, and I have no way of knowing if the Bana still have the measure of influence of which they reminded their guests, or even if they had as much political influence then as they claimed. What is important is that Bana, while unusual in its role as a minipowerhouse of wealth and influence, was not alone among Bamiléké communities in its willingness to display its ethnic pride in the accumulation of wealth or to use the multiple structures and channels of the parapolitical domain to protect and enhance its position.[11]

The Bana chiefdom, one of ninety similar Bamiléké units, is technically part of the substructures and institutions of Cameroonian local government, all of which fall under the jurisdiction of the national ministry of territorial administration and ultimately are subject to the power of the presidency of the country. Part of that power is exercised through the *fon* himself; according to Decree No. 77/245, made law in 1977, all "traditional chiefs" became auxiliaries of the administration. This was something of a trap for the chiefs because those who were seen to use the power of their office too much to advance that of the state could attract the opprobrium of their people, "who have more and more difficulty in separating the fon's incontestable power from the secular, party-political and therefore morally contestable power of the state."[12]

Although this summarily describes the formal linkages between periphery and center, it does not, and obviously cannot, encompass the multiple parapolitical ties between the Bana and those in the corridors of power; nor can it encapsulate the loose and resilient but effective network of solidarities and reciprocal obligations on which the Bana—and the Bamiléké at large—can call when needed. Needless to say, these nonformal ties and networks are as real and consequential as those described by the formal structures of politics—perhaps even more so. Clearly Bamiléké— "Bami"—is more than an ethnic identity: it represents salient membership in a socially and politically important group whose interests, demands, concerns, and national presence, manifested in both the formal and informal political domains, have to be taken seriously by any Cameroonian regime, whatever its provenance.

Political Corruption

The ubiquitous parapolitical links and networks in which ethnicity plays an empowering and active role are based ultimately on affinity, that is, personal relationships involving trust and confidence, and the obligations and ties of real or fictive kinship. Also ubiquitous, though not as dense, are those links and networks involving corrupt relationships, but these depend not so much on affinity (though trust, for example, can help reinforce corrupt links) as on mutually profitable reciprocities and exchanges.

Three important introductory points can be made about corruption. First, what is generally considered corruption in Africa involves the use of public political resources or goods for private ends, usually by people to whom these resources are entrusted.[13] Second, public-official corruption not only is endemic throughout the continent, but often reaches such proportions that the state itself becomes a criminal enterprise—what Stanislas Andreski first aptly called a *kleptocracy*, or a state run by thieves.[14] Finally, most public-official corruption, being illicit or generally considered reprehensible or both, tends to operate in the parapolitical shadows, unless, of course, the state has become so thoroughly criminalized that its managers feel free to do their looting openly. In the latter case the designation *kleptocracy* probably no longer fits; Jean-François Bayart, Stephen Ellis, and Béatrice Hibou suggest the title *felonious state,* of which the Zaire of President Mobutu Sese Seko is the paradigmatic example.[15]

If Mobutu was Africa's prime kleptocrat or thief-in-power, then Jean-

Bédel Bokassa's CAR (whose bizarre "empire" is described in Chapter 7) is certainly an example of corruption carried to odious excess, and with one unique feature: it enmeshed a European head of state—France's president Valéry Giscard d'Estaing. For that reason the story merits a brief reprise.

To summarize, Giscard and Bokassa became very good friends: Giscard's family had commercial interests in the CAR, and Bokassa had Giscard's esteem and his ear and was always welcome at the Elysée Palace when Giscard was president. Giscard not only accepted gifts of diamonds from Bokassa, but was Bokassa's frequent guest on hunting excursions and other recreational pursuits on the would-be emperor's private hunting preserve. Thus it was that the French government and Giscard helped defray the cost, estimated at about thirty million dollars, of Bokassa's coronation in 1977 and saw to it that Bokassa and the French commercial interests in the CAR were given preferential commercial and financial treatment in Paris. By 1979, however, Bokassa had turned cruelly megalomaniacal and had become too much of an embarrassment even for Giscard, who finally sent his paratroopers to remove Bokassa from his throne. Giscard, who admitted having accepted Bokassa's diamonds, never recovered from the scandal of the relationship, and he lost the 1981 presidential elections in part because of it.[16]

While the Bokassa case represents an extreme and highly embarrassing outlier in the pattern of relations between France and francophone Africa, it does serve to illuminate the fact that when francophone African rulers turned to kleptocratic ways, there was no shortage of French officials and businesspeople to encourage them and share in the spoils. François-Xavier Verschave's *La françafrique,* which describes a vast offical, private French conspiracy using bribery and violence to preserve French interests and influence in Africa, may well be a caricature, but some of his descriptions of corrupt relations do have basis in fact. Gabon is a clear case in point.

In the field of state-level corruption Bongo's Gabon ranks not far behind Mobutu's Zaire; whether one calls it a kleptocracy, a felonious state, or a *rentier* state, at least since 1967 it has operated as a family business in which President Omar Bongo and his family have been principal shareholders, along with Elf-Gabon, the French oil company that dominates the country's economy. (Bongo was also friends with Bokassa, though for reasons different from Giscard's: the Bokassa family shared hospitality and some of its loot with Bongo, and vice versa). From 1964 to the early 1990s, the French government's principal coordinator for African affairs, the shadowy but extremely powerful Jacques Foccart, who died in 1997, helped install and maintain a group of French officials—the so-called clan des Gabonais—to command Gabon's security forces and safeguard France's interests in Gabon's oil and uranium industries.

This Franco-Gabonese ensemble, much of it operating behind the scenes, became, for all intents and purposes, the ruling elite of the country. While it is probably an exaggeration to call it, as does Douglas Yates, a set of "postcolonial state institutions invented by France . . . as part of a package deal . . . to justify and perpetuate French rule in black Africa," there is some truth to Yates's characterization of it as a "secret government, occult, hidden, and behind the scenes."[17] What is more, the ensemble finds its analog, as Bayart, Ellis, and Hibou argue, in a number of other African states:

> The division of African social systems into a legal edifice which is the partner of multilateral institutions and Western governments, and the real fabric of society, which is something different, is itself an indicator of the process of criminalization. Several of the African governments which have gone the furthest in this process of deregulation are characterized by the existence of a hidden and collective structure of power which surrounds, even controls, the tenants of state power. Hidden power-brokers of this sort are able to use to their advantage the privatization of legitimate means of coercion, and even to use with impunity private and illegitimate means of coercion in the form of paramilitary organizations, or even criminal gangs. . . . In the most extreme cases these hidden structures of power function as effective boards of directors chaired by the official head of state.[18]

The profits to the Bongo family enterprise from this collaboration apparently have been enormous: money amounting to about 8.5 percent of Gabon's ordinary budget, estimated at about $111 million per annum, most of it deriving from the oil sector and disguised by shell companies and third parties, has been channeled through a variety of private Bongo family accounts in Citibank private bank offices in Bahrain, Gabon, the Isle of Jersey, London, Luxembourg, New York, Paris, and Switzerland.[19] According to the revelations of the eighteen-month corruption trial of Elf's chief executive, Loik Le Floch-Prigent, which ended on November 12, 2003, he, his deputy Alfred Sirven, and Andre Tarallo, Elf's "Monsieur Afrique," were all involved in one way or another in getting Elf's gifts to Bongo, as well as in embezzling funds from the company itself.

Bayart, Ellis, and Hibou cite as further examples of these hidden structures Cameroon's "Beti lobby"; the predatory activities of Chad's presidential guard and its Zaghawa associates; the Central African Republic, "where the Yakoma clan had such great influence on President Kolingba and where people of the ilk of Jean-Jacques Demafouth enjoy influence with President Patassé";[20] and Congo-Brazzaville, with the activities of the Nibolek elite and its several representatives in President Lissouba's office, as well as the depredations of his freewheeling Zulus.

The networks of corruption are no longer restricted by national boundaries or by ties to a former colonial metropole; today they extend transnationally and across continents, a development recently highlighted by the exposure of corrupt transactions involving diamonds and other scarce commodities. The rulers of Togo, Burkina Faso, Côte d'Ivoire, Congo-Brazzaville, Gabon, and Rwanda, and their several "boards of directors" were all directly implicated in the special March 2000 UN Security Council Report of the Panel of Experts on Violations of Security Council Sanctions Against UNITA. The panel had investigated sanctions-busting activities—involving diamonds, arms and military equipment, petroleum and petroleum products, and related financial manipulations—that were carried on by friends of Angola's rebel Jonas Savimbi and his UNITA organization. These various enterprises were fueled by diamonds mined in Angolan areas under Savimbi's control, and the proceeds were channeled directly or indirectly into the hands of presidents Gnassingbé Eyadéma (Togo), Blaise Compaoré (Burkina Faso), Pascal Lissouba (Congo-Brazzaville), Henri Konan Bedié (Côte d'Ivoire), and Bongo (Gabon), and their colleagues and coteries.

The report names Eyadéma as UNITA's "primary supplier" of end-user certificates for arms and military equipment following the downfall of Savimbi's previous patron, Zairean president Mobutu. (End-user certificates designate the final and permissible destination of restricted or embargoed goods such as arms and other military equipment. Togo, as an approved end user, imported such material for transshipment to Savimbi.) Burkina Faso became a principal nexus of illegal flights from and into UNITA-controlled areas, and Gabon the main refueling depot for these and other illegal flights. Bulgaria was named as the main source of arms, and Rwanda as a center for illicit gunrunning and diamond trading. While all those accused issued vehement denials and sharp criticisms of the report, the evidence it presented, along with that presented in non-UN corroborative reports, makes for a very strong and credible case for the existence of a highly profitable international, and particularly African, network of corrupt dealings at the highest state levels, operations deliberately kept in the parapolitical shadows.[21]

There is much more to the story; corruption is not simply an activity reserved to the wealthy or powerful. It turns out that the more venal the managers of the state and the more disengaged or disaggregated the polity, the greater the likelihood that petty official corruption will become the order of the day all up and down the social system. In 1999 Cameroon achieved the dubious distinction of being ranked ninety-ninth out of ninety-nine countries in Transparency International's annual "Corruption Perception Index."[22] The honor was well merited: for years it seemed that virtually all the country's officials were on the take. The opportunities appeared endless: for example, travelers in Cameroon encountered multiple ad hoc police roadblocks where they had to pay off officials before they were allowed to proceed (during the 1970s a 1,500 CFA note did the trick);

a post office mailbox was available only with a side-payment; only with a bribe could one obtain official certificates, licenses, permits, tax and customs vouchers, and purchase orders; and only with sizable cash payments to recruiting officers were those seeking to enter the armed forces able to do so.

In this kind of environment and in the face of such exactions, which are encountered throughout our fourteen states, civil society finds multiple ways to evade and avoid the state and its agents, in the process reinforcing the structures of the larger parapolitical domain. Unchecked corruption has a built-in multiplier effect, and all too often corruption by national leaders acts as a catalyst for the growth of corrupt networks from the top down. Even when corruption at the top seeks cover in the parapolitical shadows, it cannot hide from the informal information networks in society—the *radio-trottoir,* or "sidewalk radio," and its upper-level analog, the *radio-couloir,* or "corridor radio." Thus the greed and malfeasance of those at the top stimulates and, in the eyes of its practitioners, even seems to justify corruption at the lower echelons of the state.[23] A Cameroonian popular saying, "The goat grazes where it is tethered" *(Le chêvre brut la ou il est attaché),* nicely captures the idea.

It is important to recall that official corruption is not a late development in independent Africa, including its francophone states: it was present at independence, often in the form of a poisoned apple left over from the colonial period. African officials who stole from the colonial state often did so as a way of challenging and subverting alien rule; unfortunately and all too often, they continued their practices in their new African-ruled polities. In 1962 René Dumont's coruscating book *L'Afrique Noire est mal partie* (False Start in Africa) issued an early warning, noting that "independence is not always 'decolonization'" and that the old habits had taken on new life:

> Too many African *élites* have interpreted independence as simply meaning that they could move into the jobs and enjoy the privileges of the Europeans. . . . Since independence . . . the increase in corruption has taken on alarming proportions in certain countries, particularly the Central African Republic, the Republic of Congo (Brazzaville), Gabon, the Ivory Coast, and Dahomey. Investigating committees were established in the Cameroons to ferret out corruption, and it has been asserted that the embezzlements thus detected amount to a tenth of the budget. This figure seems high, yet it is by no means certain that the investigations reached very far up in the hierarchy.[24]

Not even Dumont could have foreseen the speed with which corruption would grow and flourish on the continent: within five years things progressed to the point where, as Andreski noted in his 1966 work, *The African Predicament,* many of the new rulers had turned into kleptocrats and had begun to despoil the patrimonies so hopefully given into their charge at independence.

The Darkest Side of the Polity: Tyranny

Political corruption and tyranny tend to go hand in hand: those who steal from the public treasury with impunity, if they are also the managers of the state, soon learn that a docile and frightened population makes easier prey, and that the institutions of the state can be easily bent to that end. So it is that the managers of the "shadow state" in Africa (as described by William Reno and by Bayart, Ellis, and Hibou)[25] not only run their system's kleptocratic operations, but also operate its "secret" prisons, "secret" police and security apparatus, and torture chambers. The parapolitical domain thus created within the interstices and "invisible" spaces of the state can encompass both corrupt and tyrannous activities. Two examples, Guinea and Chad, serve both to locate that secret face and, perhaps paradoxically, to show how the state displays it to intimidate and frighten its citizens.

The most tyrannical of the francophone African regimes, Bokassa's perhaps excepted, have always preferred to keep their most brutal machineries of repression—murder, torture, arbitrary arrest and imprisonment, extrajudicial punishment of dissenters, and the like—hidden from view, but not completely, so that when examples need to be made the victims can be put on public display. Thus, in 1971 four men convicted of plotting against Sékou Touré's regime (Baldé Ousmane, Magassouba Morita, Camara Sékou, and Ibrahima Barry, known as Barry III) were hanged from a bridge crossing the main road into Conakry and left there for several days while traffic continued to roll beneath them. While the regime denied that prisoners were maltreated in the worst of Sékou Touré's prisons, the infamous camp Boiro (located close to Conakry), the regime itself fed rumors about the camp's torture chamber and especially about the so-called *diète noir* (the black diet), whereby prisoners were starved to death. Here, of course, is where Diallo Telli, the former secretary-general of the Organization of African Unity and a close friend of Sékou Touré, was tortured and died of the *diète noir* in 1977.[26]

Similarly, while hundreds were secretly tortured and killed in former Chadian president Habré's infamous *piscine*—a series of torture chambers built into an old swimming pool at Habré's Ndjamena headquarters—and thousands more were secretly tortured and killed in other detention centers, the existence of the *piscine* and its torture chambers was generally known, and that in part through the regime's efforts. According to testimony given to the Senegalese court before which Habré was tried in July 2000, the regime occasionally released severely mutilated or traumatized prisoners to spread terror among the population and dissuade potential opponents. No one knows how many became victims of Habré's regime; fifty thousand dead, averaging between forty and fifty killed per day, is not an unreasonable estimate.[27] A Senegalese appeals court quashed the indictment in the same month, arguing that it had no jurisdiction over Habré or his alleged crimes. Idriss Déby, Habré's successor, who had sought to build his own legitimacy by demonizing Habré, protested the dismissal and agreed to help appeal the decision and to turn over additional documentation to a truth commission investigating his predecessor's regime.[28]

While the brutalities and human rights violations of Bokassa's CAR regime and those of Habré and Sékou Touré have been well publicized and visible, the daily toll of political victims created in many of the other states of our fourteen remain largely unrecorded except where prominent persons are involved or large numbers of people are killed or injured and the news cannot be kept from the international medias. However, the annual and special reports of organizations such as Amnesty International, Human Rights Watch, Reporters Without Borders, and Article 19 (an anticensorship organization), as well as the U.S. State Department's annual human rights reports on individual African states, all provide windows on the continuing operation of overt and shadow state domains of official oppression. For example, Amnesty International's *Report 2001,* which covers the year 2000, cites ten of our fourteen states for human rights violations of various kinds; the most egregious offenders, according to AI, were the regimes in Burkina Faso, Chad, Cameroon, Côte d'Ivoire, Guinea, and Mauritania, and even though the 2001 Amnesty report doesn't include listings for them, Gabon and the CAR, according to media sources and the 2000 and 2001 U.S. State Department reports, should also have been included.[29]

The principal offenders in the Amnesty violations categories (according to AI and other sources) were as follows for 2001:

- Extrajudicial executions (confirmed or possible): Cameroon, Chad (prior years), Côte d'Ivoire, Guinea, Mauritania, Senegal.
- "Disappearances" (cases in which persons missing in previous years remain unaccounted for): Cameroon, Mauritania, Senegal, CAR, Gabon.
- Torture and ill-treatment (by security forces, police, and other agents of state): Cameroon, Chad, Congo-Brazzaville, Côte d'Ivoire, Guinea, Mauritania, Niger, Senegal, Togo, Gabon, CAR.
- Prisoners of conscience (individuals detained or imprisoned for political reasons): Cameroon, Burkina Faso, Guinea, Mauritania, Senegal, Togo, Gabon.
- Detention without charge (arbitrary arrest or detention): Burkina Faso, Cameroon, Chad, Congo-Brazzaville, Côte d'Ivoire, Guinea, Mauritania, Niger, Senegal, Togo, Gabon, CAR.

- Human rights abuses by armed opposition groups: Chad, Congo-Brazzaville, Guinea, Senegal.

This list, which is similar to those for other recent years, was compiled not primarily to designate violations and violators of human rights, but to suggest the widespread impunity with which these major and petty tyrannies are committed, and that in the most repressive of the regimes, they occur almost on a daily basis. The obverse of that coin is the fact that states with democratic or at least relatively liberal regimes—Senegal, Mali, Benin—have the fewest such violations and are actively seeking to curb and punish violators. It remains, nevertheless, that some regimes unleash their regular or special security forces and then give them carte blanche, and those forces, in turn, commit egregious violations of human rights. During 2000 such sets of circumstances occurred, for example, in Cameroon, Côte d'Ivoire, and Burkina Faso.

In Cameroon, a special security unit known as the *Commandement Opérationel* (CO), or Operational Command, was set up in February ostensibly to combat street crime in Douala and Yaoundé. During the first half of the year it was reportedly responsible for killing scores of criminal suspects, as well as for carrying out beatings, rapes, and other ill-treatment of those detained. In June 2000 Cardinal Christian Tumi, the Catholic archbishop of Douala, confronted the minister for territorial administration, accusing the CO of killing at least five hundred people, but it was only in 2001, after citizens began to uncover mass graves of victims in and around Douala, that the regime took action to curb the CO.[30] The activities of the CO were also allegedly directed against opponents of the regime of President Biya, and if so, they ran parallel to those of the other security agencies, which continued to harass, detain, imprison, torture, and sometimes murder actual and suspected members of the Social Democratic Front (SDF), the Social Program for Liberty and Democracy, the Southern Cameroons National Council (SCNC), the National Union for Democracy and Progress (Union Nationale pour la Démocratie et le Progrès [UNDP]), and other opposition parties and groups.[31]

In Côte d'Ivoire, following the overthrow of President Henri Konan Bedié in December 1999, the successor regime of General Robert Gueï, which remained in power until it was replaced in October 2000 by that of President Laurent Gbagbo, was responsible for widespread killings, torture, and other violations of human rights carried out by members of the military and by allied paramilitary gangs known as the *Camora,* or Red Brigades. In October 2000 fifty-seven bodies, allegedly those of suspected sympathizers of opposition leader Alassane Ouattara, were discovered in a mass grave in Yopougon, near Abidjan. Compelling evidence adduced in 2001 implicated Gueï's gendarmerie, or security forces.[32]

In Burkina Faso the regime of President Compaoré carried out a country-wide campaign of arbitrary arrests, detentions, assaults, and beatings against members of a coalition of opposition parties, human rights organizations, trade unions, and journalists' and students' organizations known as the Collectif d'Organisations Démocratique de Masse et de Partis Politiques. The Collectif, which had organized a three-day general strike to protest the use of force by the police, which had left thirty demonstrators injured, was also involved in other strikes and protests over a five-month period.[33] Hundreds, perhaps thousands, were thereafter targeted, and there were reports that the campaign was directed particularly against ethnic Mossi and Fulani opponents of the regime.

These three cases are but the visible tip of the iceberg of petty and large-scale tyrannies visited upon the citizens of most of our fourteen states. However, these citizens are not completely defenseless against the reach of what Robert Fatton calls "the predatory state." Given the slightest opening or opportunity, the oppressed find ways not only of expressing their anger and resistance, but also of constructing useful bypasses and other structures in the parapolitical domain. The tyranny has yet to appear that completely subjugates, enslaves, or controls those it rules; during the twentieth century the Nazi, Stalinist, and Maoist regimes tried to do so and earned the title *totalitarian,* but that adjective described their aspirations, not the reality— and failures—of their politics. All three were corrupt to their core; all three sacrificed millions of people to their ambitions without ever realizing those ambitions; and all three, their most strenuously brutal efforts notwithstanding, could neither silence their internal opponents nor drive them out of existence. Perhaps only the Khmer Rouge's Kampuchea came close to being truly totalitarian, but that accomplishment came only at the price of virtual self-annihilation. The worst of the African despotisms (those of Maçias Nguéma, Idi Amin, and Jean-Bédel Bokassa) fell victim to their own excesses; the lesser ones, some of which have sponsored or countenanced brutal acts of official repression by their security agents, have been undermined by rampant corruption and by evasions, the growth of resistance, and "departicipation" in civil society.[34] Overall, while the most brutal regimes are long gone, the record is not comforting. The 2002 Freedom House ratings give the designation "free" only to Mali, Benin, and Senegal. (See Appendix J.)

The Subversive Power of Parapolitics
and Other Paradoxes and Excursions

An ongoing debate among students of African politics has been about whether the African state is getting stronger, becoming a "Leviathan" that requires "taming," or becoming weaker (soft, flabby, and receding). The foregoing discussion on corruption and tyranny could well support an argument about the attempt of African regimes to strengthen the state, and the evidence of widespread elite corruption and regime brutality could easily testify to the state's increased power. On the other hand, as Monga, Bayart, and others argue, what has here been called the parapolitical domain in its various guises and civil manifestations has the capacity to sap the authority of the strongest and most brutal state, to undermine its vitality, and to blunt if not reduce the reach of despotism. Indeed, it may arguably have already done so in a number of our fourteen states. According to Monga,

> The upsurge of informal groupings has the potential to overturn not just the existing political order, but also the surrounding moral order. . . . Most political authorities in Africa do not have a grip on the actual mechanisms of society. . . . Thirty years of authoritarian rule have forged a concept of indiscipline as a method of popular resistance. In order to survive and resist laws and rules judged to be antiquated, people have had to resort to the treasury of their imagination. Given that life is one long fight against the state, inventiveness has gradually conspired to craftily defy everything that symbolizes public authority.[35]

Goran Hyden carries the argument even further: he claims that the "economy of affection"—in effect, that of transactions based on personal, kinship, and communal ties—has overwhelmed state structures in the postindependence period. Corruption, tribalism, nepotism, collusion between civil servants and politicians, and the circumvention of laws and regulations all add up to a "softening" of the state against which postindependence regimes have been unable to mount any successful defense.[36]

It may be that one's position in the debate depends on one's perspective. Civil society may appear to have much greater strength in relation to the state when it is viewed from its grass roots than when it is seen from the elevated position of the state, in which case the state may appear the stronger. What is more likely is that, as Monga implies, there is a paradox at work here: as the state becomes stronger and, perhaps, begins to fortify itself with the institutions of despotism, it also becomes weaker because the citizenry that it seeks to control increasingly look for ways to avoid, evade, bypass, undermine, or even escape the new demands and exactions.[37]

Because even the worst tyrannies have their soft spots and because most petty despotisms in the guise of authoritarian regimes almost by definition tend to operate inefficiently, the dynamics of parapolitics can push the growth of the nonformal sector at the expense of the state. All of this is not preordained. A strong state with effective structures and agents could presumably slow or hamper the growth of the informal political sector. Nor does it occur neatly or as an action-reaction dialectic. Rather, it occurs variably, depending on the strength of civil society, the capacities of the state, and the nature of the political order. The contest is continuous in our fourteen states: as the state and its managers seek to co-opt or preempt real or symbolic political space for their own purposes, civil society often pushes back, entering and co-opting space left open in the contest or as yet unappropriated by either side. It is clear that the power of the state cannot be taken at face value, however imposing the regime or its managers; the extent and strength of that power is always an empirical question, and it remains evident that what goes on in its parapolitical shadows may turn out to be more consequential to the real power of the state—adding to it or subtracting from it—than what is visible on its formal political facade.

In the ongoing joust for political space between the state and civil society, there are few arenas of contestation where the public have a built-in advantage. The street is one such place, if only because it has the potential of overwhelming the states' agents with the sheer numerical weight of strikers and demonstrators, making such protest extremely difficult to contain. This is why strikes and demonstrations remain so frequent an expression of popular opposition and resistance. Even when the state mobilizes its coercive resources to restrain them, they have a way of evoking creative public disorder to thwart the gendarmes, soldiers, and other security forces sent against them. This is what happened in Cameroon in mid-to-late 1991, when an escalating series of labor, student, and street-people protest demonstrations and strikes grew into the national opposition's five-month *villes mortes,* or ghost town, campaign, which affected most of the country's southwestern towns and provinces.[38]

Because the Cameroonian *villes mortes* experience has apparently inspired similar attempts elsewhere, it is worth examining in summary detail. First, it is important to note that the key events triggering the campaign took place during a period of political liberalization in 1990–1991, when, for the first time since the 1960s, opposition leaders and parties were able to confront the regime. Those events led to the arrest and trial of Pius Njawe, editor and publisher of *Le Messager,* the most critical paper during the 1980s, and Célestin Monga, writer and economist, whose broadly accusatory "Open Letter" to President Biya was printed in *Le Messager* on December 27, 1990. Both were charged with bringing Biya into disrepute and disturbing public order. Their January trial, in which they were fined and drew suspended sentences, spawned the formation of defense committees for the two journalists, brought thousands of protesters and troops into the streets as far north as Garoua, and attracted international attention.

During the early months of 1990 there were demonstrations at the University of Yaoundé, during which troops were brought in and six students were killed, and at other college campuses, and labor unrest and strikes in Douala. When the opposition began agitating for a Cameroonian version of the sovereign national conference that could resolve the nation's political crisis, the government responded not only by sending in troops to put down acts of civil disobedience, but also by deploying military

Operational Command units in seven provinces considered potentially disruptive: Far North, North, Adamawa, West, Northwest, Littoral, and Southwest. In April, in an attempt to mollify the opposition, Biya appointed Sadou Hayatou, a moderate and an ostensible reformer, to the long-vacant post of prime minister. However, in a June 27 speech on projected elections, Biya categorically refused to countenance a national conference.

There was immediate violent public response on the streets of Douala, Bamenda, and other cities and towns in four provinces—Northwest, Southwest, Littoral, and West. The state immediately called out the police and the army to put down the demonstrators, but in the end it could secure only the largest northern towns and Yaoundé, the heart of Biya's Beti-Bulu support. Joseph Takougang and Milton Krieger describe the scene in mid-1991:

> Confrontations spread rapidly from Douala after Biya's June 27 speech and two more aggressive regime decisions: security personnel prevented a rally planned [for] July 5 in front of the presidential palace; six human rights groups were banned the next week (the NCOPA [the coalition of oppositional groups and parties] was already outlawed, but defied the order). Spontaneous street demonstrations, market and other economic boycotts became trenchant, fully organized civil disobedience which for three to six months depending on the locale, made massive rallies and other highly visible challenges to state authority Cameroon's dominant features. They spread from provincial capitals of North West, South West, and Littoral Provinces, and also from smaller centers like Kumbo-Nso (North West), . . . Kumba (South West), and Mbouda (West). . . . Rural people either joined actively or were drawn into the movement, some reluctantly by threats. "Villes mortes" held firm in all these four provinces for at least ten weeks, longer with some slippage in Douala, until Christmas in Bamenda and Bafoussam.[39]

The campaign sought to literally shut down the cities and towns where the opposition was able to control the streets: most schools stayed shut; all four-wheeled inter- and intracity vehicular transport stopped running; banks, shops except pharmacies on a rotating schedule, and all but the most minimal curbside markets closed Monday through Friday. Postal and health services continued to operate, but the public sector otherwise closed down. Most of the water, electricity, and telecommunications staff went on strike, and the rest stayed away. As fuel ran short, clandestine supplies from Nigeria became available. Markets opened on Saturday, as did banks, the latter somewhat chaotically, given periodic runs on available cash.

What is remarkable, aside from the opposition's ability to close down the towns, is the sheer numbers it could mobilize onto the streets. Takougang and Krieger relate that in Bamenda, a city of no more than 150,000 people, some 20,000 showed up at a rally at the governor's mansion on July 5. "Bamenda's rallies of three-four hours, three times a week, mobilized 8,000–10,000 people, 30,000 on special occasions, and 50,000 at a crisis march of defiance October 2." In all, "up to 2,000,000 unarmed Cameroonians directly or indirectly linked to *villes mortes* . . . worked striking changes in its [Cameroon's] core area's political culture. . . . They created the courage and discipline of a largely non-violent resistance movement."[40]

If some in the opposition had hoped that the *villes mortes* campaign would topple the regime, they were disappointed. Nevertheless, the demonstration of popular power shook the regime and heartened the opposition. The campaign largely ended by Christmas 1991, and its effects dissipated considerably during the legislative and presidential elections of 1992—which, amid charges of fraud and chicanery, were won by Biya and his government party. The *villes mortes* campaign may also have pushed the regime into commencing what Linda Kirschke calls "informal repression," using northern *lamibé,* or Fulani chiefs, in Rey-Bouba and Mayo-Rey to harass, arrest, imprison, and beat up opposition activists and candidates. In 1996 UNDP deputy to the national assembly Haman Adama Daouda and thirteen other UNDP party members were severely beaten by the armed guards of the *lamido* of Mayo-Rey. Adama Daouda died of his injuries.[41] What survived was an opposition that, while unable to take electoral advantage of its 1991 campaign, was strengthened by the experience and a regime that became even more repressive in the wake of the 1992 and 1997 elections. "We took the streets in 1991," an opposition leader wrote optimistically in 2001, "and we can do it again. . . . It's only a matter of time until Biya overreaches."[42]

The street as an arena of contestation between civil society and regime is, of course, nothing new in Africa, just as it is nothing new elsewhere. In 1963, for example, popular demonstrations fanned by Cardinal Zoungrana and the Mossi people's traditional ruler, the *mogho naba* Kougri, forced the resignation of Upper Volta's president Maurice Yaméogo, and during the 1960s and 1970s at least three changes of government in Dahomey were forced by striking students and civil servants. During the 1996–1997 school year in Burkina Faso, a three-month student strike pitted students and their sympathizers against the army and the police on the streets of Ouagadougou, though here the regime got the upper hand.[43]

While these events, including the *villes mortes* campaign in Cameroon, brought civil society into the streets to confront the state, less spectacular, even banal, contests take place on a daily basis involving those who use the street for commerce or simply for economic or social survival. After a period of open confrontation during the 1960s and early 1970s the Douala unemployed, organized as a loose trade union, and the municipal authorities negotiated a gentlemen's agreement to keep down rampant petty crime. Patrick Gilliard and Laurent Pédenon report that the beggars of Niamey,

Niger, many of whom live not only from the street but on it, invest it as "territory" and organize themselves and their activities into networks so as to extract maximum profit for their members. As part of the informal marketplace, the beggars apparently strike deals with legitimate merchants with whom they trade, property owners whose street space they use, and, if need be, the municipal authorities and the police, who might otherwise harass them excessively. From the point of view of city officials, the streets must be kept open for traffic and legitimate trade, and the continuing contest between the authorities and the beggars is over the appropriation and use of both marginal and profitable street space.[44]

The street is real physical space, and real blood has been shed on it in the state-society contests that characterize much of Africa's parapolitics. However, many of those contests are over symbolic as much as physical political space. Because power constitutes both dominion over the symbols and rituals of authority and control over people and resources, the state seeks to appropriate for itself as much of both as it can. Consider, for example, two such contests, one having to do with the official grandeur with which African presidents are invested, and the other, with the appropriation of religious and magical rites and symbols, both of which take place in part in the parapolitical domain and have important political impact.

Variations on the cult of personality could at one time or another be found practically everywhere in sub-Saharan Africa during the 1960s, 1970s, and 1980s. They ranged from attributions of near- or semidivinity (Equatorial Guinea's Nguéma enjoyed the title of "The Unique Miracle" and had it proclaimed as official doctrine that his mother had borne him by virgin birth; Kwame Nkrumah was consecrated by his own quasi-religious catechism and a blasphemous version of the Lord's Prayer) to the more conventional, but still grandiloquent, designations of the leader as Father of the Country, Man of the People, the Great Helmsman (one of Mao's favorites), Indefatigable and All-Knowing, and the like. Then too, there were special titles, presumably emphasizing some extraordinary virtue or characteristic: for example, The Man of Rigor (Biya's special title for himself); The Great *Sily* ("the great elephant," used by Sékou Touré; the *sily* was also Guinea's unit of currency); The Golden Voice of the North (Nigeria's Abubakar Tafawa Balewa); The Sage (Houphouët-Boigny, who also liked being called simply Le Vieux); The Redeemer (both Samuel Doe and Nkrumah, who also enjoyed the title of Messiah); and Father of Independence and Pioneer of African Unity (Ahidjo).[45]

In some countries it was difficult to avoid the image of the leader, be it in statue form, on billboards, on official and unofficial walls indoors or outdoors, on coins and currency, and, very commonly, printed on the cloth women wore as wrapping or over their dresses. The national party headquarters of the RPT (Rassemblement du Peuple Togolais) even sold a special Eyadéma windup watch on the face of which a portrait of President-General Eyadéma appeared every thirty seconds. And, of course, there was the famous "apotheosis" TV clip showing Zairean president Mobutu emerging from the clouds and descending gloriously, shining and in fully bemedaled uniform, all before the newsreaders came on camera.[46]

All of this is a matter of the state seeking to appropriate and, if possible, to monopolize yet another aspect of symbolic political space. More often than not, for all its initial splash the regimes' ideologizing made little lasting impression. The regimes did leave a limited vocabulary of targeted resentment (such as old Marxist anticolonial and anti-imperialist phrases), some ideas co-opted into nationalist programs, a number of old ideologues who washed up after their tides had gone out (e.g., Senegal's Cheikh Anta Diop, Niger's Djibo Bakary, Cameroon's Félix-Roland Moumié), some politically useful martyrs (Marien Ngouabi, Thomas Sankara), and memories of periods of exciting ideological ferment and debate. Considering the fact that homemade official ideologies in Africa have relatively short half-lives (it is doubtful that any Guinean today seriously cares about Sékou Touré's socialism, any Ivoirian about "Houphouëtism," any Cameroonian about Ahidjo's "humanism" or Biya's "rigor," or any Chadian about Tombalbaye's "authenticity"), it is not surprising that the images of leadership grandeur evoked by regimes also have trouble convincing their intended audiences.

As happens almost everywhere, when African leaders begin to glorify themselves, they quickly become targets for the deflating barbs of songwriters, poets, and playwrights, as well as those of the general public. Apparently the pretensions of certain African heads of state (Bokassa or, perhaps, Bongo) proved irresistible to noted Cameroonian songwriter Francis Bebey, whose "King of the Pygmies" (along with the protest songs of Grand Kalle and Franklin Boukaka) became popular throughout francophone Africa:[47]

> In our camp
> there's a little man
> who claims to be king.
> Everyone laughs when he says
> that his father was a king.
> Because everyone knows that in our tribe
> there has never been a king.
> We don't think that a crown
> serves much purpose on hunting trips. (1983)

Bongo, who is only about five feet, four inches tall, is rumored to have thought about becoming a king or emperor himself, as had Bokassa in

CAR, and to have retainers searching for an historical royal link; the reference to hunting trips could have been to Bongo's frequent visits to ex-emperor Bokassa's hunting preserve. Or the song could be used to deride any head of state on a monarchical ego trip. Cameroonian political scientist Luc Sindjoun observes that "pop singers mention the government only to mock it as 'Petit Pays,' [singers who] . . . Sybil-like, . . . recall that 'even Chiefs of State die'"; others castigate prominent Beti politicians who "eat"—that is, profit from the political system.[48]

Even more subversive is the trivialization of the names and titles of heads of state and political leaders, something of a pastime throughout francophone Africa. In Cameroon, President Biya becomes, derisively, Popaul and L'Homme-Lion ("lion man"); Gabon's Bongo Le Petit-Grand ("the little big man") or just Le Pygmée; and Houphouët-Boigny's name went from the respectful Le Vieux ("the old man") to the dismissive Le Vieillard ("the oldster"). As common on the street as such verbal byplay is, it becomes more serious when employed by journalists, authors, poets, and playwrights: then it is often seen as a direct challenge to those in power. When Njawe's *Le Messager* was still published in Cameroon, it poked fun at Biya and his regime, and the state's prosecution and persecution of Njawe and his writers and staff was undoubtedly due in part to the fact that many of Njawe's barbs had hit home. Njawe and Monga, tried and convicted and then immediately released, were fortunate in having mobilizable friends abroad; as Article 19 and other human rights organizations point out, journalists and writers elsewhere in our fourteen states are still in jail for alleged insults to thin-skinned presidents or their close colleagues.

Perhaps it is the fate of those who attract the state's unwelcome attention that accounts for what is perhaps the most subversive kind of popular response to those in power: the creation of what C. M. Toulabor calls "a lexicon of political derision," a set of words and phrases coined with or given insulting or even obscene meaning through double-entendre, allusion, deliberate ambiguity, or special mode of expression. In Togo the target was General Eyadéma, the self-proclaimed Guide and Savior of Togo and its ruler since he gunned down the country's first president, Sylvanus Olympio, in 1963. What seem on the surface to be quite ordinary or banal expressions in the Ewe language have, by the way they are uttered or the context in which they are expressed, become a "subterranean language" (Toulabor's term) of political insult. The words themselves (*tsala, amegan, foti,* etc.) are quite crude, but they are less so in expression than in their connotative Ewe meanings; they associate Eyadéma with a huge erect phallus and sexual excess, the head of a gorilla, and malodorous feces and flatus, and they accuse him of trying to whiten himself (*Yovovi*—"little white man"). Toulabor, himself an Ewe and able to translate the hidden meanings of the Ewe language, points out that Ewe society is given to verbal sexual hyperbole (though not to sexual excess in practice) and that sexual and scatological insult comes naturally to the lips as a weapon in the state-society contest.[49]

How general in our fourteen states is this subterranean language of political insult and derision? Students of the genre have specific evidence only such as that from Togo and anecdotal evidence from the other states, but if Monga is right—and there is every good reason to believe he is—it exists as widespread expression almost everywhere that civil society is in active contestation with the state: openly in democratic or democratizing polities, and in the parapolitical domain as deliberate ambiguity or part of James C. Scott's "hidden transcripts,"[50] where the state seeks to repress free expression. In some contexts, as Mbembe demonstrates, it manifests itself in what amounts to a contest of obscenities: however vulgar and obscene the banal symbolic displays of the state, civil society finds its own vulgarities and obscenities in reply.[51] At all events, how the contest plays itself out, or the specific forms it takes, depends on the particular dynamics of each polity.

There are other aspects of nonformal politics in our fourteen states that I did not cover in my discussion, including, for example, the role of secret societies, *fétisheurs* (masters of traditional magic), and spiritual advisors in elite politics. We know more of these matters as they relate to Gabon than to anywhere else, so the Gabonese case deserves at least brief mention here. The two most important traditional societies in Gabon are Bwiti and Ndjobi, which count Léon M'Ba and Omar Bongo among their members, and which have been used by them to reinforce their positions of power. Masonic lodges, especially the Rite Equatorial, which has important elite connections in West and Equatorial Africa, also is part of Bongo's repertory of political assets. After securing Bwiti and Ndjobi, Bongo extended his control over the Christian churches, and after his conversion to Islam, Bongo himself became a cult figure, using the African and non-African ideological spectrum to create his own personal ideology, Bongoism, and to project himself as the Guide Eclairé ("enlightened guide of the nation") who leads Gabon from tribal darkness to "national unity." Bongo has thought to preempt the terrain of symbolic politics for his own uses, and to a considerable extent he has succeeded, but his efforts have not been uncontested: François Ngolet reports that dissatisfied elements within Bwiti have tried to use their "magic" against him and that uncaptured, autonomous religious sects have become part of Bongo's opposition.[52]

Parapolitics exists in all political systems. In free societies, it operates as a benign complement to the state, its institutions, and its agents because officials understand and maintain the difference between that which is in the public sphere and that which is reserved for the private domain—in effect, the old legal distinction between *res publica* and *res privata*. All too often, those in power blur or even eliminate that distinction. The result is abuse of power—corruption, tyranny, and rule by ethnic dictators and/or religious tyrants. Our fourteen states have thus far escaped the evils of religious tyranny, but not the other excesses that attend governments operating without accountability and transparency. Only Senegal, Mali, and Benin have begun moving out of the circle of bad governance; all fourteen, however, have official parapolitical domains that sometimes bring their governments to the edge of criminality, and their populations to the politics of disobedience, evasion, and resistance. That is why it no longer suffices to speak of politics as that which transpires in the official realm.

Notes

1. See Naomi Chazan et al., *Politics and Society in Contemporary Africa,* 159–220, for applications of these concepts.

2. Bayart, *The State in Africa: The Politics of the Belly,* 55.

3. Ibid.

4. Luc Sindjoun makes this point and presents an extensive display of ethnoregional recruitment patterns in Cameroon during the forty-year 1957–1997 period in "La politique d'affection en Afrique Noire." See also Kofele-Kale, "Ethnicity, Regionalism, and Political Power: A Post-Mortem of Ahidjo's Cameroon," 53–82.

5. Mbembe, *Afriques indociles,* 169–170. My translation.

6. This is the state in crisis, when it becomes progressively unable to deliver political goods to its citizens, and the domain under its control shrinks. Ultimately such a crisis, if left unresolved, may leave the state with its government controlling little more than the presidential palace, if that. One recent example of an imploding state, Zaire under Mobutu Sese Seko during its last decade, sought to stave off complete disintegration by creating virtually autonomous satrapies around provincial capitals. That did not, of course, prevent Zaire's final collapse in 1997. The penultimate step was anarchy, which was only partially redeemed by Mobutu's death and Laurent Kabila's forces' capture of Kinshasa in May 1997 and, in 2001, by Kabila's assassination and the succession of his son, Joseph. Both Somalia and Liberia imploded, and both lapsed into anarchy. After the death of its elder statesman, President William V. S. Tubman, in 1971, Liberia was ruled first by an inept civilian (William Tolbert) and then by a hapless, brutal military man (Samuel Doe), and then, in 1989, it fell victim to civil war. Doe was murdered by one of his adversaries in 1990, and by 1996 Liberia's government was reduced to ruling only a part of the capital, Monrovia, and that only with the help of a West African peacekeeping force (ECOMOG). In 1997 it was brutally "saved" by its chief rebel tormentor, Charles Taylor, who had himself elected president by threatening to resume the civil war. Somalia, which started to implode in 1991 with the collapse of the Muhammad Siad Barre regime, still lacked an effective central government ten years later in mid-2003. Ghana during the period 1969–1982, when recurring government crises virtually left the Ghanaian countryside to its own devices, is another case in point. It was Ghana's good fortune that a strong civil society rooted in the country's towns and villages took over many of the state's functions and literally saved Ghana from slipping into anarchy and chaos. That story is told in Chazan, *An Anatomy of Ghanaian Politics: Managing Political Recession.*

7. Monga, "L'inflation du politique en Afrique: Une thèorie de la consolida-

tion démocratique," 23. My translation. In the eventual facedown between the three leaders in 1997, it was Sassou-Nguesso who won the elimination contest. An attempt by Kolelas to displace Sassou-Nguesso with elements of Kolelas's old militia and ethnically friendly regular army soldiers in May–June 2001 failed badly.

8. Sundberg, "The Struggle for Kingship: Moses or Messiah—Ethnic War and the Use of Ethnicity in the Process of Democratization in Congo-Brazzaville," 87–108. Sundberg's account is one of the best—and clearest—attempts to unravel the extraordinary tangle of ethnicity and identity politics in Congo-Brazzaville. See also *Les deux Congos dans la guerre* ("The Two Congos at War"). The fullest and most recent account of these events is "Dossier spécial: Congo-Brazzaville, entre guerre et paix." François-Xavier Verschave devotes fifty-four unsparing pages (15–69) to Congo-Brazzaville's violent 1998 and 1999 politics in his *Noir silence: Qui arrêtera la Françafrique?* The main ethnic groups of precolonial provenance were the Batéké, Bakota, Bakongo, and the Mbochi. The Lari of Brazzaville and the constructed Nibolek and Tcheks were all originally Bakongo, as were the Vili of Pointe Noire, and the Kuyu were originally Mbochi of Owando.

9. See MacGaffey and Bazenguissa-Ganga, *Congo-Paris*.

10. When I visited it, Bana probably had about fifteen thousand inhabitants, of whom about ten thousand lived in Bana town itself. My hosts said all the official demographics were wrong: they claimed at least thirty-five thousand, half of whom lived outside the chiefdom, spread around the country. Bana is one of some ninety Bamiléké chiefdoms in the densely populated Bamiléké region, which in 1954 was said to have a population of about 455,000 people, but today has at least three times that many. Bana town is located fifty kilometers due east of Bafang, the subdivisional headquarters, on the southern arc of the famous eastern "ring road," in Cameroon's West Province. The Bana speak one of the dialects of the Bafang cluster of languages, and they share a variety of sociopolitical characteristics with their coethnic neighbors in both francophone and anglophone Cameroon. Though the term *Bamiléké* has no strict ethnographic denotation, being simply a coinage designating the ensemble of a number of related so-called mountain/highland/grassfield peoples in the Cameroon southwest, their linguistic and cultural commonalities have been imprinted sufficiently that now they identify themselves as Bamiléké, or simply Bami, the old ambiguities notwithstanding. For further information on the Bamiléké, see particularly Dongmo, *Le Dynamisme Bamiléké*.

11. My point is reinforced by two studies: Miaffo and Warnier, "Accumulation et ethos de la notabilité chez le Bamiléké" (Accumulation and the Ethos of Distinction among the Bamiléké), and Rowlands, "Accumulation and the Cultural Politics of Identity"; see also Geschiere and Konings, *Itinéraires d'accumulation au Cameroun*.

12. Argenti, "Mbaya: Contemporary Masquerades and the State in Cameroon," citing Peter Geschiere's "Chiefs and Colonial Rule in Cameroon."

13. I define political corruption as "the unsanctioned, unscheduled use of public political resources and/or goods for private, that is, nonpublic ends" (Le Vine, *Political Corruption: The Ghana Case,* 2). Political corruption, in my view, is a process—at base an active dyadic relationship—in which at least one person is acting in an official capacity, involving the unsanctioned or illicit use of public goods presumably dedicated to public ends and entrusted to the official or officials concerned. The goods can include material things, like money or supplies, or nonmaterial goods, like contracts, information, privileged access, official facilitation, jobs, and the like. Such diversion of resources goes by a variety of names: *bribery, extortion, nepotism, black marketing,* and so on. In addition to the two Verschave books

(*Noir silence* and *La françafrique*), other useful books and edited collections on corruption in Africa include Péan, *L'argent noir* and *Affaires africaines;* Mbaku, ed., *Corruption and the Crisis of Institutional Reform in Africa;* and Kempe and Chikulo, eds., *Corruption and Development in Africa.* For a useful summary overview, see Médard, "Public Corruption in Africa: A Comparative Perspective."

14. Andreski, *The African Predicament,* especially 92–110, "Kleptocracy or Corruption as a System of Government." The most recent, and more sophisticated, version of that story is in Bayart, Ellis, and Hibou, *The Criminalization of the State in Africa.*

15. Bayart, Ellis, and Hibou, *Criminalization of the State.* The best of a small library of recent books on Mobutu and his regime not only trace the sordid story of Mobutu's rise and fall, but also provide insight into and analysis of how he gradually transformed Zaire into a criminal enterprise. For example, see Michela Wrong, *In the Footsteps of Mr. Kurtz.*

16. For additional details and bibliographic notes on the Bokassa period, see O'Toole, *Central African Republic;* Peau, *Bokassa 1er;* Decalo, *Psychoses of Power.*

17. Yates, *The Rentier State in Africa,* 111. See also "Le 'Clan des Gabonais,'" 129–165, 229–244, in Péan, *Affaires africaines.*

18. Bayart, Ellis, and Hibou, *Criminalization of the State,* 20–21.

19. "El Hadj Omar Bongo Case History," in U.S. Senate, *Minority Staff Report for Permanent Subcommittee on Investigations.* In addition to the charges levied against the Bongo regime by Verschave and others, the arrangement has been frequently cited as a prime example of neocolonialism. For evidence to that point, see Reed, "Gabon: a Neo-Colonial Enclave of Enduring French Interest."

20. U.S. Senate, *Committee on Governmental Affairs, Minority Staff Report,* "El Hadj Bongo Case History," 22.

21. UN Security Council, *Report of the Panel of Experts on Violations of Security Council Sanctions Against UNITA.*

22. Transparency International (TI) is a nongovernmental organization that conducts a series of annual surveys that rank countries on a set of ascriptively derived least-to-most indicators of corruption. The TI Index is generally considered highly reliable.

23. Two recent essays on corruption in Cameroon are Fombad, "Endemic Corruption in Cameroon," and Jua, "Cameroon: Jump-Starting an Economy in Crisis."

24. Dumont, *L'Afrique Noire est mal partie,* 86.

25. Reno develops this metaphor in his *Corruption and State Politics in Sierra Leone.* See also Bayart, Ellis, and Hibou, *Criminalization of the State.*

26. Camara, *La Guinée sans la France;* Rivière, *Guinea: The Mobilization of a People;* Adamolekun, *Sékou Touré's Guinea: An Experiment in Nation Building;* Kaké, *Sékou Touré, le héros et le tyran,* "Sékou Touré et la Guinée après Sékou Touré," *Jeune Afrique Plus,* no. 8 (June 1984); Charles, *Guinée,* 45–128; Le Vine, "Parliaments in Francophone Africa," 142–152; Kaba, "Guinean Politics: A Critical Historical Overview," 33; Touré, "Complot permanent," in *Défendre la Révolution,* 24–51; Biarnès, "Guinée: Le complot permanent," chapter 10, 157–182, in his *L'Afrique aux Africains.*

27. For details of the Habré indictment, prosecution, and trial, see Brody, "The Prosecution of Hissene Habré—An African Pinochet."

28. Ibid., 6. Verschave, *Noir silence,* in the chapter titled "Tchad, petrole et dictature," 151–174, argues that while Déby is not as brutally dictatorial as was Habré, he is no less corrupt. For a supporting view, see Conesa, "Les soubresauts

d'un état fictive: La Tchad des crises à répétition." Conesa argues that Déby is only the latest of the series of corrupt and brutal military adventurers who have come to power, usually with French help, since the fall of the Tombalbaye regime in 1975, and implies that Déby is not the last in this procession.

29. Amnesty International *World Report*, 2001.

30. Ibid., Cameroon Country Report. The exchanges between Cardinal Tumi and the regime can be found in the pages of Pius Njawe's Internet newspaper *Le Messager*, November 6, 11, 13, and 22, 2000. Njawe had originally published a print version of *Le Messager* in Cameroon, but beginning in 1990, after he was arrested several times, harassed (along with Célestin Mongo, who wrote for *Le Messager*), and tried for publishing "insults" to the regime, and after the paper was seized and its offices ransacked, in 1997 he began publishing on the Internet as well as in print. Withal, and despite periodic bouts of official harassment, *Le Messager* continues to operate from Douala, with both an Internet and a print version. The Internet edition is its "World Edition." The Njawe-Monga trial in 1990 was one of the sparks that set off the violent political confrontations that marked Cameroon during 1990 and 1991.

31. Amnesty International, *World Report*, 2001, Cameroon Country Report. A personal note: These allegations are also contained in five affidavits filed during 2000–2004 in U.S. immigration courts by Cameroonians seeking political asylum. I was involved in these cases as a pro bono consultant to the petitioners, and I found the petitioners' stories eminently credible: all had been accused of oppositional activity, and all had suffered arrest, imprisonment, beatings, and maltreatment up to and including torture at the hands of the authorities because of their political beliefs or activities. One of them, a woman denounced by a police informer as an SDF sympathizer, was never charged with any crime. She was raped by her jailers and suffered two years imprisonment under what can only be described as gross and inhumane conditions. Another, a student distantly related to the opposition leader John Fru Ndi, was arrested, beaten, and tortured, and saw several of his relatives killed and his parents' home burned to the ground before he was able to flee the country. All five petitioners were subsequently granted asylum. For both legal and humanitarian reasons, I cannot identify them.

32. Ibid., Côte d'Ivoire Country Report. Also, "Charnier de Yopougon: Une commission internationale accuse les gendarmes" (The Slaughterhouse of Yopougon: An International Commission Accuses the Gendarmes), *Le Monde*, July 20, 2001.

33. Amnesty International, *World Report*, 2001. Burkina Faso Country Report.

34. *Departicipation* is a coinage by Nelson Kasfir in his *The Shrinking Political Arena*. He argues that large-scale withdrawal from civic participation occurs as a result of the inroads of the predatory state; however, Bayart (*State in Africa*, 249) cautions that this not be taken as a universal trend; in fact, a collateral growth of activity in the informal sector belies it. Still, the widespread use of the "exit" option, chosen by abused citizens throughout francophone Africa, represents an important safety valve for civil society.

35. Monga, *The Anthropology of Anger: Civil Society and Democracy in Africa*, 146, 147, 148.

36. Hyden, *No Shortcut to Progress: African Development Management in Perspective*, 43 and 63. The summary of Hyden's argument is a paraphrase of Catherine Scott's précis, "Socialism and the Soft State in Angola and Mozambique," 25.

37. This is part of the argument of Wintrobe's *The Political Economy of Dictatorship*.

38. My summary of the *villes mortes* campaign is based on Takougang and Krieger's extensive and detailed account in their *African State and Society in the 1990s: Cameroon's Political Crossroads,"* 123–142 and passim.

39. Ibid., 127–128.

40. Ibid., 128–131.

41. Kirschke, "Informal Repression, Zero-Sum Politics, and Late Third-Wave Transitions."

42. Letter to the author, dated June 20, 2001, by a Cameroonian opposition leader who asked to be identified only as Monsieur K.

43. Wise, "Chronicle of a Student Strike in Africa: The Case of Burkina Faso, 1996–1997."

44. Gilliard and Pédenon, "Rues de Niamey, espace et territoires de la mendicité." The theme of the issue of *Politique Africaine* in which this article appears is "De la côté de la rue" (from street side). The authors note that during the regime of General Seyni Kountché, in periodic raids and control measures the police rounded up seasonal beggars and workers without permanent residence and forced them to return to their home villages by the truckload. Such extreme measures are apparently no longer used; however, in Niamey, as is often the case in other African capitals, the streets are temporarily swept clean of beggars when the regime expects visitors of mark or an influx of visitors for some official celebration. No contest here. Some of my comments about the beggars' relations with the authorities and local traders are from my field notes taken during visits to Ouagadougou in 1965, 1971, 1983, and 1989. In no African capital have I ever seen beggars at work on the streets through which presidential processions and official cavalcades are passing, though I have seen them removed if they had the temerity to so position themselves. I have always assumed that nonbegging mendicants standing with cheering crowds are allowed to join in the applause for passing presidents and dignitaries.

45. For an extended repertory of the adulatory titles with which leaders were endowed, or with which they had themselves endowed, see Kirk-Greene, "His Eternity, His Eccentricity, or His Exemplarity? A Further Contribution to the Study of H. E. the African Head of State."

46. Lest I be accused of propagating myths, I swear, first, that I bought one of the Eyadéma watches at RPT headquarters in Lomé in 1981 (I still have it, and when it is wound, it still runs and displays Eyadéma's head every fifteen seconds), and, second, that I was shown the "apotheosis" clip—it was no longer used—at TV headquarters in Kinshasa in 1986 after being interviewed on a live show.

47. Cited in Monga, *Anthropology of Anger: Civil Society and Democracy in Africa,* 101.

48. Sindjoun, "Le champ social camerounais: Desordre inventif, mythes simplificateurs et stabilité de l'état," 59. My translation.

49. Toulabor, "Jeu de mots, jeu de villains: Lexique de dérision politique au Togo."

50. James C. Scott, *Domination and the Arts of Resistance.*

51. The point is brilliantly argued in Mbembe, *On the Postcolony,* particularly in chapter 3, "The Aesthetics of Vulgarity," 102–141.

52. Ngolet, "Ideological Manipulations and Political Longevity."

Part 4

Connections

11

Francophone Africa in the Global Arena

Except possibly in Guinea, Cameroon, and Congo-Brazzaville, independence came to francophone West and Equatorial Africa surrounded by an aura of millennial expectations, not the least of which was that the end of French rule would bring a bountiful international future.

Guinea had been brutally cast out of the French orbit in 1958 for voting *non* to Charles de Gaulle's proposed association, Cameroon had become independent to the sound of rebel gunfire in the country's main cities and towns, and Congo-Brazzaville, which had registered francophone Africa's highest *oui* vote for the 1958 de Gaulle constitution (99.3 percent of all votes cast), had greeted independence in August 1960 with the government of Foulbert Youlou already knee-deep in political crisis.

To the rulers and the educated elites in the rest of our fourteen countries, however, independence meant that instead of being tied by France's political and economic apron strings, each of the ex-French colonies and territories could now reach out to a world waiting to embrace its products, invest in its industries, and recognize its political uniqueness. It meant walking onto the international stage carrying one's own flag, fully enabled diplomatically and entitled to the respect and status that sovereignty conferred. It meant not only enjoying in full the benefits of membership in the United Nations and other international organizations, but also finding a distinct voice and a role in the international politics of the post–World War II era. In Africa, where Soviets, Americans, Western Europeans, and Chinese actively sought friends and allies, the prospects for playing off one against the other, or others, seemed particularly attractive. The so-called nonaligned movement was in full swing, and given the visible success that Yugoslavia, Egypt, and India had had in playing the nonaligned game of being courted by the cold warriors without fully committing to one side or the other, the new African states believed they could also profit by joining in.[1]

As it turned out, independence did not bring the world flocking to the francophone African door, and it took some time for the cold-warring Americans, Soviets, and Chinese to come bearing gifts and competing for the favors of the new governments. Instead, independence generated a complicated set of arrangements—some negotiated and some imposed, and some lasting the next thirty years—that enabled France's involvement to run the gamut of major roles vis-à-vis its former colonies and territories, including those of patron, facilitator, guide, mentor, partner, creditor, investor, exploiter, protector, gendarme, and, above all, political paterfamilias. Try as several of our fourteen states might to find alternate international paths for themselves (e.g., Guinea and Mali's early temporary alliances with each other and with the more radical, *marxisant* African states, plus their dalliance with the Soviet Union and China; and the later "Afro-Marxist" internationalisms of Thomas Sankara's Burkina Faso, Marien Ngouabi's Congo-Brazzaville, and Mathieu Kérékou's pre-1990 Benin), they never really cut their connections to France; nor did they renounce their membership in the francophone family.[2]

Though the French connection dominated the external relations of our fourteen francophone African states, it was certainly not the only set of important international relations that mattered to them: the others included the connections to Europe and the European Community; those to the larger international community and its institutions; those with each other and with the other francophone African states; and those to the rest of the continent and to its regional and all-African and pan-African organizations and institutions.

The French Connection

The postindependence French connection has already appeared under several rubrics in these pages: it includes such cultural links as French education; *assistance technique* ("technical assistance," the French version of the U.S. Peace Corps); intellectual and literary production; the Francophonie organization of "states using French as a common language," which held ten meetings between 1986 and 2004; the more or less biannual Franco-African summit meetings (twenty-two summits were held between 1973 and 2003; see Appendix M), presided over by the incumbent French president; the infamous *réseaux* (networks) that several French presidents and Jacques Foccart helped to create and to put in place in order to link the French presidency and its clients to the rulers of francophone Africa and *their* clients (see Appendix O); French military interventions to reinforce, defend, or rescue regimes in trouble or even, in one case, to remove a regime that had become too embarrassing to tolerate (Jean-Bédel Bokassa's in the CAR) or, in another, to end a regime that had become too brutal to its citizens and too odious even for its French patrons (Hissene Habré's in Chad).

Mentioned in these pages are only some of the larger, more consequential sets of relationships between the francophone African states and France. It would take an encyclopedic canvas to depict the whole, which would also have to include, for example, official Franco-African cooperative links numbering in the hundreds, even thousands, both bilateral with individual states and multilateral with and through African regional international organizations;[3] connections through the more than six hundred French social and cultural nongovernmental organizations operating in Africa;[4] Franco-African commercial and trading connections annually worth literally billions of francs; and the activities not only of such French multinational giants as Elf-Total, but also of thousands of businesspeople and firms on both the African and European continents. All this, of course, must also comprise informal, and often incestuously illegal, financial relations of long duration between French companies and African rulers and elites, of which those involving Elf-Total (in its current and earlier Elf-Acquitaine and Elf-Gabon guises) are one variety, and those between Bokassa and President Valéry Giscard-d'Estaing another.

To be sure, some of these large figures are banal: bilateral interstate contacts and transactions often number into the thousands, particularly when one or both states involved are politically or economically significant. The French connection with Africa, however, is noteworthy both for the sheer volume of interactions and transactions and because France, of all the former colonial powers, not only maintained the closest ties with its former colonies but also created a qualitatively special relationship with them. How special, and whether that connection ought to be judged benign or malign, is another set of questions.

In official, and often chauvinistic, French eyes, the relationship has been almost wholly beneficent: to paraphrase Foccart (as well as various French presidents, prime ministers, ministers of finance and of cooperation, and so on), France nurtured the new states politically and financially, opened France's and Europe's markets to them, gave them copies of France's constitutions and laws to use as models, protected them from their own political excesses and the predatory designs of Moscow and Washington, created new institutions to preserve their common French cultural heritage, and gave them intimate access to the movers and shakers of French political and economic power.[5]

The other side of the coin, according to leading critic, Guy Martin, was simply and baldly French neocolonialism. According to Martin, the "family" was no family, but a tightly controlled *patronat* (an organization of bosses), with boss France calling the shots. The vaunted intimacy of the relationship, the special access to the Elysée and to the operations account in the French treasury that covered budgetary overdrafts, the Franco-African summits, la Francophonie, have all been part of a front hiding the true design of the French enterprise: a continuation of French colonial domination and the dependency of its former colonies by other means. Nor was that the end of it; according to Martin,

> In actual fact, France is acting in Africa not merely on her own account, and in the defence of her own national interests, but also as a proxy *gendarme* of the western world. . . . Operating within limits clearly defined by American imperialism, . . . France thus appears as a mere instrument—albeit vitally important—of western imperialism in Africa, whose main objective is to ensure the survival of states and leaders who act as faithful and vigilant guardians of western interests, often against those of their own people.[6]

One suspects that Martin overestimates and exaggerates American influence on France's African policymaking, but, in any event, the key instruments in that design, according to Martin (as well as to Verschave and the editorialists of the influential *Le Monde Diplomatique*), included Foccart and his *réseaux,* the Franc Zone (through its African subsidiary, the Communauté Financière Africaine—CFA), and "the maintenance in power of neo-colonial elites sympathetic to French foreign policy interests . . . assured by a web of interlocking ties that include: generous foreign aid disbursements regardless of the political orientation of the regime in question; mutual defense treaties; the stationing of French troops on African soil; . . . [and] a firm commitment to La Francophonie through the . . . holding of Franco-African summits."[7]

It remains, however, that neither Foccart's unapologetic chauvinism nor the unabashedly self-congratulatory tone of the French founders of the Francophonie organization and the conveners of its conferences—it is hard to resist the thought that all this is not much more than a refurbished, updated, and racially sensitive version of the old *mission civilisatrice*—does much to explain why the French connection so dominated the international politics of francophone Africa after 1960.

Martin's straightforward answer that France deliberately built the connection to advance its own financial and political interests makes a good deal of sense given the evidence, including Foccart's admissions to that effect. But Foccart, once characterized as *l'homme de l'ombre* ("the man of the shadows," a sort of super–éminence grise), turned out to be, as evidenced in his autobiography and his diaries, something of a braggart who was unapologetically proud of his accomplishments. To take Foccart's admissions at face value is also to accept his condescending dismissal of the African role in making the French connection: Foccart as much as says that African leaders were easily manipulated into doing France's bidding and were readily seduced by false intimacies with French power and the glitter of the Elysée. Further, to accept Foccart's version of the story is to accept at face value the image of French greed and duplicity, seconded by African greed, corruption, and unrestrained brutality, as presented in Verschave's *La Françafrique* and *Noir Silence*. Antoine Glaser and Stephen Smith are less pointed: they are prepared to concede that the Foccart-become-the-Jean-Christophe-Mitterand *réseau* may have evolved into a less dangerous "lobby" after 1995 when Jacques Chirac became president of France, but they find the connection no less repugnant and malign. (Jean-Christophe Mitterand is François Mitterand's son and was his father's choice to replace Foccart at the head of the African *cellule* in the French presidency. Foccart returned to the Elysée under President Chirac and remained until his—Foccart's—death in 1997.)[8]

Martin, as well as Foccart, Verschave, and Glaser and Smith all tend to downplay, if not denigrate, the African leaders' roles in making the connection. That view might exculpate those leaders from some of the French connection's less savory activities, but at the cost of assuming that they have been without independent will or initiative, or have simply been too stupid to know what they were getting into. With the possible exception of Bokassa (whom Foccart had labeled "an imbecile"), the evidence suggests otherwise—they were neither duped nor coerced; nor were they herded like cattle and led by their noses into the French corral. As a group the founding father generation of leaders—the so-called collaborator generation in the creation of the French connection—was not composed of stupid men. These leaders understood that genuine independence *à la Guinée* would entail economic costs none were willing to bear (which explains Malagache leader Philibert Tsiranana's famous 1958 statement rejecting immediate independence): much better to have juridical independence with monetary and economic links to France. In most cases that simply meant continuing the existing commercial and trading links, accepting French advisors and technical assistants to operate behind the scenes, and integrating finances and money into the new Franc Zone system and institutions. If it also meant French military assistance in putting down local rebellions, something that certainly provided an added benefit to the new governments, that was fine too. (See Appendix L for a list of French military interventions.)

And if the African leaders and their clients themselves profited personally from the new arrangements, so much the better as far as those leaders were concerned, particularly because the new welcome mat at the Elysée seemed to have been imprinted with a promise of the continued benefits that membership in the *pré carré* club conferred. Francophilic leaders like Léopold Sédar Senghor, Félix Houphouët-Boigny, Mokhtar Ould Daddah, Ahmadou Ahidjo, Léon M'ba, Omar Bongo, and Foulbert Youlou certainly welcomed the new arrangements, and others accepted them because they were rational solutions to the difficulties of coping with independence, including such mundane problems as the setting up of national and local civil administrations; the organization of legislative, executive, and judicial institutions; and the installation of police stations, local clinics, systems of taxation, and so on. Providentially, the French were there with a helping hand, appearing to demand little in return except a few privileges for their businesspeople, a friendly investment climate and platform, a cultural presence, and the opportunity to foster that sense of French community so dear to them.

Of the benefits of the French connection, perhaps the most valuable was the military lifeline that was available to the oldest, best, and most trusted friends of France, though not necessarily in that order. Appendix L lists some forty French military interventions. Most of them were direct, involving the use or dispatch of French troops, but one notable action was indirect: the provision of arms to the Biafran rebels in Nigeria. Shaun Gregory summarizes: "In all but a few of these interventions French action was to protect French nationals, subdue rebellion (irrespective of its legitimacy), and prop up pro-French rulers, including some of the most despotic and murderous individuals in post-colonial African history."[9] Those "some" included not only Bokassa and Mobutu, who would make most lists of infamous African rulers, but also Chad's Habré, Togo's Gnassingbé Eyadéma, and Congo-Brazzaville's Denis Sassou-Nguesso, all three credentialed despots, plus the *génocidaires* of Rwanda's Juvenal Habyarimana. And then, of course, there were those leaders whom France could have saved with its soldiers, but pointedly did not: Dahomey's Justin Ahomadegbé (1972), Burkina Faso's Maurice Yaméogo (1966), Chad's Hisseine Habré (1990), Congo-Brazzaville's Foulbert Youlou (1963) and Pascal Lissouba (1997), Mali's Modibo Keita (1968), Niger's Hamani Diori (1974), the CAR's André Kolingba (1993), and finally, at both extremes, Jean-Bédel Bokassa, whom the French had welcomed in 1966 but forcibly removed in 1979.

The list of interventions only hints at the reasons why the French intervened in some situations and not in others, and why they saved one African leader and not another. Those reasons were sometimes quite obvious, but sometimes difficult to discern. Bokassa was removed because he'd become a major embarrassment to his French patrons, and Habré was allowed to fall because he'd become too brutal to be tolerated. Also, the major French effort in Chad during the years 1968–1986 patently had as much to do with strategic considerations—the threat Muammar al-Qaddafi posed to France's Saharan interests, including Niger's uranium deposits in the Aïr Mountains, which provide most of the fuel needed for France's nuclear plants—as with the personalities who led Chad during that period. The military assistance given Mobutu and Habyarimana represented major French efforts to extend the French presence (and its *pré carré?*) to the ex-Belgian francophone countries, in part to counter American influence in Zaire and in part to draw a line between French influence in Central Africa and anglophone influence in the East and South.[10]

At the opaque end of the range of reasons for France's military intervention is the support given Sassou-Nguesso's return to power by force of arms in 1997, an event that prompted many observers to blame France for the failure of Congo-Brazzaville's experiment in multiparty democracy. Although France was ambivalent about democratic reforms in its *pré carré,* it did support those efforts, and thus it presumably should have supported the elected regime of Lissouba against its various political, military, and paramilitary challengers. A close look at the 1997 civil war reveals, however (in John F. Clark's lucid exposition), that while both French government officials and Elf (the main French oil company) sought systematically to maintain their influence in Congo-Brazzaville, "neither bears primary responsibility for the failure of the multiparty experiment." Although the French found Sassou-Nguesso easier to deal with than his opponents, Clark argues, by the time the French chose sides in the conflict, Congo-Brazzaville's "nascent democracy" had already been destroyed by its "venal politicians."[11] Simply put, it turns out that by the time Sassou-Nguesso made his move, Lissouba was beyond saving by any means, including French military intervention.

While major components of France's African military ventures do seem perplexing and even contradictory at first glance, there are thematic strands that run through all these military interventions and supports—and indeed, thematic strands in the larger relationship. These strands consist in part of French strategic interests, in part of reflexive support and habitual loyalty to a policy line established in the 1940s by de Gaulle, in part of the genuine personal commitment of French presidents to African members of the "family," and in part of the durable and self-reinforcing clientelistic networks of economic and political reciprocities that gave substance to much of the Franco-African relationship.

All of this lasted until 1995—that is, until the presidency of Jacques Chirac, who not only started to gradually dismantle the famous Gaullist *réseaux* after Foccart's "double death" in 1997 (the death of the man and end of his influence on francophone African policy),[12] but also initiated changes that resulted in the closure of military bases and the drawing down of contingents stationed in Africa, led to cooperation with African security ventures, and prompted theretofore unthinkable collaboration with American and British security programs.[13]

The March 1997 death of Foccart preceded the complete disintegration of the Mobutu regime (in May 1997) by a few months, and with that disintegration came the final collapse of the extensive French commitment to

Mobutu's survival. Foccart's death also preceded a commitment that was unhappily connected to the equally maladroit attempt to extend the *pré carré* to Rwanda, a policy that had earlier (in 1994) gone aground on the rocks of the Rwandan genocide. These embarrassments, budgetary constraints, and France's European commitments all helped persuade Chirac to change France's course in Africa. In 1997 there were some 8,700 French troops stationed in Africa; by the end of 1999 their number was down to 6,500; and by the end of 2002 they numbered about 5,200 (excepting the 1,700 on temporary military missions), with most of them garrisoned in Djibouti. The French, little given to apologizing for their mistakes, even went so far as to officially characterize the support they had given to the genocidal Rwandan regime of the late president Habyarimana as a "malfunctioning on some points of the military cooperation with Rwanda."[14]

By midyear 2003 France's security interests in Africa had been at least partially Africanized, that is, shifted to programs and activities intended, on the one hand, to reinforce African states' peacemaking and peacekeeping capabilities and, on the other, to assist subregional African organizations and the UN (e.g., in Bunia, Democratic Republic of Congo [DRC]) in meeting security crises as they arise. The exception, of course, was Côte d'Ivoire, where France almost immediately sent an elite force of one thousand troops in September 2002 when a growing rebellion began to threaten the survival of Laurent Gbagbo's elected government. Another five hundred came later that year. There is little mystery about why, after a decade of refusing to intervene militarily (mostly sending "advisors" instead), the French military was back in force. Not only is there the economic value of France's ties with the world's largest cocoa producer, but the country's port at Abidjan is one of the largest in the region and it surveys important offshore oil deposits, as well as providing a strategic naval base for French ships in the Gulf of Guinea and equatorial Atlantic waters. Then there are the old and established social and economic ties that need protection, including those involving the twenty thousand French citizens in the country, and the forty years worth of special relationships with Houphouët-Boigny's Ivoirian elite. Côte d'Ivoire is special, and the French did not apologize for their renewed intervention.

These security efforts include a French initiative, "RECAMP" (Renforcement des Capacités Africaines de Maintien de la Paix), which involves forming, training, and equipping peacekeeping forces; an American program, ACRI (African Crisis Response Initiative), which involves the training of African troops and deployment of them in multinational peacekeeping operations; and a series of British bilateral initiatives for logistical, financial, and training assistance to African states. RECAMP, now under UN auspices and coordinating with the UN's peacekeeping activities in Africa, has already been involved with several large-scale training exercises in conjunction with ACRI, as well as various peacekeeping assignments. ACRI has been involved with "battalion initial training" in Senegal, Uganda, Malawi, Mali, Ghana, Benin, and Côte d'Ivoire, plus the deployment of troops from Senegal, Ghana, Benin, Mali, Malawi, and Uganda to the CAR, Congo-Brazzaville, DRC, Sierra Leone, Guinea-Bissau, and Mozambique on peacekeeping, observer, and humanitarian assistance assignments.

The latter set of programs have included peacekeeping and peacemaking assignments under ECOWAS (the Economic Organization of West African States), operating as ECOMOG (Military Observers' Group) in Liberia, Sierra Leone, and Guinea-Bissau; under the auspices of SADC (Southern African Development Community) to help mediate in the Comoros and DRC and to dispatch a peacekeeping contingent to Lesotho; under IGAD (the East African Intergovernmental Development Authority) to seek peaceful solutions to conflicts in Sudan and Somalia and in the Eritrean-Ethiopian war; and a seminar on creating peacekeeping units sponsored by the Economic Community of Central African States (Communité Economique des Etats de l'Afrique Central, or CEEAC).[15]

Besides the security arrangements, by midyear 2002 not much was left of the obligations, reciprocities, and prerogatives of the *pré carré* (much less of the *chasse gardée*). According to Philippe Leymarie, now,

> more than forty years after independence, France no longer has its own agenda for the Black continent. . . . "Neither interference nor indifference": this is the vague, cramped slogan under which the Socialist government of Lionel Jospin has sought to epitomize its entire African policy. In the process, he [Jospin] disappointed the old-style ruling African headmen *["les caciques des pouvoirs africains a l'ancienne"]*, who now suffer the pains of abandonment: he also ended all hopes of those oppositions who had put their faith in an improbable "democratic intervention." In the name of closing down the patron-client networks and ending collusion with disreputable regimes, the Socialists have gotten the public to forget that recently France was "kingmaker" in its African *chasse gardée,* and that its ambassadors, acting more or less like secret agents in Chad, in the Central African Republic, or in Gabon, virtually shaped these countries' internal politics. So it was that Prime Minister Lionel Jospin was subsequently "one of the only outstanding French statesmen not to have a 'françafrican' network at his disposition."[16]

To be sure, the old links did not close down completely; nor did associations, friendships, and patron-client relationships forged during the forty years since 1960 simply disappear with the change in the French presidency—as the 2002 military reintervention in Côte d'Ivoire demonstrated. Nevertheless it was clear that Chirac intended to create a new *parteneriat* (institutionalized partnership) with and in Africa. The multilateral and

American-British-UN collaboration on security matters was one indication, as was a new set of diplomatic and political relationships with the post-1990 South African regime, the further restriction of bilateral assistance to democratic and democratizing states, the folding of the Ministry of Cooperation portfolio into that of the Ministry of Foreign Affairs, the putting of foreign aid into the European Union's multilateral basket for Africa, and the closing down of such old infrastructural props of Françafrique as the Center for Advanced Studies on Modern Asia and Africa (Centre des Haute Etudes sur l'Afrique et l'Asie Moderne, or CHEAAM) and the International Public Administration Institute (formerly the Ecole de la France d'Outre-Mer), which was absorbed into the National School of Administration (Ecole Nationale d'Administration). Most significant was that France now aligned itself with the June 23, 2000, Cotonou Pact, the successor to the European Union's old Lomé IV agreement on trade, aid, and cooperation. The Cotonou Pact brought together the seventy-seven states of the African, Caribbean, and Pacific Group (known acronymically as the ACP states) and the fifteen states of the European Union, and promised (certainly to considerable francophone African chagrin) a much more highly structured but less familial set of relationships between France and the old colonial metropoles.[17]

The Cold War, the Middle East, and Francophone Africa

From 1960 to 1989, when both the Soviet Union and its Communist Party collapsed as a result of their mutual internal contradictions, Africa was one of the principal arenas of the Cold War, in which, according to Peter Duignan and Lewis Gann, the "Third World countries set the West off against the East in a bidding war for their support. The West spent more than $225 billion to curry favor with often corrupt and incompetent and sometimes bloody tyrants."[18] This may be putting the case too bluntly and lacks window dressing, but it does summarize the Cold War essentials. At all events, during the same period the Soviet Union and China together probably spent at least a third, and possibly even half as much for the same purposes, including the construction and operation of the Chinese-built Tanzam railway, the construction of official buildings in over a dozen countries and roads and bridges in Rwanda and Burundi, and various and occasional subsidies, emoluments, rewards, scholarships, honors, and visits to Moscow or Beijing for favored elites.

Of our fourteen states, six (Senegal, Mali, Burkina Faso, Guinea, Benin, and Congo-Brazzaville) had regimes that claimed to be Marxist or socialist or both, and three (Senegal, Niger, and Cameroon) did not have Marxist regimes but had to confront revolutionary Marxist or *marxisant* parties. Though only ten of the fourteen were directly involved in the Cold

War, whether through official links to the Soviet Union or China as friendly socialist states or putative ideological soul mates (Mali, Benin, Congo-Brazzaville, Burkina Faso, and Guinea) or as objects of subversion (Chad, CAR, Cameroon, Niger, and Senegal), all fourteen were affected insofar as the United States, Western European countries, the Soviet Union, and China competed for their favors. That game almost invariably involved four important considerations.

First, every Western player had to play the African variant of the Cold War game against at least two communist opponents, the Russians and the Chinese, always remembering that any calculation involving either of them had to take into consideration the fact that the two communist giants were also competing against each other.

Second, a clever African player like Sékou Touré could and did simultaneously play Americans, French, Russians, and Chinese against one another, which reminds us that on top of all this, the French also played a Cold War game of their own against real or imagined encroachments by the anglophones. Moreover, while Sékou Touré, Senghor, Mamadou Dia, Abdoulaye Ly, Sankara, Ngouabi, and even Congo-Brazzaville's Pascal Lissouba (who had been Youlou's prime minister from 1963 to 1966) came honestly—out of conviction—by their socialist or Marxist credentials, some leaders, in order to take advantage of the Russian-Chinese bidding wars, acquired their socialist or Marxist labels for essentially opportunistic reasons: being considered socialists meant playing off East against West and in the process (as did the real socialist and Marxist regimes) obtaining loans and grants, military hardware for their soldiers, scholarships for their students, and trips to Moscow, Beijing, Paris, and Washington for their leaders, not to speak of invitations to ideologically oriented world meetings and congresses and the occasional Lenin or Stalin prize. Among the opportunistic socialists and Marxists could be found not only Kérékou and Didier Ratsiraka, who theatrically changed ideological sides in 1989–1990, but also such ideological poseurs as Cameroon's Ahidjo, Benin's Ahomadegbe, and Chad's N'Garta (François) Tombalbaye.[19]

Third, each Eastern player—China and its allies, including North Korea, and the Soviet Union and its allies, including Cuba, Poland, and Czechoslovakia—had to play not only against the generic Western colonialist-neocolonialist/imperialist-neoimperialist/capitalist array, but also against the other communist power and its allies and particular Western opponents, including the American superpower.

Fourth, whatever Cold War games the Americans, Russians, and Chinese played in francophone Africa, the French connection game played by African regimes and France always had the potential of trumping the other hands. For example, when Bokassa staged his coup in the CAR on New Year's Eve and New Year's Day 1965–1966, he apparently sought and obtained French support for his move, in effect playing the French card to trump both the police commandant, Izamo, and the Nzallat-Chinese conspiracies. A Cameroonian minister of state interviewed much later, in 1985, spoke directly (if indiscreetly) to the larger point: "From time to time the Russians and the Chinese and the Americans would come to us with gifts and ask us to support them at the United Nations, or some other international venue. We usually accepted the gifts but asked Paris or the French ambassador what to do about the requests. It was normal, because we always knew who was our best friend in the long run."[20]

For much of the 1960–1980s period, socialism as a developmental and governmental ideology remained quite fashionable, and almost all of our fourteen states either saw an Afro-Marxist regime installed or flirted with some variety of socialist ideology. Socialism was a "good" ideology identified with anticolonialism and anti-imperialism—as distinguished from capitalism, a "bad" ideology identified with colonialism, the West, and the United States—and one that promised early victory over the forces of reaction, neocolonialism, and the problems of underdevelopment. Only Eyadéma's Togo; Houphouët-Boigny, who bluntly rejected socialism as inappropriate for the Côte d'Ivoire; and the Mauritanians, for whom Islam sufficed ideologically, refused to join the chorus. If only the bare facts of African ideological preferences are considered, it is reasonable to conclude that the socialist and Afro-Marxist states would readily line up with the Soviet Union–Chinese camp on Cold War issues.

The reality is very much different and more complicated. For one thing, the fact that almost all African trade was with the West and that financial and other aid overwhelmingly came from there consistently tilted African policies westward, not eastward, ideological window dressing notwithstanding.[21] Add the French connection and the westward pull became even stronger, even for Mali, Guinea, Benin, and Congo-Brazzaville, all with avowed socialist or Afro-Marxist regimes and strong political ties to Moscow or Beijing. "In the late 1960s," observe Duignan and Gann, "there was still a large gap between Soviet promises and Soviet performance; less than a third of what was promised had been delivered. Between 1956 and 1960 the Soviet bloc disbursed $266 million in Africa, while France alone in the same period spent $703 million."[22]

Those proportions never changed much thereafter, and the West remained the major pole of African attraction, trade, and contact regardless of all the African socialist, Marxist, Stalinist, and Maoist rhetoric. One example is representative of the overall pattern: In 1982 the Soviet Union extended $1.1 billion in economic credits and grants to thirty-three African countries, of which the largest amounts went to Ethiopia, Nigeria, and the Afro-Marxist states; by 1986, the last year for which we have reliable data, those credits and grants amounted to only $115 million, that is, roughly one-tenth of the 1982 high, with the largest amount, a bare $70 million, going to Madagascar and Ratsiraka.[23] And, of course, after 1989–1990 and the end of the Cold War, China and Russia turned away from confronting each other and the West in Africa, curtailed their activity on the continent, and increasingly cooperated with the West on matters of aid and trade.

So much of Africa's international relations since 1960 have turned on bilateral relations with ex-metropoles (for this analysis, particularly those of the old AOF-AEF states with France), multilateral relations with Europe (with the EEC and EU via a series of treaties of association named after Yaoundé and Lomé), various maneuvers relating to the Cold War, and the problems of residual colonialism and apartheid in southern Africa, that sub-Saharan Africa's significant links with Arab North Africa and the Middle East are often overlooked. Long before Western Europe came onto the African scene during the fifteenth and sixteenth centuries, Mediterranean civilizations (both Greece and Rome), the Near and Far Eastern peoples, and Muslim and Arab societies had already impacted the sub-Saharan African world in the western Sudan, in southern Egypt and southward, and on both the east and west coasts. Arab slaving, which eventually victimized as many millions as the European trans-Atlantic trade, began perhaps eight or nine centuries before Columbus and extended well into the twentieth century. Above all, the Islamic-Muslim link continues to be salient for Black Africa's Islamic communities (see Chapter 1 for details).

For a brief eight-year period during the worldwide oil crisis of 1973–1980, sub-Saharan Africa played a major role in supporting the Arab side of the Arab-Israeli conflict and keeping international crude oil prices at nearly 1,300 percent above their January 1993 levels. During that eight-year dalliance, in exchange for promises of Arab aid and concessionary prices on oil, plus future unspecified benefits, and with some political and economic arm-twisting, all but four African states broke off formal (though not informal) relations with Israel and joined with most Arab and Muslim states in denouncing Israel at the UN and various other international venues. The promised benefits of this commitment never reached the expected levels, and decisions about the distribution of what benefits did materialize were made mostly on ideological and religious grounds, with most going to African states with large Muslim populations, Muslim rulers, or leaders willing to embrace Islam, including, notably, Idi Amin of Uganda.

Of our fourteen states, Côte d'Ivoire and Senegal, which relied heavily on imported oil to fuel their development programs, had little recompense for their embrace of the Arab position. They found the bill for their 1993–1994 oil imports up by 440 and 193 percent, respectively, their international monetary reserves significantly depleted, and their total cost, insurance, and freight import bills up by 74 and 49 percent, respectively, in those same years.[24] Although the Arab-African alliance never crystallized,

African relations with Israel, which had at one time been quite cordial, never regained their pre-October 1973 levels, and states linked to the Arab League or the Organization of the Islamic Conference (Mauritania, Senegal, Cameroon, Niger, Chad, and Somalia) have tended to side with Arab and Palestinian positions at the UN and elsewhere. Nevertheless, at midyear 2003 the future of these relations remains very much in doubt, and there are many points of Arab-African friction and confrontation.

For example, the Sudanese civil war, which, despite hopeful signs of détente and notwithstanding Western efforts to mediate between the sides (including, notably, that of ex-senator John Danforth whom President George W. Bush sent in 2002), has still not left its long, bloody path, and it continues to poison the Arab-African atmosphere, particularly as it features officially sanctioned slaving of southern Sudanese by government forces and their militia allies. In late 2003 in the southern oil region of Western Upper Nile the government and the oil companies forcibly displaced hundreds of thousands of people, and in Darfur as elsewhere similar thousands were threatened by Arab militias.

In September–October 2000 widespread violence, including some killings, in Tripoli and Zawiyah, Libya, against thousands of immigrants from sub-Saharan Africa (notably Nigerians, Cameroonians, Nigerois, Chadians, and Sudanese) ended in their organized repatriation. While officially the returnees' home governments refused to blame Colonel Qaddafi for the violence to their citizens, the incidents were a major embarrassment to Qaddafi, whose ambition is to be recognized as a statesman and champion of African unity. The events also revived charges of Arab racism against black Africans.[25]

Arab-initiated anti-American and anti-Israeli terrorism persistently intrudes into Africa, including the U.S. embassy bombings on August 7, 1998, in Nairobi and Dar es Salaam and the use of Arab diplomatic missions to harbor suspected terrorists. The nearly simultaneous blasts killed 224 people, including twelve Americans, and injured more than 5,400. Three Islamic groups—the International Islamic Front (sponsored by the Egyptian Muslim Students' Association), the Palestinian Hamas, and the Afghan Taliban—immediately praised the acts. A handful of other Arab and non-Arab Muslim sources—Iran's Official News Agency, the Muslim Brotherhood in Cairo, and the Sudanese Ummah Party—condemned both the bombings and the United States. Overwhelmingly in sub-Saharan Africa, however, the reaction was one of outrage, including anger at "the Arabs for using us as victims in their feud with the United States" (in the words of a Tanzanian colleague, who called me shortly after the Dar explosion). Overall, given the bombings and subsequent anti-African actions in Muslim and Arab countries, it is not likely that the near future will see improved relations between sub-Saharan Africa and its Arab neighbors.

Tangible and Intangible Connections

Our fourteen states—and indeed all African states—are connected to each other by dense networks of relationship on communal levels across the imaginary but official frontiers that delimit those legal fictions, the states, that are used universally and by African themselves to define the bounds of their several polities. Although the artificiality of the frontiers inherited from colonial times is periodically attacked, those imaginary lines have become real enough that the few border disputes that do break out are not only bitterly contested, but occasionally turned into bloody wars—as did the 1998–2000 Eritrean-Ethiopian conflict, in which a minor border dispute grew into a contest over regional sovereignties.[26] Still, for all their importance in giving political space a physical dimension, the borders usually fail as barriers, particularly where national frontiers figuratively traverse long-standing communal, social, cultural, and economic relationships.

The examples can be multiplied indefinitely, but two may suffice to make the point. First, in my narrative describing a 1980 visit to the small Bamiléké kingdom of Bana (Cameroon), I made much of the presence of hundreds of Bana *ressortissants* (in this context, natives) from throughout Cameroon and of their contribution to the funeral and enthronement celebrated at the time (see Chapter 10). What I did not mention in the story was the presence of a considerable number of Bamiléké from Nigeria, across the border, who are related directly to Bana on the basis of family, clan, and communal memberships. No Bana informant was able to venture an estimate of the number of these visitors, but two members of a family that had come from Takum, some twenty miles into Nigeria, indicated that they had had no trouble getting across the border and that they had in fact made the trip several times already that year, sometimes crossing at the manned border post, sometimes (apparently when carrying "unregistered" merchandise) not. And, of course, they were not alone; it is almost axiomatic that the denser the cross-border communal and ethnic relationships, the denser the informal cross-border traffic.

The second example is that of the Ghana-Togo border on the coast at and near Aflao-Lomé, which I directly observed several times in 1970 at various hours of the day. Travelers crossing by car, truck, bus, or other public conveyance dealt with customs and border police on both sides of the border, at Lomé and Aflao. Unless there was some sort of political tension between the Ghanaian and Togolese governments, passage was usually simple and brief, and any tolls or customs levied depended on the disposition of the Togolese and Ghanaian border agents or, where the crossers were regular customers (such as the truckers plying the coastal trade), whether other arrangements had been made beforehand. This being the main road between the two countries, traffic was usually brisk, and sometimes toward the end of the week it was heavy, with anywhere from two hundred to two thousand vehicles making the crossing each day.

This is the official crossing, and the volume and details of the traffic are more or less accurately recorded in both countries' government trade statistics. What is not recorded is the volume, intensity, and purposes of the cross-border activity that begins only a short distance inland from the Aflao-Lomé crossing. As a friendly observer, I myself posted for five consecutive evenings from four o'clock to seven o'clock at three different locations along the Togo-Ghana frontier just within and beyond the outskirts of Lomé and observed a total of at least seventy-five and perhaps as many as eighty uninterrupted border crossings by individuals and groups of up to six, of all ages and both sexes. Some traveled without anything in hand, but most others were carrying headloads of food, trade goods, or fuel, and some were traveling with boxes or heavy bags or even, in three instances, pushing or pulling two-wheeled carts. The points of crossing were not roads but simply areas usually flattened or worn down by constant use.

I was told that the police on both sides knew all about this illicit trade and crossing activity, but did nothing to curtail it. Why the blind eye? The simple reason, I was told, was that most people on both sides of the southern part of the Togo-Ghana border were ethnic Ewe, closely related to one another by shared social, communal, and economic ties; therefore, sealing the border—which was tried briefly by one government or the other from time to time—was bound to be futile and could even rouse the local population to further and perhaps really damaging acts of civil disobedience, if not political fury.[27]

That people on both sides of African political frontiers have not yet so differentiated themselves from one another that crossing a border takes them physically to another world is certainly a commonplace observation. And while ethnocommunal ties tend to increase the permeability of political frontiers, if not practically cause them to disappear, the francophone link has simultaneously helped to give a loose but distinct political cohesion to our group of fourteen states and to demarcate them from the anglophone, hispanophone, and lusophone states of Africa. This is not to say that our fourteen are free from conflict among themselves or with their neighbors: conflicts among the fourteen include the 1960 Mali-Senegal dispute leading to the dissolution of the Mali Federation; the 1989–1992 Senegal-Mauritanian conflict involving the black population of the Senegal River Valley; the various disputes among Mali, Burkina Faso, and Niger over disposition of the Tuareg revolt, which affected all three countries; and the six-day Burkina Faso–Mali border war in 1985 over the Agacher delimitation. Conflicts with neighboring nonfrancophone states include Senegal's several small conflicts with Guinea-Bissau; Cameroon's long and occasionally violent dispute with Nigeria over the Bakassi Peninsula; and Chad's various and periodic differences with Libya and Sudan, including those over the open Libyan military support for Goukouni Oueddei to help him capture Ndjamena (1981) and what amounted to an on-and-off war between France and Libya in Chad itself (1983–1989).

These grassroots cross-border relationships represent considerable volumes of both licit and illicit trade to local, regional, and international markets. They do not, however, include what Jean-François Bayart has called strategies of "extraversion," that is, write Thomas Callaghy, Ronald Kassimir, and Robert Latham, the "disposition of state leaders in relation to both their domestic spaces and their international realm in which "rulers build relationships with non-African states, transnational corporations, and international organizations as ways of surviving and compensating for their weak empirical stateness."[28] Strategies of extraversion are adopted to manage decline (as in Cameroon and Congo-Brazzaville, for example), or simply to reinforce what might otherwise be a shaky or weak power base (as in Gabon, Côte d'Ivoire, and other states). We have earlier come across such extraversions in the form of the Foccartian *réseaux,* the creation of durable links to the Elysée that permit calling on French military intervention in times of crisis, and corrupt networks above and beyond the *réseaux* themselves. Also worthy of note is the creation of various regional collaborative systems of more or less effectiveness and duration, including some potentially useful but still embryonic security arrangements in central Africa[29] and the possible emergence of a new regulatory authority in the Chad Basin.[30] These latter are largely transboundary institutional formations growing out of, complementing, and often expanding on associations and relationships created in informal political space.

Overall, then, the dominant pattern has been one of collaboration and cooperation, whether under the old French ambit, within the parameters of the new agreements with the European Union, or, increasingly, as part of the emerging security and interstate trading network in West and Equatorial Africa. What will also remain, thanks to its surprisingly durable political, cultural, and economic links, is a francophone African community.

Notes

1. For an excellent overview of the international politics of African states since independence, see the three editions of Harbeson and Rothchild, eds., *Africa in World Politics.* Each volume collects a new group of essays reflecting the then contemporary dimensions of Africa-related international politics. For a relatively recent, fully developed analysis, see Clapham, *Africa and the International System: The Politics of Survival.* The doctoral thesis of Cameroonian minister of state (and *agregé* in political science) Augustin Kontchou Koumegni, published as *Le système diplomatique africain,* is worthy of note because it details the complexities of intra-African relations during the first ten years of African independence.

2. The family metaphor is developed by Gellar in his "All in the Family: France and Black Africa, 1958–1960." Tamar Golan also saw the relationship between France and its former colonies as familial: "A Certain Mystery: How Can France Do Everything that It Does in Africa—and Get Away with It?" I have also frequently heard the phrase *en famille* (in the family) used by francophone Africans in reference to conferences, meetings, and relationships with France, and the verbatim accounts of the French-African summits since 1973 abound with familial metaphors and references to the conferences as "family reunions."

3. Prior to 1998 the Ministry of Cooperation was a lead player in the operation of the Franco-African network; thereafter, it was folded into the Ministry of Foreign Affairs with, as one would have expected, a considerably diminished portfolio. It turns out, however, that what is now the Direction Générale de la Coopération Internationale et du Developpement (DGCID) is still charged with a very large array of activities—cultural, economic, technical, electronic, educational, administrative—throughout both the francophone and the nonfrancophone worlds. For details, see the ministry's surprising recent report: Ministère des Affaires Etrangères (France), *Solidarité-influence, DGCID l'action 2001, rapport annuel.*

4. See, for example, Passy and Mfoumouangana, eds., *France-Afrique sub-Saharienne annuaire, 1998: Organisations sociales et culturelles.*

5. This is the tone of Foccart's interview-autobiography, compiled by journalist and old Africa hand Philippe Gaillard: *Foccart parle: Entretiens avec Philippe Gaillard.* Gaillard also helped edit the five volumes of Foccart's *Journal de l'Elysée* (Elysée is shorthand for the French presidency). According to Glaser and Smith *(Ces messieurs Afrique,* vol. 2: *Des réseaux aux lobbies),* at the demand of the government, the publisher, Fayard, took some allegedly highly compromising sections out of volume 2 of the *Entretiens* and similarly sanitized the Elysée Diaries. Foccart died in 1997, so all the subsequent Gaillard volumes were, of course, published posthumously. For a less sympathetic view of Foccart, see Péan, *L'homme de l'ombre* (Man of the Shadows).

6. Martin, "The Historical, Economic, and Political Bases of France's African Policy," 207.

7. Schraeder, "The Impact of Democratization on the Formulation and Implementation of African Foreign Policies," 13.

8. Glaser and Smith, *Ces messieurs Afrique,* vol. 2.

9. Gregory, "The French Military in Africa: Past and Present," 437.

10. For the larger picture, see Martin, "France's African Policy in Transition: Disengagement and Redeployment." See also Martin, "Historical, Economic, and Political Bases," and Gros, "Les relations franco-africaines à l'âge de la globalization."

11. Clark, "The Neo-Colonial Context of the Democratic Experiment of Congo-Brazzaville."

12. Gregory, "French Military in Africa," 441; see also de la Gorce, "La deuxième mort de Jacques Foccart."

13. The redefinition and restructuring of France's military role in Africa was due in part to the reform of France's military and the melding of the Ministry of Cooperation into the Foreign Ministry in 1998, and, in particular, to the shock of France's ignominious role in Rwanda and the public uproar over its Operation Turquoise, all of which served to persuade the Chirac government to reduce its African commitments. These moves had been foreshadowed by a series of decisions to suspend military cooperation with Zaire in 1991, with Togo in 1992, and with Niger, Burundi, Congo-Brazzaville, the Comoros Republic, and Guinea-Bissau from 1996 on. France even suspended cooperation with Côte d'Ivoire as a result of

the 1999 coup by General Gueï. (France's military return to Côte d'Ivoire in 2002 was another matter, of course.) The above summarizes part of the statement by Jean-Paul Hughes, "Military Cooperation: The Big Turnaround."

14. Gregory, "French Military in Africa," 440–443; Isnard, "Les armées françaises mènent une douzaine d'operations en Afrique." See also Leymarie, "Inexorable effritement du 'modèle' franco-africain."

15. Tessier and Gongora, "Maintien de la paix: Une Afrique bousculée en voie de réorganization sécuritaire."

16. Leymarie, "Le continent noir en quête d'un véritable partenariat: Malaise dans la coopération entre la France et l'Afrique."

17. Ibid. Also, in the same June 2002 edition of *Le Monde Diplomatique* see several useful articles on the Cotonou accords.

18. Duignan and Gann, "Communism in Sub-Saharan Africa: A Reappraisal." The $225 billion estimate may be considerably short of the actual figures, since it appears to be based on ODA (Official Development Assistance) figures and probably doesn't include the costs of military cooperation, technical assistance (including the work of the Peace Corps and its international analogs), disbursements from France's special "operations accounts," loans later forgiven or written off as grants, or the value of private aid distributed through NGOs. A more realistic estimate would add at least $100 billion to the $225 billion figure.

19. The list offered in L. V. Thomas's *Le socialisme et l'Afrique,* vol. 2, chapters 1 and 2 ("L'idéologie des leaders sénégalais" and "L'idéologie des autres leaders francophones d'Afrique Noire"), includes Senghor, Lamine Diakité, Dia, Gabriel d'Arboussier, and Ly (Senegal); Lissouba and Antoine Kithima (Congo-Brazzaville); Seydou Badian Kouyaté, Pierre Kanouté, and Modibo (Mali); Alexandre Adandé, Chabi Mama, and Ahomadegbe (Benin); Ahidjo (Cameroon); M. Adoum and Tombalbaye (Chad); and Sékou Touré (Guinea). Thomas says of these leaders that they defined their socialism "precisely and explicitly." As for the label *poseur,* it is mine. I never got to know either Tombalbaye or Ahomadegbe personally, but the monographic literature on Chad, Tombalbaye, and Benin, plus conversations with people who did know them well, strongly indicates that both men saw ideology in strictly utilitarian terms and thus produced it on demand or as needed. Tombalbaye's notorious authenticity campaign, which later inspired Mobutu's own version, was designed not as serious ideological doctrine, but as a propaganda device to enhance Tombalbaye's regime. I did get to know Ahidjo and can vouch for the fact that his ventures into ideology, including having his in-house propagandists find appealing socialist words to describe his policy, had more to do with attracting Russian and Chinese gifts, grants, and military hardware than with articulating basic political beliefs.

20. Interview, May 16, 1987, in Yaoundé; my translation. The minister refused to be identified, but allowed me to quote him. The comment was made during a tour of the magnificent facilities of the government party headquarters, which had been erected by the Chinese atop one of Yaoundé's many hills. I asked the minister how much the whole project cost, and he demurred on an exact figure: "Many millions," he said with a smile. The Chinese also gave public buildings to a number of other friendly African regimes: for example, in Kinshasa, Zaire, they built a half-sized version of the Great Hall of the People on Beijing's Tienanmen Square.

21. The point is made forcefully and with convincing evidence by Crawford Young in his *Ideology and Development in Africa,* 253–296.

22. Duignan and Gann, "Communism in Sub-Saharan Africa," 9–10.

23. U.S. Department of State, *Warsaw Pact Economic Aid Programs in Non-Communist LDCs: Holding Their Own in 1986.*

24. For a detailed examination of the political economy of the 1973–1979 Arab-African alliance and the evidence to support these propositions, see Le Vine and Luke, *The Arab-African Connection: Political and Economic Realities,* especially 31–41 and table 3 on 38. The larger picture of Israeli-African relationships may be found in Decalo, *Israel and Africa, Forty Years, 1956–1996,* and Oded, *Africa and the Middle East Conflict.*

25. Arab racism against black Africans is a reality that few educated Africans or Arabs are willing to address publicly, though such discussion did occur in the African media during the 1973–1980 oil crisis; I provide some examples in Le Vine and Luke, *The Arab-African Connection.* That racism is, of course, quite real. It is one of the unfortunate residuals of the centuries of Arab slaving in Africa, and during my own trips to and within the Arab Middle East I gathered many Arab expressions denigrating and belittling black Africans. *Abdi,* the Arab word for slave, remains a term of contempt throughout the Arab world, and it is often used patronizingly or insultingly in reference to black Africans. For informed commentary on these matters, see, notably, Lewis, *Race and Slavery in the Middle East,* and Gordon, *Slavery in the Arab World.*

26. The literature on African boundary problems is sparse. See, for example, Widstrand, ed., *African Boundary Problems,* and Shaw, *Title to Territory in Africa: International Legal Issues.*

27. I undertook these observations in April 1970 at the suggestions of a Togolese colleague, a labor economist. He selected the spots for my watch and spread the word that I was a friendly observer and would not report my sightings to the authorities. Consequently the crossers apparently felt free to pass near me without apprehension; in fact several even waved to me or said *"Bon soir!"* as they passed. Early in the evening there was some daylight; by the time I left, it was already dark, though a half-moon did provide some illumination. Much more systemic treatment and analysis of transboundary trade are found in Stary, "Cross-Border Trade in West Africa: The Ghana–Côte d'Ivoire Frontier," and Macgaffey and Bazenguissa-Ganga, "Personal Networks and Trans-Frontier Trade: Zaïrean and Congolese Migrants," both in Bach, *Regionalisation in Africa.*

28. Callaghy, Kassimir, and Latham, eds., *Intervention and Transnationalism in Africa,* 12. The reference is to Jean-François Bayart's *The State in Africa: The Politics of the Belly,* especially 20–32.

29. In 2003 René Lemarchand described an attempt to reinforce the institutional and political capacities of the CEEAC in the domain of conflict prevention and efforts involving the new African Union, the Economic and Monetary Community of Central Africa (Economique et Monétaire de l'Afrique Centrale, or CEMAC), the Great Lakes States Economic Community (Communauté Economique des Pays des Grands Lacs, or CEPGL), and the Southern African Development Committee (Committée au Développement de l'Afrique du Sud, or SADC). Lemarchand makes the strong point that while this effort is still largely embryonic and ineffective, he sees considerable potential given appropriate resources and institutional strengthening (Lemarchand, "Rapport de mission intérimaire du professor René Lemarchand su la prévention des conflits en Afrique Centrale, Libreville, 29 septembre–15 novembre 2003").

30. Roitman, "New Sovereigns? Regulatory Authority in the Chad Basin."

Appendixes

Appendix A　Principal Ethnic Groups

Country	Estimated Total Population[a] and Net Average Increase (in percentages), 1994–2002	Principal Ethnic Groups[b]	Estimated Percentage of Total[c]
Benin	6,787,625 2.91	Fon, Adja, Aizo, and related groups	58
		Bariba (Bargu)	22.5
		Yoruba	14
		Somba	5
Burkina Faso	12,603,185 2.64	Mossi	50
		Western Mande (Bobo, Marka, Samo)	14
		Gurunsi, Lobi	12
		Fulani	10
		Senufo	6
Cameroon	16,184,748 2.36	Bamiléké and allied groups	31
		Equatorial Bantu (Beti, Bulu, Bassa, Fang)	19
		Fulani (Peul, Foulah, etc.)	15
		"Kirdi" (northern "pagans")	11
		Northwest and Coastal Bantu (Douala, etc.)	8
		Eastern Nigritic (Baya, Mbum)	7
CAR	3,642,739 1.80	Baya (Baja, Gbaya)	34
		Banda and allied groups	31
		Mandjia	8.5
		Riverain groups (Yakoma, Dendi, Sango)	8
		Mbum	7
		Mbaka	6.5
		Cameroonians	3.0
Chad	8,997,237 3.27	Arabic-speaking groups	46
		Sara	23
		Maba (Quaddai)	9.5
		Masa-Musgum-Tupuri-Mundang ("Kirdi")	5
		Teda (Tubu)	5
		Kanembu-Bulala	2.3
Congo-Brazzaville	2,958,448 2.18	Bakongo (Lari, Kongo, Sundi, Vili, etc.)	48
		Teke	20
		Mbochi	12
		Bete (Mbete)	7
		Sanga and allied groups	5
Côte d'Ivoire	16,980,950 2.45	Akan (Agni, Nzima, Baoule, etc.)	27
		Kru (Bete)	18
		Mande (Malinké, Bambara, Dioula, Mahon)	15
		Senufo (Sene, Siena)	12
		Peripheral Mande (Dan, Yacuba, Guro)	9
		Lagoon cluster	8
		Lobi	5
Gabon[c]	1,233,353 0.97[c]	Fang and allied groups	33
		Shira and allied groups	20
		Bete and allied groups	18
		Bakota and allied groups	15

(continues)

Appendix A (continued)

Country	Estimated Total Population[a] and Net Average Increase (in percentages), 1994–2002	Principal Ethnic Groups[b]	Estimated Percentage of Total[c]
Guinea	7,775,065 2.23	Malinké (Mande)	48
		Fulani	28
		Soussou	16
		Kpelle	11
		Kissi and allies	7
Mali	11,340,480 2.97	Bambara	31
		Fulani	17
		Senufo	15
		Sarakole (Marka)	8
		Diuola	6
		Tuareg	6
		Songhai	6
		Malinké	5
		Minianka	5
		Dogon	5
Mauritania	2,828,858 2.92	Moors (Maurs): "white" 33%, "black" 44%[d]	77
		Fulani	10
		Toucouleur (Tukolor)	8
		Sarakole	5
Niger	10,634,746 2.7	Hausa	56
		Djerma-Songhai	22
		Fulani	9
		Tuareg	8
		Kanuri	5
Senegal	10,589,571 2.91	Wolof	38
		Fulani	22
		Serer	19
		Dioula and Bainock	7
		Mandingo (Mande)	7
Togo	6,285,201 2.48	Ewe	44
		Cabrais (Kabire, Kabre)	23
		Ouatchi	11
		Losso, Moba, Gourma	7
		Mina, Kotokoli, Akposso, and allies	9

Sources: U.S. Library of Congress, Country Study/Area Handbook series; *UN Demographic Yearbook,* 1999; *World Factbook,* 2002; *Europa Yearbook: Africa;* Murdock, *Africa: Its Peoples and Their Culture History;* Morrison, Mitchell, and Paden, eds., *Black Africa: A Comparative Handbook,* 2nd ed.; World Bank, African Development Data, 2001, 2002.

Notes: a. Estimates as of July 2002.

b. *Principal* is here used to designate groups with ca. 3 percent or more of the total estimated population of a country. *Ethnic group* names are given as they are cited in the sources listed below or, in case of doubt, as they are listed in Murdock, *Africa, Its Peoples and Their Culture History.* Some scholars, like Vincent Khapoya (*The African Experience: An*

(continues)

Appendix A (continued)

Introduction) are skittish about ethnicity, preferring to distinguish African communities of identity according to language and language groups, often using Joseph Greenberg's seminal 1955 classification (*Studies in African Language Classification*). I stay with ethnicity because distinction by language presents its own analytic problems (e.g., language is much more mutable than ethnic identity; several distinct ethnic groups may speak the same language; auxiliary languages such as Lingala and Kiswahili have become the languages of choice in various parts of Africa, etc.); and because the ethnic referent remains a contemporary fact throughout the fourteen states of this study.

c. Percentages are of indigenous ethnic groups. Both the total population figures and the percentages for Gabon should be taken with more than the usual grains of salt. According to World Health Organization officials in Libreville with whom I spoke in 1983, perhaps between 30 to 45 percent of the total Gabonese population is from neighboring countries such as Cameroon and Congo-Brazzaville, and the government regularly inflates the population estimates by at least 30 percent. The 2003 CIA *World Factbook* gives 1.32 million, which probably includes the official "inflation factor." James Barnes suggested in 1992 that the total population could range anywhere from 900,000 to the official 1.23 million (*Gabon: Beyond the Colonial Legacy*, 102). It may well be the case that Gabon's annual growth rate is flat at present, population having declined during the first twenty or so years after independence because of an abnormally high rate of infertility among Gabonese women due, I was told in Gabon 1965, to the effects of a high rate of venereal disease in Libreville and Brazzaville during the 1940s. Reliable informants in Gabon told me that it is general knowledge in the country that President Omar Bongo's estranged wife, Marie-Joséphine Assele, also known simply as Marie-Jo, was herself infertile, and that the Bongos' "official" children were in fact born of one of Mme. Bongo's village "sisters," who was brought to Libreville to give the president the offspring he needed for both personal status and political reasons.

d. The 44/33 split between Maurs (Moors) and blacks in Mauritania is contested by spokespeople for both groups, each claiming a higher percentage than the one now assigned. The Maurs believe they are largely of North African origin, and the blacks, being the indigenous populations, mostly live in the south, in or near the Senegal River Valley. Maurs, furthermore, divide themselves between "white" and "black." "White" Maurs claim "pure" Maghribi (Northwest African) Berber-Arab descent; "black" Maurs are said to be of mixed African-Moorish extraction and to include descendants of ex-slaves. Since these distinctions are cultural rather than biological and are supported by considerable social myth, no accurate count of either category of Maurs has ever been made. Also, because Mauritanian demographic statistics are themselves based on estimates made during the 1960s and 1970s, the most recent official estimates are given here faute de mieux. (A good summary explanation of these black/white distinctions is in Gerteiny, *Mauritani*, 46–56.)

Appendix B   Decolonization Timeline, 1944–1960

1944	January 30–February 8	Brazzaville Conference
	October	Constitution of 4th Republic creates French Union, provides African representation on metropolitan political bodies, sets up local African assemblies.
1946	May 7	First *Loi Lamine Guèye* grants equal civil rights to all in TOMs and colonies
	October 18–21	Bamako Congress creates Rassemblement Démocratique Africain (RDA)
1950	June	Second *Loi Lamine Guèye* grants equal pay, perquisites to African civil servants
1952	December	Overseas Labor Code passed
1955	April	Togo statute: Togo gets "Council of Government," prepares way for "autonomy"
	November	Municipal Reform statute passed
1956	May	UN plebiscite in British Togo: vote for union with independent Ghana
	June	*Loi-Cadre* adopted: introduces universal, single-college suffrage, provides cabinet government in colonies and TOM
	June	UN plebiscite: west part to Ghana, east part to (francophone) Togo
	August	Autonomous Republic of Togo set up with Grunitsky as first PM, approved by November referendum
1957	April	*Loi-Cadre* takes effect
	May	Cameroon statute makes it "state under trusteeship," with constitution and responsible government
1957–58	September–April	Federalist debates: Houphouët-Boigny et al. vs. Senghor et al.
	November–February	Political crisis in France and Africa
1958	June	de Gaulle returns to power, reopens constitutional question of relations between France and TOM
	August 20–26	de Gaulle tours Africa
	September 28	Referendum on 5th Republic: all African TOM except Guinea vote yes
	October 2	Guinea proclaims independence
	December	Cameroon statute gives Cameroon internal autonomy until independence Community comes into being
1959	January	Mali Federation proclaimed
1960	January 1	Cameroon independent
	April 27	Togo independent
	June	Senegal, Mali, Madagascar independent
	August	Côte d'Ivoire, Dahomey, Upper Volta, Niger, CAR, Congo-Brazzaville, Gabon, Chad independent
	November	Mauritania independent
1961	April 20–26	Abortive generals'/colonels' coup in Algeria: last significant resistance to decolonization crushed by de Gaulle

Appendix C General Elections in the AOF by Seats, 1945–1960

Country	First Constitutional Assembly, 1945	Second Constitutional Assembly, 1946	Territorial Assembly, 1946	French National Assembly, 1946	French National Assembly, 1951	Territorial Assembly, 1952	French National Assembly, 1956	Territorial Assembly, 1957[d]	Fifth Republic Referendum 1958	Legislative Assembly, 1959	Legislative Assembly, 1960
Senegal[a]	I-1	I-1	50[c]	2	2	50	2	60	Y97.6	80	n.a.[c]
Mauritania[a]	II-1	II-1	I-6 I-14	1	1	I-8 II-16	1	34	Y94	40	n.a.[c]
Sudan[a]	I-1	I-1	I-20 II-30	3	4	I-20 II-40	4	70	Y97.6	80	n.a.[c]
Niger[a]	II-1	II-1	I-10 I-20	1	2	I-15 II-35	2	60	Y78	60	n.a.[c]
Côte d'Ivoire	I-1 II-1	I-1 II-1	I-18 II-27	3	2	I-18 II-32	2	60	Y99.9	100	70
Guinea	I-1 II-1	I-1 II-1	I-16 II-24	2	3	I-18 II-32	3	60	N85.5	60	n.a.[c]
Dahomey	I-1 II-1	I-1 II-1	I-12 I-18	1	2	I-18 II-32	2	60	Y97.8	61	60
Upper Volta[b]			I-10 I-40	3	3	I-10 II-40	4	70	Y99.1	75	n.a.[c]
AOF Totals	10	10	265	13	20	384	20	474	Y-1 N-1	556	525
Togo[c]			I-6 II-24	1	1	30[c]	1	46	n.a.[b]	46	46

Source: Morgenthau, *Political Parties in French-Speaking West Africa*, extratextual appendices III, IV, and V.

Notes: a. The 1959 legislative assemblies continued to function into 1960.

b. Upper Volta did not become a TOM (*Territoire d'Outre Mer*—overseas territory) until 1947; prior to that year it had been administered as part of Mali and the Ivory Coast.

c. Togo, as a UN Trust Territory, did not participate in the 1958 referendum. Senegal was the first ex-AOF territory to hold elections under a single electoral college (in 1946); Togo was the second, in 1952.

d. Senegal and Mauritania constituted a single district for the election to the first and second constituent assembly; Sudan and Niger were similarly merged for those elections.

I = First "College" (French citizens' roll).

II = Second "College" (qualified African voters). The second college representatives had majorities in every local assembly from 1946 on.

n.a. = not applicable.

Minister of Colonies (governed by decree)	— advised by — Chamber of Deputies (France)
Governor-General of AOF	— advised by — Higher Council of Government
Lieutenant Governors	— advised by — Council of Government (nominated)

Dahomey · Guinea · French Soudan · Ivory Coast · Niger · Mauritania · Senegal · Upper Volta

Commandants de Cercle (French District Officers)

Gardes de Cercle

Chefs de Subdivision (French Officials)

Chefs de Canton (African Cantonal Chiefs)

Chefs de Village (African Village Chiefs)

Chefs Superieur de Province (African Provincial Chiefs)

Source: Crowder, "The Administration of French West Africa," 64.

Appendix E   Structure of the RDA

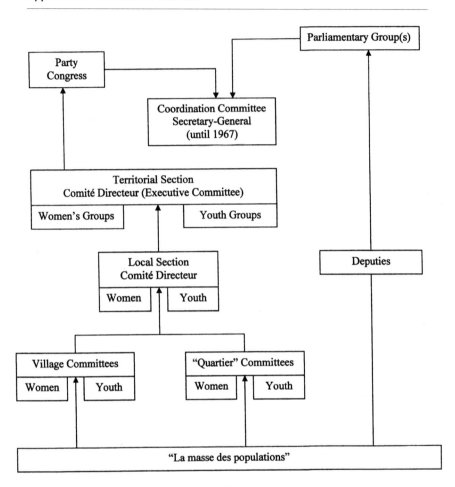

Source: Ansprenger, *Politik im Schwarzen Afrika,* extratextual table 4.

1. The people living in a colonial territory constitute a "nation," or a nation in the process of becoming one.

2. This "nation" is governed by an "imperialist" Power, which seeks its own, mostly economic, interests and advantages.

3. The relationship between the "imperialist" Power and the African "nation" is essentially one of "domination"; of "exploitation," in its economic aspect; and of "racialism," or "racial discrimination," in its human aspect. A system where such relationships predominate is called "colonialism."

4. The members of a colonial African "nation" have an "inalienable right" to govern themselves.

5. In order to gain "self-government" or "independence," a "national liberation movement" has to be generated by the African "nation."

6. The "national liberation movement" expresses itself through a political organization, whatever its name. . . . Though led by an elite, it attracts "the masses" to itself and seeks "the conquest of political power" as its primary goal.

7. The organization which serves as the instrument for national liberation has a double legitimacy. Historically it is the successor to the pre-colonial African states whose power was broken during the period of "imperialist" penetration. Morally it is the expression of the "popular will," the will of the emergent African "nation." . . .

8. In its effort to achieve "political emancipation," this organization will be bound to pursue, and is justified in pursuing a "dynamic," aggressive, strategy in its dealings with the colonial Government . . . involving, on occasion, the use of "positive action"—which should, however, as far as possible, be "non-violent." . . .

9. The "national liberation movement" . . . will be bound . . . to seek to weaken, and eventually to eliminate such "reactionary forces" as . . . restricted ethnic loyalties ('tribalism') and chiefly power, in many of its various forms . . . surviving from the pre-colonial period, but generally fostered by "colonialism," and liable to assert themselves in opposition to the organization expressing the "popular will" during . . . the transition from "colonialism" to "independence."

10. The new form of independent African state which the "national liberation movement" seeks to bring into being will be "democratic"—in the sense, particularly, that its government will be responsible to a popular assembly elected on the principle of "one man, one vote"; and "socialist," in the sense that it will develop a planned economy, in the interest of the "masses."

11. The "national liberation movement" in any given African state should cooperate with similar movements in other African states, with a view to the total elimination of "colonialism" throughout the African continent.

Source: Thomas Hodgkin, "A Note on the Language of African Nationalism."

Notes: This is as good a glossary of nationalist terminology and themes as can be found in the literature, and by and large it reflects the kind of language used by African nationalists during the 1945–1960 period. It is noteworthy that the nationalists borrowed extensively from the vocabulary of the anticolonial left in Europe, though most of them were neither Marxist nor socialist in political persuasion, nor even nominally so. Hodgkin was himself a Marxist, albeit not a doctrinaire one, and on occasion he let his own biases peek through in his work. This is the case in #10, above, where he equates socialism with a planned economy and posits that the equation is a common nationalist theme.

In francophone Africa, at least, that connection neither was inevitable nor appeared in the nationalist rhetoric of (for example) Foulbert Youlou of Congo-Brazzaville, Léon M'ba of Gabon, N'Garta (François) Tombalbaye of Chad, Ahmadou Ahidjo of Cameroon, Sylvanus Olympio of Togo, Maurice Yaméogo of Upper Volta, or Mokhtar Ould Daddah of Mauritania. Even Côte d'Ivoire's Houphouët-Boigny, whom no one could accuse of being a Marxist, occasionally flirted with socialist language; his party, the Parti Démocratique de la Côte d'Ivoire (PDCI, the local branch of the Rassemblement Démocratique Africain, or RDA), while endorsing the planned economy, specified that "a large place would be left to private initiative." All these men led their respective countries to independence or formed the first postindependence governments. Most, to be sure, were statists and endorsed the principle of a planned economy, but almost all categorically rejected the socialist state or, like Mokhtar Ould Daddah, spoke vaguely of an economy "neither capitalist nor directed."

The key elements of francophone African nationalist parties' programs are summarized in Decraene, *Tableau des partis politiques de l'Afrique au sud du Sahara.*

Appendix G   Democratic Progress (francophone states shown in italics)

Country	Population (in millions)	Last Multiparty Elections[a]	Freedom House Rating (2001–2002)[b]	Next Scheduled Elections[c]
Tier 1: Movement toward democratic consolidation				
Benin	6.4	2001	2.5 –	2006
Mali	10.7	2002	2.5	2007
Mauritius	1.2	2003	1.5	2004
Senegal	10.0	2000	3.5	2006
Tier 2: Halting progress toward democracy				
Central African Republic	3.5	1999	5.0 –	2005
Côte d'Ivoire	16.0	2000	4.5 +	2005
Gabon	1.2	1998	4.5	2005
Madagascar	15.5	2001	3.0	2005
Niger	10.1	1999	4.0	2004
Tier 3: Uncertain democratic future				
Burkina Faso	11.9	1997	4.0	2005
Cameroon	15.4	1997	6.0 +	2004
Chad	8.4	2001	5.5	2006
Djibouti	0.5	1999	4.5	2005
Mauritania	2.7	2003	5.0 +	2006
Togo	5.0	2003	5.0	2008
Comoros	0.6	2002	5.0	2006
Tier 4: Backsliding				
Burundi	6.1	1993	6.0	2008
Congo-Brazzaville	2.8	2002	4.5 +	2007
Democratic Republic of Congo	52.0	n.a.	6.0 +	2005
Guinea	7.5	2003	5.5	2006
Rwanda	7.2	1988	6.5	n.a.

Sources: Pomunyoh, "Democratization in Fits and Starts." The Freedom House ratings have been updated in accordance with Freedom House, *Freedom in the World 2001–2002*.

Notes: a. To end of 2003.

b. On a scale from 1 (most free) to 7 (least free). (+) marginal improvement from 2000–2001 rating; (–) marginal decline from 2000–2001 rating.

c. From January 2004.

n.a. = not applicable.

Côte d'Ivoire was moved into the second tier because of the reconciliation of President Laurent Gbagbo and opposition leader Alassane Ouattara and the wholesale relaxation of ethnic tensions generated by Gbagbo's two predecessors (Henri Konan Bedié and General Robert Gueï). Also, Comoros was added to the third tier because of the relatively free election of ex-colonel Azali Assoumani in April 2002 and the uncertainty surrounding the future of the newly formed Comoran Union.

Appendix H   African National Conferences: Political Events and Institutions, 1991–1993

Country	Dates of National Conference	Events of National Conference	Political Institutions Emanating from National Conference	Subsequent Events
Benin	February 19–28, 1990	National conference declares itself sovereign; President Kérékou stripped of authority; multiparty elections planned.	1990 constitution[a]; president and unicameral assembly; 6 provinces with appointed leaders and elected local councils.	Kérékou defeated by Nicéphore Soglo in 1991, but returns to win 1996 election.
Gabon	March 1–April 19, 1990	President Bongo retains control of proceedings, but agrees to multiparty elections.	Opposition parties legalized; 9 provinces, 37 departments with appointed leaders.	Bongo wins tainted 1993 election for fourth seven-year term; opposition represented in legislature.
Congo-Brazzaville	February 25–June 10, 1991	National conference declares itself sovereign; President Sassou-Nguesso stripped of authority; multiparty elections planned.	1992 constitution[a]; bicameral parliament (upper house indirectly elected, lower house directly elected); president appoints prime minister, has decree powers; 9 regions with elected leaders.	President Lissouba elected in 1992; elections marred by growing ethnic conflict and divided opposition. Sassou-Nguesso wins violent power struggle, retakes power in 1997.
Togo	July–August 1991	President Eyadéma stays in power but agrees to rewrite constitution and plan multiparty elections.	1992 constitution[a] calls for semipresidential system and unicameral assembly; 4 provinces with elected leaders.	Eyadéma wins 1993 election using military repression, then declared reelected in June 1998 in poll flawed by resignation of national election commission, widespread fraud, and harassment of opposition candidates.
Niger	July 29–November 1991	National conference declares itself sovereign, strips General Saibou of power, plans multiparty elections.	1993 constitution[a]; president appoints prime minister responsible to unicameral assembly; legislators elected by PR.	President Ousmane elected in 1993; continued problems with Tuaregs; coup by General Mainassara in 1996 because of legislative deadlock.

(continues)

Appendix H (continued)

Country	Dates of National Conference	Events of National Conference	Political Institutions Emanating from National Conference	Subsequent Events
Mali	August 1991	General Traoré ousted earlier in 1991; national conference adopts new constitution; multiparty elections planned.	1992 constitution with bill of rights[a]; president appoints prime minister and cabinet, responsible to dissolvable unicameral legislature; 8 regions with elected councils (the eighth created for Tuareg separatists).	President Konaré elected in 1992, reelected in 1997; peace brokered with Tuaregs in 1966, but continued unrest about flawed legislative elections in May 1997.
Zaire	August 7, 1991–March 17, 1993	National conference periodically suspended by President Mobutu; national conference declares itself sovereign, but Mobutu keeps power.	10 regions with appointed governors, elected local councils; opposition parties legalized.	Competing governments established: Mobutu dissolves both legislatures, appoints new body, but retains power; Mobutu overthrown in 1997; Laurent Kabila becomes new president, vaguely promises reforms, but a year later, no indications of moves toward democratization.
Chad	January 15–March 1993	National conference declares itself sovereign, but maintains President Déby in power.	New constitution adopted in 1996[a]; 14 prefectures with appointed leaders; opposition parties legalized.	President Déby's power strengthened by endorsement of NC and end of Libyan interference; end of civil war that killed 10% of population; questions persist about human rights violations of Déby regime and possible federal solution to North-South divisions.

Sources: Seely, "Transitions to Democracy"; Robinson, "The National Conference Phenomenon in Francophone Africa"; *Africa Research Bulletin,* political series, 1989–1998; Decalo, *The Stable Minority;* Wiseman, *The New Struggle for Democracy in Africa;* and Clark and Gardinier, eds., *Political Reform in Francophone Africa.*

Note: a. Approved by referendum.

Appendix I Leadership Succession, 1958–2003

Country, Year of Independence	Leaders, Years in Office[a]	Years, Months in Power (to December 2003)	Peacefulness or Violence of Succession	Circumstances of Transition	Comments
Benin, 1960 (before 1975: Dahomey)	Hubert Maga,[b] January 1960–October 1963	2 years, 10 months	peaceful	1959 Maga elected prime minister	Maga became president at independence
	Christophe Soglo (colonel, later general), October 1963–January 1964	3 months	violent	military coup	
	Sourou-Migan Apithy, January 1964–November 1965	1 year, 11 months	peaceful	elections: Apithy president, Justin Ahomadegbe vice president	
	Tahirou Congacou, November–December 1965	24 days	peaceful	military coup: Congacou, president of assembly, succeeds	Apithy and Ahomadegbe forced to resign by Christophe Soglo
	Christophe Soglo (general), December 1965–December 1967	1 year, 11 months	violent	military coup	
	Alphonse Alley (lieutenant colonel), December 1967–July 1968	8 months	violent	countercoup by Kérékou et al.	Maurice Kouandété became vice president
	Emile Derlin Zinsou, July 1968–December 1969	1 year, 6 months	peaceful	civilian chosen by military	confirmed by referendum
	Paul-Emile de Souza (lieutenant colonel), December 1969–May 1970	5 months	violent	military coup by Maurice Kouandété	three-man military directorate Maurice Kouandété, Alphonse Alley, Paul-Emile de Souza
	Hubert Maga, May 1970–May 1972	2 years	peaceful	first rotation in civilian troika	civilian rule restored in May 1970

(continues)

Appendix I (continued)

Country, Year of Independence	Leaders, Years in Office[a]	Years, Months in Power (to December 2003)	Peacefulness or Violence of Succession	Circumstances of Transition	Comments
	Justin Ahomadegbe, May–October 1972	6 months	peaceful	second rotation in troika	civilian troika dismissed
	Mathieu Kérékou (colonel, later general), October 1972–February 1991	18 years, 4 months	violent	military coup (Apithy, third in rotation, shut out of office)	
	Nicéphore Soglo, February 1991–March 1996	5 years, 1 month	peaceful	free election following National Conference	national conference removed Kérékou
	Mathieu Kérékou (general), March 1996–present	over 8 years	peaceful	two free elections	
Burkina Faso, 1960 (before 1983: Upper Volta)	Maurice Yaméogo,[b] April 1958–January 1966	6 years, 9 months	peaceful	became premier on death of Ouezzin Coulibaly, president after independence	
	Sangoulé Lamizana (lieutenant colonel), January 1966–January 1980	15 years	violent	military coup	Lamizana became president in free elections in 1978
	Saye Zerbo (colonel), November 1980–October 1982	2 years	violent	military coup	
	NCO coup, October 1982	1 month	violent	military coup	
	Jean-Baptiste Ouedraogo (major), November 1982–August 1983	9 months	violent	military coup	
	Thomas Sankara (captain), August 1983–October 1987	4 years, 2 months	violent	military coup	Sankara appointed prime minister in January 1983
	Blaise Compaoré (captain), October 1987–present	15 years, 2 months	violent	military coup	Sankara assassinated during Compaoré coup

(continues)

Appendix I (continued)

Country, Year of Independence	Leaders, Years in Office[a]	Years, Months in Power (to December 2003)	Peacefulness or Violence of Succession	Circumstances of Transition	Comments
Cameroon, 1960	Ahmadou Ahidjo,[b] 1959–November 1982	23 years	peaceful	appointed prime minister in 1959, then elected president in 1960	"re-elected" four times in "managed" elections
	Paul Biya, November 1982–present	21 years, 1 month	peaceful	designated prime minister by Ahidjo, then took power upon Ahidjo's resignation	"re-elected" twice in tainted elections, survived two attempted coups (1983, 1984)
Central African Republic, 1960 (1977–1979: Central African Empire)	David Dacko,[b] 1960–December 1965	5 years	peaceful	president at independence	Barthélemy Boganda died in 1959
	Jean-Bédel Bokassa (colonel, later field marshal), 1966–1979	13 years	violent	military coup d'état	"emperor," 1977–1979
	David Dacko, 1979–1981	3 years	violent	restored to office by French troops	Bokassa fled to France; returned to CAR in 1989
	André Kolingba (general), 1981–1993	12 years	violent	military coup d'état	Bokassa tried, condemned to death; Kolingba commuted sentence to life imprisonment, then freed Bokassa in 1993 before leaving office
	Ange-Félix Patassé, 1993–2003	9 years, 8 months	peaceful	free election; reelected after national conference	Patassé survived three army mutinies in 1996, called national conference
	François Bozize (general), 2003–present	9 months	violent	military coup d'état	ex-army chief seized power

(continues)

Appendix I **(continued)**

Country, Year of Independence	Leaders, Years in Office[a]	Years, Months in Power (to December 2003)	Peacefulness or Violence of Succession	Circumstances of Transition	Comments
Chad, 1960	N'Garta (François) Tombalbaye,[b] 1960–1975	14 years, 8 months	peaceful	president at independence	
	Felix Malloum (general), 1975–1979	3 years, 11 months	violent	military coup d'état	Tombalbaye killed
	Hissene Habré appointed prime minister 1978 (became de facto ruler)	1 year	violent	rebel pressure on Malloum	
	Mahemat Choua, 1979	4 months	?		Temporary head of state
	Goukouni Oueddei, 1979–1982	3 years, 9 months	violent	rebellion	
	Hissene Habré, 1982–1990	8 years, 9 months	violent	military coup d'état	
	Idriss Déby (colonel), December 1990–present	13 years	violent	military coup d'état	
Congo-Brazzaville, 1960	Foulbert Youlou,[b] 1959–1963	4 years	peaceful		
	Alphonse Massamba-Débat, 1963–1968	5 years, 8 months	violent	military coup d'état	Massamba-Débat was civilian
	Alfred Raoul (major), Governing National Council, 1968	4 months	violent	military coup d'état	temporary head of state
	Marien Ngouabi (captain), 1968–1977	9 years, 9 months	violent	military coup d'état	
	Joachim Yhombi-Opango (colonel, later brigadier general), 1977–1979	1 year, 4 months	violent	military coup d'état	Ngouabi assassinated
	Denis Sassou-Nguesso (colonel), 1979–1993	13 years, 10 months	violent	military coup d'état	

(continues)

Appendix I (continued)

Country, Year of Independence	Leaders, Years in Office[a]	Years, Months in Power (to December 2003)	Peacefulness or Violence of Succession	Circumstances of Transition	Comments
	Pascal Lissouba, 1993–1998	5 years	peaceful	free elections (after national conference)	Sassou-Nguesso removed by national conference
	Denis Sassou-Nguesso, October 1997–present	6 years, 2 months	violent	elimination contest, 1997, then coup	Sassou-Nguesso won contest after rounds of bloody fighting
Côte d'Ivoire, 1960	Félix Houphouët-Boigny,[b] 1959–1993	36 years, 8 months	peaceful	prime minister, 1959; president, 1960	after Houphouët-Boigny's death in December 1993
	Henri Konan Bedié, 1993–1999	over 6 years, 5 months	peaceful	constitutional succession	
	Robert Gueï (general), December 24, 1999–October 22, 2000	10 months	violent	military coup	Gueï became head of state, then proclaimed himself president, October 2000
	Laurent Gbagbo, October 2000–present	3 years, 2 months	coercive	Gueï killed during popular uprising	Gueï chased from office, Gbagbo "elected" in contest, but main opponent, Alassane Ouattara, disqualified
Gabon, 1960	Léon M'ba,[b] 1961–1967	6 years, 11 months	peaceful	appointed, then elected designated successor, repeatedly "reelected" in "managed" elections	took power on M'ba's death in November 1967
	Omar Bongo, 1967–present	over 36 years, 5 months	peaceful		
Guinea, 1958	Sékou Touré,[b] 1958–April 1984	23 years, 6 months	peaceful	appointed prime minister in 1958, elected president in 1960	Guinea independent following its *no* vote on Charles de Gaulle's constitutional referendum of 1958

(continues)

Appendix I (continued)

Country, Year of Independence	Leaders, Years in Office[a]	Years, Months in Power (to December 2003)	Peacefulness or Violence of Succession	Circumstances of Transition	Comments
	Lansana Conté (colonel), May 1984–present	18 years, 7 months	peaceful	military coup following death of Sékou Touré, April 1984	
Mali, 1960	Modibo Keita,[b] 1959–1968	8 years, 4 months	peaceful	prime minister of French Soudan, 1959; president of Mali, 1960	
	Moussa Traoré (lieutenant, later brigadier general), 1968–1991	20 years, 5 months	violent	military coup d'état	first five years as head of junta, then president
	Amadou Toumani Touré (lieutenant colonel), 1991	2 months	violent	military coup d'état	
	Alpha Oumar Konaré, 1992–2002	10 years, 4 months	peaceful	free election following national conference	1991 national conference returned to civilian government
	Amadou Toumani Touré, June 2002	1 year, 6 months	peaceful	open and free election	
Mauritania, 1960	Mokhtar Ould Daddah,[b] 1961–1978	7 years, 7 months	peaceful	free election after independence	
	Mustapha Ould Salek (lieutenant colonel), 1978–1979	11 months	violent	military coup d'état	Bouceif assassinated, May 1979
	Ahmed Ould Bouceif (lieutenant colonel), prime minister, 1979	1 month, 21 days	peaceful	appointed by junta after Salek forced to resign	

(continues)

Appendix I (continued)

Country, Year of Independence	Leaders, Years in Office[a]	Years, Months in Power (to December 2003)	Peacefulness or Violence of Succession	Circumstances of Transition	Comments
	Mohamed Khouna Haidalla (lieutenant colonel), prime minister, 1979	2 months	peaceful	appointed by junta	
	Mohammed Mahmoud Ould Louly (lieutenant colonel), 1979–1980	8 months	peaceful	Salek forced to resign by ruling junta	bloodless coup
	Mohamed Khouna Haidalla (colonel), 1980–1984	5 years	violent	military coup d'état	
	Maaouya Ould Sidi Ahmed Taya (colonel), December 1984–present	over 19 years	violent	military coup d'état	president and chairman of military committee for National Salvation
Niger, 1960	Hamani Diori,[b] 1960–1974	13 years, 8 months	peaceful	free election	
	Seyni Kountché (major general), 1974–1987	14 years	violent	military coup d'état	Diori killed in coup
	Ali Saibou (colonel), 1987–1993 (1992–1993, alliance with MNSD)	5 years	violent	military coup d'état	1992–1993 quasi-military regime
	Mahamane Ousmane, 1993–1996	3 years, 11 months	peaceful	free election one year after national conference	national conference in 1991
	Ibrahim Baré Mainassara (lieutenant colonel), 1996–1999	2 years, 3 months	violent	military coup d'état	1996 "electoral coup" "elected" Mainassara;

(continues)

Appendix I (continued)

Country, Year of Independence	Leaders, Years in Office[a]	Years, Months in Power (to December 2003)	Peacefulness or Violence of Succession	Circumstances of Transition	Comments
	Daouda Malam Wanke (major), 1999	over 3 months	violent	military coup d'état	Mainassara assassinated; Wanke promised free election by November 1999
	Mamadou Tandja, November 1999–present	4 years, 4 months	peaceful	elections sponsored by military	
Senegal, 1960	Léopold Sédar Senghor,[b] 1960–1981	21 years	peaceful	designated, then elected	
	Abdou Diouf, 1981–March 20, 2000	18 years, 3 months	peaceful	designated by Senghor; took office when Senghor resigned, then reelected	
	Abdoulaye Wade, March 20, 2000–present	3 years, 9 months	peaceful	free elections	Wade won by uncontested majority; Diouf conceded
Togo, 1960	Sylvanus Olympio,[b] 1960–1963	3 years, 13 days	peaceful	became president upon independence	
	Nicholas Grunitsky, 1963–1967	4 years	violent	military coup d'état; Grunitsky named by army	coup led by Eyadéma (seargent, later general); Olympio assassinated
	Kleber Dajdo (colonel) and military junta, 1967	4 months	peaceful	military coup d'état	bloodless coup by Eyadéma
	Gnassingbé Eyadéma (general), 1967–present	over 35 years, 8 months	peaceful	military coup d'état	Eyadéma directly assumed power, dissolved junta, nullified 2000 national conference

Sources: Jackson and Rosberg, *Personal Rule in Black Africa;* Lipschutz and Rasmussen, *Dictionary of African Historical Biography;* Wiseman, *Political Leaders in Black Africa;* *Africa South of the Sahara, 1971–1998;* Legum and Drysdale, eds., *Africa Contemporary Record, 1969–1994;* Chazan et al., *Politics and Society in Contemporary Africa,* 3rd ed., 505–525; author's country files.

Notes: a. Leader is president unless otherwise indicated.
b. Founding father.

Appendix J   Freedom House Ratings, 2001–2002

Country	Press Freedom	Civil Liberties	Freedom House Rating[a]
Mali	2	3	free
Benin	3[b]	2	free
Senegal[c]	2	3	free
Niger[b]	4	4	partly free
Burkina Faso	4	4	partly free
Côte d'Ivoire[b]	6	6	partly free
Congo-Brazzaville	6	4	partly free
Gabon	5	4	partly free
Mauritania	5	5	partly free
Togo[b]	6	5	not free
CAR	6	5	partly free
Chad	6	5	not free
Guinea	6	5	not free
Cameroon	6	6	not free

Source: Freedom House, *Freedom in the World, 2003.*

Notes: a. Freedom House combined average country ratings are from 1 (most free) to 7 (least free). Our 14 rate as follows: 2.5 = Benin, Mali, Senegal; 4.0 = Burkina Faso, Niger; 4.5 = Gabon; 5.0 = Congo-Brazzaville, Mauritania; 5.5 = Chad, Guinea, Togo, CAR; 6.0 = Cameroon. "Free" is 1.0 to 2.5; "partly free" is 3.0 to 5.5; "not free" is 5.5 to 7.0.

   b. Noticeable decline in this category since 2001–2002.

   c. Noticeable improvement in this category since last rating period (2001–2002).

Appendix K   Occupational Background: Independence Cabinets

Occupational Categories[a] (collapsed)	Cameroon	CAR	Chad	Congo-Brazzaville	Benin	Gabon	Guinea	Côte d'Ivoire	Mali	Mauritania	Niger	Senegal	Togo	Burkina Faso	Total	Category
Administration	12	5	3	5		4	7	3	4	6	3	1		6	59	30.5
Education	1	4	2	2	4	4		2	3	3	6	6	3	2	42	21.7
Public health																
Doctors		1	1	1	2		2	3	5	1	1	2	2	1	22	(11.4)
Public health workers		3		2											5	(2.6)
Veterinarians	1						1		1			2	1		6	(3.1)17.0
Law					2		1	2	2	1		3			11	5.7
"Intellectual" pursuits					1		1					1			3	1.5
Private economy																
Commerce and industry	1	1	1	1	1	3		2			1			2	13	(6.7)
Agriculture				1								1	1		3	(1.5)8.3
Chiefs, traditional and modern		1	1	1		1					2		1		7	3.6
Trade union leaders	4						1	1				2			8	4.1
Politicians	1	1													2	1.0
Engineers, scientific personnel					2		2	2	1						7	3.6
Other							1	2			1			1	5	2.6

(continues)

Sources: Adapted from *Africa Research Bulletin: Political, Social, and Cultural Series; Africa South of the Sahara,* 1971; *Afrika Biografien;* Dickie and Rake, *Who's Who in Africa; Dictionary of African Biography; Dictionnaire Bio-bibliographique du Dahomey;* Ediafric: La Documentation Africaine: *Deputés et Conseillers économiques, Gouvernements et cabinets ministeriels, Les élites africaines, Personnalités publiques de l'Afrique de l'ouest; Personnalités publiques de l'Afrique centrale; P.D.G. Afrique;* LeFevre, *Dossiers on Tropical Africa;* Taylor, *The New Africans;* Thompson, Biographical Cards on French-Speaking Africa.

Notes: a. "Administration" includes national and local-level officials; "Law" includes magistrates, advocates, and other legal professionals; "Intellectual" pursuits includes two individuals who styled themselves "writers" and one who claimed to be a journalist; "Chiefs," all of whom claimed to be Chefs *superieurs* (paramount chiefs).

Independence ministers of first government after independence, from Guinea, October 2, 1958 (first to gain independence), to Mauritania, November 1, 1960 (last of our fourteen states to gain independence).

Cabinets: Prime ministers (if constitutionally created), ministers, vice-ministers, and others designated as cabinet-level officials.

Appendix L   Principal French Military Interventions, 1960–2003

Location	Type[a]	Date(s)	General Details, Commentary
Angola	I/D	1992	Operation Addax: 50 troops to help with elections.
Biafra/Nigeria	I	1969	Indirect assistance to Biafran military forces through Gabon and Côte d'Ivoire.
Benin	I/D	1991	Troops protect free elections.
CAR	D	1967–1970	Paratroops airlifted to Bangui at request of President Bokassa to guard government from possible coups.
	D	1979	Paratroops' Operation Barracuda removes "Emperor" Bokassa, replaces him with David Dacko.
	D	1966–?	Troops suppress mutinies in CAR army, protect government.
Cameroon	D	1960–1964	Troops, equipment, supplies to help government suppress UPC rebellion.
Chad	D	1960	Assistance to Tombalbaye government against internal rebels.
	D	1968	Suppression of Toubou revolt in Aouzou Strip.
	D	1968–1972	Suppression of Front for the National Liberation of Chad (Frolinat) revolt against Habré government.
	D	1978–1980	Troops provide basic security sevice as Chad factions fight.
	D	1983–1984	Operation Manta fails to end Habré-Goukouni armed stalemate: France supports Habré regime.
	D	1986	Operation Epervier (900 men) to help guard government against Libyan attempts to invade Chad.
	I/D	1990	Support for Déby to help oust Habré.
Comoro Islands	D	1989	Two hundred troops to Moroni after assassination of President Abdallah.
	D	1995	Troops to Moroni after Bob Denard coup; President Djohar goes into exile under French protection.
Congo-Brazzaville	D	1962	Troops to Brazzaville during strikes, violence.
	D	1963	Three thousand troops positioned in Brazzaville during coup against Youlou, but do not try to save his government.
	I/D	1997	Aid to Sassou-Nguesso during civil war.
Côte d'Ivoire	D	2002–?	Fifteen hundred peacekeeping troops to help Gbagbo government against rebels and to separate rebel north from government-held south.
Democratic Republic of Congo	D	2003	Peacekeeping unit at Bunia, Ituri, to reinforce UN troops.
Djibouti	I/D	1977–?	Units stationed in Djibouti before independence remain to help new Gouled government defend against ethnic violence.

(continues)

Appendix L   (continued)

Location	Type[a]	Date(s)	General Details, Commentary
Gabon	D	1964	"Paras" rescue M'ba from rebels, restore him to power after coup.
	D	1990	Operation Requin paratroops protect government and French workers from uprisings in Libreville and Port Gentil.
	D	1992	Troops sent to protect government from violence.
Mauritania	D	1977–1978	Squadron of fighter-bombers based in Cap-Vert, Senegal, attack Polisario units in Mauritania and Western Sahara.
Morocco	D	1979–1980	Fighter-bombers attack Polisario units in Western Sahara.
Niger	D	1963	Troops to Fort Lamy to discourage plot against Diori.
Rwanda	D	1990–1993	Operation Noroît (300–1,000 troops) supports Habyarimana government against guerrillas of Rwanda Patriotic Front.
	D	1994	Operation Amaryllis: 500+ troops to evacuate French nationals and key Rwandan leaders.
	D	1994	Operation Turquoise: 2,550 French and 450 Egyptian and francophone African troops protect fleeing Hutu refugees, leaders, military, *genocidaires.*
Senegal	D	1962	Troops maintain order in wake of attempted coup against Senghor.
Somalia	D	1993	Operation Oryx: 2,100 troops for UNITAF.
	D	1993	Eleven hundred troops for UNISOM II.
Togo/Benin	D	1991	Four hundred fifty troops to Cotonou airport to foil plot against Togo prime minister.
Togo	D	1986	One hundred fifty troops guard Eyadéma against coup attempt.
Tunisia	D	1958	French planes attack villages in reprisal for attacks on French troops still stationed in Tunisia.
Zaire-Shaba	I	1975–?	French military aid channeled to Zaire to Holden Roberto, Angolan rebel (and Mobutu's son-in-law).
	D	1977–1978	Troops, planes help Mobutu repel Shaba invasion; from 1975 on, France is Mobutu regime's major arms supplier.
	D	1991–1992	One thousand troops to Kinshasa after anit-Mobutu riots.

Sources: Benchenane, *Les armées africaines;* Foltz and Bienen, eds., *Arms and the African;* "Arcanes et rouages de la coopération militaire"; Shaun Gregory, "The French Military in Africa: Past and Present"; author's files.

Notes: a. (D) direct intervention; (I) indirect intervention; (I/D) mixed indirect/direct intervention.

Given that French troops were garrisoned in a number francophone states (CAR, Senegal, Djibouti, Chad, Côte d'Ivoire, Gabon, etc.), the term *intervention* is used here to mean the use or operational deployment of those troops or of troops and material brought into Africa by France, whether at the request of an African government, unilaterally at French initiative, or in conjunction with a multilateral operation. Only the most important interventions—of well over fifty—are listed here.

Appendix M   Franco-African Summits and "Francophonie" Summit Conferences

Franco-African Summits

1st	Paris, France	November 13, 1973
2nd	Bangui, CAR	March 7–8, 1975
3rd	Paris, France	May 10–11, 1976
4th	Dakar, Senegal	April 20–21, 1977
5th	Paris, France	May 22–23, 1978
6th	Kigali, Rwanda	May 21–22, 1979
7th	Nice, France	May 8–9, 1980
8th	Paris, France	November 3–4, 1981
9th	Kinshasa, Zaire	October 8–9, 1982
10th	Vittel, France	October 3–4, 1983
11th	Bujumbura, Burundi	December 11–12, 1984
12th	Paris, France	December 11–13, 1985
13th	Lomé, Togo	November 14–15, 1986
14th	Antibes, France	December 10–12, 1987
15th	Casablanca, Morocco	December 14–16, 1988
16th	La Baule, France	June 19–21, 1990
17th	Libreville, Gabon	October 5–7, 1992
18th	Biarritz, France	November 7–9, 1994
19th	Ouagadougou, Burkina Faso	December 4–6, 1996
20th	Paris, France	November 27–28, 1998
21st	Yaoundé, Cameroon	January 14–15, 2001
22nd	Paris, France	February 19–21, 2003

Francophonie Summit Conferences (with themes)

1st	Versailles, France	February 17–19, 1986	Toward a Commonwealth, French Style?
2nd	Quebec, Canada	September 2–4, 1987	Toward an "Institutionalization" of Francophonie
3rd	Dakar, Senegal	May 24–26, 1989	Taking Root in the African Earth
4th	Chaillot/Paris, France	November 19–21, 1991	Enlargement and Maturity
5th	Grand Baie, Mauritius	October 16–18, 1993	Unity in Diversity
6th	Cotonou, Benin	December 2–4, 1995	Consolidate la Francophonie
7th	Hanoi, Vietnam	November 14–16, 1997	Economic Cooperation
8th	Moncton, Canada	September 4–6, 1999	Youth
9th	Beirut, Lebanon	October 26–28, 2001	Intercultural Dialogue
10th	Ouagadougou, Burkina Faso	November 26–27, 2004	Multilateral Francophone Cooperation

Notes: The Franco-African summits have been a key component of Franco-African political relations, in part because they functioned as "'family reunions' designed to strengthen already close personal ties between the French president and his African counterparts" (Schraeder, *African Politics and Society,* 324), in part because they served as a sounding board for African leaders, and in part because they provided French mediation between the francophone states and the markets and forums of Europe and the West. However, as France became increasingly integrated into the European Union and less directly involved in the economies and polities of the francophone states (La Baule, in 1990, marked the turning point), the summits declined in importance and effect. Since the early 1980s nonfrancophone African heads of state have come as observers to the conferences; though Nigeria was absent from Yaoundé in 2001, Morocco's King Mohammed VI and Algeria's President Abdelaziz Bouteflika did attend.

By 1993 the loose summits of "states using French as a common language" had taken on institutional form, the *Organisation internationale de la Francophonie* (OIF). Since the founding fathers of the Francophonie summits (France's François Mitterand, Senegal's Léopold Sédar Senghor, Tunisia's Habib Bourguiba, and Niger's Hamani Diori) had clearly intended that the main venue for political discussion would be the Franco-African conferences, the agendas of the early Francophonie meetings were deliberately kept to cultural matters and themes. However, with the creation of a Permanent Council in 1995 and the subsequent appointment of ex–UN Secretary-General Boutros Boutros-Ghali to head the OIF, its political aspects came to the fore. According to French president Jacques Chirac: "La Francophonie has become more political, and in that role has set up an observatory of democracy. This will permit us to observe objectively, as a physician observes a sick patient, the illness of a society or a people." ("La francophonie ne veut plus apparaître comme une 'fortresse assiegée' par l'anglais" [Francophonie No Longer Wants to Appear Like a Fortress Besieged by the English] *Le Monde,* September 6, 1999, 4, my translation). However membership was defined, by 2003 the OIF counted some fifty-six states and governments as members and observers, including fourteen where French could hardly be said to be the "common language": São Tomé and Príncipe, Cape Verde, Egypt, Moldavia, Bulgaria, Romania, Lithuania, Czech Republic, Slovenia, Slovakia, Poland, Equatorial Guinea, Vanuatu, and Vietnam. Canada was eligible for three delegations: Canada, Canada-New Brunswick, and Canada-Quebec.

Appendix N   Principal French Cooperation Accords with African and Malagache States

Principal Bilateral Pacts (fourteen francophone states in italics)

Country	Type of Pact (number of pacts signed)	Activation (Revision)	Initial African Signatory
Benin	D, DC, CA, EMF, JC, MA, TMA, TT (28)	1961, R 1963–1967	H. Maga
Burkina Faso	C, D, ED, F, JC, ST, TMA (20)	1961, R 1962–1978	M. Yaméogo
Cameroon	CA, D, DC, EMF, JC, MA, TMA, TT (31)	1961, R 1974	A. Ahidjo
CAR	C, CM, D, DC, F, MA, TMA (14)	1960, R 1972, 1976	D. Dacko
Chad	C, CM, D, DC, F, JC, MA, TMA (21)	1960, R 1962–1976	N. Tombalbaye
Congo-Brazzaville	C, D, DC, ED, F, JC, SP, TMA (28)	1960, R 1974	F. Youlou
Comoros	MA (1)	1978	A. Soilih
Côte d'Ivoire	C, D, ED, EMF, F, JC, G, TF, TMA (21)	1960, R 1963–1972	F. Houphouët-Boigny
Djibouti	D, JC, TMA (3)	1978	H.G. Aptidon
Gabon	C, D, DC, ED, EMF, F, JC, MA, TA, TMA, TT (28)	1960, R 1961–1972	L. M'ba, O. Bongo
Guinea	C, TA, TP (6)	1962, 1963, 1978	S. Touré
Madagascar	CM, D, DC, ED, EMF, F, JC, SP (44)	1960, R 1973, 1975, 1977	P. Tsiranana
Mali Federation	CM, D, ED, EMF, SP (11)	1960	L.S. Senghor
Mali (Republic)	C, D, EMF, F, G (14)	1962, R 1963–1972	M. Keita
Mauritania	C, D, F, JC, MA, TA, TMA, TP (28)	1961, R 1963, 1972–1976	M. Ould Daddah
Mauritius	C/TA (joined accord), MA (2)	1974	S. Ramgoolam
Niger	C, CA, D, EMF, F, G, MA, TMA, TP (28)	1961, R 1962–1977	H. Diori
Rwanda	C, ED, EMF, G, MA (6)	1962, 1971	J. Habyarimana
Senegal	Mali Fed., accords accepted, 1960; plus CA, D, DC, ED, G, SP, TMA (35)	1961, R 1962–1976	L.S. Senghor
Togo	C, D, DC, EMF, F, JC, SP, TMA (18)	1963, R 1976	N. Grunitsky
Zaire	C, MA, TC (4)	1963–1975	Mobuto Sese Seko

(continues)

Appendix N (continued)

Multilateral Pacts (fourteen francophone states in italics)

Countries (France plus)	Type of Pact	Activation	Signatories
Gabon, Côte d'Ivoire, Benin, Niger	Five-country Defense and Strategic Products accords (DSP)	1961	Heads of state
Cameroon, CAR, Congo-Brazzaville, Côte d'Ivoire, Benin, Gabon, Burkina Faso, Mauritania, Madagascar, Niger, Senegal, Chad	Thirteen-country Joint French-African Insurance Companies Accord (IC)	1962	Heads of state or government
Mali, Madagascar, CAR, Congo, Gabon, Chad	Seven-country Conciliation and Arbitration Accord (CAA)	1960	Heads of state or government

Sources: Viaud and Lestapis, *Afrique: le souverainétés en armes*; Plantey and Broyer, "Les accords de cooperation entre la France et les états africains et malagaches"; Dabezier, "La politique militaire de la France en Afrique noire sous le Général de Gaulle; author's files.

Notes: (C) cultural; (CA) civil aviation; (CAA) conciliation and abitration accords; (CM) community membership; (CO) consular; (D) defense; (DC) diplomatic and consular; (DSP) defense and strategic products; (ED) higher education; (EMF) economic, monetary, and fiscal; (F) fiscal; (G) general cooperation; (IC) insurance companies; (JC) judicial cooperation; (MA) informal accord; (R) revised; (SP) strategic products; (TA) technical assistance, personnel; (TMA) technical and military assistance; (TP) technical personnel; (TT) treasury to treasury.

Appendix O   Political and Entrepreneurial Power Connections: "Françafrique"/Paris-Village Networks

Principal Official African Client Patrons	Participating French MNCs	Local Networkers (*Ces messieurs Afrique*)	Net Operators (Elysée "Cellules," Officials)	Principal Official French Patron/Clients
F. Houphouët-Boigny (Côte d'Ivoire) 1959–1993		J.-P. Prouteau[a] (B) V. Ballore[a] (B) M. Bouygues[a] (B)		C. de Gaulle 1959–1969
H. Konan Bedié (Côte d'Ivoire) 1993–2000	ADEFI International	A. Tarallo[a] (B) P. Barril[a] (F, O) J. Verges[a] (F, L)		
O. Bongo (Gabon) 1967–?	Elf/Total	H. Bourges[a] (B, J) J. Y. Ollivier[a] (O, B) J. Lorgeoux[a] (M, O)		G. Pompidou 1969–1974
G. Eyadéma (Togo) 1967–?		S. Versano[a] (B) J.-P. Fleury[a] (B)	J. Foccart (1958–1974)	
Mobutu Sese Seko (DRC) 1965–1997	Sucden	G. Kentler (M, B) Gen. J. Lacaze (F, O)		V. Giscard-d'Estaing 1974–1981
J. Habyarimana (Rwanda) 1973–1994	BNP-Paribas	G. Vidal (M, O) P. Martini (P, O) C. Debbasch (F, O)	C. Pasqua (1986–?)	
J.-B. Bokassa (CAR) 1966–1979	Castel	D. Schuller (F) J.-C. Marchiani (F, O, B)		F. Mitterand 1981–1995
A. Kolingba (CAR) 1981–1993	Bouygues	Bros. Feliciaggi (F, B) P. Jaffra T. Mailler		
P. Biya (Cameroon) 1984–?		C. de Peyron (F, B) J. P. Bondil (F, O, B)	J. C. Mitterand (J) (1982–1995)	J. Chirac 1995–?
S. Djohar (Comoros) 1989–1995	SCOA	C. Sabbe (F, L) P. Moussa (F, B) J. Rossignol (F, B) P. Voita (F)		
D. Sassou-Nguesso (Congo-Brazzaville) 1979–1992, 1997–?		Y. Omnes (M, O) Col. J. Mantion (P, O) D. Leandri (P, O, B)	J. Foccart (1995–1997)	
I. Déby (Chad) 1990–?		M. Tomi (P, O, B) J.-P. Tosi (P, O, B) J. Filipedu (P, O, B)		H. Vedrine→D. de Villepin C. Josselin→P.-A. Wiltzer
H. Gouled Aptidon (Djibouti) 1977–?		Y. Challier (P) T. Luciani (P, B) P. Lefranchi (P, L)	F. Wibaux (F) M. Dupuch	
F. W. de Klerk (South Africa) 1989–1994		A. Blanc (P, O, B) M. Melin (P, B) P. Dijoud (M) J. N. Tassez (M)		

Sources: Glaser and Smith, *Ces messieurs Afrique: Le Paris-village du continent noir*; Smith and Glaser, "Les reseaux africains de Jean-Christophe Mitterand"; "Les liaisons mafieuses de la Françafrique"; Verschave, *Noir silence: Qui arrêtera la Françafrique* and *La françafrique.*

Notes: a. Main actors described in Glaser and Smith, *Ces messieurs Afrique.*

(B) businessmen, entrepreneurs; (F) mainly identified with Foccart networks; (J) journalists; (L) lawyers *(avocats)*; (M) mainly identified with J.-C. Mitterand network; (O) active or retired officials, including military, diplomatic, and security personnel; (P) mainly identified with Pasqua network.

(——) direct links; (– – –) indirect links.

This is a rough approximation of the (figurative) informal networks—the so-called *réseaux*—that linked the French political and entrepreneurial power centers of France and Africa (mainly francophone). The *réseaux* were created, operated, and maintained under five French presidencies, from de Gaulle to Chirac. They were usually identified by the names of the net operators (Foccart, Pasqua, J.-C. Mitterand). The table identifies the principal African "client/patrons," usually heads of state/government who became both number-one clients in the networks and (less frequently) patrons, providing soft money for elections and other favors to French officials and notables. The French MNCs identified here all did business—often under preferential terms—in francophone Africa and were represented by some of what are here called "local networkers." French businessmen, retired officials, and, often, active officials acting as intermediaries in the networks. For details of the connections, see the sources cited above. After the death of Foccart in 1997[6], Chirac deemphasized the importance of the networks, placing greater responsibility for French-African relations with the Foreign Ministry, first under Vedrine then de Villepin, and moved the cooperation portfolio under Foreign Affairs (Josselin, then Wiltzer). While the networks are journalistic metaphors, such authoritative francophone Africanists as J.-F. Bayart, Médard, and Guy Martin have testified that they do appear to have accurately evoked the informal nature of the relations they portray.

**Appendix P   Relationship of the Democratic Party of Guinea
to the Government Organizational Structures, 1961**

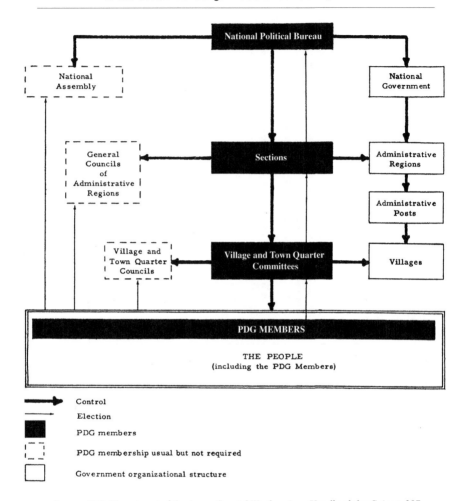

Source: U.S. Department of the Army, *Special Warfare Area Handbook for Guinea,* 287.

Bibliography

Adamolekun, Ladipo. *Sékou Touré's Guinea: An Experiment in Nation Building.* London: Methuen, 1976.

Adinkrah, Mensah. "Political Coercion in Military-Dominated Regimes: A Subcultural Interpretation." Ph.D. thesis. Washington University, 1988.

Adjovi, Emmanuel V. *Une élection libre en Afrique: La presidentielle du Bénin (1966).* Paris: Karthala, 1998.

Adloff, Richard. *West Africa: The French-Speaking Nations, Yesterday and Today.* New York: Holt, 1964.

Africa Research Bulletin: Political, Social, and Cultural Series. London: Blackwell, 1960–2004.

Africa South of the Sahara, annual publication since 1971. London: Europa.

Afrika Biografien. Bonn: Friedrich-Ebert Stiftung, 1967–1971.

"Afrique: Images incertaines." *Afrique Contemporaine* (fourth quarter, 1992): 22–31.

Akinoa, M. G. A. "The French and East Africa." Unpublished paper prepared for the Institute of African Studies, University of Ghana, 1966.

Alexandre, Pierre. "The Problem of Chieftaincies in French Africa." Unpublished paper, Conference on West African Chiefs, University of Ife (Nigeria), 16–21 December 1961.

———. "Social Pluralism in French African Colonies and in States Issuing Therefrom: An Impressionistic Approach." In Leo Kuper and M. G. Smith, eds., *Pluralism in Africa,* pp. 195–210. Berkeley, CA: University of California Press, 1969.

———. "A West African Islamic Movement: Hamallism in French West Africa." In Robert I. Rotberg and Ali A. Mazrui, eds., *Protest and Power in Black Africa,* pp. 497–512. New York: Oxford University Press, 1970.

Allen, Chris. "Benin." In Chris Allen, ed., *Marxist Regimes: Benin, the Congo, Burkina Faso,* pp. 1–144. New York: Pinter, 1989.

———. "Restructuring an Authoritarian State: Democratic Renewal in Benin." *Review of African Political Economy* 54 (1992): 42–58.

———. "Understanding African Politics." *Review of African Political Economy* 56 (1996): 301–320.

Almond, Gabriel, and James S. Coleman, eds. *The Politics of the Developing Areas.* Princeton, NJ: Princeton University Press, 1960.

Amnesty International. "Climate of Terror in Casamance." AFR 49/01/98. New York: Amnesty International, 1998.

———. *World Report,* 2001. Available at http://amnesty.org/web/ar2001.nsf.home/home/home. 2001.

Andereggen, Anton. *France's Relationship with Sub-Saharan Africa.* New York: Praeger, 1994.

Andrain, Charles F. "The Political Thought of Sékou Touré." In W. A. Skurnik, ed., *African Political Thought: Lumumba, Nkrumah, and Touré,* pp. 103–147. Denver, CO: University of Denver Monograph Series, 1968.

Andreski, Stanislas. *The African Predicament.* New York: Atherton Press, 1968.

Andriamirado, Sennen. *Il s'appelait Sankara.* Paris: Présence Africaine, 1989.

———. *Sankara le rebelle.* Paris: Jeune Afrique, 1987.

Annuaire des dioceses d'expression française, delegations apostoliques pour l'Afrique occidentale, l'Afrique centrale, et Madagascar. Paris: Presses Apostoliques de France, 1994.

Ansprenger, Franz. *Politik im Schwarzen Afrika: Die modernen politische Bewegungen im Afrika französischer Prägung.* Cologne: Westdeutscher Verlag, 1961.

Apter, David. *The Politics of Modernization.* Chicago: University of Chicago Press, 1965.

Apter, David E., and James S. Coleman. "Pan-Africanism or Nationalism?" In American Society of African Culture, *Pan-Africanism Reconsidered.* Berkeley: University of California Press, 1962.

"Arcanes et rouages de la coopération militaire." In *Présence militaire française en Afrique: dérives* . . . . Dossier noir numero 4/Agir et Survie/L'Harmattan, 1995. Available at http://www.reseauvoltaire.net/rubrique12.html.

Argenti, Nicolas. "Mbaya: Contemporary Masquerades and the State in Cameroon." Unpublished paper, Universities of Hull and London, October 23 and 31, 1996.

Asso, Bernard. *Le chef d'état africain: L'éxperience des états africains de succession française.* Paris: Editions Albatross, 1976.

Augagneur, Victor. *Erreurs et brutalités coloniales.* Paris: Montaigne, 1927.

Bâ, Amadou Hampaté. *The Fortunes of Wangrin (Etrange destin de Wangrin).* Translated by Abiola Irele. Ibadan, Nigeria: New Horn Press, 1987.

———. "Les traditions Africains, gages de progrès." In Rencontres Internationales de Bouaké, *Traditions et modernisme en Afrique Noire,* pp. 31–48. Paris: Editions du Seuil, 1965.

Bach, Daniel C., ed. *Regionalisation in Africa: Integration and Disintegration.* Oxford, UK: James Currey, 1999.

Bakary, Tessy. *La démocratie par le haut en Côte d'Ivoire.* Paris: L'Harmattan, 1992.

Bala, Henri. *J'aime mon pays: Le Cameroun.* Yaoundé: Centre d'édition et de production de manuels de l'enseignement, 1970.

Balandier, Georges. *Ambiguous Africa.* New York: Pantheon, 1966.

———. "La situation coloniale—Approche théorique." *Cahiers Internationaux de Sociologie* 11 (1951): 44–79. Reprinted in I. Wallerstein, ed., *Social Change: The Colonial Situation,* pp. 34–57. New York: Wiley, 1966.

———. *Sociologie actuelle de l'Afrique Noire,* 2nd ed. Paris: Presses Universitaires de France, 1963.

Ballard, John A. "The Colonial Phase in French West Africa." In J. F. Ade Ajayi and Ian Espie, eds., *A Thousand Years of West African History,* pp. 380–404. London: Thomas Nelson for Ibadan University Press, 1969.

———. "Four Equatorial States." In Gwendolen Carter, ed., *Nationalism and Regionalism in Eight African States,* pp. 231–335. Ithaca, NY: Cornell University Press, 1966.

———. "Nationalist Movements in West Africa, (ii) The French Territories." In J. F. Ade Ajayi and Ian Espie, eds., *A Thousand Years of West African History,* pp. 461–474. London: Thomas Nelson for Ibadan University Press, 1969.

———. "The Porto-Novo Incidents of 1923: Politics in the Colonial Era." *ODU/African Studies* 2, no. 1 (July 1965): 52–75.

Bamouni, Babou Paulin. *Burkina Faso: Processus de la révolution.* Paris: L'Harmattan, 1987.

Barbier-Wiesser, François-George, ed. *Comprendre la Casamance.* Paris: Karthala, 1994.

Barnes, James F. *Gabon: Beyond the Colonial Legacy.* Boulder, CO: Westview, 1992.

Baulin, Jacques. *La politique interieure d'Houphouët-Boigny.* Paris: Eurafor-Press, 1982.

Baxter, John, and Keith Somerville. "Burkina Faso." In Michel Radu et al., eds., *Marxist Regimes: Benin, Congo, Burkina Faso,* pp. 237–286. New York: Pinter, 1989.

Bayart, Jean-François. *L'état au Cameroun.* Paris: Presses de la Fondation Nationale des Sciences Politiques, 1979.

———. *La politique africaine de François Mitterand.* Paris: Karthala, 1984.

———. *The State in Africa: The Politics of the Belly.* New York: Longman Group, 1993.

Bayart, Jean-François, Stephen Ellis, and Béatrice Hibou. *The Criminalization of the State in Africa.* Bloomington, IN: James Curry/Indiana University Press, 1999.

Bazenguissa-Ganga, Rémy. "The Spread of Political Violence in Congo-Brazzaville." *African Affairs* 98 (1999): 37–54.

———. *Les voies du politique au Congo: Essai de sociologie historique.* Paris: Karthala, 1997.

Beck, Linda. "Senegal's 'Patrimonial Democrats': Incremental Reform and the Obstacles to the Consolidation of Democracy." *Canadian Journal of African Studies* 31, no. 3 (1997): 1–31.

Behrman, Lucy. *Muslim Brotherhoods and Politics in Senegal.* Cambridge, MA: Harvard University Press, 1970.

Benchenane, Mustapha. *Les armées africaines.* Paris: Publisud, 1983.

Benjamin, Jacques. *Les Camerounais occidentaux.* Montreal: Les Presses de l'Université de Montréal, 1972.

Bénot, Yves. *Idéologies des indépendences africaines.* Paris: François Maspero, 1972.

Berg, Elliot J. "The Economic Basis of Political Choice in French West Africa." *American Political Science Review* 54 (1960): 341–405.

Berg, Elliot J., and Jeffrey Butler. "Trade Unions." In James S. Coleman and Carl G. Rosberg, eds., *Political Parties and National Integration in Tropical Africa,* pp. 340–381. Berkeley: University of California Press, 1964.

Beti, Mongo [Alexandre Biyidi]. *Main basse sur le Cameroun.* Paris: Editions Peuples Noirs, 1984.

Betts, Raymond. *Assimilation and Association in French Colonial Theory, 1890–1914.* New York: Columbia University Press, 1961.

Biarnès, Pierre. *L'Afrique aux Africains.* Paris: Armand Colin, 1980.

Bigo, Didier. *Pouvoir et obéissance en Centrafrique.* Paris: Karthala, 1988.

Bill, James A., and Robert Springborg. *Politics in the Middle East,* 4th ed. New York: Harper Collins, 1994.

Billet, Brett L. "The Precipitants of African Coups d'Etat: A Case Study of the 1968 Malian Coup." Unpublished paper, 1988 International Studies Association meeting, St. Louis, MO.

Blanchet, André. *L'itinéraire des partis africains depuis Bamako.* Paris: Plon, 1958.

Boni, Nazi. *Histoire synthétique de l'Afrique résistante.* Paris: Présence Africaine, 1971.

Boubacar, Diabaté. *Porte Ouverte sur la Communauté Franco-Africaine.* Brussels: Editions Remarques Congolaises, 1961.

Bouquet, Christian. "Côte d'Ivoire: Quatre consultations pour une transition (décembre 1999–mars 2001)." In *L'Afrique politique 2002,* pp. 313–342. Paris: Karthala, 2002.

Braeckman, Collete. "Le feu court sur la région des Grands Lacs: La présence militaire française au Rwanda." *Le Monde Diplomatique* (September 1994): 10–11.

Brass, William. "The Demography of French-Speaking Territories." In William Brass, et al., *The Demography of Tropical Africa,* pp. 342–439. Princeton, NJ: Princeton University Press, 1968.

Bratton, Michael. "Second Elections in Africa." *Journal of Democracy* 9, no. 3 (1998): 51–66.

Bratton, Michael, and Nicolas van de Walle. *Democratic Experiments in Africa: Regime Transitions in Comparative Perspective.* New York: Cambridge University Press, 1998.

Brockway, Fenner. *African Socialism.* London: The Bodley Head, 1963.

Brody, Reed. "The Prosecution of Hissene Habré—An African Pinochet." *New England Law Review* 35 (2001). Available at Human Rights Watch, http://hrw.org/hrw/editorials/2001/habre0515.htm.

Brunschwig, Henri. *French Colonialism, 1871–1914.* London: Pall Mall, 1966.

———. *Noirs et blancs dans l'Afrique Noire française.* Paris: Flammarion, 1983.

———. "Politique et économie dans l'empire français d'Afrique Noire, 1870–1914." *Journal of African History* 11, no. 3 (1970): 402.

Buell, Raymond Leslie. *The Native Problem in Africa.* 2 vols. New York: Macmillan, 1928.

Burkina Faso, Direction de la Presse Presidentielle. *Le Burkina Faso du Front Populaire, An I.* Ouagadougou: D. P. P., ca. 1989.

Callaghy, Thomas, Ronald Kassimir, and Robert Latham, eds. *Intervention and Transnationalism in Africa.* Cambridge: Cambridge University Press, 2001.

Camara, Sylvain Soriba. *La Guinée sans la France.* Paris: Presses de la Fondation Nationale des Sciences Politiques, 1976.

Carter, Gwendolen. *Independence for Africa.* New York: Frederick Praeger, 1960.

Chafer, Tony. *The End of Empire in French West Africa.* New York: Berg, 2002.

Chaffard, Georges. *Les carnets secrets de la décolonisation,* vols. 1 and 2. Paris: Calmann-Lévy, 1965–1967.

———. "La longue marche des commandos nigériens." In Georges Chaffard, *Les carnets sécrets de la decolonisation,* vol. 2, pp. 269–342. Paris: Calmann-Lévy, 1967.

Charles, Bernard. *Cadres guinéennes et appartenances ethniques (thèse de doctorat).* Faculté des Lettres, Sorbonne, Paris, 1968.

———. *Guinée.* Lausanne: Editions Rencontre, 1963.

———. "Le socialisme africain, mythes et réalités." *Revue Française de Science*

Politique 15 (1965): 856–884.

"Charnier de Yopougon: Une commission internationale accuse les gendarmes." *Le Monde* (July 20, 2001). Available at http://www.afrik.com/afp/general/0101720154757.9hms8ug5.html.

Charpy, Jacques. *La fondation de Dakar, 1845–1861*. Paris: Larose, 1958.

Chazan, Naomi. *An Anatomy of Ghanaian Politics: Managing Political Recession*. Boulder, CO: Westview, 1983.

Chazan, Naomi, et al. *Politics and Society in Contemporary Africa*, 3rd ed. Boulder, CO: Lynne Rienner, 1999.

Chege, Michael. "Between Africa's Extremes." In Larry Diamond and Mark Plattner, eds., *The Global Resurgence of Democracy*, 2nd ed., pp. 350–364. Baltimore, MD: Johns Hopkins Press, 1996.

Cherlonneix, Bernard. "La voie burkinabé vers le socialisme." *Le Mois en Afrique,* nos. 247–248 (August–September 1986): 4–14.

Chipman, John. *French Power in Africa*. London: Blackwell, 1989.

CIA. *World Factbook, 2003*. Available at www.cia.gov/cia/publications/factbook.

Clapham, Christopher. *Africa and the International System: The Politics of Survival*. New York: Cambridge University Press, 1998.

Clark, John F. "The Neo-Colonial Context of the Democratic Experiment of Congo-Brazzaville." *African Affairs* 101 (2002): 171–192.

Clark, John F., and David E. Gardinier, eds. *Political Reform in Francophone Africa*. Boulder, CO: Westview, 1997.

Cohen, Michael A. "The Myth of the Expanding Centre: Politics in the Ivory Coast." *Journal of Modern African Studies* 2, no. 2 (1975): 227–246.

Coleman, James S. "Togoland." *International Conciliation,* no. 509 (1956).

Coleman, James S., and Carl Rosberg, Jr., eds., *Political Parties and National Integration in Tropical Africa*. Berkeley, CA: University of California Press, 1964.

Collier, Ruth Berins. *Regimes in Tropical Africa: Changing Forms of Supremacy, 1945–1975*. Los Angeles: University of California Press, 1982.

Colson, Elizabeth. "Competence and Incompetence in the Context of Independence." *Current Anthropology* 8, nos. 1–2 (1967): 92–111.

Commissariat aux Colonies. *La Conférence Africaine Française, Brazzaville*. Algers: France Libre, Commissariat aux Colonies, 1944.

Comte, Gilbert. "Le Marxisme et l'Afrique." *Le Mois en Afrique* (March 1967): 85.

Conesa, Pierre. "Les soubresauts d'un état fictive: La Tchad des crises à répetition." *Le Monde Diplomatique* (May 2001): 23.

Congolese Human Rights Observatory. "Congo-Brazzaville: l'Arbitraire de l'Etat, le terreur des milices." International Federation of Human Rights Leagues/FIDH Report, June 17, 1999. Available at http://www.fidh.imaginet.fr/rapports/brazza.htm.

Conklin, Alice. *A Mission to Civilize*. Stanford, CA: Stanford University Press, 1997.

Constantin, François G. "The Foreign Policy of Francophone Africa: Clientelism and After." In Anthony Kirk-Greene and Daniel Bach, eds., *State and Society in Francophone Africa Since Independence*, pp. 183–199. New York: St. Martin's, 1995.

Copans, Jean. *Les marabouts de l'arachide*. Paris: L'Harmattan, 1988.

Corbett, Edward M. *The French Presence in Africa*. New York: Black Orpheus, 1972.

Cornevin, Robert. *Histoire du Dahomey*. Paris: Berger-Levrault, 1962.

————. *Histoire du Togo.* Paris: Berger-Levrault, 1962.

————. *Le Togo, nation-pilote.* Paris: Nouvelles Editions Latines, 1963.

Cornewell, Richard. "Africa Watch, Côte d'Ivoire: Asking for It." *African Studies Review* 9, no. 1 (2000). Available at http://www.iss.co.za/Pubs/ASR/9.1/ Africa%Watch.html.

"La Côte d'Ivoire, rejet du modèle, retour du réel." *Le Monde Diplomatique* (November 1992): 10–11.

Coulon, Christian. *Le marabout et le prince (Islam et pouvoir au Senegal).* Paris: A. Pedone, 1981.

————. "Senegal: The Development and Fragility of a Semidemocracy." In Larry Diamond et al., eds., *Democracy in Developing Countries,* vol. 2, *Africa,* pp. 141–178. Boulder, CO: Lynne Rienner, 1988.

Coussy, Jean. "The Franc Zone: Original Logic, Subsequent Evolution, and Present Crisis." In Anthony Kirk-Greene and Daniel Bach, eds., *State and Socety in Francophone Africa Since Independence,* pp. 160–180. New York: St. Martin's, 1995.

Crowder, Michael. "The Administration of French West Africa." *Tarikh* (Ibadan) 2, no. 4 (1969): 54–62.

————. "Independence as a Goal in French West African Politics." In William Lewis, ed., *French-Speaking Africa,* pp. 15–41. New York: William Walker, 1965.

————. *Senegal: A Study of French Assimilation Policy.* London: Oxford University Press, 1968.

————. *West Africa Under Colonial Rule.* Evanston, IL: Northwestern University Press, 1968.

Cultru, Paul. *Histoire du Sénégal du XVe siècle à 1870.* Paris: E. Larose, 1910.

Cumming, Gordon. "French Development Assistance to Africa: Toward a New Agenda?" *African Affairs* 94 (1995): 390–401.

Cuoq, Joseph. *Histoire d'islamisation.* Paris: Librairie Guthner, 1984.

Dabezier, Pierre. "La politique militaire de la Françe en Afrique Noire sous le Général de Gaulle." In Dimitri G. Lavroff, ed., *La politique africaine de Général de Gaulle,* pp. 229–262. Paris: A. Pedone, 1980.

Dahl, Robert Alan. *Who Governs? Democracy and Power in an American City.* New Haven: Yale University Press, 1961.

D'Arboussier, Gabriel. *L'Afrique vers l'unité.* Paris: Editions Saint-Paul, 1961.

————. *Lettre ouverte à Félix Houphouët-Boigny par Gabriel d'Arboussier.* Paris: private publisher, 1952.

Davis, Shelby Collum. *Reservoirs of Men: A History of the Black Troops of French West Africa.* 1934. Reprint, Westport, CN: Negro Universities Press/ Greenwood, 1970.

Dawson, Richard, and Kenneth Prewitt. *Political Socialization.* Boston: Little, Brown, 1969.

Decalo, Samuel. *Coups and Army Rule in Africa: Motivations and Constraints,* 2nd ed. New Haven: Yale University Press, 1990.

————. "Full Circle in Dahomey." *African Studies Review* 13, no. 3 (1970): 445–457.

————. "Ideological Rhetoric and Scientific Socialism in Benin and Congo/Brazzaville." In Carl Rosberg and Thomas Callaghy, eds., *Socialism in Sub-Saharan Africa: A New Assessment,* pp. 231–265. Berkeley: University of California Press, 1979.

————. *Israel and Africa, Forty Years, 1956–1996.* Gainesville: Florida Academic

Press, 1998.
———. *Psychoses of Power: African Personal Dictatorships*. Boulder, CO: Westview, 1989.
———. "Regionalism, Political Decay, and Civil Strife in Chad." *Journal of Modern African Studies* 18, no. 1 (1980): 47–58.
———. *The Stable Minority: Civilian Rule in Africa*. Gainesville: Florida Academic Press, 1997.
Decoudras, Pierre-Marie, and Mamadou Gazibo. "Niger: Démocratie ambigue, chronique d'un coup d'état annoncé." In *L'Afrique Politique 1997*, pp. 155–189. Paris: Karthala, 1997.
Decraene, Philippe. *Tableau des partis politiques de l'Afrique au sud du Sahara*. Paris: Fondation Nationale des Sciences Politiques, 1963.
Defosses, Helen, and J. Dirck. "Socialist Development in Africa: The Case of Keita's Mali." In Helen Defosses and J. Levesques, eds., *Socialism in the Third World*, pp. 163–179. New York: Praeger, 1975.
de la Gorce, Paul-Marie. "La deuxième mort de Jacques Foccart." *Jeune Afrique* no. 1990–91 (1997): 40–42.
DeLancey, Mark, and H. Mbella Mokeba. *Historical Dictionary of the Republic of Cameroon*. Metuchen, NJ: Scarecrow, 1990.
Delavignette, Robert. *Freedom and Authority in French West Africa*. London: Oxford University Press, 1950.
———. "Resurgences tribales dans les régimes présidentiels en Afrique Noire Francophone." *Le Mois en Afrique* (June 1967): 24–36.
Delpey, Roger. *Affaires Centrafricaines: Quand Centrafrique bougera, l'Afrique explosera*. Paris: Jacques Grancher, 1985.
———. *La Manipulation*. Paris: Jacques Grancher, 1981.
De Lusignan, Guy. *French-Speaking Africa Since Independence*. London: Pall Mall, 1969.
Deschamps, Hubert. "La F.O.M. et la Communauté." *Fascieule 1, Amicale I.E.P.* Paris: Cours d'Institut d'Etudes Politiques, 1958–1959.
Les deux Congos dans la guerre. Special issue of *Politique Africaine* 72 (December 1998).
Development Data Group, 2001. New York: World Bank, 2002.
Dia, Mamadou. *African Nations and World Solidarity*. Translated by Mercer Cook. New York: Praeger, 1961.
Diallo, Siradiou. "Haute-Volta: Qui sout les nouveau dirigeauts?" *Jeune Afrique* 1146 (December 22, 1998): 50–53.
Diarrah, Oumar. "Les deux morts de Modibo Keita." In *Dossiers secrets de l'Afrique contemporaine,* tome 3, pp. 151–171. Paris: Jeune Afrique, 1991.
———. *Le Mali de Modibo Keita*. Paris: L'Harmattan, 1986.
———. *Vers la troisième République du Mali*. Paris: L'Harmattan, 1991.
Dickie, John, and Alan Rake. *Who's Who in Africa*. London: African Buyer and Trader, 1973.
Dictionary of African Biography, 1st and 2nd eds. London: Melrose Press, 1970 and 1971.
Dictionnaire bio-bibliographique du Dahomey. Porto Novo: Institut de Recherches Appliqués de Dahomey, 1969.
Diop, Cheikh Anta. *The African Origin of Civilization: Myth or Reality*. Translated by Mercer Cook. New York: L. Hill, 1974.
———. *Nations nègres et cultures*. Paris: Editions Africains, 1955.
Diop, Majhemout. *Contribution à l'étude des problèmes politiques en Afrique*

Noire. Paris: Présence Africaine, 1958.

———. "L'unique issue: L'indépendance totale; La seule voie: Une large mouvement d'union anti-imperialiste." *Présence africaine* 14 (1953).

Docking, Timothy. "Mali: The Roots of Democracy's 'Success.'" In *L'Afrique Politique 1997,* pp. 191–212. Paris: Karthala, 1997.

Dongmo, Jean-Louis. *Le Dynamisme Bamiléké,* vols. 1 and 2. Yaoundé: University of Cameroon, Ministry of Education, General Delegation for Scientific and Technical Research, 1981.

"Dossier spécial: Congo-Brazzaville, entre guerre et paix." *Afrique Contemporaine.* Paris: Documentation Française, April–June 1998.

Du Bois, Victor D. "Catholicism's Problems in French Black Africa." *American Universities Field Staff Reports Service,* West African Series, vol. 5, no. 3 (1962).

———. "The Decline of the Guinean Revolution." *American Universities Field Staff Reports Service,* West African Series, vol. 8, nos. 7–9 (1965).

———. "Guinea." In James S. Coleman and Carl G. Rosberg, eds., *Political Parties and National Integration in Tropical Africa,* pp. 186–215. Berkeley: University of California Press, 1964.

———. "The Struggle for Stability in Upper Volta." *American Universities Field Staff Reports Service,* West African Series, vol. 12, nos. 1–3 (1969).

Duchêne, Albert Paul André. *La politique coloniale de la France: Le Ministère des colonies depuis Richelieu.* Paris: Payot, 1928.

Dugue, Gil. *Vers les Etats-Unis d'Afrique.* Dakar: Lettres Africaines, 1960.

Duignan, Peter, and Lewis H. Gann. "Communism in Sub-Saharan Africa: A Reappraisal." In *Hoover Essays,* pp. 1–49. Stanford, CA: Stanford University, Hoover Institution, 1994.

Dumont, René. *L'Afrique Noire est mal partie.* Paris: Editions du Seuil, 1962.

———. *Démocratie pour l'Afrique.* Paris: Editions du Seuil, 1991.

Eboussi Boulaga, Fabien. *Les conférences nationales en Afrique Noire: une affaire à suivre.* Paris: Karthala, 1993.

———. *La démocratie de transit au Cameroun.* Paris: L'Harmattan, 1997.

Echenberg, Myron. *Colonial Conscripts: The Tirailleurs Sénégalais in French West Africa, 1857–1960.* Portsmouth, NH: Heinemann, 1991.

Ediafric: La Documentation Africaine. *Deputés et Conseillers économiques.* Paris: Editions africaines, 1962 and 1963.

———. *Les élites africaines.* Paris: Editions africaines, 1971.

———. *Gouvernements at cabinets ministeriels.* Paris: Editions africaines, 1962.

———. *P. D. G. Afrique.* Paris: Editions africaines, 1969.

———. *Personnalités publiques de l'Afrique centrale.* Paris: Editions africaines, 1969 and 1974.

———. *Personnalités publiques de l'Afrique de l'ouest.* Paris: Editions africaines, 1970 and 1973.

Ehrhard, Jacques. *Communauté ou sécession?* Paris: Calmann-Lévy, 1959.

Engberg, Holger L. "The Operations Account System in French-Speaking Africa." *Journal of Modern African Studies* 11, no. 4 (1973): 537–545.

Englebert, Pierre. *Burkina Faso: Unsteady Statehood in West Africa.* Boulder, CO: Westview, 1996.

———. "Recent History [of Niger]." In *Africa South of the Sahara 1996,* pp. 687–693. London: Europa, 1997.

———. *La révolution burkinabé.* Paris: L'Harmattan, 1986.

———. *State Legitimacy and Development in Africa.* Boulder, CO: Lynne Rienner,

2000.

Etoga-Eily, Florent, et al. *Paul Biya ou l'incarnation de la rigeur.* Yaoundé: Editions SOPECAM, 1983.

"Les étudiants noirs parlent." *Présence africaine* 14 (1953): 145–184.

Fall, Boubacar. "Economie de plantations et main-d'oeuvre forcée en Guinée-Française: 1920–1946." *Travail, Capital, et Société* 20, no. 1 (1976): 8–33.

Farah, Douglas. "Diamonds Are a Rebel's Best Friend." *Washington Post* (April 17, 2000).

Fatton, Robert, Jr. "Clientelism and Patronage in Senegal." *African Studies Review* 29, no. 4 (1986): 61–78.

———. *The Making of a Liberal Democracy: Senegal's Passive Revolution, 1975–1985.* Boulder, CO: Lynne Rienner, 1987.

———. *Predatory Rule: State and Civil Society in Africa.* Boulder, CO: Lynne Rienner, 1992.

Fauré, Y. A., and Jean-François Médard, eds. *Etat et bourgeoisie en Côte d'Ivoire.* Paris: Karthala, 1982.

Feit, Edward. *The Armed Bureaucrats: Military-Administrative Regimes and Political Development.* Boston: Houghton-Mifflin, 1973.

Ferguson, Gregor. *Coup d'Etat: A Practical Manual.* New York: Sterling, 1987.

Ferkiss, Victor C. "Religion and Politics in Independent African States: A Prolegomenon." In Jeffrey Butler and A. A. Castagno, eds., *Boston Univesity Papers on Africa: Transition in African Politics.* New York: Frederick Praeger, 1967.

Fernandez, James A. "Microcosmogony and Modernization in African Religious Movements." *Occasional Papers,* no. 3, Center for Developing Area Studies. McGill University, Montreal, 1969.

Foccart, Jacques. *Tous les soirs avec de Gaulle, Journal de l'Elysée I: 1965–1967,* ed. Philippe Gaillard. Paris: Fayard, 1997.

———. *Journal de l'Elysée II: 1968–1959, Le Général en mai,* ed. Philippe Gaillard. Paris: Fayard, 1998.

———. *Journal de l'Elysée III: 1969–1971, Dans le bottes du Général,* ed. Philippe Gaillard. Paris: Fayard, 1999.

———. *Journal de l'Elysée IV: 1971–1972, La France Pompidolienne,* ed. Philippe Gaillard. Paris: Fayard, 2000.

———. *Journal de l'Elysée V: 1973–1974, La fin du gaullisme,* ed. Philippe Gaillard. Paris: Fayard, 2001.

Foliet, Joseph. *Le travail forcé aux colonies.* Paris: Editions du Cerf, 1936.

Folson, B. D. G. "Ideology and African Politics." *Transition,* no. 43 (1973): 13.

Foltz, William J. *From French West Africa to the Mali Federation.* New Haven: Yale University Press, 1965.

———. "Senegal." In James S. Coleman and Carl G. Rosberg, eds., *Political Parties and National Integration in Tropical Africa,* pp. 16–64. Berkeley: University of California Press, 1964.

Foltz, William J., and Henry S. Bienen, eds. *Arms and the African.* New Haven: Yale University Press, 1985.

Fombad, Charles M. "Endemic Corruption in Cameroon." In Ronald Hope Kempe, Sr., and Bornwell C. Chikulo, *Corruption and Development in Africa,* pp. 234–260. New York: St. Martin's, 2000.

Foster, Phillip, and Remi Clignet. *The Fortunate Few.* Evanston, IL: Northwestern University Press, 1967.

Fottorino, Eric. "France-Afrique, les liaisons dangereuses: La démocratie à contre-coeur." *Le Monde dossier, Sommet Franco-Africain à La Baule,* June 1990. Available at www.lemonde.fr/dossiers/afric/1003.htm.

Fougeyrollas, Pierre. *Modernisation des hommes: L'exemple du Sénégal.* Paris: Flammarion, 1967.

"La France en Afrique." *Politique Africaine* 2, no. 5 (February 1982): 8–110.

Freedom House. *Freedom in the World 2001–2002.* Washington, D.C.: Freedom House, 2002.

Freeman-Grenville, G. S. P. *The French at Kilwa Island: An Episode in Eighteenth-Century East African History.* Oxford: Clarendon, 1965.

Fugelstadt, Finn. *A History of Niger.* New York: Cambridge University Press, 1983.

Gaffarel, Paul. *Histoire de l'expansion coloniale de la France dépuis 1870 jusqu'en 1905.* Marseille: Baratier, 1906.

Gaillard, Philippe. *Foccart parle: Entretiens avec Philippe Gaillard,* vols. 1 and 2. Paris: Fayard/Jeune Afrique, 1995 and 1998.

Galy, Michel. "Le Burkina-Faso à l'ombre de Sankara." *Le Monde Diplomatique* (December 1994): 4–5.

Gann, Lewis H., and Duignan, Peter. *Burden of Empire.* Stanford, CA: Hoover Institution Press and Frederick Praeger, 1967.

Gardinier, David. *Cameroons: United Nations Challenge to French Policy.* New York: Oxford University Press, 1963.

Gbagbo, Laurent. *Le Côte d'Ivoire: Pour une alternative démocratique.* Paris: L'Harmattan, 1983.

Geertz, Clifford. "The Integrative Revolution: Primordial Sentiments and Civil Politics in the New States." In Clifford Geertz, ed., *Old Societies and New States,* pp. 163–194. New York: Free Press, 1963.

Gellar, Sheldon. "All in the Family: France and Black Africa, 1958–1960." *Asian and African Studies* 26 (1992): 101–117.

———. *Senegal: An African Nation Between Islam and the West.* Boulder, CO: Westview, 1982.

Gendreau, R. "Les Populations des pays d'Afrique Noire d'expression française et de Madagascar." *Revue Economique de Madagascar,* nos 3–4 (1968–1969): 195–208.

Gerteiny, Alfred. *Mauritania.* New York: Frederick Praeger, 1966.

Gervais, Myriam. "Niger: Regime Change, Economic Crisis, and Perpetuation of Privilege." In John F. Clark and David E. Gardinier, eds., *Political Reform in Francophone Africa,* pp. 86–108. Boulder, CO: Westview, 1997.

Geschiere, Peter. "Chiefs and Colonial Rule in Cameroon." *Africa* 63, no. 2 (1965): 151–171.

Geschiere, Peter, and Piet Konings, eds. *Itinéraires d'accumulation au Cameroun.* Paris: Karthala, 1993.

Gilliard, Patrick, and Laurent Pédenon. "Rues de Niamey, espace et territoires de mendicité." *Politique Africaine,* no. 63 (October 1996): 51–60.

Glaser, Antoine. *L'Afrique sans Africains: Le rêve blanc du continent noir.* Paris: Stock, 1994.

Glaser, Antoine, and Stephen Smith. *Ces messieurs Afrique,* vol. 1: *Le Paris-village du continent noir.* Paris: Calmann-Lévy, 1992.

———. *Ces messieurs Afrique,* vol. 2: *Des réseaux aux lobbies.* Paris: Calmann-Lévy, 1997.

Glélé, Maurice. *Naissance d'un état noir: L'évolution politique et constitutionelle du Dahomey de la colonisation à nos jours.* Paris: Librairie Générale de Droit et de Jurisprudence, 1969.

———. *Religion, culture, et politique en Afrique Noire.* Paris: Economica—

Présence africaine, 1981.

Golan, Tamar. "A Certain Mystery: How Can France Do Everything that It Does in Africa—and Get Away With It?" *African Affairs* 80, no. 318 (1981): 3–11.

Goldsmith, Arthur A. "Donors, Dictators, and Democrats in Africa." *Journal of Modern African Studies* 39, no. 3 (2001): 411–436.

Gonidec, P. F. *L'état Africain.* Paris: Librairie générale de droit et de jurisprudence R. Pichon & R. Durand-Auzias. 1970 and 1985.

———. *La République Fédérale du Cameroun.* Paris: Berger-Levrault, 1969.

Gordon, April A., and Donald L. Gordon. *Understanding Contemporary Africa,* 3rd ed. Boulder, CO: Lynne Rienner, 2001.

Gordon, Murray. *Slavery in the Arab World.* New York: Amsterdam Books, 1989.

Gouilly, Alphonse. *L'Islam dans l'Afrique Occidentale Française.* Paris: Larose, 1952.

Greenberg, Joseph Harold. *Studies in African Linguistic Classification.* Reprinted from the *Southwestern Journal of Anthropology* for the Language and Communication Research Center, Columbia University, and the Program of African Studies, Northwestern University. Branford, CN: Compass. 1955.

Gregory, Shaun. "The French Military in Africa: Past and Present." *African Affairs* 99 (2000): 435–448.

Grimal, Henri. *Décolonisation: The British, French, Dutch, and Belgian Empires, 1919–1963.* Boulder, CO: Westview, 1965.

Gromyko, Anatoly, and C. S. Whitaker, eds. *Agenda for Action: African-Soviet-U.S. Cooperation.* Boulder, CO: Lynne Rienner, 1990.

Gros, Jean-Germain. "Les relations franco-africaines à l'âge de la globalization." *Revue Africaine de Sociologie* 2, no. 2 (1998): 1–9.

Grubb, Kenneth G., and E. G. Bingle. *World Christian Handbook.* London: World Dominion Press, 1998.

Grundy, Kenneth W. "Mali: The Prospects for 'Planned Socialism.'" In William H. Friedland and Carl G. Rosberg, Jr., eds., *African Socialism,* pp. 174–193. Stanford, CA: Hoover Institution, 1964.

Guena, Y. *Histoire de la Communauté.* Paris: Fayard, 1952.

Guernier, Eugène, and G. Fromont Guieysse, eds. *Afrique Equatoriale Française et Côte française des Somali.* Vol. 5 of *Encyclopédie coloniale et maritimes.* Paris: Encyclopédie de l'Empire Français, 1950.

Guilbot, J. *Petite étude sur la main d'oeuvre à Douala.* Yaoundé: IFAN Centre du Cameroun, 1948.

Guinea, Government of. *L'agression portugaise contre la République de Guinée: Livre blanc.* Conakry: Impr. nationale Patrice Lumumba, 1971.

Guirma, Frederic. *Comment perdre le pouvoir? Le cas de Maurice Yaméogo.* Paris: Editions Chaka, 1991.

Hamon, Léon. "Introduction à l'étude des partis politiques de l'Afrique française." *Revue Juridique et Politique d'Outre-Mer,* no. 2 (1959).

Hanotaux, Gabriel, and Alfred Martineau, eds. *Histoire des colonies françaises.* 6 vols. Paris: Société de l'Histoire Nationale, 1929–1933.

Harbeson, John W., and Donald Rothchild, eds. *Africa in World Politics.* Boulder, CO: Westview, 1991, 1995, and 2000.

Hargreaves, John D., ed. *France and West Africa.* London: Macmillan, 1969.

———. *Prelude to the Partition of West Africa.* London: Macmillan, 1963.

———. "Toward a History of the Partition of Africa." *Journal of African History* 1, no. 1 (1960): 100–121.

———. *West Africa: The Former French States.* Englewood Cliffs, NJ: Prentice-

Hall, 1967.

Harmand, Jules. *Domination et colonisation.* Paris: Flammarion, 1910.

Hasek, Jaroslav. *The Good Soldier Svejk and His Fortunes in the World War.* New York: Heinemann/Penguin, 1973.

Hauser, André. *Absentéisme et instabilité de la main d'oeuvre.* Paris: CCTA-CSA, Publ. #69, 1961.

Hazard, John N. "Marxian Socialism in Africa: The Case of Mali." *Comparative Politics* 2, no. 1 (1969): 1–16.

Hazoumé, Paul. *Doguicimi: The First Dahomean Novel (1937).* Translated by Richard Bjornson. Washington, D.C.: Three Continents, 1989.

Herskovits, Melville J. *Dahomey, an Ancient West African Kingdom,* 2 vols. New York: J. J. Augustin, 1938.

Hiskett, Mervyn. *The Development of Islam in West Africa.* London: Longman, 1984.

Hobbes, Thomas. "Of Punishment." In *A Dialogue Between a Philosopher and a Student of the Common Laws of England.* London: J. Cropsey, 1971.

Hodges, Tony. *Angola: Anatomy of an Oil State.* Bloomington: Indiana University Press, 2004.

Hodgkin, Thomas. *African Political Parties.* New York: Penguin, 1962.

———. "Background to AOF 3: African Reactions to French Rule." *West Africa,* no. 1925 (January 16, 1964): 31–32.

———. 'The Metropolitan Axis." *West Africa,* no. 1924 (January 9, 1954): 5–6.

———. *Nationalism in Colonial Africa.* London: Frederick Mueller, 1956.

———. "A Note on the Language of African Nationalism." In Kenneth Kirkwood, ed., *St. Anthony's Papers No. 10: African Affairs, Number One,* pp. 23–24. Carbondale: Southern Illinois University Press, 1961.

———. "Political Forces in French-Speaking Africa." Unpublished manuscript, 1959.

———. "Political Parties in French West Africa." *West Africa,* no. 1930 (February 20, 1954): 157.

Hodgkin, Thomas, and Ruth Schachter Morgenthau, "Mali." In James S. Coleman and Carl G. Rosberg, eds., *Political Parties and National Integration in Tropical Africa,* pp. 216–258. Berkeley: University of California Press, 1964.

Hoover Institution. *Yearbook on International and Communist Affairs.* Stanford, CA: Hoover Institution Press, 1991.

House, Arthur, H. "Brazzaville: Revolution or Rhetoric?" *Africa Report* 16, no. 4 (1971): 20.

Hughes, Arnold, and Janet Lewis. "Beyond Francophonie? The Senegambian Confederation in Retrospect." In Anthony Kirk-Greene and Daniel Bach, eds., *State and Society in Francophone Africa Since Independence,* pp. 228–243. New York: St. Martin's, 1995.

Hughes, Jean-Paul. "Military Cooperation: The Big Turnaround." In Ministère des Affaires Etrangères, *Dossiers, Pays Afrique.* Available at http://www.france. diplomatie.fr/actu/impression.asp?ART=31861.

Hugon, Philippe. *Analyse du sous-développement en Afrique Noire.* Paris: Presses universitaires de France, 1968.

Human Rights Watch. "Weapons Sanctions, Military Supplies, and Human Suffering: Illegal Arms Flows to Liberia and the June–July 2003 Shelling of Monrovia," a Human Rights Watch Briefing Paper. New York: Human Rights Watch, November 3, 2003.

Huntington, Samuel P. *The Third Wave: Democratization in the Late Twentieth*

Century. Norman: University of Oklahoma Press, 1991.

Hyden, Goran. *No Shortcut to Progress: African Development Management in Perspective.* Berkeley: University of California Press, 1983.

Imperato, Pascal James. *Mali: A Search for Direction.* Boulder, CO: Westview, 1989.

International Crisis Group. "Côte d'Ivoire: 'The War Is Not Yet Over.'" *ICG Africa Report,* no. 72 (November 28, 2003).

International Federation of Human Rights Leagues, Congolese Human Rights Observatory. "Congo Brazzaville: L'arbitraire de l'état, la terreur des milices." *FIDH Report,* June 17, 1999. Available at http://www.fidh.imaginet.fr/rapports/brazza.htm.

Irele, Abiola "Negritude or Black Cultural Nationalism." *Journal of Modern African Studies* 3, no. 3 (October 1965): 321–348.

Isnard, Jacques. "Les armées françaises mènent une douzaine d'operations en Afrique." *Le Monde* (December 29, 1999). Available at http://www.lemonde.fr/article/0.2320.seq-2037-36401-QUO.00.html.

Jackson, Robert H., and Carl G. Rosberg. *Personal Rule in Black Africa.* Berkeley: University of California Press, 1982.

Jemie, Onwuchekwa. "Biafra." In Edris Makward and Leslie Lacy, eds., *Contemporary African Literature,* pp. 315–325. New York: Random House, 1972.

Johnson, G. Wesley. "The Ascendancy of Blaise Diagne and the Beginning of African Politics in Senegal." *Africa* 36 (1966): 235–252.

———. "Blaise Diagne, Master Politician of Senegal," *Tarikh* 1, no. 2 (1969): 51–57.

———. *The Emergence of Black Politics in Senegal.* Stanford, CA: Stanford University Press, 1971.

Johnson, R. W. "The Parti Démocratique de Guinée and the Mamou 'Deviation.'" In Christopher Allen and R.W. Johnson, eds., *African Perspectives: Papers in the History, Politics, and Economics of Africa Presented to Thomas Hodgkin,* pp. 347–370. New York: Cambridge University Press, 1970.

Johnson, Thomas, Robert O. Slater, and Patrick McGowan. "Explaining African Coups d'Etat." *American Political Science Review* 78, no. 3 (1984): 622–640.

Johnson, Willard R. *The Cameroon Federation.* Princeton, NJ: Princeton University Press, 1970.

Joseph, Richard. "Democratization in Africa After 1989: Comparative and Theoretical Perspectives." In Lisa Anderson, ed., *Transitions to Democracy,* pp. 237–260. New York: Columbia University Press, 1999.

———. *Radical Nationalism in Cameroun: Social Origins of the U.P.C. Rebellion.* Oxford: Clarendon Press, 1977.

Jua, Nantang. "Cameroon: Jump-Starting an Economy in Crisis." John Mukum Mbaku, ed., *Corruption and the Crisis of Institutional Reform in Africa,* pp. 85–112. Lewiston, NY: Edwin Mellen, 1998.

Julien, Charles A. "From the French Empire to the French Union." *International Affairs* 26, no. 4 (1950): 487–502.

Kaba, Lansiné. "Guinean Politics: A Critical Historical Overview." *Journal of Modern African Studies* 15, no. 1 (1977): 25–46.

Kaké, Ibrahima Baba. *Sékou Touré, le héros et le tyran.* Paris: Jeune Afrique, 1987.

Kalck, Pierre. *Central African Republic.* World Bibliographical Series, vol. 152. Santa Barbara, CA: Clio Press, 1993.

———. *Réalités Oubanguiennes.* Paris: Berger-Levrault, 1959.

Kasfir, Nelson. *The Shrinking Political Arena.* Berkeley: University of California Press, 1976.

Keller, Edmond. *Revolutionary Ethiopia.* Bloomington: Indiana University Press, 1988.

Keller, Edmond, and Donald Rothschild. *Afro-Marxist Regimes.* Boulder, CO: Lynne Rienner, 1987.

Kelley, Michael P. *A State in Disarray: Conditions of Chad's Survival.* Boulder, CO: Westview, 1986.

Kempe, Ronald Hope, Sr., and Borwell C. Chikulo, eds. *Corruption and Development in Africa.* New York: St. Martin's, 2000.

Kester, Gérard, and Osumane Oumarou Sidibé, eds. *Trade Unions and Sustainable Democracy in Africa.* Translated by Michael Cunningham. Aldershot, U.K.: Ashgate, 1997.

Khapoya, Vincent B. *The African Experience: An Introduction.* Englewood Cliffs, NJ: Prentice Hall, 1994.

Kilson, Martin. "The Politics of African Socialism," *African Forum* 1, no. 3 (1966): 17–26.

Kirk-Greene, Anthony H. M. "His Eternity, His Eccentricity, or His Exemplarity? A Further Contribution to the Study of H. E. the African Head of State." *African Affairs,* no. 90 (1977): 163–187.

———. "'Le roi est mort! Vive le roi!': The Comparative Legacy of Chiefs After the Transfer of Power in British and French West Africa." In Anthony Kirk-Greene and Daniel Bach, eds., *State and Society in Francophone Africa Since Independence,* pp. 16–33. New York: St. Martin's, 1993.

Kirk-Greene, Anthony, and Daniel Bach, eds. *State and Society in Francophone Africa Since Independence.* New York: St. Martin's, 1993.

Kirschke, Linda. "Informal Repression, Zero-Sum Politics, and Late Third-Wave Transitions." *Journal of Modern African Studies* 38, no. 2 (2000): 383–405.

———. "Northern Cameroon: Attacks on Freedom of Expression by Governmental and Traditional Authorities." Report. London: Article 19, 1995.

Ki-Zerbo, Joseph. *Le monde africain noir—histoire et civilisation.* Abidjan-Paris: CEDA-Hatier, 1954.

Ki-Zerbo, Joseph, Ali Mazrui, and Christophe Wondji, with A. Adu Boahen. "Nation-Building and Changing Political Values." In Ali A. Mazrui, ed., *UNESCO General History of Africa,* vol. 8: *Africa Since 1935,* pp. 468–498. Berkeley, CA: UNESCO, James Currey, and University of California Press, 1999.

Klein, Martin. *Islam and Imperialism in the Sine-Saloum.* Berkeley: University of California Press, 1968.

Kofele-Kale, Ndiva. "Ethnicity, Regionalism, and Political Power: A Post-Mortem of Ahidjo's Cameroon." In Michael G. Schatzberg and I. William Zartman, eds., *The Political Economy of Cameroon.* New York: Praeger, 1986.

Koumegni, Augustin Kontchou. *Le système diplomatique africain.* Paris: A. Pedone, 1977.

Kritzeck, James, and William H. Lewis, eds. *Islam in Africa.* New York: Van Nostrand-Reinhold, 1969.

Labouret, Henri. *Colonisation, colonialisme, décolonisation.* Paris: Larose, 1952.

Lacouture, Jean. *Cinq hommes et la France.* Paris: Seuil, 1961.

Lavroff, Dimitri G. *La politique africaine du Général de Gaulle, 1958–1969.* Paris: A. Pedone, 1980.

———. *La République du Sénégal.* Paris: Librairie Générale de Droit et de

Jurisprudence, 1966.

Lefevre, Robert. *Dossiers on Tropical Africa.* Paris: n.p., 1962.

Legum, Colin, and John Drysdale, eds., *Africa Contemporary Record: Annual Survey and Documents,* annual publication. London: Africa Research, 1969–1994.

Lemarchand, René. "Rapport de mission intérimaire du professor René Lemarchand su la prévention des conflits en Afrique Centrale, Libreville, 29 septembre–15 novembre 2003." Unpublished manuscript, used by permission of the author, 2003.

———. "The Venomous Flowers of Ivoirité." *WARA (West African Research Association) Newsletter* (Spring 2003): 21–22.

Le Vine, Victor T. "Ahmadou Ahidjo Revisited." In Jean-Germain Gros, ed., *Cameroon: Politics and Society in Comparative Perspective,* pp. 33–60. New York: University Presses of America, 2003.

———. *The Cameroon Federal Republic.* Ithaca, NY: Cornell University Press, 1971.

———. *The Cameroons from Mandate to Independence.* Berkeley: University of California Press, 1964.

———. "Changing Leadership Styles and Political Images: Some Preliminary Notes." *Journal of Modern African Studies* 15, no. 4 (1977): 631–638.

———. "Conceptualizing 'Ethnicity' and 'Ethnic Conflict': A Controversy Revisited." *Studies in Comparative International Development* 32, no. 2 (1997): 45–75.

———. "The Coup in the Central African Republic." *Africa Today* 15, no. 2 (April–May 1968): 12–15.

———. "The Coups in Upper Volta, Dahomey, and the Central African Republic." In Robert Rotberg and Ali A. Mazrui, eds., *Protest and Power in Black Africa,* pp. 1035–1071. New York: Oxford University Press, 1970.

———. "The Fall and Rise of Constitutionalism in West Africa." *Journal of Modern African Studies* 35, no. 2 (1997): 181–206.

———. "Leadership Transition in Black Africa: Elite Generations and Political Succession." *Munger Africana Library Notes.* California Institute of Technology, Pasadena, CA. May 1975.

———. "Military Rule in the People's Republic of Congo." In John W. Harbeson, ed., *The Military in African Politics,* pp. 123–140. New York: Praeger, 1987.

———. "Parapolitics and the Terrain of Informal Politics." Unpublished manuscript, 1997.

———. "Parliaments in Francophone Africa: Some Lessons from the Decolonization Process." In Joel Smith and Lloyd Musolf, eds., *Legislatures in Development: Dynamics of Change in New and Old States,* pp. 125–154. Durham, NC: Duke University Press, 1979.

———. *Political Corruption: The Ghana Case.* Stanford, CA: Hoover Institution Press, 1975.

———. "Political-Cultural Schizophrenia in Francophone Africa." In Isaac James Mowoe and Richard Bjornson, eds., *Africa and the West: Legacies of Empire,* pp. 159–174. New York: Greenwood, 1986.

———. "The Political Cultures of French-Speaking Africa." *Ghana Social Science Journal* 1, no. 2 (November 1971): 1–17.

———. *Political Leadership in Africa: Post-Independence Generational Conflict in Upper Volta, Senegal, Niger, Dahomey, and the Central African Republic.*

Stanford, CA: Hoover Institution Press, 1967.

———. "The Politics of Partition in Africa: The Cameroons Myth of Unification." *Journal of International Affairs* 18, no. 2 (1964): 198–210.

Le Vine, Victor T., and Timothy Luke. *The Arab-African Connection: Political and Economic Realities.* Boulder, CO: Westview, 1979.

Levtzion, Nehemia, and Randall L. Pouwels, eds. *The History of Islam in Africa.* Athens: Ohio University Press, 2000.

Lewin, André. *Diallo Telli, le tragique destin d'un grand Africain.* Paris: Jeune Afrique, 1990.

Lewis, Bernard. *Race and Slavery in the Middle East.* New York: Oxford University Press, 1990.

Lewis, David Levering. *The Race to Fashoda: European Colonialism and African Resistance.* New York: Weidenfeld and Nicolson, 1987.

Lewis, I. M., ed. *Islam in Tropical Africa.* Studies presented and discussed at the Fifth International African Seminar, Ahmadu Bello University, Zaria, Nigeria, January 1964. London: Oxford University Press, 1966.

Lewis, Martin D. "One Hundred Million Frenchmen: The Assimilation Theory in French Colonial Policy." *Comparative Studies in Society and History* 4 (1962): 129–153.

Lewis, W. Arthur. *Politics in West Africa.* Westport, CN: Greenwood, 1981.

Leymarie, Philippe. "Le continent noir en quête d'une véritable partenariat: Malaise dans la coopération entre la France et l'Afrique." *Le Monde Diplomatique* (June 2002): 18.

———. "En Afrique, Dieu n'est plus français." *Le Monde Diplomatique* (May 1995): 26–27.

———. "En Afrique, la fin des ultimes 'chasses gardées.'" *Le Monde Diplomatique* (December 1996): 4–5.

———. "Gendarmes et voleurs en Centrafrique." *Le Monde Diplomatique* (June 1966): 5–6.

———. "Inexorable effritement du 'modèle' franco-africain." *Le Monde Diplomatique* (January 1994): 4–5.

"Les liaisons mafieuses de la Françafrique." *Dossier Noir,* no. 2, *Agir ici et Survie.* L'Harmattan, 1995. Available at http://www.sources-ouvertes.net/rubrique256. html.

Lipschutz, Mark R., and R. Kent Rasmussen. *Dictionary of African Historical Biography.* Berkeley, CA: University of California Press, 1989.

Lloyd, Christopher. *The Navy and the Slave Trade: The Suppression of the African Slave Trade in the Nineteenth Century.* London: Cass, 1968.

Lonsdale, John. "Political Accountability in African History." In J. D. Fage and Roland Oliver, eds., *The Cambridge History of Africa,* vol. 6: *From 1870 to 1905,* pp. 680–766. New York: Cambridge University Press, 1975–1986.

Loubat, Bernard. *L'Ogre de Berengo: "Bokassa m'a dit."* Nice: Editions Alain Lefeuvre, 1981.

Lubabu, Tshitenge. "Idris Déby: Le déclin . . ." *L'Autre Afrique Hebdomadaire,* no. 18 (March 1999): 9–16.

Luttwak, Edward. *Coup d'Etat: A Practical Manual.* New York: Penguin, 1968.

Ly, Abdoulaye. *La Compagnie du Sénégal.* Paris: Présence Africaine, 1958.

MacGaffey, Janet, and Rémy Bazenguissa-Ganga. *Congo-Paris.* Bloomington: Indiana University Press, 2000.

———. "Personal Networks and Trans-Frontier Trade: Zaïrean and Congolese Migrants." In Daniel Bach, ed., *Regionalisation in Africa,* pp. 179–188.

Oxford: James Currey, 1999.

Mahiou, Ahmed. *L'avenement du parti unique en Afrique Noire.* Paris: R. Pichon & R. Durand-Auzias, 1969.

Makonnen, Ras. *Pan-Africanism from Within.* New York: Oxford University Press, 1973.

"Le Mali, la transition." *Politique Africaine* 47 (1992): 3–42.

Mali, Ministère d'Information. "Discours historique de Général de Gaulle de 14 Juin 1960." Mimeographed copy, 1965.

Manning, Patrick. *Francophone Sub-Saharan Africa, 1880–1985.* New York: Cambridge University Press, 1988.

———. *Slavery, Colonialism, and Economic Growth in Dahomey, 1640–1960.* New York: Cambridge University Press, 1982.

Mannoni, Dominique Octave. *Prospero and Caliban: The Psychology of Colonization.* Ann Arbor: University of Michigan Press, 1991.

Marchesin, Philippe. *Tribus, ethnies, et pouvoirs en Mauritanie.* Paris: Karthala, 1992.

Mariol, Henri. *La chronologie coloniale.* Paris: Larose, 1921.

Markovitz, Irving Leonard. *Léopold Sédar Senghor and the Politics of Negritude.* New York: Athenaeum, 1969.

Marshall, D. Bruce. *The French Colonial Myth and Constitution-Making in the Fourth Republic.* New Haven: Yale University Press, 1973.

Martens George. *Trade Unionism in French-Speaking West Africa During the Colonial Period.* Lomé, Republic of Togo: Regional Economic and Documentation Center, 1981.

Martin, Guy. "Continuity and Change in Franco-African Relations." *Journal of Modern African Studies* 33, no. 1 (1995): 1–20.

———. "France's African Policy in Transition: Disengagement and Redeployment." Unpublished paper, Center for African Studies, University of Illinois, Champaign-Urbana, 2000.

———. "The Historical, Economic, and Political Bases of France's African Policy." *The Journal of Modern African Studies* 23, no. 2 (1985): 189–208.

———. "Ideology and Praxis in Thomas Sankara's Revolution of 4 August 1983 in Burkina Faso." *Issue: A Journal of Opinion* 14 (1987): 77–90.

Marty, Paul. *Études sur l'Islam au Sénégal.* Paris: Ed. Leroux, 1917.

———. *Études sur l'Islam en Côte d'Ivoire.* Paris: Ed. Leroux, 1922.

———. *Études sur l'Islam au Dahomey.* Paris: Ed. Leroux, 1926.

———. *Études sur l'Islam et les tribus du Soudan.* Vol. 3, no. 21. Paris: Ed. Leroux, 1920–1921.

———. *Études sur l'Islam et les tribus maures: Les Brakna.* Paris: Ed. Leroux, 1921.

———. *Les Mourides d'Amadou Bamba.* Paris: Larose, 1913.

Matloff, Judith. "New Kids on Trade Bloc: Portugal and Ex-Colonies." *Christian Science Monitor,* July 16, 1996.

Mbaku, John Mukum, ed. *Corruption and the Crisis of Institutional Reform in Africa.* Lewiston, NY: Edwin Mellen, 1998.

M'baye, Sanou. "Alternance historique dans l'ex-pré carré français: Au Sénégal, les chantiers du changement." *Le Monde Diplomatique* (April 2000): 22.

Mbembe, Achille. *Afriques indociles.* Paris: Karthala, 1988.

———. *La naissance du maquis dans le sud-Cameroun (1920–1960).* Paris: Karthala, 1996.

———. *On the Postcolony.* Berkeley: University of California Press, 2001.

McGowan, Patrick, and Thomas Johnson. "African Military Coups d'Etat and Underdevelopment: A Quantitative Historical Analysis." *Journal of Modern African Studies* 22, no. 4 (1984): 637–666.

McNamara, Francis Terry. *France in Black Africa.* Washington, D.C.: National Defense University, 1989.

Médard, Jean-François. "Public Corruption in Africa: A Comparative Perspective." *Corruption and Reform,* no. 1 (1986): 115–131.

Mehler, Andreas. "Cameroun: une transition qui n'a pas eu lieu." In Jean-Pascal Daloz and Patrick Quantin, ed., *Transitions démocratiques africaines,* pp. 95–138. Paris: Karthala, 1997.

Memmi, Albert. *The Colonizer and Colonized.* Translated by Howard Greenfield. Boston: Beacon, 1967.

Mercier, Paul. "Remarques sur la signification de tribalisme actuel en Afrique Noire." *Cahiers Internationaux de Sociologie* 21, no. 1 (1961): 61–80.

Merkl, Peter. "Political Cultures." In P. Merkl, *Modern Comparative Politics,* chapter 3. New York: Holt, Rinehart, and Winston, 1970.

Miaffo, Dieudonné, and Jean-Pierre Warnier. "Accumulation et ethos de la notabilité chez les Bamiléké." In Peter Geschiere and Piet Konings, eds., *Itinéraires d'Accumulation au Cameroun,* pp. 33–69. Paris: Karthala, 1993.

Milcent, Ernest. *L'A.O.F. entre en scène.* Paris: Editions de Temoignage Chrétien, 1958.

———. "Senegal." In Gwendolen Carter, ed., *Five African States.* Ithaca, NY: Cornell University Press, 1964.

Ministère des Affaires Etrangères (France). *Solidarité-influence, DGCID l'action 2001, rapport annuel.* Paris: Ministère des Affaires Etrangeres, 2002.

Mitterand, François. "Discours de François Mitterand devant au XVIème sommet franco-africain La Baule." Paris: La Documentation Française, 1990.

Mombat, Blaise. "Verités sur le 'Complot Mockey.'" In *Dossiers sècrets de l'Afrique contemporaine,* tome 3, pp. 49–64. Paris: Jeune Afrique, 1991.

Monga, Célestin. *The Anthropology of Anger: Civil Society and Democracy in Africa.* Boulder, CO: Lynne Rienner, 1996.

———. "L'Inflation du politique en Afrique: Une théorie de la consolidation démocratique." Boston University Francophone Africa Research Group, *Monographs/Occasional Papers.* 1997.

Monteil, Vincent. "La decolonisation de l'histoire." *Preuves,* supplement to no. 142 (1962).

———. *L'Islam noir.* Paris: Editions du Seuil, 1964.

———. "Marabouts." In James Kritzeck amd William H. Lewis, eds., *Islam in Africa,* pp. 87–100. New York: Van Nostrand, 1969.

Moore, Gerald. "Literary Protest in French-Speaking Africa." In Robert Rotberg and Ali Mazrui, eds., *Protest and Power in Black Africa,* pp. 807–822. New York: Oxford University Press, 1970.

Morgenthau, Ruth Schachter. *Political Parties in French-Speaking West Africa.* London: Oxford University Press, 1964.

Morrison, Donald George, Robert Cameron Mitchell, and John Naber Paden, eds. *Black Africa: A Comparative Handbook,* 2nd ed. New York: Paragon, 1989.

Mortimer, Edward. *France and the Africans, 1944–1960: A Political History.* London: Faber and Faber, 1969.

Moyo, Ambrose. "Religion in Africa." In April Gordon and Donald Gordon, eds., *Understanding Contemporary Africa,* 3rd ed., pp. 299–329. Boulder, CO: Lynne Rienner, 2001.

Mphalele, Ezekiel. *The African Image.* New York: Praeger, 1974.

Mumford, W. Bryant, with G. St. J. Orde-Browne. *Africans Learn to Be French.* New York: Negro Universities Press/Greenwood Press, 1970.

Mundt, Robert J. "Côte d'Ivoire: Continuity and Change in a Semi-Democracy." In John F. Clark and David E. Gardinier, *Political Reform in Francophone Africa,* pp. 182–203. Boulder, CO: Westview, 1997.

Murdock, George Peter. *Africa: Its Peoples and Their Culture History.* New York: McGraw-Hill, 1959.

Mveng, Engelbert. "L'Afrique: Emergence d'un continent, peuples, et civilisations de l'Afrique antique." In *La culture africaine—Symposium d'Alger,* pp. 275–294, from the First International Pan-African Cultural Festival, Algiers, July 21–August 1, 1969. Algiers: Société Nationale d'Edition et Diffusion, 1969.

N'Diaye, Jean-Pierre. *Enquête sur les étudiants noirs en France.* Paris: Editions Réalités Africaines, 1962.

———. "Sénégal: L'heure de verité," *Jeune Afrique,* no. 540 (May 11, 1971): 14–19.

Néra, Georges. *La Communauté.* Paris: Presses Universitaires de France, 1960.

Neres, Phillip. *French-Speaking West Africa.* London: Oxford University Press, 1962.

Newbury, Colin. "The Formation of the Government-General of French West Africa." *Journal of African History* 1, no. 1 (1960): 11–128.

———. "The Government-General and Political Change in French West Africa." In *African Affairs No. 1 (St. Anthony's Papers 10),* pp. 41–59. London: Oxford University Press, 1961.

Ngayap, Pierre Flambeau. *Cameroun: Qui Gouverne?* Paris: Editions Harmattan, 1983.

Ngolet, François. "Ideological Manipulations and Political Longevity: The Power of Omar Bongo Since 1967." *African Studies Review* 43, no. 2 (2000): 55–71.

Ngongo, Louis. *Histoire des forces religieuses au Cameroun: De la Première Guerre mondiale à l'Indépendance (1916–1955).* Paris: Editions Karthala, 1982.

Nyerere, Julius K. *Ujamaa—Essays on Socialism.* Dar es Salaam: Oxford University Press, 1968.

Nzouankeu, Jacques Mariel. "La transition démocratique au Mali." *Alternative Démocratique au Tiers-Monde,* nos. 3–5 (January 1991–June 1992): 223–316.

———. "The Role of the National Conferences in the Transition to Democracy in Africa: The Cases of Benin and Mali." *Issue: A Journal of Opinion* 21, nos. 1–2 (1993): 44–50.

O'Brien, Donal Cruse. *The Mourides of Senegal.* London: Oxford University Press, 1971.

Oded, Arye. *Africa and the Middle East Conflict.* Boulder, CO: Lynne Rienner, 1987.

Orlova, A. C. *Afrikanskyie Narodi: Kultura, Khosaistvo, Byit.* Moscow: Publishing House of Oriental Literature of the Soviet Academy of Science, Oriental Affairs Institute, Ethnographic Institute, 1958.

O'Toole, Thomas. *The Central African Republic: The Continent's Unsteady Heart.* Boulder, CO: Westview, 1986.

———. "Jean-Bedel Bokassa: Neo-Napoleon or Traditional African Ruler?" In Joseph Held, ed., *The Cult of Power: Dictators in the Twentieth Century,* pp. 95–106. New York: Columbia University Press, 1983.

Ottaway, David, and Marina Ottaway. *Afrocommunism.* New York: Africana. 1986.

Pakenham, Thomas. *The Scramble for Africa.* New York: Aron, 1991.

Palmer, Robert R. *The World of the French Revolution.* New York: Allen and Unwin, 1971.

Paringaux, Roland-Pierre. "D'autres voies pour le developpement: Coopération su-sud au Sénégal." *Le Monde Diplomatique* (March 2001): 12.

Passy, Aubert Macaire, and Jean-Médard Mfoumouangana, eds. *France-Afrique sub-Saharienne annuaire, 1988: Organisations sociales et culturelles.* Paris: L'Harmattan, 1988.

Péan, Pierre. *Affaires africaines.* Paris: Fayard, 1983.

———. *L'argent noir.* Paris: Fayard, 1988.

———. *Bokassa 1er.* Paris: A. Moreau, 1977.

———. *L'homme de l'ombre: Eléments d'enquête autour de Jacques Foccart, l'homme le plus mysterieux et le plus puissant de la Vème République.* Paris: Fayard, 1990.

Person, Yves. "Les syndicats en Afrique Noire." *Le mois en Afrique,* nos. 172–173 (1980): 22–46.

Piquemal-Pastre, Michel. *La République islamique de Mauritanie.* Paris: Berger-Levrault, 1969.

Plantey, Alain, and Philippe Broyer. "Les accords de cooperation entre la France et les états africains et malagaches." In Dimitri G. Lavroff, ed., *La politique africaine de Général de Gaulle,* pp. 200–228. Paris: A. Pedone, 1980.

Pomunyoh, Christopher. "Democratization in Fits and Starts." *Journal of Democracy* 12, no. 3 (2001): 37–50.

Potholm, Christian. *Four African Political Systems.* Englewood Cliffs, NJ: Prentice-Hall, 1970.

Pouquet, Jean. *L'Afrique Equatoriale Française et le Cameroun.* Paris: Presses Universitaires de France, Editions "Que Sais-Je?" 1954.

Pye, Lucian, and Sidney Verba, eds. *Political Culture and Political Development.* Princeton, NJ: Princeton University Press, 1965.

Quinn, Charlotte, and Frederick Quinn. *Pride, Faith, and Fear: Islam in Sub-Saharan Africa.* New York: Oxford University Press, 2003.

Quinn, Frederick. *The French Overseas Empire.* Westport, CN: Praeger, 2000.

Radu, Michael, and Keith Somerville. "Congo." In Chris Allen et al., *Marxist Regimes: Benin, the Congo, Burkina Faso,* pp. 160–205. New York: Pinter, 1989.

Ray, Donald I. *Dictionary of the African Left.* Brookfield, VT: Gower, 1989.

Raynal, Jean-Jacques. "La démocratie au Niger: Chronique inachevée d'une accouchement difficile." In Gérard Cognac, ed., *L'Afrique en transition vers le pluralisme politique,* pp. 357–368. Paris: Economica, 1985.

Le RDA dans la lutte anti-impérialiste. Undated pamphlet. Paris: no publisher given, ca. 1948.

Reed, Michael C. "Gabon: A Neo-Colonial Enclave of Enduring French Interest." *Journal of Modern African Studies* 15, no. 3 (1987): 283–320.

Reno, William. *Corruption and State Politics in Sierra Leone.* Cambridge: Cambridge University Press, 1995.

"Report" (on Muslims in each country), Islamic Web, 1998. Available at www.islamicweb.com/begin/population.html.

Rivière, Claude. *Guinea: The Mobilization of a People.* Ithaca, NY: Cornell University Press, 1977.

———. "L'intégration des ethnies guinéennes." *Afrique Documents,* no. 101, 1er cahier (1969): 3–46.

Rivkin, Arnold, ed. *Nations by Design.* Garden City, NY: Doubleday-Anchor, 1968.

Robinson, Kenneth. "Political Development in French West Africa." In Calvin Stillman, ed., *Africa in the Modern World,* pp. 140–181. Chicago: University of Chicago Press, 1955.

Robinson, Pearl T. "Democratization: Understanding the Relationship Between Regime Change and the Culture of Politics." *African Studies Review* 35, no. 1 (1994): 39–67.

———. "Grassroots Legitimation of Military Governance in Burkina Faso and Niger: The Core Contradictions." In Goran Hyden and Michael Bratton, eds., *Governance and Politics in Africa,* pp. 143–166. Boulder, CO: Lynne Rienner, 1992.

———. "The National Conference Phenomenon in Francophone Africa." *Comparative Studies in Society and History* 36, no. 3 (1994): 575–610.

Robinson, Ronald, and John Gallagher, with Alice Denny. *Africa and the Victorians.* New York: Macmillan, 1961.

Roitman, Janet. "New Sovereigns: Regulatory Authority in the Chad Basin." In Thomas Callaghy et al., eds., *Intervention and Transnationalism in Africa,* pp. 240–266. Cambridge: Cambridge University Press, 2001.

Ronen, Dov. *Dahomey.* Ithaca, NY: Cornell University Press, 1975.

———. "People's Republic of Benin: The Military, Marxist Ideology, and the Politics of Ethnicity." In John Harbeson, ed., *The Military in African Politics,* pp. 93–122. New York: Praeger, 1987.

Rosberg, Carl G., and Thomas Callaghy, eds. *Socialism in Sub-Saharan Africa: A New Assessment.* Berkeley, CA: University of California Press, 1979.

Rowlands, Michael. "Accumulation and the Cultural Politics of Identity." In Peter Geschiere and Piet Konings, eds., *Itinéraires d'accumulation au Cameroun,* pp. 71–97. Paris: Karthala, 1993.

Rubin, Neville. *Cameroun: An African Federation.* New York: Praeger, 1971.

Sanneh, Lamin. *Christianity in West Africa: The Religious Impact.* Maryknoll, NY: Orbis, 1983.

———. *The Crown and the Turban: Muslims and West African Pluralism.* Boulder, CO: Westview, 1997.

Sarraut, Albert. *La mise en valeur des colonies françaises.* Paris: A. Payot, 1923.

Sassou-Nguesso, Denis. *The Mango-Tree, the River, and the Mouse (Le manguier, la rivière, et le souris).* Paris: Editions J. C. Lattés, 2001.

Schachter, Ruth. "Single-Party Systems in West Africa." *American Political Science Review* 55 (1961): 294–307.

Schatzberg, Michael G. "The Coup and After: Continuity or Change in Malian Politics?" *Occasional Paper #5,* African Studies Program, University of Wisconsin, Madison, 1972.

———. *Political Legitimacy in Middle Africa: Father, Family, Food.* Bloomington: Indiana University Press, 2001.

Schnapper, Bernard. *La politique et le commerce français dans le Golfe de Guinée de 1838 à 1871.* Paris: Mouton, 1961.

Schraeder, Peter J. *African Politics and Society: A Mosaic in Transformation.* Boston: Bedford/St. Martin's, 2000.

———. "France and the Great Game in Africa." *Current History* (May 1997): 206–211.

———. "The Impact of Democratization on the Formulation and Implementation of African Foreign Policies." Unpublished paper, African Studies Association, Nashville, TN, November 2000.

Scott, Catherine V. "Socialism and the Soft State in Angola and Mozambique."

Journal of Modern African Studies 26, no. 1 (1988): 25–63.

Scott, James C. *Domination and the Arts of Resistance.* New Haven: Yale University Press, 1990.

———. *Weapons of the Weak: Everyday Forms of Peasant Resistance.* New Haven: Yale University Press, 1985.

Seely, Jennifer C. "It's All Relative: The Importance of Ethnicity in Benin's Elections." Unpublished paper, American Political Science Association meeting, Philadelphia, PA, August 25–32, 2003.

———. "Transitions to Democracy in Comparative Perspective: The National Conferences in Benin and Togo." Ph.D. dissertation, Washington University, St. Louis, 2001.

———. "Transitions to Democracy: Overcoming Ethnic Conflict." Unpublished manuscript, 1996.

Segal, Ronald. *Political Africa.* London: Stevens, 1961.

"Senegal's Slide from 'Model Economy' to 'Least Developed Country.'" Misanet.com/IPS. Available at http://www.afrol.com/Countries/Senegal/back-gr_ldc.htm.

"Senegal: Ten Years After." *West Africa,* no. 2767 (June 26, 1970): 664.

Senghor, Léopold Sédar. *Chants d'ombre, suivis de Hosties noirs,* 2nd ed. Paris: Seuil, 1956.

———. "Latinité et négritude." *Présence Africaine,* no. 52 (1964).

———. "Negritude and the Concept of Universal Civilization." *Présence Africaine,* English edition (2nd quarter, 1963).

———. "Negritude et civilisation Greco-Latine ou democratie et socialisme." *L'Unité Africaine* (Dakar), November 26, 1964.

———. "Oxford Statement." *West Africa,* no. 2318 (November 4, 1961): 1211.

Serge, Saint-Michel. *Histoire du Togo: Il etait une fois—Eyadema.* Paris: Afrique Biblio Club, 1976.

Shaw, Malcolm N. *Title to Territory in Africa: International Legal Issues.* Oxford, UK: Clarendon, 1986.

Shoumatoff, Alex. *African Madness.* New York: Vintage/Random House, 1988.

Sik, Endre. *Histoire de l'Afrique Noire.* Budapest: Academic Presses, 1961.

Sindjoun, Luc. "Le champ social camerounais: Desordre inventif, mythes simplificateurs et stabilité de l'état." *Politique Africaine,* no. 62 (June 1966): 57–67.

———. "La politique d'affectation en Afrique Noire." Francophone Africa Research Group (GRAF), occasional papers, Boston University, 1998.

Skinner, Elliott. *The Mossi of Burkina Faso.* Stanford, CA: Stanford University Press, 1989.

———. "Sankara and the Burkinabe Revolution: Charisma and Power, Local and External Dimensions." *Journal of Modern African Studies* 26, no. 3 (1988): 437–455.

Smith, Stephen, and Antoine Glaser. "Les reseaux africains de Jean-Christophe Mitterand." *Liberation,* no. 2836 (July 6, 1990): 14–17.

Snyder, Francis G. "The Political Thought of Modibo Keita." *Journal of Modern African Studies* 5, no. 1 (1967): 79–106.

Snyder, Gregory Frank. *One-Party Government in Mali: Transition Toward Control.* New Haven: Yale University Press. 1965.

Stary, Bruno. "Cross-Border Trade in West Africa: The Ghana–Côte d'Ivoire Frontier." In Daniel Bach, ed., *Regionalisation in Africa,* pp. 169–178. Oxford: James Currey, 1999.

"Statistics by Country by Population." Available at www.catholic-hierarchy.org/country/sc1.html.

Sundberg, Anne. "The Struggle for Kingship: Moses or Messiah—Ethnic War and the Use of Ethnicity in the Process of Democratization in Congo-Brazzaville." In Einar Braathen et al., eds., *Ethnicity Kills? The Politics of War, Peace, and Ethnicity in Sub-Saharan Africa,* pp. 87–108. New York: St. Martin's, 2000.

Suret-Canale, Jean. *Afrique Noire: L'ère coloniale.* Paris: Editions Sociales, 1964.

———. "The End of Chieftaincy in Guinea." In Irving Leonard Markovitz, ed., *African Politics and Society: Basic Issues and Problems of Government and Development,* pp. 96–117. New York: Free Press, 1970.

———. "La fin de la chefferie en Guinée." *Journal of African History* 7, no. 3 (1966): 459–493.

"Le sursaut du PDCI." *Africa International* 230 (September 1990): 31–32.

Sy, Seydou Madani. *Recherches sur l'éxercise du pouvoir politique en Afrique Noire.* Paris: A. Pedone, 1965.

Takougang, Joseph, and Milton Krieger. *African State and Society in the 1990s: Cameroon's Political Crossroads.* Boulder, CO: Westview, 1998.

Tardits, Claude. *Porto-Novo: Les nouvelles générations africaines entre leurs traditions et l'Occident.* Paris: Mouton, 1958.

Taylor, John. *Christianity and Politics in Africa.* Westport, CN: Greenwood, 1979.

Taylor, Sidney, ed., *The New Africans.* New York: Putnam, 1967.

Tessier, Manon, and Thiery Gongora. "Maintien de la paix: Une Afrique bouscoulée en voie de réorganization sécuritaire." Université Laval, Institut Quebecois des Hautes Etudes Internationales, *Bulletin,* no. 44 (2000).

Thiam, Doudou. *La politique étrangère des états africains.* Paris: Presses Universitaires de France, 1963.

Thomas, L. V. *Le socialisme et l'Afrique.* 2 vols. Paris: Le livre africain, 1996.

Thompson, Virginia. Biographical Cards on French-Speaking Africa. Hoover Institution Library, Stanford, CA.

———. "The Ivory Coast." In Gwendolen Carter, ed., *African One-Party States,* pp. 237–324. Ithaca, NY: Cornell University Press, 1962.

Thompson, Virginia, and Richard Adloff. *The Emerging States of French Equatorial Africa.* Stanford, CA: Stanford University Press, 1960.

———. *French West Africa.* London: Allen and Unwin, 1958.

Thompson, W. Scott. *Ghana's Foreign Policy, 1957–1966: Diplomacy, Ideology, and the New State.* Princeton, NJ: Princeton University Press, 1969.

Titley, Brian. *Dark Age: The Political Odyssey of Emperor Bokassa.* Montreal: McGill-Queens University Press, 1997.

Toulabor, C. M. "Jeu de mots, jeu de villains: Lexique de dérision politique au Togo." *Politique Africaine,* no. 3 (September 1981): 55–71.

———. "Naissance du démocratie Africain." *Le Monde Diplomatique* (October 2001): 4.

Touré, Sékou. *Défendre la Révolution.* Conakry: publisher unknown, 1969.

Transparency International. *Corruption Perception Index, 1999–2003.* October 7, 2003. Available at http://transparency.org.

Traoré, Bakary, Mamadou Lô, and Jean-Louis Alibert. *Forces politiques en Afrique Noire.* Paris: Presses Universitaires de France, 1966.

Trimingham, J. Spencer. *A History of Islam in West Africa.* London: Oxford University Press, 1970.

———. *Islam in West Africa.* London: Oxford University Press, 1959.

Tripp, Aili Marie. "The New Political Activism in Africa." *Journal of Democracy*

12, no. 3 (July 2001): 141–155.

Tsebendal, Yumjagin. "The Revolutionary Party and Social Changes." *World Marxist Review* 9, no. 2 (February 1966): 3–11.

Ulam, Adam. *The Unfinished Revolution.* New York: Random House, 1960.

UN Demographic Yearbook, 1999, 2000. New York: United Nations Press, 2002.

UN High Commissioner for Refugees. *The State of the World's Refugees.* New York: Oxford University Press, 2000.

United Kingdom, Foreign and Commonwealth Office. "The Casamance Conflict 1982–1999." *Research and Analytical Papers.* London: HMSO, 1999.

UN Office for the Coordination of Humanitarian Affairs. "Côte d'Ivoire: UNSG Releases First Report on Côte d'Ivoire." IRIN News Organization, April 2, 2003.

UN Security Council. *Report of the Panel of Experts on Violations of Security Council Sanctions Against UNITA.* UN Doc. S/2000/203. March 10, 2000. Available at www.un.org/news/dh/latest/angolareport.htm.

———. *Report of the Security Council Special Mission to the Republic of Guinea, Established Under Resolution 289.* UN Doc. S/100009. December 3, 1970.

U.S. Department of State. *Warsaw Pact Economic Aid Programs in Non-Communist LDCs: Holding Their Own in 1986.* Washington, D.C.: GPO, 1988.

U.S. Department of the Army, Special Operations Research Office, Foreign Areas Studies Division. *Special Warfare Area Handbook for Guinea.* Washington, D.C.: GPO, 1962.

U.S. Library of Congress, Country Study/Area Handbook series. Washington, D.C.: GPO, 1988.

U.S. Senate. Committee on Governmental Affairs. *Minority Staff Report for Permanent Subcommittee on Investigations, Hearing on Private Banking and Money Laundering,* November 9, 1999. Available at http://levin.senate.gov/issues/psireport2.htm, downloaded 11/12/99.

Vengroff, Richard. "Governance and the Transition to Democracy: Political Parties and the Party System in Mali." *Journal of Modern African Studies* 31, no. 4 (1993): 541–563.

Vengroff, Richard, and Lucy Creevey. "Senegal: The Evolution of a Quasi Democracy." In John F. Clark and David E. Gardinier, *Political Reform in Francophone Africa,* pp. 204–224. Boulder, CO: Westview, 1997.

Verschave, François-Xavier. *Complicité de génocide? La politique de la France au Rwanda.* Paris: La Decouverture, 1994.

———. "Connivences françaises au Rwanda." *Le Monde Diplomatique* (March 1995): 10.

———. *La Françafrique.* Paris: Editions Stock, 1998.

———. *Noir silence: Qui arrêtera la Françafrique?* Paris: Editions des Arènes, 2000.

Viaud, Pierre, and Lacques Lestapis. *Afrique: Les Souverainétés en armes.* Paris: Fondation pour les Etudes de Défense Nationale, 1987.

"La vie parlementaire et son évolution au Sénégal d'hier à aujourd'hui." *Le Rayon du Soleil, Le Soleil en Ligne,* no. 3 (1998). Available at http://www.primature.sn/lesoleil/lg_histo.htm.

Vieyra, Christian. "Structures politiques traditionelles et structures politiques modernes." In Rencontres Internationales de Bouaké, *Tradition et modernisme en Afrique Noire.* Paris: Editions du Seuil, 1965.

Villalón, Leonardo A. *Islamic Society and State Power in Senegal: Disciples and Citizens in Fatick.* New York: Cambridge University Press, 1996.

Villalón, Leonardo A., and Ousmane Kane. "Senegal: The Crisis of Democracy and the Emergence of an Islamic Opposition." In Leonardo A. Villalón and Phillip A. Huxtable, eds., *The African State at a Critical Juncture,* pp. 143–166. Boulder, CO: Lynne Rienner, 1998.

Villard, Andres. *Histoire du Sénégal.* Dakar: Maurice Viale, 1943.

Wagret, Jean-Michel. *Histoire et sociologie politique du Congo-Brazzaville.* Paris: Librairie Générale de Droit et de Jurisprudence, 1963.

Wallerstein, Immanuel. "Elites in French-Speaking Africa: The Social Bases of Ideas." *The Journal of Modern African Studies* 3, no. 2 (1965): 1–33.

————. "Ethnicity and National Integration." *Cahiers d'Etudes Africaines* 3 (October 1960): 129–139.

Waterbury, John. *The Political Economy of Risk and Choice in Senegal.* London: Frank Cass, 1987.

Wauthier, Claude. *L'Afrique des Africains, inventaire de la négritude.* Paris: Editions du Seuil, 1964.

————. *The Literature and Thought of Modern Africa.* London: Pall Mall, 1956.

Welch, Claude. *Dream of Unity: Pan-Africanism and Political Unification in West Africa.* Ithaca, NY: Cornell University Press, 1966.

Whiteman, Kaye. "The Gallic Paradox." *Africa Report* (January–February 1991): 19.

Widner, Jennifer A. "Political Reform in Anglophone and Francophone Africa." In Jennifer A. Widner, ed., *Economic and Political Liberalization in Sub-Saharan Africa,* pp. 49–79. Baltimore, MD: Johns Hopkins University Press, 1994.

————. "The Rise of Civic Associations Among Farmers in Côte d'Ivoire." In John Harbeson et al., eds., *Civil Society and the State in Africa,* pp. 191–211. Boulder, CO: Lynne Rienner, 1994.

————. "Single-Party States and Agricultural Policies: The Cases of Côte d'Ivoire and Kenya." *Comparative Politics* 26, no. 2 (1994): 127–148.

Widstrand, Carl Gosta, ed. *African Boundary Problems.* Uppsala: Scandinavian Institute of African Studies, 1969.

Willner, Ruth Ann. *The Spellbinders: Charismatic Political Leadership.* New Haven: Yale University Press, 1984.

Wintrobe, Ronald. *The Political Economy of Dictatorship.* New York: Cambridge University Press, 1998.

Wise, Christopher. "Chronicle of a Student Strike in Africa: The Case of Burkina Faso, 1996–1997." *African Studies Review* 41, no. 2 (1998): 19–36.

Wiseman, John A. *Democracy in Black Africa: Survival and Revival.* New York: Paragon House, 1990.

————. *The New Struggle for Democracy in Africa.* Brookfield, VT: Avebury, 1996.

————. *Political Leaders in Black Africa.* Brookfield, VT: Edward Elgar, 1991.

Wolpin, Miles. "Dependency and Conservative Militarism in Mali." *Journal of Modern African Studies* 13, no. 4 (1975): 600–618.

Woods, Dwayne. "Côte d'Ivoire: The Crisis of Redistributive Politics." In Leonardo A. Villalón and Phillip A. Huxtable, eds., *The African State at a Critical Juncture,* pp. 213–232. Boulder, CO: Lynne Rienner, 1998.

World Bank. "African Development Data, 2001, 2002." *World Bank Africa Database.* CD-ROM. Washington, D.C.: World Bank, 2002, 2003.

————. *World Development Report, 1996, 2001.* Washington, D.C.: World Bank.

Wrong, Michela. *In the Footsteps of Mr. Kurtz.* New York: HarperCollins, 2001.

Yates, Douglas Andrew. *The Rentier State in Africa.* Trenton, NJ: Africa World,

1996.

———. "The Rentier State in Gabon." Unpublished paper, "Brazzaville + 50" Conference, African Studies Center, Boston University, 1994.

Youlou, Foulbert. *J'accuse la Chine*. Paris: La Table Ronde, 1966.

Young, Crawford. *The African Colonial State in Comparative Perspective*. New Haven: Yale University Press, 1994.

———. *Ideology and Development in Africa*. Princeton, NJ: Princeton University Press, 1972.

———. "Zaire: The Anatomy of a Failed State." In David Birmingham and Phyllis Martin, eds., *History of Central Africa: The Contemporary Years Since 1960*, pp. 97–130. New York: Addison Wesley Longman, 1998.

Zartman, I. William, ed. *The Political Economy of Ivory Coast*. New York: Praeger, 1984.

Ziegler, Jean. "Dans la Haute-Volta du capitaine Sankara." *Le Monde Diplomatique* (March 1986): 10–11.

———. *Thomas Sankara: Un nouveau pouvoir africain*. Paris: P. M. Favre, 1986.

Zolberg, Aristide R. *Changing Political Order: The Party-States of West Africa*. Chicago: Rand-McNally, 1966.

———. *One-Party Government in the Ivory Coast*. Princeton, NJ: Princeton University Press, 1964.

———. "Patterns of National Integration." *Journal of Modern African Studies* 5, no. 4, (1967): 449–467.

Index

Gentil, Emil, 38
Goldsmith, Michael, 228
Governor, ambiguity of role, 68
Groupes d'études communistes
(GECs), 74
Gueï, Robert, 194, 212–213
Guèye, Lamine, 66, 79, 128, 205, 211
Guinea: as exception to referendum
vote, 70; plots in, 222; retribaliza-
tion of, 173; Stalinist socialism in,
224; unity in, pre-1961, 173
Guinean National Assembly, 221
Guineans, exile of, under Touré
regime, 223
Gum arabic, 31

Habré, Hissein, 318–319, 342
Hammallist Brotherhood, as protest
movement, 183–184
Hapi (Happi), 311
Hapi, Daniel Kemayou, 312
Hapi, Jean-Claude, 312
Hapi, Louis Kemayou, 312
Hargreaves, John, 31, 35
Harmand, Jules, 42
Hazoumé, Paul, 124
Heads of state, as national unity sym-
bol, 140
Herders, 20
Heterogeneity, cultural and social, 161
Hodgkin, Thomas, 98–99, 125
Houphouët-Boigny, Felix: attempted
arrest of, 77; decline of regime,
255–256; defense of Franco-
African Community, 71; medical
background of, 287–288; percep-
tions of, 273–274; role in drafting
Loi-Cadre, 79; ruling style,
206–211
Human rights violations: in francoph-
one Africa, 319; by special security
forces, 320
Human Rights Watch, 235*n36,* 319
Hunters, 20

Ideology, 120–126
IMF. *See* International Monetary Fund
Imperial acquisition, post-1880, 40
Imperial citizenship, 63

Incivisme (civic responsibility), 98,
107, 109
Independence: economic implications
of, 122; hesitance toward, 126; as
partial autonomy, 122
Indépendents d'Outre-Mer (IOM), 78
Indigénat, 44, 48, 50, 63–64
Indigenous Savings Societies, 188
Indirect rule, British system of, 52
International Monetary Fund (IMF),
247
Internet, as medium for opposition
parties, 112–113
Interterritorial parties, 78, 80
IOM. *See* Indépendents d'Outre-Mer
Iron ore, 22
Iron surgeons, 142. *See also* Marxism
Islam, 12; in Mauritania, 348; role in
uniting ethnic groups, 172. *See
also* Organization of the Islamic
Conference
Islamic law, 176
Islamic opposition, 206
Islamic Republic of Mauritania, 13,
175, 180
Ivoirians, violence against non-
Ivoirians, 167
Ivoirité, 16, 193–194

Jehovah's Witnesses, 186
Jeune Afrique, 4, 251
Julien, Charles A., 38

Kakism, 188
"Kamerun myth," 131
Kautsky, Karl, 35
Keita, Modibo, 164, 273
Kérékou, Mathieu, 146, 169, 253–255,
258–259, 292–293
Kimbangu, Simon (prophet), 74, 187
Kleptocracy, 313–314, 317–318
Kolingba, André, 229–230
Kountché, Seyni, 276

La Baule conference, 247–250, 259.
See also Franco-African Summit
Labor tax, 48
La Françafrique, 314, 341
La Francophonie, 3, 90, 246, 340

About the Book

The fourteen countries in West and Equatorial Africa that form the heart of what was once France's African colonial empire—all independent now for more than four decades—still retain French as an official language, remain attached to French culture, and maintain political links with France. Each country, however, has developed its own distinctive brand of politics. Victor Le Vine traces the political evolution of these countries, exploring the elements that have shaped their particular political dynamics while allowing them to remain part of a unique francophone sociopolitical community.

Le Vine's provocative discussion of topics ranging from the colonial context, political culture, and religion to redemocratization, informal politics, and international relations offers a comprehensive, unique perspective on the workings of this relatively little-known group of states.

Victor T. Le Vine, professor emeritus of political science at Washington University in St. Louis, has been following the political fortunes of the French-speaking African states since their independence.